Memoirs from Eldred, New York, 1800–1950

Book 3

Farewell to Eldred

Stories of Families and Boarding Houses in the Town of Highland, New York

1920–1950

Louise Elizabeth Smith

HALFWAY BROOK

Eldred sign courtesy of Cynthia Leavenworth Belllinger.

Published by Halfway Brook
Cave Creek, Arizona

Family information online:
halfwaybrook.com: Halfway Brook community blog, on-going projects, resources

weezy.info: Stories and information about the Crabtree-Higginson, Austin-Leavenworth, Smith-Corbridge, and Fallin-Williams families

Photo and text contributions:
Mary Briggs Austin, Melva Austin Barney, Cynthia Leavenworth Bellinger, Katherine Calkin Traxler, Ken Bosch, Kevin Marrinan, Chuck Myers, Christene Stevens Myers, Bill Ihlo, and Gary D. Smith

Cover, interior design, and maps:
Gary D. Smith (PerformanceDesign.net)

Editing:
Gary D. Smith, Cynthia Leavenworth Bellinger

Copyright © 2013 by Louise E. Smith
Printed in the United States of America
ISBN: 978-0-9826374-3-2

Cover photos are repeated and credited in the book. Map on Title Page courtesy of Sullivan County Historical Society.

Other books by Louise Elizabeth Smith, available through halfwaybrook.com:
Echo Hill and Mountain Grove
The Mill on Halfway Brook
Grandma and Me
Aida Austin's 1881 Diary

I would like to thank:

Richard O. Eldred for permission to quote from his book, *The Eldred Family: Elisha Eldred of Minisink, New York, and His Descendants*, Baltimore: Gateway Press, Inc., 1988.

John Conway for permission to quote: *Retrospect*, *Sullivan County Democrat*, January 13, 2006 and July 14, 2006; *Times-Herald Record*, September 26, 2003.

Shawn Younger (wwiiarchives.net) for photos of the 5th Army in Rome.

All rights reserved. Please contact the author for permission to reproduce any part of this book.

Disclaimer: Information and sources were recorded as accurately as possible. Incorrect information is unintentional. Please notify the author regarding errors so they can be corrected in the next edition.

Table of Contents

Preface and Acknowledgments iv

Map of Northeast United States vi

Town of Highland Boarding House Locations viii

Dedication and Ecclesiastes 3 x

Farewell to Eldred Introduction xi

Map of the Town of Highland xii

Chapter 1: Most Pleasant Time of All, 1920 1

Chapter 2: The First Real Sorrow, 1921–1924 21

Chapter 3: A Fortunate Occurrence, 1925–1926 45

Chapter 4: Lights, Toasters, Radios, 1927–1929 67

Chapter 5: Better Life in the Country, 1929 87

Chapter 6: The Foot of the Class, 1930–1933 107

Chapter 7: The Breezy Westerner, 1934–1936 139

Chapter 8: Prosperity Dampened, 1937–1939 171

Chapter 9: Newspapers and Oatmeal, 1940–1941 207

Chapter 10: Human Nature Observed, 1942 251

Chapter 11: Correspondence, 1943–1944 277

Chapter 12: "I Do," 1945–1946 321

Chapter 13: Old Home on the Hill, 1947–1950 351

Chapter 14: Epilogue, 1950 and Beyond 375

Bibliography 390

Appendix 391

Index 473

About the Author 506

Preface

Farewell to Eldred is the culmination of the fifty-page booklet turned three-volume series, about Mort and Jennie Leavenworth Austin, my grandparents.

The Mill on Halfway Brook introduced us to my relatives, their friends, and neighbors who settled on either side of Halfway Brook in the years 1800 to 1880. *Echo Hill and Mountain Grove* continued the story. *Farewell to Eldred* follows the descendants of the early settlers as well as newcomers to the area in the third and final volume of *Memoirs from Eldred, New York, 1800–1950*.

Since the *Memoirs from Eldred, New York Series* began in the year 1800 and included the ancestors of the future spouses of the Leavenworths and Austins, a high percentage of the townsfolk who settled on either side of Halfway Brook, became part of the story.

The initial family treasure troves from my mother Mary Briggs Austin, my cousin Melva Austin Barney, and my second cousin Cynthia Leavenworth Bellinger, were added to by Austin descendants, Dorothy Calkin Hale and Katherine Calkin Traxler.

Melva's collection contained a few loose pages of our great-aunt Aida Austin's early 1940s Diary. Aida's day-to-day accounts often mentioned the help and care she and her brother received from Howard and Emily Stevens and their daughter Teenie; and Herman and Mary Horton Bosch.

The search to find the descendants of the Stevens and Herman Bosch families (and offer my appreciation) was unexpectedly rewarded with major archives of photos from Christene Stevens Myers (Teenie) herself. Herman and Mary Horton Bosch's vast assortment was shared by Victoria Kohler, the granddaughter of Herman and Mary Bosch, thanks to Ken Bosch. Ken also supplied his extensive array of Bosch Family photos and research.

A list of the numerous other contributors, both family and friends (new and old), can be read in the Acknowledgments.

Acknowledgments

Where do I start to say thank you to so many who have made this third book possible. The gargantuan array of information and photos shared and questions answered by numerous generous relatives and friends (new and old) have helped to make this narrative a historical resource on the Town of Highland and its townsfolk from 1920 to 1950.

Special mention goes to the original three contributors: my mother Mary Briggs Austin, my cousin Melva Austin Barney, and my second cousin Cynthia Leavenworth Bellinger. These three women have stuck with the project from the outset. Their combined resource of photos, information, and answered questions has been the backbone of the *Memoirs from Eldred, New York, 1800 to 1950* Series.

This book would have been absolutely impossible to write without Cynthia's incredibly enthusiastic help. Cynthia was my "feet-on-the-ground" in getting first hand information from so many folks who still live in Eldred or nearby. She scanned umpteen quad zillion photos, not only of her family, but also those from contributors in Eldred. She proofed way too many rough drafts, always graciously.

Cynthia tracked down birth, marriage, and death dates, boarding house photos, and answers to at least a quadrillion questions I asked. She also typed the diaries of her grandmother Ella Sergeant Leavenworth, her aunt Anna Leavenworth Meyers, and our great-aunt Anna Leavenworth—a time consuming endeavor.

Melva and my mom have continued to answer my queries. Cynthia's mother Gisele Rouillon Leavenworth joined the troop of question answerers. Who knew there would be a "test" about what happened sixty to eighty years ago?

Christene (Teenie) Stevens Myers gladly answered a barrage of unending questions from Cynthia and myself. Chuck Myers was also a major resource. "Ask Chuck Myers. He will know," my mom often said.

Ken Bosch joined the research network and diligently unearthed photos, mega information, and stories about the Highland Lake area (including a detailed map of boarding house locations) and Bosch family descendants.

Quite a few people served as a resource for their family data.

A number of folks volunteered information and shared photos. This included guests who had fond memories of staying at one of the Town of Highland Boarding Houses and folks who had grown up in the area, possibly in one of the Boarding Houses mentioned in the book.

Without the technical and design expertise of my husband Gary, there would be no book. Once again Gary's professional touch can be seen in the interior design and yet a third superb cover. Gary again created maps, retouched some 1,200 photos in photoshop, and edited the book. He encouraged me that this gargantuan project could actually be completed! Thank you Gary!

Thank You to Family and Friends
The following list includes family and friends who sent photos or information, answered questions, or helped in some other way. It does not include friends and other family whose encouragement has also been most appreciated. Hopefully I have included the names of all the generous folks whose contributions have been so necessary to the writing of *Farewell to Eldred*. My thanks and appreciation to all!

Austin Relatives
Carol J. Austin, Charles A. Austin, Mary M. Austin, Mary Briggs Austin, Melva Austin Barney, Darren Foster, Kathleen Baker Foster, Elizabeth Geier, Walter Geier, Joan Austin Geier, Tania Leigh Gaete, Ricardo Gaete, Karen M. Gibson, Dorothy Calkin Hale, John D. Hull, Marjorie Hull Huwa, Richard James, Andy Maglione, Margie Austin Maglione, Joanna Smith Meyer, Dawn Lee Austin Segarra, Barbara Kate James Stowell, Augustus Austin Thompson Family, Katherine Calkin Traxler.

Eldred Relatives
Marnette Hart Click, Richard O. Eldred, Martha Eldred Worzel.

Leavenworth Relatives
Brad Bellinger, Richard Bellinger, Cynthia Leavenworth Bellinger, Norman Bohs, Linda Leavenworth Bohs, Gerald Koenig, Marialyce Koenig Kornkven, David and Diane Leavenworth, Gisele Rouillon Leavenworth, Nancy Leavenworth Leo, Charlee Hirsch Schroedel, Matt Schroedel, Ric Schroedel, Edythe King Westerfield, Pamela Westerfield, Marion Connor Woods.

Jane Ann Webb Myers Relatives
Clifford Crandall Family, George Crandall, Christene Stevens Myers, Helen Crandall Pisarski, Magdala Trautsch Ray, Timothy C. Rizzuto, Pat Myers Toaspern.

Friends Who Contributed
Mary Purcell Abele, Alice M. Aber, Linda Guenther Anderson, Carol Dunlap Brandau, Howard Barnes, Arlene Wolff Bennett, Frederick Bosch, Ken Bosch, Dennis J. Carroll, James C. Clark, Vernon Clark, Carolyn Hallock Clark, Sue Horton Cloud, John Conway, Lorraine West Daniels, Pam Fischetti DeFeo, Ruth Ann Wilson Donovan, Mary Agnes Wilson Dorney, Chris Doyle, Betty Ann Mulvihill Doyle, ECCE Bed & Breakfast (Alan Rosenblatt, Kurt Kreider), Ron Flieger, Kathy Hulse Frisbie, George J. Fluhr, Dorothy Knecht Foster, Christopher Frey, Edward Grotecloss III, Marion Lass Guenther, Alan Gothard, Berniece Wells Haas, Darlene Sutherland Haas, Richard (Dickie) Haas, Emily Knecht Hallock, Wayne Hansen, William E. Horton, Bill Ihlo, John Ihlo, Marion Doeller Kistner, Victoria Kohler, Bronwyn Kyte, Earl Lilley, Sharon Stewart Lilley, Russell MacKechnie, Peggy Gilmore MacKechnie, Mary Ellen Busse Mackinder, Kevin Marrinan, Sandy Sergeant McBride, Ed Mellan, Joseph Mellan, Mary Paulik Mellan, Betty Ihlo Morganstern, Chuck Myers, Ruth Worzel Myers, James Nieke, Helen Hensel Oset, Virginia West Palmer, Diane Pankow, Sandy Parker, Sue Parker, William H. Parker Jr., Charles Paulus, Joan Polishook, James Purcell, James Purcell (son of Edward Purcell), Stuart Russell, Geraldine Mills Russell, Barbara Ihlo Sardone, Frank V Schwarz, Kathy Wilson Scofield, Dale and Tricia McDowell Smith, Christiane Lorphelin Stolte, Sunshine Hall Free Library, Judy Guamer Testa, Ivan J. and Jana Tether, Doris Doeller Toaspern, Town of Highland (Doreen Hanson), Jeanie Staubes Turner, Janith Boyd Vogt, Nancy Vonderhorst, Christina Watts, Dorothy Brodmerkel Weber, David Weidner, Edey LaBarr Werman, Barbara Waite Wilkinson, Randy Drum Williamson, Alice Willis, Gladys Moran Wilson, Edward Wolff, Herb Wolff, Lillian Hainzl Wolff, and Marjorie Hess Worzel.

VI • FAREWELL TO ELDRED

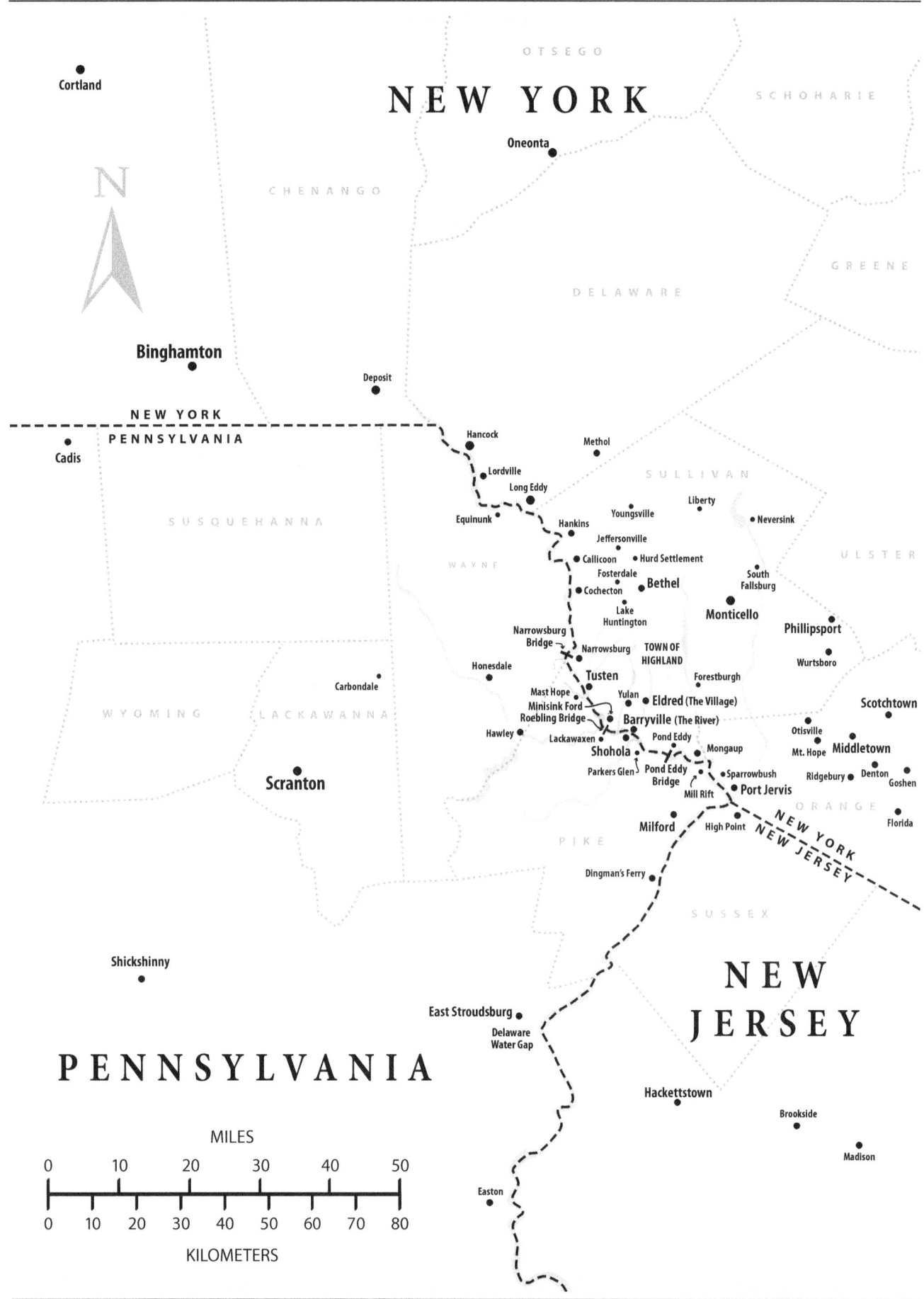

MAP OF NORTHEAST UNITED STATES • VII

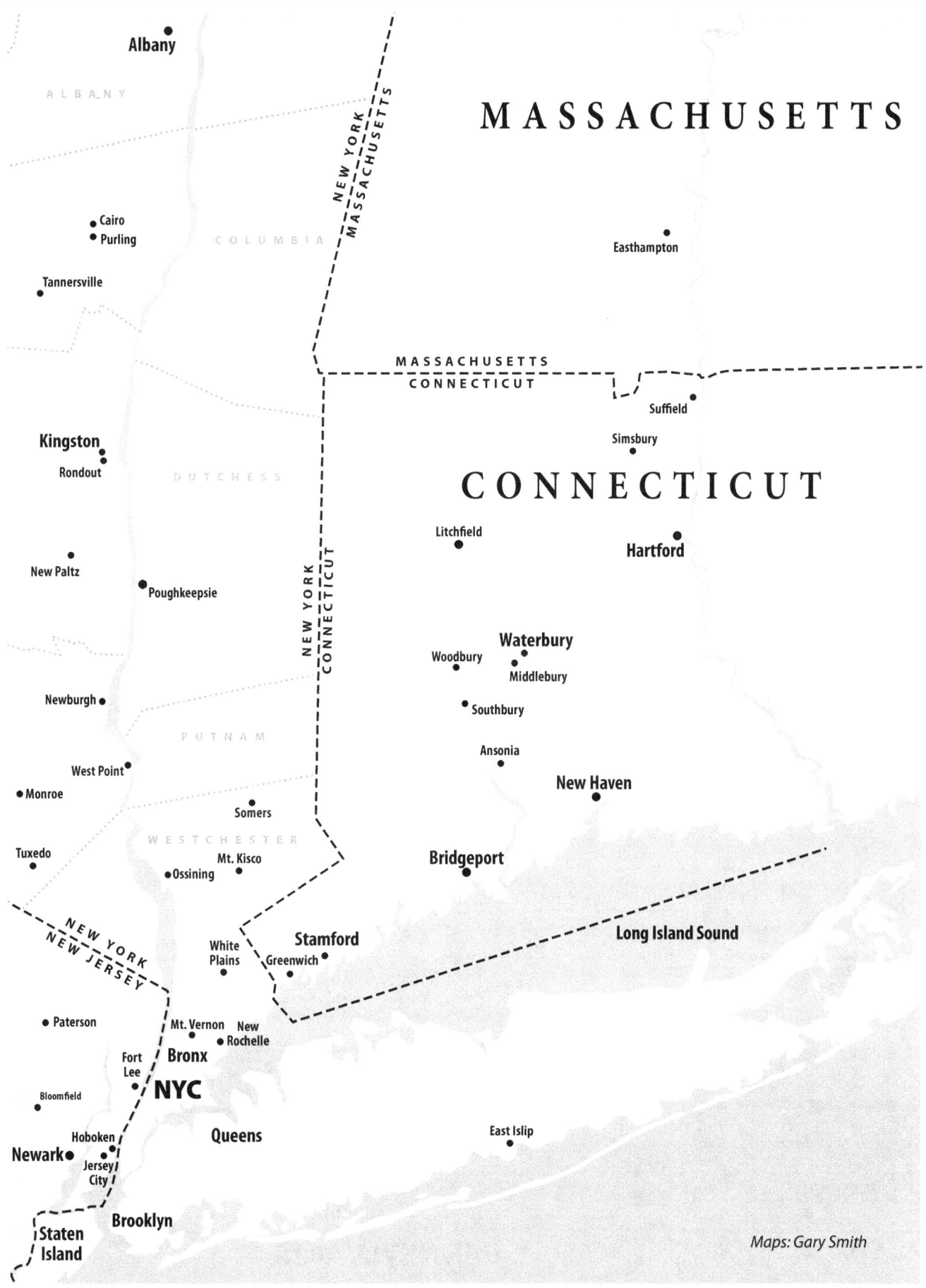

Maps: Gary Smith

VIII • FAREWELL TO ELDRED

Yulan, Washington Lake, and West Eldred

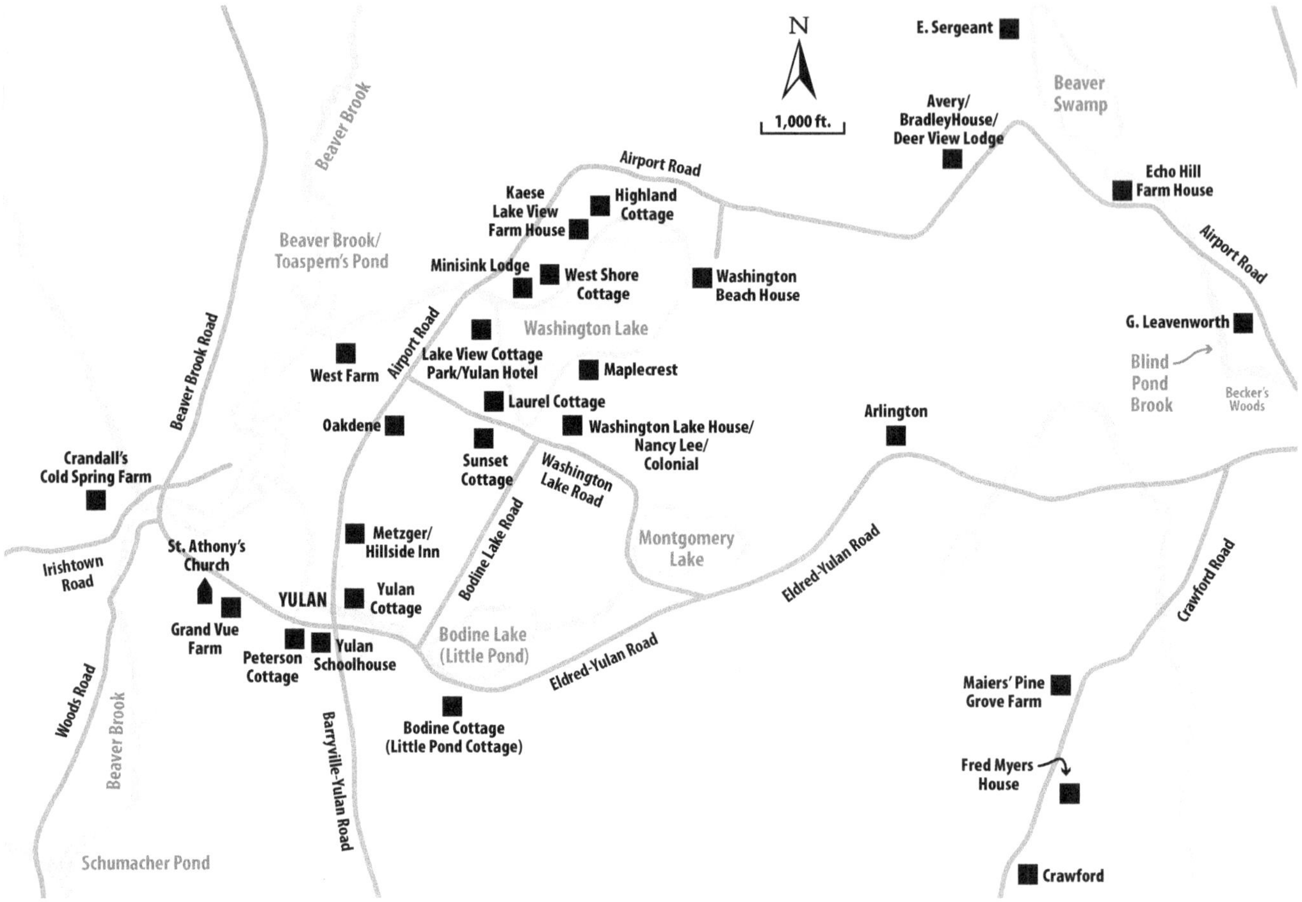

Corkscrew Road

Barryville, New York and Shohola, Pennsylvania

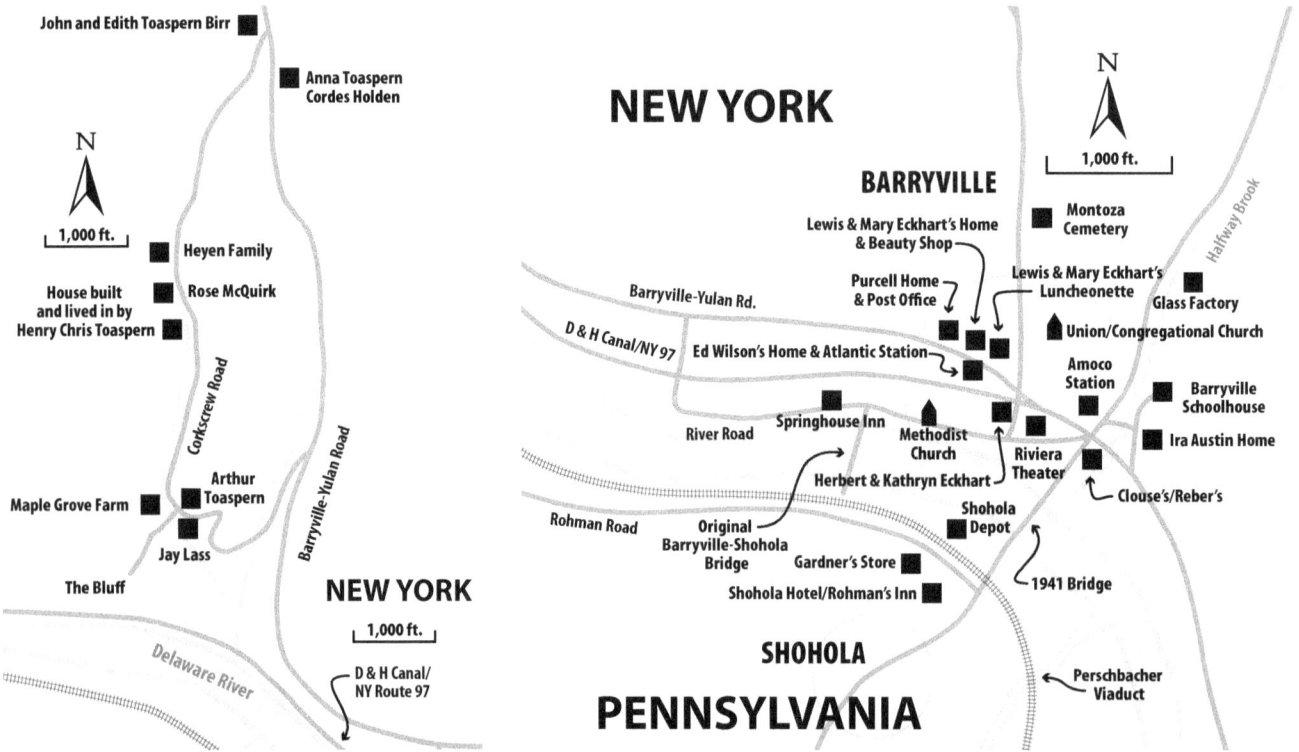

TOWN OF HIGHLAND'S BOARDING HOUSE LOCATIONS • IX

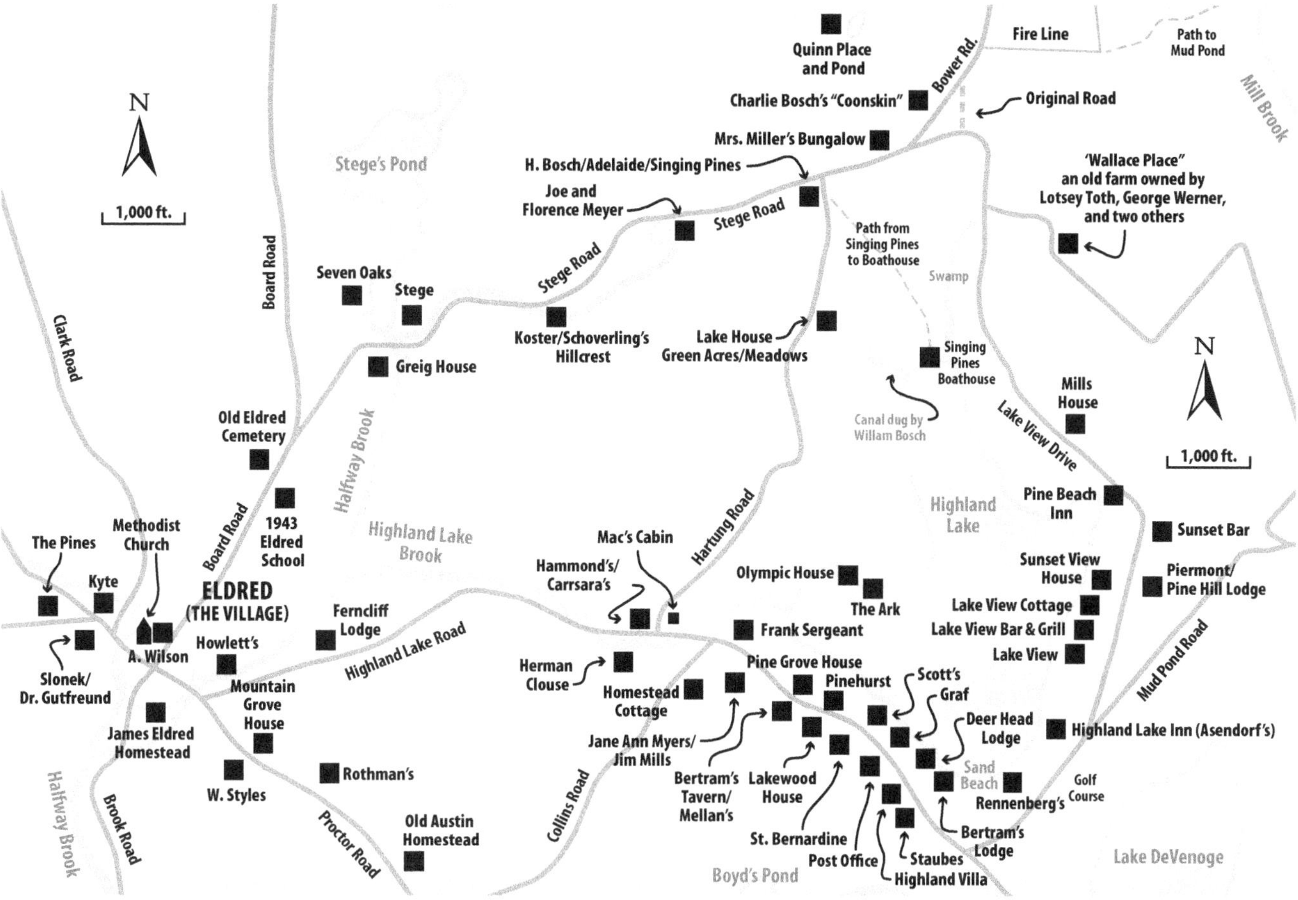

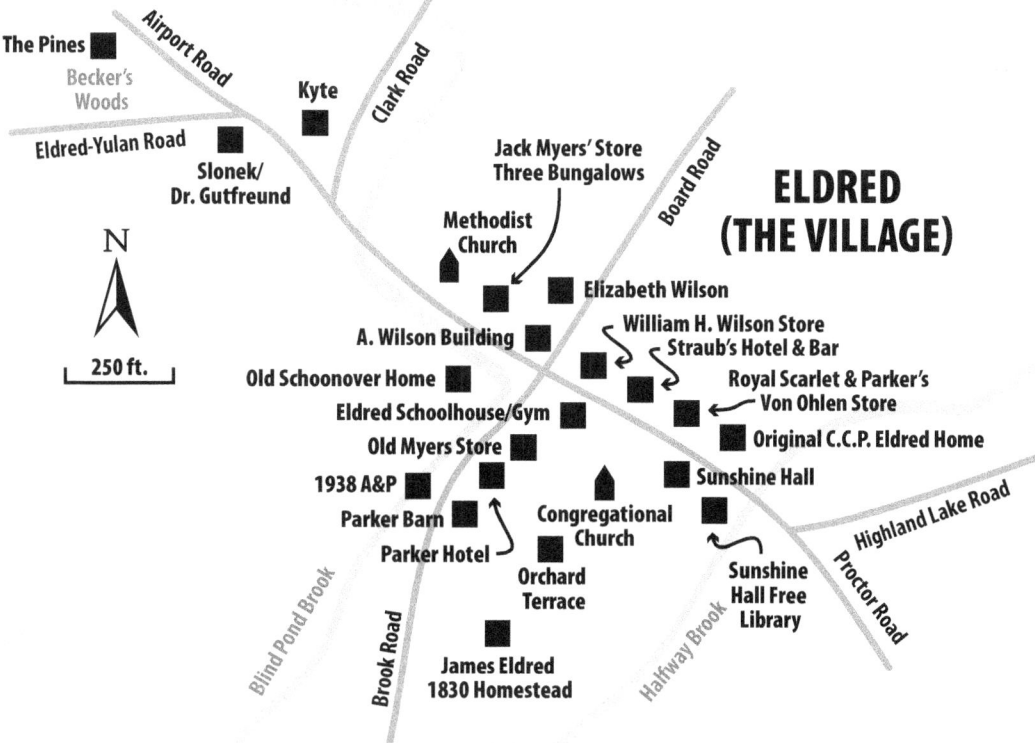

Maps: Gary Smith

Dedicated To:

The memory of my Austin grandparents,

Charles Mortimer Austin, 1865–1937

and

Jennie Louisa Leavenworth, 1880–1940

To Everything There is a Season

To every thing there is a season, and a time to every purpose under the heaven:
A time to be born, and a time to die; a time to plant, and a time to pluck up that which is planted;
A time to kill, and a time to heal; a time to break down, and a time to build up;
A time to weep, and a time to laugh; a time to mourn, and a time to dance;
A time to cast away stones, and a time to gather stones together; a time to embrace, and a time to refrain from embracing;
A time to get, and a time to lose; a time to keep, and a time to cast away;
A time to rend, and a time to sew; a time to keep silence, and a time to speak;
A time to love, and a time to hate; a time of war, and a time of peace.

What profit hath he that worketh in that wherein he laboureth?
I have seen the travail, which God hath given to the sons of men to be exercised in it.
He hath made every thing beautiful in his time: also he hath set the world in their heart, so that no man can find out the work that God maketh from the beginning to the end.
I know that there is no good in them, but for a man to rejoice, and to do good in his life.
And also that every man should eat and drink, and enjoy the good of all his labour, it is the gift of God.
I know that, whatsoever God doeth, it shall be for ever: nothing can be put to it, nor any thing taken from it: and God doeth it, that men should fear before him.—Ecclesiastes 3:1–14

Farewell to Eldred
Introduction for Book 3

"If you are raised on Halfway Brook water, you will always come back."—Bertha Boyd Wilson to Melva Austin, 1943.

Hawk's nest photo courtesy of Bill Ihlo.

Farewell to Eldred resumes the narrative of *Echo Hill and Mountain Grove*, in the year 1920.

Over a hundred years have passed since Charles Mortimer (Mort) Austin's grandparents James Eldred and Hannah Hickok first settled near Halfway Brook in what was then the Town of Lumberland.

Almost ninety years previous the Leavenworth grandparents of Jennie Austin had put down roots near Blind Pond Brook, west of Halfway Brook, in what became Eldred, in the Town of Highland.

Farewell to Eldred, the last book in the *Memoirs from Eldred, New York, 1900–1950* Series, continues the story of the Town of Highland's five hamlets: Eldred, Highland Lake, Yulan, Barryville, and Minisink Ford; and the descendants of the original settlers—relatives, friends, and neighbors—first read about in Book 1, *The Mill on Halfway Brook*.

When *Farewell to Eldred* commences in 1920, Mort and Jennie Austin, my grandparents, managed Mountain Grove House on the east side of Eldred. Jennie's father and three of her siblings resided at the Leavenworth's Echo Hill Farm House on the west side of Eldred.

In the next thirty years newcomers, often from New York City, join the story. Some run Boarding Houses which continued to be the backbone of the area's economy. Work was also available at the Erie Railroad, bluestone quarries, and private sawmills. And most unfortunately there is another war.

A phenomenal amount of photos, letters, postcards, diaries, old newspapers, and first hand stories from family and friends, tells the story of daily life—its joys and sorrows—in the Town of Highland from 1920 until 1950. Soon after 1950 my parents would depart from the home of my Hickok, Eldred, Leavenworth, Austin, and Myers ancestors.

Please join me as we return to Halfway Brook in 1920 and say a long farewell to the descendants of the original settlers and the newcomers in the Town we have come to love.

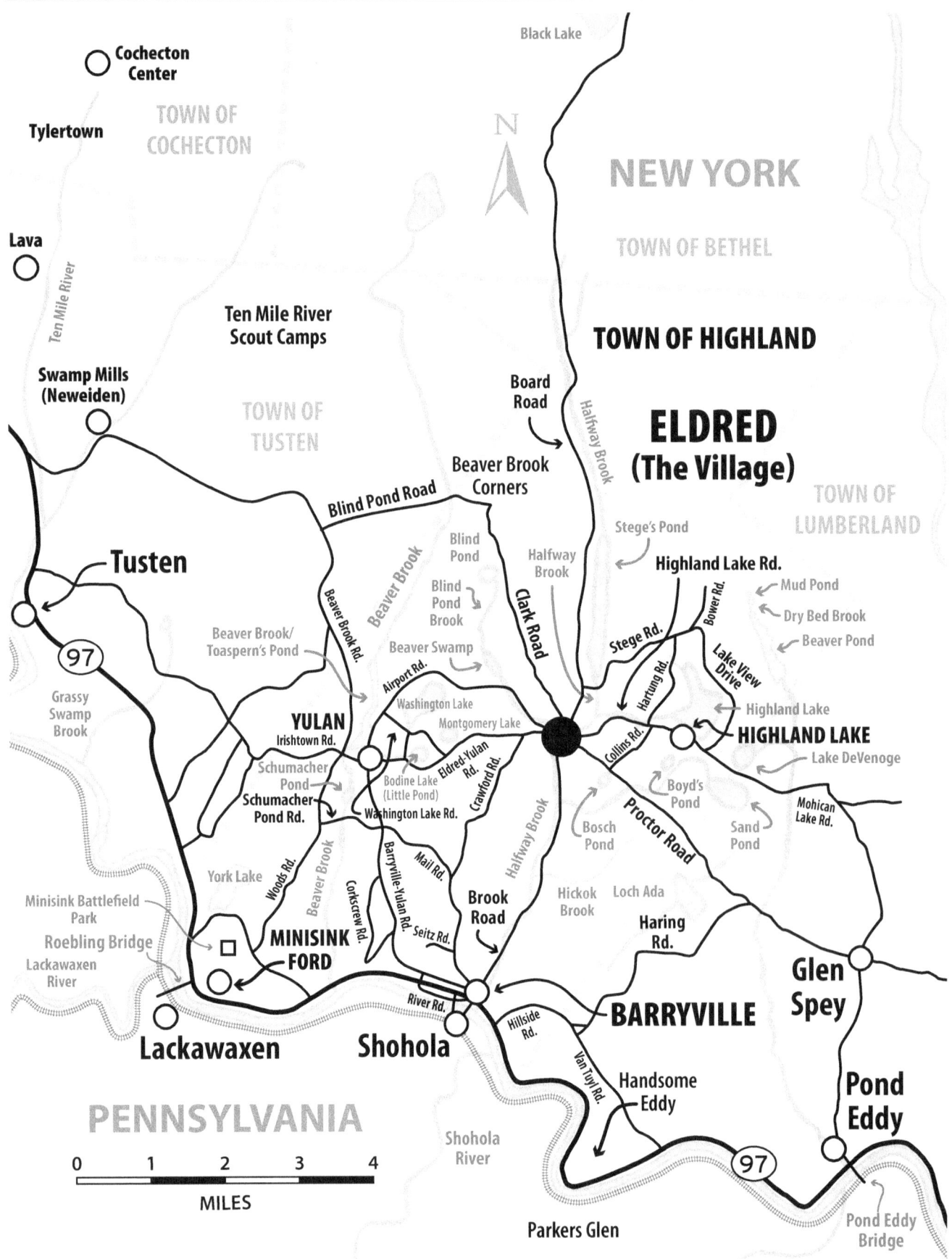

The Town of Highland's hamlets: Eldred (the Village), Highland Lake, Yulan, Barryville, and Minisink Ford; and nearby Towns of Bethel, Tusten, and Lumberland. Map: Gary Smith.

Chapter 1
Most Pleasant Time of All
The Town of Highland, 1920

I always looked forward to the time when school would be out, for I never was too fond of studying and, besides, my parents ran a small summer boarding house to which a few families brought their children year after year.

The summer season was the most pleasant time of all, for then the school bell did not interrupt the baseball games or the hours spent swimming with my city friends.—Arthur Austin.

Bob and Arthur Austin during the summer season. Photo courtesy of the Austin Family.

It was the last day of school and the start of the anticipated summer season in the picturesque Town of Highland, New York.

Arthur Austin, 7, his sister Elizabeth, 9, and his brother Bob, 5, walked home from the Eldred Schoolhouse near the southeast corner of Eldred. It was less than a half mile walk (Bob and Elizabeth probably ran) east towards the Austin Mountain Grove House.

Art, Elizabeth, and Bob Austin weren't the only children looking forward to a time uninterrupted by the school bell. Youngsters in the Town of Highland's five hamlets—Eldred, Highland Lake, Barryville, Yulan, and Minisink Ford—also had counted down the days to the best of all seasons and visits from their city friends.

They looked forward to fishing, boating, and swimming (called bathing); ice cream socials; church bazaars; fourth of July sparklers and fire crackers; catching lightning bugs; making slingshots; playing baseball; and countless other summer delights.

The adults were geared up for summer visitors. Reservations had been made ahead of time. (Some families continued to vacation in Highland for two and three generations.)

Ice had been cut and packed in sawdust in the winter months and stored in the ice house for the summer. In the spring the gardens had been planted as many of the boarding house owners also farmed—so there was fresh produce for the guests.

The Boarding Houses sprinkled among the rolling hills, lakes, and rivers of the Town of Highland, provided the perfect setting for a summer retreat. They also supplied a foundation for the community's economy.

The out-of-town guests (both sportsmen and vacationers), mostly from New York City, stayed in boarding houses near or on large bodies of water on either the east or west side of the town; or along the Delaware River.

On the east side of town was hand-shaped Highland Lake, and the nearby hamlets of Highland Lake and Eldred (where the Austins lived); and Glen Spey in the Town of Lumberland.

This is the view the Austins had on their way to school. Eldred Schoolhouse on the left. Von Ohlen's store on the right. In the middle: Charles Wilson's and later Arthur Wilson's. Jack Myers' store after Wilson's. Slonek's House is on the hill. Photo courtesy of Chuck Myers.

Fish-shaped Washington, Montgomery and Bodine Lakes were on the west side of town—close to Yulan and Eldred's west side (where the Austin's Leavenworth relatives lived).

Barryville or Minisink Ford Houses were situated on or close to the Delaware River.

Summer Houses and some townsfolk had telephones. It would be a few more years before electricity would arrive in the Town's Houses and homes.

Original and New Owners
Some of the boarding houses had been in the area since around 1880. In the next 27 years, new families (each with their own story) would move to the area. The Frey, Hensel, Theuer, Pankow, Hainzl, Bertram, Lorphelin, and Mellan families would purchase and run established boarding houses. Several would be renamed.

Though brochures and ads touted each House as the best, there didn't seem to be any rivalry. Owners helped each other out. If there was no vacancy, guests were referred to a nearby location.

Quite a number of folks met or would meet their future bride or groom during the summer at the various boarding houses.

Running a boarding house was an incredible amount of hard work, shared by the family and hired help, as well as children who carried water and helped with the dishes. But that still left lots of time for the youngsters to play.

Austin's Mountain Grove House
Art, Bob, and Elizabeth's parents Mort and Jennie Leavenworth Austin ran Mountain Grove House, a three-story boarding house on Proctor Road. Their Homestead Cottage on Collins Road had burned down around 1915 and they had moved to Mountain Grove House, the same house Mort and his brother Lon built around 1893.

As he had for many years, Mort picked their summer guests up at the lovely Shohola Railway Station in Pennsylvania, across the river from Barryville.

Post Offices and Schools
Each of the five hamlets: Eldred, Barryville, Highland Lake, Yulan, and Minisink Ford, had a Post Office. Since mail was not delivered to homes, residents picked their correspondence up

Barryville Schoolhouse. Photo courtesy of Linda Guenther Anderson.

On the right is the Eldred Post Office in the Parker Hotel around 1920. In the middle of the photo is William H. Wilson's Store on the northeast corner of Eldred. Postcard of Aida Austin courtesy of Mary Briggs Austin.

at the local Post Office, which was (and continued to be) a general meeting place for news and gossip.

Postmasters were still required to have the same party affiliation as the U.S. President. Emily Parker Stevens, Eldred's Postmaster in 1920, left when Warren Harding became president in 1921. Mr. Sparks, a Republican, served as Postmaster until 1933, when Emily Stevens returned as the Postmaster. (My father Art Austin would work for Mrs. Stevens in the 1930s.) When Emily Stevens was Postmaster, the Post Office was housed in the Parker Hotel that her father James Y. Parker had built around 1900.

Barryville, Yulan, and Eldred each had a two-room schoolhouse and at least one general store. Main shopping continued to be in Port Jervis, New York—even into the 1950s and 1960s. The scenic, winding Hawk's Nest Road on the way to Port Jervis, was not yet paved in the 1920s. Barryville, Eldred, and Highland Lake had at least one gas station.

Congregational and Methodist
In 1799 Isaac Sergeant helped establish what became the

Mary Horton Bosch with her children Herman Jr. and Marjorie on Hawk's Nest Road around 1923 when the road was not yet paved. Photo courtesy of Victoria Kohler.

The Congregational Church in Eldred was built in 1835 when Felix Kyte was the pastor. In back on the right is Abel Myers' Orchard Terrace. Photo courtesy of Chuck Myers.

Barryville Glass Factory, Dam, and workers around 1920. Photo courtesy of Ed Wolff.

Eldred Congregational Church. Descendants of Rev. Isaac and his wife Mary Richards Sergeant resided in the Town of Highland in 1920. As did several relatives of Felix Kyte.

Rev. Felix Kyte was the well-respected pastor when the Eldred and Barryville Congregational Churches were built in 1835.

Five years earlier Mr. Grace and Mr. Street, Methodist circuit riders, had preached every two weeks in the Town of Lumberland. In 1859 the Methodists built a church in Eldred. Later, Barryville and Pond Eddy each had a Methodist Church.

St. Bernardine Catholic Church in Highland Lake and St. Anthony's Catholic Church in Yulan were conveniently located for summer boarders. Shohola, Pennsylvania was home to both a Lutheran and a Catholic Church.

Families Who Settled by 1850
The Mill on Halfway Brook introduced us to many families who settled in the Town of Highland (originally Lumberland) by 1850. Many of those families were represented in 1920. Some of the surnames included: Eldred, Barnes, Crawford, Myers, Mills, Clark, Gardner, Sergeant, Kyte, Austin, Bradley, Boyd, Collins, Owen, Parker, Tether, Dunlap, Horton, Leavenworth, Quick, Van Tuyl, Hallock, Wilson, West, and Wells.

Town of Highland Occupations
Boarding houses were the main "industry" in the area, but there were still sawmills (belonging to Harry Wormuth, John Love, and others) and bluestone quarries which needed workers. The Erie Railroad employed many men.

The Barryville Glass Factory

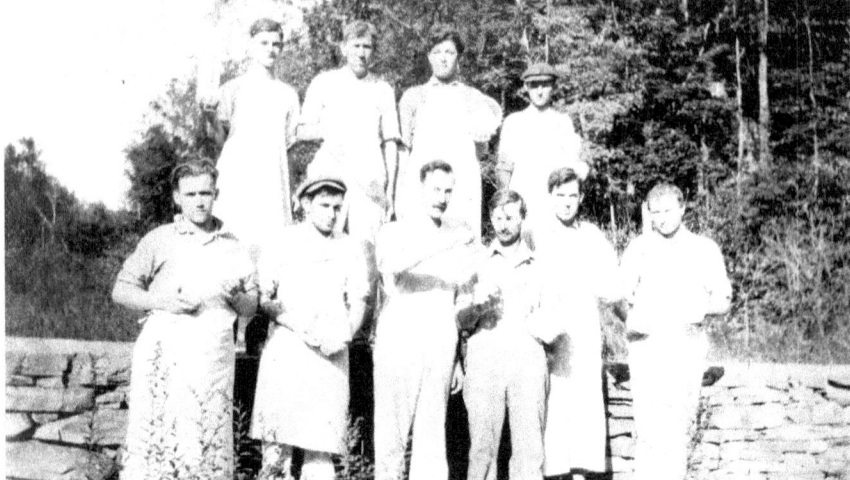
Glass cutters top row: George Liebla, Pat Palmer, Albert Wolff, Norm Wolff; bottom row: Harold Quick, John van Eastenbridge, Howard Pelton, Irving Quick, Frank Wolff, and an unknown man. Photo courtesy of Ed Wolff.

William H. Gibbs and the Barryville Glass Factory

William Henry Gibbs learned the glass cutting trade as an apprentice at the leaded crystal factory in White Mills, Pennsylvania, beginning in 1882. From there, he traveled to New York, Pittsburgh, Wheeling, West Virginia, Toledo, Ohio, and Corning, perfecting his craft. By 1895 he had formed a partnership with Irish immigrant Michael J. Kelly, operating a plant in Honesdale under the name of Gibbs, Kelly & Company. By 1909 Gibbs was operating a plant in Hawley [Pennsylvania] and in 1910 built the Barryville enterprise.

The two-story wooden structure on Halfway Brook in Barryville was powered by the stream and employed about fifteen workers, who etched, engraved and cut glass blanks supplied by Libbey and other manufacturers. Punch bowls, salt and pepper shakers, nappies, stemware, and many other types of glassware were cut and polished there. Gibbs sold the plant to Krantz & Sell Company in 1912 and it operated through the 1920s.

The late Austin Smith, longtime Highland Town Historian, remembered when the plant was operational, and often related stories about the glass shop, which employed many of the men in his neighborhood, including his father, Edward.

Barryville had fallen on hard times after the closing of the D&H Canal and the demise of the timber industry. The local economy was heavily reliant on the shop and the shop was heavily reliant on the weather, since sufficient rainfall was necessary to keep the stream running high enough to run the wheel.

"The plant was run by a water-powered turbine," Smith once recalled, "and that meant it was dependent upon the water level of Halfway Brook, which varied quite a bit, depending on the weather and the time of year.

"One day, the plant manager comes to the workers and tells them that he was shutting down the plant because the water level of the brook

Water going over the dam beside the Barryville Glass Factory. Photo courtesy of Linda Guenther Anderson.

had dropped so low, and they were all going to be laid off until it rained enough to raise the stream.

"Needless to say, that didn't sit too well with the boys, so they got the idea that they could go up to Highland Lake, where Halfway Brook originates, and take a couple of boards off the dam there, to let more water over it. That raised the level of the brook up enough that the plant could operate even without the rain. By the time the plant manager figured out what had happened, it was too late to do anything about it."

Although he only operated the Barryville shop for two years, William Henry Gibbs spent most of his life in the cut glass industry. He was a talented craftsman, and his work is highly prized by collectors to this day. In his 1965 book, American Cut and Engraved Glass, Albert Christian Revi notes that "on November 7, 1899, a design patent for a beautiful cut glass bowl was registered by William Henry Gibbs of Honesdale, Pennsylvania. The pattern consists of three large brilliantly cut rosettes with panels of bright cut buttons arranged four in a panel between the rosettes.

"The bottom of the bowl is decorated with another large and brilliantly cut rosette." It is not clear whether Gibbs had any of these patented bowls produced while he operated the Barryville shop.

By 1930, the Barryville Cut Glass Shop had closed, and the building disappeared some time after that.
—John Conway, Retrospect, Sullivan County Democrat, July 14, 2006.

Side view of the Barryville Glass Factory. Photo courtesy of Linda Guenther Anderson.

Spring House Garage near the Spring House owned by Chris and Meta Meyer during a major flood time in the 1920s. Photo courtesy of Ed Wolff.

employed some 15 local people. Earl Palmer (who also was the bridge tender for the Barryville and Pond Eddy bridges) was a polisher and his wife Kate worked in the Glass Factory Showroom showing glassware for sale. The glass cutters included Albert, Norm, and Frank Wolff, sons of Charles and Janette Kerr Wolff. (We first met the Wolff family in *Echo Hill and Mountain Grove.*)

The Delaware River

The Delaware River had been a major player in the growth of the Town of Highland. Spring and fall flooding continued to cause major disasters. The Barryville-Shohola Bridge built in 1856 still spanned the Delaware River.

Barryville-Shohola Bridge

By the 1920s some summer guests arrived at their favorite summer vacation place by automobile. Others still traveled by railway to the Shohola Station in Pennsylvania. After disembarking from the train, the vacationers crossed the Barryville-Shohola Suspension Bridge to get to the New York side. On the New York side, bridge access was near Chris and Meta Meyer's Spring House (which also had the Spring House Garage); and the James K.

Barryville, Delaware River. The house with the two A-shaped roofs was Clouse's Casino. It would become Reber's. Photo courtesy of Kevin Marrinan.

The Ira Austin House where Minerva Drake Austin, Minnie Austin, and Ed and Mabel Austin Smith and their son Austin Smith lived. Photo courtesy of Lillian Hainzl Wolff.

Handsome Eddy Farm would be owned by Albert Fischer and Fred Doeller. Photo courtesy of Marion Doeller Kistner.

Gardner residence.

James K. Gardner was a descendant of both the Eldred and Gardner families who had settled in the area very early in the 1800s. James K. and Ella Gardner's daughter Edna lived with them. Edna, a music teacher, would give piano lessons to children in the area for many years. More than one child would sit on the steps of Edna's home waiting for a lesson, concerned because they hadn't practiced that week in spite of Miss Gardner's instructions.

The Spring House on the Delaware River originally belonged to George Layman and was advertised in 1885.

There were two Clouse buildings in Barryville. One would become the Riviera Theater; the other, Reber's Restaurant. Ira Austin's old house was a short distance east of the future Reber's restaurant; just south of the Barryville schoolhouse. Ira's widow Minerva Drake Austin, 74, lived in the historic house with her daughter Minnie Austin; and daughter Mabel, her husband Ed Smith, and their son Austin Smith. Ed Smith worked at the glass factory.

Southeast of the Austin abode was another boarding house. Handsome Eddy Farm had a view of Handsome Eddy, the area where long ago logs had been collected and made into rafts, before their trek southeast on the Delaware River. Handsome Eddy Farm was originally owned by the Schwab family. In 1920 Agnes Schwab was the proprietor. Soon Albert

View from the Bluff of a train traveling along the Delaware River. Photo by Irwin Briggs courtesy of Mary Briggs Austin.

The Lass Home a quarter of a mile from Maple Grove House. Photo courtesy of Linda Guenther Anderson.

Fischer, a chef, and Fred Doeller would own and run the Schwab Boarding House.

West of Barryville, Minisink Ford also offered some boarding house options. In 1917 Charles and Martha Draxler from New Jersey had built their York Lake Mountain House on a large parcel of land in Minisink Ford.

On the way to Yulan from Barryville was the aptly named Corkscrew Road. On this twisting road was Maple Grove Farm, the Bluff (a tourist spot), and the homes of the Toaspern, Birr, Cordes, and Lass families (descendants of Henry Christian Toaspern); and the Heyens and McQuirks.

The Toasperns
Henry Christian Toaspern, the patriarch of the family, made cogs (which ground grain and seeds) for gristmills. He traveled west by train to find work, but did not get very far. Chris got off the train at Shohola, and ended up settling in the area. He built the cogs for the Barryville Gristmill which was constructed in 1895.

Chris also lumbered and built the home they lived in. He owned a large amount of land on Corkscrew Road (which included the famous Bluff). Chris had run Maple Grove Farm, which was south of the home he had built.

When Chris and Ida Heyen Toaspern died (1909 and 1912), their land was divided amongst their children: Edith Birr, Anna Cordes, Meta Lass, Arthur C. Toaspern, and Walter Cole Toaspern. These families play a part in this story.

John and Edith Toaspern Birr did not run Maple Grove but may have helped. He was a carpenter and she was quite deaf. Walter built them a house on the Yulan-Barryville Road. Across the road was a smaller boarding house owned by Anna (Toaspern) Cordes' family which Edith may have helped with at times.—Linda Guenther Anderson.

John and Meta Toaspern Lass' children: Jay, Charles, Helen, and Harry. Arthur C. and Emma Rueger Toaspern's sons: Royden Arthur and Walter (Bub) Toaspern.

Walter Cole Toaspern would

Barryville Gristmill was built in 1895. Henry Christian Toaspern built the cogs used to grind grain and seeds. Photo courtesy of Linda Guenther Anderson.

Maple Grove dog near one of the buildings at Maple Grove House. Photo courtesy of Linda Guenther Anderson.

soon marry Emma Straub, daughter of Fridolin and Juliana Straub, owners of Straub's Hotel in Eldred. Walter and Emma Straub's children Frances and Ed have a role in this narrative.

Yulan was less than three miles north of Maple Grove Farm.

Yulan Boarding Houses
Yulan had so many guests from New York City that the Four Corners of Yulan—which housed a Post Office and Souvenir/Tourist store—was dubbed Times Square for its New York City counterpart. Summer guests had vacationed in several of the hamlet's nearby Summer Houses in the 1880s.

Justin Bodin(e) had advertised his Little Pond Cottage on Little Pond (Bodine Lake) in 1880. In 1920 Henry's son and his wife, Henry and Blanche Bodine, were proprietors of Bodine's Cottages.

William Owen's four-story Oakdene was first advertised around 1900. William and Phoebe Middaugh Owen's children: Pearl, Basil, and Russell. Pearl was married to Fred DeFeo Sr. They

1920 Halfway Brook News

1920 Town of Highland Occupations

Blacksmith, boarding house owner, book keeper, brass worker, bridge keeper, carpenter (bridgework and houses), chauffeur, clergyman, dairy farm worker, doctor, dog kennel keeper, dress maker, electrician, automotive engineer, farmer (including at least one woman, Margaret Greening), fireman, garage mechanic, worker at hat factory, house keeper, ice plant worker, periscope maker, general laborer, hotel keeper, IRS collector, lawyer, librarian, mail carrier, driver, clerk, embossing for a manufacturer, stone masonry, musical instructor, nurse, officer on sailing vessel, druggist at pharmacy, railroad worker (carpenter, signal man, switchman, trackman), lumber worker (sawmill worker, log cutter, edger, engineer, laborer, lumberman, lumber truck driver, millwright, sawyer, superintendent of lumber mill, wood chopper), seamstress at underwear factory, servant, shoemaker, worker at steel corporation, store keeper, merchant, student, trucking teamster, telegraph or telephone operator, truck driver, waitress, and watchman.—*1920 Town of Highland Census.*

1920 Baseball

- Baseball was a popular sport. The Town of Highland would become the home of the Barryville Braves.

1920 Marriages

- Stella Boyd married Stoddard Van Etten.
- Bertha M. Hill, daughter of Thomas and Alice Sergeant Hill, married George Ely Eldred, son of Herbert and Eliza Post Eldred.
- Morgan Sergeant married his second wife Alice Spiers.
- Justina Schoonover, daughter of Rowlee and Emily B. Schoonover, married S. Deyo Hull.
- Hazel Alice Leavenworth married

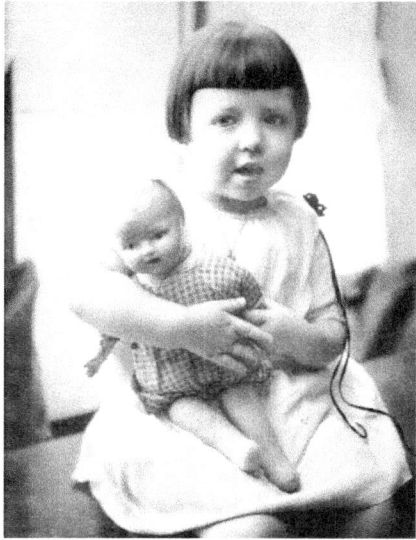

Stella Clark, daughter of Ernest and Eunice Hallock Clark. Photo courtesy of Vernon Clark.

Eugene Charles Koenig in Colorado.
- Raymond Myers married Gladys (Jake) Hill.

French Memorial Certificates

- Monticello, N.Y., March 14, 1920: presentation of the French Memorial Certificates of those who died in France in WWI. This seems to have included McKinley Austin.

1920 Births

- Stella Adelaide Clark born to Ernest and Eunice Hallock Clark in Tylertown.
- Eleanor Mildred Myers born to Charles C. and Elizabeth Ferguson Myers.
- Martin David Myers Jr. born to Martin D. and Mary Fee Myers.
- Clifford M. Hulse born to Chester and Catherine Hulse.
- Charlie Kerr born to John G. and Katherine Greening Kerr.
- Emily Christene Stevens born to Howard and Emily Christene Parker Stevens.
- Laura Margaret Briggs born to Irwin and Myrtle Crabtree Briggs.
- Raymond Clouse born to Fred and Emma Clouse.

1920 Deaths

- Tom K. Collins, 1844–1920.
- William Owen, 1857–1920.
- Charles Wilson, 1853–1920.
- Fridolin Straub, 1863–1920.
- Helen Bradley, 44, wife of Atwell L. Bradley, died of tuberculosis. Surviving: two sons, a stepson and her husband; sister Mrs. J. Guenther of Shohola, and one brother and two sisters in Germany. Buried in Eldred.
- Cora Sisson Eldred, wife of Lewis Laforde Eldred, died during the Spanish influenza epidemic. Lewis was left with 10 children also sick with the Spanish flu. Lewis moved to Honesdale.
- Helen Horton, 14, died at her home in Eldred after a month's illness. She was the daughter of Walter David and Cleta B. Myers Horton. She had always lived in Eldred where she attended the public school and the Congregational Church and Sunday School. The surviving relatives are her parents, two sisters, Bessie and Theo, and two brothers, Walter J. and LeRoy. —*Republican Watchman Jan. 23, 1920, p. 5.*

Elizabeth Myers on the left. Daughter Eleanor third from left. Photo courtesy of Timothy C. Rizzuto.

William and Phoebe Owen's charming Oakdene. Photo courtesy of Pam Fischetti DeFeo.

lived in New York City with their young daughter Alice. William Owen, a postman, died in 1920.

In 1920 Edith Miller Kalbfus managed Highland Cottage, a large hotel on Washington Lake which had been in existence since the 1890s.

Kaese's Lake View Farm on Washington Lake was first owned by Edward Prange in 1886.

Atwell Bradley's Park Hotel on Washington Lake was originally Lake View Cottage. Atwell's second wife Helen died of tuberculosis in 1920. He was left with three sons to care for: Clifford, George, and Clarence.

Atwell's sister Viola and her husband Abel Hazen ran Laurel Cottage, south of Atwell's Park Hotel, near the southern tip of Washington Lake's fishtail.

To the east, on the other side of the fishtail, was Washington Lake House which Joseph Tether had advertised in 1885. Joseph also seems to have built Washington Beach Hotel northeast of his Lake House. Joseph and his wife Anne moved to Hawley, Pennsylvania, around 1915. Anne died the next year. Their son Walter, his wife Meda, and their son Ivan, 14, lived north of Barryville in 1920. Perhaps for a few years Walter hired someone else to run the two Tether Houses. Walter would eventually operate Washington Beach House. The Washington Lake House would have new owners.

Walter's sister Jessie and her

Isaac M. and Joanna Bradley holding their Avery grandchildren, Laura, Beatrice, and Arthur, around 1909. Photo courtesy of Mary Ellen Busse Mackinder.

husband Isaac N. Bradley lived in Brooklyn, with their son Clifton.

Isaac M. Bradley

The Bradley patriarch, Isaac M. Bradley, lived in the original Bradley House on the west side of Eldred. The Bradleys had settled in Eldred by the 1840s. In the early 1880s the Bradley House was advertised as a boarding house.

In 1920 Isaac M. lived with his daughter Norah and her husband Erwin Avery. The Averys had run the boarding house since the death of Isaac's wife Joanna, in November 1909. Isaac's half brother John Bradley also lived with the Averys. The Avery children: Laura, Beatrice, Arthur, and Gladys play a part in this story.

Isaac M.'s daughter Lottie and her husband Charles Colville ran Woodland Cottage in Barryville.

The Bradleys were long time neighbors of the Leavenworths.

Sherman S. Leavenworth

Echo Hill Farm House continued as the residence of Sherman S. Leavenworth, his daughter Charlotte, a teacher, and sons Truman and Martin. Daughter Christina lived in the Bronx with her husband Anthony Hirsch who had a bakery there.

Sherman's daughter Jennie Austin lived on the east side of Eldred with her family.

Sherman's son Garfield Leavenworth and his wife Ella Sergeant and their three children: Clara, Clinton, and Anna, lived in Easthampton, Massachusetts. They would soon move back to Eldred where many of Ella's Sergeant relatives still lived.

The Sergeants of Eldred

In 1797 Reverend Isaac Sergeant, a Congregational minister from

1920–1921 Boarding Houses and Owners

Barryville
- Spring House, Christian Meyer
- Woodland Cottage, Colville
- Handsome Eddy, Agnes Schwab
- Maple Grove Farm
- Anne Toaspern Cordes
- Torwood Farm, Kerr
- Delaware View Inn (Side Hill), Eggers and Rothenback
- Riverside Cottage, Louis and Mildred Warshauer
- Rose McQuirk

Yulan
- Bodine's Cottages, Henry and Blanche Bodine
- Grand Vue, Bornstein
- Park Hotel, Atwell Bradley
- Cold Spring Farm, Crandall
- Washington Beach Hotel, Henri Darriensecq. Impts.; elec. light. Bathing, fishing, dancing free. First-class cooking: $18 up.
- Laurel Cottage, Abel Hazen
- Lakeview Farm, Kaese
- Highland Cottage, Edith V. Kalbfus. On Washington Lake. Dancing, bathing, fishing, garage, $16–20 week.
- Minisink Lodge, M.A. McCormick, Homelike, on Washington Lake; bathing, fishing.
- Max and Minnie Vonderhorst
- West Farm, Theodore West
- Oakdene, Phoebe Owen
- Pine Grove Cottage, Frank Owen

Minisink Ford
- York Lake Mountain House, Draxler

Eldred
- Bradley House, Avery
- Echo Hill Farm House, Leavenworth
- Fred and Mary Myers
- Ferncliff Lodge, Jackson Myers, soon to be Bischof's
- Seven Oaks, Beck

Barth's Highland Cottage, Eldred. Photo courtesy of the Town of Highland.

- Greig' House
- Straub Hotel/Bar, Juliana Straub
- Parker Hotel, Emily Parker
- Mountain Grove House, C.M. Austin

Highland Lake
- Highland Lake Inn, Henry Asendorf
- Highland Cottage, Peter and Mary Barth
- Lake Side Cottage, Mary Wait
- Lake House, Bosch
- Piermont Hotel, Boyd
- Otto and Amanda Hartung
- Sunset View House, Catharine Loerch and Matilda Loerch
- Stephen A. and Charlotte Myers
- Mills House, Elizabeth Mills
- Lake View, Charles Myers
- Anton and Mary Rennenberg
- Mountain Lake House, Staubes

- Hillcrest, Chris and Freida Koster
- Theodore and Thekla Kassner

Rooms in Farmhouse to Let
Furnished for housekeeping; week, month or season; on the mountains; beautiful view; fishing, boating, bathing; lake on property; Sullivan County, Box 54, Eldred, N.Y.
—*Brooklyn Daily Eagle,* August 1, 1920.

Brooklynites and Long Islanders Enjoy a bit of Country in Sullivan County
At Yulan there has been no letup in the season since it began in earnest, about the middle of July. Although many guests went back the end of July, August vacationists are more than filling the places vacated.

Yulan: Bodine Cottages, Yulan Cottage, Park Hotel, and Highland Cottage.

Eldred: Bradley House, and Mountain Grove House.

At Highland Lake the fish are biting better than they did in previous years and many anglers are summering at the resorts to partake of their favorite sport.

Highland Lake: Sunset View, Mills House, and Park View.—*Brooklyn Daily Eagle,* August 8, 1920.

Washington Lake in 1920. Highland Cottage in the background. Photo courtesy of Kevin Marrinan.

Sergeant Descendant Photos

Sergeant Family photo, about 1911. Top row (standing) left: Charles Edgar Sergeant, his second wife Henrietta Halstead; Frank Roberts Sergeant, his second wife Anna Hull; Morgan Sergeant (a widower at the time); Alma Luella Sergeant Kelley, her husband Frank Kelley; Alvah Thomas Sergeant, his wife Margaret Clemens. Sitting on chairs: Isaac Sergeant, his wife Elizabeth Persbacher; Unita Jane Sergeant Livingstone (a widow); Phebe Owen Sergeant (a widow); and three unknown people. The man and woman closest to Phebe may be Thomas Hill and his wife Alice Sergeant. The people sitting on the ground are unknown. Photo courtesy of Alan Gothard.

Christianna (Chris) Livingstone. Chris was the daughter of William and Unita Jane Sergeant Livingstone. She and her husband William Flieger had a son William who was three in 1920. Photo Courtesy of Ron Flieger.

Several of the Sergeants were skilled carpenters. Morgan Sergeant working on the roof. Photo courtesy of Alan Gothard.

Alvah Thomas Sergeant, Charles MacKechnie, Morgan Sergeant, and Mr. Geisler, 1920. Photo courtesy Alan Gothard.

Ridgebury, New York, held services for the few settlers scattered along the Delaware River. Two years later Rev. Sergeant helped organize the Narrows Falls Congregational Church, which became the Eldred Congregational Church.

The Sergeants in Eldred were descended from Rev. Isaac and Mary Richards Sergeant's grandson Ethel Sergeant and his wife, Lettie Gardner.

Children of Alvah Sergeant and Isaac Sergeant (sons of Ethel and Lettie Sergeant) lived in Eldred or nearby in 1920.

Alvah and Phebe Owen Sergeant's children: Unita Jane Livingstone, Charles Edgar Sergeant, Alice Hill, Frank Sergeant (Ella Leavenworth's father), Luella Kelley, Morgan Sergeant, and Alvah Thomas Sergeant (who died in 1921).

Minnie Sergeant (daughter of Isaac and Elizabeth Persbacher Sergeant) had married Archie Myers. Archie and Minnie would be the parents of Chuck Myers.

Surnames of the Sergeant descendants included: Hill, Livingston(e), Flieger, Kelley, and Leavenworth. Several of the Sergeant men were skilled carpenters, including Frank Sergeant, father of Ella Leavenworth.

Starting in 1931, we hear more about the Sergeant family in Eldred from the diaries of Ella Sergeant Leavenworth.

There was at least one boarding house on Crawford Road on the west side of Eldred.

Crawford Road
Charles Fred and Mary Frances Bradley Scott Myers ran a boarding house on Crawford Road. Mary Frances was also a daughter of Isaac M. Bradley. She married

Fred Myers' Family. Mary Frances' grandchildren Bill and Dorothy Meyers standing. From left: Lottie Scott Meyers, Mildred Myers, Ada Myers, Fred Myers, and his wife Mary Frances Scott Myers (daughter of Isaac M. Bradley). Photo courtesy of Mary Ellen Busse Mackinder.

Fred Myers (a widower with children) after her first husband died. Fred and Mary's daughter Ada Wells was the only child living at home with them in 1920. Their son Bradley had died at age 12, when he caught diphtheria from boarders who didn't mention they had the contagious disease.

Mary Frances' daughter (from her first marriage) Lottie Scott was married to Bill Meyers Sr. and they had two children: Bill Jr. and Dorothy. Bill and Lottie would also run a boarding house. The Meyers family lived in Garfield and Ella's home in Eldred.

Joseph Maier and his adult children Julius and Annie Maier also lived on Crawford Road. Joseph rebuilt a smaller version of his Pine Grove House which had burned down in 1903. It is uncertain if he continued running it as a boarding house. Joseph was the father of Mary Maier, Wilhelm Bosch's first wife who had died in 1904. Many of Joseph Maier's Bosch descendants lived or would live in Highland Lake.

William and Victoria Simpson Parker, parents of James Y., William H., Elsie, and Andrew Parker. Photo courtesy of William H. Parker Jr.

Von Ohlen's store in Eldred. Photo courtesy of Ken Bosch.

From Barryville to Eldred

Mort Austin had been chauffering guests to and from the Shohola Station almost 30 years in 1920. From Shohola Mort drove to Barryville, and took Brook Road north past the Barryville Schoolhouse and the Barryville Glass Factory.

Almost four miles north of Barryville, Mort would pass through the village of Eldred. On the east side would be the Parker Hotel, the second one built by James Y. Parker. (The first one had become Straub's Hotel.)

James Y. Parker's widow Emily Christene Payne Parker still lived in the Parker Hotel. Her daughter Emily Christene Parker Stevens and her husband Howard also lived in the Hotel (which some years included a Post Office). Howard and Emily's delightful daughter Emily Christene Stevens arrived in the fall of 1920.

Emily Parker Steven's brother William and his wife Victoria Simpson Parker had four children: James Y., William H., Elsie, and Andrew Parker, who play a part in this account. William H. Parker, the son, would soon meet his future wife Eleanora Alston. For a short time Eleanora, a widow with three children, would run a boarding house in the triangle where the Eldred-Yulan and Airport Roads connected.

Set back behind the Parker

Emily Christene Payne Parker, Howard and Emily Christene Parker Stevens and Emily Christene Stevens. Photo courtesy of Christene Stevens Myers.

Barn, south of Abel Myers' Orchard Terrace House, was the home where Mort's grandparents James and Hannah Hickok Eldred once lived—near the sawmill on Halfway Brook.

Most likely Mort Austin had been born in that house built in 1830 by James Eldred. One room in Temperance Tavern (as the house was once called) was the Post Office. James Eldred was Postmaster from 1830 to 1850.

On the northwest corner of Brook and Proctor Roads was a structure built by Charles Wilson. Arthur Wilson's A&P would be housed in his father's building sometime in the 1920s.

The road to the west passed the Methodist Church (of 1859) and headed towards Leavenworth's Echo Hill Farm where Jennie Austin had grown up.

On the northeast corner of Eldred was the store of William H. Wilson, the brother of Charles Wilson. William and his wife Bertha Boyd had a son Forrest who was nicknamed Pat.

If Mort continued north of Eldred, on Board Road, he would pass the Eldred Cemetery on the left (west). If he took Stege Road

1920 World and National News

- The United States population topped 100 million in 1920.
- George Gershwin wrote *Rhapsody in Blue* and *An American in Paris*.

January 1920
- The Treaty of Versailles, which ended World War I, went into effect.
- Babe Ruth traded by Red Sox for $100,000.
- Prohibition (18th Amendment to the U.S. Constitution) January 17, 1920. Chicago's Al Capone would become a famous bootlegger.

February 1920
- Nazi Party born.

March 1920
- U.S. Congress refused to ratify the Treaty of Versailles and to join the League of Nations.

June 1920
- The Red Army retook Kiev from Poland.

July 1920
- Mexican Revolution: Pancho Villa signed his surrender on July 28.

August 1920
- Radio broadcast by Scripps' WBL, predecessor of WWJ, Detroit.
- The 19th Amendment gave women the right to vote.

September 1920
- Wall Street bombing.

At noon, on September 16, 1920, a bomb in a horse wagon exploded in front of the J.P. Morgan Bank. It killed 38 and injured at least 300. Shortly before the bomb went off a warning note was placed in a mailbox at the corner of Cedar Street and Broadway. The FBI rendered the file inactive in 1940 without ever finding the perpetrators.—wikipedia.org.

- American Professional Football League formed with 11 teams; Jim Thorpe president.

- The first domestic radio sets in the U.S. A Westinghouse radio cost $10.

October 1920
- League of Nations headquarters moved to Geneva, Switzerland.
- KDKA in Pittsburgh, Penn. received its license October 1920. It went on the air as the first U.S. licensed commercial broadcasting station.

November 1920
- Republican Warren G. Harding won Presidential election.

1920s
- Flappers, Charleston, bob haircut, marathon dancing, mah-jong, Yahtzee, crossword puzzles and pole-sitting.

1920s Musicians
- George Gershwin, Al Jolson, Louis Armstrong, Irving Berlin, Eddie Cantor, Duke Ellington, Jelly Roll Morton, Fats Waller, Cole Porter, Rudy Vallée, Bela Bartok.

1920s Filmmakers, Entertainers
- Cecil B. DeMille, Alfred Hitchcock, Buster Keaton, Charlie Chaplin, Roscoe "Fatty" Arbuckle, Mary Astor, Ethel, John, Lionel Barrymore, Joan Crawford, Douglas Fairbanks, Greta Garbo, Dorothy Gish, Lillian Gish, Harry Houdini, Tom Mix, Will Rogers, Mary Pickford, Gloria Swanson, Rudolph Valentino.

1920s Sports Personalities
- Babe Ruth, Ty Cobb, Lou Gehrig, Jack Dempsey, Knute Rockne, Johnny Weismuller.

Some 1920s People in the News
- F. Scott Fitzgerald, A.A. Milne, Ernest Hemmingway, Wilder, Tolstoy, Kahlil Gibran, George Bernard Shaw, T.S. Eliot, Joyce, Aldous Huxley—writers.
- Pablo Picasso, Salvador Dali, Georgia O'Keefe, Piet Mondrian—artists.
- Albert Einstein, Sigmund Freud, Nikola Tesla, Alexander Fleming, Niels Bohr, Robert Goddard—scientists.
- Frank Lloyd Wright—architect.

World and National News taken mainly from wikipedia.org timelines, and from WWII Day by Day, published by Dorling Kindersley Limited, 2004.

Actress Lillian Gish would vacation in Eldred. Photo in Public Domain.

Lillian Diana Gish (1893–1993)
Lillian Gish was an American stage, screen and television actress whose film acting career spanned 75 years, from 1912 to 1987. She was a prominent film star of the 1910s and 1920s, and one of America's best-loved actresses.—*wikipedia.org*.

When Lillian, her sister Dorothy, and their mother moved to New York, their next door neighbor was Gladys Smith. Gladys later took the stage name, Mary Pickford.

Lillian Gish vacationed in Eldred in the "bungalow" Guido Bischof built specially for her. This "bungalow" is part of the story in 1933–4, though Lillian herself was not part of the anecdote.

Sunshine Hall Free Library built around 1920. Photo courtesy of the Sunshine Hall Free Library.

Charles Myers' Lake View House courtesy of Timothy C. Rizzuto.

at the Y, he could view the Greig's magnificent house, the Beck's stately Seven Oaks, and pass by the property of Ed and Kate Stege.

The Greig household in 1920: Kate Greig, 60, a widow; her son Robert, 29, a civil engineer; her daughter Isabel (Belle) Kelso, 27, a widow; and her son Bennett Greig, 25, a general carpenter. A relative Sarah Greig, 87, also lived in the huge, grand Greig House. Belle would soon meet and marry Edward Grotecloss Jr.

Ed Grotecloss Jr. went to Cornell University where he met Belle's uncle and that is how he came to Eldred. He loved to hunt for anything, especially ducks. There were plenty of ducks on Mill Pond because the Greigs had planted wild rice that ducks are fond of at the north end of the pond.—Ed Grotecloss III.

East Eldred
At Eldred's Four Corners, Mort Austin turned right (southeast) onto Proctor Road. On the right or south side was the schoolhouse, the Congregational Church, Sunshine Hall, and what would soon be the Sunshine Hall Free Library. Mort and Jennie had received a letter from Fred Lewis requesting funds for the new building (see p. 439).

On the north side (left) of Proctor Road (at Eldred's Four Corners going east) was the William H. Wilson Store and next the Straub Hotel owned by Fridolin and Juliana Straub. Their five children: Fridolin (Fred) Jr., Julia, Emma, Rosa, and Ida, play a part in this story. (Fridolin Sr. died in 1920 and his wife Juliana then ran the Hotel.)

The Von Ohlen Store was after Straub's. Then the home (next to Halfway Brook) where Mort's uncle C.C.P. Eldred had once lived.

C.C.P. Eldred, son of James Eldred, had become Postmaster in 1850 and the Post Office had also been in his home. A grandson and his family, Herbert and Eliza Post Eldred and their children may have lived in the house in 1920. They would move the next year.

Hillcrest House Owners

When Henry Koster bought the Marquet Farm, it consisted of 80+ forested acres and about 20 cleared acres, a two-story log cabin with the logs set vertical, a barn, and outbuildings with a brook in back.

The boarding house built in 1888 consisted of a main section with full cellar, 24' × 36', a 16' × 18' wing on the south side, and a porch all along the north side. The first floor contained a 14' × 24' parlor, central hall and stairway, a 14' × 24' dining room, and a 16' × 18' kitchen. There were nine bedrooms on the second floor; and six on the third floor.

Henry Koster, a skilled woodcarver, carved furniture in New York City during the winter, returning each spring to help his wife and son Christian with the farming and operating the Hillcrest. During the 1890s, about 20 acres from the bottom to the top of what is now known as Stege's Hill was sold to allow installation of a waterline to provide water under high gravity pressure to the Sidwell, later Stege, complex at the bottom of the hill.

The Kosters continued operating the Hillcrest and farm. But while Henry Koster was bringing a load of hay down the very steep slope across the brook, the leather strap that pulled the brakes against the rear wheels broke, the wagon over rode the horses, and Henry Koster was killed.

The Hillcrest was purchased by Frederick Schoverling in September 1920 and he immediately had renovations made. He added a larger wrap-around porch in the front, a much larger kitchen in the rear, converted the former kitchen into an office, installed a 32-volt DC Delco electric system with electric water pump, electric lights in every room and converted a second floor bedroom into a bathroom with sink, claw foot tub, and flush toilet.—Ken Bosch.

Bosch Pond Herman built around 1925. In winter it was a place to skate and get ice for the summer. In summer it was a place to swim. Photo courtesy of Victoria Kohler.

Herman's brother Ed Bosch driving guests around at the Lake House. Photo courtesy of Ken Bosch.

After crossing Halfway Brook, Proctor Road continued southeast; Highland Lake Road branched off to the northeast.

Mort Austin continued a short distance after the Y to his Mountain Grove House across the road from Walter Styles' house.

Walter Styles, 58, a librarian, his second wife Georgia Clark, 30, a teacher, and Walter's elderly parents Charles and Sarah Styles lived in a home built by Frank Sergeant—perhaps with help from his brothers. Frank did all the beautiful trim work inside.

Proctor Road continued past the house where Mort grew up on the old Austin homestead. His sister Aida Austin lived in one of the houses and his brother Lon lived in the one next to her.

Herman and Mary Horton Bosch would soon be country neighbors of Lon and Aida Austin.

Herman and Mary Horton Bosch
In 1920 Herman and Mary Horton Bosch lived in a small boarding house on their property at the corner of Hartung and Stege Roads, near Highland Lake. The place was built by Wait and Boyd.

Herman Bosch was a plumber and dairy farmer. Their son Herman was 1. Herman and Mary had quite a house full: Mary's sister Maude Kalin and Maude's children (ages 2–8): Robert, Eugene, Harold, and Kenneth Kalin; Mary's mother Anne Elizabeth Horton, 60, and Mary's brother John Horton, 27, a teamster on a dairy farm.

Herman and Mary sold the boarding house, and moved to their Proctor Road property (southeast of Collins Road) in 1923, on what was Dan Hallock's property.

Albert Schoverling seems to have bought Herman and Mary's House and called it the Adelaide. At some point Otto Seel would buy the Adelaide house and rename it "Singing Pines."

Around 1925 Herman would build Bosch Pond on his Proctor Road property. In the summer the Austin children (and others) went swimming in the Bosch Pond. In the winter Herman cut ice blocks and stored them in the ice house he built. He sold the ice in the summer. On the same property Herman, at some point, established a dairy, a sawmill, and a permanent home.

Herman and Mary Bosch would become like family to their near neighbors Aida and Lon Austin, and play a major part in this story in the early 1940s.

Proctor Road continued on to Glen Spey, after Collins Road.

Collins and Highland Lake Road
Collins Road connected Proctor and Highland Lake Roads. East of the Collins and Highland Lake Roads T, was the original home of Jennie Austin's grandmother Jane Ann Van Pelt Myers. The two-house building was owned by Jennie's uncle Gus Myers in 1920.

A short way west of the T was Hartung Road which went north and led to the Bosch Lake House.

The Bosch Relatives
Wilhelm Bosch and his second wife Mary van Eastenbridge retired from running Lake House sometime in the 1920s. Wilhelm's son Ed Bosch took ownership of the boarding house at some point, but did not run it on a day-to-day basis.

When I got out of the army in August 1919, Webb LaBarr and I cut logs for John Love until the snow got so deep, 30 inches in the woods. So I went to New York, got a job building pool tables and bowling alleys for Wagner and Adler Company in New York City.—Ed Bosch.

Wilhelm and Mary Bosch's daughter Tina, 14, and Wilhelm's son Ralph lived with them. Ralph would marry Paula Schreib in 1922. Paula's parents Otto and Maria Schreib may have been operating the Lake House. They had for several summers starting around 1915.

Mary Bosch's daughter Florence van Eastenbridge and her husband Joe Meyer ran the Lake House sporadically. They had their own place a bit northwest of Lake House and took in boarders for several years. Joe and Florence Meyer's children in 1920: Raymond, John, and Anna. (Joe Meyer was a brother to William Meyers Sr. who lived on the west side of Eldred.)

Wilhelm's son Charlie Bosch and his family lived on his 300 acres of property off Bower Road.

Soon after Bower Road, Stege became Lake View Drive, turned south, then made a slight curve to go around Highland Lake's little finger. Just before the little finger was the Mills House which had been there since 1840.

Lake View, Highland Lake Inn
Lake View Drive continued on along the east of Highland Lake and passed Charlie Myers' Lake View House and Henry Asendorf's Highland Lake Inn.

Charlie Myers, Jennie Austin's first cousin, had been a union carpenter in Westchester, but

1920 Hickoks, Eldreds, Leavenworths, Austins, Myers

Some descendants of families referred to in *The Mill on Halfway Brook*:

Asa and Esther Hinman Hickok
The Hickok descendants (except for the Austins) seem to have moved to Middletown, N.Y. or Pennsylvania by 1920.

James and Polly Mulford Eldred
In 1920 there were still a few descendants of James and Polly Mulford Eldred in the area: Maria Gardner Calkin, 87, Susan Gardner, 55, Kate M. Gardner, 56, James K. Gardner, 59, Edna Gardner, 30, Ann Eliza Gardner Cuddeback, 76, and Herbert L. Eldred, 52, and his family.

Herbert Eldred's daughter Bertha was married to Norman Myers. Herbert's son George Ely married Bertha Hill, in April 1920. Herbert's mother Marietta West Eldred Hoatson (widow of George W. Eldred), was a second time widow of Samuel Hoatson. Marietta lived with her stepdaughter Elizabeth Hoatson Clark Wilson.

Lewis Laforde Eldred was a recent widower with ten children. The family lived in Pennsylvania. Within ten years Lewis' son Harvey Eldred would live in Minisink Ford. Lewis' brother John Franklin Eldred and his wife Minnie Sears and their son Orvis R. Eldred lived in Pennsylvania as did Frank Eldred, father of Lewis and John.

Augustus Alonzo and Phebe Maria Eldred Austin's known descendants are listed under Ralph and Fanny Knapp Austin.

Augustus and Phebe's children (the Eldred-Austin Cousins) were half cousins of Lon, Aida, Dory, Ell, and Mort Austin, descendants of James Eldred and his second wife Hannah Hickok.

Ralph and Fanny Knapp Austin
The known descendants of Ralph and Fanny Austin included the children of William Henry and Mary Ann Eldred Austin just mentioned; and the children and grandchildren of the Eldred-Austin Cousins: Mortimer B. and Mary Millspaugh Austin; Archie and Rand Austin Paton; and Thomas J. and Addie Austin Thompson. Dr. Alonzo Eugene Austin (son of cousin Rev. Alonzo Eugene Austin) owned the Austin houses and much of the original Austin property, which Lon and Aida Austin would rent.

Mortimer B. and Mary Millspaugh Austin; and their son Charles Augustus Austin, his wife Mary Johnson, and their children Alden and Mabel Austin, lived in Middletown, New York.

John Mortimer Austin (son of Mort B. and Mary Millspaugh) was married to Mary Hoatson (sister of Elizabeth Hoatson Clark Wilson).

Dorothy Paton, 2, was the daughter of Archie R. and Mabel Slagle Paton, and granddaughter of Archie and Rand Austin Paton.

Augustus Austin Thompson and his wife Gertrude Cotton were the parents of Elward Austin Thompson, 17, Gertrude R. Thompson, 13, and Elbert Paul Thompson, 2. Augustus (Gussie in *Aida Austin's 1881 Diary*) was the son of Thomas J. and Addie Austin Thompson.

Bradley/Leavenworth Relatives
Isaac M. Bradley's daughter Amelia Bradley Leavenworth Gregory lived in Colorado. Her daughter Lottie Leavenworth was married to Len Andeway. Amelia's daughter Hazel Leavenworth married Eugene Koenig in 1920.

Amelia and her second husband Eber Gregory had two children: Charlie and Nora Gregory. Amelia, Hazel Koenig, and Lottie Andeway play a part in this story.

Jane Ann Van Pelt Webb Myers
Charles and Charlotte (Lottie) Myers Darling lived in Binghamton, N.Y. Their daughters: Agnes Curtiss, Ida Whitmarsh, and Edith Sears.

Henry Webb (Jane Ann's grandson) and at least two of his children were living in 1920.

returned to run the Lake View when his parents George W.T. and Martha Mills Myers died in 1917. Charlie built a "Cottage," a six-bedroom, four-square house, to handle the overflow from the Lake View, in 1920.

Charlie's first wife had died in childbirth in 1914 leaving Charlie with son Harold and his newborn son, George. (Henry and Belle Boyd Asendorf adopted George.)

In 1916 Charlie had married Elizabeth Ferguson. Charlie's son Harold lived with them. In April Charlie and Elizabeth's pretty daughter Eleanor was born.

Charlie's brother Martin D. Myers was a chauffeur for Asendorf's Highland Lake Inn—getting guests at the Shohola Station. Martin and his wife Mary Fee had two young daughters.

Boyd's Piermont Hotel, across and north of Lake View Cottage, had been there since at least the turn of the century. It would change names and ownership in later years.

Henry Asendorf had become the owner of Highland Lake Inn around 1916. The huge boarding house was on the property that Mary DeVenoge Miller had inherited from her father Dr. Leon DeVenoge.

Louis and Mary Miller had run the Highland Lake Inn since 1900. "Hard times fell upon the couple in 1916, and Mary left a portion of the estate and the inn buildings to the care of a neighbor, Henry Asendorf, in exchange for the management of her financial affairs, personal well-being, and funeral expenses." —John Conway, The deVenoge Family and its Legacy are Rediscovered, Retrospect. *Sullivan County Democrat, January 13, 2006.*

Perry and Mary Murray Parker Schoonover Descendants

Perry Schoonover had first married Ann Mary Austin, Ralph and Fanny Austin's daughter. Ann Mary died young and Perry married Mary Murray Parker, a widow with three children: George, Laura, and Kate Parker. Perry and Mary Parker Schoonover had two children who lived: Emma (Waidler) and Daniel Rowlee Schoonover.

Aida Austin called all five children "cousin." They have been and continue to be part of this story.

Laura Parker Britt had three young children when she died at the age of 32. Mary and her daughters Kate Parker and Emma Waidler helped to raise Laura's daughters, Ada and Kitty Britt. (John Britt raised their son.)

By 1920 Kate Parker and Emma Waidler were great-aunts. Kitty and her husband William James had a son Elwood (born 1911); and Ada and her husband Arthur Wood had a daughter Norma (born 1915).

Aida Austin continued to correspond with Emma Waidler. Around 1920 Emma and her husband Will sold their farmland at Green Farm in Cairo, New York, but kept 100 acres. Some of the property would continue in the family. Emma became a housekeeper for Mrs. Blauvelt, a wealthy woman who owned a big house on Catskill Creek near the Hudson River. Emma and Will may have lived in a caretaker's house on the Blauvelt property.

Daniel Rowlee Schoonover
Rowlee Schoonover whose lively raft story started off *Echo Hill and Mountain Grove,* couldn't find work when he returned from World War I. He took a job as a car mechanic for six months in Haiti.

When Rowlee returned, he and his wife Emily Banner and their children: Justina, William, Ethel, and Mary Murray Schoonover (born 1916),

Back left: Justina Schoonover (soon to be Hull) and Ada Wood; children: Elwood James and Norma Wood. Photo courtesy of Richard James.

stayed with Arthur, Ada, and Norma Wood, while he looked for work. Mrs. Douglas, wife of Dr. Douglas (the minister who was impossible to work for), wanted Rowlee to be her husband's chauffeur again. There had been 12 drivers hired during Rowlee's absence. An agreement was made that was acceptable to Rowlee's wife Emily. Rowlee would chauffeur for the next 18 years.

Rowlee and Emily Banner Schoonover's daughter Justina married Solomon Deyo Hull in 1920.

Justina had attended Cooper Union but did not finish. She met the handsome sailor S. Deyo Hull looking quite dapper in uniform and got a Mrs. instead of a BFA. They spent their honeymoon on the farm in Cairo. —John D. Hull.

George and Kate Parker, Emma Waidler, Ada Wood, Kitty James, and Deyo and Justina Hull are part of our story. We'll meet Rowlee and his wife Emily Banner Schoonover, in Eldred, around 1940.

Myrtle Crabtree Briggs and Harry Irwin Briggs would move to Barryville in 1934. Photos courtesy of Mary Briggs Austin.

The golf course built on Louis and Mary DeVenoge Miller's land plays a part in World War II.

Irwin and Myrtle Briggs
Irwin and Myrtle Briggs (my maternal grandparents) play a role in this story, but not until 1934, when they arrive in Barryville with their four children. (Irwin would pastor the Eldred, Pond Eddy, and Barryville Methodist Churches.) Irwin and Myrtle attended seminary at Taylor University in Indiana, in 1920. Their first child Laura was born in July.

Job Possibilities
Through the years Mort Austin's friend Charles Dassori repeatedly tried to find a job elsewhere and often coaxed Mort to join him. In August Charles wrote Mort again about job possibilities.

Chas. Dassori, Scranton, Penn., to Mort Austin, Eldred
August 30, 1920
Dear friend Mort,
Well here I am again Mort, in Scranton, Pa. Say Mort, do you think there is any prospects of my securing a position in Yulan, N.Y.? I do not like it here in Scranton, Pa., and Gussie (his wife) said she is willing to go to Yulan if there is any way of my making a living.
I am also stuck on Eldred. I think between you and I, we ought to be able to dope out some kind of business to go into and make good. Have you anything in mind Mort we could venture in?
California is a pretty state of what I have seen. The climate there is just grand.
Mort, I have the name and address of the Land Commisioner for Atchison, Topeka, and Santa Fe in Kansas. Mr. Howell Jones has charge of the sale of land at very reasonable prices and terms—from Kansas to Arizona.
How is things going with you Mort? How is the family? We are all enjoying good health, thank God, and trust you are all doing the same. Trusting to hear from you soon. I remain, Your true friend, Chas. S. Dassori

But Mort Austin, who had worked in Kansas with his brothers Lon and Ell, and then gone to seminary in New Jersey for a year, remained in Eldred.

Eldred (Halfway Brook Village) was where Mort's grandparents Ralph and Fanny Knapp Austin had settled 80 years previous; and James and Hannah Hickok Eldred over 100 years. It was where Sherman Buckley and Charlotte Ingram Leavenworth, Jennie's grandparents, had settled at least by 1835; and Martin D. and Jane Ann Van Pelt Myers had built their home in the early 1850s.

Mort and Jennie continued to run Mountain Grove House. Their oldest son McKinley Austin had died in France during World War I. In 1920 Raymond Austin attended Business School at Eastman Gaines in Poughkeepsie, New York. Bill Austin, 16, worked as a wood chopper. Art, Elizabeth, and Bob, who we met at the beginning of this chapter, were still in school. Mort's brother Dory, a farmer, lived with them.

In the early 1930s Mort would no longer chauffeur guests back and forth from Shohola. He would retire his horses.

Mort Austin driving to get boarders at Shohola. Photo in Austin Collection.

Chapter 2
The First Real Sorrow
The Austins, 1921–1924

My oldest brother was killed in the closing months of World War I, and although I was too young to fully realize the loss, the grief that it caused my parents and older brothers made an indelible impression on my mind. A few years later, my sister, the only girl among five remaining children, died during a tonsillectomy.

Leaving for school in the morning with my sister as well and happy as ever and coming home at noon to be told that she had died, was the first real sorrow that I had known.—Arthur Austin.

Elizabeth Austin sitting on her mother Jennie Austin's lap. Photo in Austin Collection.

Some years of our lives contain times of deep heartache. Such was 1921 for Mort and Jennie Austin and their sons, Raymond, Bill, Art, and Bob.

Thursday, March 24, Dr. Smith arrived at the Austin home to take out Elizabeth's tonsils. The operation took place on the family's kitchen table.

Still perhaps recovering from the death of their son McKinley in France during World War I, one can imagine the deep sorrow of the family when the unthinkable happened—Elizabeth died from a "heart clot following an operation for tonsils and adenoids."

Elizabeth, the only daughter of Mort and Jennie Austin, died four days before she turned 10.

Mort Austin wrote down his thoughts. Many friends offered sympathy.

Mort Austin's Letter
March 24, 1921
Our only daughter died on the 24th day of March, 1921. My dear Elizabeth. I did not know how much we loved you until now. I hope that it will not be long before I meet you in Heaven. I know you are happy there and I hope through the goodness of God, in a few years to be with you.
Father

A. Gedeone, to Mr. and Mrs. Austin, Mountain Grove House
March 28, 1921
My dear Mr. and Mrs. Austin,
These are just a few words of sympathy for your loss. Yet we trust in a God who we know does all for the best. So trusting in the loving memory of our dear one, we think of her as a cherub in God's home.
With sincere and heartfelt sympathy, Anna Gedeone

W.M. Baumgartner, Madison, N.J., to Mr. and Mrs. C.M. Austin
March 31, 1921
My dear Brother and Sister in Christ, I have learned from Mr. Ether of your very great sorrow.

What a blow is yours, so sudden and scarcely expected! My heart goes out to you in sympathy and prayer.

I realize my human words are powerless to bring consolation; and yet I want you to know that I have not forgotten you and I am feeling for you in your grief and praying that the everlasting arms may be beneath you.

*Yours in deepest sympathy,
William M. Baumgartner*

The Collins family had been friends of the Austins since the mid-1800s when James and Isabella Collins and their children: Annie, Robert, and Thomas lived on Collins Road near to Mort's folks, Henry and Mary Ann Austin. Thomas had died, but Robert, a Methodist pastor, continued to keep in touch.

Robert Collins, Madison, N.J., to Mort and Jennie Austin, Eldred
April 7, 1921
My dear Mort and Mrs. Austin,
We learned by telephone from your pastor of the sudden and unexpected death of your dear and only little daughter Elizabeth, while undergoing an operation for

Elizabeth Austin. Photo in Austin Collection.

the removal of her tonsils. This was an unusual occurrence.

You surely have our deepest sympathy and prayers in this very sad bereavement. I know you both will greatly miss Elizabeth, but especially your wife, an only daughter, and in her youth. She must have been a great help and comfort to her mother in the home, and growing more necessary every day and more of a companion as well. How sad. But such is life often and its experiences with all its terrible losses and failures.

Our only consolation in such sorrows are the assurances of the word of the dear Lord, "Like as a father pitieth his children, so the Lord pitieth those who trust in him."

"Cast thy burden on the Lord and he shall sustain thee, he shall never suffer the righteous to be moved."

These are words for us to think upon in such a great sorrow as yours. May they give your aching hearts relief and rest.

*Cheer up amid the gloom. Lizzy is safe. With best wishes,
Sincerely yours, R.B. Collins*

Guenther and Vonderhost Deaths
The year 1921 was also a year of terrible sadness for Freida Meyer Guenther and Louise Vonderhorst.

Joseph Guenther, a butcher, had a meat market in Lackawaxen and Shohola where he worked with his friend Fritz Suessman.

On a foggy March morning as Joseph and his dog Spot crossed the railroad tracks to the Shohola Depot, they were struck by an Erie train. Joseph, 35, died about two weeks later as a result of his injuries. Spot also died.

Joseph's wife Frieda was

Memorial Day 1921

Veterans of the Civil War and Residents Remember the Dead

Impressive memorial exercises were held in the Shohola, Barryville, and Eldred Cemeteries on Memorial Day.

The Veterans of the Civil War, Valentine Hipsman of Shohola; Theodore West of Yulan; and David Crandall and Sherman Leavenworth of Eldred, formed a guard of honor and identified the graves of their comrades; the school children decorated the graves of our heroes with flowers, after which the G.A.R. service was rendered. Jay Lass sounded taps. A community memorial service was held at Sunshine Hall, Eldred in the evening. H.J. Rixton was chairman.

Program:
Overture: Orchestra

Star Spangled Banner and *Battle Hymn of the Republic*: community singing.

Invocation: Rev. Fidor Ether, Barryville; Rev. Balmer, Glen Spey.

Violin solo: F.A. Schwarz, Glen Spey.

Lincoln's Gettysburg Address: F.J. Lewis, Barryville.

Vocal solo: Mrs. Minnie Myers, Eldred.

Reading: Rev. Fidor Ether, Barryville.

Violin and Piano Duet: Franz Schwartz and Miss Beatrice Covart, Glen Spey.

Address: Hon. Guernsey T. Cross, Callicoon.

Mr. Cross gave a complete history of Decoration Day, now called Memorial Day. He laid special emphasis on the character of its observance and on our duty to perpetuate its memory by living for the country our war heroes made possible.—*Republican Watchman.*

now a widow with five children: Freida, 11, Edith Vera, 10, Clinton Joseph, 7, Helen Katherine, 6, and Viola, 2.

Louise and Eric Vonderhorst were building a boarding house up above Washington Lake when Eric, still in his twenties, died of typhoid fever. Louise Vonderhorst would raise their children: Carl, 6, Walter, 3, and Elsie, 1; and run Lake View Inn for at least another twenty years.

The Austin Siblings
Five of the ten Austin siblings were still living in 1921. Aida, Albert Alonzo (Lon), Mort, Henry Ladore (Dory), and James Eldred (Ell) Austin play a part in this account. Lon, Mort, and Ell had all worked on the Parmenter farm in Solomon, Kansas. Their sister Emma (Edith Emogene) Austin had moved to Solomon for her health, but died there of tuberculosis. Emma was buried in a nearby cemetery. Lon had also worked in California. But both Lon and Mort had settled back in Eldred.

Ell (James Eldred) Austin and his daughter Lillie Calkin
Ell Austin had married Emily Parmenter, the daughter of Henry Parmenter, the farmer he worked for in Kansas. Ell, Emily, their daughter Lillie, and Emily's son Henry (adopted by Ell), eventually moved back to Eldred. The family then moved to Bethel. By 1921 Ell and Emily Parmenter Austin were separated or divorced.

For a few years Ell was a wanderer looking for and finding odd jobs. His daughter Lillie Calkin, a teacher, and her children: Robert Dale, 10, and Dorothy, 7 (in 1921), exchanged letters.

(You may remember the newsy letters of Lillie's friend Jennie Crawford Crandall in *Echo Hill and Mountain Grove*. Lillie and Jennie continued as best of friends, but there are only hints of Jennie in a few of the letters.)

Lillie, her husband Burt, and their children lived in Bethel, New York. Burt was a carpenter and built the houses that they lived in. Their home, farm, and the apple trees Dale planted were next to the property that would be the location of the Woodstock Music Festival in 1969.

Lillie taught grades one to eight in Bethel when her children were in the early grades. As Dale and Dot's teacher, Lillie was harder on them than the other children. They had to "toe the mark." Burt backed up Lillie and warned the children that they would be in big trouble if their mother sent them home from school. Which was the reason Dale didn't want to go home one day when he got in a wrestling match. He stayed in the swamp.

Emily Austin lived with her sister Sophorina, and later with her daughter Lillie, but not at the times when Ell Austin lived with Lillie's family.

Emily Austin was apparently a challenging person to live with. She seems to be a very different person than the one who wrote such endearing letters (which can be read in *Echo Hill and Mountain Grove*) to her husband Ell in the late 1880s; and later to Lillie in college. Dorothy (Dot) Calkin had some fond memories of her grandfather Ell Austin.

I grew up in Bethel and remember skating on White Lake. Grandfather James Eldred Austin lived with us at times. Grandpa told me I was his favorite granddaughter. I loved horses and loved to be outside with Grandpa

Joseph and Freida

Joseph and Freida Meyer Guenther's wedding photo taken in 1909. Photo courtesy of Linda Guenther Anderson.

Joseph Guenther Sr. arrived in the U.S. from Hamburg, Germany in the fall of 1903 on the *S.S. Fürst Bismarck*. He was 17 years old.

In 1909 Joseph married Freida Meyer. They would have five children. Freida became a widow in 1921 when Joseph and his dog Spot were struck by an Erie train on a foggy March morning. Joseph's meat market was bought by his friend Fritz Suessman who hired Louie Moniserra.

In happier March 1921 news, Charles Howard Lass son of John and Meta Toaspern Lass, married Veronica A. Campbell. Charles and Veronica's daughter Marion Helen Lass (born May 1922) marries Joseph's son, Clinton Joseph Guenther, in 20 years.

in the fields. I liked Grandfather, but he was kind of a stickler that girls' ankles had to be covered— you couldn't show your ankles.
—Dot Calkin Hale.

Ell Austin wrote for work

Christina Leavenworth Hirsch visited Echo Hill with her stepson Tony Hirsch Jr. Photo courtesy of Cynthia Leavenworth Bellinger.

Martin Leavenworth and his nephew Tony Hirsch Jr. Photo courtesy of Cynthia Leavenworth Bellinger.

in 1921 and received letters and brochures regarding picking peaches in North Carolina.

Seaboard Airline Railway Co., Aberdeen, N.C., to J.E. Austin
June 15, 1921
Sir,
 If you would care to work at peaches, you might write the Sand Hill Fruit Growers Association, Aberdeen.
 A great many cars of peaches are to be shipped from this section in the next 60 days and I am sure you could get work here as more help will be required. There are approximately 10,000 acres now planted in peach trees in the Sandhill section of North Carolina…Near 4,000 of those 10,000 acres will be bearing this year…conservative estimate of 700 car loads to be shipped. The average car contains 480 crates. Last year these sold for $3.00 per crate…

Coop Extension in Agriculture, Pinehust, N.C., to J.E. Austin
June 18, 1921
Dear Sir:
 We are needing quite a bit of help but not until the first of August in harvesting the peach crop and I believe there is a chance for you to get employment. You might write Mr. Thad S. Page, Secretary of the Fruit Growers Association, and see what he has to offer. Yours very truly, W.W. Wall, County Agent

More Sorrow for Mort and Jennie
Mort and Jennie experienced what must have been a repeat of sorrow for them when McKinley's body was shipped back to the States in September. A funeral was held at their home and he was buried in the Eldred Cemetery next to Elizabeth. The U.S. Government had offered to bring back the bodies of soldiers who had died and were buried overseas during World War I. It is curious as to who asked that McKinley's body be shipped back, as the family story had been that Aida Austin went over to France in 1923 specifically to bring the body back.

Augustus Myers Dies
There was yet another funeral for the Austin family to attend in October, when Jennie Austin's uncle Augustus "Gus" Waterman Myers, 65, died. Gus was the son of Martin D. and Jane Ann Van Pelt Webb Myers. His siblings Maria Leavenworth (Jennie Austin's mother) and George W.T. Myers had died before him. His sister Lottie Darling, 63, lived near Binghamton, New York.

Jennie Austin's Siblings
In the fall of 1921 Jennie Austin's sister Charlotte Leavenworth began teaching first through fourth grade at the two-room

Tony Hirsch Jr. drives in the country. Photo courtesy of Ric Schroedel.

1921 Halfway Brook News

Moved in 1921
- Eugene and Hazel Leavenworth Koenig moved to Milwaukee.
- Garfield and Ella Sergeant Leavenworth and their three children moved back to Eldred.
- Herbert Lincoln and Eliza Eldred moved to Middletown, New York.
- Lewis Laforde Eldred and his children moved to Honesdale, Pa.
- Katherine Hensel bought Yulan Cottage.

1921 Births
- Frederick Meyer born to Joseph and Florence van Eastenbridge Meyer.
- Mildred Briggs born to Irwin and Myrtle Briggs in Indiana.
- Daniel Deyo Hull born to S. Deyo and Justina Schoonover Hull.
- Everett Charles Frey born to Charles and Gertrude Frey.
- Clara Wolff born to Carl and Freida Kloss Wolff.
- John E. Myers born to Raymond and Gladys (Jake) Hill Myers.

1921 Marriages
- Charles H. Lass married Veronica A. Campbell in March.
- Walter C. Toaspern married Emma Straub.
- Earl Wells married Ada Myers.
- Charlie MacIntyre married Lena Hill.

1921 Deaths
- Elizabeth Austin, daughter of Mort and Jennie Austin, died in March.
- Joseph A. Guenther, husband of Frieda Josephine Meyer, died leaving Freida a widow with five children.
- Eric Vonderhorst died of typhus.
- Marietta West Eldred Hoatson died when she was visiting her stepdaughter Mrs. John Mortimer Austin. Marietta was buried in the Eldred Cemetery beside her first husband, George W. Eldred.

Earl and Ada Myers Wells. Photo courtesy of Berniece Wells Haas.

Irwin and Myrtle Briggs with Mildred and Laura. Photo courtesy of Mary Briggs Austin.

Independent Republican, Nov. 8, 1921.
- Alvah T. Sergeant, 1873–1921.
- Jean Charles Rouillon, husband of Blanche Olga Malinge, died in 1921, in France. He was a baker by trade and the grandfather of Gisele Rouillon who marries Jim Leavenworth.
- Martin van Buren Austin, 1835–1921, was a brother of Ira Austin.
- Bennett Greig died in October from an infection after an amputation.
- Evaline S. Dunlap, 1883–1921.

- Augustus "Gus" Waterman Myers, 1856-1921, was the son of Martin D. and Jane Ann Van Pelt Myers.
- Mortimer McKinley Austin
  The body of private McKinley Austin, who died in France October 14, 1918, arrived at the home of his parents, Mr. and Mrs. C.M. Austin, in Eldred on Saturday. The funeral was held at his home in Eldred at 1:30 on Wednesday. Rev. Mr. Ether, pastor of the Barryville M.E. Church, officiating.—News article, September 16, 1921.

Eugene and Hazel Leavenworth Koenig moved to Milwaukee in 1921. Photo courtesy of Marialyce Koenig Kornkven.

Around 1922, Kate Parker and Danny Hull, son of Deyo and Justina Schoonover Hull. Photo courtesy of Richard James.

Charlie and Lena Hill MacIntyre. Photo courtesy of Alan Gothard.

Gladys Myers and her friends. Gladys top left. Photo courtesy of Joan Austin Geier.

Eldred schoolhouse.

Charlotte lived with her father Sherman Leavenworth and brothers Martin and Truman Leavenworth. Charlotte and Jennie's sister Anna Leavenworth lived in E. Islip, New York, where she was apparently a math tutor. In the early 1900s Anna had taught in both the Yulan and Eldred schoolhouses.

The fourth Leavenworth sister, Christina Hirsch, lived in the Bronx with her husband Anthony and stepson Anthony Hirsch Jr. Christina played the organ in a large New York City Church. Anthony Sr. had a bakery which would close down later, partially due to the depression.

Christina and Charlotte had always been very close. The Hirsch family continued to visit at Echo Hill Farm House, which still had summer boarders.

Christina and Anthony Sr. had first met at Echo Hill. There are photos of Christina, Tony Jr., and Martin Leavenworth during visits to Eldred. (Martin's mental ability was that of a five-year-old due to a high fever he had as a baby. The family continued to care for him as we will see in Ella Leavenworth's diaries.)

Gladys Myers

It was the *Twenties* and Gladys Myers and her friends were enjoying those years. Gladys was the daughter of Edwin and Mabel Owen Myers. She had three brothers: Raymond who was married to Gladys (Jake) Hill, Clifford, and Orville who would marry Leversa (Lee) Beisel.

Gladys had helped at the Austin's Mountain Grove House for some time and had become like family to the Austins whose sons were a bit of an enigma to her. Though Raymond teased her unmercifully, they continued to be friends and kept up a correspondence when he was in school. She would be the future Mrs. Raymond Austin.

1922

It was a new year. Jennie Austin wrote to her son Raymond in early 1922. He worked on Governor's Island, one-half mile from the southern tip of Manhattan Island.

Gladys Myers and her friends. Gladys is in the middle. Photo courtesy of Joan Austin Geier.

Cute Teenie Stevens stands beside Jennie Austin and quite a stack of lumber. Photo courtesy of Christene Stevens Myers.

Jennie Austin, Mountain Grove House, to Mr. Charles R. Austin, Governor's Island, N.Y.C.
January 1922
Dear Raymond,
At last I will try and write a few lines to you. The kids have both been under the weather. Arthur seems to have an ulcer or something like one in the upper part of his throat and a low fever. Dad is pretty well again.

I see the "flu" is raging again so be very careful of yourself and don't expose yourself more than necessary.

Marcella Flood was up for one week with us. Mrs. Tuzza wrote for your address.

We had quite a snowstorm here last night and the beginning of last week very cold weather. By Thursday night the thermometer fell to 24 degrees below zero. I imagine you must have felt it at Governor's Island.

Chapter 2: The First Real Sorrow, 1921–1924 • 27

Emily and Teenie Stevens. The home of William and Victoria Parker (brother of Emily Stevens) is on the left, across from the Parker House, down by the brook. Photo courtesy of Christene Stevens Myers.

We received Annie Eldred's marriage announcement last week. Yesterday we sent you the Gregg Magazine. Hope you get it alright. Did you get the books we sent—the arithmetic and grammar?

Bill is helping Harold in the "wood business." I believe tomorrow Dad and he start to finish Mr. Sergeant's logs.

Warren Parker has been very sick. He had an operation for appendicitis.

Why don't you write to Harold Fraley? Likely he would go over to see you.

Pat Morgan called up to see us last Sunday evening to get your address and during the evening he told us many interesting things. He said when he was in the Army hospital with the "flu", they came and tied a red tag on the foot of his bed. Of course I was curious and asked what they did that for *and he said, "to show I was near death." He said he would go back in the Army in a moment, only he thinks too much of his folks.*

Well will close and write a few more letters. Be very careful and not catch cold.

Bobby is going to charge you one dollar the next time you make him mad.

With love from all, Mother

Warren Parker and his wife Anna had ten children. Warren, 6, and Harvey, 3, in 1921, are part of the story during World War II.

Annie Eldred was the daughter of Herbert and Eliza Post Eldred. Herbert and Eliza moved to Middletown, New York, in 1921. Herbert and Eliza sold some of their property to Mort and Jennie.

With washing dishes, making beds, cleaning house, washing clothes, grocery shopping, and all the other housework required for everyday life—and even more so with summer guests, help was very needed and appreciated at the boarding houses. Miss Marcella

Letterhead for Howard Stevens' Taxi and Express Service in the 1920s, courtesy of Christene Stevens Myers.

Teenie Stevens helps Marcella Flood (a tireless worker for Jennie Austin) do the wash at Mountain Grove. Photo courtesy of Christene Stevens Myers.

Flood, mentioned by Jennie in her letter, was just such a tireless helper for Jennie Austin.

There is a photo of young Teenie Stevens with Marcella Flood doing laundry on the Austin porch.

Howard and Emily Parker Stevens

Teenie (Emily Christene) lived with her parents Howard and Emily Christene Stevens, and grandmother Emily Christene Parker in the Parker Hotel built by James Y. Parker, Teenie's grandfather. Howard ran a taxi service in the 1920s.

In the 1940s Howard, Emily, and Teenie would be very helpful neighbors to Aida and Lon Austin.

Teenie (two years old in 1922) was a delightful child. She most likely was a comfort to Jennie Austin with the loss of Jennie's only daughter the year before.

Anna, Jim, and Clara Leavenworth in winter. Photo courtesy of Cynthia Leavenworth Bellinger.

There are a number of photos of Teenie with different townsfolk who play a part in this story. Besides Marcella Flood (who has been mentioned), there was Everett Kelley, a Sergeant relative (*see p. 112*); and Claude Angell, husband of Hazel LaBarr (*see p. 126*).

Garfield and Ella Leavenworth
Garfield and Ella Sergeant Leavenworth had been in Massachusetts since August of 1910. Their youngest daughter Anna was born there. Garfield, Ella and their children: Clara, Clinton (Goldie), and Anna arrived back in Eldred (where they would stay), at least by 1922. In the spring of 1922 Garfield and Ella welcomed their fourth child, James Roberts Leavenworth.

Bill and Lottie Scott Meyers
While Garfield and Ella were in Massachusetts, their home was rented by Bill and Lottie Meyers. Now that Garfield and Ella were back in Eldred, Bill and Lottie built a house on the property they had bought next door. Bill and Lottie would also have summer boarders. Bill and Lottie's children, Bill Jr. and Dorothy. Bill Jr. would be the husband of Anna Leavenworth.

Ell Austin, 1922
In 1922 Ell Austin, 67, lived in Bethel, perhaps with his daughter Lillie Calkin. Ell received several letters from a Mr. G.W. Travis, representative for E.A. Strout Farm Agency, "Largest in the World." Mr. Travis needed a helper on his farm in Hopewell Junction. After a few letter exchanges to get wages he wanted, Ell moved to Hopewell Junction, New York.

G.W. Travis, Hopewell Jct., N.Y., to J.E. Austin, Bethel
April 21, 1922

Bill Meyers Jr., son of Bill and Lottie Meyers, neighbors of Garfield and Ella. Photo courtesy of Mary Ellen Busse Mackinder.

Clara and Jim Leavenworth in the spring. Photo courtesy of Cynthia Leavenworth Bellinger.

Dear Mr. Austin,
I am in need of a man at once. Are you open for a position, if so would like to have you. Will hire plowing done if you wish and try not to make it too hard for you. Have 300 hens and 600 baby chicks, will only milk one cow this summer.
If you want to come, please advise me at once when you can come and what pay you will expect. Telephone me at my expense as I must know as soon as possible.
Yours very truly,
G.W. Travis

April 26, 1922
Your letter received and am glad to note that you will come on May 22. Wages I had in mind is $25 and board. If you would rather you could board yourself. In that case would give you $10 a month more and furnish eggs, milk, potatoes,

1922 Halfway Brook News

Yulan Social Club
*Last Saturday night the Yulan Social Club held its regular monthly dance and supper at the Yulan Cottage. The affair was well attended and was a large success both socially and financially. Dancing, singing and games were played. The feature of the evening was the elaborate supper which was served at midnight…Much credit is due Chef Cantwell and his able assistants, the young ladies of the Club…The people started for home at 2 a.m. All…eagerly looking forward to the next social event…in May.
—Republican Watchman, April 25, 1922.*

Eldred Retaliates over Yulan in Second Game this Spring
The Eldred baseball team, undaunted by their defeat at the hand of the Yulan team on April 16, again met the Yulan team on the Eldred diamond and defeated them 12–8. Although the day was raw and chilly, with occasional snow flurries, many spectators turned out to root for both teams. The game featured the fast base running of Johnny Steward of the Eldreds. Both teams now have won a game from each other this season. Yulan's star pitcher "Speed B. Hazen," having left his speed home, retired early in the game. Louis Hensel, having thoughtfully brought his speed with him, took to pitching, making a creditable showing and would no doubt have won the game had the rules permitted more than eight men to assist him. Eldred Pitcher Timmerhoff and Catcher Myers, did splendid work considering this was the first game together.—Republican Watchman.

Land Deed
- A deed from Herbert L. and Elizabeth Eldred to Jennie L. Austin, Dec. 19, 1922, was recorded at the Sullivan County Clerk's office on Jan. 29, 1923.

1922 Births
- James Roberts Leavenworth born to Garfield and Ella Leavenworth.
- Marion Helen Lass born to Charles and Veronica Campbell Lass.
- Milton Ort born to William and Bertha LaBarr Ort.
- Frances Toaspern born to Walter C. and Emma Straub Toaspern.
- Elizabeth Whitmarsh born to Walt and Ida Darling Whitmarsh.

1922 Marriages
- Anna Eldred married Benjamin Ferguson.
- John Weber married Eva Kalin.
- Oliver L. Hallock married Edna Hill, daughter of Thomas and Alice Sergeant Hill. Oliver was the grandson of Oliver Blizzard and Emma Hallock.
- Edward A. MacIntyre married Helen A. Lass in Barryville.
- Hazel Sergeant, daughter of Frank and Clarissa Clark Sergeant, married Walter Connor.
- Ed Grotecloss Jr. married Isabelle Greig Kelso.
- Ralph Bosch married Paula Schreib.
- Ernest Timmerhoff married Edith May Sergeant, daughter of Charles Edgar and Elizabeth Clark Sergeant.
- William H. Parker married the widow Eleanora Alston.

1922 Deaths
- Herman J. Rixton of Barryville died.
- Maria E. Gardner Calkins, 89, daughter of James K. and Eliza Eldred Gardner, died in Barryville.
- Frank Kelley, 1847–1922, was the husband of Luella Sergeant.
- Warren H. Parker, husband of Anna, died.
- John W. Johnston, 1841–1922, of Barryville was the nephew of John W. Johnston who wrote *Reminiscences*.

Eleanora Alston Parker. Photo courtesy of William H. Parker Jr.

Hazel Sergeant married Walter Connor. Photo courtesy of Cynthia Leavenworth Bellinger.

Jim Leavenworth was born in April 1922. Photo courtesy of Cynthia Leavenworth Bellinger.

Warren H. Parker died in 1922. Photo courtesy of Alice M. Aber, granddaughter.

Jeanne Lair, the new Mrs. Rouillon. Photo courtesy of Gisele Rouillon Leavenworth.

Cyrus Rouillon. Photo courtesy of Gisele Rouillon Leavenworth.

and anything else that grows on farm and fuel. I'm sure we can arrange to our mutual benefit. Will expect to hear how you feel about it. Yours Truly, G.W. Travis

May 3, 1922
Dear Mr. Austin,
I have your letter of April 30th and note that you want $30 per month this summer which I am willing to pay you. If we can get things going with a few cows for next winter and about 300 hens we won't argue about the price. Will expect you May 21st or 22nd. If you could get here earlier, why come along and I'll pay you Bonus.
I have a man coming tomorrow with team to draw the manure and start plowing for the corn. Wish you might be here now to plan the work.
Have 600 chicks, 200 month-old and 400 two-week old. This is all I will raise. Have a hatch off every 10 days. Last hatch had 950 chicks from 1250 eggs set. With all this work and the other business, I have my hands nearly full. Can't get a man by the day that I can trust. Sold five farms in April.
Hope to keep things going until you arrive. Yours very truly, G.W. Travis

Eldred School 1922
In 1922 only eight grades were available in Eldred. Students either stopped at eighth grade or went to another community such as Monticello, and boarded there. That is what Beatrice Avery did. She was the daughter of Erwin and Norah Bradley Avery who ran the Bradley Boarding House.

Laura and Mildred Briggs in Harrison, Nebraska. Photo courtesy of Mary Briggs Austin.

Beatrice Avery graduated from the eighth grade in 1922. In the fall she boarded with the Schineman family in Monticello, to attend Monticello High School. While there, she met my dad, Charles Horton. In the fall of 1923, she went to live with an aunt and uncle in Salamanca, N.Y., and went to school there.—William Erwin Horton.

1923
And another new year. There were some families who would live in the Town of Highland (some years in the future) who lived elsewhere in 1923.

France 1923
Cyrus Marries Jeanne Lair
Cyrus Albert Rouillon married the lovely Jeanne Marguerite Marie Lair January 11, 1923, in Asniere, France. Their daughter Gisele Jeannine Rouillon (born in a few years) would marry Jim Leavenworth.

Nebraska 1923
The future Methodist pastor, Irwin Briggs and his wife Myrtle and daughters Laura and Mildred, moved from Taylor University (where Irwin had gone to seminary) to Harrison, Nebraska, where Irwin had accepted a pastorate.

The Harrison Congregation of 98 people represented a dozen different denominations. Irwin's salary of $700 in cash and produce was paid by the church. The Board of Home Missions paid $300. The cattle industry collapsed the next year and one of the town banks failed, but the citizens added $100 to Mr. Briggs's salary. We'll join the Briggs family in 1925 when they head east for Irwin to attend Drew Seminary.

A couple of long time Town of

1921–1923 World and National News

1921
- Russian famine: 5 million die.

March 1921
- Warren G. Harding inaugurated.

April 1921
- WWI Allies Commission reduced Germany's reparations to 132 billion gold marks ($33 trillion) in annual installments of 2.5 billion.

May 1921
- Emergency Quota Act in U.S. restricted immigration; Eastern Europe (Jews) drastically limited.

July 1921
- Communist Party of China founded.

August 1921
- First radio baseball game broadcast: Harold Arlin announced the Pirates-Phillies game over KDKA.

September 1921
- In Atlantic City, N.J., Margaret Gorman won the title Golden Mermaid (later Miss America).

October 1921
- Albert Einstein awarded the Nobel Prize in Physics for his work with the photoelectric effect.

November 1921
- Tomb of the Unknown Soldier dedicated by President Harding.

1922

January 1922
- First successful insulin treatment of diabetes.

February 1922
- Five Power Naval Disarmament Treaty signed between United States, United Kingdom, Japan, France, and Italy, to curtail warship construction, outlaw poison gas, restrict submarine attacks on merchant ships, and respect the integrity of China. Ratified in 1925.

March 1922
- Mohandas Gandhi sentenced to six years in prison for sedition in India;
- The *U.S.S. Langley* was commissioned as the first U.S. Navy aircraft carrier.

April 1922
- Joseph Stalin appointed General Secretary of the Central Committee of the Soviet Communist Party.

May 1922
- Construction began on Yankee Stadium.
- Lincoln Memorial dedicated in Washington, D.C.

June 1922
- President Harding made his first speech on the radio.

August 1922
- Palestine became a British League of Nations protectorate.

October 1922
- British Broadcasting Company formed.
- Benito Mussolini appointed Premier in Italy.

November 1922
- The Ottoman Empire's last sultan abdicated.
- Howard Carter and Lord Carnarvon first in over 3,000 years to enter the tomb of Pharaoh Tutankhamun, in the Valley of the Kings, Egypt.

December 1922
- Union of Soviet Socialist Republics created; The Irish Free State officially came into existence; Hyperinflation in Germany.

1923

March 1923
- *Time Magazine* first published in the United States.

April 1923
- First sound on film motion picture "Phonofilm" was shown in N.Y.C.
- Yankee Stadium opened.
- Prince Albert, Duke of York (later King George VI) married Lady Elizabeth Bowes-Lyon in Westminster Abbey. They would be the parents of Queen Elizabeth.

May 1923
- The Irish Civil War ended.
- The Ku Klux Klan in the United States defied a law requiring publication of its members.

June 1923
- Mount Etna erupted in Italy—60,000 homeless.

July 1923
- The Hollywood Sign in California originally read Hollywoodland.
- Pancho Villa assassinated.

August 1923
- President Harding died. Calvin Coolidge became President.
- Clarence Birdseye invented frozen food with his quick-freezing process (patented in 1930).

September 1923
- Major fire in Berkeley, California, consumed some 640 structures, including 584 homes.
- Newspaper printers strike in N.Y.

October 1923
- Roy and Walt Disney founded The Walt Disney Company.
- The Ottoman Empire dissolved in Turkey.

Undated:
- Hyperinflation continued in Germany.

Photo from Aida's ride across the Atlantic to France. Aida is in the hat. Photos in Aida's album courtesy of Mary Briggs Austin.

Postcard Aida sent to Lon showing the second class dining room aboard the ship. "We are near Plymouth, England..."

Highland residents died in 1923: Daniel Hallock and Mary Frances Bradley Scott Myers.

Daniel Hallock Dies
Daniel Hallock, son of William and Mary Brodt Hallock, lived quite an adventurous life. He lived not far from the Austins. Daniel had given his farm to Herman and Mary Bosch, asking that they take care of him as long as he lived. He died at the age of 83, in March of 1923.

Mary Frances Myers Dies
Mary Frances Bradley Scott Myers had been ill for some time when she died at age 56. Mary Frances Myers was survived by: her husband Fred; sons Fred Jr. and Harvey; daughters Ada Wells, Della Howlett, and Lottie Meyers; father Isaac M. Bradley; sisters Amelia Gregory, Viola Hazen, Lottie Colville, and Norah Avery; and brothers Atwell and Isaac N. Bradley, most of whom have played a part in this story.

Aida Austin Sails to France
In June of 1923 Aida Austin went to France, possibly to see where McKinley fought and died in World War I. She had studied up on her French with Clark's *French Course for Americans*.

Aida taught in Barryville. One of her students was Jessie Kerr, daughter of William and Mary Kerr. William and Mary Kerr had five daughters including Ruth Kerr (who later married Robert Nelson) and a son John (Jack), 6, in 1923. The Kerrs lived on land by Lock 68 of what was once the D&H Canal. Jessie Kerr would marry Clarence Bradley (son of Atwell) and at some point would be the Barryville Postmaster.

Aida Austin wrote and received letters/cards from Jessie Kerr during her trip to France. Aida also wrote her brother Lon Austin.

Aida Austin, N.Y.C., to Lon Austin, Eldred
June 6, 1923
Dear Lon,
I did not stop for my check, but wrote to Mrs. Quick to send it to you. You can endorse my name on it and send it to the bank. We just called Dr. Austin's folks on the phone and they are coming to the dock to see me off. Mrs. Tuzza

Panorama of Eight Bridges in Paris. Postcard of Aida Austin courtesy of Mary Briggs Austin.

and Nettie are going to the boat with me, too. I will write as soon as I reach France. Yours, Aida

Aida Austin, to Lon Austin, Eldred
June 12, 1923 Tuesday
Dear Lon,
We are near Plymouth England. They will send this from there. We reach Havre tonight and leave for Paris eleven o'clock tomorrow. Yours, Aida

Aida Austin, Paris, France, to Lon Austin, Eldred
June 16, 1923
Dear Lon,
I was up to the American Bank yesterday and deposited what money I don't need. Then I went to the depot and hunted up my trunk. Of course, I took a cab because I didn't know how to find the places.
But today I took quite a little walk. I think I could soon find my way anywhere around Paris, but I am too tired to do much of anything. I was terribly sick all the way over.
I have certainly struck a good hotel. I shall hate to leave it although I feel anxious to get out to where I am going. I don't dare start until I feel like myself again.
I will write to you when I leave here and just where I am going to stop when I know more.
I haven't been disappointed in my opinion of the French people, and have got along fine so far. I don't think you would have regretted it if you had come.
I was so glad I was able to be on deck when we were at Plymouth. The English coast along there was beautiful. But I didn't catch a glimpse of poor old Ireland. Tell Mr. Scott I was so sorry about that. And tell Mrs. Barth I am going to write to her soon.

Hôtel des Invalides, Paris

Hôtel des Invalides postcard in Aida Austin's Collection courtesy of Mary Briggs Austin.

Les Invalides in Paris, France, is a complex of buildings in the city's 7th arrondissement containing museums and monuments, all relating to the military history of France, as well as a hospital and a retirement home for war veterans, the building's original purpose. The buildings house the Musée de l'Armée, the military museum of the Army of France, the Musée des Plans-Reliefs, and the Musée d'Histoire Contemporaine, as well as the burial site for some of France's war heroes, notably Napoleon Bonaparte.
—wikpedia.org.

Paris. Hôtel des Invalides: Tomb of Napoleon. Postcard in Aida Austin's Collection courtesy of Mary Briggs Austin.

I don't know but that I left my key in my door. I wish you would see, and if I did, put the key where I told you I was going to put it. If you see Emma Stevens, tell her I forgot about my Post Office Box, but I don't need it anyway. Will write soon again.
With love, Aida

Mt. Etna Erupts
On June 18, some 1,363 miles from Paris, Mount Etna erupted in Italy, making 60,000 homeless.
Aida would soon visit Dun-Sur-Meuse, the area where McKinley had died.

Aida Austin, Paris, France, to Lon Austin, Eldred
Sunday afternoon, June 24, 1923
Dear Lon,
I expect to leave Paris for Dun-Sur-Meuse tomorrow evening. I would have gone sooner, but had to go to the U.S. Lines Office to change my order for my return ticket, and another day I went to the American Passport Office, and yesterday I went down to the American Consulate General to report as an American Citizen. So you see I have had quite a little to attend to since I got over feeling the effects

Postcard showing The Great Street, Romagne-sous-Montfaucon, in the area where McKinley was killed. Five years after the war, the area still looked devasted. Postcard in Aida Austin's Collection courtesy of Mary Briggs Austin.

Envelope of letter Aida sent Lon from Hotel D'Angleterre, 91 Rue de la Boetie, Paris. Letter courtesy of the Austin Family.

of my voyage, and I didn't want to hurry and get tired before starting on.

I take the ten o'clock train tomorrow night and will reach Verdun early Tuesday morning and will have to wait there a little while for the train to Dun-Sur-Meuse. The man at the U.S. Lines said I would be at Verdun long enough to get breakfast. Then I will go on to Dun-Sur-Meuse, and will have to look up a hotel there. I saw by the paper you were having such hot weather over there. It has been very cool here.

We haven't had a hot day since I came. I am so thankful that it has kept cool. I am feeling good and hope all are well at Eldred. Remember me to Mrs. Barth and family. I will try to write as soon as I get on to Dun-Sur-Meuse. Give my kind regards to Mrs. Rothman and household.

With love, Aida

Jessie Kerr, Barryville, to Miss Aida A. Austin, Hotel D'Angleterre, 91 Rue De La Boetie, Paris, France
July 1, 1923
Dear Miss Austin,

I received your letter last week and was very glad to hear from you. I am sorry you had so much trouble getting your trunk, but as long as you got it, it is alright.

Jack received the card you sent him and was delighted to get it. He showed it to everybody.

Helen Ether, Elma Liebla, and Kenneth Sheen passed their examination. Royden [Toaspern] had the measles during that time, but he is over them now.

We had our spelling contest and Horace and I go to Monticello to the contest there. I do not know if I passed my regents or not.

Doloros is at Middletown and expects to go to Jersey City. Madeline is working at Highland Lake Inn again.

Frances and Eleanor Williams have a little brother. They named him John Daton.

Many men who were working on the roads are going to be working at Pond Eddy on the road there.

Yesterday the boys for Camp Dalinque came on the 11:23 train. We had only three boarders so far and do not expect many this season.

Everyone here is well and hopes you are the same.

Will close with lots of Love, as ever a Friend, Jessie Kerr

Isaac Bradley and Amelia Gregory
Isaac Bradley's daughter Amelia lived in Dunton, Colorado, with her second husband Eber Gregory and their two children.

Two of Amelia's daughters from her first marriage with John Leavenworth were still living, Lottie Leavenworth Andeway and Hazel Leavenworth Koenig. Eugene and Hazel Koenig's first child (Amelia's first grandchild), John Emery Koenig, was born in Wisconsin, in August of 1923.

Proud of being a "Great-Grand Paw," Isaac, 86, wrote Amelia a letter after his daughter Mary Frances (Amelia's sister) had died. You may remember that Isaac lived at the original Bradley House with Erwin and Norah Avery and their children: Laura McBride (was or soon would be married); Beatrice was in school elsewhere; Arthur and Gladys Avery.

Isaac M. Bradley, Eldred, to Amelia Gregory, Dunton, Colo.
July 24, 1923
My Dear Daughter Amelia and all,

I have not written you or any of my family since my dear daughter Mary, Mrs. C.F. Myers passed away. It was the first of my children to go to their Eternal home. If your Mother Amelia had lived until today, she would have been 81 years old today. And if I live 14 more I will be about 100. I do not think I will reach that mark.

As a family we are as well as we are generally. Since Mary died, Fred Myers has had a married woman keeping house for him. I have not been there since the funeral.

I took dinner once this year with Atwell [his son] and once with Lottie Colville [his daughter]. I don't go around much. Home is good enough for me and I have a good home and good attendances [at the boarding house].

Averys have three hired girls from N.Y. City. One boy, Arthur's age, a man, and their four children all work about the house. Arthur runs his Chivelee [Chevrolet] car for the mail and some other errands. He goes to Eldred and back in 15 minutes. When he does not half to do many arents [errands] he drives his car quite a lot, takes fat ladies over to the lake to bathe and some lean lasey [lazy] ones who have more money than brains.

We have had from 30 to 50 guests since May. I think we have over 50 now at $2 per day. You see that is $100 per day besides rides for pleasure and to and from Shohola. Avery has the old price $1 each way. Last Sunday they had three cars to take the guests to the Catholick Church. The Church is at Yulan two miles away. Each car made three trips over and then they had to go three times each to bring them back. About 40 people went to church at 50 cents each. Commenced at 8:30 a.m. and all back at 10:30 a.m.

Our hay crop was good this year. It is very dry here now and pasture is all drying up. John [his brother] is cutting oats for the cows. We use all the milk from seven cows in the cichen (kitchen). Don't churn at all.

Fred Myers is trying to sell his farm. He has it advertised. I hope he don't sell. He was over here but did not see me or did not speak to me. He was in a car and I was on the front stoop. I did not know it was him untill he had gone.

We have a verry nice class of Irish people here and they call me Grand Paw. I have not tasted any intoxicating drinks in 10 years. Gave up smoking sigars (last October when I got a box of poor ones) and pipe and never smoked sigerets. I weigh 196 pounds and quite well built. My feet are verry week and also my hands are week.

Hoping to hear from you all soon. I remain Father and Grandpaw and Great-Grand Paw.
Isaac M. Bradley

> # Work Costs, 1923
>
> Taking care of brush 17 hours 8.50
> Drawing wood 14 hours 7.00
> Drawing logs 7 hours 4.72
> Drawing logs 6 hours 4.00
> Drawing wood 3 hours 2.00
> Drawing wood 1/4 day 1.50
> Work with team 8 hours 5.32
> Work with team 6 hours 4.00
> Work with one horse 4 hours 2.00
> Work on garden 6 hours 4.00
> Drawing stone/slate 6 hours 4.00
> Drawing slate one day 6.00
> Drawing slate 1/2 day 3.00
> 1 cake ice..50
> —From Mort Austin's work log, 1923.

Esther Grinnell Hill Dies
It was a very sad day in August for John Edward Hill, a Sergeant descendant. His wife Esther Grinnell Hill of 28 years, died at age 50. Five of their seven children were married, leaving the twins Alvin and Alfred Hill at home. Many in this family are a part of this narrative.

The surviving relatives were her husband John Hill; four daughters, Mrs. Agnes Ernst,

Bradley Avery Boarding House courtesy of William E. Horton.

John and Esther Grinnell Hill and their children some years before Esther died: John, Esther, Agnes (Ernst), Edgar Charles Hill, Gladys/Jake (Myers), Lena (MacIntyre), Alfred Hill and his twin Alvin Hill, and Edna (Hallock). Photo courtesy of Alan Gothard.

Charles and Elizabeth Ferguson Myers. Photo courtesy of Timothy C. Rizzuto.

Mrs. Raymond Myers, Mrs. Charles MacIntyre, and Mrs. Oliver Hallock, of Eldred; three sons, Edgar, Alfred, and Alvin, of Eldred; and one brother, Edgar Grinnell of Belleville, N.J. The funeral will be held at the Eldred Congregational Church, where the services will be conducted by the Rev. Bennett.—Port Jervis Union, *August 17, 1923.*

Estate of Augustus Myers
Charlie Myers, son of George and Martha Mills Myers, was the executor of the boarding house where his uncle Gus had lived (the original house of Jane Ann Myers).

In December 1923 the Estate of Augustus (Gus) Myers was settled. Gus' sister Charlotte (Lottie) Darling, who had also grown up in the Jane Ann Myers Home, received the largest amount, over $3,500, and paid a tax of $71.80. The Myers nephews Charlie and Martin D. Sr. each paid $89.75 tax on the $1,794.91 they each received. The Leavenworth nieces and nephews: Jennie Austin, Christina Hirsch, Garfield, Truman, Martin, Anna, and Charlotte Leavenworth each paid $25.64 on $512.83.

Frank Sergeant bought the Jane Ann Myers House initially, but then Frank and his wife Anna moved to a house across Highland Lake Road. By 1924 Jim Mills, a relative of Charlie and Martin D. Myers Sr., bought the house. Jim and his wife Sophia would manage the house, which Jim renamed, Highland Lake House.

Charlie and Martin D. Myers Sr.
Charlie Myers and his wife Elizabeth ran Lake View where he and his brother Martin Sr. had grown up. Charlie's son Harold from his first marriage lived with them, and Charlie and Elizabeth's daughter Eleanor.

Charlie's brother Martin D. Myers Sr. had worked at nearby Asendorf's since before 1914. They lived in the Asendorf Cottage until their oldest Mary was school age, then moved to Eldred. Martin Sr. continued to work for Henry Asendorf. In August Helen Zita Myers was born to Martin D. and Mary Myers. Helen's siblings, Mary Martha and Martin D. Jr., welcomed the new little one. Martin D. Myers Sr. was a first

Eleanor Myers with her nanny Theresa Burns. Photo courtesy of Timothy C. Rizzuto.

1923 Halfway Brook News

1923 Land Deed
- A deed from William Bosch and wife to Edward H. Bosch, dated November 13, 1923.

1923 Births
- Margo Bosch born to Menzo and Lena Miller Bosch at Red Bank, New Jersey, where they worked at the Herbert N. Straus Estate.
- John Emery Koenig born to Eugene and Hazel Leavenworth Koenig.
- Helen Zita Myers born to Martin D. and Mary Fee Myers.
- Ed Schroedel born to Leopold and Louise Schrimpe Schroedel on Long Island. He would grow up on a farm in Flemington, N.J. Ed would stay at Echo Hill Farm run by Anthony and Christina Leavenworth Hirsch, and marry their daughter Charlee Hirsch.
- William H. Parker Jr. born to William H. and Eleanora Alston Parker.
- Elizabeth Whitmarsh born to Walt and Ida Darling Whitmarsh. Grandparents: Charles and Lottie Myers Darling. Little Elizabeth would research the family line of her great-grandmother Jane Ann Van Pelt Myers, when she was older.

1923 Marriages
- Alexander Randolph married Kathryn Myers, both of Clifton, N.J.
- Cyrus Albert Rouillon married Jeanne Marguerite Marie Lair, in Asniere, France.
- George F. Dunlap married Elizabeth Justina Eldred, daughter of James and Elizabeth Hardcastle Eldred.

1923 Deaths
- Sarah Schoonmaker Styles, 1839–1923, was Walter Styles' mother.
- William Wait, 1849–1923.
- Frederick Schwab, 1843–1923, died at his home in Barryville after a long illness. Frederick was born in Switzerland, but had lived in the U.S. most of his life. He was a boatman for the D&H Canal Company. Surviving relatives: his wife, formerly Margery Kerr, and a sister. The funeral was conducted by the Rev. F.C. Ether.
- Charles Hickok, son of Justus and Mary Wells Hickok, died in November.
- Mary DeVenoge Miller died in 1923.
- Daniel Hallock, 1840–1923, an old resident of Eldred, was the son of William and Mary Brodt Hallock, and nephew of Oliver Blizzard Hallock. His wife was Elvira Horton. After his illness he gave the farm to Herman Bosch, with the understanding that he should take care of him as long as he lived, but he didn't live many months to enjoy the care. He is survived by one brother, Stephen Hallock and two sisters, Mrs. Kate Meyers of Monticello, and Miss Martha Hallock, of Eldred.—*Republican Watchman, March 30, 1923, p. 2.*
- Mary Frances Bradley Scott Myers, 1865–1923, wife of Fred Myers, died at her home after a lingering illness. She was born at Eldred. She was survived by her husband, sons Charles F. Myers Jr. and Harvey B. Myers; daughters Mrs. Ada Wells, Mrs. Della Howlett, and Mrs. William Meyers; and her father Isaac M. Bradley.
- Esther Grinnell Hill, 1872–1923, married around 1895 to John Edward Hill and they had seven children together. The surviving relatives were her husband; daughters Agnes Ernst, Gladys Myers, Lena MacIntyre, and Edna Hallock of Eldred; sons Edgar, Alfred, and Alvin of Eldred; and one brother Edgar Grinnell of N.J. The funeral was held at the Eldred Congregational Church and conducted by the Rev. M. Bennett.—*Port Jervis Union*, Aug. 17, 1923.
- Benjamin Franklin Eldred, 1840–1923, son of Abraham Mulford Eldred and Elizabeth Wheeler, was born in Halfway Brook Village.

"Frank was a kind and generous man and was known for helping his neighbors. He was always well-groomed with a neatly trimmed, white beard. Eldred, Richard O., The Eldred Family, p. 71.

Frank died at the home of his son Judson, "surrounded by his three daughters and five sons."—The Honesdale Citizen, March 30, 1923.

---

cousin of Jennie Austin, so the Myers' children were second cousins to the Austin brothers.

Highland Lake Boarding Houses
By 1924 there were a number of boarding houses in the Highland Lake area near the Myers' Lake View and Asendorfs' Highland Lake Inn. Peter Barth managed a boarding house. Harry Sulzbach ran Pinehurst. Fred Schoverling still operated Hillcrest Cottage. Mountain Lake House was run by Gustave Staubes. Mrs. J. Dennehy was the proprietor of the new, modern Highland Villa.

Lake Shore House was owned by Chris and Kathryn Scott. Carl and Minnie Bosch Benedict ran Charlie Bosch's place near Highland Lake as Eagle House. It offered boating, bathing, and fishing. Herman and Mary Bosch's

The Draxlers stored ice cut from York Lake in their hexagonal shed to use in the summer. Elsa Draxler, in front, getting ready to feed the chickens. Photo courtesy of Martha Eldred Worzel.

The Nancy Lee was run by sisters Helen Hughes and Clara Davies in 1924. Nancy Lee had been Tether's Washington Lake House. It would become the Colonial. Postcard courtesy of Helen Hensel Oset.

boarding house at Hartung and Stege Roads may have become the Adelaide, operated by Albert Schoverling, Fred's brother.

Barryville Boarding Houses
Barryville Boarding Houses included: Delaware View Inn (was Side Hill Farm) owned by Eggers and Rothenback; Handsome Eddy Farm owned by the Doellers and Albert Fisher; Washauer's Riverside Cottage; Kerr's Torwood Farm; Meyer's Spring House Inn, and Outlook Cottage run by Holmes and Livingstone.

Yulan Boarding Houses
Edith Kalbfus continued to operate Highland Cottage on Washington Lake. Walter Tether started managing Washington Beach Hotel by 1924.

M.A. McCormick ran Minisink Lodge; Atwell Bradley still supervised Park Hotel.

The Nancy Lee, first known as the Washington Lake House, was run by two sisters, Helen Hughes and Clara Hughes Davies, at least by 1922. Joseph Tether had built the boarding house in the mid-1880s. At some point the Washington Lake House and quite a bit of acreage was owned by Cyrus and Ella Walter and their sons Donald and Reginald. Cyrus may have rented Washington Lake House to Helen and Clara. Soon Jacob Hensel and his wife Lisette would purchase the Nancy Lee, and rename it the Colonial.

Jacob's mother Kathryn Hensel had run Yulan Cottage for three years in 1924. Later her son (Jacob's brother) Fred would own Yulan Cottage. Cantwells owned West Shore Cottage. Lake View Inn on Washington Lake was managed by Mrs. E. Vonderhorst.

Minisink Ford Houses
A William Taeterow ran Highland Bridge House in Minisink Ford.

York Lake Mountain House was owned by Charles and Martha Draxler. Their daughter Emmy was 13 in 1924. The Draxler's stored ice cut from York Lake in a hexagonal-shaped building near the chicken pen.

Some Eldred Boarding Houses
The Averys were still proprietors of the Bradley House. Anna Zauner managed Oanna Mountain

Gustave and his son Art Staubes around 1923. The Staubes ran Mountain Lake House. Photo courtesy of Jeanne Staubes Turner.

1920s Lake View Dock. People thought to be Top: Betty Williams, Harold Myers; Below: Theresa Burns, Anna Dwyer. Photo courtesy of Timothy C. Rizzuto.

Farm, and offered campsites on Lake Montgomery. The Arlington was near Montgomery Lake. Mrs. M. Dunlap ran Lynn Brook Farm.

What is Ell Austin's Address?
Ell Austin was hard to find in 1924. He lived in several places before he settled again at Hopewell Junction. His brother Mort updated Ell in a letter which was first sent to Cross River, N.Y.; then readdressed to Mt. Kisco, N.Y. Lillie also wrote him a letter.

Mort Austin, Mountain Grove House, Eldred, to J.E. Austin, 402 Main St., Mt. Kisco, N.Y.
April 7, 1924
Dear Brother,
Raymond left here last Monday. Will and me are very busy. Tuesday it snowed hard all day. We had about 12 inches of snow. Yesterday it rained very hard here all day. This morning it is snowing.
I am glad you like your place and hope you do well. I hope you will excuse me for not writing sooner for I get so tired that I do not feel much like writing, but am always glad to hear from you. After I get through with the lumber, I will not work so hard.
If I can get Bill and his mother to agree to it, and the roads get in good shape, I will take a trip up to see you and the country. I think you should make good where you are if you stick at it. The first year is usually the hardest. I would like it much better than working by the month.
It has stopped snowing. So I will go to work. I will be glad to hear from you often.
With love from Mort

Lillie Calkin, Bethel, to Mr. J.E. Austin, Mt. Kisco, N.Y.

Art Austin, an unidentified woman, Bob Austin, Jennie Austin. Photo in Austin Collection.

June 1, 1924
Dear Dad,
I am so busy this spring I don't have time for anything. Burt is working on the road and leaves early and gets home late so I look after the chickens before and after school, and Saturday. There is always so much to do.
We have about everything planted. Burt finished putting in corn yesterday. Everything is planted in the garden except melons and okra.
We finished papering the sitting room yesterday. Friday night we went to Jeffersonville to the movies.
I think you must have a very good place. You are getting the equivalent of $75 a month at least. Much love, Lillie

Eldred School Bond Sale
As mentioned earlier in this chapter, there was no high school in the Town of Highland. In July of 1924, Henry Asendorf, Trustee of the Town of Highland's Common School District No. 4., placed the notice of a Bond Sale in the Monticello, *Republican*

Watchman. Finally a high school would be available in the area.

Notice is hereby given that the trustees of common school district No. 4, Town of Highland... will receive sealed proposals at Sunshine Hall Free Library in the village of Eldred, N.Y. until 1:30 o'clock in the afternoon on the 28th day of July 1924 for the...

Ell Austin, Mt. Kisco, N.Y., to Mort Austin, Eldred
July 20, 1924
Dear Brother Mort,
I came very near not being here when your letter came. It was only three days before my month was up that I decided

An unidentified woman stands in front of Mountain Grove House. Photo courtesy of the Austin Family.

Sunshine Hall Free Library where the School Bond Sale took place. Photo courtesy of Sunshine Hall Free Library.

The New Paltz School Lillie Calkin attended. Postcard courtesy of Katherine Calkin Traxler.

to stay longer. I may stay until October 1st or I may go any day. It depends on how the spirit moves me. My first check was $50, second check $55, and the last one $60, and I expect a bonus if I stay until October. I am offered a good job for the winter and begin any day at $50 per month with far better accommodations and board than I get here.

I have a chance to buy a good five-year-old horse weighing about 1,100 pounds, a kind and good worker. Do you think you could sell it for $125 if I brought it up?

It is very cold here nights. We have had peas for about a month; canned 25 two-quart cans of beans. Have had beets and carrots and will soon have corn.

I am enclosing you one of the old man. Best wishes and love to all, Ell

Ell apparently sent the same photo to his daughter Lillie. The photo is in both Lillie's collection and that of Mort's children.

Lillie Calkin, New Paltz, to J.E. Austin, Mt. Kisco, N.Y.
July 23, 1924
Dear Dad,
The picture of you is fine. I got it when I was home last week.
Did I tell you mother rented some of her rooms this summer? She gets $60 for the season. Just furnishes two beds, a table, an oil stove, and I guess some dishes.

I think you have been very lucky to get such good wages. You make more than I can make teaching.

I must stop now and get at some of my work. It is very hot here and rain is needed very badly. With love, Lillie

Lillie Austin Calkin had taught in Bethel when her children Dale and Dot were young. They were getting older and in 1924 Lillie furthered her education at the Normal School in New Paltz and taught school nearby. Dot and Dale, her mother Emma, and sister-in-law Hannah lived in New Paltz with her. Some of that time Burt stayed in Bethel to take care of the farm. When they moved, Dale rode his horse from Bethel to New Paltz, some 57 miles. Some of this Lillie mentioned in a letter.

Lillie Calkin, Bethel, to Mr. Jas. E. Austin, Bedford Village, N.Y.
August 29, 1924
Dear Dad,
I was waiting for your address because I didn't know where you would get your mail. We are closing up the house this winter. I have a position in Ohioville which is 1-1/2 miles out of New Paltz on the trolley line. We will live in New Paltz and the children will have the advantage of the New Paltz school. There is a good deal of carpenter work, so Burt will have plenty of work.

We are renting a seven-room house very close to the Normal School. Hannah is going to keep house for me and we want to take a couple of girls from the Normal to board.

There is a hen house on the lot that will accommodate about 150 hens. There is some fruit as well.

Mother will stay with us through the winter. I expect to

Photo of "the old man" Ell Austin. Photo courtesy of Katherine Calkin Traxler.

1921–1924 Boarding Houses

Barryville

Delaware View Inn, formerly Side Hill Farm, Eggers & Rothenback
The finest location in Sullivan Co. overlooking Delaware River: modern improvements; electric lights; newly furnished; under new management; Elevation 1,800 ft.; Fishing in the Delaware River.

**Handsome Eddy Farm
Fischer & Doeller**
Most comfortable farmhouse on Delaware. Boats free. Excellent table. $12 and up, 1921–2. ($13–$15, 1924.)

Riverside Cottage, L. Warshauer
Banks of Delaware. High elevation. Home cooking; own farm products. Boating, bathing, fishing. Shohola Station. Booklet, 1922–1924.

Torrwood Farm, Kerr
Healthful summer resort on top of the mountains. Own farm and dairy. Catholic church nearby. Rates $12 per week and up, 1923.

**Outlook Cottage
Holmes & Livingstone**
Overlooks Delaware. Boating, bathing fishing; own garden, 1924.

Yulan

Highland Cottage, E.V. Kalbfus
Splendidly situated on Washington Lake. Acc. 125. Good roads. Dancing, bathing, fishing. Garage. Own farm products. Rates on application. Booklet, 1921-2, 1924.

Washington Beach House, W. Tether
Bathing beach on lake. Excellent table; large, airy rooms; modern Improvements: Booklet, 1924.

Minisink Lodge, M.A. McCormick
Homelike Hotel on Washington Lake, 1,800 ft.; bathing, fishing, 1921-4.

**Brookside Farm
Carl and Anna Vonderhorst**

Park Hotel, A.L. Bradley
Open for season. Modern impts.; on Washington Lake. Rates reasonable, 1922-3: $16 up; 1924: $18 up.

Nancy Lee, N. Hughes & C.H. Davies
Overlooking Washington Lake; boating; bathing; fishing; excelllent home cooking; reasonable. 1922-3.

Yulan Cottage, Mrs. K. Hensel
Boating, bathing, fishing; good table; home cooking, 1922.

Lake View Inn, Louise Vonderhorst
Washington Lake. Comfortable rooms; electric lights: excellent table: boating, bathing. Acc. 60. 1924.

West Shore Cottage, M. Cantwell
Excellent boating, bathing, fishing; electric; Catholic church. $14, 1924.

Minisink Ford

Highland Bridge House, W. Taeterow
5 minutes from depot and village, on Delaware; boating, fishing, bathing; $10 week up; farm products, 1923.

Eldred

Bradley House, E.D. Avery
Large airy rooms; excellent table; everything fresh from own farm. Circular, 1922, 1924.

The Arlington
On the mountain; beautiful view; large porch, large lawn; plenty shade. Montgomery Lake on property. Fishing, boating, bathing. Excellent table. Own farm products. Easy access to movies, dancing, etc., 1922.

The Adelaide
Excellent table; reasonable rates. 1924.

The Oanna, Anna Zauner
Mountain farm, Eldred, N.Y. Acc. 60. Bathing, boating, fishing; fine plentiful table; $15 per week. Camp sites on Lake Montgomery, 1923.

**The Lynn Brook Farm
Mrs. M. Dunlap**
Situated in mountains of Sullivan County. Accommodates 16 guests. Circular, 1922, 1924.

Highland Lake

The Lake Shore House, P.C. Barth
Modern; electric light; excellent table; near Catholic Church. Accommodates 30. Rates, apply. Booklet, 1924.

Eagle House, C.J. Benedict
Situated on Highland Lake. Boating, bathing, fishing. Moderate rates.

**Hillcrest Cottage
Fred and Annette Schoverling**
Boating, bathing, fishing, dancing; excellent table; comfortable rooms; new beds; moderate. Booklet, 1924.

Highland Lake House, James Mills
Ideal location, overlooking lake. 1,400 feet elevation: modern; own farm produce. Booklet, 1924.

Highland Villa, Mrs. J. Dennehy
New, modern house on lake; excellent table; farm products; all amusements; bathing, fishing; churches; $18 up. Booklet, 1924.

1922 Summer Season
The season at Highland Cottage on Washington Lake, Yulan, this year, is the most successful in the history of that establishment. Probably the greatest night was an ambitious show and lawn party held at the end of last week…Estella Waterman performed the diving Venus act from the center cupola on the cottage roof.

At Eldred, the whortleberry season is on and thousands of the summer vacationers spend their time in picking the delicious fruit from the blue laden bushes. Although the season is just beginning, so plentiful is the crop that it is drawing hosts of summer folk who otherwise would not go to the wooded region.—The Brooklyn Daily Eagle, Sunday, July 30, 1922.

Yulan Cottage 1921. Postcard courtesy of Kevin Marrinan.

leave for New Paltz Tuesday or Wednesday. With love, Lillie

By September Ell Austin lived in Hopewell Junction. He had taken a job as a caretaker/boarder for two ladies, Mrs. Forman and Mrs. Cole, who lived there.

Charles M. Colville Dies
In October Charles Colville, husband of Lottie Bradley, died of stomach ulcers following an illness of two days.

Their daughter Ruth, who wrote to McKinley during World War I, was married to Herbert Devireaux. Their daughter Esther would marry Walter Hess. Their son Leslie would have a small electronics shop. Lottie continued to manage their Woodland Cottage.

Lillie Calkin, New Paltz, N.Y., to J.E. Austin, Hopewell Jct., N.Y.
December 7, 1924
Dear Dad,
Your letter received tonight. Instead of coming up Saturday, come Christmas Day. I have to go to Extension School on Saturday, so won't be home. I want you to come up Xmas anyway.
I have most of my shopping done. I had both children down to Poughkeepsie on Saturday and they had a great time doing their Xmas shopping and visiting the toy departments.
Burt and I slipped up to Kingston one night last week to shop for the kids. I believe I'd rather trade in Poughkeepsie.
I think your hens are doing fine. Ours are not doing anything.
Be sure to come up Xmas.
With love, Lillie

Electricity at Mountain Grove
By December 1924, there were electric lights at the Austin home.

Mort Austin, Eldred, to J.E. Austin, Hopewell Junction, N.Y.
December 16, 1924
Dear Brother,
I am very glad to hear you have a good place to work. I am sure that you feel to home with the ladies and doubtless you will be well cared for.
I have electric lights in our house. I tell you, they are just the thing for a boarding house. I have paid one thousand dollars on the mortgage.
I did not get as much for my lumber as I expected to, but it was a right good investment. I have not forgotten what I owe you. If you do not need it now, I would rather pay you in the spring, but if you need it at any time, let me know and I will send it to you.
Bert Eldred and wife spent a few days with us and went home yesterday. Mr. West's wife was buried yesterday. We are all well

1924 National News

January 1924
- Vladimir Lenin died and was buried in the Mausoleum in Moscow's Red Square.
- 1924 Winter Olympics opened in the French Alps.

February 1924
- A radio time signal was broadcast for the first time from the Royal Greenwich Observatory.
- IBM founded in New York State.
- Calvin Coolidge first U.S. President to deliver a radio broadcast from the White House.

April 1924
- American media company Metro Goldwyn Mayer (MGM) founded in Los Angeles, California.

May 1924
- The 1924 Summer Olympics opening ceremonies were held in Paris, France.
- J. Edgar Hoover appointed head of the Federal Bureau of Investigation.
- Mercedes-Benz formed by merging companies owned by Gottlieb Daimler and Karl Benz.
- The Immigration Act of 1924 was signed into U.S. law, including the Asian Exclusion Act. National quotas curbed most Eastern and Southern European nationalities, further enforced the ban on immigration of East Asians, Indians and Africans, and put mild regulations on nationalities from the Western Hemisphere (Latin Americans).

June 1924
- Citizenship granted to all Native Americans born within the territory of the United States.
- American Russell Maughan flew from New York to San Francisco in 21 hours and 48 minutes on a dawn-to-dusk flight in a Curtiss PW-8.

August 1924
- The Dawes Plan was accepted. It was an attempt in 1924 to solve Germany's reparation problem following World War I.
- France began to withdraw its troops from Germany.

September 1924
- U.S. Army pilots John Harding and Erik Nelson completed the first round-the-world flight in 175 days with 74 stops.

November 1924
- Calvin Coolidge elected U.S. President.
- First Macy's Thanksgiving Day Parade held in N.Y.C.

1924 Halfway Brook News

1924 General News
- Last raft carrying goods down the Delaware. The first one was in 1764.
- A fire destroyed Brookwood in 1924. The lions were sold to Mr. Reber and were in the front of his restaurant until the 1980s.
- New York first assigned its state highways with route numbers.

1924 Land Deeds
- Being the same premises described in a deed from Sherman S. Leavenworth to Jennie L. Austin dated March 24, 1924 and recorded in the Sullivan Co. Clerk's office June 19, 1924.
- A deed from Frank R. Sergeant and wife to Edward Bosch, dated November 3, 1924.

1924 Moved
- William and Christianna Flieger and son William moved to Port Jervis, N.Y.

1924 Births
- Edward W. Toaspern born to Walter and Emma Toaspern.
- Fred DeFeo Jr. born to Fred and Pearl Owen DeFeo.
- Orville Ernest Clark born to Ernest and Eunice Hallock Clark.
- Ruth Worzel born to Herman and Blanche Quick Worzel.
- Robert Clinton Hallock born to Oliver L. and Edna Hill Hallock.
- Kenneth McBride born to Buck and Laura Avery McBride.
- Marjorie Ruth Connor born to Walter and Hazel Sergeant Connor.
- Louis Norman Maudsley was born in Binghamton, New York, to Ellis S. Maudsley and Edna Adele Rauner. Louis and his wife Edith (born in 1927) would be friends of my parents. Louis is a descendant of Eliza Ann Gardner Young whose family settled in Pond Eddy around 1800.

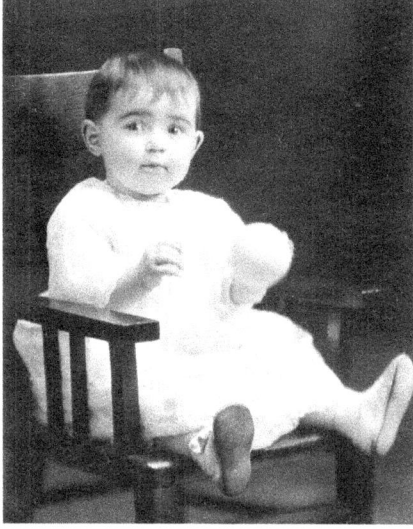

Adorable Ruth Worzel. Photo courtesy of Ruth Worzel Myers.

- Frank Colony Kyte was born to Frank Crouch Kyte and Hazel Robinson in Lansing, Michigan.
- Charlotte (Charlee), daughter of Christina and Anthony Hirsch, born in December in Bronx, New York.

1924 Marriages
- James Lewis Hazen married Elsie Parker. Elsie was the daughter of William H. and Victoria Simpson Parker. Lewis Hazen was the son of Abel and Viola Bradley Hazen who owned Laurel Cottage on Washington Lake.

1924 Deaths
- Sarah Ida Clark Crandall, 1856–1924, wife of David Crandall, mother of George Crandall (husband of Jennie). Sarah was the daughter of Mary/Mercy Harding Brown and George Case Clark.
- Maggie Dunlap, 1838–1924.
- Frank Ort, 1858–1924, was the husband of Mary Crandall and father of William, Frank, George, and Charles.
- John Bogert, husband of Amanda Hogencamp, died at the age of 90. They lived on a farm and John sold milk and had milk cans with the letters JB on them at Little Egypt, between Youngsville and White Sulpher Springs. Survived by: his wife Amanda; children: Edgar and Irving at home; Mrs. John Kniffin of Liberty; Carrie Bogert Clark of Narrowsburg; Mrs. Jacob Sander of Callicoon; Charles of Binghamton; Lester of Callicoon Center; brother, Isaac Bogert of McKeesport, Pa.; sister Mrs. Esther Hardenburgh of Youngsville; ten grandchildren; and five great-grandchildren.
- Charles M. Colville, 1860–1924, moved to Barryville 27 years ago. He was a farmer and from 1916 to 1918 he filled the Justice of the Peace. He was a member of the Methodist Church.

Fred DeFeo Jr. Photo courtesy of Pam Fischetti DeFeo.

The newest cousin Charlee Hirsch held by her mother Christina Hirsch. Photo courtesy of Ric Schroedel.

and hope these few lines will find you the same.

Love from all, Mort

Charlotte Hirsch Born
The third week of December Mort and Jennie Austin had a new niece. Charlotte (Charlee) Hirsch was born to Anthony and Christina Leavenworth Hirsch, in Bronx, New York. Charlee was the last of the Austin-Leavenworth cousins to be born. The other cousins: Mort and Jennie Austin's sons: Raymond, Bill, Art, and Bob; and Garfield and Ella's children: Clinton, Jim, Clara, and Anna.

Burt and Lillie's Christmas 1924
The Calkin family celebrated Christmas in New Paltz. Dot turned 10. Lillie's father Ell was not able to be at their house, but sent a check and package instead. Lillie, Dale, and Dot wrote Grandpa thank you notes.

Lillie, Dorothy, and Dale Calkin, New Paltz, N.Y., to Mr. J.E. Austin, Hopewell Junction, N.Y.
December 28, 1924
Dear Grandpa,
Thank you for the dollar you sent me. Thanks for the doll and book. I like my book very much. I read it through already. I like my doll very much, too. I play with it everyday. I like my dollar, too.
I got a doll's bed, a doll's carriage, two games, two pairs of beads, a pair of slippers, some handkerchiefs, a loose leaf notebook. I got some other books and some other things.
I hung up my stocking and received a pickle, a banana, some candy and some nuts, and the rest was paper.
We just bought some straw for our horse Dick, and he thinks he needs it all. He is fat as a pig. I don't think of anything else, just now, so will close.
What did you get for Christmas?
Love from Dorothy

Dear Grandpa,
Thank you for the check. Did you get our package yet? What did you get? I got an erector set, jackknife, five books, a number of games, slippers, and different things. I hung up my stocking and got a pickle and a lot of candy and a banana. The rest was full of paper.
We go skating every day.
Will close with love from Dale

Dear Dad,
Thank you for all the Christmas you sent us. I wish you wouldn't be so extravagant. Dorothy's doll is a beauty. Dot is delighted and says she is the nicest doll she ever had. We bought her a doll carriage and Burt made her a doll bed. Mother has been sick again. She hasn't done anything since Wednesday morning.
Was sorry you could not get up Christmas. Come when you can. With love, Lillie.

Leavenworth cousins of Charlee Hirsch: Clinton, Jim, Clara. In back Anna. Photo courtesy of Cynthia Leavenworth Bellinger.

Able Myers' Orchard Terrace was remodeled and became Eldred Union School. The view is from the Parker Hotel. Photo courtesy of Christene Stevens Myers.

Chapter 3
A Fortunate Occurrence
Start of Eldred High School, 1925–1926

The year before I completed grammar school, a high school was built in our town. Without this fortunate occurrence, my education would probably have ceased at the grammar school level.—Arthur Austin.

Arthur Austin with his St. Bernard dog, King. Photo in the Austin Collection.

The Orchard Terrace Boarding House, which once belonged to Abel Myers, was being remodeled into the new high school in 1925. Arthur and his brother Bob could keep track of the construction progress on the new school on their way to and from the old one.

In the fall of 1925 Art would begin the eighth grade (his last year of grammar school) at the new school.

While Art and Bob attended school, their brother Bill helped out their dad. Besides the work of running a boarding house and growing a garden, Mort did side jobs such as drawing wood for neighbors, haying, clearing brush, or gardening.

Raymond Austin seems to be working at a Barge Office (possibly under the direction of the Coast Guard) in New York City. He lived on Staten Island and corresponded with Gladys Myers. Raymond's family often wrote him. But he does not keep in touch by letter often enough for his mother Jennie.

Lillie Austin Calkin, the only Austin cousin of Raymond, Bill, Art, and Bob, attended College and taught in New Paltz, New York.

In 1925 Lillie, 41, her husband Burt (a carpenter), their children Dorothy (Dot) and Dale, and Emma Austin (Lillie's mother) lived in New Paltz until Easter break. Burt and Dale then went home and tended their farm in Bethel, New York. Lillie and her children continued to exchange letters with Lillie's father, James Eldred Austin (Uncle Ell).

Lillie Calkin, New Paltz, N.Y., to J.E. Austin, Hopewell Junction, N.Y.
January 3, 1925
Dear Dad,
  All are well except Dorothy who has sore eyes, pink eye, I guess. She is getting better.
  With love, Lillie

Bob Austin, Eldred, to Raymond Austin, Staten Island
February 9, 1925
Raymond,
  The snow up here is melting fast. In the morning it is frozen so we go sleigh riding. We both got

Winter in Eldred. From left: Orchard Terrace, Congregational Church, Sunshine Hall, and Sunshine Hall Free Library. In the center of the photo, the old Eldred Schoolhouse. Von Ohlen's was the dark building. Straub's set behind Von Ohlen's. Photo courtesy of the Austin Family.

sleighs for Christmas. We saw the total eclipse of the sun. We have our wood sawed. Mrs. Cox hurt her leg sleigh riding and she came to school with a cane.

I am sick and I can not go to school. I had to stay in bed all day Sunday. I felt dizzy when I stood up. I hope you are feeling well. I am feeling better.

I hope you can come up on Lincoln's birthday. The rest of the family are feeling well. Arthur is as fat as ever.

Your brother, Bob

In the letters of Lillie Calkin in the rest of this chapter, she often mentions Hannah Calkin, her sister-in-law, the current health status in their family, the weather, her teaching, their garden, and an update on their hens and eggs. A number of folks sold eggs as a source of income (including Garfield and Ella Leavenworth, who we will read more about later).

Lillie Calkin, New Paltz, N.Y., to J.E. Austin, Hopewell Junction, N.Y.
January 21, 1925
Dear Dad,
Hope you are well. Mother has been very sick. Grippe and pleurisy. She is around now.
Hannah came a week ago Saturday. The children and I have had pink eye. My eyes are not strong yet. Dorothy is looking fine. I lost four days of school the first week in January. We had a rousing snowstorm yesterday, but I got to school by taking the trolley.
With love, Lillie

February 10, 1925
Dear Dad,
We are alive and well and it is thawing. The fog today has been thick enough to cut and part of the time it has rained. I did not miss a day because of bad

1925 Valentine from Dot Calkin to her grandfather Ell Austin. Card courtesy of Katherine Calkin Traxler.

weather, though one morning I was quite late.
Our hens are beginning to lay now, got 34 today.
Burt had a letter from his mother. They sold $300 worth of eggs last; feed cost $90. They have about 500 hens. Burt has not worked for a few days, but started again today. They are building a barn.
Hope you are well and that your chickens are laying.
With love, Lillie

J.E. Austin, Hopewell Jct., N.Y., to Lillie Calkin, New Paltz, N.Y.
February 15, 1925
Dear Lillie,
Glad to hear you were all well. I see in the N.Y. paper the ice has gone out of the Hudson and Delaware Rivers. The rivers did quite a lot of damage in places on account of the ice damming up, but saw no account of any damage being done above the waters on the Delaware.
It's about time your hens began to lay eggs. We took a crate of eggs to Poughkeepsie yesterday and only got 48 cents a dozen. The most we got for eggs was $1 per dozen. Our best month for the hens was December with $65 clear for about 187 hens. 100 of the hens about paid for their feed in December.

I have not heard from Mort since November. Hoping you are all well. With love, Dad

Mort Austin, Eldred, to Mr. J.E. Austin, Hopewell Junction, N.Y.
February 20, 1925
Dear Brother,
I received your valentine yesterday. I have been going to write you for sometime, but have been busy. We are having a very good winter and are all feeling well. I will write you a letter soon.
With love from all, Mort

Lillie Calkin, New Paltz, N.Y., to J.E. Austin, Hopewell Junction, N.Y.
March 1, 1925
Dear Dad,
Thanks for the box of fruit and candy.
Burt has had the grippe. Just as he was getting over it, Dorothy had three days of croup. Last night she came down with grippe, not very bad. She's pretty good today, but was burning with fever last night.
Hannah came back last night to look after Dorothy while I am in school. I have 13 weeks and four days to teach yet. I do not think I shall teach next year. This teaching all day, nursing all night, and working Saturdays and Sundays is too much like work, and I've done a lot of it all since Xmas.
We are making our hens lay with an ax. That being the only way in which they will lay. Dorothy and Hannah have been working crossword puzzles.
Hope you keep well.
With love, Lillie

Jennie Austin, Eldred, to Raymond Austin, Staten Island
Friday noon, April 1925
Dear Ray,
We all have been straining our eyes in looking for a letter from you.
I have been going to write and ask you to go and call on Dr. Smith. He has had an operation in some hospital in the city, this morning. I called up his residence and Edith Pelton was there. I think she said he expected to leave the hospital today, but they wanted to get a room in Aunt Christina's neighborhood for a few days before undertaking the trip home. She said if you called up Aunt Christina she could tell you where to find him.
So if you have time Sunday, it would be nice for you to look him up and take him some corn cob pipes and tobacco and Mrs. Smith some flowers, but of course the flowers would not be necessary.
It is reported one of Eldred's widows with six children is to marry one of our widowers with seven children, but his children are all grown up, so she has the best of it.
The boys are getting along fine in school. The boys in Bob's class tried to smoke one day, but fortunately it was after school and Bob had come home before the boys got hold of the tobacco. Archie Von Ohlen said afterward that his mother was going to give him something nice if he didn't smoke again until he was 19, but the poor Parker boys, their mother didn't wait at all and from the sound, it wasn't very nice.
Well, try and write soon and take care and not to catch cold for it is good pneumonia weather.
Lovingly, Mother

John E. Hill Marries Harriet Classen Eldridge
The wedding Jennie Austin referred to took place on April 10, 1925. John Edward Hill, the

"It is reported one of Eldred's widows with six children is to marry one of our widowers with seven children." John and Hattie Classen Eldridge Hill were married in April. Photo courtesy of Alan Gothard, grandson.

widower with seven children, married Harriet Classen Eldridge, the widow with six children. These two families play a part in this story.

Jennie Austin, Eldred, to C.R. Austin, Staten Island
6 a.m. Monday, April 1925
My Dear Raymond,
I wonder if you realize that we have not heard from you since you were home in February, so it is time you should spare a few moments and write to us. The reason for writing so early in the morning is that I have just got Bill off to work. They are building another dam on the Mongaup stream and about 35 men from this side of Mongaup go over nearly every morning.
Harold Dunlap is married. The event happened on Easter Sunday [April 12, 1925]. The first day he went back to work he was nearly killed by a large

"The boys have a bicycle so have falls and fights galore." Art and Bob Austin on Austin property off Proctor Road. Austin barn on left. Photo in the Austin Collection.

branch falling on him. Quite a few of the Eldred boys have met with accidents over there. None serious.

As yet, Clinton Leavenworth [Raymond's cousin] cut his foot quite badly and they took him to Port Jervis to have it attended to, but then they are working nearer Port than home.

Mrs. Tuzza, Nettie, Margaret, Anna, and a friend were up for the Easter week. It really seemed good to have them for we could or had to get out of our winter rut of living.

It keeps very cool and we still have snow and ice in spots. Now try and send us a letter within a day or so as we cannot help but feel anxious at times.

Love from all, Mother

Wed. morning, April 22, 1925
Dear Raymond,
We have not heard from you in quite some time. Now I am writing by request of Mrs. Hattie Liebla in regards of the soldiers' bonus. She wanted me to find out if you could get her a blank to fill out.

I think you stated you had wrote to Washington D.C. to find out the details, but now I think it

Bill Austin worked on Mongaup Dam. Photo courtesy of the Austin Family.

would be to Albany where your Bonus came from as this is a state and now a Federal bonus. Do what you can anyway.

We thought we would use Mac's bonus to pay for the markers for his and Elizabeth's graves which we expect soon, having been uneasy about ordering them, but likely some other way of paying will turn up.

We are having the house painted and will certainly look like a different place.

So far the prospects for the summer appear good. Am up to my neck in house cleaning.

The boys have a bicycle so have falls and fights galore.

Lovingly, Mother

Lillie Calkin, New Paltz, N.Y., to Mr. J.E. Austin, Hopewell Junction, N.Y.
April 27, 1925
Dear Dad,
Was going to write you today, but have had a splitting headache all day. Better tonight.

Thank you for the fruit. Mother and I were alone when it came. The kids were on their Easter vacation. Burt has gone up home to look after the spring work. Dale is with him.

I expect Burt down Tuesday and we will move up Wednesday. Mother went up last Monday. Dorothy is with me.

We will take a couple of furnished rooms till my school closes.

Will come and see you some Saturday in May.

With love, Lillie

At his mother's request, Raymond did write regarding the information on compensation for McKinley from his death in WWI and Jennie received a response and a form in May.

War Department, to Mrs. C.M. Austin, Eldred
May 18, 1925
Dear Madam:
I am in receipt of a letter of April 29, 1925, from Mr. Charles R. Austin, Staten Island, N.Y., requesting that you be advised of the necessary steps to obtain compensation for deceased veterans of the World War.
The World War Adjusted Compensation Act provides that if a veteran died without making application for the benefits thereof, his compensation will be payable only to his dependents and in the following order of preference: Unmarried widow, children, mother, father. If the dependent is a father or mother the law requires that a statement of dependency under oath be submitted.
I am enclosing a blank application form with instructions for the dependent of Mr. Austin who is entitled to apply and upon its receipt in this office, it will be given prompt consideration.
Very truly yours,
The adjutant General

Ell Austin continued to board at the home of Mrs. Forman and Mrs. Cole, and helped them out with home maintenance.

Lillie and Dorothy Calkin, New Paltz, N.Y., to J.E. Austin, Hopewell Junction, N.Y.
May 19, 1925
Dear Dad,
If it is a nice day next Saturday, Dorothy and I will be down and stay all night since Mrs. Forman is kind enough to ask us.
My school will be out June 5th and I want to go home on the 6th. They have 1,000 baby chicks up home. Dale sprained his ankle and Burt is having trouble with his rupture. There is a new bus line from Newburgh and Bloomingburg. You can go from New Paltz to Monticello now for $1.81 if you go by train to Montgomery or $2.30 all the way by bus by way of Newburgh. We are going back by Kingston on account of my trunk.
I am sorry you are having such bad luck with your chicks.
With love, Lillie

Dear Grandpa.
We are coming down next Saturday if it is a nice day. We went home last Friday. Daddy sent for 1,000 little chicks, white ones. He lost a few. Hannah has got a new Chevrolet car. I got more to write about, but have no more room to write it, so will close.
Love from Dorothy

Burt Calkin Bethel, to Lillie
May 24, 1925
Dear Lillie,
It is raining hard up here, has all day. I went to Eldred yesterday with hay. I took three loads down.

Gravestones for McKinley and Elizabeth Austin paid for from Mac's bonus. Photos: Gary Smith.

Now I got a check of $113 for it and have about three more loads to take. I saw Dave Crandall. He wants us to come and see him. He said that George and Jennie would not speak to him and he did not want us to go back on him. I told him he done just right if he felt that way.
Did you go to Hopewell Junction today? Our chicks are doing fine...With Love, Burt

Dave Crandall was the father of George Crandall, Jennie's husband. Dave's wife (George's mother) Sarah had died in 1924. Jennie and Lillie continued to be best of friends. Burt Calkin sounds like a peacemaker from the letter. Burt also wrote to his daughter.

Burt Calkin, Bethel, to Dorothy Calkin
May 25, 1925
Dear Dorothy,
How are you getting along? Did you go to see Granddad? Does it rain down there? We had a hard shower last night. Dale and I was coming home from Eldred. It has rained ever since.
You and Mother will soon be home now. I hope so, don't you?
The little chickens felt awful bad today. They had to stay in all day and they did not like it.
I haven't got a cow yet. I think I will go down and see how the chicks are. With love, Daddy

Lillie Calkin, New Paltz, N.Y. to, J.E. Austin, Hopewell Junction, N.Y.
May 26, 1925
Dear Dad,
We got here safely on the next to the last trolley at about seven o'clock. I think you have struck a place in a thousand. They [Mrs. Forman and Mrs. Cole] are certainly fine people.

How are the chickens? I hope you have better luck than with the others.

I had a letter from home last night. The chicks are doing well, they say. I hope we are able to raise 500 pullets, but that is rather too much to expect.

I'm going to write a "thank you" to Mrs. Forman and then tackle my school work.

With love, Lillie

Lillie Calkin, Bethel, to J.E. Austin, Hopewell Junction, N.Y.
July 2, 1925
Dear Dad,

If I were to hunt much longer for the ink, I wouldn't get any letter written tonight, so I guess I'll use pencil. We came home on the 6th of June.

We get up at 5 or 6 in the morning and go just as hard and fast as we can until 8 or 9, generally 9. I am keeping very well though, save that I have been 'enjoying" an ulcerating tooth, which is about well now.

The chickens have done very well—probably lost about 150 from various causes. We sold 120 roosters tonight. So many of ours seem to be pullets. It seems likely that we will have 450 or 500 of them. It's too bad you had such bad luck with yours. I think the yards must be infected.

Our garden is fine this year. We have had onions, radish, lettuce, turnips, and we have chard and peas big enough to use.

We set out about 500 cabbages. Our sweet cherries bore only a few. We will have quite a good many plums and peaches too as well as some grapes, also a good many raspberries and blackberries.

Burt is building a new porch. He tore down the old one. This one is 10 feet by 35 feet.

Mother has had her house painted gray with white trim. It looks fine; also a new chimney laid in the sitting room from the cellar up. Her roomers are there this summer.

Malcolm Hadden lost all his cows in the TB test except three or four young heifers. Harry Tyler lost all or nearly all his.

I am going to teach again next winter in Fosterdale.

Burt bought a three-year-old heifer from Julius Maier this spring. She is certainly a dandy. Gives six to eight quarts at a milking, very rich.

We use all the cream we want. Dorothy drinks a small cup every meal. We use it on cereals, berries, lettuce, coffee, etc. We have all the butter we want for mother and ourselves and I hope to have one to five pounds a week to sell. Mrs. Schneider wants all the sweet butter I can make. Don't you think that is a pretty good heifer?

I am going to make currant jelly and jam and sour cherries tomorrow. Remember me to Mrs.

Julius Maier with a calf by Maier barn. "Burt bought a three-year-old heifer from Julius Maier this spring. She is certainly a dandy." Photo courtesy of Ken Bosch.

Amelia Bradley Gregory and grandchildren John and Deloros Koenig. Photo courtesy of Marialyce Koenig Kornkven.

Forman, Mrs. Cole, and Mrs. Dodgson. With love, Lillie

Isaac Bradley Letter
Isaac M. Bradley on the west side of Eldred wrote to his daughter Amelia Gregory who lived with her daughter Hazel Leavenworth Koenig in Wisconsin. Her other daughter Lottie Andeway lived, or soon would live, in Iowa.

Isaac M. Bradley, Eldred, to Amelia Gregory, Wisconsin
July 8, 1925
Dear daughter and family,

I have hurd from you and yours several times since I have written. Will say I am a lisey [lazy] man!

As a family we are well. Lottie C. [his daughter] is as well as she has been. I think all the rest are OK. Averys [run the Bradley boarding house] have 40 guests and they have a man cook. He has only been here about four days and so far he suits me and should suit anyone!...I begin to feel old this year. You see, I have three great-grandchildren born

John and Deloros, children of Eugene and Hazel Leavenworth Koenig. Photo courtesy of Marialyce Koenig Kornkven.

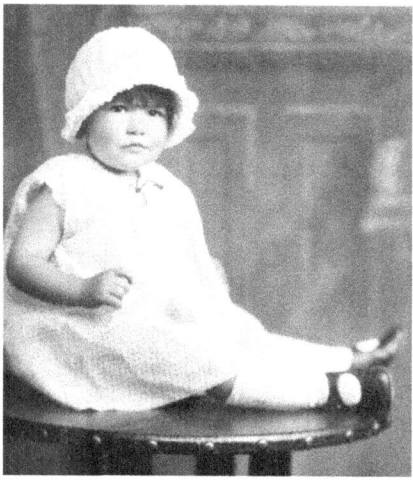

Charlee Hirsch, daughter of Anthony and Christina, granddaughter of Sherman Leavenworth. Photo courtesy of Ric Schroedel.

news. How Charley and Nora [Gregory] are. I hear from Lottie [Andeway, Amelia's daughter] quite often.

Remember me to all the family. Your Father, I.M. Bradley

Sherman Leavenworth

Isaac Bradley mentioned Sherman Leavenworth. Sherman had been a neighbor of the Bradleys for many years. Sherman was also an uncle to Amelia Bradley Gregory's daughters Hazel and Lottie.

Amelia was an aunt to Sherman Leavenworth's children: Jennie Austin, Christina Hirsch, Martin, Garfield, Truman, Anna, and Charlotte Leavenworth.

In 1925 Sherman had nine grandchildren: Raymond, Bill, Art, and Bob Austin; Charlee Hirsch; and Clara, Clinton, Anna, and Jim Leavenworth.

Sherman's grandson Clinton Leavenworth turned 16 in July of 1925. Garfield taught his son Clinton to shoot.

Clinton had saved his money for a long time and bought a rifle—the Savage 300—a real

this year. Don't you think I ought to feel quite old. And two more expected soon and Laurie's boy [Kenneth McBride] has three teeth and old women used to say when they began to have teeth the next one began to have toe nails! So look out for Bradleys by the score soon.

Avery commenced haying last Monday. Cut the field back where the old house was and all around this house and got in four loads of hay yesterday and today it is raining so haying stops...It is now 11 a.m. and no signs of clearing.

I have not seen Sherman Leavenworth in a long time.

My feet and legs have been week but are coming around ok now. They ar just getting the frost thawed out of them.

Hazens have 13 boarders; Lottie Meyers [his granddaughter] has 8; and Averys 40. So you see we hold our own. Don't hear how many Atwell Bradley had.

You must have a fine time with your grandson John [Koenig, son of Hazel Leavenworth Koenig]. I would like to see him and all of you. Write me all the

Garfield taught his son Clinton, 16, how to shoot his Savage 300. Photo courtesy of Cynthia Leavenworth Bellinger.

prize to have.

On his first time out hunting, Clinton was very disappointed when he took a shot at a running deer and missed and told his dad something was wrong with the gun.

In Garfield's typical style he said, "There's nothing wrong with the gun. It's the man pulling the trigger that's the problem."

Garfield took Clinton out behind their house. It was very rocky going from the hill down to the barn. Garfield put a piece of cardboard inside a tire and had Clinton start rolling the tire from the top of the hill.

As the tire rolled down the hill, it of course built up speed and bounced from rock to rock. Garfield shot at it and put a bullet hole right in the cardboard and said, "Nothin' wrong with this gun," and handed it to his son.

"Don't shoot at it until it is at the bottom of the hill at full speed and bouncing around."

Not surprisingly, Clinton missed. "Keep practicing until you put a hole in the cardboard."

Garfield had Clinton take the tire with the cardboard insert back up the hill and roll it down

Jim Leavenworth. Photo courtesy of Cynthia Leavenworth Bellinger.

Clinton, Jim, and Garfield Leavenworth. Photo courtesy of Cynthia Leavenworth Bellinger.

the hill again. When the tire was at the bottom of the hill, Garfield shot and put a hole in the rubber of the tire.

"When you can do that, you'll never miss another running deer."

Dad used boxes of bullets and practiced all summer until he got it; and he never missed another running deer. He killed at least 300 bucks and didn't remember how many does. But that's how they ate all winter. It took at least seven to feed the family a winter.
—Linda Leavenworth Bohs, daughter of Clinton Leavenworth.

Dr. A.E. Austin, 14 Central Park, N.Y.C., to Lon Austin, Eldred
July 30, 1925
Dear Lon:

I am sending a couple of packages of papers which I will ask you to place upstairs in our little house. I will send a few more copies of the Geographical Society magazine for you to have. We leave here for 15 Claremont Avenue, Wednesday. I was glad to receive your letter. I have read the letter you sent me many times. It was full of music and a beautiful poem about the old place driving the cattle home.

With much love from us all to all,
 Lon [Dr. Alonzo E. Austin]

The Briggs Family Drives East
In Harrison, Nebraska, the Briggs Family welcomed Mary Rosamond Briggs (the future wife of Arthur Austin) in July of 1925.

Three weeks later, Irwin and

Anna Leavenworth, daughter of Garfield and Ella, and granddaughter of Sherman Leavenworth. Photo courtesy of Cynthia Leavenworth Bellinger.

Myrtle Briggs, Laura, 5, Mildred, 4, and little Mary (3 weeks old) headed east in their Model-T to Drew Seminary in New Jersey. (Irwin and Myrtle would be back near the area where the Briggs and Crabtree ancestors had lived in the 1750s.)

The Briggs' came east in a "rattlety bang" Ford, camping across the continent with two older children and a two-month-old baby. They were caught in a terrific rainstorm and the only thing they were able to keep dry was the baby, Mary Rosamond.
—*News article,* The Breezy Westerner.

Besides the occupants of the car...the Ford contained three extra tires, a wash tub, 57 varieties of kitchen utensils, bedding, three suitcases, a score of bundles, a doll and doll carriage, a pair of cow horns... and a donated tent from friends in Chicago. The pair of cow horns was presented to them as a souvenir of their send off by their Nebraska Church.

The Ford covered 2,073 miles an average of 172 miles a day. They passed through nine states, two Indian reservations and two mountain ranges.

The baby of the party, Mary aged six weeks, gained one pound on the trip.—News article titled, Eastward Ho!

We packed everything on our Model-T Ford. Mary was three weeks old. We stopped in Nebraska to see our folks (John and Ida Crabtree; Clint and Indy Briggs) first.

Three weeks later we arrived in the middle of the night. Not knowing where to go, Irwin pitched the tent right in the middle of the campus. Next morning it caused no small stir. In fact it was in all the papers, even over to London, England.
—*Myrtle Crabtree Briggs.*

The Briggs family arrived a day late at Drew Seminary, too late for the church that had been promised to Irwin. Eventually other arrangements were made.

In nine years the Briggs Family would move to Barryville. Irwin would be the pastor of the Pond Eddy, Eldred, and Barryville Methodist Churches.

Lillie Calkin (who Mary Briggs would one day meet) wrote her dad in August, and tried to talk him out of moving.

Lillie Calkin, Bethel, to J.E. Austin, Hopewell Junction, N.Y.
August 4, 1925
Dear Dad,

Just a line to let you know we are alive. Burt is all through haying and has the porch nearly done. Dorothy is visiting at Fosterdale and Dale is with a friend in New Paltz.

We have a swarm of bees which Horton gave Burt.

They are building a reservoir for the Mongaup Falls plant on the Black Lake Brook.

I think you would be very, very foolish to leave the place you have. They are remarkably nice people and you do just as you please, when you please. Jobs like that don't grow on every bush.

How are the chickens and ducks getting on? Our chicks are fine. It still looks as though we would have 450 or 500 pullets.

With love, Lillie

Lillie Calkin, Bethel, to J.E. Austin, Hopewell Junction, N.Y.
Sunday, September 13, 1925
Dear Dad,

We have had a fine time as from about the 13th of August until Sept. 3, some one was sick most of the time.

First Dorothy, then Dale, then Burt, and I. We all had tonsillitis, but none of us were very bad except Burt. He had the worst looking throat I ever saw. It gathered and broke in two places. He doesn't feel just right yet.

My school started Tuesday. I have 25 pupils, all eight grades.

The wind blew hard for about two minutes here tonight. It blew Olsen's hen house clear across the road onto Bernas' fields. It would hold about 1,000 hens beside a two-story feed house. A boarder was seriously hurt, windows blown out, wires down, car ran into a tree. A tree was blown across the road.

We must have just got the edge of it. We have had a few very hot unseasonable days and I thought this afternoon that if we lived in the west I'd be afraid of a cyclone.

Our grapes are ripening.

The Briggs Family on Drew Seminary's campus. Irwin, Laura, Myrtle holding Mary, and Mildred. Photo courtesy of Mary Briggs Austin.

Raymond Austin visited Gladys Myers. Photo in the Austin Collection.

The white grapes are turning red.

I think you are very sensible if you stay where you are this winter. You won't find a better place.

There are bright northern lights tonight.

Have some school work to do so must quit. Love, Lillie

Mort Austin, Eldred, to Mr. J.E. Austin, Hopewell Junction, N.Y.
September 14, 1925
Dear Brother,

Just a few lines to let you know I have not forgotten you. I am not sure that this letter will find you. I should have wrote to you long ago. But we have been very busy this summer. The summer is almost passed away before I knew it. We all have been quite well and business very good.

I hope you are still taking good care of the three ladies that you were with when I last heard from you. I will send you a money order for what I owe you just as soon as you let me know where to send it.

We have a few people here yet. I think we will have most of this month. It will seem good when we are alone again. It has been a long time. We have had a few people since the middle of May. For a while we had 45. That kept us busy. Write soon. Let me know where you are.

Love from all, Mort

New School
It was fall 1925. The former Abel Myers Orchard Terrace Boarding House had been completed, and Art Austin started eighth grade.

Charles E. Lewis was the principal. There were five faculty; two years of high school were offered. The two high school classrooms and three grade school rooms were attended by 116 students—29 were in first and second; 39 were in third through fifth; 24 in sixth through eighth grades; and 24 in High School.

The college entrance course choices: English I, English II, history A, biology, civics, Latin I, Latin II, plane geometry, and elementary algebra.

Jennie Austin, Edred, to Raymond Austin
October 1925
My dear Raymond,

I wonder if you ever thought that we have not heard a word of you since Labor Day which seems a long time ago. So we are beginning to think about your welfare.

We are counting on your vacation being the first two weeks in November and hope you will not disappoint us at that time. I think you are registered up here, so you can vote if you are here at election time which I hope you will be. Let us know what your plans are as soon as possible.

We have had a few days of winter here, but tonight it begins

Gladys Myers who Raymond Austin visited. Photo courtesy of Joan Austin Geier.

to warm up again. I suppose you see Gladys each weekend. I think Aunt Minnie and Charlotte are down there now. For some reason or other, my relatives keep far away. I have only seen grandfather twice this fall.

Burma-Shave

Clinton Odell, owner of the Burma-Vita Company, in Minneapolis, Minnesota, introduced a brush-less shaving cream product he called Burma-Shave in 1925. It was hoped that Burma-Shave would have more appeal than the company's original liniment product and would increase sales. The advertisement scheme was novel—a series of signs with quips (and later poems) were placed along roadsides across the U.S. Sales took off. In the 1950s our family (in Michigan) enjoyed the rhyming jingle signs similar to this one:

Every shaver now can snore
Six more minutes than before
By using Burma-Shave (1929).
—Rawsome Jr., Frank, *the verse by the side of the road*, S. Greene Press, 1965.

1925 Halfway Brook News

1925 Births

- Deloros May Koenig born to Hazel Leavenworth and Eugene Koenig.
- Thomas Emmet Myers born to Martin D. and Mary Fee Myers.
- Mary Rosamond Briggs born in Harrison, Nebraska.
- Robert Wolff born to Carl and Freida Kloss Wolff.

Mary Briggs, daughter of Irwin and Myrtle Briggs. Photo courtesy of Mary Briggs Austin.

1925 Marriages

- Harold Dunlap married on Easter Sunday.
- Herbert Kinne married Mildred MacKechnie in June.
- Beatrice Avery married Charles W. Horton. After they were married at the farm in Eldred in 1925, they moved to the Binghamton area where Charles got a job with the Johnson City Publishing Co. The following June they were back living in Monticello in a very small bungalow on Summit Avenue. —*William E. Horton.*
- Raymond Sherwood Hallock, son of Samuel and Anna Hallock, married Ida Mary Schwarz.
- Leavenworth descendant Elliott Swanell Ewart, son of Albert and Edith Palmer Ewart, married Vera Jones in Detroit, Michigan.
- Atwell Bradley married Frieda Meyer Guenther (a widow) the day before Christmas. Her children: Freida, 15, Edith, 14, Clinton Joseph, 11, Helen, 10, Viola Guenther, 6. Atwell's sons: Clifford Bradley, 23 (may have been elsewhere), George Bradley, 17, Clarence Bradley, 16.

1925 Deaths

- Robert Crandall, 1871–1925, was the husband of Nellie M. Simpson, and father of Clifford, Verna, and, Stanley.
- Charles H. Styles, 1836–1925. Charles was the father of Walter Styles.
- Minerva Wells, wife of Willard Wells, died December 11, 1925. She was the daughter of Hiram and Prudence Racine. Their daughter Maude Wells married Duane Hulse.
- Thomas Alvin Hill Sr., 1851–1925, an old and highly respected citizen died at his home, near Barryville, after a long illness. Mr. Hill was born in England and came to this country with his parents at the age of ten years and settled in Barryville, where he followed the occupation of farming. At the time of his death, he was 75 years of age. He was united in marriage to Miss Alice Sergeant (his second wife), of Eldred, and had he lived until next September, he and his wife would have celebrated their 50th wedding anniversary. The surviving relatives: his wife; three daughters, Mrs. James Crowe, Mrs. Myron Carpenter of this city, and Mrs. George Eldred of Middletown; six sons, Walter of Binghamton, Alvin and John of Eldred; Thomas, Matthew, and William of Barryville; and 19 grandchildren. Funeral services were held in the Congregational Church and conducted by Rev. John Bennett. —*Port Jervis Union Gazette*, March 1925.

Bobby has not been very well lately and from now on I must watch his diet very careful. He has had glasses for about three weeks. As school began the boys got the rope off the old flag pole and were having hanging parties. Bobby was one of the chief horse thieves and certainly had a close call from the scar on his neck. Sometimes, I think his trouble with his head might come from that western necktie party.

Last night we were settled for a quiet evening when one of our city boarders walked in on us. I believe he goes back tomorrow night.

Mr. Shubert went back last week. He had a very bad cold when he started home and we feel rather anxious as we have not heard from him as he said he would send a card.

The electric line is going up quite fast. I believe they are putting up the wire through the village now.

1925 Shohola Barryville Baseball Team. Standing: Charles Lass, Walt Coursen, Bill Coursen, Art Toaspern, Jay Lass. Sitting: Harold Black, Prosper Yozag, Peddler Liebla, Carl J. Vogt. Photo courtesy of George J. Fluhr.

Art with his dog King. Photo courtesy of Mary Briggs Austin.

I heard the boys say that Raymond Myers had moved to Port Jervis this last week so he must have a winter's work down there.

Dad and Bill are busy getting out wood. They have quite a lot ordered ahead, I suppose on account of the coal strike.

Arthur is still as robust as ever and seems to enjoy life very much.

We want to walk down to the village and mail this tonight so it will be sure to go tomorrow.

Let us know when you are coming home. The boys watch the mail to hear from you.

Love from all, Mother

Lillie Calkin, Bethel, to Mr. J.E. Austin, Hopewell Junction, N.Y.
November 15, 1925
Dear Dad,
   Burt finished the new hen house and we put the pullets in a week ago yesterday. Burt puts the lights on them and today we got six pullet eggs. How are your hens doing? Mother [Emma Austin] doesn't get any eggs from hers. She bought 15 ready-to-lay pullets this fall at $2.25 each. She can't take care of chickens, but you might as well talk to the wind. She will probably come up here to stay after a little. She can't stay there alone this winter. [Emma's sister must have died.]
   With love, Lillie

December 15, 1925
Dear Dad,
   Will you come up for Xmas this year? Don't send us any

Jennie's father Sherman S. Leavenworth, on his property. "I have only seen Grandfather twice this fall." Photo courtesy of Cynthia Leavenworth Bellinger.

presents, but come on yourself. Surely, someone can be found to do the chores for a few days.

I want you to see the house since it is finished, the hen house, etc. We have a dandy bunch of pullets, about 375 good ones and about 75 old hens. Today the pullets laid 181 eggs, yesterday, 187. With Love, Lillie

Atwell Bradley Marries Freida Meyer Guenther
You may remember Atwell's second wife Helen Heinekamp died in 1920 and that Freida Guenther's husband Joseph Guenther died in 1921. On December 24, Atwell Bradley married Freida Meyer Guenther.

Lillie Calkin, Bethel, to Mr. J.E. Austin, Hopewell Junction, N.Y.
December 27, 1925
Dear Dad,
   So you have a car, too. Well they are a hard thing to do without. I wish you could have come up for X-mas.
   Our pullets are doing well. The most we have had in one day from the pullets was 203; from the hens, 34. We have sold $108 worth of eggs this month and have three crates out and will fill three or four more this week.
   With love, Lillie

The Kelso Family
The Kelso family lived in Eldred in 1860 and were good friends with Henry and Mary Ann Austin—until Robert Kelso Sr. and Henry Austin got into a lawsuit. The children however remained friends.

There are several Kelso folks mentioned in this book who were most likely related to the original Kelso family: Emma Kelso Collins, Belle Greig Kelso Grotecloss (her first husband), and Murie Kelso.

Murie Kelso was probably a brother to Emma Collins (widow of Tom Collins). Lon Austin kept up Emma's property on Collins Road. In this next letter, Murie writes to his friend Mort Austin who was caring for Murie's horse. Edgar Sergeant had been feeding and housing the horse, but Edgar was sick in December.

M.C. Kelso, 16 Horatio St., N.Y.C., to Mort Austin, Eldred
December 1925
Dear Friend Mort,

You will think I am a careless person to simply put my horse over on you and make no further arrangements as to his expenses. I will leave the matter of how you feed him to you. He did not get many oats, as he was doing no work. Just how much Edgar fed him, I don't know, and once a week he was to have a bran mash.

Whatever his oats and hay cost you, send me the bill and I will send you a check and add to that what you want for his care. It has been a great relief to me to know he is with you and I hope you may find some little use for him so he can get exercise.

You know what it means to pity a helpless animal and I could not turn him away. And I also know that you more than any person I know can understand my feeling about him. If I could find time to learn how to run the car, we could see Eldred a little oftener. Give my love to Jennie.

I am sincerely, M.C. Kelso
Kelso and Company, Inc.
Pianos & Player Pianos

M.C. Kelso, 16 Horatio St., N.Y.C., to Mort Austin, Eldred
January 1926
Dear Friend Mort,

It was good of you to write me again. I am enclosing a check for the bill sent me, but I feel guilty in letting you take so little for the care of the horse. It is worth more and I am willing to pay you more for his keep, as I think that too is very little.

When Emma was up that last time she met Mr. Kinne and he said he had loose hay for sale, so she ordered some to be sent to Lon and I think a ton to be sent to you for the horse.

If it comes, you will please take it in, that is if you have the room.

Emma had a letter from Mrs. Sergeant telling her of Edgar's death, but she gave no particulars. When Mrs. Sergeant wrote me about two weeks ago, she said Edgar was still at the hospital, but had not been operated on. So I imagine his trouble was of a hopeless nature, since he could not get well, it was far better he was not called to bear his pain and trouble longer. It is a very sad case, almost seems incredible for he was so strong and well such a short time ago.

Emma is looking forward to getting back to the farm. These last few days have been so warm it almost fools you in thinking winter is gone, but we know better.

We had some fiercely cold days Christmas week, seven degrees above zero. I used to like winter and how I used to drag that sleigh up the hill and ride down all the way from the top of the hill of your father's farm to the foot of the hill before your home now.

I can't say I pine to go up and down those hills for the sake of a sleigh ride.

Emma and I were sorry we could not get down to see you that last trip we made out…But spring and summer will come again and we will look forward to seeing you all again. I am so content when I think of poor Dick in your care. I wish all animals had so good a place. I never worry about him.

Send me the bill each month. You should not lay out your money. You are doing a good deal for me in keeping the horse.

With best regards to Jennie, and wishing you both a Happy New Year.

I am ever your old friend,
Murrie Kelso

1925–1926 National News

1925
- The 1925 Locarno Pact committed Britain and Italy to come to France's aid.
- Field Marshal Paul von Hindenburg elected president of Germany.
- John T. Scopes convicted of teaching Charles Darwin's evolutionary theory at a Tennessee High School, fined $100.
- The Grand Ole Opry transmitted its first radio broadcast.

1926
- Warner Brothers produced the first movie with a sound track.
- Pilot Floyd Bennett with Richard E. Byrd as his navigator, guided a three-engine monoplane to the North Pole and back—the first flight to the North Pole.
- Robert H. Goddard demonstrated the first liquid-fueled rockets in Auburn, Massachusetts. The rocket flew 184 feet in 2.5 seconds.
- Germany joined the League of Nations in September.
- The NBC Radio Network was formed by Westinghouse, General Electric, and RCA in November.
- December 25, 1926, Hirohito became Japan's 124th emperor.

Dog walks past Sunshine Hall and Sunshine Hall Free Library. The old schoolhouse is in the distance. Photo in the Austin Family Collection.

Dot Calkin, Bethel, to Mr. J.E. Austin, Hopewell Junction, N.Y.
January 7, 1926
Dear Grandpa,
　How is your tin horse [car]? Can you get on it yet? Just as quick as you can run it, come up. I wish I could come down and see you. Thank for the beads. They are the only pair I got this Xmas. I got a doll and this writing paper and two or three boxes of handkerchiefs and 1/2 dozen books, a pair of garters, a pair of slippers, a vanity bag, a pair of bloomers, an under skirt and a bottle of perfume and a box of powder, and a game of old maid. I got another little doll about 3-1/2 inches tall. Mama gave it to me for a joke, but I like it just about as good as the rest of my gifts.
　I have got a cold. I am not going to school today, the 7th of January.
　I haven't sent your present yet. I got it late so I could not send it and have it get there by Xmas. Mother said that she was going to send something with it so I have waited. I will send it on soon. Love from all, Dorothy

Mort Austin, Eldred, to J.E. Austin, Hopewell Junction, N.Y.
January 8, 1926
Dear Brother,
　We received the cards and were glad to hear from you. I know you must think it shaming I have not sent you a letter before this. I seem to be so busy all the time. But to tell you the truth, I have so little ambition, I can not get a long with my work very fast. I have just got my winter's wood cut up, but now I have got a lot of brush to cut and a little lumber to get out for a new hen house. We are having very good winter weather so far.
　Ed Sergeant passed away Saturday about seven o'clock; was buried Tuesday.
　If you stay where you are, I may in the spring come to see you and the country. I will try to get away for two or three days. I do not feel very well this winter. My folks are all feeling quite well. I hope this few lines will find you well. With love from all, Mort

Charles Edgar Sergeant Dies
Edgar Sergeant had been a caretaker and watchman at the Cahoonzie Club for several years before he died at age 70. Edgar and his first wife Elizabeth Clark had several children who are a part of this story: Alvah and Mary Hulse Sergeant and their sons Grant and Charles Arthur; Anna Pearl Sergeant Brague; and

J.P. Morgan's Shell Cottage

Herb and Margo Bosch, cute children of Menzo and Lena Bosch, in 1925. Photo courtesy of Ken Bosch.

From about 1926 to 1941, Menzo and Helen "Lena" Bosch and their children Herbert and Margo lived and worked on the J.P. Morgan Estate in Glen Cove, Long Island.
　Menzo was a groundskeeper and gardener; and Lena cooked for the help who boarded upstairs at their residence, the Tudor-style "Shell Cottage."
　Lena's sons Charlie L. and Willie (from her first marriage to Charlie Bosch Sr.) later lived with Menzo and Lena. Willie worked as a chauffeur in the late 1920s and early 1930s, driving for Jerome Kern and other luminaries. "Shell House Cottage," its ceilings covered with sea shells, is now in the National Register of Historic Places.—*Ken Bosch.*

Edith Sergeant Timmeroff.

Lillie Calkin, Bethel, to Mr. J.E. Austin, Hopewell Junction, N.Y.
February 14, 1926
Dear Dad,
    I did not know about Ed Sergeant.
    We have had quite a spell of weather. I got to school both days of the big storm, but no one else did on Friday. Dorothy is going to school with me now. We both stay in Miss Story's house over to Fosterdale from Monday to Friday. I could not drive from here the way the roads are now.
    Our chickens are not doing very well, range from 130 to 177 a day. Only cleared about $65 in January. I think we crowded them too hard, too young.
    I meant to send you a check on what we owe you this month and maybe I will yet, but Burt expects to go to the city to have his rupture operated on, and I will want a little spare cash if he goes before I get my next check. I'll send you some then, if not before. I hope you will keep well. How is the sore hand? We have to leave early in the morning. We have had an ice storm today and the roads will be heavy tomorrow.
    Don't think I bought this paper. I detest pink writing paper, but I received two boxes for Xmas.
    With love, Lillie

Dot Calkin, Bethel, to Mr. J.E. Austin, Hopewell Junction, N.Y.
February 20, 1926
Dear Grandpa,
    Have you tried to run your car yet or haven't you had a chance to? We can't run ours. It's all we can do to get down through the field with the horses.
    I go over to mother's school now. We can't get through anymore, so we stay over there.
    How are your hens laying? Daddy says our hens are laying pretty good. He has got about 320 and he gets around 175 eggs every day.
    I think I got 27 valentines this year. Thanks for the valentine you gave me. It is the nicest one I got. Daddy has got all of his wood out of the woods and some sawed up.
    Love from all, Dorothy

Lillie Calkin, Bethel, to Mr. J.E. Austin, Hopewell Junction, N.Y.
April 13, 1926
Dear Dad,
    Have been even busier than usual with Burt in the hospital, Dale sick, and school. Burt is home again. Came Tuesday. Is feeling and looking fine, but will have to be very careful for some time. Dale is better, too. Had a real croupy cold for a week and is not really well yet. We got 194 eggs today. Got 30 cents and 32 cents for the last we have returns from. Hope you are keeping well.
    With love, Lillie

Mort Austin, Mountain Grove House, Eldred, to J.E. Austin, Hopewell Junction, N.Y.
April 13, 1926
Dear Brother,
    Your card received a few days ago. As ever, glad to hear from you, and that you are still in the same place for that is good since you like the place.
    I was in hopes I would be able to take a trip this spring up to see you, but I will not be able to get away for I have so much to do.
    The snow has been so deep and lasted so long I did not get my wood yet. It looks now as if spring had come and I am way behind with my work.
    Bill has a steady job, so I will be very busy.
    We are all feeling quite well.

> ## J.C. Penney Marries Caroline Autenrieth
>
> Perhaps you remember that around 1900 the Autenrieth's ran the Hotel in Eldred that James Y. Parker had built, and that it was owned by the Straubs by 1910. Caroline Autenrieth was in Anna Leavenworth's class at the Eldred schoolhouse in 1906.
>
> In the 1920s Caroline Autenrieth worked a short time as secretary for Mr. James Cash Penney, founder of Penney's Department Store. In 1925 Caroline went to France to study voice. She married Mr. Penney in 1926 in Paris, France. It was her first marriage. Mr. Penney had been widowed twice.

Hope you are the same.
    Mrs. Collins (Emma) has moved back. I think Lon is going to help her out this summer. Lon has sold all of his cattle except two cows. It is dinner time, so I must close.
    With love from all, Mort

Lillie Calkin, Bethel, to Mr. J.E. Austin, Hopewell Junction, N.Y.
June 13, 1926
Dear Dad,
    School closed the 11th! I thought I'd get down this week, but Burt has carpenter work and I'll have to stay and look after the chicks. It will probably be early in July when I can get away.
    I have got to get busy and clean house, too. We got another 500 chicks, but lost over 120 of them. They are doing well now. Our garden is very belated. Have had radishes, lettuce, and onions, but that is all (except asparagus).
    With Love, Lillie

Mort and Jennie Austin, unknown lady, Raymond and Gladys, Sherman Leavenworth, (possibly) Anna Leavenworth. In front: Rev. Bennett, Bob Austin, unknown man, Johnny Myers, the ring bearer.

Bill Austin, Raymond Austin, Gladys Myers, Betty Horton Bennett, Rev. Bennett. Photos courtesy of the Raymond Austin Family.

Raymond Austin Marries Gladys Myers

In June Raymond Austin married Gladys Myers. Mr. Bennett, pastor of the Congregational Church, performed the ceremony.

"I'll love, honor, and cherish, but not obey," Gladys had told the pastor. *Obey* was not included in their vows.

Raymond left for Venezuela to work for Gulf Oil, after a three-day honeymoon. He had to sign the contract as a single man. Raymond was to be gone for two years but would be back after one because he was so ill with malaria.

Jennie Austin, Eldred, to Mr. C.R. Austin, c/o Gulf Oil Co., Apartado 234, Maracaibo, Venezuela, S.A.
Sept. 12, 1926, Sunday afternoon
My dear Raymond,

We all feel guilty in not writing before and we certainly would of, but we knew Gladys was keeping you informed of our welfare. We have been very busy, but only have Mr. Shubert and Mr. Baque here now and a girl from Beaver Brook who is attending High School here in Eldred.

Dad is on the jury and goes back and forth to Monticello every day. Mr. Howlett is also on the jury so it makes it good for Dad as he rides with him.

I have not seen Grandfather since your wedding, but know he is alright. Aunt Anna has been home with him most of the summer. As soon as Dad is home again, I will go over someday. It is quite a walk for me as I have not walked much lately.

Dory came in the other day to inform me that our town clerk had skipped the country. From all accounts, the poor fellow got so deeply in debt that he has had to make himself scarce for awhile and besides he is quite a sport and drinks too much for his own good. Of course Dory is delighted.

Gladys helped us out during our rush. We had a good lot of help and I do not feel nearly as tired as other years. Even Dad has come through without a sick spell. He gives all the credit to the "pep" he eats so much of.

Bob has a new teacher (Mrs. Styles). He said he never knew anyone could talk so much and so fast before.

Arthur has started in the first year in high school. Sometimes he is quite discouraged. He is the only one of the beginners that they put in the Latin class and he don't like it one bit.

I suppose it will be two weeks or more before you receive this letter and so much can happen between now and then.

We had quite a smash up out on our hill the other day. Some crazy fool was going like the wind down the hill and just below the

Raymond and Gladys Myers Austin on their wedding day. Photo in Austin Collection.

first entrance to our house, the car somersaulted twice and came back on its wheels. Mr. Shubert and Mr. Baque said they would not have believed that such a thing could happen if they had not seen it with their own eyes. The man driving was the only one in the car. His face was only scratched, but they took him back to the city as he seemed to think he was hurt inwardly. Talk of looping the loops, he certainly did it in his car.

Sometime in August the Federal officers raided our booze joints at Highland Lake. Claude Angell lost his two booze trucks and his drivers are under bonds.

Mrs. Straub died in the early part of the summer. Although the family is grown up, they surely will miss her.

"Uncle Dave" caused some amusement to the town by buying a bathing suit and going in bathing with the young folks this summer. Soon after you left, he tried driving his car and they found him under it one day, a few miles from Eldred. So he sold it and bought the bathing suit. And by the way Arthur swam across Highland Lake, but it was unbeknown to me, until later. He will be wanting to try the English Channel next.

I watch the paper to see when there is an incoming vessel from South America, and then for a day or so watch for letters.

I suppose you have heard from Gladys that Winiford and Betty are married…

Gladys told me you had a touch of the fever. I hope it don't get such a hold on you as it did when you were in Panama.

Be sure and take good care of yourself and write as soon as possible for we all are anxious to hear from you and from now on I will be able to write oftener.

Love from us all, Mother

Franz August Schwarz Dies
Franz A. Schwarz, town clerk of the Town of Lumberland died suddenly at Glen Spey in September, following an illness of three weeks. An experienced musician, he had farmed and had owned Pine Terrace in Glen Spey. He would have a grandson Frank V Schwarz who would one day be historian for the Town of Lumberland.

School Fall 1926
In fall 1926 an English 3 class was added to the curriculum. Charles C. Pierce was the principal; there were still five faculty and two years of high school available. There were 106 pupils: Arthur Austin was one of the 25 in High School; 27 were in first and second; 30 in third, fourth, and fifth; and 24 in sixth through eighth grades.

In April the New York State Education Department had granted permission for the eighth grade common school in Eldred to add a secondary department. The eighth grade students of that year continued their studies for the next three years, completing the freshman, sophomore, and junior courses of studies.

In the first grade class of 1926 was Eleanor Myers, second cousin of the Austins and Leavenworths. Most likely Eleanor's teacher was Miss Charlotte Leavenworth, a first cousin of Eleanor's father, Charlie Myers. Charlie's brother Martin D. Myers Sr. and family lived in Eldred. We'll talk more about Martin's family in the next chapter.

Arthur Austin, High School
As mentioned in his mother's

"Arthur has started in the first year in high school." Arthur Austin and King. Photo in Austin Collection.

"Dory came in the other day to inform me…" A formal photo of Ladore (Dory) Austin, Mort's brother. He sometimes lived with Mort and Jennie Austin. Photo in Austin Family Collection.

Students at the Eldred School in 1926. Adorable Eleanor Myers is in the middle of the first row. Photo courtesy of Timothy C. Rizzuto.

letter, my dad (Art Austin) started high school in the fall of 1926.

In high school I took an academic course, and received a state regents' diploma with credit.

Arthur Austin's 1926 Health Club and Reading Certificates, courtesy of the Austin Family.

My participation in a number of High School plays helped to break down a reserve inherited from English ancestry and developed by country life.

During my school years, I read a wide variety of books, ranging from wild west stories and the Rover Boys *to Dickens and Dumas. Much of this reading was of questionable value, but it did give me an interest in a wide range of subjects.—Arthur Austin.*

Arthur's Reading Certificate of June 1926 recorded books he read in eighth grade: Longfellow, *Hiawatha*; Lincoln, *Gettysburg Address*; Tappan, *In the Days of William the Conqueror*; and Cooper, *The Pilot*.

There are a number of photos of Art dressed as Uncle Dudley, a character in one of the High School plays. There are so many photos *(see p. 406)* that most likely Art's Aunt Aida Austin was the photographer. After McKinley died in WWI, Art became Aida's favorite nephew, and suffered through many photo sessions.

Arthur Austin, Eldred, to C.R. Austin, c/o Gulf Oil Co., Venezuela, S.A.
September 20, 1926
Dear Raymond,

Arthur Austin as Uncle Dudley in a play. Photo courtesy of Mary Briggs Austin.

1926 Halfway Brook News

Oakland Hotel Burned

- 1926 saw a spectacular fire in which the Oakland Hotel was totally consumed.—*Tusten History*.

Arrivals on Ship from Germany

- Alfons, Johanna, and Irene Theurer arrived in June. Within ten years they would run the Sunset View House on Highland Lake.

1926 Weddings

- Leavenworth descendant Rolland Ewart, son of Albert and Edith Palmer Ewart, married Rhoda Crean.
- Harry Lass, son of John Charles and Meta Toaspern Lass, married Elizabeth (Bessie) MacIntyre.
- Charles Raymond Austin married Gladys Myers.
- Joseph Mulvihill married Elizabeth Ford *(see pp. 92–93)*.

1926 Births

- Charles (Chuck) Myers born to Archibald and Minnie Ethel Sergeant Myers.
- Hazel Parker born to William H. and Eleanora Parker.
- Richard F. Haas born to Richard E. and Louise Haas.
- William F. Horton born to Charles W. and Beatrice Avery Horton.

1926 Deaths

- Charles Edgar Sergeant, 1856–1926, son of Alvah Sergeant and Phoebe Owen Sergeant, was survived by his second wife Henrietta Halstead.
- Charles S. Darling, 70, husband of Charlotte (Lottie) Myers, died in April. He was survived by his wife, three daughters: Ida Whitmarsh, Edith Sears, and Agnes Curtiss; two sisters; two brothers; and two grandchildren: Elizabeth Whitmarsh and Charlotte Curtiss. (Lottie Myers Darling was the sister of Maria Leavenworth).
- Mary J. Kerr, 1843–1926, widow of John Kerr, died at the home of her son, William Kerr, in Barryville. She was a member of the Barryville Methodist Church. The surviving relatives: two daughters, Mrs. James MacIntyre and Mrs. Charles Wolfe; Three sons: William, John, and Lewis. *Republican Watchman*, June 4, 1926.
- Franz A. Schwarz, 1859–1926, was town clerk of the Town of Lumberland. He was born at Hamburg, Germany. He married Anna Eckstein and moved to Sullivan County in 1910. The Glen Spey folks thought so much of him that they elected him…as town clerk, and in that capacity he was an expert. He was an experienced musician and was heard at Monticello on two occasions. He was a farmer by occupation. Besides his wife he was survived by three sons: Victor, Walter, and Frank; and two daughters, Irena and Margarett. Burial at Glen Spey. *Republican Watchman*, Sep. 10, 1926.
- Howard Pelton, 1882–1926, died at his home in Barryville, after a six weeks' illness from a complication of diseases. He was a son of Asher and Carrie Westfall Pelton. For the greater part of his life he lived at Barryville. For 14 years he was the foreman in the Barryville Glass Cutting Factory. He was survived by his wife Edith Pelton; his mother Carrie Pelton and brother Edward.
- Amanda Hogencamp Bogert, 83, was survived by four sons, three daughters, one brother, ten grandchildren, and seven great-grandchildren.
- Charles Howard Lass, husband of Veronica Campbell, died from pneumonia at the age of 29. Charles liked to hunt. He worked for a Bower's Lumber Co. from Pennsylvania, and worked locally lumbering. His children: Marion Helen Lass, 4-1/2, Jean Lass, 3, Meta Lass, 1-1/2. His son Charles Howard Lass would be born February 1927.

Katherine Wiest Miller. Photo courtesy of Ken Bosch.

- Katherine Wiest Miller, 1859-1926, died of stomach cancer at the home of her son, Ben Miller, in Matamoras, Penn. Her daughter Lena was married first to Charlie and then Menzo Bosch.
- Juliana Straub died in 1926.
- Joseph Maier, 91, was a grandfather to Minnie, Charlie, Lulu, Herman, Ed, Ralph, Menzo, and Tillie Bosch.
- Charles Scheniman, 1875–1926.
- Emma Amelia Schwab Hallock, 1852–1926. She was buried in the Van Tuyl Cemetery, Lumberland.

Joseph Maier. Photo courtesy of Ken Bosch.

Bob, Raymond, and Bill with Ned the donkey. Photo courtesy of Joan Austin Geier.

As I have nothing to do, I guess I might as well tell you a lot of junk. I am taking Latin, biology, civics, and algebra in high school. Next year I think I will take Spanish and German. Latin and Algebra are kind of hard, but civics and biology are easy. Friday in biology, we had to pick a grasshopper apart. Some of the girls did not like it very much. Mr. Pierce teaches biology, and civics and Miss Hartmon teaches Latin and Algebra. I have to study pretty hard.

We are trying to make up a baseball team. Mr. Baque and Mr. Shubert are up here now. We are having nice weather here. How do you like South America? Is it very hot? I wish I could come down and stay with you.

Mother, Dad, Bill, and Bob are feeling good. Mr. Shubert, Mr. Baque and I play cards every night. They are going away Wednesday. That's all the junk I can think of, so I will close.

Arthur

Mort Austin, Eldred, to C.R. Austin, c/o Gulf Oil Co., Venezuela, S.A.
September 26, 1926
My dear son,

I have come home from church, the boys are all in bed. Your mother is reading a book. We are all very glad to get a letter from you. We have had a good summer and made good. It is good to be alone. We have one woman here yet. I think she will go this coming Saturday.

I am very busy trying to get my work done before winter. Arthur is in high school and Bob is getting on good. I think they have sent you a letter. I suppose your mother and Gladys tell you all the news. I do so little writing that it is hard work for me to write a letter. So I do some of your mother's work and get her to do the writing.

I think about you everyday, and I pray that God will take care of you and keep you from all harm. I know when we are young, we do not see things as we do when we get older. I know it pays best to do right here and I am sure it will be better for us in the next world if we have done the best we can in this world.

I hope you will write home as often as you can. I am getting sleepy. So good night.
With love, Father

Bob Austin, Eldred, to C.R. Austin, c/o Gulf Oil Co., Venezuela, S.A.
October 22, 1926
Dear Raymond,

I bought a donkey from Mae Parker. I can ride him. Last night I rode it up to Uncle Lon's and tonight after school, Clifford Crandall came up and we rode him up to Uncle Lon's. I'm going to get a harness and a pair of shafts for him to pull my wagon.

I am in the fifth grade and Arthur is in high school. Last Saturday night, Gladys came up to our house. Last weekend Ed Myers went up to Collins and got all of her apples.

Mrs. Styles is my teacher. Last Saturday I went nutting. I have the nuts drying by the stove. I'm going nutting tomorrow. Bob

P.S. Mae Parker gave me the donkey. We got a radio. It's name is Ned. I mean the donkey's name.

Lillie Calkin, Bethel, to Mr. J.E. Austin, Hopewell Junction, N.Y.
November 14, 1926
Dear Dad,

We are having pretty fair weather for November. We have had some very cold days, but much better than last year.

Our pullets lay about 35 eggs now and are gaining steadily. Got about 8 or 10 from old hens. Burt is building an addition to the hen house. When done the whole house will be 18 feet by 90 feet. We have about 350 pullets from the first thousand; the latter ones have not begun to lay yet.

Burt saw a power washer there which belongs to Volk's who wanted to sell it as they had a new electric machine. Burt told me about it. My old machine being about worn out, I told him he might get it, but I advised him not to pay more than $10 for a temporary makeshift. He told Frank what I said and Frank told Volk, who said that he ought to have $20. Rather than store it he told Frank to take $10. So this is what we have; a Thor washing machine, for either engine or electric drive, a power wringer, reversible, only used one season for $10. If I had seen the machine, I would never have had the nerve to make such an offer. Our gas engine pumps the water and runs the washer.

Hope you keep well and that

Homemade Brew from Highland Lake

Left: Charlie Bosch (in dark sweater, standing) with the thirsty entourage of city folks he took to Patsy Clark's brew house. Patsy on right in front row. Right: Patsy's brew house around 1930. Note the craftsmanship in the building. Photos courtesy of Ken Bosch.

Patsy Clark and puppy. Photo courtesy of Victoria Kohler.

Patsy and customers. Photo courtesy of Ken Bosch.

Charlie Bosch (left) hosts a party with his own home brew. Photo courtesy of Ken Bosch.

Jennie Austin mentioned in a letter to Raymond that the "Federal officers raided our booze joints at Highland Lake."

The 18th Amendment to the U.S. Constitution prohibited the manufacture, sale, and importation of intoxicating liquors from January 17, 1920 to December 5, 1933 when it was repealed.

During Prohibition Patsy Clark (well-known for skirting the law in such activities as illegal trapping for hides) made home-brew and sold it to the city boarders.

Patsy brewed his illicit beverage in a crock in his shack near Highland Lake under less than hygienic conditions. While "the booze" was brewing Patsy covered the crock with his very dirty old hunting coat. Besides being filthy, the coat was full of dog hairs because his dog slept on it at night.

Aside from buying alcohol from illicit brewers and still operators, many people brewed their own beer. Charlie Bosch brewed large quantities of beer and even grew his own hops. —Ken Bosch, from memoirs of Ed Bosch.

One of several photos Aida Austin took of Arthur Austin as Uncle Dudley in a play. Photo courtesy of Mary Briggs Austin.

your chickens do well.
    Kindest regards to the ladies.
    With love, Lillie

Jennie Austin, Mountain Grove House, Eldred, to Raymond
Sunday evening [after Dec. 10]
My dear Raymond,
    We have been a very wicked family today, not one of us have been to church and the reason, Dad, Arthur, and Bobby are just recovering from the grippe. It has been the worst siege that we have had in a long time. They were all quite sick for a couple days, but will be alright if they do not catch more cold. I suppose you heard of the death of Charley Lass and Harold Quick. Next it will be Nate Dailey. He has had one hemorrhage after another, the last week or two.
    Mrs. Tuzza and Nellie have been here for two weeks. They returned to the city yesterday. Nellie had pneumonia and the doctor told them to get out of the city a couple weeks. She seemed alright when she went back.
    My electric washer and radio have certainly taken some of the loneliness and hard work out of the winter months. I only wish I could remember one quarter of the things I hear over the radio. I certainly would be a wise one if my memory was good.
    There has been a lot of sickness in Eldred. Part of the time Dr. Smith has been away. I think one of his brothers has been sick. We had Dr. Gutfruend. He lives on the Becker place. He seems very good at his practice. He came to Eldred for his health and does not go out very much.
    I am expecting quite a few of the N.Y.C. school teachers up for their Easter vacation. We gave our room downstairs to Nellie and her mother so it made it hard when Dad and the boys were sick to run up and downstairs. Arthur certainly grew.
    I was expecting Gladys Tuesday. But her father told me she went to Binghamton instead.
    Harold Dunlap has turned to be a hermit—at least I have not seen him all winter. His wife and mother stopped and had coffee with me the day of George LaBarr's funeral.
    From all accounts, Harold has settled down to be an old steady married man.
    We hear some fine sermons over the radio, also lectures, music, etc. It seems that I must have heard almost everything worth hearing. Of course a lot of nonsense comes along with the other. Jacksonville is the farthest south and Kansas City, West. We have heard California, but it was relayed. Also London has been relayed through a Canadian station. Davenport, Iowa, has a fine station, but it comes on late at night.
    Dory is as busy as ever and everybody keeps stringing him continually. Just now, it is over some girl. I know Harry Lang is the girl, but cannot make Dory believe it. Harry writes the letters and sends them to someone in the city and they mail them back to Dory and of course he answers them. They say the letters are very funny.
    Dad had a nice letter from Robert Collins last week. When you, or better still take time and send him some cards from South America. Send them to Rev. Robert Collins, Madison, N.J., care of Mrs. Louis Noe.
    Well, must close. Bob has a letter somewhere around to put in.
    Love from all, Mother

Jennie Austin, in east Eldred, had written in October 1925 that the electricity was being put up quickly. It had not reached her brother Garfield's place yet. In this next chapter Jennie's nephew James (Jim) Leavenworth tells about the electricity which finally arrived at their house in 1927.

Men's Clothing

Sinsheimer, the Store of Quality, Court Street Brooklyn, N.Y.

In Fall 1926 Louis Sinsheimer quoted Ell Austin the following costs:
- Rubber Knee Boots $3.45/pair.
- Good overalls $1.25/pair.
- Heavy socks (size 10) 19 cents/pair.
- Oil slickers $3.75.
- Rain coat $2.75.
- Good work shirts 75 and 85 cents.
- Good work pants $1.50.
- Heavy ribbed winter underwear 85 cents/garment.
- Heavy ribbed union suits $1.35/garment.

Chapter 4
Lights, Toasters, Radios
The Leavenworths, 1927–1929

Electricity was something for the future and when I was about five years old they gave us electric on this road. Some people had it in town, but it was not common at that time.—James Leavenworth.

Electricity arrived at James Leavenworth's home when he was 5. James (Jim) Leavenworth, 8, in the photo. Photo courtesy of Cynthia Leavenworth Bellinger.

When we first got electric it was something; one ceiling light in each room, and one receptacle in each room. Everybody put a few receptacles in each room as the electric company advised it. No one knew what they were for, but then everyone got radios and toasters and then later the refrigerator and washers came.

Our electric bill those days was 90 cents a month and sometimes that was hard to come up with.

Money in those days was nice, but no one had any and it didn't seem to bother them. People would barter. Many people in the winter time lived off the land, cut wood in the winter, or worked in the woods logging or icing. Most everyone had an ice house in those days to keep things fresh in the summer.

As for the electric line I'm not sure, but think it came to Yulan from Narrowsburg. In Narrowsburg there was a man by the name of Huebner who put a generator in the brook and he had light that supplied all of Narrowsburg. The light company bought him out and then they came to Beaver Brook and then to Eldred.

When I worked for the Lumber Company, Bob Huebner worked there too, and he gave me the history of electric that supplied Narrowsburg. It was his father that started it, and said he was paid well, and couldn't refuse to sell out to the light company.

When it got to Yulan, they started putting power to Yulan and all the boarding houses which were many at the time. I have been told that there were as many as 600 to 800 boarders in the summer, and it was a busy place.

They then came to Eldred and hooked up houses there and then they started a line to Highland Lake as Highland Lake had more boarding houses than Yulan.

When the electric line got to Highland Lake, everybody hooked on including my grandfather Frank Sergeant. He got a radio that would plug in electric. He already had a radio that he bought from Montgomery Ward that played off a car battery.

He gave that to us. It was the first radio that came into town, so they tell me. It had ear phones and we got the fight between Jack Dempsey and Gene Turney. It came in from Pittsburgh on KDKA. At the time I had no interest in boxing, but can remember that they split the ear phones and four people could listen at once.

On our road there were no cars, but plenty of horses and bicycles.—James Leavenworth.

As Jim Leavenworth indicated, the boarding houses of Yulan, Eldred, and Highland Lake had electricity by 1927. We will visit the Town of Highland's Boarding Houses in the next chapter.

This chapter continues with anecdotes, news accounts, and letters of former, current, and future residents of the Town of Highland; Eldred Union School; new businesses; and the Town itself in the years 1927–1929.

Gisele Rouillon Born
Gisele Rouillon, the future wife of Jim Leavenworth, was born in Paris, France, at the beginning of 1927. Gisele was the daughter of Cyrus A. and Jeanne Marguerite Marie Lair Rouillon. The family were bakers and had a bakery in Paris. Cyrus fought in WWI and would also fight in WWII.

New Organizations, 1927
The Narrowsburg Lumber Company, and the Ten Mile River Scout Camp in Tusten began in 1927.

Narrowsburg, New York was the first location of the Narrowsburg Lumber Company organized by Fred Hendricks, E.O. Barnes, and Arthur Van Schoick. Jim Leavenworth and many others from the area would work for the

Gisele Rouillon was born in 1927 in Paris, France. Photo courtesy of Gisele Rouillon Leavenworth.

Narrowsburg Lumber Company, which would eventually open two more locations.

Jim's father Garfield and brother Clinton would work at the Ten Mile River Scout Camp—10,000 acres near the Ten Mile River in Tusten. The property was sold to the Boy Scouts of New York City for summer camps in 1927.

You may remember that Raymond worked in South America for the Gulf Oil company after he was married in fall 1926.

Certificate for the Electrical Installation Paul Knorr did at the Garfield Leavenworth home in December 1928. Certificate courtesy of Cynthia Leavenworth Bellinger.

Jennie Austin, MGH, Eldred, to C.R. Austin, Maracaibo, Venezuela, S.A.
Sunday evening, January 9, 1927
My dear Ray,

I am staying home from church on purpose to make a special effort to answer some of my correspondence.

We are having quite severe weather, but before we know it, summertime will be here once more with all its work and worries. It is hard to tell which is the more agreeable of the two, summer or winter. Still winter does not hold the hardships that it used to for most of us. Likely you are sweating just at present.

Gladys called us up from Port Jervis last night and said she had heard from you. She as well as ourselves were growing anxious for it had been four weeks since she had heard from you.

We are all well but Bobby. He has a sore throat; a number have chickenpox here.

Do they have radios where you are? If so, do you get any U.S. stations? They say KDKA from Pittsburgh is heard in Australia.

It looks as though Uncle Sam might have some little trouble with Mexico and the Central American Countries. Today's paper stated that China had asked the other powers for help to protect their citizens from the rebels who ever they are. Do you get any N.Y. papers? If not, we could send you some; of course the news would be old, but still new to you.

The people who usually go south are down there again, lucky ones.

Howard Pelton is dead and Charley Lass. Howard died of typhoid fever and Charley of pneumonia.

Eddie Crail's mother died

leaving him a few thousand, so he built a house or bungalow up at the Lake. He took Leon Parker up there as caretaker and partly out of sympathy, for they say Leon is nearly dead of consumption.

Last fall old Bischof took a monkey up to Leon and Eddie to take care of for a few days, and told them he would come back and get it again, but never showed up. So it was on their hands about a week ago when Eddie found it with a box of matches trying to strike them. He hit it over the head with stove poker and killed it. Leon began to swear at Eddie. So poor Leon was chased out.

Right after that, Eddie and Patsy Clark were celebrating and got in some kind of a dispute, then they had trouble, so the other night, Bill [Austin] saw Eddie Crail and he told him that "the surroundings were so crude here in Eldred," that if he could sell his house here, he would "move to where the society was more congenial."

Fred Morgan decided he would buy Eddie's house. He wrote out a check for $4,500. He did not sign it, but said he would as soon as Eddie gave him the deed of the house.

Stacked wood from the sawmill at Narrowsburg Lumber Company in Narrowsburg, New York. Photo courtesy of Howard Barnes.

The best of all, I thought, was when Fred told him that his wife had received a check for $10,000 for some lumber land. They asked him what bank the check was on, and he said the custom house. So they all told him the money must be safe. Eldred certainly has its share of foolish characters.

Dory does not come in very often. They only have the movies once a week and they are not well attended which make the ruling ones sore.

When you are sending cards, send some to Rev. Robert Collins, Madison, N.J. He will be surprised to hear you are in South America.

Be sure and take good care of yourself and remember that we think of you every day and are looking forward to the time when you will return.

Love from all, Mother

Lillie Calkin, Bethel, to Mr. J.E. Austin, Hopewell Junction, N.Y.
February 13, 1927
Dear Dad,

Our hens are picking up a bit now. Only a few show the disease and we get as high as 171 eggs.

Hope you are keeping well. I have had a fine cold and now Burt has it. I enclose a picture of each of the kids (who are well). That mark across Dale's forehead is not dirt, but a scar acquired this year. The pictures were taken in the schoolhouse in December. Will close. With love, Lillie

Robert Collins, a Methodist preacher, wrote his long time Eldred friend Mort Austin a nostalgic letter in March. Robert, his brother Tom (who had died in 1920), and his sister Annie, had lived on Collins Road.

Stacked logs containing 1 million board feet of lumber for the sawmill at Narrowsburg Lumber Company in Narrowsburg, New York. Photo courtesy of Howard Barnes.

"That mark across Dale's forehead is not dirt, but a scar acquired this year." Dale and Dot's photos mentioned in their mother's letter. Photos courtesy of Katherine Calkin Traxler.

R.B. Collins, Madison, N.J., to Mort Austin, Eldred
March 9, 1927
Dear Mort,

How are all you dear folks? You like myself are getting to be an old man, I will be 87 in July next and you can't be far behind.

I had a letter from Tom's wife Emma Kelso, saying that she thought of going up to Eldred this summer, just for a change of climate. She thought it would do her a lot of good to breathe again the sweet, strong, healthy air of that dear old place.

I have not been up to the nice old place for some time. Dear old Eldred, I shall never forget the years I spent there, and the acquaintances I made there. I often think of the services in the old church. That was long ago.

I left Eldred in the Spring of 1862—during the Civil War, for New Jersey, to begin my life work as a Methodist Preacher, and for 37 years I faithfully and joyfully tried to do my work and I had good success. Then my voice failed me, and I had to stop.

I have been living with my dear daughter and her husband in a delightful home among the roses.

Remember me to all the members of your family who still live and I loved. Best wishes,
R.B. Collins

Robert Collins' sister-in-law Emma wrote to Mort's brother Lon regarding her home and cows on Collins Road, not far from the Herman Bosch residence.

Emma K. Collins, Tenafly, N.J., to Lon Austin, Eldred
March 18, 1927
Dear Friend,

Thank you for taking my cattle for a while. We hear the roads are very bad, so I am afraid to risk sending a moving van full of furniture up until later, for fear they should get stuck in the road in front of my place.

The same man that brought the cows down is going to take them back. Be careful of the cows. Feed them well—they will be pretty well shaken after the long ride.

Now Lon, about the second week in April, I would like you to open up the house and have Herman Bosch fix the pump in the kitchen. I will settle all bills with you when I get there. I am feeling better, but am not real well yet.

Hope this finds you and Aida well. With kind regards. Your friend, Emma K. Collins

The Herman Bosch Family
Herman and Mary Horton Bosch were a very industrious couple. Herman had built Bosch Pond and sold ice from it; he had or would have a sawmill; he was a plumber, and he also had a dairy. Herman and Mary and their children Herman Jr., 9, Marjorie, 4, and Robert, 2, play a part in this story.

Raymond Austin's aunt Charlotte wrote him a nice long letter in May.

C. Leavenworth, Eldred, to R. Austin, Maracaibo, Venezuela
Sunday May 8, 1927
Dear Raymond,

Grandfather Sherman S. Leavenworth. "It pleases him to be remembered." Photo courtesy of Cynthia Leavenworth Bellinger.

This letter in lead pencil is quite different from your business like ones, but I think you will pardon pencil when you know I'm away from home and have no pen with me and don't like to ask an old gentleman to move away from the writing desk where materials are kept. I am spending the weekend with Mrs. Smith. The doctor's older sister and brother are also visiting them.

Grandfather [Sherman Leavenworth] was very pleased to get both your nice, long, descriptive letters. He was also glad to get your photo—it is splendid of you, I think, and you surely look no thinner. Gladys brought it to him with a box of cigars for his birthday, I believe.

Your folks were all well the last time I heard. I see the boys each day at school.

I have often wondered if you went on that surveying and geological expedition last fall—it must have been a wonderful experience. Did you ever think, Raymond, what stories you'll be able to tell your grandchildren when you are old? When you are young surely is the time to travel and see the world—you seldom do later in life.

I have seen Gladys only once or twice this winter. She looked very well the last time I saw her in Eldred. She keeps busy, I guess.

Grandfather has been exceptionally well for him during this winter. Usually his rheumatism bothers him so in cold weather, but he has had very little this year. His chief trouble is not being able to read and being alone so much of the time, and which can't very well be helped as matters stand.

I'd be glad to send you magazines or papers from time to time if you need reading material.

Emma Collins asked Lon Austin to have Herman Bosch fix the pump at her house on Collins Road. Mary Bosch with son Bob. Herman Bosch Sr. with children Marjorie, Bob, and Herman Jr. Photo courtesy of Victoria Kohler.

There have been quite a few deaths in this vicinity since you left—Howard Pelton, Charles Lass, Harold Quick, Nathan Dailey and just lately, Bert Kyte from an enlarged spleen. So you see it is just as hazardous to stay at home as go abroad.

It is very quiet here at home. We are just beginning to hear the noise of the 1928 Presidential Campaign. Just now Al Smith is making the most noise. He has written all sorts of open letters in magazines to be answered by him concerning his views on religion and prohibition.

Aunt Christina and her folks were all well the last time I saw them. Little Charlotte is growing up so fast you won't know her. She helps wash dishes all ready—that is, she carries dishes from tubs and puts them in the dish closet, and she doesn't waste time doing it. She has never broken any yet, but I think they must be good strong dishes. She keeps saying, "Arly hep Mama way dishes." She is too cute for anything, but she has a will of her own and sometimes is so obstinate that it is hard to know what means to take with her.

I expect to go to summer

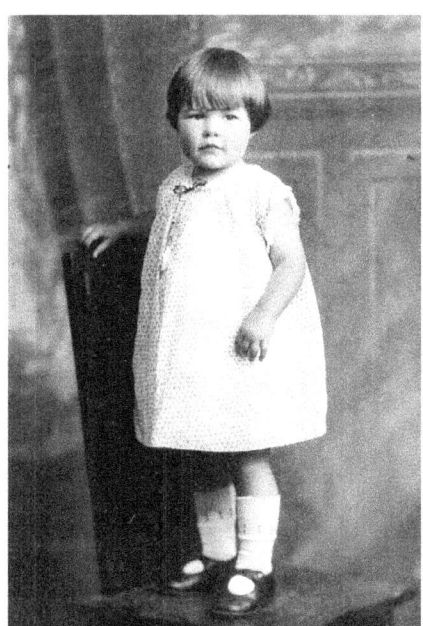

"Too cute" Charlee Hirsch. Photo courtesy of Ric Schroedel.

Martin D. Myers and family, 1927: Mary, Tom sitting on his dad Martin's lap, Martin Jr., Helen standing next to her mother Mary. Photo courtesy of Christene Stevens Myers.

school again. I have not studied much since January as I have had a spell of indigestion, etc. which seemed to use up all my spare energy; but hope to start anew next fall. I passed Biology in January with 99%, so I have gained five credits anyway this year.

Write when you can to Grandfather for I read his letters and that will do for me too. It pleases him to be remembered.

Just think, Raymond, next year this time, we will be making plans for your homecoming. Time does fly, doesn't it?

With love, Aunt Charlotte

Nathan Dailey Dies

Just as Charlotte Leavenworth said, Nathan Dailey, 45, had passed away Monday morning, March 14, 1927, after a long illness, suffering from a complication of diseases. The pall bearers mentioned in his obituary: John Hill, Howard Stevens, John Love, Harry Wormuth, Norman Myers, and Archibald Myers.

Myers Relatives

Charlotte Leavenworth and Charlee Hirsch were related to Charlie Myers who ran Lake View in Highland Lake, and Martin D. Myers Sr. who lived in Eldred, but worked at the Asendorf Hotel in Highland Lake.

Around 1927 there was a charming photo taken of the Martin D. Myers family. Martin D. and Mary Fee Myers' children: Helen, Mary, Martin Jr., and Tom. Sadly their daughter Ethel had died young.

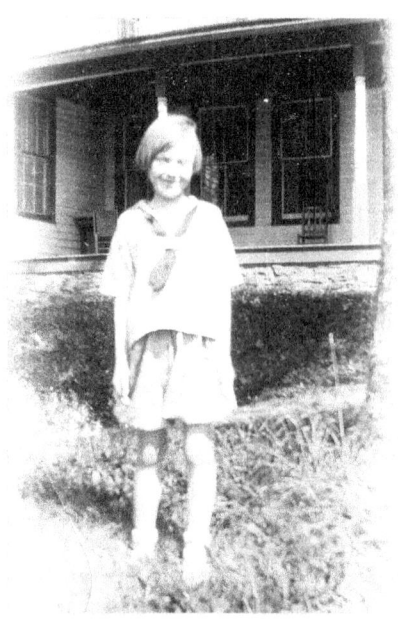

Eleanor Myers at Lake View summer 1927. Photo courtesy of Timothy C. Rizzuto.

There was also a cute photo of Eleanor Myers, daughter of Charlie and Elizabeth Myers, which was taken around 1927.

Raymond Austin Returns

Raymond Austin was supposed to have worked in South America for two years, but because of illness returned home at least by September of 1927. He may have been home in time to help with haying on the Austin property.

Harry Lass Dies

An unexpected and sad event happened in September when Harry Lass, husband of Bessie, was electrocuted while moving a steam shovel. Harry and Bessie would have been married one year in October. Their son William Lass would be born at the end of February 1928. Bessie was good friends with Jennie Austin and plays a role in this story.

The High School in Eldred

Howard K. Moore was the school principal in 1927. There were five faculty and 106 pupils—39 in first through third; 29 in fourth through sixth; 16 in seventh and eighth grades; and 22 students in High School. The school rating was raised. Latin III, History B, physical geography, and commercial arithmetic were added. Activities included the interclass track meet and Science Club. It was the year of the first high school play and working for the first Washington D.C. Class Trip.

From New York City Murie Kelso wrote Mort Austin in December. His sister Emma had apparently been ill. Mort was still caring for Murie's horse.

Murie Kelso, West 28th Street, N.Y.C., to Mort Austin, Eldred

*December 27, 1927
Dear Friend Mort,*

I was glad to read your letter and that you were all well. That after all is the greatest blessing and one we do not appreciate until we lose it.

Emma is feeling quite a little better, but is still confined to her room and we must be very careful. The weather is intensely cold down here. Ten above this morning; the dampness cuts right through.

I saw by the Tri-States Union *that you have begun work on the church and I hope it is coming along nicely. I will send you a little donation, $50.00, and increase it a bit later on.*

Poor Teddy, I wish he could go happily to Horse Heaven without pain or suffering. I feel guilty in keeping him when what it cost would help some human being. But you know how it is, and you are the person that does understand that feeling for a helpless dumb animal. I am so thankful he is with you. It is a debt I shall never be able to repay you. I can only tell you that I shall never forget your kindness.

Give my love to Jennie. I always see in her the little blue-eyed girl I did so love to tease.

*Hoping you may all have a very Happy New Year and to see you all again when summer comes. I am sincerely your friend,
Murie Kelso*

Mary Paulik Returns to the U.S.
We met Mary Paulik (the future Mrs. Mellan) in *Echo Hill and Mountain Grove*, when she was born in Garfield, New Jersey, November, 15, 1911.

Mary's parents Josef and Theresa Paulik were immigrants from Transylvania. They had met and married sometime after each

Eldred News, September 1927

Mrs. Charles Scheineman, who has been visiting friends and relatives here, has returned to her home on Long Island. Rev. and Mrs. E.S.J. Patterson were entertained at the home of Mr. and Mrs. Jackson Myers on Wednesday and at the home of Mrs. George Mills, Highland Lake, on Saturday.

Raymond Austin and brother, William, Orville Myers, Rev. and Mrs. E.S.J., Patterson attended a patriotic meeting on Friday evening, August 26, which was held in the Mechanic's Hall, Port Jervis. Mr. Patterson was the speaker for the evening.

The annual supper and fair of the Congregational Church was held on August 25 and 26 in the Community Hall. The booths were very attractive with their various designs worked out with crepe paper, of very beautiful colors. The committee on decoration, deserve a great deal of praise. Many very beautiful pieces of hand work were disposed of. The mystery bags were a great source of amusement for both young and old. Candy, peanuts, fruits and soft drinks were on sale. A very delicious supper was served both evenings. The sum of $570 was the result of two days of work by the ladies. Mrs. Otto Schroeder, Mrs. Mary Wormuth, Mrs. Mary Kyte, Mrs. F. Williams and Mrs. C. Scheineman were the committee in charge of decorations. Mrs. W.B. Styles, Mrs. W. Horton, Mrs. Norman Myers, Mrs. M. Wormuth and Mrs. H. Van Ohlen were the committee in charge of the supper.

Rev. E.S.J. Patterson preached his farewell sermon at Barryville and Eldred on Sunday, August 28. At the close of the service at Eldred a farewell reception was tendered the pastor and Mrs. Patterson by members of the Y.P.C. Society at the home of Mrs. F. Williams.

Mrs. James Morgan is ill at her home. Mrs. James Clark is convalescing nicely from a severe illness.—*Republican Watchman*, Sep. 1927.

The Austins during haying time. Gladys Myers Austin on the left. Photo courtesy of Joan Austin Geier.

had immigrated to the United States around 1905.

Josef, Theresa, and Mary returned to Transylvania when Mary was about 16 months old, as Josef Paulik had been summoned by his family to return and run the family cattle farm.

Shortly after the family's return, World War I broke out. Josef was conscripted to serve in the army of the Austro-Hungarian Empire. A talented mechanic, Josef served in the motor pool.

The map of Europe was redrawn after the war and the area of northern Transylvania where the Paulik family lived was awarded to Romania.

Josef Paulik operated a bus business picking up passengers from rail stations and transporting them to their destinations. With the new political alignments in the post-war period, Josef found it increasingly difficult to obtain the parts to keep his Fiat bus in good running order and his business failed.

In 1927 Josef and Theresa sent Mary (15-1/2) back to New Jersey. Josef and Theresa wanted to return to America, but were placed on a waiting list, so they remained in Romania.

Mary lived in Paterson, New Jersey, with her aunt Rance (who had arrived in 1905 with Mary's mother Theresa) and Rance's husband Lotsey Toth. Sadly, Josef and Theresa Paulik were never able to rejoin their daughter.

Mary attended trade school, studying pattern and dressmaking.—As told by Mary Paulik Mellan to Ken Bosch.

Mary Paulik sewed dresses for a Jewish couple in Manhattan who sold wedding dresses. The wife was upset because Mary's Romanian accent sounded too much like a German accent. Since most of their clients were Jewish, she was asked not to speak to them.

But Mary needed to talk to the future brides in order to ask them if the dress was too tight or the right style, etc. So she left that job and went to work for the Bronx Home News.

The Bronx Home News *purchased the most recent dresses designed in Paris. Mary was the head pattern cutter. The dresses were taken apart and Mary would make patterns of these styles. The patterns sold for a nickel a piece. That way the everyday woman could sew her own dress of the latest style.—As told by Ed Mellan to Cynthia Leavenworth Bellinger.*

Mary worked over ten years in New York City for the Bronx Home News *producing the fashion pattern that appeared on the woman's page each day.*

Mary regularly vacationed in Highland Lake, beginning in 1928. Her uncle Lotsey owned a share of the Wallace Place, northeast of Highland Lake. —As told by Mary Paulik Mellan to Ken Bosch.

Joseph Mellan
Though she did not know it at the time, Mary Paulik had met her future husband Joe Mellan at the elementary school in Romania.

Joseph's family immigrated to the United States after 1918 and settled in Trenton, New Jersey. Joseph's father George Mellan Sr. worked for John A. Roebling Sons. Joe and his brother George Jr. would both work for Roebling Sons. To help support his family during the depression, Joe worked weekends driving a truck which served as a floral, bakery delivery truck, ambulance, or hearse.

Though both Mary Paulik and Joe Mellan lived in New Jersey, in 1927, it would be 15 years before they would meet again.—Ken Bosch.

Eva Purcell, New to Barryville
Eva Purcell and her sons—Ed, Jack, Jim, and Andy—play a part in our story. Eva's husband James had been in the Navy when he became ill with tuberculosis and died. Eva was left with four sons to raise.

In 1927 Eva and her sons lived at Handsome Eddy Farm, and Eva worked for the Doellers. After about a year, Eva was appointed Barryville Postmaster, and the family moved to a new home, half of which was the Barrvyille Post Office.

1928
January 1928 started off very sad for two different families with a connection to the Leavenworths.

In Milwaukee, Wisconsin, Deloros May Koenig, daughter of Eugene and Hazel Leavenworth

---

Charles Lindbergh

May 20, 1927, Charles Lindbergh left Roosevelt Field, on Long Island, New York, in his aircraft, the *Spirit of St. Louis*. He reached LeBourget Field in Paris, France, 33-1/2 hours later, on the first non-stop transatlantic solo flight in history. It was nearly 3,600 statute miles in a single-seat, single-engine purpose built Ryan monoplane. A ticker tape parade was held in his honor in New York City, after his return on June 13.—wikipedia.org.

1927 World, National, and Local News

John Briggs born 1927. His grandparents, John and Ida Higginson Crabtree. Photos courtesy of Mary Briggs Austin.

Charles and Janette Kerr Wolff. Photo courtesy of Ed Wolff.

1927 National and World News
- American Philo Taylor Farnsworth invented an electronic TV system.
- Selective Jukeboxes introduced by Automated Musical Instrument Co.
- Stalin became leader of the party. He continued the abolition of private property.

March 1927
- Civil War in China; 1,000 U.S. Marines landed in order to protect property of U.S. interests.

April and May 1927
- Mississippi Flood affected over 700,000.

August 1927
- Sculptor Gutzon Borglum began chiseling the busts of four presidents on Mount Rushmore.

October 1927
- Talking pictures; Al Jolson debuts in N.Y.C.

1927 Halfway Brook News
- Amoco, one of the first drive in stations in the area, was built in Barryville around 1927.

1927 Births
- Giselle Rouillon born to Cyrus Albert and Jeanne Marguerite Marie Lair Rouillon, in Paris, France.
- Vernon Clark born to Ernest and Eunice Hallock Clark.
- Audrey E. Kyte born to Frank Crouch and Hazel Robinson Kyte.
- John Briggs born to Irwin and Myrtle Crabtree Briggs in October.

1927 Marriages
- Jay Lass married Tillie Flynn.

1927 Deaths
- Thomas E. Thompson, son of Thomas J. and Addie Austin Thompson, died. (Addie was an Eldred-Austin Cousin.) Thomas E. was mentioned in Books 1 and 2.
- Phebe Simpson Parker, 1848–1927.
- Janette Kerr wife of Charles Wolff, died. Their children: Norman, Carl, Frank, Anna, Agnes, and Albert.
- Regina S. Metzger, 1841–1927.
- Nathan Dailey, 1881–1927, the son of Mr. and Mrs. Henry Dailey, lived most of his life in Eldred. Survived by: his wife, daughter Alice Dailey, aged father in Eldred, brothers George and Stephen Dailey, half brother William Dailey, and sisters Mrs. Frank Ort and Mrs. Webster LaBarr.—*Republication Watchman*, March 1927.
- John George Lewis Crabtree, 72, died in Long Pine, Nebraska, in September. John was the father of Myrtle Briggs, my grandmother.
- Harry Lass, husband of Bessie MacIntyre, died.
- Herbert W. Kyte, 1877–1927, son of William and Mary A. Whitney Kyte.

Koenig, died on January 1, just before she turned 3. Eugene and Hazel's son John Koenig was 8.

In Asniere, France, Jeanne Marguerite Marie Lair Rouillon, the mother of one-year-old Gisele Rouillon, died. Gisele was cared for by her grandmother, Blanche Rouillon, the mother of Cyrus, Gisele's father.

February 1928, Eldred
Emma Collins sent Lon Austin a check for taking care of her cows and directions for the care of her trees and barn on Collins Road.

Pretty Meta Toaspern Lass had some sad years. Her husband John Charles Lass died in 1928. Her son Charles Lass died in 1926. Son Harry Lass died in 1927. Photo courtesy of Linda Guenther Anderson.

Emma K. Collins, Tenafly, N.J., to Lon Austin, Eldred
February 14, 1928
Dear Friend,

I enclose a check for January 15 to February 15. Now, Lon, I wish you would send me your bill for what hay you have used. If there is no hay at my barn, I wish you would see that there is a ton put in there before the road is too bad to get any taken over it.

When you trim the fruit trees, be sure and trim those down at the old place.

I will need new floors in all the stalls of the barn now. Do you think you could get Willie Austin or Rob Clark [Lon's cousin] to help you do the work.

Hope you and Aida are well. The winter has not been severe, but cold enough and we long for the spring time. Be sure and send feed bills. With kind regards from us and ever your friend,
Emma Collins

John C. Lass Dies
John Charles Lass, 59, husband of Meta Toaspern Lass, died in February 1928. John Lass had been a bicycle cop in Brooklyn. When he broke his leg, he had to retire, and the whole family had moved up to the Toaspern homestead.

The last few years have been quite sad ones for Meta Lass. Her son Charles died in 1926, her son Harry in 1927, and now her husband of 33 years, died in 1928. Meta's grandchildren were most likely a comfort to her. We hear more about her son Jay Lass at the end of Chapter 7.

Willard Wells from Eldred occasionally wrote Ell Austin. He and his wife Minerva Racine (who had died in 1925) were the parents of at least seven children which included Earl Wells, Maude Hulse, and Marjorie Hill.

W. Wells, Eldred, to J.E. Austin, Hopewell Junction, N.Y.
February 18, 1928
Mr. Austin,

I thought I would answer your letter rec. at Christmas time as we are all closed in today with a big snowstorm. Times seam rather dull this winter. Many are out of work. Trust it will liven up in the spring.

I am lumbering and usually working every day driving my own team. I have started a good many logs and hauled to the mill until we have a good stack in and many more to haul yet.

When I sold my land to the club, I reserved the lumber and I have yet four years to get it.

I suppose you heard our oldest son died three or four months ago. That threw a lot of responsibility on me. We miss him verry much. I am verry well. Much to be thankful for. I hope you are well and have a good place.

From your friend, W. Wells

Blanche Rouillon who cared for one-year-old Gisele Rouillon (her granddaughter), after Gisele's mother Jeanne died. Photo courtesy of Gisele Rouillon Leavenworth.

Anne Elizabeth Stanton Horton with two of her grandchildren: Marjorie and Bobby Bosch, children of Herman and Mary Horton Bosch. Photo courtesy of Victoria Kohler.

1928 World, National, and Local News

1928 World and National News
- John L. Baird invented the first color television.
- American Col. Jacob Schick, patented the first electric razor.
- Richard E. Byrd Jr. began his first expedition to the Antarctic with two ships, and three airplanes.

May 1928
- Mickey and Minnie Mouse first appeared on film.

June 1928
- Amelia Earhart became the first woman to fly over the Atlantic Ocean.

August 1928
- 15 countries, including the U.S., Britain, France, Germany, Italy, and Japan signed the Kellogg-Brian Pact, to renounce aggressive war and look for peaceful ways to settle international disputes.

November 1928
- Herbert Hoover won the U.S. Presidential Election.

December 1928
- U.S. Congress approved Boulder Dam construction; later named Hoover Dam.
- U.S.S.R.: Stalin ordered a campaign of forced collectivization. From 1928 to 1933, an estimated 9 million peasants suffered. Soviet Union would suffer a man-made famine of staggering proportions.
- Mussolini became absolute dictator.

1928 Halfway Brook News
To Build Road to Minisink Battlefield
Port Jervis, Oct. 3: Members of the Board of Supervisors of Sullivan County met with the Sites and Roads Division of the Minisink Sesquicentennial Celebration Committee at the Minisink Battlefield Saturday to look over the ground prior to building a road from Yulan to the site. The road will be about three miles long and has been laid out…it will form an easy approach to the battlefield and will provide ample room for the parking of automobiles.

For the actual clearing of the field itself in preparation for the ceremonies July 22, 1929, workmen will be engaged for several weeks in cutting and removing trees and brush from the site.—Republican Watchman, *1928.*

1928 Births
- Shirley Parker born to William H. Parker and Eleanora Alston.
- Berniece Wells born to Earl and Ada Myers Wells.
- Katherine S. Hensel was born at her grandmother Kathryn Hensel's Yulan Cottage. Kate's parents Jacob and Lisette Hensel had most likely moved into the Colonial.
- Marion Connor born to Walter and Hazel Sergeant Connor in June.
- Herb Wolff born to Carl and Freida Kloss Wolff.

1928 Marriages
- Claude Angell, 32, married Hazel Labarr, 28, in October.
- Belle Mills, 34, married Tom Stalker.
- Alvin Hill married Harriet MacKechnie.

The wedding supper was given at the home of the bride. Waitresses were Miss Harriet Kinne and Miss Ruth Parker. Wedding gifts included linens, silver, money, cut glass and many other articles. Mr. Hill is a mechanic at the Wait and Boyd Garage. Both are popular in the community and their many friends wish them happiness.
—From Republican Watchman.

1928 Deaths
- Ernest Timmerhoff, 1860–1928.
- Edward Pelton, almost 50, died. He was the son of Asher and Carrie.
- John Charles Lass, 1868–1928.
- Jeanne Lair Rouillon, 1896–1928, was the mother of Gisele Rouillon.
- Anne Elizabeth Stanton Horton, 1860–1928.
- William Horton, 1876–1928.
- Will Waidler, husband of Emma Schoonover, died. Will was buried in Cairo, New York Cemetery.
- In Milwaukee, Wisconsin, Deloros May Koenig, daughter of Hazel Leavenworth and Eugene Koenig, died. She was almost 3.
- Alice Rose Bye, 4, daughter of Fred and Jeanette Bye, died.
- David E. Crandall, 1846–1928, had served with Co. C., 8th Regiment, N.Y. Cavalry Volunteers during the Civil War.
- Lewis Laforde Eldred died leaving several young children orphans.
- Margery Kerr Schwab, 1848–1928.

She died at the home of her niece, Miss Agnes L. Schwab, in Barryville. Marjorie was born in Scotland, the daughter of John and Marjorie Kerr.

For many years she had been a resident of Barryville. She was united in marriage with Mr. Frederick Schwab at Port Jervis in 1870. The surviving relatives are several nephews and nieces. The funeral will take place at the house on Sunday, February 19, at 1:30 and at 2, in the Barryville M.E. Church. Published: February 1928.

William and Catherine Sutherland Horton. Photo courtesy of Victoria Kohler.

"Sunshine Hall was used as an auditorium." Photo courtesy of Ken Bosch.

Sideview of the former Orchard Terrace Boarding House as a school. Photo courtesy of Christene Stevens Myers.

Anne E. Stanton Horton Dies
Perhaps you remember the remarkable Anne Elizabeth Stanton Horton of Highland Lake, and the photo of her with her white handled revolver in *Echo Hill and Mountain Grove*. Anne, a widow for 21 years, died at age 68, in March. Several of Anne's children have played a part in this story. Anne Elizabeth's children at the time of her death: William, Walter, John, and Ernest Horton; Mary Bosch, Edith Maney, Maude Kalin, and Mabel Wormuth.

Harvey Eldred and the Draxlers
Harvey Eldred was orphaned in April 1928, when his father Lewis LaForde Eldred died. Harvey's mother had died in 1920, when he was only three years old. Harvey, his brother Cecil, and sister Elsie were raised by their older sister Eleanor and her husband Art Barnes in Minisink Ford. Minisink Ford was also where Charles and Martha Draxler had their York Lake Mountain House. When Harvey was a bit older, he would work for Charles Draxler, and guess who Harvey would meet?

Mort's Cousin Olin Hickok
It has been 47 years since the last brief mention of Olin Hickok in *Echo Hill and Mountain Grove*. Olin was Mort Austin's cousin as well as a best friend (along with Edwin Myers). They shared the same great-grandparents, Asa and Esther Hinman Hickok who had arrived in Lumberland in 1811.

Olin (who had worked in the oil fields) wrote his friend Mort from Oklahoma. Olin included a clipping from a Texas newspaper about the Austins of Texas.

Olin Hickok, Seminole, Okla., to Mort Austin, Eldred
May 6, 1928

I will surprise you I know with a few lines. I got a letter from Jim Boyd not long ago and he told me that your son had been in South America. Please tell me what part of the country and for which oil company he went, for my son Arthur was in Venezeula, South America, at Meracaibo for the Carter Oil Co., which is a branch of the Standard Oil Co. He was there for two years.

How are all your family? Give them all my kindest regards.

Enclosed is a clipping from a Texas paper which mentions the Austin Family. These Austins came from Connecticut to Tennessee and then moved to Texas. Stephen Austin's Statue stands at the front door of the state capitol at Austin, life-size. Just about the size and build of your father. I saw it there 22 years ago. These Austins are said to be distant relatives of yours. Do you know anything about them? Moses and his son Stephen died there, but Moses had a daughter who is married and lives in Houston, Texas. Will close for this time. With love to all.

Please write soon.
Your Friend, Olin Hickok

Gladys Austin holds her daughter Melva Elizabeth Austin. Photo courtesy of Melva Austin Barney.

Mort and Jennie's Granddaughter

Melva Elizabeth Austin, daughter of Raymond and Gladys Myers Austin, arrived in July 1928—Mort and Jennie Austin's first granddaughter. How exciting for Mort and Jennie!

The following letter to Mort's brother Ell Austin, was from one of the ladies Ell boarded with and helped out. Laura's letter included some motherly advice for him.

L. Forman, Manasquau, N.J., to J.E. Austin, Hopewell Jct., N.Y.

*September 2, 1928
Dear Mr. Austin,
We reached N.Y. City safely. We went to the Ocean Grove M.E. Camp meeting last night. Billy Sunday preached. The auditorium holds 10,000, and it was filled. The collection last night amounted to $1,700. They always have the best of meetings.*

We had some corn for supper tonight, but, oh, how I wished for some of our golden bantam.

*Do take it as easy as possible, Austin, and don't overdo, and don't forget to take your medicine. Hope to receive a line from you that all is well. Mrs. Cole joins me in sending regards to you. Sincerely yours,
Laura P. Forman*

Eldred School News, Fall 1928

Once again fall came and it was time for school. Howard K. Moore was the Principal. There were six faculty in the school year 1928–1929. Arthur Austin was one of the 31 students taking High School classes. Art's second cousin Eleanor Myers was in an elementary class.

Classes available included four years of English, physics, solid geometry, German I, and four years of Latin. A room was added for the library and a science laboratory was set up. This would be the first class to graduate (June 1929) and the first class to have class rings. It was also the first class trip to Washington D.C. Jesse Kerr would send a postcard to Aida Austin from Washington D.C.

William H. Parker Jr.

William H. Parker Jr., son of William and Eleanora Parker, was 4-1/2 years old when he started first grade in 1928.

I can remember when I first went to school. I jumped out the window and ran home. That was when Charlotte Leavenworth was teaching. I don't remember it, but they used to tell me I got mad at something and jumped out.

I can still remember the building up there. If you look at the building from the Barryville Road, that addition was built on to the main building.

The first three grades were on the right; grades four, five, and six on the left.

When you got out of those first six grades, you went down a hall and seventh and eighth grades were in a room by themselves. Then high school classes were held upstairs and down in the basement.

There was no cafeteria. For gym we would walk down the hill to where the Town Hall is now. Sunshine Hall was used as an auditorium. They very rarely would have a movie and show it there. Any assembly or play was there. As was Graduation.

The highway department was behind the library. My dad William H. Parker worked for the Town. He was a grader operator. He worked out of there. The driveway for that went right between those two buildings.

When I first went to school there, the high school on the side that faced Barryville, was all kind of gullies and ditches. Then they

Arthur Austin standing on a hill east of Proctor Road and south of Highland Lake Road, just as it leaves Eldred. Left: Al Randolph's house. The hollow behind the houses was the path of Halfway Brook. Photo in the Austin Collection.

Time for school for Eleanor Myers in the Lake View driveway, 1928. Photo courtesy of Timothy C. Rizzuto.

Eldred's Four Corners, looking south on Brook Road which heads to Barryville. On far right Arthur Wilson's General Merchandise Store. The next building was Wait and Boyd's Garage. Across the road was a store that belonged at one time to Abel Myers. Next was the Parker Hotel that sometimes had the Post Office. Postcard courtesy of Mary Briggs Austin.

leveled it off and made a ball field out of it.

My dad and many other men from around the area would play softball there once a week. Us kids got a big hoot watching them play. They were all working guys and it just seemed funny to see them playing ball.—William H. Parker Jr.

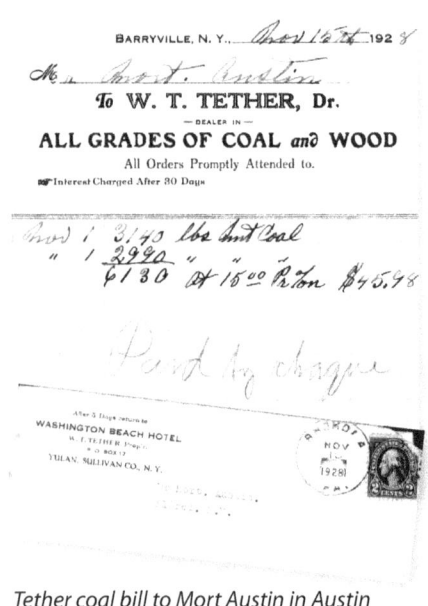

Tether coal bill to Mort Austin in Austin Collection.

Tether Coal Bill
Walter and Meda Breen Tether lived in Barryville, but ran the Washington Beach House on Washington Lake. Their son Ivan was in his early twenties. Walter also sold coal and wood as there is a paid bill from November 15, 1928, in my Austin grandparents' collection. The cost of 6,130 pounds of coal at $15 per ton was $45.98.

Robert Collins wrote Mort again in December. He missed Eldred, but also wondered if Mort had heard from his brother Tom's widow, Emma.

R.B. Collins, Madison, N.J., to Mortimer Austin, Eldred
December 25, 1928
Dear Mortimer Austin:

It is a long time since I wrote you a letter of inquiry concerning old Eldred, Sullivan County, N.Y.

We have not heard from Mrs. Thomas Collins [Emma] for nearly a year. We were not sure if she were alive or had left Eldred, and gone away.

We were interested in the old Place, and often think of it as our early home and of the acquaintances we made there and loved. Is the old farm still in the possession of Mrs. Collins? If it has changed hands, who is the owner?

That dear old spot has to me many blessed memories. My dear old father, mother, brother, and sisters lived for many years there, and it was from the front door of the old house that my dear mother kissed me good bye when I left home in 1862 to enter the Christian ministry.

We kept up an acquaintance with the family until this year and for some reason, Em has ceased to write us and I fear something has happened to her, is the reason I write you.

How are you all? I have not been in Eldred for two years. I have not been well since last July, when I reached my 88th birthday.

Still I am not confined to the bed all the time; simply getting old.

I shall be greatly pleased if you can tell me how the old place is and how its folks are. It is a dear spot to my heart, full of delightful memories, not only of the place itself, but of the people whom I knew and loved and still remember. With best wishes for your happiness. I am yours,
R.B. Collins

Eldred 1929

Wait and Boyd built their Garage on the southwest corner of Eldred at least by 1929. There was a 1929 envelope from Wait & Boyd to Mort Austin in the Austin Collection.

North of Wait and Boyd's Garage, at Eldred's northwest corner, was a store run by Arthur Wilson. The building was built by Arthur's father, Charles Wilson.

Arthur Wilson got the A&P to come in, which was a big thing for Eldred. The A&P was on the lower end. In the center there was a butcher shop owned and operated by various people—Claude Angell, Ralph Hessberger, and Archie Myers. On the upper end the Post Office was moved by John Sparks from the Parker House while he was Postmaster for the eight years between Emily Parker Stevens' appointments.—Christene Stevens Myers.

Eldred's Four Corners showing the Art C. Wilson Store in 1928. Photo courtesy of Ken Bosch.

Yulan Times Square 1929

As mentioned earlier, Yulan's Four Corners was often called Yulan's Times Square because of the number of summer guests from the original Times Square in New York City. From Yulan's Times Square (Four Corners) you could drive to Washington Lake, Eldred, Barryville, Highland Lake, Glen Spey, and Narrowsburg, in New York; or Shohola or Honesdale in Pennsylvania.

Mabel Hazen Parker was the Yulan Postmaster from 1928 until 1938, when Fred Hensel would become the Postmaster. We meet Fred in a future chapter.

Henry Ladore (Dory) Austin Dies

In January of 1929 Dory Austin died of a shotgun wound as he tried to go under a barbed wire fence with a loaded gun. Dory was a brother of Mort, Aida, Ell, and Lon Austin. Now only four of the ten Austin siblings were still living. Henry Ladore Austin was buried in the old Eldred Cemetery with his sister Maria Austin who had died in 1916.

In March 1929 Ell Austin wrote to his brother Lon who was planning a visit to Kansas.

Ell wrote that he had paid for the plot where their sister Edith Emogene (Emma) Austin was buried, in Solomon, Kansas.

Emma had died from tuberculosis, in Solomon, Kansas, in 1879, when Lon, Mort, and Ell Austin worked there for Henry Parmenter. Henry was a farmer with quite a few acres in the

Sign to locations near Yulan's Times Square. Photo courtesy of Dennis J. Carroll.

Front and back of Wait & Boyd envelope sent to C.M. (Mort) Austin. Envelope courtesy of Mary Briggs Austin.

Entrance to Prairie Mound Cemetery, Solomon, Kansas. Emma Austin's gravesite was on the right, in the area behind the tree with the curved trunk. Photo: Gary Smith.

Solomon area. Ell had stayed and married Henry's daughter Emily. Their daughter Lillie Calkin was born there in Solomon, Kansas. Ell had gone back to the area on at least one occasion, probably more.

Ell Austin, Hopewell Junction, N.Y., to Lon Austin, Eldred
March 31, 1929
Dear Brother Lon,

I was glad to learn you were all well. We are having real spring weather. The farmers are plowing and getting ready to sow oats and make gardens. One neighbor planted garden peas a week ago.

The old must die and I am getting old very fast. I will soon be 74, but at heart do not feel older than when I was at 40. Every morning I kneel and thank God for health and strength as I have it.

Sometime in April I will go to Ossining to live. I wish it was so I could go to Kansas with you in June, but it will be impossible to get away from my work this summer.

I paid for and got a certificate for the plot where Emma is buried. The plot is 25 feet north and south, and 12-1/2 East and west. My wife and her sister bought the other half of the plot and buried Father Parmenter in.

Your brother, Ell

My great-aunt Emma Austin had been buried in Prairie Mound Cemetery in Solomon, Kansas *(see p. 402).*

Several folks who we first met in *The Mill on Halfway Brook* died in 1929. Dory Austin has already been mentioned. Others who died included Elizabeth Kyte, daughter of Felix and Eliza Gregier Kyte; Jackson Myers; Ella Clark Howe; and Fred Myers.

Ella Clark Howe Dies
Ella Clark Howe the daughter of George and Harriet Covert Clark, died of a fractured hip at age 75, in January 1929. (George and Harriet's children have been a part

Dot Meyers by Glass Factory Pond, 1928. Dot was the granddaughter of Mary Frances Scott Myers. Photo courtesy of Ed Wolff.

of this story starting with, *The Mill on Halfway Brook*.)

Ella Clark Howe had lived in Massachusetts. She was an aunt to Georgia Clark Styles, Ella Sergeant Leavenworth, and Hazel Sergeant Connor. Hazel Sergeant had lived with Ella Howe when her mother Clarissa Clark Sergeant had died.

Apparently Ella Howe had some money when she died, which was unusual in those days. Ella Howe had no children. The will dated 26 March 1926, left proceeds to found an old aged home on her property in Easthampton, Massachusetts. Ella Howe's funds were most likely eaten up in legal proceedings and the old age home doesn't seem to have become a reality.

Some personal belongings were left to: Hazel Sergeant Connor of Easthampton; and Georgia Clark Styles and Ella Leavenworth, both of Eldred.

Charles Frederick Myers Dies
Fred Myers, 72, died in March. He was the widower of Mary Frances Bradley Scott Myers. Fred and Mary Myers had run a boarding house on Crawford Road.

Della Myers, Fred's daughter from his first marriage, was married to Harry Howlett. Harry and Della had or would have a boarding house on Highland Lake Road, not far from Proctor Road.

Mary's daughter from her first marriage, Lottie Scott Meyers, had two children: William Meyers Jr. and Dorothy Meyers. In a year Bill Sr. and Lottie would have an adorable surprise bundle, Madelyn.

Fred and Mary's daughter Ada and her husband Earl Wells had several children including Berniece who was about a year old.

Eldred Union School, 1929–30

In September 1929 my dad, Arthur Austin, started his senior year. He was one of 26 high school students. Ralph Stanley was the principal. There were six faculty and a total of 113 students.

Mr. Stanley had his own office, but no clerical help. His job description was quite extensive. His salary of $1,700 a year included: 15 hours a week of office duties; teaching algebra, geometry, geography, and biology; and his advice as guidance counselor.

Erwin Avery was the Board of Education president. Fredrick J. Lewis was the Superintendent of Schools. Mr. Lewis would continue as Superintendent until 1950.

Charlotte Leavenworth had attended summer school at Oneonta in August. In the fall she taught first and second; Georgia Styles taught third through fifth; and Mary Twichell Lewis, wife of the superintendent, taught sixth through eighth grades. The average secondary salary: $1,350; average elementary salary: $1,283.

Dorothy Calkin, Bethel, to Mr. J.E. Austin, Ossining, N.Y

In October Dorothy (Dot) Calkin wrote her grandfather Ell Austin. Dot loved horses and helped her father out on the farm with their horses Dan and Ted.

October 29, 1929
Dear Grandpa,
You said I should write oftener so I am writing now. I hear you were surprised to see Dale down there begging for some dinner.
Dad had Ted hooked up with Dan in a team on the stone boat with a load of manure and he pulled good. I was driving him single Sunday and again today.

1929 World, National, and Local News

1929 World and National News
- Stalin's political purges and terror continued to intensify.
- Martin Luther King born in the U.S.
- St. Valentine's Day Massacre: Al Capone gangsters in Chicago killed seven rivals.
- Herbert Hoover became the 31st U.S. President in March.
- Two weeks before the stock market crash, J.C. Penney opened a store in Delaware, the last state in the Union to have a J.C. Penney Store.
- October 29, 1929, the N.Y. Stock Exchange collapsed and triggered a worldwide economic depression.
- Arthur Wesley Wheen translated, *All Quiet on the Western Front*, the story about WWI. It was a movie in 1930.
- Port Jervis had a hospital. The closest one had been in Monticello or Middletown.

1929 Halfway Brook News
1929 Eldred Seniors
- Fred Fracke, Mary Kerr, Klelah Kirby, Richard Palmer, Marie Roberts, Roger Sheen, Donald Walter, Forrest Wilson.

1929 College
- Mabel E. Austin (Eldred-Austin relative) graduated from Cornell University with a Bachelor's of Science Degree.
- Charlotte Leavenworth took a summer class at Oneonta College.

1929 Births
- Florence Meyer born about 1929.

Oneonta College where Charlotte Leavenworth went to summer school. Photo courtesy of Cynthia Leavenworth Bellinger.

Russell and Ina Owen were married around 1929. Photo courtesy of Pam Fischetti DeFeo.

Jesse Kerr's postcard to Aida Austin from Washington D.C., June 1929. "Miss A. Austin, Eldred, Am here with the graduating classes of Shohola and Matamoras. Jessie Kerr." Postcard in collection of Mary Briggs Austin.

1929 Marriages
- Christina Bosch married William Brodmerkel around 1929.
- Pamela (Millie) Ewart married Edward King. Millie was the granddaughter of Harriet E. Palmer, sister of Sherman S. Leavenworth.
- Russell Owen married Ina Hazen around 1929.

1929 Deaths
- Ella Clark Howe died in January.
- Henry Ladore Austin, 1866–1929.
- Fred Myers died in March.
- Mary E. Nelson, 1850–1929.
- Jackson Myers, 1876–1929.
- Elizabeth Terry Kyte, daughter of Felix and Eliza Gregier Kyte, died.
- Clinton Lane Briggs, 71, died. He was the father of Irwin Briggs.

Everyone I see says they like him. John Coots wants to buy him but I won't sell him. If I sell any horse, it will be Nelly. He won't let me catch him very well in the pasture but I get him anyhow. I am all over the appendicitis now and I think I'll go back to school tomorrow.

I've been doing history all day today and have still got a lot to do. Dale sets here peeling an orange. It's the first nite that he's been home since you left. We are all well except for a few colds and I hope you're no worse for your trip. I will close, because I have to do history. Love, Dorothy

Black Tuesday
And then it happened. The stock market began to fall on Thursday, October 24, 1929. It continued to plummet and bottomed out on "Black Tuesday," October 29, 1929.

The economic boom of the 1920s was over. The Great Depression years, the worst ever in America, were ahead. It would be hard times and a continual search for work for many in the Town of Highland. Most families at least could grow their own food.

The Leavenworth Family
In 1929 Garfield and Ella's children were Clara, 22, Clinton, 20, Anna, 16, and Jim, 7 (whose memoir started off this chapter). Garfield Leavenworth would have a number of jobs in the next ten years trying to keep his family with enough money to live on.

Garfield Leavenworth may have gone back to Massachusetts to work for a time or perhaps he had jury duty when he wrote a delightful letter to his son Jim, who must have taken a spill on his bicycle.

Dale and Dorothy Calkin, grandchildren of Ell Austin. Photo courtesy of Katherine Calkin Traxler.

My Dear James,
I wonder how the hurt is coming on. One must be more careful just how they ride.

How are you coming with your studying; hope that I will soon get a real man to man letter from you.

I wonder how soon we can get out in the garden and get to growing things. Have you made up a list of things that you would like to grow and sell this coming fall? Now would be a good time to think over this matter.

Do they keep you going much of the time gathering the eggs? It must be fun carrying in so many eggs in one dish. My how I wish that I was a little boy along with you. What fun we could have.

Do the cats catch many mice these days or have they got them all caught? I wonder if the frost has got in the cellar and frozen anything. I hope not.

We have just had a three-inch snowstorm here last night, but the day is fine so far, and hope that the next thing we see will be the green grass coming up and nice warm weather to enjoy. I think when a fellow can lay on the ground is fine, don't you?
Daddy

Starting in 1929, Garfield worked for the Ten Mile Scout Camp. His son Clinton worked there some and would work there full time in the future.

In 1929 the stock market crashed and then there was no work and many people were destitute. We never lost any money as we had none to lose. We ate good because we had our own eggs, meat, milk, and a large garden and always had a warm house as we burned wood.

The year the stock market crashed, the Boy Scout Camp started up and my father got a job for $5 a day for a seven-day-week which lasted for about six months and then they let most of the help go. But my father was working for Elijah Moore and he kept three of his best men for the winter. My father [Garfield] was one of them.—James Leavenworth.

The Briggs Family
Irwin Briggs pastored Broadway Methodist Church, in New Jersey in 1929. In five years the Briggs family would move to Barryville.

During the depression years, we lived across the river from the railroad. Men (called Bums at the time) getting off the train knew where the parsonages were and that they might get something to eat there. My dad would talk to them and my mother always found something good for them to eat.—Mary Briggs Austin.

Irwin and Myrtle's son Robert Briggs born in January 1929, had

Bosches Build Bowling Alleys

Charlie Bosch Sr., Andy Anderson, and Ed Bosch arrived on the job in Richmond, Virginia, in June 1931, to build 27 bowling alleys for Wagner & Adler Co. Ed built bowling alleys up and down the East Coast. Charlie often worked with him. Photo courtesy of Ken Bosch.

Will and Lulu Bosch Lansmith. Photo courtesy of Ken Bosch.

Charlie Bosch working in Virginia clearing the field for a bowling alley. "Lovely vacation we are having." Photos courtesy of Ken Bosch.

Lulu Bosch met her husband Will Lansmith when he was a boarder at the Bosch Lake House. Will Lansmith was a partner in the Wagner and Adler Company, manufacturers of billiard tables and bowling alleys.

Lulu's brothers Ed and Charlie Bosch benefitted from this relationship and worked for years building bowling alleys for Wagner and Adler up and down the Eastern United States. Ed worked for them for about 30 years. His brother Charlie often worked with him. Charlie took many photographs and made some travelogue books documenting the bowling alley work.

The photos here are from one such book, Believe it or Not: Building Bowling Alleys at Richmond, Virginia, June 1931. The memoirs and photos in the book documented the construction of a bowling alley complex in Richmond, Virginia.

When the crew arrived, the building was complete, but the lumber and other materials necessary to construct the alleys had not arrived. The crew was put to work on the grounds surrounding the building, cutting and baling hay and plowing for the next crop. When the materials arrived, they went to work on constructing the 27 bowling alleys.
—Ken Bosch.

Charlie takes a spin on a motorcycle. Photo courtesy of Ken Bosch.

The Briggs children. Top photo: Mary holding doll, Laura and Mildred holding cats, and Johnny. Lower photo: Johnny with the cat, Mildred with Dimples, Mary with Virginia, and Laura with Rosebud. Photos courtesy of Mary Briggs Austin.

Getting Claude Angell's Whippet out of Highland Lake. Photo courtesy of Cynthia Leavenworth Bellinger.

only lived 11 days. He had a cleft palette and they probably didn't know how to do the surgical closure. He had a hard time nursing, caught pneumonia, and died. I don't think my grandmother Myrtle ever got over his death.

Our Old Farm, Aida Austin
November 13, 1929, 2:10 p.m. It is a drizzly, dark day, but Lon and Willie are working on our plot in the cemetery. Lon did not come to dinner until about one o'clock.

Cousin Van Wyck Young [from the James Eldred family] called for a few minutes. The first we have seen him since they moved from Eldred, over 50 years ago. The family are all dead except him, but his wife and children are living. We were certainly glad to see him.—Aida Austin's Diary.

Claude Angell's Whippet
In the winter of 1929–1930, Claude Angell and his Whippet broke through the ice on Highland Lake. Claude (about 5'6" and 300 pounds) kicked the door off the hinges and got out. There are photos of rescuing the car from Highland Lake.

1929 Boarding Houses
There were many Boarding Houses advertised in the summer of 1929, before the stock market crash.

Christopher Frey's engaging narrative of his grandparents' Maple Grove Farm (bought in the early 1920s from the Toaspern family) begins the next chapter.

Christopher's fascinating and detailed description of both the day-to-day and yearly work involved in managing Maple Grove Farm, was repeated with some variation in the many boarding houses in the Town of Highland.

Chapter 5
Better Life in the Country
Town of Highland Boarding Houses, 1929

Maple Grove Farm: *Overlooking Delaware River. Accommodates 50. Excellent table. Own farm products. Boating, fishing, and bathing 10 minutes from house. Tennis Court. Modern improvements. Protestant and Catholic churches nearby. Double, $15; Single, $17; Transients, $3 day. Tel. Barryville 1-3F-15. Nitzsche & Frey.—Ad summer 1929.*

"The view down to the Delaware and across the dense forests of Pennsylvania from 'The Bluff' were—and are—remarkable and in many ways made up for the lack of a lake front location."—Christopher Frey. Photo courtesy of ECCE Bed & Breakfast.

The Maple Grove property on the wonderfully named "Corkscrew Road" just outside of Barryville was owned and operated by the families of Charles and Gertrude Frey and Fred and Minnie Nitzsche for over forty years.

Like so many other residents of the area, the Freys and Nitzsches had grown tired of the boroughs of New York and sought a better life in the country.

Gertrude Frey's father had been an energetic New York Assemblyman from Woodhaven (Queens) who introduced bills on topics ranging from creating a boxing commission to urging an exception to Prohibition to enable the sale of wine and beer in New York. But even this interesting political environment was not enough to keep Gert in Queens.

The Freys and Nitzsches teamed up to purchase the Maple Grove property from the Toaspern family in the early 1920s and launched their business.

Typical of local boarding houses, Maple Grove Farm catered to working class families from the New York Metropolitan area. The main amenity was its spring-fed concrete swimming pool—in later years refinished in brick and upgraded with a water purification system. There was a tennis court, handball court, horse shoe pit, swings, and almost forty acres of pasture and orchards for the guests to explore.

The huge red barn, testimony to the property's agricultural past, housed a variety of indoor amusements and became a more important amenity once the pool side "rec hall" was converted to additional rooms in the late 1950s.

Since Maple Grove Farm was also open in hunting season, the barn occasionally filled the role of "trophy room" for successful hunters. Over the years many a deer and the occasional bear ended their visit to the property hanging from the rafters.

The guest rooms were typically small, furnished with iron beds, a single straight back chair, a dresser and a wall-mounted rack for hanging clothes. Cold water was available

Maple Grove Farm owned by Nitzsche and Frey. The Annex, the Main House, the "washhouse" where laundry was done, the Barn (behind the kids on the cart). In front of the Annex is the swimming pool. 1928 photo taken by H.S. Motschenbacher, courtesy of Christopher Frey.

in every room at the tiny corner sink—barely big enough to fit one hand at a time. Bathrooms with hot water were down the hall and were shared with fellow guests. Though lacking in a certain level of privacy, this plumbing was a welcome upgrade from the chamber pots and outhouses that guests used in the early days of the property.

The main house and "The Annex" rooms had transoms over the doors—the sole concession to the heat of July and August.

Guests found their escape from the heat on the broad covered porches; the rocking chairs were always in motion. Adirondack chairs graced the lawns; other casual chairs surrounded the pool, and sturdy multi-colored umbrellas fabricated from sheet metal shaded several round tables that bracketed the driveways. These were favorite spots for prolonged card games and marathon sessions of Dominoes.

Some families enjoyed the relative privacy of tiny bungalows away from the main house—these two-room buildings with shared bath cost a little more, but the soothing sound of the babbling brook just a few feet away was included for free.

The clean country air of Barryville was a big draw of course, but the food served up by Gertrude Frey was a huge attraction too. Like many neighboring boarding house operators, the meal plan at Maple

Maple Grove Farm Main House (with laundry on the line) as viewed from the Annex. It was later expanded to include a dining room. At the time of this photo, they used the living room of the main house to serve meals. When they expanded MGF by renovating the "rec room" by the pool and could accommodate more guests, they built the dining room and extended the porch. 1928 photo taken by H.S. Motschenbacher, courtesy of Christopher Frey.

This photo predates the expansion of the main house to include two more bathrooms; that addition extended the front of the building toward the sign. 1928 photo taken by H.S. Motschenbacher, courtesy of Christopher Frey.

Grove was simple: three family style meals a day. The menu repeated itself every week—you could count on enjoying a steak to celebrate your Saturday arrival and a Friday fish meal the night before you left.

Breakfasts were the only opportunity to ask for a custom order; Gert had a phalanx of small bowls with freshly cracked eggs lined up at her stove so she could scramble, fry, or poach on demand. Sixty people crowded the dining facilities three times a day, and about a dozen staffers had to be fed too. She never let them down—she cooked, she baked, she did the ordering. She even washed her own pots and pans—allowing the teenaged dishwasher to concentrate on the dishes, glasses, and silverware.

Minnie Nitzsche was in charge of laundry, staffing, bookkeeping, and marketing. In an era when the only clothes dryer available rose and fell each day, Minnie and her helpers were baked brown by the sun as they wrestled hundreds of pounds of linens onto and off the clotheslines each day. "Turnover day" on Saturday meant even more work as all the sheets and pillow cases were stripped, washed, dried, folded and distributed to the chambermaids in the rush to get ready for the new guests.

Despite the workload, every Saturday the entire work force gathered on the porch to wave good bye to the rested, well-fed, city-bound guests heading out. The brass hand bell that woke everyone up every morning of their vacation was rung in farewell as the big sedans wound down the driveway and headed down the impossibly curvy Corkscrew Road.

For many vacationers the week consisted largely of sitting, rocking, swimming, eating, drinking, sleeping, and reading. Daily strolls to "The Bluff" were common—Maple Grove's next door neighbors were generous and receptive as they opened their grounds to guests. The view down to the Delaware and across the dense forests of Pennsylvania from "The Bluff" were—and are—remarkable and in many ways made up for the lack of a lake front location.

Many guests came back again and again—their vacation preferences and reservations were recorded on a board above Minnie's desk. In her own early version of an Excel spreadsheet, Minnie managed the occupancy of Maple Grove Farm and ensured that there would be no disappointments the following summer.

Though the season was short, the work of running a boarding house was endless. July, August, and hunting season meant seven days of work per week—no respite.

When there were no guests,

From the left: a small bungalow attached to the shed, which in turn, was attached to the barn. Then the washhouse and main house. Far right is The Annex. There was an ice house in the woods just beyond the Annex. The second bungalow (by the brook) is not visible. 1928 photo taken by H.S. Motschenbacher, courtesy of Christopher Frey.

the maintenance, planning, and marketing tasks loomed. Painting, for example, was much more difficult in the era before latex made clean up easy and safer.

All the plumbing had to be drained for winter—at Maple Grove only the main house, where the Freys and Minnie lived year round, was heated. This was accomplished through a single kerosene heater that required tending every day. A giant glass bottle was refilled from a larger tank in a shed, lugged back into the house and flipped upside down to deliver the gurgling golden fluid to the flame. All this took place under the watchful eye of the German cuckoo clock that graced the nearby wall and announced the hours.

The tennis court fence on the left. Annex on right, looking down the drive to the main house. Pool would have been on the right across from main house with the "rec room" building adjoining the pool. It featured an attic where my grandparents actually slept when they had to accommodate overflow and gave up their room! 1928 photo taken by H.S. Motschenbacher, courtesy of Christopher Frey.

Minnie and Gert were skilled in many areas. Aside from the work involved in running this business for over forty years, they sewed, crocheted, and knitted clothing and afghans for family and friends. They teamed up with other Methodist ladies in Barryville to sew cancer dressings and help out in fundraising.

Charlie Frey was in charge of maintenance and helped in the kitchen. He had a giant workshop in the red barn with every tool imaginable. He kept the motorized reel lawn mower going and made sure the classic handoperated Berkel slicing machine in the kitchen functioned smoothly. Perfectly calibrated slices of luncheon meats fell off that spinning blade every day as his wife prepared lunches.

Charlie was a creative and self-reliant mechanic; he jury-rigged repairs in the middle of summer storms and winter blizzards and tended the ingenious spring-loaded faucets in the guest rooms so they didn't

The Doeller Handsome Eddy Farm was two miles southeast of the Shohola Railway Depot. Photo courtesy of Marion Doeller Kistner.

waste a drop of water. He figured out how to attach an electric motor to a hand operated potato peeling machine to ease the task of preparing heaping piles of potatoes every day.

He did the shopping in town—as did most other men in the local boarding house industry. Maple Grove Farm was typical in that most purchases were local—for many years the butcher in Clouse Brothers' store in Barryville fulfilled all the weekly meat orders. A rickety truck piled high with vegetable crates wheezed up the Corkscrew Road all the way from Port Jervis several days a week to restock the cool root cellar with fresh food.

The local garbage man even enjoyed a special relationship with Maple Grove—as the kitchen staff cleaned up after meals, food scraps went into a special bucket for daily delivery to the trash man's pigs.

Maple Grove ordered milk from the Yulan Dairy in large milk cans delivered every day. Classic metal pitchers holding cold milk were on every table in the dining room—at least until the Health Department decreed that Gert had to use wax milk cartons.

In perhaps the most perfect example of the local boarding house economy, Minnie Nitzsche handled the weekly payroll for employees. Each tiny pay envelope included her precise accounting of hours, payroll deductions, and net pay. Many Maple Grove employees worked there every summer for years. Family bills were paid; waitresses saved for college tuition; and the business partners managed to get through a lifetime without having to work for anyone else.

Maple Grove Farm was not unique—unless of course you were a family from Brooklyn that looked forward every July to leaving the noisy, grimy confines of their cramped city for a week of rest, good food, fields of wildflowers, starry nights, and a daily dip in the cool spring water pool. For them, it was Paradise.
—Christopher Frey.

Summer Homes in 1929
Maple Grove was one of many Boarding Houses advertised in the summer of 1929. The rest of this chapter visits the known Boarding Houses and some of the families in Barryville, Yulan, Minisink Ford, Eldred, and Highland Lake during the summer of 1929.

Barryville Boarding Houses
The Barryville Houses were on or near the Delaware River. They were also the closest to Pennsylvania's Shohola Depot, usually within a mile. Maple Grove Farm, though, was a 2-1/2 mile ride, west and a bit north. Handsome Eddy Farm, also in New York, was located about two miles east and a bit south.

Albert Fischer and Fred Doeller owned Handsome Eddy Farm. Fred and his wife Gertrude Doeller's daughters Doris and Marion grew up at the House and attended the Barryville school. Mr. Fischer was still the chef and made three meals each day for the guests.

Mary Hankins' Rosemary

Barryville House Ads, Summer 1929

Handsome Eddy Farm. Photo courtesy of Marion Doeller Kistner.

Handsome Eddy Farm
Fischer & Doeller
2 miles from Shohola. Opened all year. Accommodates 50. Most comfortable farmhouse on the shore of Delaware River. Well known for its beautiful scenery and excellent fishing, bathing; boats free; modern improvements; tennis, dancing. Excellent table. The whole country affords no finer spot to fully enjoy your vacation days. Rates—Double, $15 each; single $17.

Glendella postcard courtesy of the Town of Highland.

Fred Doeller, owner of Handsome Eddy Farm, and his daughter Doris. Photo courtesy of Marion Doeller Kistner.

Riverside Cottage, Warshauers
Open all year. Situated on the banks of the Delaware, 100 feet from the river; 1,500 feet elevation. Excellent table, supplied with products from our own farm. Home cooking. Fine old fashioned well water. All large, outside rooms. All modern improvements, including running hot and cold water in every room. Ideal boating, bathing, and fishing. Tennis, piano and Victrola. Amusements, including dancing and beautiful new tennis court. Churches of all denominations. Auto accommodations. Rates $18. Fine golf course 15 minute ride from house.

Rosemary Lodge, Mary Hankins
A beautiful healthful location on the banks of the Delaware. Substantial home cooking, products from my own farm. Large tennis court, boats free, bathing directly in front of house, dancing in my own private dance hall. Fine bathroom. Spring water right in house. Free auto service to and from station. Finest maple grove anywhere. Churches of every denomination positively within five minutes walk. You will be delighted with the magnificent scenery and excellent roads. Open all season. Reasonable rates. Booklet.

Glendella, Ed and Hazel Carroll
Accommodates 60. All improvements; hot and cold water in rooms; electricity. Bathing, tennis, handball. $15–20. Booklet.

—*All ads in Brooklyn Daily Eagle, summer 1929.*

Lodge was only 1/4-mile from the Shohola Station. It was about a 1/2-mile ride to Louis and Mildred Warshauer's Riverside Cottage or Chris and Meta Meyer's Spring House which they had owned since 1909.

Four Houses were within a mile of the railroad depot: Ed and Hazel Carroll's Glendella; Seitz's Delaware View Inn (possibly Side Hill Farm in the early 1930s); William Kerr's Old House at Home; and Holmes & Livingstone's Outlook Cottage.

Mrs. Edward Schumacher's Pinehurst Cottage was closer to Yulan and listed as four miles from the station.

Yulan Boarding Houses
The Yulan Houses were four to six miles from Shohola and on or near one of three lakes: Bodine, Washington, or Montgomery.

Lawrence Crandall's Cold Spring Farm, west of Beaver Brook Road, was the furthest from both the depot and water.

Many romances began in the summer at the various boarding houses. Chris Doyle, a third-generation summer boarder, relates the story of how his grandparents met at Crandall's.

My grandfather Joseph Mulvihill vacationed with his family at Crandall's and other boarding houses starting in the early 1900s. He once told me that he remembered hearing about the start of the war in the summer of 1914 on the front porch of Crandall's.

Joseph met my grandmother Elizabeth Ford at a dance on Airport Road. Elizabeth was staying at a boarding house with a friend. They started dating and were married in 1926. Later on, starting in 1945, they used to spend the whole month of July at Kaese's on Washington Lake. They became good friends with the Fours who helped run Kaese's and also owned a restaurant in Queens, New York.—Chris Doyle.

Ed and Georgiana Bornstein's Grand Vue was between Cold Spring Farm and Yulan's Four Corners. Georgiana was rather sickly and at some point Edward would hire Mary Oset, a chef for the Pennsylvania governor, to do the cooking at Grand Vue. (In 1930 though, Mary Oset was in Michigan with her husband Stanley and their five sons: Joseph, Stanley Jr., Chester, Walter, and Henry.)

Henry and Blanche Bodine ran Bodine's Cottages on Bodine Lake. Henry's father Justin Bodine had started the boarding house business, Little Pond Cottage, in 1880. (Little Pond was the original name of Bodine Lake.) Henry kept the pond stocked with pickerel, bass, and perch and still served excellent American-French cuisine.

Lillian Stidd, a widow, ran Montgomery Lake Cottage on the lake of the same name, northeast of Bodine's. Her father Louis Acor was 94 in 1930.

Kathryn Hensel had lived at Yulan Cottage, close to Yulan's northeast corner, since 1921. Yulan Cottage was sometimes called "Little Colonial" because they would take the overflow from Jacob Hensel's Colonial. By 1930 Kathryn's son Fred Hensel managed Yulan Cottage.

Oakdene was north of Yulan Cottage, on the way to Washington Lake. Phoebe Owen, a widow, ran the picturesque four-story house. Phoebe had three children: Basil, Pearl DeFeo, and Russell. Pearl and her husband Fred DeFeo Sr.

Town of Highland, Summer 1929

1929 Brooklyn *Daily Eagle's* Summer Resort Directory Section
Shohola, Pa. Station 107 miles; Elevation 1,000; Fare: $6.97

Barryville

House	Guests	Water	Terms	Season	Proprietor
Riverside Cottage	75	On	$18	All year	L. Warshauer
Delaware View Inn	65	1/2	—	Ma–Oc	C. Seitz
Glendella	60	On	$15–20	Ma–Oc	E.H. Carroll
Handsome Eddy Farm	50	On	$15–17	All year	Fischer & Doeller
Maple Grove Farm	50	1	$15–17	—	Nitzsche & Frey
Pinehurst Cottage	40	1	—	All year	Mrs. E. Schumacher
Rosemary Lodge	35	On	—	Jy–Se	Mary Hankins
Outlook Cottage	20	—	—	—	Holmes & Livingston
Old House at Home	20	On	—	Je–Se	Wm. Kerr

Yulan

House	Guests	Water	Terms	Season	Proprietor
Highland Cottage	125	On	$22–25	Ma–De	Mrs. E.V. Kalbfus
Bodine's	75	On	$18–28	All year	H. Bodine
Minisink Lodge	75	On	—	Je–Oc	McCormick
Washington Beach Hotel	60	On	$18 up	Ma–No	W.T. Tether
Colonial	60	On	—	Je–Oc	Jack Hensel
Lake View Inn	60	On	—	Ma–Oc	L. Vonderhorst
Grand Vue Inn	50	Near	$22–28	Ma–Oc	Edw. Bornstein
Park Hotel	50	On	—	Je–Oc	A.L. Bradley
Oakdene House	50	Near	—	Ma–Oc	Phoebe Owen
Laurel Cottage	50	On	$16–18	Je–Se	A.A. Hazen
Pine Grove Cottage	40	Near	—	Je–Oc	F.B. Owen
West Shore Cottage	40	Near	$20 up	Je–Oc	Mrs. M. Cantwell
Cold Spring Farm	35	1	—	Je–Se	L.G. Crandall
Yulan Cottage	30	Near	—	All year	Mrs. K. Hensel
Brookside Farm	30	Near	—	—	Mrs. A. Vonderhorst

Eldred

House	Guests	Water	Terms	Season	Proprietor
Bradley House	50	1	$15	Je–No	E.D. Avery
The Adelaide	30	1/4	$17 up	Ma–Se	A.A. Schoverling
Hillcrest Cottage	25	1/2	—	Ma–Oc	F. Schoverling

Highland Lake

House	Guests	Water	Terms	Season	Proprietor
Highland Lake Inn	200	On	—	Ma–Oc	Henry Asendorf
Lake View House	100	On	—	Ma–Oc	C. Myers
Highland Villa	100	On	—	Ma–No	M.J. Dennehy
Piermont Hotel	75	On	—	Je–Oc	Geo. Boyd
Lake Shore Hotel	60	On	$18 up	—	Chris G. Scott
Pine Grove House	60	On	—	—	H. Graf
Sunset View House	50	On	—	Ma–No	Mrs. H.J. Loerch
The Pinehurst	50	On	$18–25	Ma–Oc	Mrs. H. Sulzbach
Pine Beach Inn	50	On	$20–25	Ma–Oc	Michael Weber
Mills House	40	On	—	Ma–Oc	Mrs. Geo. Mills
Highland Lake House	35	On	—	All year	James G. Mills
Sunset House	14	—	$18	All year	Mrs. Jos. P. Gibney
Deer Head Lodge	—	On	—	—	Karl Eggers

Oakdene photo taken by H.H. Holcombe, courtesy of Pam Fischetti DeFeo.

Phoebe Owen in the middle of the photo. Granddaughter Alice DeFeo sitting in front of her. Photo courtesy of Pam Fischetti DeFeo.

The Colonial in the 1930s. Part of the bungalow with three rooms that was rented out can be seen. Photo courtesy of Kevin Marrinan.

Kaese's where Joseph and Elizabeth Ford Mulvihill would spend the month of July in 1945. Photo courtesy of Betty Ann Mulvihill Doyle and Chris Doyle.

lived in New York City and had two children: Alice, 10, and Fred Jr., 5. Russell Owen married Ina Hazen around 1929. There are a few letters written by Phoebe in Chapter 7; and by her grandson Fred DeFeo Jr. in Chapter 11.

Phoebe Owen's brother-in-law Frank Owen ran Pine Grove Cottage on the Barryville-Yulan Road south of Yulan.

Charles and Selma West operated West Farm—west and a bit north of Oakdene. They had quite a household: Charles and Selma's children, Theodore, Selma, Daniel, Ralph, and Paul; Charles' father Theodore West; and Selma's mother, Selma Werner, a widow. We'll read a letter Ralph West wrote to his parents in Chapter 12.

On Washington Lake
At least eight Houses had been built on Washington Lake.

Hensel's Colonial, close to the southeast corner of Washington Lake, was originally Joseph Tether's Washington Lake House. At some point Cyrus Walter had bought the House and a large amount of property. Cyrus may have rented the original Tether

Yulan House Ads, Summer 1929

Washington Lake Casino photo courtesy of Joan Polishook.

At Washington Lake the casino of the Washington Beach Hotel has been the main center of social activity. Nightly dances are given and once each week there is a novelty dance or mask ball at which prizes are awarded.

At Yulan the outdoor sports are the main order of the day. Situated in the midst of a mountainous district that abounds in beautiful forest country, hiking has grown to be one of the chief pastimes. Many parties set out for overnight or week-end jaunts. A campfire and a bed under the stars appeal to many a summer vacationer.

Guests are summering at the Highland Cottage on Washington Lake, the Colonial House, Yulan Cottage, the West Farm, and Washington Beach Hotel in Yulan.

Fishing, bathing, boating, and canoeing are the chief sports at the Riverside Cottage in Barryville, where a host of Brooklyn and Long Island vacationers are making their summer home. Card parties and dances fill the evenings.—Brooklyn Daily Eagle, August 11, 1929.

Bodine's on Bodine Lake, H. Bodine
Accommodates 75. All improvements. Double tennis, basketball, baseball diamond. French American cooking. Boating, bathing, fishing, farm products. $18 up. Open all year.

Montgomery Lake Cottage, L. Stidd
Lake on the premises. Boating, fishing; superior table. Rates $14 to $16.

West Farm, Charles and Selma West
West Farm, pleasantly situated among the mountains of Sullivan Co., accommodating 35 guests, offers an ideal spot for a pleasant vacation. Convenient to Catholic and Protestant churches. Its cozy nooks, lawn swings, pretty walks, croquet, piano, radio, etc., afford the opportunity to while away many happy hours.

Near amusement hall and casino. Beautiful views of the country may be had. Boating, bathing, fishing. Baseball diamond. An ideal trout stream runs through our property.

Just a short distance from the house are two fragrant pine groves with swings and seats.

We are sure you will find it a good place for rest and recreation. Good, wholesome, home cooking. Pleasant airy rooms. Electric lights. Good roads leading to and from make West Farm easy of access by auto.

West Shore Cottage, M. Cantwell
Accommodates 40. Private boating, bathing, fishing, electric, modern, improvements. Catholic church. Rates $20 and up.

Photo of West Farm courtesy of Lorraine West Daniels.

Atwell Bradley's Park Hotel. Postcard courtesy of the Town of Highland.

Park Hotel, Atwell Bradley
Accommodates 50 guests; 5 miles from Shohola. On Washington Lake. Boating, bathing, fishing; all amusements. Rates $18 up.

Laurel Cottage, Abel & Viola Hazen
On Washington Lake. Overlooking Lake. Good boating, bathing and fishing for pickerel, bass and trout. Table supplied with our farm products. Electric lights and running water. Two in room $16 a week; single, $18 week; transients, $3 a day. Accommodates 30.

Yulan Cottage, Kathryn Hensel
Accommodates 30. Apply all year. Modern; electric lights. Boating, bathing, fishing.

Washington Beach, Walter Tether
Accommodates 60. Only bathing beach on Lake. Excellent table; large, airy rooms; modern improvements; $18 up.

Minisink Lodge, M.A. McCormick
On Washington Lake. Good table. Accommodates 75. Bathing, boating, fishing. Electricity.

Highland Cottage, Edith Kalbfus
Modern, up-to-date summer hotel. 125 guests. 5 miles from Shohola. On Washington Lake. Electric lights. Good roads. Dancing, bathing, fishing, tennis. Own farm products. Rates $22-$25. Booklet. Telephone: Barryville 4–F–5.

Lakeview Farm, A. Kaese
On Washington Lake. Hot and cold running water in every room. Tennis, handball, boating; other outdoor sports. Known for its excellent meals. Accommodates 75. Apply for booklet.

Washington Beach House

Washington Beach Hotel. Photo courtesy of Ivan J. and Jana Tether.

For healthful and leisure vacations, Yulan is the one resort section in Sullivan County that caters to the most discriminating persons. With an elevation of 1,800 feet above sea level, surrounded by lakes, Yulan is "air-conditioned" by nature and almost invariably there is a breeze—made cool by the waters of the lakes.

Washington Lake is spring fed and is two miles around and one mile in length, and is known to fishermen for the bass, pickerel, and perch to be found in its waters. Boating and bathing are favorite recreations of our guests.

You will find everything about Washington Beach Hotel attractive, clean, spacious, and in good taste. Make Washington Beach Hotel your summer headquarters this year. Spend a few days or several weeks, and then go back a new person.

The Hotel is complete with all improvements. Electric lights, hot and cold running water in rooms, from the artesian well. All outside large, airy rooms with good beds and clean bedding. The hotel is three-stories and can accommodate 120 guests. Has a double front porch overlooking the Lake.

The hotel is amidst all amusements for young and old. Boating and bathing a specialty. The only natural sandy beach on the Lake. The large beach is of white sand. Bathing free to guests. Shower baths 10 cents each. Pleasures for guests include a large parlor with two pianos, radio as well as dance hall, bar and grill with electric Victrola and piano.

Handball court and quoits, table tennis and badminton. Golf course and saddle horses within 15 minutes by auto from the Hotel.

Excellent meals served with fresh vegetables and the best of farm products and meats obtainable.

We assure you it is our aim to see that our guests have service and do not leave the dining room hungry. All churches nearby. Good roads and shady walks make the summer holidays at the Washington Beach Hotel days to be remembered.

Washington Beach Hotel is situated 107 miles from New York via Erie Railroad to Shohola, Pa. Station, then by auto over the mountains to the hotel. Or take the bus from New York City to the Hotel.

Auto parties accommodated. We meet trains when notified.

Rates: All persons boarding by the week will please pay in advance. Rates are based on size and location of rooms. All rates include meals. No consumptives or dogs taken. We will be pleased to hear from you. W.T. Tether, Proprietor. Phone: Barryville 2145.

home to two sisters who had run it as the Nancy Lee for a few years.

By 1927 Cyrus had sold the Nancy Lee to Jacob and Lisette Hensel who renamed the house, the Colonial. The Colonial will be featured in Chapter 13.

Cyrus, a lumberman, and his sons Reginald and Donald, lumbered the land north of the Colonial. They also had cows in their fields by Montgomery Lake.

A sad event for the Walter family happens in February 1935, when a tree falls on Cyrus as he lumbers and breaks his back. Reginald and Donald take him out on a skid to the hospital, but Cyrus dies. Reginald, Donald, and their mother then live on the second floor of the Colonial's garage. In the late 1930s Reginald Walter would build the Maplecrest north of the Colonial.

Walter and Meda Breen Tether managed Washington Beach Hotel, on the northeast side of the Lake.

Summer guests had stayed at Abel and Viola Bradley Hazen's Laurel Cottage, since before 1900. Hazen's was near the Colonial on the other side of the fish tail.

Abel and Viola's son Lewis and his wife Elsie Parker (daughter of William and Victoria Simpson Parker) had their own boarding house by 1930. Sunset Cottage was built across the road from the elder Hazen's House. Lewis and Elsie Parker had two daughters, Viola and Marcella.

North of Laurel Cottage was Atwell Bradley's Park Hotel which had been called Lake View Cottage at one time. Atwell was twice a widower with sons, Clifford, George, and Clarence. George would own a restaurant in Yulan sometime in the future.

Atwell had married Frieda Guenther, a widow with five children. In 1930 Clarence Bradley;

and Edith, Clinton, Helen, and Viola Guenther lived with Atwell and Freida.

North of Park Hotel was Minisink Lodge which was run by M.A. McCormack for many years. Much later the Lodge may have become part of West Shore Cottage/Lodge.

Margarite Cantwell managed West Shore Cottage (also called Cantwell's). Her son George was a chauffeur early on. Later Margarite's son Joseph Cantwell managed the large boarding house.

Lake View Farm House (north of West Shore Cottage) was most likely owned by Ed Prange in the late 1880s. Ahrend and Sophia Kaese owned the House in the early 1900s. Albert Kaese seems to be the owner by 1930.

Next to and north of Kaese's was Highland Cottage. Edith Kalbfus managed Highland Cottage, a large hotel that had its start before the turn of the century.

Other Yulan Houses
Carl and Anna Vonderhorst ran Brookside Farm. Their daughter-in-law-Louise Vonderhorst, a widow, managed Lake View Inn—the house her husband Eric was building when he died of typhoid in 1921.

Carl and Anna Vonderhorst were my great-grandparents. Opa came over from Germany first (perhaps before 1900) and then Oma came later, and they built the house in Yulan. It is the big house on Beaver Brook or Toaspern's Pond.

I grew up there as my father did and his father did before me. The house has a wonderful sun porch and a total of 49 windows. Lots of memories changing the storm windows to screens in the spring and back to storm windows in the autumn. When my mom did spring and fall cleaning she washed the curtains and hung them on curtain stretchers.

My grandmother Louise Vonderhorst had a boarding house in Yulan, and later on the coffee and gift shop opposite the gas station in Yulan.—Nancy Lee Vonderhorst.

Lewis Hazen's Sunset Cottage

Sunset Cottage is located in Sullivan County about 1,800 feet above sea level overlooking beautiful Washington Lake where our guests spend many enjoyable hours in boating, bathing, and fishing. The location of our house with its spacious lawn and apple orchard makes it an ideal summer resort.

Sunset Cottage is a new house with all modern improvements, including hot and cold running water in every room.

The Post Office and St. Anthony's R.C. Church are within walking distance from the house. All casinos nearby.

The meals are clean, wholesome and plentiful. Strictly fresh eggs, milk, fruit, and vegetables served daily.

We can comfortably accommodate 40 people in large rooms, well kept and equipped with

Sunset Cottage photo courtesy of Christene Stevens Myers.

electric lights. Two meals daily. Piano and radio.

Let us make reservations for you and your friends at your earliest possible convenience.

The rates for adults are $18 to $20 per week. No reduction for children.

Take Erie R.R. to Shohola Station. Auto transportation to and from Shohola, Erie R.R. Station, $1.00 per person each way. Trunks, $1.00 each way. Telephone Barryville 4-F-4.

Charles and Martha Draxler's York Lake Mountain House in Minisink Ford. Photo courtesy of Martha Eldred Worzel.

There was one known boarding house in Minisink Ford.

Minisink Ford
The York Lake Mountain House was owned by Charles and Martha Draxler and their family. The family had run the house since about 1917. Their daughter Emily had or soon would meet her future husband Harvey Eldred. Harvey helped out at the Draxler Place. He

Martin D. Myers Jr. riding his horse around 1930. Photo courtesy of Christene Stevens Myers.

had lived with his sister Eleanor Barnes since 1927 when his father had died and he was orphaned.

Minisink Ford folks crossed the Roebling Bridge to get to Lackawaxen where they shopped. Many of the men in Minisink Ford worked for the Railroad.

West Eldred
The Avery House, on the west side of Eldred, was east and somewhat north of Washington Lake. Norah and her husband Erwin D. Avery ran the original Bradley House her father Isaac M. Bradley had first advertised in the early 1880s. Isaac, 91, lived with them. Arthur and Gladys Avery may also have resided with their parents.

Laura Avery and her husband Buck McBride had three children: Kenneth, Frances, and Virginia. Beatrice Avery and her husband Charles W. Horton had two sons: William Erwin and Clifford (born January 1931).

Avery House Ad: *Among the hills of Sullivan County beautiful pine and maple shade. Elevation 1300. Lakes and streams nearby. Acc. 50. $15. Table is abundantly furnished with fresh produce from our own farm. An ideal spot for rest and recreation. Telephone, piano, electric light.*

Guests will be met with auto when notified. No consumptives.

The Bradleys had always been country neighbors of the Leavenworths and their Echo Hill Farm on Blind Pond Brook. Sherman S. Leavenworth and his children, Charlotte, Truman, and Martin, lived there. Both Isaac M. Bradley and Sherman Leavenworth were quite elderly.

The old Slonek home where Dr. Gutfruend lived was closer to Eldred's Four Corners. Near Dr. Gutfruend's house was a House on what was once Becker's Woods. It would be called "The Pines" in 1936. Margaret Hellman owned it in 1930.

Eleanora Alston, a widow with three children, had managed the Becker's Woods' House around 1920. In the early 1920s Eleanora married William H. Parker, son of William and Victoria Simpson Parker. William H. and Eleanora Parker and their children, William Jr., Hazel, Shirley, and Howard, resided in several different homes, including southeast of central Eldred—in the area of the old James Eldred house built in 1830.

Central and North Eldred
Near William H. Parker's household, on Brook Road before Eldred's Four Corners, was the Parker House managed by Emily Payne Parker, William H. Parker's grandmother. Emily Parker's daughter Emily, her husband Howard Stevens and their daughter Teenie lived upstairs. Teenie could walk out the door and up the hill to school.

Christene (Teenie) Stevens and her grandmother Emily Christene Parker, around 1926. Photo courtesy of Christene Stevens Myers.

During the 1920s Howard ran a taxi service with Pete Callahan. In 1928 Howard was elected Superintendent of Highways.

The Martin D. Myers family lived near the Stevens which gave opportunity for Teenie Stevens and Martin D. Myers Jr. to race wagons in their growing up years.

When we were kids, all of us in "downtown Eldred" were friends and were together doing things. Tracey Myers (my dad's cousin) had a truck and in the winter would take everyone up to Bosch's Pond to skate. When there was sleigh riding, everyone got out and yes, we went on the roads, like the school hill, Highland Lake Hill, and down our hill. We did get our exercise.

Martin and I were probably 10 or 11 and we had wagons and would put one knee in and use the other leg to push and go as fast as we could. We were coming down through the Four Corners and I upset. Jim Wade, the barber, came

out and picked me up and always kidded me that through my tears and bleeding leg I said, "I beat him anyway, Jim."
—Christene Stevens Myers.

Greigs, Seven Oaks, and Steges
North of Eldred's Four Corners—past the Eldred Cemetery, on Stege Road—were the Seven Oaks, Greig, and Stege houses.

When Mrs. George Beck was older, she sold Seven Oaks to the Greigs. Seven Oaks seems to have burned down in the mid-1930s.

Kate Greig was a widow. Her daughter Isabel was married to Edward Grotecloss Jr. and lived or would live in the huge Grotecloss home that was built a bit south of the Greig Place. Isabel and Ed had three sons—Edward III, Robert, and Bennett.

East Eldred
On the east side of Eldred was the Straub Hotel. Fred Straub, (who we met in World War I) became the proprietor after his mother Juliana died.

Proctor Road went southeast from Eldred's Four Corners. The road passed Straub's Hotel and crossed Halfway Brook. Highland Lake Road veered left and Proctor Road continued to Glen Spey.

The Austin Mountain Grove House was on Proctor Road. Anna Rothman's boarding house was next door and had been there since at least since 1917.

Highland Lake Road headed towards Highland Lake when it left Proctor Road.

Harry and Della Howlett owned the first and second houses on the left. They boarded school teachers for many years. At that time teachers had to live in the area.

Continuing on Highland Lake Road, Ferncliff Lodge was on the

Ferncliff Lodge. Photo courtesy of Chuck Myers.

Bischof's Ferncliff Lodge. Photo courtesy of Christene Stevens Myers.

Teenie Stevens on her horse Bess. Her friend Janith Boyd rides Sailor. The photo was taken in front of Fred Lewis' house. Photo courtesy of Christene Stevens Myers.

Highland Lake House Ads, 1929

View of Highland Lake, N.Y., seen from the North Beach. Postcard courtesy of Kevin Marrinan.

Highland Lake is one of the prettiest lakes in Sullivan County, a couple of miles from Eldred, N.Y. Magnificent scenery along the road. Elevation 1,800 feet. Nothing would be more invigorating than a stay around here during September, a truly marvelous month.

Highland Villa, M.J. Dennehy
The Villa amongst the pines—noted for its excellent cuisine. Bathing, golf, tennis, handball, saddle horses, bowling, casinos. Reduced rates in June and September. Accommodates 100. New, modern house; located 100 feet from Lake. Home cooking; fresh vegetables, butter, eggs, and poultry. Bathing at Sand Beach. Rowing, canoeing, fishing, regattas. Short distance to the golf course. Dancing, bowling and other amusements at six casinos nearby. Convenient to Catholic and Protestant churches. Terms $18 a week and up. Descriptive booklet on request.

Mountain Lake House, G. Staubes
New house and new furnishings. All improvements. Private bath. Excellent table.

Highland Lake Inn, H. Asendorf
200 guests. 7 miles from Shohola; 1,800 feet elevation; long distance telephone, Barryville 209; telegraph station, Pa. Special rates for September; new golf course; beautiful lake and scenery; running hot and cold water in all rooms; bathrooms on floors; excellent table and service. Apply for rates.

Piermont Hotel, George Boyd
Accommodates 100 guests. Overlooking lake. Altitude 2,000 ft. All improvements (including running water in every room). Canoeing, bathing, fishing, dancing, tennis, golf. Rates $18 up.—July 1928.

Pine Beach Inn, Michael Weber
Accommodates 50. Located on the shore of lake; private bathing beach; large, airy rooms; large porches; German cooking; dancing; modern improvements. $20–25. Write for booklet.

Lake Shore House, Chris Scott
Accommodates 60. Located on the shore of beautiful Highland Lake, in the hills of Sullivan County. Modern improvements. Electric light. Excellent table, fresh vegetables. Near all churches. Amusements of all kinds nearby. Four new bowling alleys attached to casino near house. Boating, bathing, fishing, and dancing. Write for booklet. $18 and up per week.

Deer Head Lodge, Eggers
New. Running hot and cold water in each room. Private lake shore. Golf course. Dancing, entertainment. Catholic Church. Booklet on request. Deer Head Lodge extends a cordial welcome and offers the ideal spot for a happy vacation of relaxation and healthy recreation. Here you will meet the kind of friendly clean cut people you'll enjoy knowing and keeping as friends over the years to come. Plan now to spend a vacation here with your family and friends. Modern buildings equipped with every comfort and convenience. Spacious, well ventilated rooms, all with hot and cold running water. Cozy, homelike furnishings amid which our guests spend their happiest hours. Food here is tops in both quality and quantity. Meals prepared and served under the personal supervision of Mr. and Mrs. Eggers are satisfying to the most exacting guest.
—Deer Head Lodge Brochure.

Pine Grove House, H.E. Graf
All improvements. Running water in every room. Rates $17 up. Elevation 2,000 feet. Excellent table. Near golf links. All amusements. Churches nearby.—Ads from Brooklyn Daily Eagle, August 1929 (unless noted otherwise).

Boyd's Piermont Hotel was on Highland Lake. This is the Boyd's Boathouse. Postcard courtesy of Ken Bosch.

left. Later photos of Ferncliff look quite different than the original Lodge built by Jackson Myers.

Bischof's Ferncliff Lodge

Guido Bischof owned Ferncliff Lodge by the early 1920s. Early on he had built a "bungalow" for the actress Lillian Gish. The bungalow (but not Lillian) plays a part in our story. Prohibition lasted from 1920 to the end of 1933 and there was quite a bit of activity at the bungalow.

Mr. Bischof served an annual Venison Dinner as shown in this 1927 invitation.

You are cordially invited to attend the Fifth Anniversary Venison Dinner to be held at Ferncliff Lodge, Eldred, Sullivan Co., N.Y. at 2 p.m. Sunday, November 13, 1927, under direction of Guido Bischof. Dinner De Luxe $5.00 per person.

Herman Clouse's Bungalows

There were two boarding houses at the juncture of Highland Lake and Hartung Roads.

The Hammond Boarding House to the north, had been there at least since 1920. Bill Hammond, his sister Mae Hammond Parker, and her daughter Ruth managed the House. We meet all three in the early 1940s.

Herman and Veronica Clouse and their children resided in a large house across the road from the Hammonds. Herman Clouse built four bungalows on his property to rent to summer boarders.

In the summer of 1925 the Gilmores from New York City rented one of the bungalows. Peggy Gilmore (the future Mrs. Russell MacKechnie) was 18 months old. Peggy, her parents, five siblings, her mother's parents, and father's mother all stayed at Clouse's square-shaped bungalow. The large room in front was the dining/living room. There was one large room in the center. In the back was a very big kitchen with a wood burning stove, but no running water. On each side were three small bedrooms (total of six). When they first rented there was an outhouse, and no bathroom.

On one side the maternal grandparents had the last bedroom; then two brothers; and the front bedroom was for the

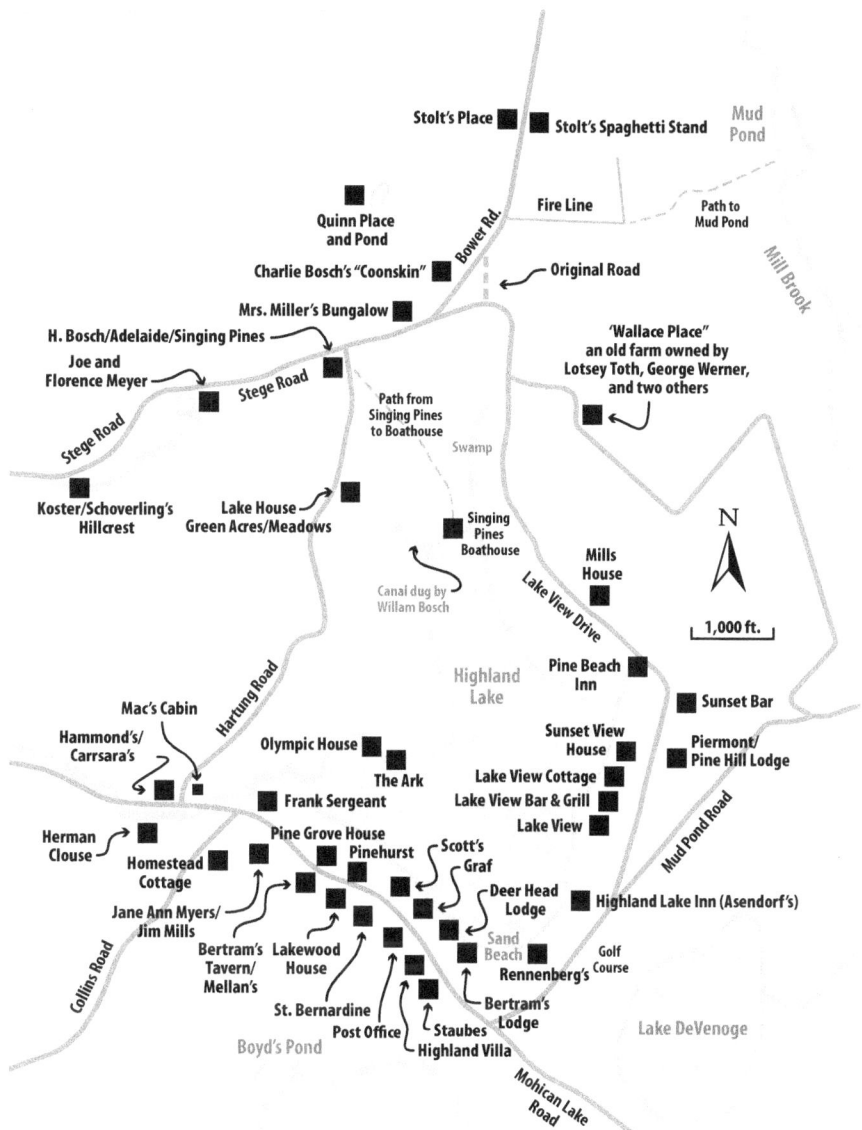

Boarding houses near Highland Lake from the research of Ken Bosch. Map: Gary Smith.

parents. On the other side the paternal grandmother (a widow of many years); the other brothers in the middle room; and Peggy and her sister shared the last room.

The Gilmores rented that bungalow for 17 consecutive summers. Over the years Herman Clouse did away with the middle bedroom and turned it into a bathroom with a toilet and sink, but no shower or tub. In those days they washed their hair and bathed at Sand Beach.

The Clouse children (in the 1930 Census) ranged in age from 2–21: Ida, Gertrude, Herman,

Sunset View House owned by Matilda Loerch would be sold to the Theuers. Photo courtesy of Jeanie Staubes Turner.

Highland Villa run by Mrs. Dennehy in 1929. Photo courtesy of Kevin Marrinan.

Helen, George, Katherine, Theodore, Veronica (Peggy), and Girard. The Clouse and Gilmore children were friends. Peggy Gilmore and her sister were close in age to Peggy Clouse. They wrote each other during the winter.—*As told to Louise Smith by Peggy Gilmore MacKechnie.*

Highland Lake Houses

You may recall that Jim Leavenworth said that there were more boarding houses in Highland Lake than Yulan. And such seems to be the case, when trying to reconstruct where these many houses were most likely located.

We'll tour the Houses north of Hammond's after visiting the houses on or closer to Highland Lake.

After passing Hartung Road to the north and Collins Road on the south, Highland Lake Road traveled past Jim Mills' Highland Lake House. The house built around 1850, originally belonged to Jane Ann Myers.

Jim Mills had grown up in the Mills Boarding House on the opposite side of the lake. The Mills House had been built around 1840 by Jim's grandparents Alexander and Margaret Gillies Mills. Jim's father had died in 1909 and his mother Elizabeth Gillespie Mills continued to run the Mills House which housed 40 summer guests.

Southwest Highland Lake Houses

Frank and Anna Sergeant and Anna's sister Jennie Hull lived across the road from Jim Mills' Highland Lake House—near the bottom of the Lake's "thumb."

Frank Sergeant rented rowboats. He gave permission to the Gilmores (mentioned earlier) to leave their rowboat on his property to make it more convenient for them. Mr. Gilmore only came on weekends and his wife and their five children couldn't afford to drive the two-mile round trip from Clouse's to Sand Beach each day. Gilmores were very appreciative to Frank Sergeant for allowing them to store their boat on his property.

Along the side of the "thumb and palm" of Highland Lake were the following Houses: Graf's Pine Grove House (which burned down around 1930), Sulzbach's Pinehurst Casino, Chris Scott's Lake Shore House, Karl and Elsie's Eggers' Deer Head Lodge, and what would be Bertram's

Pine Grove House owned by the Grafs. Postcard courtesy of Ed Mellan.

Staube's Mountain Lake House. Photo courtesy of Jeanie Staubes Turner.

Brochures of Eggers' Deer Head Lodge on Highland Lake and Cantwell's West Shore Lodge on Washington Lake courtesy of Kevin Marrinan. Washington Beach Hotel Brochure courtesy of Ivan J. and Jana Tether.

Lodge in a few years.

Mrs. J. Dennehy's Highland Villa Hotel, near the Post Office, was not on Highland Lake. Staubes' Mountain Lake House was south of Highland Villa, opposite Deer Head Lodge.

Rounding the "palm" of Highland Lake was Rennenberg's by Sand Beach, and the nearby Golf Course on the original property of Dr. DeVenoge.

North of Rennenberg's was Asendorf's Highland Lake Inn, Charlie Myers' Lake View, and Matilda Loerch's Sunset View House.

Houses on East of Highland Lake
Henry and Belle Asendorf and their son George ran Highland Lake Inn. The Asendorfs wintered at least one year in Florida.

Martin D. Myers Sr. had worked for Henry since before 1914. Along with his many duties, he chauffeured Highland Lake Inn guests to and from Shohola. Asendorfs' Hotel was south of Lake View which Martin's brother Charles C. Myers ran, and where both brothers had grown up.

Charlie Myers' Lake View could accommodate 100 guests. In the 1920s Charlie built an ice cream/snack bar for the summer visitors. Charlie and his second wife Elizabeth had a delightful daughter Eleanor. Charlie's son Harold may have completed college by 1929.

The Boyd's Piermont Hotel, opposite Sunset View House, was another old established summer home. The Piermont, run by George Boyd as late as 1929, would be owned by Charlie Myers for a short time. Charlie lost the Hotel due to taxes during the Depression. The Piermont would become Pine Hill Lodge at some point.

Florence Ort and Eleanor Myers at Charlie Myers's ice cream/snack bar in 1927. Courtesy of Timothy C. Rizzuto.

Sunset View House, on the Lake north of Lake View, could accommodate 50 guests. It also offered home cooking. It had been operated by Matilda Loerch for some time. Theuers, the next owners, would also own Sunset Bar, north of Piermont Hotel.

Perhaps the Sunset Bar was first called the Sunset House and run by Mrs. Joseph Gibney. It could house 14 guests and was open all year.

Martin D. Myers Sr. stands beside a gas pump. Asendorf's Highland Lake Inn is in the background. Photo courtesy of Christene Stevens Myers.

At the top of Highland Lake's "little finger" was Michael Weber's Pine Beach Inn.

Hartung Road and the Bosches
The original Wilhelm Bosch Lake House was on Hartung Road, a bit north and west of the top of Highland Lake. It would soon be called Green Acres.

Ed Bosch, who had assumed ownership of Lake House in the early 1920s, built a small house for Wilhelm and Mary across from the Lake House. Several others had managed Lake House since 1915, including Joe and Florence van Eastenbridge Meyer. Joe and Florence had built an addition to their house on Stege Road about 1920 to accommodate their own boarders.

Some of Wilhelm Bosch's descendants lived nearby. Ralph and Paula Schreib Bosch and their family lived in a small cabin in back of the Lake House barn. Herman Bosch lived on Proctor Road. Carl and Minnie Bosch Benedict operated a chicken farm on Hartung Road. Further north, off Bower Road, Charlie Bosch had property nick-named *Coonskin*, which Carl and Minnie had run as a boarding house in the mid-1920s. The Bosch brothers hunted

Get Around that First Turn and It's Downhill All the Way

The "wonderfully named Corkscrew Road" provided great winter adventure. Christopher Frey reminisced about a 1950s perilous excursion, some 30 years later in a River Reporter *article.*

This poor excuse for a winter is sufficient reason to haul out all the old stories about how rough winters used to be in the Delaware River Valley. But in the yin and yang world of what used to be, those difficult winters created great opportunities for play. Among the most memorable was the death-defying toboggan run down the Corkscrew Road.

The spiraling section of this town road that gave rise to its name is now officially closed in winter and rarely travelled in the best of weather. But in the days before Suzy Chapstick, assorted hardware-wielding thugs, and the Jamaican bobsled team kept our attention glued—or maybe frozen—to televised winter sports, the kids of Barryville used to create competitions of their own. These cold weather outings were done without benefit of internal combustion engines or motorized ski lifts. All it took were wooden toboggans, some Monkey Ward boots, and those one-of-a-kind sweaters and mittens that Grandma used to knit.

The toboggan run down the Corkscrew was truly difficult. Starting up by Weber's house you could get some real momentum going by the time you reached the first turn, a hairpin baby banked on the left by a huge boulder that was the Moby Dick to all us slipsliding Cap'n Ahabs. If only we could master that first turn—steer up and off the boulder at just the right angle not to fall sideways off the slippery wooden apparatus in a tangle of frozen dungarees and dammits.

Most of the time we couldn't and so had to reassemble the team and continue down from there. The thrill diminished, but only slightly. A less-steep stretch of about 100 feet just after Boulder Turn was enlivened by rocks jutting out from the ditches on both sides; we played a kind of Russian Roulette with these hazards, which, if we wobbled off the trajectory, occasionally resulted in snow tinted with little red badges of courage—er, recklessness.

But after the straightaway came more great turns and steep inclines; the hoots and hollers must certainly have been heard in the village a mile downwind as we rocketed through the powder clinging to our pals like so many hunched-over circus elephants. When our weight shifted the wrong way and confounded the elaborate steering mechanism, we risked launching ourselves headlong into the woods and making a more intimate contact with the evergreens than we had counted on.

Just before the brook at the bottom of the Corkscrew Road the inevitable happened. The physics of fun could no longer overcome the force of gravity, and the toboggans stopped. Moments later the giggling did too, as we reluctantly got up and began the bargaining over whose turn it was to pull the streamlined slabs back up the hill for the next run.

These climbs were inevitably accompanied by elaborate schemes and Rube Goldberg-ian plans to harness the energy of the Toasperns' fabulous tractor to haul us effortlessly back up to the pinnacle on some kind of rope tow. Like Jules Verne with his submarine we fantasized about the advent of snowmobiles and skidoos—anything to keep us from having to make those quadricep-searing scrambles back up the hill.

But, even then, pint-sized thrill seekers and speed-merchants though we were, the beauty of winter in the woods did not go unnoticed; we would pause at the summit to look down the river valley and squint into the sun. We looked for deer hoofprints and the strange little cuneiform footprints of birds as well as other more pungent traces of the animal life all around us.

As we proved ourselves to our parents, we were eventually permitted to indulge in that oldest of rituals—firemaking. The promise of a small campfire crackling in the snow helped spur us on as we grunted and tugged our way back up the hill.

Fortunately, on the coldest of winter days on the Corkscrew, my brothers and I had the luxury of Grandma's house just a shout away from the starting point. When we got too cold and even the little wood fire couldn't restore the feeling to our fingers, we could escape to the warmth of her kerosene stove and listen to the bottle of amber fuel gurgle as it fed the flame that dried the gloves that went back on the hands of the refried Freys as we went back outdoors, fortified by hot chocolate and sticky buns, to the challenge of tobogganing around Boulder Turn.

Back when winter was winter and Florida was just another town in Orange County.—*By Christopher Frey, River Reporter.*

Left: Group at Lake House around 1925: Starting fourth from left, Christina Bosch, Mary van Eastenbridge Bosch, in front of her, Katherine Miller with grandson Whipple Bosch, Florence Meyer. Standing in back of Mrs. Miller and Florence is Joe Meyer. Others unknown. Right: Ed Bosch, front right, with hunting group. Photos courtesy of Ken Bosch.

on Charlies' property and took others on hunting trips.

Charlie Bosch had built a small bungalow (known to the family as Mrs. Miller's Castle for her beautiful curtains, lamps, and decor) near the fork of Stege and Bower Roads for his widowed mother-in-law, Katherine Wiest Miller. (Katherine died in 1926.)

Other Bosch children—Will and Lulu Bosch Lansmith; Ted and Tillie Bosch Wicks; Menzo and Lena Bosch; and Will and Tina Bosch Brodmerkel, and their families—lived on Long Island.

Stolts and Schoverlings
Six-tenths of a mile north of Charlie Bosch, on Bower Road, Joseph and Sadie Stolt had a small boarding house. Mrs. Stolt was Italian and had a spaghetti stand which attracted strolling boarders. The boarding house burned down in the early 1930s.

The Adelaide owned by Al Schoverling was likely the House at Stege and Hartung Roads which was first owned by Herman and Mary Bosch. At a later time Otto Seel would own the building and call it, Singing Pines.

Frederick and Annette Schoverling's Hillcrest Cottage sat on Stege Road closer to Stege's Pond. Fred and Annette had purchased the House in 1920 from the Kosters. The 1930s would be hard on folks everywhere, but the Schoverlings had some unexpected help.

The Schoverlings continued operating the Hillcrest, and during the tough times of the 1930s, Fred Schoverling discovered some money under the newspapers under the oilcloth on the kitchen table of the log cabin and in a hollowed out section of one of the logs. The log cabin was dismantled looking for more. He also found some money behind a loose board between the horse stalls and the barn was dismantled. The nearest bank was 20 miles away, so going to a bank was not a convenient thing.
—Frederick Bosch.

Not many found cash hiding under a kitchen tablecloth or in their horse stall during the Depression. Much of the 1930s found townsfolk searching for work and taking a variety of jobs to make ends meet. The graduating class of 1930 entered a world where the "depression was on in full force." Eldred Union, though, had only one graduate.

The main building of Lake House, soon to be Green Acres. It housed the kitchen and all the dining rooms as well as waiters and waitresses on the third floor. Photo courtesy of Diane Pankow.

Chapter 6
The Foot of the Class
Arthur Austin, 1930–1933

My name led the list of the 1930 graduates of the Eldred Union School. That year's class, it should be noted, was composed of one member. Some have been so unkind as to point out that I also graduated at the foot of my class.—Arthur Austin.

Arthur Austin's graduation photo, 1930. Photo courtesy of Mary Briggs Austin.

It was January 1930. In six months Arthur Austin would be the lone graduate from Eldred Union. Classes had been in Abel Myers' old Orchard Terrace House for almost five years.

As mentioned in Chapter 4, the principal Ralph Stanley wore many hats, including that of a teacher. There were two other high school teachers for the 40 students in grades nine to twelve. Edna Woolsey taught English, civics, and history; Adeline Diessler taught Latin and German. All three teachers had degrees and taught subjects they majored or minored in.

The high schoolers attended eight classes, each 45 minutes long. German II had been added. The 1926 New International Encyclopedia was part of the 444 volumes of books owned by the school. There were maps and a biology chart, but no typewriters or phonographs.

1930s Eldred
A previous chapter referred to the Wilson building on the northwest corner of Eldred which included the A&P (owned by Art Wilson) on the lower end, a butcher shop in the center, and a Post Office (which would change locations before 1935) on the upper end. John Sparks was the Postmaster in 1930. On the southwest corner was Wait and Boyd's Garage. Jim Wade's barbershop was in the lower level of the garage with some other businesses.

Pat's Stand
On the northeast corner would eventually be Pat's Stand. It would extend out onto the street from the William H. Wilson Store. Forrest, or Pat as he was called, was the son of William H. and Bertha Boyd Wilson. Pat would become a lawyer.

Mort and Jennie Austin's Family
Mort and Jennie Austin still ran Mountain Grove House each summer. Sometime around 1930 Mort, 65, retired from over 30 years of driving his horse and carriage to get guests from the Shohola Railway Station.

Raymond Austin worked at a U.S. Barge Office in

Pat's Stand at Eldred's Four Corners. Photo courtesy of Christene Stevens Myers.

New York City. Raymond and his wife Gladys Myers' daughter Melva turned two the summer of 1930. Gladys' mother Mabel Owen Myers had died at the beginning of January, a sad time for Edwin Myers and his family.

Bill Austin, 27, worked or would work, for the County. Bob, 15, was still in school.

Wilhelm Bosch Dies

In May of 1930, Wilhelm Bosch, "country neighbor" of the Austin family, died of a stroke.

According to family legend, Wilhelm had walked to town to pick up his mail twice on the day he died.

Toward the end of his life, Wilhelm made his peace with God, became a professing Christian, and stopped drinking. He could be seen praying in the woods and fields. Family members said, "He got real religious" and "went on the wagon."

Wilhelm became a member of the Eldred Methodist Church. He was awarded their old church organ in recognition of his donations toward the purchase of a new one.

Wilhelm was buried in the same plot as his first wife Mary Maier Bosch, in the old Eldred cemetery.—Ken Bosch.

Arthur Austin Graduates

Arthur Austin, as he pointed out at the start of the chapter, was Eldred's only graduate in 1930.

After graduating from high school, I took a business course at Baker's Business School on Staten Island. When I was graduated, the depression was on in full force. —Arthur Austin.

Baker Business College

While attending Baker Business School, Arthur stayed with Raymond, Gladys, and Melva Austin in Staten Island.

I could not play or make noise in the living room in the evening when Uncle Art and my dad studied. I could sit in my little chair and watch them, which I found quite fascinating. Uncle Art was "writing" in the air (practicing shorthand); and my dad Raymond was staring at the wall opposite him, moving only his eyes up, down, and side to side again and again, doing eye exercises.—Melva Austin Barney.

The Empire State Building

In March construction had started on the Empire State Building. Up to 3,000 men worked on the framework which rose at a rate of four to five stories per week. The masonry work started in June and was completed in November.

Ted Wicks Sr. was one of the construction workers. He was the husband of Tillie Bosch who had grown up in Highland Lake. Ted Jr. visited where his dad worked.

Lon Austin

Lon Austin, a lay preacher, was asked to speak at the service in Glen Spey for Founder's Day, the 146th anniversary of the Methodist Church.

Baker Business College that Arthur Austin attended after high school graduation. Students are unknown. Photo courtesy of Mary Briggs Austin.

1930 World, National, and Local News

1930 World and National News
- Chinese Civil War, 1927–1949.
- End of the League of Nations.
- 1930 U.S. Census: 123,202,624.
- The Great Depression.
- The Great Plains devastated by severe dust storms as a result of extreme drought and heavy winds.
- The analog computer invented at MIT in Boston by Vannevar Bush.
- Ruth Graves Wakefield accidentally invented the chocolate chip cookie.
- Warner Brothers' first All-Talking, All-Color, wide-screen movie.

January 1930
- Excavation for Empire State Building.

February 1930
- C. Tombaugh discovered (un) planet Pluto at Lowell Observatory, Flagstaff, Arizona.

March 1930
- First frozen foods of Clarence Birdseye sold in Ringfield, Massachusetts.

April 1930
- London Naval Reduction Treaty signed into law by the U.S., Great Britain, Italy, France, and Japan.

September 1930
- Nazi Party received 20 per cent of the vote in German elections.

December 1930
- President Hoover sent Congress $150 million Public Works Project request.

1930 New York State News
- A section of N.Y. Route 97 was constructed. Much of it was built on the D&H Canal bed.

1930 Halfway Brook News
Eldred School News 1930–1931
- The school had eight faculty; 99 students in first through eighth grades; 58 students in High School. There was a new school office and a new coal bin. German III, music, and plane trigonometry added to the curriculum. New activities included: some inter school basketball; Glee Clubs; and basketball games for girls and boys.

1930 Fire
- Barryville Methodist Church burned.

1930 Moved
- Hirsches moved to Connecticut.

1930 Births
- Helen Hensel born to Jacob and Lisette Galm Hensel at the Colonial.
- Gerald Koenig born to Eugene and Hazel Leavenworth Koenig.

1930 Marriages
- Alfred Hill married Elizabeth (Bessie) MacIntyre Lass in June.
- James Gibson married Mabel Austin (Eldred-Austin relative).

1930 Deaths
- Frances Payne Eldred, 1852–1930.
- John Perry Bradley died in March.
- Henry Webb, 1861–1930, grandson of Jane Ann Van Pelt Webb Myers.
- Mabel Owen Myers, 1873–1930.
- Wilhelm Henry Bosch, 1849–1930, was born in Germany and came to the U.S. in 1870. He had a summer hotel business for 30 years in Highland Lake. His first wife Mary Maier died in 1904. Surviving relatives: Minnie Benedict, Lulu Lansmith, Matilda Wicks, Edward, Ralph, Herman, Charles, and Menzo Bosch; his second wife Mary van Eastenbridge and their daughter Christina Brodmerkel.
- William H. Parker, 1872–1930, son of James Y. and Emily C. Payne Parker. Surviving relatives: his wife Victoria Simpson Parker; their children: James Y., William H., Andrew, and Elsie Hazen; sisters Emily Stevens and Adelaide Brett; and mother Emily C. Parker.
- Joseph W. Tether, 1844–1930. Surviving children: Jessie Bradley and Walter Tether.
- Mrs. Ella G. Campbell, 1862–1930. Mrs. Campbell was gate tender at the Lackawaxen-Minisink Ford toll bridge for several years.

Wilhelm Bosch photo courtesy of the Bosch Family.

Rev. John Ralph, Glen Spey, to Mr. Alonzo (Lon) Austin, Eldred
July 18, 1930
Dear Brother Austin:
We are celebrating "Founder's Day," the 146th anniversary of the church at the Glen Spey Church on Sunday. We would be very pleased to have you favour us with an address knowing you to be connected in an integral way with the Church History.
The Service begins 2–3 p.m. and you will be the first speaker. Hoping you can come. I thank you in anticipation of your kindness. Very Sincerely Yours,
John R. Ralph

Chicago World Fair Preparation
Lon's brother Ell Austin also

Ted Wicks Sr. and co-workers at the Empire State building around 1930. Ted is the second from the left. The N.Y.C. skyline is obscured by a haze. Photo courtesy of Ken Bosch.

Ted Wicks Jr. at the construction site of the Empire Building where his father worked around 1930. Photo courtesy of Ken Bosch.

received a letter in July. The Chicago World Fair of 1933 was three years off, but the following letter to Ell Austin indicated the work had already begun.

Adelaide Hamlin, Chicago, Ill., to Mr. Austin, Ossining, N.Y.
July 26, 1930
My dear Mr. Austin,
    We do not forget your many and usual kindnesses.
    I am wondering if I might interest you a little in up-to-date Chicago?
    They are soon to build an Island out in the Lake and are now getting ready for the World's Fair in 1933. Some of the people here do not care to have another fair, but one cannot hinder enterprising Chicago from anything or everything.
    Very sincerely,
    Adelaide Hamlin

Sherman S. Leavenworth
Sherman Leavenworth had been sick with gangrene in his foot which led to hardening of the arteries. He had suffered several strokes. In the summer before his death, Sherman's great-granddaughter Melva Austin and granddaughter Charlee Hirsch visited him with their parents.

One of the rooms on the first floor of Echo Hill Farm House, was Great-Grandfather Leavenworth's bedroom during his last illness. I can remember visiting him there when I was a babe in arms—my father carrying me. He had such snowy white hair and a jar of hard candies on his dresser.
I think I must have been reaching for it and my dad restraining me. I remember the tense moment when Great-Grandfather said "Let her have one." I wasn't sure whether I would get it. Guess I must have, as I don't remember any terrible disappointment. Other things I remember about that day was white sheer curtains moving in the breeze of an open window.
—Melva Austin Barney.

We lived in the Bronx and came home summers. I remember the summer I was six. Grandpa Sherman had a big white mustache and fed me gingersnaps. That winter he died. Grandpa Sherman was quite a gentleman.—Charlee Hirsch Schroedel.

Garfield and his sons Clinton and James went to visit his father Sherman at Echo Hill Farm House the Saturday before Sherman died.

Sherman S. Leavenworth Dies
Sherman died five days later at one in the afternoon, January 8, 1931. He was buried in the old Eldred Cemetery with his wife Maria Myers who had died in 1918.

Sherman and Maria's children: Jennie Austin, Charlotte, Truman, Martin, and Garfield Leavenworth of Eldred; Christina Hirsch of Bronx; and Anna Leavenworth of E. Islip, New York.

Sherman's grandchildren:

Sherman S. Leavenworth 1843–1931

Mr. Leavenworth was a life long resident of Eldred. He was born February 14, 1843, at Eldred, the son of Sherman B. Leavenworth and Charlotte Ingraham Leavenworth.

His ancestors came from England and first settled in Connecticut and later moved to the Eldred section, which was then called Halfway Brook.

Sherman married Maria Myers in 1874. Mr. Leavenworth was a Civil War Veteran, Co. B, 56th Infantry of New York. He was one of the few remaining Civil War veterans.

During the time he was in the Union Army, he took part in 24 important engagements, including the siege of Yorktown and Seven Oaks. This, however, did not include many minor engagements that are recorded on his service record.

The funeral was held at the home in Eldred, on Sunday, January 11, at 1 p.m.; the Rev. John Ralph, pastor of the Eldred-Barryville Methodist Churches, officiated.—*Port Jervis Union Gazette*, Jan. 9, 1931.

Mr. Leavenworth was a member of the Congregational Church at Eldred.

Members of the Delaware Valley Post attended the funeral with their colors and gave full honors at the grave by firing a salute and the blowing of taps. The detail was in command of George W. Seibert, Post Commander; Jay H. Lass acting as bugler. Legion men also acted as pall bearers.—*News article.*

Sherman S. Leavenworth. Photo courtesy of Cynthia Leavenworth Bellinger.

Melva Austin, great-granddaughter of Sherman, with her mother Gladys. Photo courtesy of Melva Austin Barney.

Art, Bill, and Bob Austin, grandsons of Sherman S. Leavenworth. Photo courtesy of Mary Briggs Austin.

Charlee Hirsch, granddaughter of Sherman S. Leavenworth. Photo courtesy of Ric Schroedel.

Raymond, Bill, Art, and Bob Austin; Clara, Anna, Clinton, and Jim Leavenworth; and Charlee Hirsch. Melva Austin was his only great-grandchild at the time.

I remember Great-Grandfather's army discharge framed and hanging on the wall. It was while pointing it out to me that Great-Aunt Christina told me the provisions made in his will, though I had never seen it before. He was certainly a very thoughtful and caring man.

Reminds me of a story my father told about some local fellow who said that he had never heard of Sherman Leavenworth doing a spiteful thing to anyone but "he could give you the worst leaving alone you ever had in your life."—Melva Austin Barney.

Ella's Diary

Sherman's daughter-in-law Ella, wife of his son Garfield, kept diaries of daily local and national events from 1931 to 1950.

We get a glimpse of life in the Town of Highland in those years as Ella mentioned her Sergeant, Austin, and Myers relatives; and

Charlotte Leavenworth and Christina Hirsch, daughters of Sherman S. Leavenworth. Photo courtesy of Cynthia Leavenworth Bellinger.

Around 1922 Everett Kelley, Marcella Flood (who helped at the Austin's), and Teenie Stevens. Photo courtesy of Christene Stevens Myers.

the many neighbors and friends that visited their home.

In 1931 Garfield and Ella's children, Clara, 24, and Clinton (Goldie), 22, were out of school; Anna, 17, and Jim, almost 9, still attended Eldred Union.

Garfield was a carpenter. He gave music lessons, made and repaired string instruments, and farmed. He did numerous side jobs during the depression.

There always was a lot of music in our house as my father Garfield taught most any kid that wanted to learn music. He was very good on the violin and learned most of it from my mother's father and uncles as they were musically inclined.
—James Leavenworth.

In 1931 Garfield enlarged their house by building a kitchen addition, a larger living room and entry way, and a bathroom.

Ella kept busy making clothes and meals. In the summer she canned farm produce non-stop.

January 1931, Ella's Diary
Thursday, January 1, the first evening of the year had started off playing cards with Ella's relatives Charlie Sergeant and Everett Kelley. Friday Herman Bosch (from Proctor Road southeast of Eldred) joined Charlie and Everett when they visited the Leavenworths.

After visiting his father on Saturday, Garfield had put a new "floor in the incubator room." (Perhaps he was getting ready to start his business selling eggs.) His father Sherman had died the following Thursday.

Monday, January 12, Anna and Jim were back in school. Clinton started to work for John Love (who had a sawmill) on Tuesday. That evening, Herman Bosch again stopped by for a visit.

Wednesday Garfield went up to Echo Hill Farm to say good-bye to his sister Christina Hirsch. Everett Kelley, 45, stopped by Ella's in the evening. Everett often stopped by.

Everett Kelley
Everett, the son of Frank and Luella Sergeant Kelley, was a cousin of Ella, and quite a character. Everett was seven feet tall. He never married and would stop in at the homes of neighbors at meal time.

One morning Everett stopped in at the Garfield residence when Ella was making pancakes on a round griddle—the type that sat on top of a wood cook stove.

Everett kept eating pancakes which didn't seem to fill him up. So Ella poured the remaining batter onto the round griddle filling it completely. She thought it would embarrass Everett when they put the pancake on his plate and it hung over the plate all around. Instead he said, "That is just the way I like them."

Everett made a living by selling the junk steel he collected as scrap metal.

Mid-January 1931 at the Leavenworths
Charles and Betty Timmerhoff were over on Saturday to play with Jim. Everett and Garfield worked on the wood machine.

A group of men got together to play music at the Leavenworth home on Sunday. Monday Anna went to a basketball game in Milford.

Saturday, January 24, Jim went up to Edith Timmerhoff's. Monday Clara and Ella sewed; Garfield fixed the chicken coop.

Paul Knorr the electrician

Ella Sergeant Leavenworth's Diary

Ella Sergeant Leavenworth (wife of Garfield Leavenworth) left a diary record of her life in Eldred from the years 1931 to 1950.

A number of Ella's neighbors and relatives (or soon-to-become relatives) were mentioned in Ella's daily accounts.

Garfield's Austin Relatives
- Mort, Jennie, Raymond, Bill, Art, and Bob Austin.

Garfield's Leavenworth Relatives
- Charlotte, Martin, Truman, and Anna Leavenworth; Anthony Sr., Christina, Tony Jr., Charlee Hirsch.

Ella's Sergeant Relatives
- Luella and Everett Kelley; Frank and Raola Daiber and children: Frank and Lillian.
- Walter, Hazel, Marjorie, and Marion Connor.
- Unita Jane Sergeant Livingstone.
- Alvah, Mary, Charlie, and Grant Sergeant.
- Frank and Anna Hull Sergeant; Jennie Hull.
- Elizabeth Hoatson Clark Wilson.
- Georgia Styles.
- Ernest and Edith Sergeant Timmerhoff; children Charles and Betty.
- Alice Amelia Hill.
- Morgan Owen Sergeant.
- Thomas and Myrtle Labarr Hill and children: Thelma and Frank Hill.
- Edward and Kate Livingstone Kuen, Clareta and Helen Kuen.
- Archie and Minnie Sergeant Myers.

Garfield's Myers Relatives
- Charlie Myers and son Harold.

Jim Leavenworth's Friends
- Frank Bartle, Bobby Bosch, Vernon and Orville Clark, Ken Crandall Jr., Carl Dunlap, William and Charles Eldridge, Charles Foster, Robert Hanck, Holbrook boys, Hulse boys, Kenneth McBride, Nick Rohman (nephew of Art Rohman), Frances and Ed Toaspern, Herb and Bob Wolff.

Near Neighbors
- Erwin and Norah Bradley Avery, Doctor Gutfruend, Laura McBride, Meyers (Bill Sr., Lottie Scott Meyers, Bill Jr., Dorothy, Madelyn), Chester Middaugh.

Other Neighbors/Friends
- Claude Angell, Herman Bosch Sr. and Jr., Ed Bosch, Ralph Clouse, Comstocks, Ed Crail (boarder at Kelley's), Dorothy Dunlap, Charlie Dunlap, John Dunlap, Selma Dunlap, Jess Derheimer, Lewis Hazen, Chet Hulse, Maude Hulse (Duane's wife), Paul Knorr, Mr. Krause, Anna Kyte, Frank Kyte, John and Kate Love, MacIntyres, William McBride, Maria Myers, Mildred and Lynn Myers, Lena Myers (daughter of Jackson and Jessie Myers), Stan Myers, Henry Von Ohlen, Andrew Parker, Harvey Parker, Mr. Sidwell, Austin and Dorothy Kuen Smith, Ed and Mabel Smith, Walter Tether, Mr. Toaspern, Bertha Wilson, Alfred Wolff, Albert Wolff, Carl Wolff and sons Herb and Bob, Frank Wolff, Rev. Wood, Harry and Mary Kyte Wormuth.

Boy Scout Camp
- Elijah Moore; Ken Crandall, and Ken's brother Robert.

Cover of one of Ella Sergeant Leavenworth's Diaries. Photo courtesy of Cynthia Leavenworth Bellinger.

was there on Friday. Saturday, the last day of the month, neighbor Bill Meyers Jr. was over for the evening. Garfield, Ella, and Anna would be seeing Bill Jr. more often.

The Bill Meyers Sr. Family
Bill and Lottie Meyers and their children were neighbors of Garfield and Ella. Bill Meyers Sr. was a brother of Joseph Meyer (who dropped the "s" from his name) who lived in Highland Lake. Bill Sr. was a truck farmer and Bill Jr. worked road construction in 1930. Lottie Scott Meyers was a granddaughter of Isaac M. Bradley.

Bill and Lottie had quite a surprise (and a relief Lottie did not have a tumor) in August, when their delightful daughter Madelyn Meyers was born. Their daughter Dorothy was 19 years old. Bill Jr., 23, would marry Anna Leavenworth.

Aunt Lizzie Wilson
Aunt Lizzie—Elizabeth Hoatson Clark Wilson—lived in the house behind the Wilson building on the northwest corner of Eldred. Teachers and others often boarded there. Elizabeth had been widowed twice and was Ella Leavenworth's aunt as Lizzie's first husband

George Malcome Clark was a brother to Ella's mother Clarissa.

George Clark had died after a year of marriage and a few months later their daughter Georgia Clark (Styles) had been born.

Elizabeth later married Charles Wilson who also had been widowed and had two children, Arthur and Julia. Charles Wilson had died in 1920.

February 1931
Sunday, February 1, was a busy day. Ella sold Lottie Meyers 1-1/2 quarts of milk. Kate Love was there in the afternoon and Garfield gave music lessons in the afternoon and evening.

Thursday Anna went to school, but not Jim as the schoolhouse was too cold.

A few days later, Clara went to work for Aunt Lizzie Wilson. Anna went to Beach Lake with the basketball team the day before Valentine's Day.

Thursday evening, February 19, was a house full of company—Grant Sergeant, Billy Meyers, and the Wolff brothers.

The Wolff Brothers
Carl, Frank, Albert, and Norman Wolff who play a part in this story, were the sons of Charles and Janette Kerr Wolff. Carl Wolff was married to Freida Kloss. Freida's brother Lou Kloss' engaging memoirs were included in *Echo Hill and Mountain Grove*. Carl and Freida's children were Clara, Bob, and Herbert Wolff.

Ella thought the last week of February felt like spring. She sent in an order for 100 chicks to arrive in May.

Though the weather was clear and felt like spring to Ella, Grant and Clara skied over at Alvah Sergeant's. Clinton was working; Anna and Jim were in school. Bill

Bill Meyers Jr., Leavenworth neighbor, would marry Anna Leavenworth. Photo courtesy of Mary Ellen Busse Mackinder.

Meyers Sr. helped Garfield with his Ford engine.

At the end of the month, Mr. Elijah Moore (a carpenter at the Boy Scout Camp) had dinner with the Leavenworths.

March 1931
Sunday Jim started the month off at his friend Ken Crandall's house. (Ken Crandall Sr. was a carpenter at the Scout Camp. Later he was a caretaker.)

Grant and Charlie Sergeant, and Herman Bosch were at the Leavenworth home in the evening. (Herman's uncle Julius Maier and his sister aunt Annie lived nearby on Crawford Road.)

The Wolff brothers visited on Monday evening. Friday Anna was down to the MacIntyres. Garfield bought a ton of hay from Averys for $15 and also fixed the brooder coop.

Frank Wolff was over the third week of March for advice on buying a house.

Ella finished Mary Sergeant and Bertha Wilson's dresses on Tuesday, March 24. Charlotte, Garfield's sister, was there for supper later that day. She visited

Anna Leavenworth would marry Bill Meyers Jr., a neighbor of her family. Photo courtesy of Cynthia Leavenworth Bellinger.

them again the next day as did Minnie and Archie Myers.

The end of the month, Charlie Dunlap stopped by for a visit.

April 1931
Wednesday, the first day of April, Clinton started working for Mr. Toaspern at the County. The High School students left for Washington D.C. on Saturday.

Garfield started work on the mess hall for the Scouts the following Monday. Thursday Clinton took his driver's test and got his license on Friday.

Jim Leavenworth and Madelyn Meyers. Photo courtesy of Cynthia Leavenworth Bellinger.

Wednesday, April 15, Chester Middaugh called (stopped by).

In March Ella had put 300 eggs of their own in a new incubator. The ones that hatched went into the brooder. Of those 300 eggs, only 143 chicks lived.

Clinton, Clara, Anna, and Bill Meyers Jr. went to the "talkies" at the end of the month.

May 1931
May 1, 1931, President Hoover pressed a button in Washington, D.C. which turned the lights on and officially opened the Empire State Building.

The first week of May in Eldred, Garfield finished his job at the Scout Camp. A few days later he went to see Doc Gutfruend to see what work he had for him to do.

Monday, May 11, Garfield, Ken Crandall, and his brother Robert started a new carpentry job at the Scout Camp.

Friday Mary Sergeant and Bertha Wilson visited. Garfield and Ella visited her dad Frank Sergeant in Highland Lake.

June 1931
Monday, June 1, Jess Derheimer plowed the garden. Jess boarded in town and did odd jobs.

Wednesday Kate Love visited. Ella's order from the A&P arrived. She planted three rows of corn, some peas, and squash by the end of the first week.

"Old Mrs. Maria Myers" died on Wednesday, June 10.

Maria had been the second wife of Abel Myers and a widow for some years. She and Abel had had six children: Lulu Scheniman, Lila Von Ohlen, Cleta Horton; and Jackson, Archie, and Norman Myers.

Wednesday was exam day for Jim. Garfield kept Jess busy

Herman Bosch's uncle Julius Maier, kneeling on left; aunt Annie Maier, behind the third man from the left. Others unknown. Photo courtesy of Ken Bosch.

skidding logs and clearing the meadow. Anna finished school for the year on Friday, June 18. The following Monday, Garfield's birthday, Herman Bosch Sr. and Bill Meyers Sr. called in evening.

Wednesday, June 24, Clara, Clinton, Anna, and Jim went to graduation exercises. Ella's stepmother Anna Hull Sergeant and Anna's sister Jennie Hull visited Ella Friday evening.

July 1931
The first week of July, Jess planted millet. His wife joined him for dinner with Garfield and Ella.

Kate Love and her niece visited Saturday evening, July 11.

Ella spent Wednesday with her dad Frank. Since Clinton had his license, he drove his mother home in the evening.

Raola Kelley Daiber's son and daughter spent a couple days in July with Ella. (Raola was Everett's

Clara, Jim, and Anna Leavenworth. Photo courtesy of Cynthia Leavenworth Bellinger.

sister.) The girls went berrying and got over two water pails full.

Ella canned 18 quarts of veal. Garfield finished working for the Scouts for a while.

Walter Tether, owner of Washington Beach Hotel. Walter was superintendent of the Town of Highland at one time. Photo courtesy of Ivan J. and Jana Tether.

Hazel Sergeant Connor, her daughters Marjorie and Marion, and her father, Frank Sergeant. Photo courtesy of Cynthia Leavenworth Bellinger.

Hazel Sergeant Connor, Anna Hull Sergeant, and Jennie Hull. Photo courtesy of Cynthia Leavenworth Bellinger.

Ella's sister Hazel, husband Walter, and their daughters Marjorie and Marion arrived at Ella's the last week of July. They visited Frank and Anna Sergeant that day and the next. At 7 p.m. that evening, the Connors left for their home in Massachusetts.

August 1931

In August Ella ordered a stove, windows, etc. from Sears, for her new kitchen.

September 1931
Isaac M. Bradley Dies

Isaac M. Bradley, 93, died at his home, Tuesday, September 1, 1931. Isaac has been part of the story since *The Mill on Halfway Brook*. Isaac's children still living: Norah Avery, Viola Hazen, Lottie Colville, Amelia Gregory; Newton (Isaac N.), and Atwell Bradley.

After great-grandpa Bradley died in 1931, I remember that his bedroom (off the parlor on the first floor) became a bathroom. The outhouse disappeared. The well house in the front yard was replaced by a large flagstone, with a hand pump.—William E. Horton.

Sherman Leavenworth's Will

Thursday, two days after Isaac M. Bradley died, the will of Isaac's life long neighbor Sherman S. Leavenworth was read. His seven children shared in the $4,000 estate. The daughters, Anna, Charlotte, Christina Hirsch, and Jennie Austin, were left equal shares in bank accounts; the farm, livestock and household furnishings were left in a trust; the income was to go to son Martin.

Anna M. Leavenworth was the executrix of the will written December 28, 1918. Earlier Sherman had given each of his children some property.

Ella's new stove arrived the second week of September. School started for Jim and Anna. A few days later Kate Love stopped by when Clara and Ella made catsup.

On the weekend Jim went to Averys to play with Ken McBride. Ken, his mother Laura McBride, and his two sisters lived with their grandparents Erwin and Norah Bradley Avery who ran Averys, the original Bradley House.

The first killing frost arrived just before the end of September. Charlotte Leavenworth had supper with Ella and Garfield that day.

October 1931

John Love finished a driven well (machine pounded rather than by hand) on Thursday, October 1.

Ken McBride was over to play with Jim on Saturday. They often got together in October.

Saturday afternoon, October 9, the Connor family arrived again for a short visit. They spent Sunday at "the lake" (Highland Lake) with her parents, and left for Massachusetts at 7:30 a.m. on Monday.

The middle of October Garfield started remodeling their kitchen for Ella's new stove. Three days later, Ella had moved into her kitchen and the new stove was set up. Kate Love visited again.

Garfield started work for Walter Tether. At the end of October Garfield worked for Dr. Gutfruend. Dr. Gutfruend and his granddaughter Shirley Sanders lived in the old Slonek house that would one day be called, *Under the Pines*. Perhaps Garfield did some repairs on the old house. Garfield did put shingles on his own porch.

There is a photo of Shirley Sanders with several children

1931 World, National, and Local News

1931 World and National News
- RCA Victor introduced the first long-playing phonograph record.
- Chinese Communist Party leader Mao Zedong formed the Chinese Soviet Republic in 1931.

March 1931
- *The Star-Spangled Banner* by Francis Scott Key was the national anthem.

May 1931
- Construction completed on the Empire State Building in N.Y.C.

September 1931
- Japan invaded Manchuria in China.

1931 Halfway Brook News
Candidates nominated in the Town of Highland on September 28:
- Supervisor: Elias A. Sheen, Barryville.
- Town Clerk: Fred Hensel, Yulan.
- Justices of the Peace: Frederick Bye, Highland Lake; John J. Marren, Yulan.
- Superintendent of Highways: Carl J. Wolff, Barryville.
- Assessors: John Weber, Yulan; Harry Wormuth, Eldred; Harold Beufve, Yulan.
- Collector: Charles Flieger, Yulan.
- Constables: William Parker, Eldred; William Clouse, Eldred; Orville Myers, Eldred; Peter Callahan, Barryville; Henry Koch, Lackawaxen.
- School Director: Herman J. Rixton and Frederick J. Lewis, Barryville.

Rebuilding
- Methodist Church rebuilt. It had burned down in 1930.

1931 Eldred Seniors
- Herman Fracke, John Holbrook, Josephine Holbrook, Gertrude Peirano, Lillian Seitz, Reginald Walter, Kenneth Sheen, Charles Sergeant.

Eldred School News 1931–1932
- Charles D. Coutant was the principal. There were nine faculty; 83 students were in first through eighth grades; 70 were High School students. The old school building had been remodeled and was used as a gym and a community center, with a kitchen and serving room. There was first league baseball and basketball.

Merchant Marines
- Edward Wilson, a licensed taxi driver in New York City in the 1920s, grew up in Tusten. In 1931 Ed joined the Merchant Marines and worked as oiler, wiper, and fireman on the *S.S. President Harding*, *S.S. President Monroe*, and *S.S. President Van Buren* which traveled around the world. We'll meet Ed in the 1940s.

1931 Births
- Dorothy Brodmerkel born to William and Tina Bosch Brodmerkel.
- Cliff Horton born to Charles and Beatrice Avery Horton.
- Barry Owen born to Russell and Ina Owen.

1931 Marriages
- Gladys Avery married George Dobbs.
- Olliamus D. Smith married Wilna Fallin in Oklahoma City, Okla.
- Walter Hess married Esther Colville.

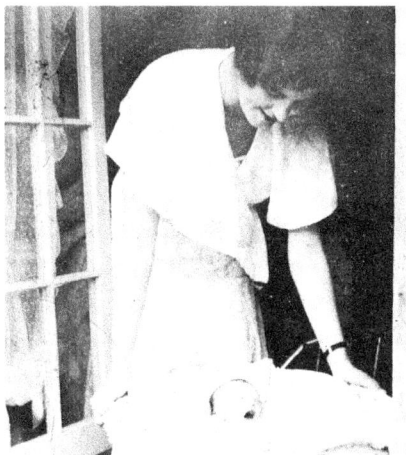
Ina Owen with Barry. Photo courtesy of Pam Fischetti DeFeo.

1931 Deaths
- Sherman S. Leavenworth, 1843–1931.
- Alfred McCann died.
- Robert B. Collins died.
- Frank Owen, 1858–1931, was the son of Robert and Elizabeth Tether Owen. Frank had conducted the Pine Grove Cottage. The surviving relatives: his wife Catherine; daughters Catherine, Helen, and Maude Barnes; sons Frank, Ernest, and Earl; four grandchildren and several nephews and nieces.
—From the *Republican Watchman*, *April 17, 1931*.
- Daniel Deyo Hull, 10, son of Deyo and Justina Schoonover Hull, died in February, following an operation for appendicitis. He was survived by a younger brother John. Daniel Hull was the grandson of Rowlee and Emily Banner Schoonover.
- Maria Hankins Myers, second wife of Abel Myers, died.
- Isaac M. Bradley died in September.

---

from Eldred with my dad and his St. Bernard dog King. The group had gone swimming behind the library one day when King got in the water and they had a hard time getting him out.

November 1931
Starting Tuesday, November 3, Garfield worked 11 days for Walter Tether. As that job was ending, Garfield went to the Scouts to see if they had work for him. Mid-month Garfield worked some more on his own home. He took

Dr. Gutfruend and his granddaughter Shirley lived in the house which was originally Sloneks. Photo courtesy of Christene Stevens Myers.

the partition out of the front room and laid some floor. He bought sheetrock and worked on the front room, including on a bay window.

On Thursday, November 19, Garfield and Bill Meyers Sr. put the roof on Garfield's garage. Mary Sergeant, Kate Love, and Kate's mother stopped by.

Friday Garfield put the entry on his new back porch. Paul Knorr's man changed the lights around on the porch.

Saturday, November 21, started off as a clear, warm day. It had been many years since there had been such a warm fall. A week later the first snow of the year fell. Garfield did some more work for Doc Gutfruend.

December 1931

Ella's dad Frank Sergeant gave her some dahlia bulbs when he visited on Tuesday, December 1.

Jim went up to Averys to play on Saturday. The following Tuesday Bill Meyers, Garfield, and Clinton cut firewood for the Leavenworths.

The chickens must have been laying as Kate Love stopped by for eggs on the Sunday, December 13.

In the middle of the month Garfield made two chairs. Ella made some Christmas candy. A package arrived for Ella from her sister Hazel, four days before Christmas. Garfield was still making chairs on Tuesday, December 22. Ella and Clinton visited her father Frank at Highland Lake.

Friday, Christmas Day, Garfield and the children visited their Sergeant grandparents to say Merry Christmas. Ella stayed home and cooked a two-year-old turkey for dinner. Saturday they made 55 pounds of sausage.

Monday the men cut more wood for 1932. Clareta Kuen and Charlie Sergeant visited. Clara and Anna spent the evening with Clareta. (Charlie and Clareta would marry in 1937.)

1932
January 1932

Busy times at Ella and Garfield's home on the first day of 1932. Garfield helped Ken Crandall. The girls went skating; the boys went after bait fish. Dorothy Meyers was there for dinner.

Bradley Family Connections

Dorothy's grandmother Mary Frances Bradley Scott Myers was a daughter of Isaac M. Bradley, and a younger sister of Amelia Gregory who had first married John Leavenworth. Amelia, who had lived out west, had visited Eldred with her second husband Eber Gregory around 1928. (My uncle Bob Austin remembered meeting them.)

Amelia seems to have been back in Iowa by 1931. Her daughter Lottie Leavenworth Andeway lived there. Amelia's daughter Hazel Leavenworth and her husband Eugene Koenig lived in Wisconsin with their children: John, Gerald, and Marialyce (born in August 1932).

Hazel Koenig's mother Amelia Bradley Gregory had married her third husband Byron Thomas when she was about 70 years old (around 1931). Amelia knew Byron from Colorado, but at the time of the marriage lived in Oscaloosa, Iowa, where her daughter Lottie Andeway and her husband ran a grocery store.

I remember visiting them there. She took care of him until he died.—Marialyce Koenig Kornkven.

Lucille Wait, Betty Boyd, Shirley Sanders, Dorothy Wait, Janith Boyd, Arthur Austin, Billy Boyd and King. Photo in Austin Collection.

At the beginning of 1932, Amelia Bradley Thomas received a family news update from her niece Laura Avery McBride. Laura's mother Norah Avery was also a sister of Amelia and Mary Frances.

Laura Avery had married Buck McBride, but had left him sometime after their third child was born. Laura and her children: Virginia, Frances, and Ken McBride went back to live with Laura's parents Erwin and Norah Avery. The Averys ran the Avery/Bradley House where Laura and her siblings: Arthur Avery, Beatrice Horton, and Gladys Dobbs; and aunts and uncles had grown up.

Laura McBride, Eldred, to Amelia Bradley Thomas, Oscaloosa, Iowa
January 7, 1932
Dear Aunt Amelia,

We were all so glad to hear from you at Christmas time, and I will try to write you a short letter.

Little Frances has just had bronchial pneumonia but seems to be on the gain now. She is so terribly weak, but if nothing else sets in she will come along O.K. She was taken sick the day after Christmas and it was a couple of days before we realized she had more than a bad cold.

Dr. Smith is in the hospital, so we had Dr. Gutfruend, from the village. He did everything that could be done for her, and we are all so relieved that she is on the gain. I could not help but think of the little girl [Deloros Koenig] Hazel lost three years ago.

I bought a typewriter last fall, and typed this old family record of Grandpa's for you. I know you will be interested in the family history, although you may have read this before.

Mama had such a nice letter from Aunt Jessie [wife of Isaac N.]

Amelia Bradley and daughter Lottie Leavenworth Andeway. Photo courtesy of Cynthia Leavenworth Bellinger.

this week. She doesn't write so often since Grandpa is gone. We miss him so much this winter.

We have a new radio, also new furniture for the living room. Frances is in the bedroom just off the living room that mamma used to have. We have a new Heatrola which circulates heat and burns coal in it.

This surely has been a funny winter. We have only had one snow that amounted to anything, and the ground is bare now, and the cars are getting stuck in the mud on the hill above the house everyday. The thermometer stopped at 45 today, and we have only had a few cold days, and no zero weather at all. I guess not many people will go to Florida, if this lasts.

I guess Mamma [Norah Avery] told you that my little girls had their tonsils and adenoids out on December 2. I think Frances would have been worse off if she had had them in when she was so sick.

Amelia Bradley and daughter Hazel Koenig holding son Gerald Koenig, 1930. Photo courtesy of Marialyce Koenig Kornkven.

It looks as if Buck [her husband] has forgotten the children entirely. He has not sent any money for about 2-1/2 months, and at Christmas he never even sent a card. I did not trouble to let him know when Frances was so sick.

Aunt Lottie [Colville] thinks she has found a buyer for her place [Woodland Cottage], and I hope she can get rid of it, the taxes and upkeep are so high.

Beatrice [Horton, her sister] certainly has a nice baby [Clifford]. He is such a good natured little fellow. He was a year old January 1. I think Beatrice has much better health since he was born. She is stronger than she has been in years.

Gladys [her sister] came up night before last. She has a goiter in the inside of her throat, and sometimes it bothers her a lot.

Arthur [Laura's brother] married such a nice girl [Marian Ayers]. She has a good job, and I think they will get along good.

Arthur Avery, first wife Marian Ayers Avery, and niece Virginia McBride. Photo courtesy of William E. Horton.

She seems to be so sensible.

Kenneth [Laura's son] gets along so well in school. He can hardly wait to get started in the mornings. He has grown a lot this winter. I suppose little John [Koenig born 1923] is quite grown up too. It doesn't take long. Virginia will be 5 in February, and Frances will be 4 the same day.

I hope to get up my ambition and make a quilt. The children have been sick so much I haven't had much time.

I have spent a good many evenings practicing on my typewriter. I have also learned how to make all kinds of artificial flowers. I love to make them.

Truman [Leavenworth] must lead a lonesome life. He isn't able to work, and he lives on his side of the house alone. Sometimes Dad [Erwin Avery] takes him a can of milk, or pork or cottage cheese. I guess he gets pretty sick of his own cooking.

Please write again soon, and keep this record, as I have copied it especially for you.

Sincerely yours, Laura

The Leavenworths, January 1932
Garfield cleaned the ice house for the Scout Camp the second week of January. Clinton went hunting, but Anna, a senior, and Jim, 10, were still in school.

Mid-January was very unseasonable weather—"75 degrees in the shade." They had yet to have some cold weather. Garfield remodeled the pantry.

Harold (Bud) Myers Dies
Harold (Bud) Myers was hurt in an automobile accident and died the next day. Harold, the son of Charles Cripps Myers and his first wife Lena Schoonmaker, died three months before he turned 25. His half sister Eleanor was 12.

Bud was a relative of the Leavenworths and Austins as Charles Myers, Harold's father, was a cousin to Jennie Austin and Garfield Leavenworth.

Laura Avery McBride around 1945. Photo courtesy of William E. Horton.

The funeral of Harold C. Myers was conducted Wednesday afternoon at the home of Mr. and Mrs. John Love of Eldred by the Rev. J.J. Wade. Pallbearers were Stanley Myers, Alvin Hill, Walter McBride, Hugh Myers, Lynn Myers, and Oliver Dunlap. Flower bearers were Archie Von Ohlen, Forrest Wilson, Orville Myers, Clifford Crandall, Alfred Hill, and Stanley Crandall. Buried in Eldred Cemetery.—Middletown Times Herald.

Snow squalls threatened on Friday, the 25th. Saturday was colder, but still beautiful, clear and warm. No snow had stuck to the ground yet.

Paul Knorr was busy at the Leavenworth home at the end of the month. He fixed the door bell and buzzer, put in sidelights, two plugs, and finished the wiring.

Kate Love, and Alvah and Mary Sergeant stopped by to see the Leavenworths.

The last day of the month, Clinton and Jim headed to Port Jervis to get a radio fixed.

The international news was not good.

February 1932
"The Japanese and Chinese are fighting," Ella wrote on February 1 and 6.

What little snow was on the ground was gone by the end of the first week of February.

Bill Meyers Jr. stopped by a few evenings the second week, perhaps to see Anna. Clara Leavenworth went to a bridal shower for Bill's sister Dorothy who was engaged to Norman Wolff.

On a clear, warm day, in mid-February, Jim played with Carl Dunlap. Garfield started porch screens and did a little work for John Love. Grant Sergeant stopped by for supper and the evening. He was joined by Bill Meyers.

Garfield made Ella a flower stand and started on a table. Clinton and Garfield worked at the Scouts cutting ice for four days.

At the end of the month, Clinton and Herm Bosch went fishing at Montgomery Lake.

March 1932
National news Tuesday evening, March 1, contained the upsetting story of the abduction of Charles Lindbergh Jr., 20 months old.

Tuesday at the Eldred School, Mrs. Styles gave her student Jim Leavenworth a certificate saying he had passed the New York State Test for the first semester of fourth grade.

At the beginning of March, Ella was given an electric washer from Lottie Meyers who had gotten the machine from Mrs. Sidwell, a neighbor. The next day Ella and Anna dressed 19 hens for the High School supper. Anna would help serve at the supper.

Friday, March 19, the men went to Henry Graf's on Highland Lake to play for the first dance.

Harold Myers' half sister Eleanor Myers (second from the left) with some friends at Highland Lake. Photo courtesy of Timothy C. Rizzuto.

Harry (Bud) Myers, son of Charlie Myers. Bud died in a car accident in January 1932. Photo courtesy of Timothy C. Rizzuto.

Austin Smith and Dot Kuen spent the evening at the Leavenworths.

Monday Clinton went for Doc Gutfruend as Ella's Aunt Lou Kelley was very sick. Aunt Lou was a sister to Frank Sergeant, and the mother of Everett Kelley and Raola Daiber.

"They haven't found Lindy's (Lindbergh) baby yet," Ella wrote on Wednesday, the day the Highland schools were closed because of scarlet fever.

Aunt Lizzie Wilson stopped by to pick up her two roosters on Thursday.

Friday Austin Smith was in for a violin lesson. Stan Myers and William McBride were at Leavenworths for the evening.

The last Sunday of March, Nick Rohman was up to play with Jim; Austin Smith and Tom Hill were there for violin lessons.

Towards the end of March Albert Wolff married Ruth Foster, daughter of George and Jennie Hallock Foster.

Albert and his brother Norman would soon buy the house near the old Ira Austin house where Ed and Mabel Austin Smith and their son Austin Smith lived. The Wolff's "new" home had been sold to Charles Frace in 1868. John W. Johnston mentioned it in his book *Reminiscences*.

Close to and adjoining the premises of Mrs. Frace is the house and premises of Ira M. Austin a wagon maker, blacksmith and general mechanic. The house was first erected by Abraham Russel…
—Johnston, J.W., Reminiscences, p. 328.

April 1932
The first week of April, Bill Meyers bought a new Dodge car. Clinton worked on the Methodist Church Hall. Tom Hill and family and Austin Smith visited one evening.

Mid-April Austin Smith and Frank Hill were in for lessons. Jim played all day with the Eldridge boys—perhaps William and Charles, the sons of Harriet Hill from her first marriage.

Garfield started on a contract barn building job. Clinton worked for the County at Hurleyville.

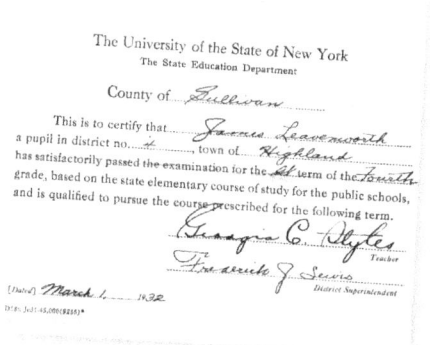
Certificate of James Leavenworth saying he passed the examination for the first term of fourth grade. Signed by Georgia Styles and Frederick J. Lewis, March 1, 1932. Certificate courtesy of Cynthia Leavenworth Bellinger.

Norman and Albert Wolff's new home in Barryville. Ira Austin's house, not showing, was to the left. Photo courtesy of Ed Wolff.

Austin Smith drives the car he bought for his 21st birthday in 1931. Car in front of Ira Austin's house. Wolff house to the right. Photo courtesy of Christina Watts.

May 1932

Ed and Mabel Smith (Austin Smith's parents) called on Monday, the second day of May.

Tuesday Ella did some spring cleaning. She washed quilts and more quilts and cleaned two bedrooms. Clara helped her clean the rest of the upstairs.

Kate Love's mother called one day and another day Claude Angell stopped by and bought six hens.

Saturday Martin (Garfield's brother) was at Garfield and Ella's for the day.

Martin Leavenworth

Martin Leavenworth had had an extremely high fever as a baby. His mental development was that of a four- or five-year-old. After his father died, Martin lived mainly at Echo Hill with Truman and Charlotte. He rotated living with his siblings Jennie Austin and Garfield. Echo Hill would still be home base for Martin when the Hirsches moved back in 1940.

Aunt Christina Hirsch told me their father Sherman had made some sort of agreement with his children to see that Martin always had a home with family. Seems that whoever he was staying with always arranged for him to have some sort of work to do.

He was certainly an important member of the team in the summer at the Austin boarding house. When I was small Great-Uncle Martin Leavenworth was dishwasher and general kitchen assistant. When I was there as a small child, I was sent to "help" Uncle Martin.

The dish washing room was just off the kitchen and contained two big sink tubs.

Sometimes Uncle Martin gave me a little stool to stand on. I can't imagine what a "help" my splashing away would have been. Sometimes he told me that I didn't have to work, I could just talk to him, which as I recall, I did endlessly, anyway.

There were a few times when he told me, "Don't do that," but I can't remember what "that" was. Mostly I remember him just washing, rinsing, and stacking dishes endlessly and smiling. I thought he had the best job I could think of. Since his mental development was arrested at four or five years old, maybe he really did enjoy my company. At the time I was "helping" him we were "intellectual" equals.—Melva Austin Barney.

Sunday evening, May 8, Kate and John Love, and Everett Kelley visited the Leavenworths.

Tuesday on the east side of Eldred, Aida Austin received a postcard from her nephew Arthur.

Arthur Austin, San Juan, to Miss Aida Austin, Eldred
May 10, 1932
Dear Aunt Aida,
Arrived here this afternoon and will leave tomorrow at 2 p.m. It is the rainy season down here and it has been raining all day.
Arthur

Arthur Austin, Yeoman

Art had received a 90.9% average on a Civil Service Clerical test to qualify as a Steward's Yeoman (a petty officer performing clerical duties on board ship). The pay was $1,032 per year.

I took a few extra courses in high school, and worked on a few temporary jobs—the most interesting was as yeoman on an army transport which plied between New York and the Panama Canal.—Arthur Austin.

Art resigned when he returned from the 16-day round trip (4,800 miles, New York to the Panama Canal) on the *U.S.S. Chateau Thierry*. Art had gotten quite seasick, but there were things happening in the upper echelon that he didn't think were right. Art was discharged from Brooklyn, with a "very good" rating.

Sometime in the early 1930s, Art and some of his Eldred and Barryville friends visited Coney Island and had their picture taken.

Thursday, May 12, the body of the Lindy baby was found.

Mid-May at the Leavenworths
Mid-May the Leavenworths' old Model-T Ford was back from the garage. Garfield was learning to drive. His license plates arrived a week later. That day Garfield fought a fire from 1 to 7. Everett went with Garfield when he drove his Ford for the first time.

Friday, May 27, Anna left on a trip with the high school at 7 p.m.

Saturday Clinton was home for the weekend. He boarded during the week to be close to his job.

Hazel, Walter, Marion, and Marjorie Connor arrived from Massachusetts. They visited Frank and Anna Sergeant on Sunday and started for home Monday.

Clinton and Jim went to the ball game at Glen Spey. Tuesday, the last day of May, Clinton went back to work. Kate Love visited.

June 1932
June was very busy. At the start of the month, Garfield and Ella lost 16 turkeys because the fire went out in the brooder.

A week later 105 chicks arrived in the afternoon mail.

Ella and Garfield finished planting the garden. They set out 55 tomato plants and 30 pepper plants. The frost mid-month didn't seem to hurt the garden as Garfield and Ella got up early and put water on the beans and tomatoes.

In June two couples were

Friends at Coney Island. Bud Smith, Bill Warden at the wheel, Charles Geissler, Ian Warden, and Arthur Austin. Next to Art, Bub Toaspern, in front of Bub, Royden Toaspern. Photos courtesy of Mary Briggs Austin.

married: Norm Wolff and Dorothy Meyers; and Austin Smith and Dorothy Kuen. After they were married Norm and Dorothy lived with his brother Albert and his wife Ruth.

Jim Leavenworth took regents exams and went to the school picnic. Anna graduated from High School. Her aunt Charlotte stopped by on her graduation day. Her grandfather Frank Sergeant bought her a class ring.

Bill Meyers, Clinton, and Jim took in a couple baseball games. Clinton was home for the weekend a couple times. One week he worked for the County. Garfield worked six hours for the Scouts one day. He was laid off for a few days and built a new run for the dogs. Garfield and Clara played for a dance at Beaver Brook.

July 1932
Friday, July 1, Ella noted that the Democratic Convention was going on.

Monday, July 4, Clinton and Jim went to ballgames. Mr. Sidwell, their neighbor, visited for the evening. Tuesday Clinton went back to work, but was home on the weekends.

Thursday, July 7, Kate Love and Charlotte visited with Ella.

Friday Garfield and Ella paid the balance on their barn lumber to John Love.

Jim had played with a number of friends throughout the month: the Holbrook brothers, Nick Rohman, the Hulse boys, Ed Toaspern, and Frank and Lillian

Lovely Anna Leavenworth at graduation time. The new porch Garfield built is in the background. Photo courtesy of Cynthia Leavenworth Bellinger.

Art & Kate Hess Rohman

Kate Hess Rohman, Art's better half, on their wedding day in the early 1900s. Photo courtesy of Gladys Moran Wilson.

Arthur Rohman became proprietor of the hotel [Shohola Glen at the time] on February 10, 1909. He was to be active there for 64 years, becoming "legend in his own time." His ever-present cigar became his personal trademark. Most noticeable in the hotel were the 54-foot Brunswick bar, the pull-out barstools, the embossed metal sheeting on the ceilings and walls, the polished wooden tables and chairs, and over 100 telephone books in the corner.

Art obtained a portion of the bar from Vogt's old German Hotel... and the pull-out stools were Art's way of satisfying his customers who preferred to stand, when the state passed a law requiring stools at bars. The telephone books became almost a necessity for customers from so many areas, and once they began to accumulate, many visitors would bring one from their home cities...

Rohman's customers over the years included novelist Zane Grey, ball players Smokey Joe Wood and his friend from Red Sox days Babe Ruth, boxers Jim Stewart and Jack Britton, swimmer Gertrude Ederle, and aviator Charles Lindbergh. Movie stars who have visited include Mary Pickford, John Gilbert, Barney Google, Jean Harlow, Clara Bow, Bette Davis, Gloria Swanson, Ronald Coleman, and Paul Newman.

In addition to local residents who found Rohman's a gathering place at the end of the day, thousands of visiting hunters, fishermen, weekenders, and tourists, visited Rohman's each year and found it exactly the same year after year.

In 1937, prominent musician, and local vacationer, Dick Robertson wrote the lyrics to "Springtime in Shohola." He recorded it with his orchestra for Art Rohman's jukebox, and for over sixty years the words, "We'll be buying beer at Rohman's...while the trains come crashing through," have been listened to and sung to by thousands.

During his 64 years at the bar, Art Rohman saw many men leave for, and return from, several wars, buying them drinks coming and going. He operated through prohibition; his slot machines were famous. He not only survived the Great Depression but also helped many of his neighbors to do the same.

Under Art Rohman, the old hotel, which had served as a polling place and election headquarters since the days of Chauncey Thomas and George Layman, continued to be a powerhouse in state, county, and local politics. They celebrated Roosevelt's election, the repeal of prohibition...
—George J. Fluhr, *Rohman's Inn, Shohola Glen Hotel: Shohola, PA; 1849–1999*, pp. 4,5.

Katie Rohman died around Christmas. Until his death Art would never allow a Christmas tree in the place. He would of course wish everyone a Merry Christmas and give out cigars and complimentary drinks. The bar room was festooned with hundreds of Christmas cards hanging from strings on the ceiling and of course the place was decorated and jam packed on New Year's Eve each year. But no tree.—*George J. Fluhr.*

Daiber (Raola's children).

Nick Rohman was the nephew of Art Rohman. We met Art in 1909 in *Echo Hill and Mountain Grove* when he became the owner of the old Shohola Glen Hotel.

Mid-July Garfield made a cart to draw hay on. Clinton and Jim went to a ball game on the weekend, then to Highland Lake to see their Sergeant grandparents.

Garfield and Everett cut Kelley's hay and worked on the Leavenworth driveway. Ella canned 18 quarts of greens and gave her aunt Lou three bushels of endive to can.

August 1932

The first day of August Anna and Clara got the cabbage rose slip from the Leavenworth farm. The original bush came from Holland. "Grandmother's grandmother brought it over," wrote Ella. (Elizabeth Lazerlier Van Pelt's family had once lived in Holland.)

During August Garfield worked on Lou Kelley's porch. Frank Sergeant screened the porch. Garfield put steps in and rails, which Ella painted. Garfield also put in the front walk.

In August the Ladies' Aide Auxiliary held Church Fairs.

"Clara got the Cabbage Rose slip from the Leavenworth Farm." Rosa centifolia foliacea" (Cabbage Rose) by Pierre-Joseph Redouté (1759–1840) in public domain.

Some of Jim's friends, August 1932. In back: Gilbert Holbrook and Jim. Sitting: Robert Hanck and George Holbrook. Photo courtesy of Cynthia Leavenworth Bellinger.

Blanche Malinge Rouillon Dies

You may remember that Blanche Rouillon (in France) was the grandmother who took care of little Gisele Rouillon after Gisele's mother died. Blanche had a stroke when she was walking, and died soon afterwards. Gisele's father Cyrus had a business and couldn't care for Gisele. She was put into a convent and raised by the nuns for about a year.

The bedroom with all the cots lined up and the nun's bed behind curtains in the corner of the room was just like in the children's book Madeline.*—Gisele Rouillon Leavenworth.*

September 1932

During the month of September Ella canned: 124 quarts of peaches, 76 quarts of tomatoes from their garden, and 27 quarts of apples. Garfield cut the millet and sowed grass seed on the front lawn close to the house. He cut down the cornstalks. They had picked 2,034 ears of corn total for the season.

Garfield and Ella's neighbors, the Sidwells, left for their home in Michigan. Garfield and John Dunlap drew hay from Kelley's. They also plowed a garden patch in Garfield's meadow.

Garfield worked on the walk to the back door, put curbing by the bay window, and cut wood in their woods.

Doily crocheted by Ella. Photo courtesy of Cynthia Leavenworth Bellinger.

Bob, Marjorie, and Herman Bosch Jr. ready for the first day of school, fall 1932. Photo courtesy of Victoria Kohler.

Ella and the ladies in town worked all year making items to sell. When Mary Sergeant stopped by, Ella sent some of her crocheted work to be sold at the fair.

One day Charlotte spent the day with her sister-in-law Ella. Another day Lena Myers spent the day with Anna. Ella put edges on three pillowcases for Jessie, Lena's mother.

Mid-August Jim and Bob Bosch played all day.

Towards the end of the month Ella canned 32 quarts of corn. Anna and Clara got a few apples from the old Echo Hill Farm which were not much good. Aunt Anna Leavenworth was at the Leavenworths for the day on Tuesday. They canned 68 quarts of corn. Garfield and Aunt Anna husked it. (Garfield put more shelves in the cellar for the cans.)

Anna took her mother's film to Mr. Krause in Port Jervis. (She got the photos back September 1.) The last day of August, an eclipse covered 95% of the sun.

Clinton worked some distance from home and boarded there.

Ella received a package from Sears with sport shoes for her girls and Garfield's chambray shirting.

School started on Monday, September 12. Ella painted the kitchen.

Towards the end of the month Garfield's sister Charlotte had dinner with Garfield and Ella. Mr. Avery was in to pay the balance of $2.15 on his egg bill, Rev. Wood called, and Ella bought two small hams from the A&P.

October 1932

Garfield cut wood and Ella continued to can in October.

Tuesday, October 4, Ella and her girls canned pumpkin and tomato soup. Garfield and John Dunlap drew wood out of the woods for at least four days. "We have 21 loads—such a pile," commented Ella in her diary.

Saturday John Dunlap, Everett Kelley, Ed Crail (boarder at Kelley's), Walter Horton, and Garfield cut wood in the morning.

Marcella Flood, Claude Angell (the butcher in 1933), and Emily Christene Stevens around 1922. Photo courtesy of Christene Stevens Myers.

Walter left at noon. There was still a very large pile of wood and not all of it was cut.

Wednesday Garfield, Everett, and Ed Crail finished cutting wood.

Thursday the Leavenworths gathered 11-1/2 bushels of carrots. They would pull up a total of 47 bushels of carrots.

Mid-October Garfield and his children went up to the lake. They found a bee tree but only got one pail of honey in the comb. They gathered hickory nuts at Kelley's and picked apples at the Wait place. Clara made a night gown for her mom and pajamas for Anna.

Garfield helped Ella's dad Frank Sergeant with his wood.

A week or so before Halloween, Jim went to his uncle Mort Austin's to get a pumpkin.

Monday, October 24, Mabel Smith's mother (Austin Smith's grandmother), Minerva Drake Austin died.

Monday evening, October 31, Jim went to a Halloween party.

November 1932

Garfield was still helping his father-in-law Frank Sergeant with his wood at the beginning of November. Clinton went hunting.

At the end of the first week, there was a half-inch of ice on the pails in the entry way. Ella put the carrots in the cellar. She paid the October electric bill of $3.74.

Clinton voted for the first time on November 8, election day.

Franklin Roosevelt was elected President by a large majority. Because the Democrats were now in the majority, the Postmaster would change when Roosevelt was inaugurated. Emily Parker Stevens would be the Eldred Postmaster again.

Friday Ella bought 20 bushels of potatoes from the A&P at 49 cents a bushel. Saturday Ella started crocheting a rug for Jim's bedroom. Jim, Clinton, and Bill Meyers went to the pictures.

Sunday, November 20, Laura Avery and her children visited with the Leavenworths. Anna went for a walk with Laura.

Tuesday Ella sold five turkeys and four chickens to Claude Angell, the butcher, for $17.48.

Wednesday Anna and Clara went to town and got a bowl from Henry Von Ohlen for 49 cents. Thursday Clinton had to work so the Leavenworths had their Thanksgiving dinner at night.

Friday Madelyn Meyers fell in the brook and nearly drowned. Garfield helped Frank Sergeant out at Highland Lake.

Sunday, November 27, Garfield, Clinton, Jim, and Bill Meyers went to help Frank Sergeant some more.

On Monday Clara worked at Lizzie Wilson's for the day.

December 1932

The first snow of the season fell on Saturday, December 10. Sunday Clinton hunted rabbits and got three.

Thursday Garfield and Jim went to the Christmas program practice at the Methodist Church. Friday night it was 12 degrees below 0. Jim was sick with an earache and Clara sat up all night to the keep fires going.

Garfield played violin at the Hall for the Library, Saturday, December 17. Monday and Tuesday evenings Garfield was at the church for practice.

Jim was still sick Tuesday and the doctor was called for three times. Wednesday Jim was better.

Thursday Clinton and Bill Meyers went to get a Christmas tree for the Leavenworths.

Friday, two days before Christmas, Clinton and Bill Meyers took Clara and Anna to have their teeth pulled. Clara had six removed and Anna two. Garfield played for the Methodist Christmas program in the evening. Poor Anna was sick all night.

Christmas Eve day Clinton took a turkey and other food to his grandfather Frank Sergeant.

Christmas was not that much fun for Jim who was "miserable yet" and Anna as her jaw still ached. It was such a warm day that they let the fires out for about three hours.

Jim and Anna were some better the day after Christmas, but "still miserable with ears and jaw."

The last day of the year Bill Meyers Jr. stayed late at the Leavenworth home listening to the radio. (And maybe enjoying Anna's friendship?)

1932 World, National, and Local News

1932 World and National News
- Japan occupied Manchuria.
- Nazi party largest single party in the German Reichstag (parliament).
- 12 million unemployed.
- Aldous Huxley's *Brave New World*.

May 1932
- Charles A. Lindbergh Jr., infant son of Charles and Anne Morrow Lindbergh, kidnapped and later found dead not far from his home.
- Amelia Earhart's transatlantic flight in her single engine Lockheed Vega 5B from Newfoundland landed in Northern Ireland instead of Paris due to winds, icy conditions, and mechanical problems.

November 1932
- Franklin D. Roosevelt won the presidential election.

1932 Halfway Brook News
1932 Eldred Seniors
- Anna Leavenworth, Delia (Blanche) Parker, Roger Quick, Vivian Shaffer, Arthur Staubes, Harry Sulzbach, Veronica Thiesen, Doris Vogt, William Warden.

Eldred School News 1932–1933
- Howard K. Moore was the Principal. There were eight faculty. There were 87 students in first through eighth grades; High school had 67 students. Text books were provided by the district. Dishes and silverware were purchased for the gym. Economics, geography, physical education, and chemistry were added. General science replaced biology. There were class advisors and homerooms. Boys and girls entered track teams in League meets. The Alumni Players was organized.

1932 Births
- Arthur E. Avery Jr., born to Arthur and Marian Ayers Avery.
- Marialyce Koenig born to Eugene and Hazel Leavenworth Koenig.
- Marjorie Hess born to Walter and Esther Colville Hess.

1932 Marriages
- Orvis R. Eldred married Selma Myers in Pennsylvania. Orvis, a descendant of James and Polly Mulford Eldred, attended Coyne Electrical School in Chicago in 1930. *Eldred*, p. 124.
- Walter J. Horton Jr. married in March.
- Albert Wolff married Ruth Foster in March.
- Norm Wolff married Dorothy Meyers in June.
- Austin Smith married Dorothy Kuen in June.
- Orville Myers married Leversa Beisel.

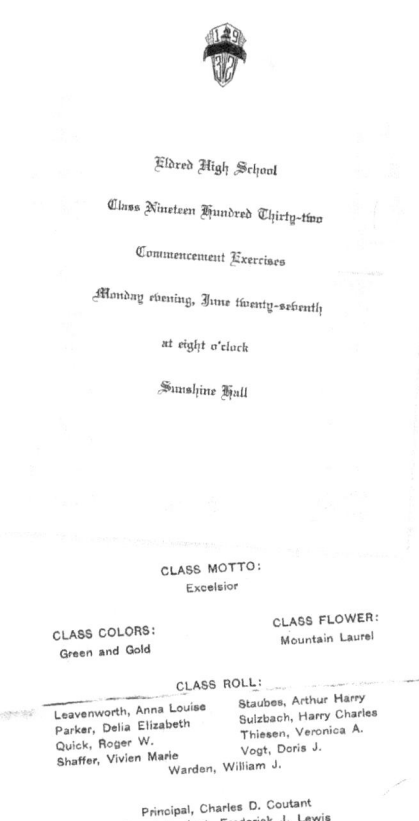

1932 Graduation Exercises courtesy of Cynthia Leavenworth Bellinger.

1932 Deaths
- Minerva Austin, 1845–1932, was the widow of Ira Austin. Children at the time of her death: Mabel Smith, Nellie, Frank, and Ralph W. Austin.
- Harold C. Myers, 1907–1932.
- Blanche Olga Malinge Rouillon died in France.
- Lottie Bradley Colville, 1870–1932.
- Henrietta C. Halstead, 1857–1932, was first married to Seely Crawford and then to Edgar Sergeant. The funeral was held at the Eldred Congregational Church. Pallbearers were Charles Dunlap, John Love, Harry Howlett, Martin Myers, Tracey Myers, and Howard Stevens. Henrietta was survived by her brother Oscar Halstead, daughter Mrs. Anna Hill, a granddaughter, and several nieces and nephews. —From *Middletown Times Herald*.
- Bertha Hulse, 49, died in Deerpark Hospital from burns received in an explosion on Sunday at the home of her brother Ami Hulse in Eldred. Both Ami and his wife were severely burned. Survivors: mother Ella Hulse; brothers Duane, Ami, George, Abraham, Dewey, Joseph, and Nelson; sisters Belle Hulse and Elizabeth Hulse. Funeral services were held at the Congregational Church in Eldred.—*News article*.
- Maude Wells Hulse, 48, died in October. Born near Liberty, she lived her whole life in Eldred. She and her husband Duane had a restaurant in Liberty, N.Y. Survivors: her husband Duane, father Willard Wells, sisters Mrs. Chester Kewley, Mrs. Edgar Hill, and Mabel Wells; brothers Earl, Ray, Emil, and Everitt; sons Raymond, Willard, Russell, Elmer, Harold, and Melvyn; and daughters Ruth and Lillian.

1933
January at the Leavenworths

Friday, January 6, Garfield played at the Hall for Dr. Smith's send off.

Monday Austin and Dorothy Smith were at the Leavenworth's for the evening.

Mid-January Anna and Jim

Unita Jane Sergeant Livingstone was very ill in January 1933. She was well enough to visit her brother Frank in April when he was so sick. Photo courtesy of Ron Flieger.

"Every Saturday night we were home and Mary and Alvah Sergeant and family were here." Mary and Alvah Sergeant courtesy of Sandy Sergeant McBride.

skated on Bosch's Pond. Anna also skated on Highland Lake. The men hunted rabbits, but no luck.

Jim didn't make it to school the day it started. He fell in the brook and had to go home.

Friday, January 20, Clinton took Aunt Lou Kelley to see her sister Jane (Unita) Sergeant Livingstone who was very sick. Monday evening Unita's daughters were at the Leavenworth home.

Narrowsburg Lumber's New Store

The Narrowsburg Lumber Company in Narrowsburg opened a retail store in Shohola, in 1933. It was located by the Shohola Railway Depot and made for easy delivery of building materials from Canada and western U.S.

February 1933

On Friday, February 3, Jennie Austin spent the day with Ella.

The following Tuesday Clara and Anna went to town to get slab bacon from Claude Angell, the butcher. It cost $1.59.

Thursday night 12 inches of snow fell. Mid-February Lawrence Crandall was in an auto accident. He died the next day. Lawrence Crandall had run Cold Spring Farm with his wife Matilda. The Leavenworth men went to Larry Crandall's funeral.

The next day Austin Smith was at the Leavenworth's for his violin lesson.

Saturday Lynn and Mildred Hill Myers were at Garfield and Ella's for the evening. Clinton went to visit the Wolff's.

The last day of February, Garfield got a piece of sawdust in his eye.

March 1933

Wednesday, March 1, Garfield took Frank Sergeant to the doctor. Clinton drove John Love's team of horses when the Leavenworth men drew their wood.

Franklin Delano Roosevelt was inaugurated on Saturday. It was a clear, warm day in Eldred. Ken McBride played with Jim. In the evening Mary and Alvah Sergeant were at the Leavenworths until after midnight. Alvah was Ella's cousin.

Every Saturday night we were home and Mary and Alvah Sergeant and family were here or we were there to visit and listen to the Grand Old Opera. The older ones would play pinochle until around eleven o'clock and then the women would go in the kitchen and make a pot of coffee and usually oyster stew.
—James Leavenworth.

Tuesday March 7, 1933, Thelma Hill started taking mandolin lessons from Garfield.

Friday there was a magnitude 6.4 earthquake in Southern California; 120 people died and there was about $50 million of damage.

Wednesday, March 15, Anna and Kate Love went to Jennie Austin's. The Leavenworth men went to see Hawk's Nest Road, a section of N.Y. Route 97 which was being constructed.

Saturday Jim went to Avery's to play with Ken McBride. Henry Graf's Pine Grove House on Highland Lake and the Davis houses burned.

Homes burning down may have meant that old wood needed to be cleared from the wooded properties.

At some point in 1933, the Civilian Conservation Corps cut firebreaks and cleared land on the Boy Scout properties.

Tuesday, March 21, Chet Hulse, Charlie Sergeant, and

Some Boarding House Ads 1930–1933

Guests at Maple Grove Farm run by the Nitzsche and Frey families, 1932. Photo courtesy of Christopher Frey.

Barryville

Glendella, Ed & Hazel Carroll
All impts; hot and cold water in rooms; electricity. Bathing, swimming pool, tennis, handball. Booklet.

Maple Grove Farm, Nitzsche & Frey
Overlooking Delaware River. Modern impts. Running water in every room. Swimming pool, recreation hall, tennis courts. Own farm products. $15/$17.

Mount Pleasant House
Riding, tennis, other entertainments. All improvements. Reasonable rates. Accommodations for weekenders.

Side Hill Farm, C.E. Seitz
Ideally situated. Modern impts. Tennis. Swimming pool. $14. Booklet.

Riverside Cottage, Warshauer
On Delaware. All modern impts., hot and cold water every room; boats free, bathing, fishing, tennis, handball. Bklt.

Handsome Eddy Farm Fischer & Doeller
On Delaware, Modern. Booklet.

Yulan

Colonial, Jacob & Lisette Hensel
On Lake, boating, bathing, fishing; running water in rooms; modern improvements. Booklet. $18.

Bodine's on Bodine Lake, Bodine
Modern improvements; French-American cooking, Frigidaire; Sports.

Lake View Inn, Mrs. Vonderhorst
Bathing boating, fishing; excellent table; improvements, tennis, handball.

Sunset Cottage, L. Hazen
On Washington Lake. Hot and cold water every room. Farm products. Request rates. Barryville 4-F-4.

Park Hotel, Atwell Bradley
Modern impts. Artesian well. Water in all rooms. References on request. Catholic Church nearby.

Highland Cottage, Edith Kalbfus
Modern, up-to-date summer hotel. Acc. 125. On Washington Lake. Electric lights, running water in every room. Good roads. Dancing, bathing, fishing, tennis, golf. Bklt. Barryville 4-F-5.

Washington Beach Hotel, W. Tether
On Washington Lake. Large airy rooms with running water; home cooking; farm products. Only sand beach on lake; all amusements. Booklet.

Minisink Lodge, M.A. McCormick
On Washington Lake. Hot, cold water in rooms; bathing, boating; good table.

Laurel Cottage, Abel Hazen
On Washington Lake. Boating, bathing, fishing. Own farm products. Electricity, running water.

Pine Grove Cottage, Mrs. K. Owen
Large, airy rooms. Improvements. Acc. 50. Near lake and Catholic Church. Hot and cold running water; homelike atmosphere. Bathing, fishing. $16 up.

Highland Lake

Deer Head Lodge, K. Eggers
On Lake. Known for excellent meals. New, up-to-date house; modern in all respects. Open fireplace, hot and cold water. Boating, bathing, fishing golf, dancing. Booklet. Barryville 8-F-2.

Lakeshore Hotel, Chris Scott
On Lake, modern impts; electric lights: unexcelled table; near all churches; all amusements; boating, bathing, fishing, bowling, dancing, golf. Booklet. $17.

Highland Lake Inn, H. Asendorf
Capacity 200. Beautiful surroundings. Hot and cold water in all rooms. Golf Course opposite hotel. Booklet.

Highland Villa, M.J. Dennehy
Accommodates 100. Plentiful table. Dancing, sports. $18 up. Hot and cold running water all rooms. Booklet.

Mountain Lake House, Staubes
All impts; running water in rooms. Boating, bathing, fishing, dancing. Bklt.

Pine Grove House, H. Graf
All impts. Running water, bath. Golf. Water sports. Dancing. German-American table. Bklt. Barryville 8-F-23.

Pinehurst, Sulzbach
Acc. 50. Improvements. Boating, bathing, dancing, fishing; good table; churches close by. Barryville 8-F-51.

Noble House, Robert Forster
Home atmosphere, all country amusements. Excellent table. Free rowboats. Rates $18–$20 per week.

Austin Smith were at Garfield and Ella's in the evening for lessons.

There was no school on Wednesday. The electric light line was broken so the school had no water.

Thursday the Leavenworths celebrated Frank Sergeant's birthday at his house. He was 72.

The next week Clinton and Ella visited with her dad. Clinton started working for the County.

Emily Christene Parker Stevens
Now that the Democrats were in office, Emily Stevens was re-appointed Postmaster in Eldred.

In the 1920s the Post Office had been moved from the Parker Hotel to the northwest corner of Eldred where Arthur Wilson's A&P store and the butcher shop were. Emily kept the Post Office at that location for awhile, but later moved it back to the Parker Hotel.

The Eldred Post Office was the gathering place. We had no deliveries; everyone came to the Post Office. My mom [Emily Stevens] had a table and chairs in the big lobby and there was always a morning gathering waiting for the mail.—Christene Stevens Myers.

April 1933
In April Jim turned 11. Bill and Ken McBride were over to play with Jim several times during the month.

Tuesday, April 4, the *U.S.S. Akron*, the enormous U.S. Navy dirigible, was buffeted by ferocious winds off the coast of New Jersey. It crashed and at least 73 men died.

The second week of April Clinton took his grandparents Frank and Anna Sergeant to Bethel.

Ella sent a letter to Anna Kyte

"Wednesday, March 15, the Leavenworth men went to see Hawk's Nest Road in the afternoon." Photo courtesy of Bill Ihlo.

(perhaps the wife of Herbert Kyte, brother of Mary Wormuth). Anna Kyte replied a week or so later.

Garfield went to Highland Lake with John Love to look for a job. Mid-April Anna started work cleaning Sunset Cottage for Lewis Hazen. Anna boarded there when she was working. She earned $12 the first week.

Frank Sergeant is Very Sick
Garfield and Ella visited her dad as he was very ill with cancer. The Leavenworths, their relatives, and neighbors spent the rest of the month helping out Frank and Anna Sergeant in Highland Lake.

Thursday, April 20, Ella and Garfield took Frank to the hospital. Frank was some better when he returned home that day.

Friday the Leavenworth men, and Frank's sisters: Lou Kelley and Jane (Unita) Livingstone, stopped by, but Frank wasn't much better.

Sunday Frank was very sick when Clinton, Anna, Clara, and Ella visited him. Monday Howard Stevens (husband of Emily) drove Frank Sergeant to the hospital in Middletown. Garfield went also.

Clara Leavenworth stayed with her grandmother Anna Sergeant and Anna's sister Jennie Hull for three days. Clara went home for a bit, then returned to stay with Anna and Jennie.

Friday Harry Wormuth drove Garfield and Anna to Middletown to see Frank. Mary Wormuth stayed with Ella. Clara was still with her grandmother. Sunday Frank went home from the hospital.

May 1933
May was an intense month for Ella and her family. Garfield was at Frank and Anna's all Monday afternoon, May 1. Ella and the children visited that evening and the next.

Wednesday evening Ella wrote, "dad is very, very bad and mother [Anna] is suffering awful." Clara went to stay with her grandparents on Thursday.

Thursday Garfield worked for Averys. Jim went to school. Clinton worked. Anna and Ella stayed home.

Friday Jim was home from school as Ella thought he might have mumps. Clara was home for the day, but went back to help her grandfather who was not doing so well.

Saturday Clinton and Ella went to see Frank and Anna. Garfield and the men in his combo played at a dance in Shohola in the evening.

The following week was a bit more normal for Ella, though Frank was still feeling miserable. Garfield worked at Averys. Jim was at school. Anna cleaned the two bedrooms and the hall for her mother. Clara did the washing and Ella ironed. Ella thought Frank seemed a little better when they visited him on Saturday.

The Leavenworth brothers went to a ball game Sunday, May 14. Clara was at her grandparents home when Garfield stopped in to give Frank a shave.

Tuesday Frank's sister Aunt Lou Kelley was sick again.

The Leavenworths were at

the Sergeant home Wednesday evening as Frank was very bad.

Thursday Garfield worked at Avery's. Friday he started working on Route 3A with Andrew Parker.

Saturday Ella's sister Hazel Connor and her family arrived from Massachusetts for the weekend. Hazel and Ella and their families spent time with Frank and Anna Sergeant that weekend.

The following Saturday Clara worked at Hazen's Sunset Cottage for a few days. Anna helped out her grandparents. Decoration (now Memorial) Day, Tuesday, May 30, Jim played at Avery's. Clara worked at Hazen's.

June 1933
The first two days of June all the Leavenworths were at Highland Lake to be with Frank Sergeant.

Saturday, June 3, Clinton bought a new Chevy Coupe (he had smashed his Whippet) and took his grandfather Frank for a ride.

The next week Garfield painted the row boats Frank Sergeant rented out. Anna and Clara alternated working for Hazens during the month.

One day after working, Clinton drove his grandfather to the Leavenworth home. The heat was really bothering Frank.

Wednesday, June 14, Ella sent a check of $8.95 for the electric bill.

Thursday Clara set out the rose slips they had gotten from Georgia Styles and her mother.

Friday, June 23, Frank's throat closed and they took him to the hospital in Middletown again. It was Jim's last day of school and time for his summer vacation.

Saturday Clinton and Anna visited their grandfather at the hospital.

Monday, June 26, Hazel and her family were back to see her dad. They went with Garfield and Ella to see Frank at the hospital Monday and Tuesday.

Frank Sergeant Dies
Wednesday the Connors and Leavenworths were at the hospital while Frank was operated on for cancer of the stomach and chest cavity. He died at 12:30, shortly after the operation was over.

Frank Roberts Sergeant was the son of Alvah and Phebe Owen Sergeant. Frank's great-great-grandfather had been Rev. Isaac Sergeant whose preaching in 1799 was the start of what became the Eldred Congregational Church. Frank's siblings still living: Unita Jane Livingstone, Alice Amelia Hill, Luella Kelley, and Morgan.

Friday Anna continued to work at Hazen's. Hazel and her family decided to stay until after the funeral. Hazel and Clinton went to Port Jervis for flowers for Frank's funeral that both families attended.

July 1933
Saturday, July 1, Hazel and her family went home. Anna worked at Hazen's.

Wednesday Clinton worked. Jim played with Ed Toaspern. (Ed

Frank Sergeant on the steps of his house before he became so ill. Photo courtesy of Cynthia Leavenworth Bellinger.

was the son of Walter and Emma Straub Toaspern and plays quite a part in World War II.)

Wednesday, July 12, Garfield was haying at Avery's. Jim played at Avery's with Ken McBride. In the evening the boys went back to Jim's house and slept outside in a tent.

Thursday Clara worked for Hazens again. Garfield was still haying at Avery's.

Saturday, July 15, Garfield was haying at Avery's. Both Clara and Anna were working at Hazen's.

The following Thursday Garfield put in stone abutments

Emma Straub Toaspern (right) with her sister Rose Straub Myers (wife of Hugh Myers), in 1932. Emma was the mother of Ed and Frances Toaspern. Photo courtesy of Bill Ihlo.

The Leavenworths weren't the only ones haying. Left: Mary Horton Bosch. Right: These men are most likely haying on nearby Crawford Road, on the Maier property. Photos courtesy of Victoria Kohler.

for the meadow bridge, in his own meadow.

Garfield is Hurt
A week later Garfield went to the doctor for his leg which he had hurt working at the Scout Camp.

My father worked at the Boy Scout Camp for about three more years and one day he got hurt by getting hit in his knee with a rusty nail, and developed blood poisoning. It got quite bad and in those days they didn't have the medicines of today.

There was an old retired doctor that owned the home that they now call Under the Pines Restaurant, and he came up and took care of my father. He came up twice a day for two or three weeks and finally my father started to get better.

The doctor told us later that he was doubtful that he could save him. My father did get better, but never was as good as he was after that. He was in this shape for a long time and things were really getting rough. We had at the time about 300 laying hens and were selling eggs in the City.

Nelson Hulse had a job in the city and took our eggs down every Sunday when he went back to work. Things got so bad that eggs dropped to 10 cents a dozen and there was no way that you could make anything.

Meantime, my father had bought five tons of feed from Joe Barnes who had Narrowsburg Feed Company. When the eggs dropped, no way could he pay the feed bill.

Joe Barnes and my father were good friends and Joe never pressed my dad for money. He would stop by every once in a while and he would say, "I'm not after money, but stopping by to visit."—James Leavenworth.

(Jim Leavenworth would eventually be able to pay the feed money his family owed to Joe Barnes.) Friday, July 28, Tony Hirsch Jr. and his wife spent the evening at Garfield and Ella's home.

August 1933
Tuesday, August 1, Garfield went to a school meeting. Jim went fishing with Robert Hanck.

Wednesday, August 9, John Dunlap gave Garfield and Ella some cucumbers and lettuce.

Sunday Jim went over to Washington Lake to see the airplane and stunt jumping.

Saturday, August 26, there were terrible hurricanes on the Atlantic Ocean.

Sunday Anna (Aunt Annie) Leavenworth was at her brother Garfield's house and gave her nephew Jim $5.

September 1933
Saturday, September 2, Jim's school clothes arrived from Montgomery Wards.

"Aunt Annie" Leavenworth gave $5 to her nephew Jim. Photo courtesy of Cynthia Leavenworth Bellinger.

1927 Rear view of Ferncliff Lodge and its up-to-date cottages. Courtesy of Christene Stevens Myers.

Tuesday Robert Hanck was over to play with Jim. "Robert Hanck went back to the city on Wednesday and James is lost," wrote Ella.

Wednesday, September 6, there was a terrible wreck on the Erie Railroad near Binghamton—23 were killed and 100 injured.

Thursday a large shovel went through the bridge near Barryville. No one was hurt.

Monday, September 11, Jim started back to school.

Tuesday, September 19, Harvey Parker started lessons on the cello with Garfield.

Saturday Anna went to High Point on a picnic. Jim played ball. Clara worked at Hazen's.

Sunday Charlotte was at her brother Garfield's in the evening.

Tuesday the stores closed at 6 p.m.

Wednesday the town started a new road by Garfield's house. Thursday Jim was home sick. He had been sick several days.

The Still
Many famous gangsters operated in Sullivan County during Prohibition which lasted from 1920 to December of 1933. The Town of Highland had its share of illegal brewery operations. Jennie Austin mentioned a raid in a 1926 letter.

There is a "Still Story" in my Austin family that coincides with that of several others who lived in Eldred at the time. This story took place between 1933 and 1934—before Emily Stevens the Postmaster moved the Post Office from the northwest corner of Eldred to the Parker Hotel.

There was a major liquor operation (not run by locals) at one of the nice two-story bungalows of Ferncliff Lodge which was owned by Guido Bischof.

Guido Bischof had originally built the bungalow for the actress Lillian Gish who had rented it from him. Her bungalow was set by itself on the hill (behind what would become the school in 1943), away from the other bungalows which were inside a fence. Since it could not be seen from the road, it offered some protection to the shady characters who stayed there.

Inside the building were huge vats of mash. Fifty-gallon barrels of molasses used for making the illegal brew were stacked up outside. They had five-gallon cans in which they evidently put the alcohol when they were done.

In the area was a gate (which led to the house) where the trucks came for the barrels of liquor.

Lillian's building became The Still. It was ruined when they cut the floors to accommodate the big wooden vats which held the mash.—Christene Stevens Myers.

The most foolish thing they could have done was to build a still on a hill near a creek because whatever waste there was would flow into the creek and kill everything. And then the revenue men would find it.—William H. Parker Jr.

The still was in operation during prohibition. It was all fenced in, and when my dad Archie delivered meat, they would meet him at the gate. He wasn't allowed to enter the property.

When I was in fifth grade, the Feds raided the still and smashed all the cans of alcohol, which ran into Halfway Brook. We saw dead fish floating down the brook. —Chuck Myers.

The Still was raided by the Feds. Government men (G-men) had been stationed in the area to spy on the operation. There was a little room at the back of the Post Office (a federal building) which

The Still building some years later. Photo courtesy of Chuck Myers.

housed their headquarters. One of the men often sat on the bench in front of the Post Office on the northwest corner of Eldred, and posed as a tourist.

The men boarded at the Austin's Mountain Grove House. Mort and Jennie were unaware of the work the men did at the time.

When the G-men raided the Still, they poked holes in everything, even the 50-gallon barrels of molasses.

This caused some excitement in town as the molasses ran downhill and into Halfway Brook. Ed Grotecloss' mother sent him to scrape up leftover molasses to give their cows. (Mrs. G. had 1,000 acres of farmland and had bought many cows from the Proctors. One of them cost $2,400.)

Bill Parker and his friends found a barrel without holes.

I told my mother, "You know that molasses barrel got to be good."

So we would go over and tap it and Mom would make molasses cookies and everything else. But what a mess they left that in. The revenue men poked holes in everything, including the five gallons of alcohol.

My brother Howard, Jack Williams, Bud Timmerhoff, and myself used to go there just for the sport of it, and my mother would give us the devil for going over there.

We would get those barrels on the top of the hill which were half full of molasses, and roll them down the steep hill to the creek. They were heavy, and would flop a sapling two-three inches around right over. We thought that was the greatest fun.—William H. Parker Jr.

After the still was raided, one of the G-man from the Austin house took Raymond Austin and his daughter Melva (4 or 5) to look at the Still. They went upstairs to the second floor (the place was still structurally sound at the time) where they could look down and see the still with what looked to be large vats and tubing of some sort.

A news article dated May 1934 matches this story, though the original source of the article could not be found.

A 2,000-gallon still, valued at $28,000, was seized by Federal, State and County officials when they closed in on the Sandhill Hunting Lodge at Eldred last Tuesday afternoon.

Two men were arrested for operating the still. The still was said to be the most complete ever found in Sullivan County. Besides the equipment, agents found 500 gallons of manufactured alcohol, 300 empty five-gallon cans, a large vat partly filled with manufactured alcohol and ten vats of 5,000 gallon capacity each, partly filled with mash. Outside the lodge were 100 drums of molasses.

October 1933

Sunday, October 1, Clara came home for a while. Monday Clara was back working at Hazen's. Jim was well and back in school. The kitchen flooring arrived. The turn in the road between Leavenworths and Meyers was cut.

Tuesday Garfield and Ella papered the kitchen and put new flooring down. Harvey Parker was there for his lesson.

Friday Anna and Ella cleaned the rooms and made peach syrup. Clara was home from Hazen's for good for the season.

Saturday Jim went over to the Parker's. The New York Giants won the World Series.

Sunday, October 8, the boys killed two rattlesnakes.

Wednesday Anna worked at Avery's.

Thursday was Columbus Day.

Melva Austin helping her grandpa Edwin Myers with his garden which didn't have any smelly geraniums. Photo courtesy of Melva Austin Barney.

The men drew truck loads of stone for the road. Anna worked at Avery's. Ken McBride spent the day with Jim. Friday Garfield's sisters Christina and Charlotte called. Anna was still working at Avery's. Ken McBride and Jim played.

Saturday Jim went to play at Echo Hill Farm where his Aunts Charlotte and Christina were.

Anna still worked at Avery's. Garfield spent the evening with his sisters Charlotte and Christina. Clinton went to the pictures to see *New Prince*.

The following Saturday (October 21) Clara and Jim went to town to get some plant slips from their aunt Jennie Austin.

Grandma Austin loved her flowers and plants and busy as she was she managed to have some flowers growing near the house that she tended herself. In the fall she brought in some plants either to keep over or make cuttings.

I remember particularly begonias and geraniums. I liked the look of geraniums but hated the smell so of course I repeatedly stuck my face in them and said "yuck." I remember Grandma rolling her eyes and shaking her head.—Melva Austin Barney.

Sunday Austin Smith and Harvey Parker were in for lessons.

Tuesday, Garfield worked for Wait and Boyd. Tuesday was Anna's last night at Avery's for the season.

Thursday Jim was up to Wells'. Comstocks were at the Leavenworths for the evening.

Friday Ella wrote, "Beatrice Avery Horton is worse."

Tuesday, the last day of October, Anna and Jim went out "for Halloween pranks."

Dorothy Calkin. Photo courtesy of Dorothy Calkin Hale.

Dorothy Calkin
It's been a while since we heard from the Calkin family. Dorothy (Dot) Calkin, the granddaughter of Ell Austin, had graduated from High School in Monticello. That summer Dot had done all the haying with her team of horses, as her dad was busy with carpentry work. Dot loved horses. At the fair she raced the neighbor's horse against all men and came in second. The next year she raced her own horse and it died on the race track. Her dad bought her another horse before they left the fairgrounds.

Dot was at college when she wrote the following letter to her grandfather Ell. Dot explained why taking a Physical Education major course was a good thing. Ell Austin was a stickler for young ladies dressing modestly, so Dot also told her grandfather that he didn't need to worry about skirt length or drinking at the college she was attending.

Dorothy Calkin, Brookline, Mass., to Mr. J.E. Austin, Ossining, N.Y.
October 30, 1933
Dear Grandpa,
　I like it a lot here. You say I'm not taking a practical course. Don't you think this country needs good healthy bodies and minds? Besides that, it is necessary for a person to be able to help others when they're ill. Why, I'll be as good as a trained nurse when I get through. We study all about the body and different kinds of disease and their cures. Do you believe a person can be much help to his country if he does not have health? I don't, he's only a drawback.
　There is no drinking in this school at all. And we're not even allowed to gymnasium classes without long stockings. So don't worry.
　I go to school at "Posse Nissen School of Physical Education." It certainly is building me up. I've gained 8-1/2 pounds since my first day of school. I have a mile walk every night and morning to and from school and often I walk into the center of Boston which is about three miles. This walking is something very unusual for me.
　I was very surprised to find that the girls here are very different than you hear the average college girls are, but I suppose if a girl wants to be strong and healthy, she can't drink, smoke, etc. Oh, yes, they don't permit any vile language either. Well, I've got to study.
　Love, Dot

November 1933
Saturday, Jim went to visit his Aunt Jennie Austin.

Monday it snowed seven inches and promised to snow more on Tuesday when the four Leavenworths went to vote.

Adorable Gisele Rouillon and her best friend Marie Therese. Photo courtesy of Gisele Rouillon Leavenworth.

Gisele Rouillon. Photo courtesy of Gisele Rouillon Leavenworth.

with two young sons, William, 6, and Clifford, 2, to care for.

Wednesday was the coldest November 15, in 50 years—according to the radio. Anna went to Avery's to help out. Garfield dug the grave for Beatrice Horton. The same day John Love's sled and truck burned.

Beatrice Avery Horton was buried Thursday, November 16. Anna and Clara Leavenworth went to the cemetery.

Monday, November 27, was another horrid accident. Roy Foster's leg was cut off in the track of the tractor.

Wednesday Anna and Clara went skating on Bosch's Pond.

Thursday was a splendid, warm Thanksgiving for the Leavenworths. Alvah, his family, and Charlotte Leavenworth had dinner with them.

Sunday, November 12, Jim went to Sunday School and then sliding with his friends.

Monday Anna went to Avery's to work. Perhaps it was to help out Erwin and Norah Avery whose daughter Beatrice had died at only 26 years of age. Beatrice had never been a real hearty individual and died from a weak heart. Her husband Charles Horton was left

Gisele Rouillon in Paris

You may remember that Gisele Rouillon was placed in a convent after her grandmother had died. After Gisele's father Cyrus Rouillon married a woman also named Gisele (who had a lingerie shop in Paris), he found a kind of foster care home for Gisele.

It was not like our foster care homes, but long term care in a private home of an older couple, Mr. and Mrs. Cailloux. "Mama and Papa Cailloux" as Gisele called them, took care of the children whose parents worked in Paris. The children would stay for the week and go home on weekends and vacations. But there were some like Gisele (who had no mother) who were there most of the time. (Cyrus paid for his daughter to stay with them.)

Gisele met her best friend, Marie Therese at the home of Mama and Papa Cailloux. The girls grew up as sisters and continue to stay very close.

Mama and Papa had two children of their own—a son Pierre and a daughter Mathilde—who were very nice to Gisele.

Being the oldest girl in the home, Gisele had to do a lot of extra work. She helped care for the younger children, scrubbed floors, etc. Gisele learned how to knit with wooden sticks before she was allowed real knitting needles.

A friend of the family, Mathilde, Gisele in front, Mama Cailloux, friend of the family, Marie Therese and Papa Cailloux. Photo courtesy of Gisele Rouillon Leavenworth.

1933 World, National, and Local News

1933 World and National News
- The 3M Company marketed Scotch Tape.

February 1933
- Japan in control of Manchuria and northern China. Japan withdrew from the League of Nations.

March 1933
- Japan, China, the Dutch East Indies, and Siam formed the Great Asia Association. It was under Japanese leadership.
- Hitler became Chancellor of Germany. He withdrew Germany from the League of Nations.
- President Franklin D. Roosevelt was inaugurated. His speech included, "We have nothing to fear, but fear itself." Roosevelt's *Fireside Chats* began. He also introduced the New Deal (social and economic legislation) from March to June.
- The Civilian Conservation Corps was authorized under the Federal Unemployment Relief Act.

April 1933
- U.S. gold standard was dropped.

May 1933
- After Japan and China signed a truce; Japan controlled the part of China north of the Great Wall.
- The Century of Progress World's Fair opened in Chicago, Illinois, on 427 acres. It lasted for two seasons and drew over 39 million visitors.

November 1933
- U.S. granted diplomatic recognition to the Soviet regime.

December 1933
- The 21st Amendment to the U.S. Constitution ended prohibition.

1933 Halfway Brook News
1933 Fire
- Henry Graf's Pine Grove House burned in March.

1933 Eldred Seniors
- Robert Austin, Clifford Crandall, Ernest Owen, Carl Vonderhorst, Marie Wait, Archie Warden, John Zurowsky. June graduates faced 25% unemployment.

Eldred School News 1933–1934
- Howard K. Moore was Principal. Seven faculty; 164 students. Boys won the baseball league championship. School purchased Sunshine Hall. Magazines added to school library.

1933 Births
- Joan Hill born to Alfred and Bessie Hill.

1933 Marriages
- Charles L. Bosch (son of Charles W. Bosch) married Karin Nielsen (a Norwegian) in Norway about 1933. Karin worked as a domestic servant and cook in area of Glen Cove, L.I.
- Iva Eldridge married Herbert Foster in September.

1933 Deaths
- Mary Grace Nelson Deats, 1876–1933.
- Frank R. Sergeant, 1861–1933.
- Mrs. Carrie Wait died in July.
- Beatrice Avery, 1907–1933, wife of Charles W. Horton.

From the left: Mr. Nielsen, Karin Nielsen Bosch, Charles L. Bosch, Mrs. Nielsen, Ad Nielsen (Karin's brother in Norwegian Army uniform) in Norway. Photo courtesy of Ken Bosch.

- Theodore West, 1845–1933. Theodore was a drummer boy in the Civil War.
- Mary Mills Wait died at the age of 78 in November. She had been a widow since 1906 when her husband George Wait had died. Mary was the mother of Alexander Wait.
- Lawrence Crandall, 1892–1933.
- John Eldred, son of Frank and Almira Barnes Eldred, died in July.
- Sam Simpson, brother of Victoria Parker and Nellie Crandall was killed in a tractor accident.
- Kate Hess Rohman, 1888–1933.

December 1933 in Eldred
December was a month for skating, visiting, and getting ready for Christmas. Jim and Anna skated on Bosch Pond.

Laura McBride stopped and visited with Ella. Clinton and Ella visited with her stepmother Anna at Highland Lake. Ella also mailed a Christmas box to her sister Hazel. Garfield fixed a viola.

Austin Smith, Jim, and Garfield went to at least three Christmas Program practices in Barryville. The program took place at the Methodist Church three days before Christmas.

Two days before Christmas the Leavenworths trimmed their tree which Clinton had brought home. Anna and Jim went to the

Arthur Austin standing in front of the Post Office at the Parker Hotel. The building behind Arthur was possibly Ray Ryman's electrical business. Pete Callahan would own an appliance store there around 1940. Photo courtesy of Christene Stevens Myers.

cemetery and put wreaths on graves.

Christmas Eve afternoon, the Sergeants visited. Bill Meyers was there for dinner. The family opened their presents.

The Leavenworths feasted on a 22-1/2 pound turkey for Chrismas dinner.

Garfield gave Bertram his first mandolin lesson the day after Christmas. Thursday, December 28, it was 14 degrees below zero. It warmed up to six degrees below by four on Friday afternoon.

And it was time for a new year. Ella mentioned Garfield working for the TCWA in her diary. The organization seems to be related to the construction jobs created by the CWA (Civil Works Administration) in November 1933.

1934
January at the Leavenworths

Monday, the first day of January 1934, Garfield started work on some roads for the TCWA and continued into February. Howard Stevens was in charge of the project. Garfield was paid "his first $15 for road work" a week later.

Two bad accidents happened in January. Ed Crail, a boarder at Lou Kelley's, fell and shot his leg off while hunting. Clinton Leavenworth, Morgan Sergeant and his family, Lou Kelley, and Bill Meyers visited Ed Crail in the Port Jervis Hospital.

Alice Sergeant Hill (Ella's aunt) smashed her new car into a tree on the road between the Leavenworth home and Eldred.

The last day of January, Mary Kyte Wormuth and Cleta Myers Horton called at the Leavenworth home. Austin Smith was there at some point for his lesson.

February and March 1934

Garfield got his oak boards from John Love to make chairs. Clinton had finished his County job before Christmas and worked several days for John Love in March. Clinton also hunted foxes with Bill Meyers Jr. Bill Jr. took Clara and Anna to visit his sister Dorothy Wolff one evening. And then, Anna went out with Bill Meyers Jr. for the first time alone. The second date they went to the pictures.

Jim visited his aunt Charlotte Leavenworth one day and another time stopped by the Austin's, perhaps to play baseball with his cousin Bob.

Austin Smith continued violin lessons. Carl Wolff had his first violin lesson.

Joan Louise Austin Born

Joan Louise Austin was born to Raymond and Gladys Myers Austin in March of 1934. Joan's sister Melva had been staying with Jennie Austin, their grandmother.

During the times that Joan and Margie were due to be born, I stayed with Grandma Austin. Sometimes I spent some time with the Austin Grandparents, just to visit. I started school there in primary grade (there was no kindergarten). Aunt Charlotte was my teacher and I was instructed to call her "Miss Leavenworth" while in school.

Before I was old enough to start school, Aunt Charlotte would stop into Grandma's when I was there. She would bring a bag full of pennies and I could have all that I could count. I sure learned to count at a young age! Probably good for Great-Aunt Charlotte's penny supply that I was not there for very long on that stay!—Melva Austin Barney.

Arthur Austin, Eldred Post Office

Arthur Austin had taken another Civil Service test in July 1933. His average percentage as typist was 84.30.

By the spring of 1934, Arthur Austin worked at the Eldred Post Office for Postmaster Emily Stevens. The Eldred Post Office had been moved back to the Parker Hotel, or it would be soon.

Arthur was unaware that Mary Briggs (who had arrived with her family in Barryville in the spring of 1934) would be his future bride. Mary's father Irwin would pastor the Methodist Churches. Irwin would soon meet Garfield Leavenworth and Mort, Aida, and Lon Austin. The Briggs family had finally arrived in the Town of Highland.

Chapter 7
The Breezy Westerner
The Briggs Family Arrives, 1934–1936

Mr. Briggs, a "breezy Westerner," is a man of action. He was brought up on a ranch; educated himself for a school teacher; went to Taylor University; became a "cowboy preacher;" and later, a Home Missionary in Nebraska. Mrs. Briggs, a former Nebraska school teacher, has been his "right hand man" and proficient pardner in the work, since 1919.
—Newspaper article.

Irwin and Myrtle Briggs standing on the Bluff. Photo courtesy of Mary Briggs Austin.

Harry Irwin (H.I.) Briggs, definitely a man of action, and his "pardner" Myrtle Briggs arrived with their family in Barryville, in the spring of 1934. Irwin would be the pastor of the Methodist Churches in Eldred, Pond Eddy, and Barryville.

Many a tale of the West Mr. Briggs draws from his hundreds of experiences and uses to interest his Eastern audiences.
Mr. Briggs had a reputation to live down at his first charge. A tenderfoot parson from the East had been there a year before and made some mistakes in Western etiquette. Unknown to the reception committee, Irwin had lived on a ranch and knew the life.
First his gentle host set him on an insane vicious "locoed" horse. Mr. Briggs thought he was just bad and did not know the horse had partaken of loco weed. He rode the horse well enough to satisfy his host. Next, six cowboys hitched a couple of wild broncos to a mowing machine and told Irwin to mow the lawn. It was a somewhat hazardous task, but after a wild ride of a mile or so the broncos were finally subdued and driven back to the corral. The parson gained the admiration of the cowboys.—Newspaper article.

Irwin was very friendly and outgoing. He often visited the people in his congregation which would include, Mort and Jennie Austin; Mort's siblings, Aida and Lon Austin; and Garfield and Ella Leavenworth.

Irwin was very musical and played violin, the potato bug (mandolin), and a musical saw. He made several instruments including a dishpan "cello."

The Briggs family of six all played instruments and sang for churches and shutins—people who couldn't get out to church.

Soon Irwin and Garfield Leavenworth would discover their common musical interest.

Irwin (he didn't like the name Harry) and Myrtle (she didn't like Myrtie), and their four children: Laura, 13, Mildred, 12, Mary, 8, and John, 6, lived in the parsonage beside the Barryville Methodist Church, near the Delaware River.

The Briggs Family: Myrtle with a mandolin, Laura, violin; Mary, guitar; Mildred, trumpet; Johnny, drums; and Irwin with his musical saw. Photo in collection of Mary Briggs Austin.

We lived by the Delaware River. In winter, we ice skated on Glass Factory Pond. That's where I learned to skate.

Squares of ice were cut out of the lakes, then they put sawdust around them and stored them in an ice house. The ice blocks kept all summer. In summer we used the squares of ice for our icebox. When we got a fridge, we didn't need the ice blocks anymore.

My dad Irwin Briggs made whistles. He took the bark off a half-inch-round branch, and made three holes to play different sounds. He also made us stilts.

Mr. Deats, one of the men at church that I remember well, made silver jewelry. One time he brought me flowers wrapped in a dollar. Minnie Nelson was Mr. Deats' sister-in-law.

We had party lines—ten people with ten different rings, one for each person. You had to get the operator before you could talk to anyone. The phone office was to the right, before Edna Gardner's place.

We always had electricity in Barryville and a bathroom. My family raised rabbits to eat and saved skins and stretched the skins to make things like mittens.

For bread or milk we went

The Barryville Parsonage and Methodist Church in winter. Photo courtesy of Mary Briggs Austin.

"We walked past the old mill which was not working." Postcard in Austin Collection.

Burt Calkin, father of Dorothy and Dale. "Dad has got a barn to build now." Photo courtesy of Katherin Calkin Traxler.

to the A&P store in Eldred which also had meat and other groceries. There was also an ice cream place. We went to Eckhart's when we ran short of something. Milk was delivered in half gallon pails.

Port Jervis had grocery and clothing stores, Woolworths, and a 5 and 10 cent store. Material was 10 cents a yard. Mr. Deats went to town with our family. We went to the ice cream parlor and he bought each of us a half pint of ice cream—three scoops for 5 cents. Bread was 10 cents.

We ordered every thing from the catalog—single beds and even mattresses.

If a car needed work, Dad went to the Ford garage in Port Jervis. One time my dad went to Port Jervis to get his car fixed, and he came back with a brand new car.

In fourth grade I met my good friend Gracie at school. She was in first grade, and her family had moved to Barryville from New York City where Gracie's father had been an insurance agent. He had bought property next to the Gardners.

To get to school, we would walk past the Old Mill, which was not working, across the little bridge. We would go home for lunch and then back, about a quarter mile I guess. There was a steep hill with rocks and trees behind the school where we played the game Dog and Deer. If you got to the designated place you would be home free.

There were two rooms and four grades. Miss Winecoop had first through fourth grade, and Mr. Crispell had fifth through seventh. Mr. Stewart taught eighth grade. One year Mr. Crispell gave me a tennis racket for perfect attendance and took a friend and me to play tennis.
—Mary Briggs Austin.

The Calkin Family
Burt and Lillie Austin Calkin lived in Bethel. Their son Dale would marry Nellie Hill from White Sulphur Springs in September.

John and Harriet Hill with their delightful daughter Peggy. Photo courtesy of Alan Gothard.

Dorothy Calkin with her dog. "There isn't anything to do up here now but study." Photo courtesy of Katherin Calkin Traxler.

Their daughter Dot still attended college. In the summer Dot sometimes worked at Jewish Hotels. Her grandfather Ell Austin still helped out two older ladies.

Dorothy Calkin, Boston, Mass., to Mr. J.E. Austin, Ossining, N.Y.
April 8, 1934
Dear Grandpa,
I received your two cards. I went home March 30th for a few days. Everyone is well although Mother is taking a course in Kingston now every Saturday.

I guess Dad has got a barn to build now up toward Liberty. Dale is making syrup. I guess he has about five gallons made.

There isn't anything to do up here now but study, so I get along pretty good. I think I will be home for a week around May 19. I am going to church this morning, so I'll have to get ready. Take care of yourself and give my regard to the ladies. Love, Dot

Soon after the letter, Dot had an operation for appendicitis. Lillie wrote her father Ell Austin.

Anna Leavenworth. Photo courtesy of Mary Ellen Busse Mackinder.

Lillie Calkin, Waltham, Mass. to Mr. J.E. Austin, Ossining, N.Y.
April 17, 1934
Dear Dad,
The doctor told us today that Dorothy is out of danger. We expect to go home Wed. a.m. and get Dot when she is well. Her address is Waltham Hospital, Waltham, Mass. Just write her something cheerful. Love, Lillie

April 1934 at the Leavenworths
At the beginning of April, Aunt Anna Leavenworth called to wish Jim a happy twelfth birthday. During the month Jim of course went to school. After school and on weekends he played with Ed Toaspern, Nick Rohman, or Charles Foster. Sometimes Jim played ball in Glen Spey.

Clara started a flower bed. Bill Meyers Jr. and Clinton hunted rattlesnakes.

They picked them up with their hands. I guess it was a daredevil game."—Linda Leavenworth Bohs, daughter of Clinton.

Clinton worked for Ray Wells and then started work for the County. Garfield worked on a CWA project.

Anna and Jim went to Bill and Lottie Meyers' for supper once and Anna and Bill went to the pictures a couple times. Hmmm…this is starting to get serious?

Thursday, April 18, delightful Esther (Peggy) Hill was born to John and Harriet Classen Eldridge Hill. Peggy received a lot of love from her seven Hill and six Eldridge siblings.

Monday, April 30, Anna started working for Hazen's again.

May 1934
Anna and Bill went to the pictures several times in May.

Garfield and Clinton helped to fight the forest fire in back of Bill Meyers' home. There were several fires "in back of the house in the woods," in May.

Clara worked for a family in Shohola for two weeks. Garfield built four steps for Walter Tether. At the end of the month he worked for Wait and Boyd.

Saturday, May 12, Frank Kyte called. "We haven't seen him for about 27 years," wrote Ella. Frank Crouch Kyte, son of Charles Colony and Elizabeth Bliss Kyte, was a descendant of Felix Kyte (1800–1878). Felix had been the Congregational preacher in Eldred for 46 years.

Garfield played in church for Mother's Day. Mary Sergeant made a Mother's Day cake. Jim played ball at his aunt Charlotte's place.

The new preacher and his wife, Irwin and Myrtle Briggs, visited the Leavenworths the third

Bill Meyers Jr. Photo courtesy of Mary Ellen Busse Mackinder.

week of May. The next week the whole Briggs family stopped by.

Garfield and Jim went to practice at the church.

June 1934
In June Jim's friends Charlie Foster and John Williams visited him.

Saturday Anna and Lottie

Frank Kyte who visited Garfield and Ella. "We haven't seen him for about 27 years." Photo courtesy of Barbara Waite Wilkinson.

Garden behind the parsonage. "After swimming, we would stop by the garden and eat a tomato off the vine." Photo courtesy of Mary Briggs Austin.

Mary's brother John Briggs with the pike he caught. Photo courtesy of Mary Briggs Austin.

Mary Briggs with a big smile. Photo courtesy of Mary Briggs Austin.

Arthur Austin on the merry-go-round at High Point. Photo courtesy of Mary Briggs Austin.

Meyers visited Della Howlett, Lottie's half sister who ran a small boarding house on Highland Lake Road.

Anna went to Middaugh's a couple times. Perhaps she helped out Florence, the wife of Chester, as Florence was not feeling well. Clara worked at Hazen's.

Anna and Bill went to the commencement exercises. Another time they went to the pictures.

Mid-June Garfield bought a calf from Hazen's for $10. Oliver Dunlap stopped by Garfield's. His sister Isabelle Dunlap was very sick.

The first day of summer vacation, Jim mowed his aunt Charlotte's lawn, then visited Freddie Meyer at Highland Lake.

Charlotte Leavenworth took classes at Oneonta sometime that summer. The last day of June Anna worked at Avery's and Clara at Hazen's.

Summertime
It was summertime, a favorite for many including Mary Briggs who was new to the Town of Highland.

Summer was a wonderful time. Besides the fact that there was no school, there were picnics in Pond Eddy, Shohola, Pennsylvania, and Stege's Pond. There were boats that we used to go fishing and caught sunfish which we would eat.

We lived by the Delaware River near John Traver's beach and he kept his lawn mowed so we would have a nice place to go swimming. In the summer we went swimming there everyday except Sunday or when it rained. After swimming, we would stop by the garden and eat a tomato off the vine.

Every year there was a Sunday School picnic at High Point, New Jersey, a lookout place with a beautiful view. There was swimming, swings and slides, and a merry-go-round. It was an all day affair.

Every fourth of July the Pond Eddy Church had a big deal for dinner. Tables were set up with covers. There was a watermelon eating contest and burlap sack races. At night there was a baseball game and then fireworks.

We made ice cream in a six-quart size ice cream freezer.

I went with my mom when she visited Nellie Austin. We gave

Nellie bouquets of flowers Mom had picked. Nellie had a yard goods store in Olean, New York. I think Nellie gave mom four yards of material.—Mary Briggs Austin.

July 1934
In July Clara started working

November, "Bill works for the County on the Road." Photo in the Austin Collection.

November, "Arthur is in the Post Office." Photo courtesy of Mary Briggs Austin.

for Avery's. Anna still worked for Hazen's.

Jim's friends Frances and Ed Toaspern, Ken McBride, Madelyn Meyers, and Nick Rohman were often over at the Leavenworth home. Sometimes Jim, Ed, and Frances played at Madelyn's house.

Saturday the men worked on the upkeep of the cemetery and did some cement work.

The Hirsches were in town. Anthony, Christina, and Charlee stopped by Garfield and Ella's a couple times.

During the month Ella canned 5 pints of blueberries; 18 quarts of peas from the 2-1/2 bushels of pea pods she and Garfield had picked; and 14 quarts of beans.

Mid-July Isabelle Dunlap died. The next day, around eleven p.m., Henry Von Ohlen's store burned.

After Jim mowed his aunt Charlotte's lawn, he, Bill, and Clinton went swimming and to the pictures.

Friday, July 27, Ella's sister Hazel Connor and her family arrived from Massachusetts. Walter, Hazel, Margie, and Marion, visited Anna Sergeant (Hazel and Ella's stepmother) in Highland Lake. They left for home Monday morning at nine.

August 1934
Summer was in full swing, or at least canning time was for Ella.

Ella canned: 21 quarts of beans; 15 quarts of Swiss chard; 13 quarts of peas; 25 quarts of beans; 4 quarts of sauerkraut; 22 pints of sliced pickles; 35-1/2 quarts of Applesauce, from a bushel and a half of apples she bought from Haas' Orchard for $1.25; 48 quarts of beans and carrots; 10 quarts of corn; and 5 more quarts of beans.

John Dunlap; Garfield's sisters Charlotte, Anna, and Christina, Charlee Hirsch; Kate Love, and others stopped by for a visit while Ella canned. Ella managed to find time to go to Port Jervis with Garfield's sisters Charlotte and Christina, to get fitted for glasses.

The Congregational Church had a its yearly two-day fair. (Jim bought his mom a comb tray at one of the Church Fairs.)

Jessie Dunlap Myers (widow of Jackson Myers) died Friday, August 24, at 1 p.m. Jessie was the mother of Hugh, Lynn, and Lena Myers.

Saturday Garfield and Charlie Ort dug Jessie's grave. Jessie Myers was buried on Sunday.

The last week of August Walter Horton Jr. borrowed the Leavenworth's barbed wire stretcher.

September 1934
During September, the month Ella turned 45, she canned 130 quarts of tomatoes (they cost .50 per bushel), beets, and carrots; turned 1/2 bushel of grapes into jelly; churned 4-1/2 pounds of butter; made ground pickles, some tomato soup, and also sewed.

Ella earned $3 from the coats she made for Laura McBride's daughters Virginia and Frances. She also sewed a red silk dress for Clara.

The day before school started Frances Toaspern and Madelyn Meyers were over to play with Jim.

Mid-September Jim had a new bike. Ken McBride and Charlie Foster stopped by to play after school sometimes.

Garfield started digging up the potatoes. He was laid off work, but was able to get a job in town which started October 1.

Clinton started to move to Crystal Lake, where he would work at Camp Manhattan, one of

1934 World, National, and Local News

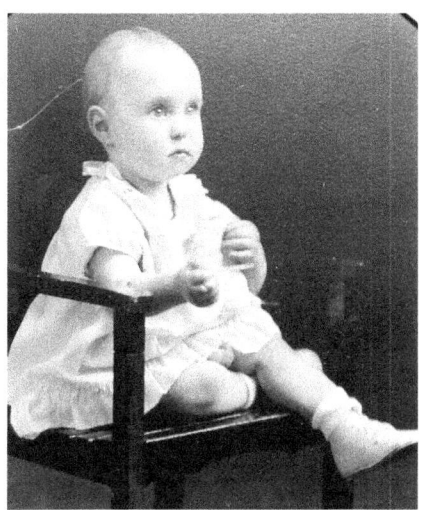

Esther (Peggy), daughter of John and Harriet Hill. Photo courtesy of Alan Gothard.

1934 World and U.S. News
- Sergei Rachmaninoff, *Rhapsody on a Theme of Paganini*.
- First Master's Golf Tournament at Augusta National Golf Club.
- The Soviet Union joined the League of Nations.

January 1934
- Germany and Poland signed non-aggression pact.

March 1934
- Mussolini signed agreement with Hungary and Austria.

August 1934
- German President Hindenburg died; Hitler proclaimed himself supreme leader (Fuhrer).

December 1934
- Japan renounced Naval Treaties of 1922 and 1930.

1934 Halfway Brook News

1934 Eldred Seniors
- Leslie Dunlap, Mildred Hill, Adolph Kalin, Ruth Kerr, Norman Myers, Warren Parker, Mary Stanton, Lucille Wait, Caroline Weber.

Eldred School News 1934–1935
- Sunshine Hall was purchased to be the auditorium. The *Green and Gold* news was organized and published by students. The first yearbook was mimeographed and had no pictures. There were 171 students; 82 were in high school. Mimeograph, Underwood and Royal typewriters purchased. Howard K. Moore was the Principal. There were eight faculty.

1934 Newcomers
- Briggs family: Rev. H.I. Briggs, wife Myrtle, and children: Laura, Mildred, Mary, and John.

1934 Births
- Alberta Elaine Brodmerkel born to William and Tina Bosch Brodmerkel.
- Esther (Peggy) Hill born to John and Harriet Classen Eldridge Hill.
- Joan Louise Austin born to Raymond and Gladys Myers Austin.
- Emily Knecht, future wife of Doug Hallock, was born to Francis (Red) and Margaret Harder Knecht. Red and Margaret had lived in Barryville for two or three years after they married; then moved to Narrowsburg.
- Geraldine Mills was born to Jim and Sophia Mills around 1934.

1934 Marriages
- Lynn Myers married Mildred Hill.
- Robert Dale Calkin, son of Burt and Lillie Calkin, married Nellie Hill.
- Emerson Lilley married Eleanor Ort.
- Alden Austin (Eldred-Austin relative) married Gertie Horton.

1934 Deaths
- John Sparks, 1864–1934, retired as Postmaster of Eldred in July of 1933. He lived in Eldred 13 years and was Postmaster for 8 years.
- Maggie Bauer Dunlap, 1873–1934, was the widow of Walter Dunlap.
- Isabelle Dunlap died in July.
- Henry Asendorf, 1874–1934, died of pneumonia in December.
- William Clouse, 1889–1934.

September 19, 1934, Robert Dale Calkin married Nellie Hill. Photo courtesy of their daughter, Katherine Calkin Traxler.

- Jessie Dunlap, widow of Jackson Myers, died in August. Jessie was the mother of Hugh, Lynn, and Lena Myers.
- Charlotte (Lottie) Leavenworth Andeway, died in October.
- John Eldred, son of Frank Eldred, was severely injured while "hay was being put in the mow of his barn. Within two weeks he had a serious heart attack and died."—*Eldred*, p. 96.
- George Parker, son of Mary Murray Parker Schoonover, died. He was buried in a cemetery in Cairo, N.Y.
- Emma Wagner Clouse, 1864–1934, was the widow of Jacob V. Clouse.
- Anna Eldred Ferguson, 1901–1934, was the daughter of Herbert Lincoln and Eliza Post Eldred. Herbert L. Lincoln was the son of George W. Eldred and Marietta West.

Mrs. Claudia Hickok Freeman Rixton, wife of Joseph W. Rixton of Barryville, died.

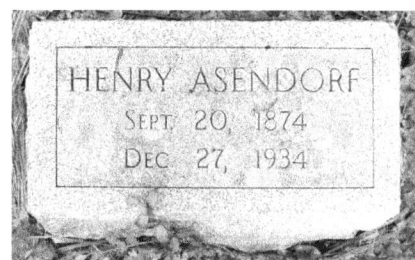

Stone marker for Henry Asendorf. Photo courtesy of Cynthia Leavenworth Bellinger.

Florence Middaugh, wife of Chester Middaugh. Photo courtesy of Pam Fischetti DeFeo.

the Boy Scout Camps.

Towards the end of the month Walter, Emma, Ed, and Frances Toaspern stopped by the Leavenworths for the evening.

October 1934
Monday, October 1, Garfield started working in town for Howard Stevens.

Thursday Clara made a white and a dark fruit cake. Clinton got two large pumpkins from Hazen's.

Saturday Anna was done working for Hazen's for the year. She would soon turn 21.

Wednesday, October 17, Garfield put potatoes in the cellar—3 bushels for seed and 17 for winter use. Thursday Eva Wormuth was at the Leavenworths for the evening. They hadn't seen Eva in 23 years.

Saturday Carl Wolff took his sons Herb and Bob for music lessons with Garfield.

The next week Garfield did some work for Dr. Gutfruend. He also gathered rutabagas. Clara gathered celery.

November 1934
On Sunday, November 11, Mort Austin wrote his brother Ell.

Mort Austin, Eldred, to Ell Austin
November 11, 1934
Dear Brother,
I was very glad to hear from you. I have been going to write to you for a long time, but I am busy all the time, and have not been feeling any too good, so when night comes, I am tired and sleepy.

But tonight I will write you a few lines. Bob is in the C.C.C. Camp way out in California. Bill works for the County on the road. Arthur is in the Post Office.

We will be glad to see you at any time. It is getting late and I have to get up at 4:30. Everyone here is in bed and asleep.

I am always glad to hear from you. With love, Mort

Tuesday, November 13, Maggie Dunlap, 61, died at the home of her sister Miss Emma Bauer at Beaver Brook. Maggie was the widow of Walter Dunlap. Her three sons: Charles and Harold of Eldred, and George of Middletown, New York.

There was a thank-you card from the Dunlaps sent to Lon Austin in the Austin Collection. The Austin and Dunlap families had known each other at least as early as 1856. In a January 1857 letter Lon's grandmother Fanny Knapp Austin wrote (from Halfeway Brook) about the marriage of Walter's parents "Oliver Dunlap and Caty Devenport" on New Year's Eve.

On Wednesday Garfield applied for relief work. The following Tuesday he started working for Ray Wells.

Sunday, November 25, Lewis and Elsie Hazen called on the Leavenworths. Elsie brought a dress for Ella to alter. Tuesday Elsie was back to get her dress fitted.

December 1934
Wednesday, December 5, Bill Meyers Jr. turned 26. Anna went to the Meyers for supper and the evening.

To Mr. A.A. Austin, Eldred. Thank you card from the sons of Maggie Dunlap who had died in November 1934. Card courtesy of Melva Austin Barney.

Barryville Braves and Diamond Triumphs, 1934

An action shot of a play at the plate. Right: View of the field from the railroad tracks in front of Rohman's. Photos courtesy of Bill Ihlo.

Barryville Braves Continue Diamond Triumphs, was a headline in the Monday, July, 16, 1934 *Middletown Times Herald*, which included a photo of the team taken by H. Mallison, a photographer in Barryville.

The Barryville Braves were a quality team and played traveling teams from the "Colored" leagues who were no slouches. My grandfather Walter Toaspern was manager. It seems Art Rohman used to arrange the games and then he was the bookmaker taking bets on the games.—Bill Ihlo.

Back in those days every hamlet in these parts worth talking about had its own baseball team, and Sunday afternoon all summer was "family baseball" afternoon.—Comment in 1984 paper.

When I was growing up, they had a baseball team in Barryville—Barryville Braves. My brother in-law, Dick (Pat) Palmer, was centerfield. —William H. Parker Jr.

Barryville Braves Continue Diamond Triumphs: left to right, bottom row: Johnny Genegal, Bill Givens, Johnny Mertz, Manager Walter Toaspern, Linn Dixon, Gippy Nanis, Dick Haas. Top row: Nicky Whitiak, Bill Worden, Albert Smith, Joe Dixon, Fritz Williams, Pat Palmer, and Mac Wagner. 1934 Photo of the Barryville Braves taken by Barryville photographer, H. Mallison. Photo courtesy of Christene Stevens Myers.

The ballfield in Shohola was the one Eldred Central School used when my brother Orville was playing. The "field" in Highland Lake was actually just an open area where we played ball and not a regulation field. We used to play ball on the fields of various boarding houses—Sulzbachs,' Jim Mills', George "Doc" Mills', and Scottys'.—Vernon Clark.

Ella sent a Christmas box to her sister Hazel on Monday.

Wednesday, December 12, Jim went to the High School play. Anna and Bill also went. The Leavenworths made ice cream.

Friday, December 21, Jim and Clara went to the Christmas party given for school children.

Christmas Eve, Anna and Bill went to the town Christmas play.

Tuesday, Christmas Day, Bill was at the Leavenworths for supper and for the evening.

Thursday Mr. Henry Asendorf died of pneumonia. He was 60 years old. Mrs. Fox also died.

The last day of the year Bill Meyers and Charlie Sergeant were at Leavenworths until after 1 a.m.

Owen, DeFeo, Middaugh
At the end of the year, Florence Middaugh wrote a letter to her husband Chester's niece, Pearl Owen DeFeo and her family: husband Fred Sr., and children

John Briggs, Freddy Dieckhoff, and Mary Briggs next to the Delaware River. The river is at flood stage and the ice is breaking up. Photo courtesy of Mary Briggs Austin.

Fred Jr. and Alice, in New York City. Pearl's mother Phoebe Middaugh Owen was visiting Pearl. Phoebe Owen was a sister of Chester Middaugh, Florence's husband. Chester and Florence had a son Herbert.

Florence Middaugh, Eldred, to Pearl and Fred DeFeo, N.Y.C.
December 27, 1934
Dear Pearl, Fred, and All,
I am thinking of you and wondering if Phoebe's feet is warm yet. I hope so, and that you are all well, and do not get the flu cold that seems to be chasing around.
Now I want to thank you for your kind remembrances to Chester and myself. I hope Santa was good to all of you, he certainly remembered us all very generously. Well, Herbert was certainly overjoyed with his trip and visit to N.Y. at holiday time, and I wish to thank you all for your kindness to him. He got back to his place around three o'clock, and then came down home for breakfast and the rest of the day, except for having to go up and do his chores.
It snowed all day Christmas day until evening and then turned to rain, cleared off yesterday afternoon with a terrific wind, which fell and broke its neck about ten o'clock this morning. It is very clear now, but cold, and I suppose another storm brewing.
The saddest news is Mr. Asendorf died last night or this morning. Willie Clouse told me of it about noon.
Chester and Herbert have had that cold that is going the rounds. I use extra-strength musterole on Chester. He says he is coming down to see you when Herbert has slack time. I can imagine him in N.Y. never having seen the city.
It is nearly 35 years since I passed through it, but then I never had any desire even before I came to America, to be in any City or place where there is so much commotion. It is nice for those that like it, for it takes all kinds of people to make a world, but give me the country.
Now all of you be good and take care of yourselves and not get this cold.
With love and best wishes for a Happy and prosperous New Year. Chester and yours Truly,
Florence Middaugh

January 1935
Tuesday, January 1, eight inches of snow fell and drifted. Bill Meyers Jr. plowed. Anna took the mail over to Bill and Lottie Meyers.

Erwin Avery delivered the milk with a tractor Wednesday and Thursday. Thursday the snow plow finally got to the Leavenworths.

Thursday, January 10, Clara went to see Laura McBride. Friday Clinton took Clara and Jim to the dentist in Monticello. Clara had three teeth pulled. Jim had his teeth cleaned and a tooth pulled.

Mort Austin had written to his brother Ell that his son Bob was in the C.C.C. in California. The Civilian Conservation Corps was part of the Roosevelt's New Deal. It was a public work relief program from 1933 to 1942 for unemployed, unmarried men, ages 18–25. Around January Raymond Austin received a letter from Bob in California, with his take on C.C.C. Camps. The first page was missing.

Bob Austin, Calif., to Raymond Austin, Staten Island
January 1935
The work is about 20 miles from Camp. If it wasn't for the long ride in the morning, it would be very nice out here as we don't have to work very hard. I have become used to the Camp, but I can't get used to the cold.
We are quartered in barracks, but we have to sleep in double deck bunks in which there is a bag that we stuffed with straw the first day we came. It was very uncomfortable at first, but I can sleep on them just as well as if I were in a bed.
The barracks are very unclean since they raise quite a dust in the morning which settles on the two by fours and the boards which the beds are made out of.

We have to eat out of mess kits and it is very hard to get them clean as sometimes the water we have to wash them in is not very warm. They promised us table service over a month ago, but we haven't got it as yet.

I guess we had about the same food (on the train) as they gave you during the war. But I didn't feel very hungry. Some of the fellows ate in restaurants when the train stopped, but as I didn't feel very hungry, I didn't bother to eat in any.

We had it much nicer traveling as we had Pullmans to sleep in and we were always seeing new country.

The country around here is very beautiful and I think I wouldn't mind it if we could live like human beings. It certainly gets monotonous lining up every night for supper and making our beds every morning. However, I guess it isn't near as bad as the Army. But when I get out, I never want to get in another C.C.C. Camp.

We seem to be in about the worst part of California as we haven't got any of the things that you associate with California.

The trees here are very large, but we haven't got any of the real big redwoods that you read about. The biggest tree that I have seen yet was about 7 foot through and about 250 to 300 feet high. Most of the wood here is red pine, fir, and cedar trees. There are a few oak trees here and they also raise apples here. The trees however have altogether different leaves and bark than the ones back home.

I guess we missed sunny California by about 80 miles as our boss tells us that the Orange County starts about 80 miles southwest from here in

Parker, Waidler, Wood, and James

Left: Kate Parker. Right: Kate's brother George Parker. Photos courtesy of Richard James.

Left photo: Will and Kitty Britt James. Right photo: Emma Schoonover Waidler and her half sister Kate Parker. Photos courtesy of Richard James.

George Parker, 76, brother of Kate Parker, 74, and half brother of Emma Schoonover Waidler, 64, died in 1934.

We first met George and his sister Kate in *The Mill on Halfway Brook*, when his widowed mother Mary Murray Parker married Perry Schoonover, a widower.

When the Parker sister Laura Britt died young, Kate Parker, her half sister Emma Schoonover Waidler, and their mother Mary Murray Parker Schoonover, helped to raise Laura's daughters, Kitty and Ada Britt.

Before Will Waidler (Emma's husband) died in 1928, 17 acres of the Waidler property near Cairo, New York, had been conveyed to Arthur and Ada Britt Wood; and Will and Kitty Britt James. The bungalow built on the property, continues in the family.

The "Bungalow" built on the Waidler/James property. Photo courtesy of Richard James.

In the 1930s Kate Parker most likely lived with Arthur and Ada Wood's family in Brooklyn. Emma Waidler most likely lived in Cairo, but stayed with Will and Kitty James in Brooklyn during the winters.

In 1940 we meet Emma Waidler in Eldred when she visits her brother Rowlee and his wife Emily Banner.

Mort and Jennie Austin's Mountain Grove House which burned down in May 1935. Photo courtesy of Mary Briggs Austin.

the Sacramento Valley. I don't think I will be able to get to San Francisco as it is over 269 miles and it would be very cold riding on freight trains now and when the weather gets warmer, we will just about be starting home.

Some of the fellows were thinking of bumming to Sacramento which is about 170 miles, but they changed their mind.

I got a package from home Thanksgiving and I just got a letter from Mother asking me why I didn't write. So wrote to her this morning. I guess she didn't know that you wrote to me as she gave me your address.

How do you like the new place where you moved? It certainly must seem good to you and Gladys to be living by yourself again. How is Melva's throat? Does it bother her much?

I suppose Gladys and the baby [Joan] are both well. Mother tells me you are having nice weather back home. The weather here would also be called nice back home, but it don't seem to me like sunny California. I will close now as it is nearly time for supper. I must get my mess kit and go to the mess hall. Your brother, Bob

February 1935
Monday, February 4, was cloudy and colder in Eldred. Clinton cut ice blocks for Perry Foster. Garfield went to Greig's to butcher a pig for them (the Leavenworths) to eat. Friday, February 8, Ella started a star bouquet quilt.

On Friday Arthur Austin received his assistant typist score of 86.53 on the June 1934 test he had taken at the New York Department of Civil Service in Albany. Art worked for Emily Stevens at the Post Office. His next job, clerical in nature, would be for the Sullivan County Highway Department.

Monday, February 11, Ella started a feather fan quilt. The following Monday she made Anna a dress.

March 1935
Monday, March 11, Clinton and Garfield started carpentry work for Elijah Moore at the Scout Camps.

Clara had been helping Mrs. Kestler in Shohola. The Kestlers brought Clara home for a while Wednesday, March 20. (Mary Kestler's baby girl was born the last day of March.)

Wednesday, March 27, Mr. and Mrs. Hazen, Lottie, and Bill Meyers were at the Leavenworths for the evening. Jim got a baseball glove and ball.

Sunday Madelyn and Frances Toaspern were over at the Leavenworth home to play with Jim.

April 1935
Tuesday, April 2, Ella made Jim a cake for his 13th birthday.

Monday, April 8, Clara went to help Mrs. Kestler again. Tuesday Garfield went to work for Henry Von Ohlen.

The following Tuesday Ella made Easter boxes for her nieces, Marjorie and Marion Connor.

Florence Middaugh, Eldred, to Pearl Defeo and family, N.Y.C.
April 17, 1935
Dear Pearl and All,
Your welcome letter received and was glad to know you was all well.

Yes, Herbert said he saw Fred the Sunday you brought your mother home. Herbert was so surprised to meet New York right in Eldred, that he forgot everything except that he was so dirty.

By the looks of the weather now, winter loathes to leave.

How is it down your way? I hope you are not having a dust storm. I feel heart sorry for those poor farmers in the west and for anyone living in those terrible dust sections. What a lot we have to be thankful for when we hear of people in such distress.

I have not seen Aunt Chat [Charlotte Middaugh Myers] or your mother since last December. I look for them up if the weather ever gets warm enough.

I am so lame myself this weather. At times it's all I can do to get around and do my work. It's worse when my hands get lame. It's all in a lifetime, and we can be thankful we are as we are.

Herbert is home and works to Monticello when the weather permits.

Today looks more as if Xmas was coming than Easter. I hope it will warm up by Sunday so those that have new Easter outfits will not be disappointed.

Of course you have heard Mr. Von Ohlen has his new store up and enclosed and expects to open in May. I wish him lots of good luck.

I suppose you saw Marie's baby [Marion Hulse] when you were up. She will be 11 weeks old Friday. I have not seen her yet.

How are the kiddies? Hope well. U. Chester has a bad cold, but trudges along. How is Russ and Family? I hope well. I hope Russ still has his job and makes out good.

Will close with our sincere good wishes for a happy Easter and love to all and lots of good luck. From all as always,
C. & F. Middaugh

Thursday, April 25, Ella set out the new rose bushes Clinton had bought at the A&P. Friday Garfield went to see his sister. Jennie and Ella went to Kelley's.

Tuesday Anna started work for Mrs. Hazen. It was time to get ready for summer boarders. Clara still helped out Mrs. Kestler.

May 1935

Sunday May 12, Eileen Wolff was born to Norman and Dorothy Meyers Wolff.

Monday Garfield went to the Scouts, probably to look for work. Friday men staked out the road for telephone poles and new telephone lines.

Mountain Grove House Burns
Wednesday, May 22, Mort and Jennie Austin's big boarding house burned. Everyone got out safely including my dad Arthur Austin who was sleeping at the time. The problem had something to do with the electric wiring.

This was the second boarding house of Mort and Jennie's to burn. Homestead Cottage on Collins Road had burned down around 1915.

Martin Leavenworth must have been staying at the Austins. He would be staying at Garfield and Ella's for some time.

Thursday Anna went to help her aunt Jennie Austin.

Friday Jennie gave Anna a table cloth, most likely for helping her.

Mort and Jennie moved to the house that they called *The Pines* on the west side of Eldred. The house had been built in what was once called Becker's Woods. They rented it from Margaret Hellman, and purchased it in December.

The Pines house was a big home, but plain and utilitarian. The kitchen floor was plain wood. There was some carpet in the living room. There were porches around the house and a lovely gazebo. A bedroom on the first floor was where Grandma and I slept when I visited.

Upstairs were many small rooms with white iron beds for guests. Jennie was still running a boarding home.

There was no indoor plumbing, but a hand pump in the kitchen and you could get cold water.

The dining room sat 13

Arthur Austin was still working at the Post Office when Mountain Grove House burned. He was sleeping at the time, but got safely out. Photo courtesy of Mary Briggs Austin.

or 14 people and was warm, comfortable and pleasant. There was a pot bellied stove. The guests enjoyed themselves and there was lots of laughter.—Joan Austin Geier.

Anna helped her uncle Mort and aunt Jennie move in on Monday, May 27. Wednesday the Ladies Aide from church gave Jennie a shower to help replace items lost in the fire. Thursday Clara worked at Avery's and Anna continued at Hazen's.

June 1935

Ell Austin wrote his brother Mort in June. The Austin (and Leavenworth) siblings had strong political feelings and Ell included his thoughts with the letter.

Ell Austin, Ossining, N.Y., to Mort Austin, Eldred
June 9, 1935
Dear Brother Mort,

Left: "It is hot as mustard." Phoebe Owen on left, Fred DeFeo Jr., Pearl DeFeo sitting up higher with Alice. Other child unknown. Right, 1940: Back left: Paul Knorr (the electrician), Fred DeFeo Sr., Fred DeFeo Jr., unknown. Row 2 left: Hazel LaBarr Angell, Frances LaBarr Knorr (Hazel's sister) holding Arlene, Pearl DeFeo. Front left: Gordon Knorr (son of Frances and Paul), unknown. Photos courtesy of Pam Fishchetti DeFeo.

I was very sorry to read in the paper your house was burned. I hope you was well insured. Even if you were insured, it is a terrible loss and especially to one as old as you and Jennie and you have spent so many years of hard labor to get a home and then lose it by fire is mighty tough to hear. When you get time and feel like it, I hope you will write and tell me about it and what you are going to do. How is Jennie and the boys coming on? I hope they are all well and the boys have got work.

Where is Raymond living? How much of a family has he? Is Will married?

I suppose Lon and Aida are on the old place.

Just after FDR was elected, Lon wrote me he was glad we had a Roosevelt to lead us out of the wilderness. Well, I think FDR has led us out of the wilderness into the jungle or the mire into the quagmire.

Love to all, Ell

Monday, June 10, Clara and Ella went to help the Austins. After school on Wednesday, Charlie Foster went home with Jim. They cooked their supper outside.

Dorothy Calkin, Bethel, to Mr. J.E. Austin, Ossining, N.Y.
June 18, 1935
Dear Grandpa,

The 29th of June is Mother's and Dad's 25th wedding anniversary. They are getting up a surprise party for them and want you to come up. You could come up and stay all night and go back the next day if you couldn't stay any longer.

Everyone here is well. I hope your folks are, too. I had the measles but am pretty well over them now.

Mother finished her school year up with a picnic last Saturday. We have quite a large garden in this year but something ate nearly all our cauliflower plants. Well, try to come up.

Love from, Dorothy

Saturday, June 22, Ella made Garfield a cake, for his 53rd birthday.

Monday Ella canned a bushel of strawberries—25 quarts cold packed; and made Anna two dust caps. Wednesday, Ella bought another bushel of strawberries for $4.00.

A tree was planted in front of Eldred Central School in memory of Henry Asendorf who had died in December. Henry had been the clerk of the Board of Education from the start of the organization of the high school.

The last day of June, Phoebe Owen wrote to her daughter Pearl DeFeo in New York City.

Phoebe Owen, Eldred, to Pearl Defeo, N.Y.C.
June 30, 1935
Dear Children,

I received your letter and was glad to hear you were all well.

Alice said that you people was coming up to spend the fourth. Let me know if you are so that I will have something to eat.

It is as hot as mustard. It must be terrific down there. I feel like putting on my birthday suit.

Today is Paul Knorr's birthday so they are giving him a party. Twenty invited. Sorry you are not here to join the party. Frances said if you drove up we would go on a picnic somewhere while you were here. We had hard thundershowers yesterday. It begins to look showery today.

I will bet Alice and Sunny [Fred Jr.] will be glad when school is out and they can come to the country. Let me know if you are coming.

With lots of love.
Lovingly, Your Ma

Ed Bosch Marries Eleanor Schroeder

Ed Bosch was mentioned several times in Ella Leavenworth's Diary. Ed had been very successful building bowling alleys along the east coast of the U.S., but often returned to Highland Lake and the Lake House where he and his siblings, Ralph, Herman, Charlie, Menzo, Minnie Benedict, Lulu Lansmith, Tillie Wicks, and Tina Brodmerkel had grown up.

Like most of Ed's siblings, Ed most likely met his wife at the Lake House. Eleanor Schroeder, a delightful looking lady, was a granddaughter of Mary van Eastenbridge Bosch, Ed's stepmother.

There was quite a crew of Schroeder and Bosch relatives at Ed and Eleanor's wedding

The wedding of Ed Bosch and Eleanor Schroeder in Laurella, Pa., around 1935. Seated on the ground, second from left: unknown lady holds Dorothy Brodmerkel; Florence Meyer with daughter Florence; unknown. Middle row, third from left: Eleanor Bosch, unknown, Tina Brodmerkel holds daughter Alberta, Mary van Eastenbridge Bosch, unknown. Behind Mary Bosch is Willie Brodmerkel. Standing, left to right: Charlie Bosch, William N. Schroeder, Charles Schroeder, Bill Schroeder, George Schroeder, Ed Bosch, Charles L. Bosch, unknown, Karen Bosch, Henry Schroeder, remainder unknown.

in Pennsylvania. Cute young Florence Meyer would one day marry a grandson of Garfield and Ella Leavenworth. William and Tina Brodmerkel and their delightful daughters Dorothy and Alberta, were in the photo.

Tina Brodmerkel was Ed's half sister. She and her husband William had moved to Highland Lake after her father Wilhelm had died. William would own a garage in Eldred, which he would buy from Norman Myers. Norman

Myers had bought the gas station from Stanley and Stephen Myers, and had run the building as a gas station. Since William Brodmerkel was a mechanic, he also worked on cars at the station.

Ed and Eleanor lived at Lake House, after they were married. Ed may have renamed the House, Green Acres. There would be new owners in three years.

George Andersen

George Andersen rented two

The delightful Brodmerkel sisters: Alberta and Dorothy. Photo courtesy of Victoria Kohler.

William Brodmerkel's Garage owned previously by Norman Myers; and Stanley and Stephen Myers. Photo courtesy of Christene Stevens Myers.

Charlee was in to play with her cousin Jim. Charlee Hirsch, fall 1935. Photo courtesy of Ric Schroedel.

rooms and a shared kitchen from Charlie Bosch, Ed's brother. This was Charlie's house on his Coonskin property on Bower Road. George had been born in the Town of Highland in 1907. But his family moved away. By 1935 George, a confirmed bachelor at the time, returned to live in Highland Lake. George, a family friend of Charlie Bosch, was also a friend of Bill Austin. George spent the remainder of his life in Highland except for the years he was in the service in WWII, which we will read about in a later chapter.

July 1935
Monday, July 1, The Town's electric light line was being worked on. Anna and Clara went to Kestler's. Garfield, Jim, and Ella stayed home.

Wednesday Carl Wolff was at Leavenworth's. His son Bob had a lesson.

Thursday, July 4, Clara worked at Avery's; Anna at Hazen's.

Monday Garfield went to a school meeting. Charlotte stopped by the Leavenworth home.

Wednesday, July 10, Ella made strawberries into wine. Martin was back to stay for a month and then went home with his sister Charlotte.

"Thursday Jennie Austin was at Ella's for the afternoon." Jennie (third from the right) with friends. Photo in Austin Collection.

Saturday and Sunday Mort stopped by the Leavenworth's. Jennie visited on Monday. The Leavenworths were much closer neighbors since the Austins had moved just down the road.

Sunday, July 21, Emile Four went to the Leavenworths and paid $20 for his right of way. (Across from Garfield's was a road. Four's property, may have originally been Leavenworth's.)

Tuesday, July 30, Ella canned 15 quarts of beans.

August 1935
It was August again, and time for Ella to can summer produce for winter eating. Garfield helped her can 13-1/2 quarts of peas. Ella canned another 9 quarts of peas, 22 quarts of spinach (Clara helped), 19 quarts of corn, 7 quarts of applesauce from crab apples, and 6 quarts of peaches. She would continue canning in September.

During August friends and relatives stopped by as usual. One evening John Dunlap was there for dinner. The Hirsches visited from East Islip where they lived with Aunt Anna Leavenworth. Anthony and Christina called on

---

Dempsey and Braddock

William Harrison "Jack" Dempsey (1895–1983) was an American professional boxer who held the World Heavyweight Championship from 1919 to 1926. Dempsey's aggressive style and exceptional punching power made him a popular boxer. Many of his fights set financial and attendance records, including the first million dollar gate. He is #10 on The Ring's list of all-time heavyweights; and #7 among its Top 100 Greatest Punchers.

In 1935, Dempsey opened Jack Dempsey's Broadway Restaurant directly across from the third Madison Square Garden.
—wikipedia.org.

Arthur Austin would take Mary Briggs there on a date in 10 years.

James J. Braddock "Cinderella Man" started as a poor local fighter and became the heavyweight boxing champion of the world. Braddock, had a powerful right hand and turned pro in 1926. After he lost the light heavyweight championship title in 1929, Jimmy struggled to win fights so he could provide for his family.

In 1934 Jimmy's two wins gave him a shot for the Heavyweight title, June 1935, in Long Island, N.Y. Braddock, a 10 to 1 underdog, won the heavyweight championship. He would lose his heavyweight title in 1937, to Joe Louis. Jimmy Braddock retired after a win in 1938.
—wikipedia.org.

Jimmie Braddock, Great-Aunt Anna Leavenworth's cat, was appropriately named.

Garfield and Ella a couple times. Charlee was in to play with her cousin Jim. There was also a fair in town.

Other events Ella recorded in her diary: Dorothy Dunlap came home from the hospital. Jim went on a trip with the Toasperns. Jim and Clara went to town and to Lizzie Wilson's.

Garfield started shingling on the back of his house. He was adding on to the back of his house which included a 'real' bathroom. Garfield put soil pipes in for the bathroom and dug drains. Another day the men drew stones to fix the addition on the Leavenworth kitchen.

September 1935
Tuesday, September 3, Ella canned two bushels of peaches which made 57 quarts. Wednesday Ella got two more bushels of peaches. She had a total of 109 quarts of peaches by the end of the day.

Thursday, Jim started school. Garfield worked on the house addition. He bought windows, a door, and roofing for $15.15.

Mid-September Jim rode his bike to see his sister Clara who worked at Hazen's.

The third week of September Garfield worked half days building a garage for Emile Four. The end of the month Garfield laid the floor in the addition to his house.

October 1935
Tuesday, October 1, Ella made jam. Wednesday Clara and Anna pulled the paper off the walls in the kitchen. Ella canned seven quarts of tomatoes.

Jennie Austin was at Ella's Thursday afternoon. Clara, Anna, and Ella papered the kitchen. They finished on Friday.

Sunday, October 6, Everett and his sister Raola Daiber

1935 Eldred Union News

1935 Eldred Baseball Team. Photo courtesy of William H. Parker Jr.

1935 Eldred Basketball Team. Photo courtesy of William H. Parker Jr.

The 1935 *Green and Gold,* Eldred's School Newspaper, announced information about parties, dances, photography club, dramatics, science club, basketball, baseball, and track.

Music
Old rooms were converted into a larger music room There were two pianos. Mr. Titus directed glee club and orchestra. The school purchased a bass violin and assembly song books.

Sports
Fred Fehling was the first full time gym teacher in 1935. Additional seating space was added to the gym. The athletic field was enlarged and leveled. The school bus was used for basketball games. Boys won League championship in baseball for third time. They had a good showing in track. Tumbling teams were added.

New Activities
First high school orchestra, Glee Club resumed, Home Nursing Club (one year only), Yearbook mimeographed with pictures added, Boy Scouts organized, and first intensive decorations for school parties.

Morgan Sergeant visited the Leavenworths in December 1935. Photo courtesy of Alan Gothard.

Della Myers Howlett, stepsister of Lottie Scott Meyers. Photo courtesy of Mary Ellen Busse Mackinder.

and her family were at the Leavenworths. Everett and Raola's mother (Ella's aunt Lou Kelley) was quite sick.

Monday, the Detroit Tigers won the World Series! [Go Tigers!]

Saturday, Jim went to the Austin's.

Sunday, October 13, Everett called. Raola, who lived around Middletown, was home with their mother Luella who was still very sick.

Tuesday Ella baked five apple pies. Saturday Jim shot his first partridge.

Monday, October 28, "Old Mr. Jim Boyd died." He was buried on Thursday.

November 1935

Saturday, November 2, Jim went to Austin's. Charlotte visited with Garfield and Ella.

"Terrible tidal waves in Florida. Earthquakes in Montana. Aunt Lou Kelley died," Ella wrote in her diary on Monday, Nov. 4.

Ella's aunt Luella A. Sergeant Kelley was born in 1863, and died November 4, 1935. She was buried on Thursday. Friday Garfield went to the Kelley's for the evening.

The following Friday Garfield hung the bathroom door.

Saturday Jennie Austin and Cleta Horton were at the Leavenworth home.

Sunday was the first snow of the year; eight inches fell. Monday Garfield started making the China closet.

Saturday, November 30, Garfield and Ella went to Mort and Jennie's place.

December 1935

Tuesday, December 3, Garfield went to see Mort Austin and also went to the Kelley's for a while. Friday Jennie visited Ella for the afternoon.

Monday, December 9, Garfield went to the Austins again. Ella sent a package to her sister Hazel.

Wednesday Garfield went down to Austin's to butcher pigs.

Morgan Sergeant visited the Leavenworths on Thursday.

Both Garfield and Ella went to Austin's on Saturday. The following Friday Garfield went to see Mort and Jennie.

Friday evening Jim went to a party at the school.

Saturday, December 21, Anna and Bill went to the pictures in Port Jervis. Sunday they went to see some Christmas entertainment.

Monday Garfield went to Austin's; Anna and Bill went to the Methodist Church Christmas Program.

Tuesday, Christmas Eve, Garfield worked on a violin.

The Leavenworths had a nice Christmas. All their family was home for dinner. Bill Meyers Jr. joined them for supper. Thursday, the day after Christmas, Alvah and Mary Sergeant visited the Leavenworths for the evening.

Saturday Jim went to see his Uncle Mort and Aunt Jennie Austin. Garfield worked on a violin.

Tuesday, the last day of December, Jim sent six muskrat furs to Sears Roebuck.

Most everyone that could get one had a trap line, including me. I used to trap muskrats in the brook which was good for six or seven muskrats a year.

Bill Meyers Sr. and my brother would not trap the brook, and left it to me.

I would cure the hides and send them to Sears Roebuck and would get $1.50 to $2.00 for each skin. That is how I would pay for my school clothes as my mother would then make out an order to Sears.

In those days the mail would be good and you would have the order back in three or four days. In fact we sent an order to Montgomery Ward in the morning and had the order the next night. They had two mails in those days.—James Leavenworth.

1935 World, National and Local News

1935 World and U.S. News
- George Gershwin's *Porgy and Bess* opened in New York City.
- Babe Ruth (the greatest hitter in the history of baseball) retired from Major League Baseball.
- Workers began contributing to Social Security system: 2% of the first $3,000 in earnings, half paid by the employee and half paid by the employer.
- A team of scientists headed by Sir Robert Alexander Watson-Watt developed the first radar in 1935.

February 1935
- Bruno Hauptmann was found guilty of kidnapping and murdering the Lindbergh baby.

March 1935
- Nuremberg Laws increased the persecution of Jews in Germany.

April 1935
- Works Project Administration created.

May 1935
- U.S.S.R. and France made a mutual assistance pact.

June 1935
- The Anglo-German Naval Agreement allowed Germany to build fleets as large as 35% of the Royal Navy. U-boats were permitted.

August 1935
- Social Security Act signed by President Roosevelt who also signed the Historic Sites Act which was to preserve historic sites and landmarks.
- Congress passed the Neutrality Act. It was designed to keep U.S. out of a European war; banned supply of arms or financial backing to the combatant countries; and forbad U.S. citizens from traveling on belligerent vessels.

October 1935
- Italian forces invaded Abyssinia (Ethiopia).

September 1935
- Hoover Dam dedicated by President Roosevelt.

1935 Halfway Brook News
- Route 97 was completed from Port Jervis, over the Hawk's Nest. It reached Hancock, N.Y. in 1939.

1935 Eldred Seniors
- Blanche Bodin, Paul Bodin, Joseph Clouse, Gordon Comstock, Annabelle Kalin, Lena Myers, Mary Myers, Eleanor Quick, Rowland Ramsey, Gwen Rohman, Lillian Stanton, Clifford Sulzbach, Walter Toaspern, Raymond Weber, Troward Wells, Eleanor Williams.

Eldred School News 1935–1936
- Howard K. Moore was the principal with ten faculty. There were 100 students in first through eighth grades; and 81 in high school. New courses: mechanical drawing I, and French I and II replaced German. It was the first year for caps and gowns at commencement.

1935 Enlisted in the Army
- Harvey Parker enlisted in the Army on December 3.

1935 Land Deed
- A deed from Margaret M. Hellman to Charles M. Austin, Dec. 26, 1935.

1935 Births
- Doug Hallock born to Raymond and Mary Schwarz Hallock.
- Doug Foster born to George and Iva Eldridge Foster.
- Eileen Wolff born to Norman and Dorothy Meyers Wolff.
- Richard Orvis Eldred born to Orvis R. and Selma May Myers Eldred. Richard would write *The Eldred Family* book which has been so helpful.
- Leavenworth descendant Edythe King born to Edward and Millie (Pamela) Ewart King.
- Robert (Bob) Calkin born to Dale and Nellie Hill Calkin.

1935 Marriages
- Ed Bosch married Eleanor Schroeder about 1935. They lived at Green Acres (the former Bosch Lake House) for about three years.

1935 Deaths
- Nathaniel Brague, husband of Anna Pearl Sergeant, died of multiple sclerosis of the spine. Anna Pearl Sergeant Brague later married Charles Ort.
- Jim Boyd, 1848–1935.
- Luella Sergeant Kelley, 1863–1935, was the daughter of Alvah and Phebe Owen Sergeant. Survivors: son Everett Kelley; daughter Raola Daiber.
- George James Clark, 1885–1935, was the son of Martin Dominick and Mary Costello Clark.
- Joseph Rixton, 1872–1935, drowned in the Delaware River, Barryville.
- Cyrus Walter died.

Ed Bosch and his bride, Eleanor Schroeder. Photo courtesy of Bosch Family.

Samuel Jesse and Anna May Buchanan Hallock. Photo courtesy of Emily Knecht Hallock.

January 1936, the Leavenworths
Wednesday was the start of a new year. Anna Leavenworth went with the Meyers to Harry and Della Howlett's for dinner. (Della was Lottie Meyers' stepsister.)

Thursday Garfield fixed a cello in his shop. Ella worked on a sweater for Bill. Jim went to school and Clinton hunted.

Friday the roads were so icy there was no school. Bill took Anna, Clara, and Jim to Hawley, Pennsylvania. Clinton went hunting.

Saturday Anna and Bill drove to the pictures. Garfield went to town. Carl and Freida Wolff and their children Bob, Clara, and Herb were there in the evening.

Jim received $5.60 from Sears for the hides he had sold. He now had money to buy school clothes.

Wednesday, February 8, music practice started again at the Leavenworth home. Friday Garfield started remodeling Austin Smith's fiddle.

Saturday afternoon Jennie Austin went to visit Ella. They continued to see each other more often now that they lived closer.

The following Thursday (16th), Clinton took Anna and Jim to Dr. Spaulding to have their teeth filled.

Saturday it started snowing. Bill Meyers Jr. drove the Town snow plow and had a big job. Sunday some 18 inches of snow had fallen.

There was no school for at least two days as the roads were closed. It was 10 degrees out.

Finally the roads opened. Five a.m. Tuesday Clinton started shoveling roads for the County.

Wednesday, January 22, Ella finished a tablecloth for Anna. Clinton was back home. Jim was back to school. He and Charlie Foster were home at noon for a few minutes. Austin Smith, his dad Ed, and Bill Meyers were at the Leavenworths for the evening.

Thursday Clinton was back plowing snow for the County. Friday Clinton was home for breakfast before he went back to plowing. He stayed at his parents that night and Saturday was back plowing again.

Saturday Ella wrote, "Austin Smith and his Pa here in the afternoon for a lesson."

Sunday morning, January 26, a week after the snow started falling, Clinton was apparently still plowing snow. He arrived home at 2:30 a.m., but went back to work at 8:00 a.m. He was home that evening.

Friday, the last day of January, Clara and Anna went skiing, and Jim went to school. How fair is that?

Samuel Jesse Hallock
Samuel Jesse Hallock died in January. He was the grandfather of Stella Clark who would one day be Clinton's wife. The Hallocks had been in the area a very long time and there were many descendants in the area. Samuel J. Hallock's surviving relatives: his wife Anna Buchanan; and children Eunice Clark, Oliver L., Wilbur, Raymond, John Merlin, Edgar, Charles, and Elmer.

Raymond Hallock's wife Mary

Kate Stege

Kate Stege died in February of 1936. Ed Stege, her third husband, had died in 1932. Katie had been willed the entire 800-acre estate, and this would become a problem.

Ella's Diary entries indicated that there was an estate sale at the Stege Property.

Eccentric was what the natives of Eldred, New York, called Katie Stege while she was alive. The tiny crossroads settlement had plenty to gossip about when the old woman who talked to the birds was still living. And ever since she died, their conversation's been centering around the strange will that she left behind.

Written on the back of the faded, encyclopedia advertisement, the will of Mrs. Stege, who died in February 1936, at 86 years of age, startled the natives of Eldred. To this day it has been the bone of contention in a series of court battles as well as furnishing the major item for the gossip of the village.

Katie Stege was not a native of Eldred. But for 42 years she lived on a magnificent 800-acre estate, just a mile or so from the settlement. In all that time, few of the neighbors ever got to know her well. She seldom visited the "Corners." Rarer still were her trips to nearby Monticello, the county seat.
—From the Sunday Mirror *Magazine Section, February 27, 1938, p. 2.*

Barryville and Yulan Boarding Houses 1934–1936

Barryville

Maple Grove Farm, Nitzsche & Frey
Overlooking Delaware River. Running water in every room. Swimming pool, recreation ball, tennis. Own farm products. $15.

Riverside Cottage, L. Warshauer
On the Delaware River. All modern improvements; hot and cold water in every room; boats free; bathing, fishing, tennis, handball. Booklets. $16.

Yulan

Bodine's, H. Bodine
French-American cooking. On Bodine Lake. Modern improvements. $16 up. Sports.

Colonial, Hensel
On Washington Lake. Boating, bathing, fishing; running water in rooms; modern improvements. Booklet. Rate $15–$17.

Highland Cottage, E.V. Kalbfus
Accommodates 125. On the lake. Modern. Tennis, bathing, golf, dancing. Rates $18–$23.

Lake View Farm House, A. Kaese
On Washington Lake. Accommodates 75. Hot and cold running water in every room. Tennis, handball, boating; other outdoor sports. Known for its excellent meals. Apply for booklet.

Lake View Inn, L. Vonderhorst
Washington Lake. Modern improvements; excellent table; tennis; all water sports.

Laurel Cottage, A.A. Hazen
On Washington lake. Boating, bathing, fishing. Table supplied with own farm products. Electricity, running water. $14–$16. Barryville 4-F-14.

Park Hotel, A.L. Bradley
On Washington Lake. Modern improvements. Catholic Church nearby. References.

Sunset Cottage, Lewis Hazen
On Washington Lake. New building. Hot and cold water every room. Farm products. Rates $14–$16.

Washington Beach Hotel, W. Tether
Large, airy rooms with running water; only sand beach on Lake; free bathing to guests; amidst amusements, near churches. Rates reasonable.

Twin Oak Cottage, Flieger
Washington Lake. Near churches. Boating, bathing, fishing, handball. Running water every room. $15 to 20. (Charles Flieger built Twin Oaks Cottage. He married Freida Guenther, daughter of Freida Guenther Bradley.)

West Shore Cottage, M. Cantwell
Catholic Church; modern improvements; $15–$18.

Minisink Lodge, M.A. McCormack
On Washington Lake. Hot, cold water in all rooms; bathing, boating; good table.

Oakdene, P. Owen
Oakdene, run by Phoebe Owen for many years, is thought to have burned down sometime in the mid-1930s.

Yulan Restaurants

Bradley's Restaurant
Sometime in the 1930s George Bradley, son of Atwell, started his Bradley Restaurant that would later be called, Blue Ribbon.

Chinese Food
In the 1930s, there were several places that served Chinese food in Yulan. Harry and Edna Beufve Miller owned the Chinese-American Restaurant. George Bradley's restaurant near Yulan Corners served Chinese food, as did the Casino by Washington Lake. There was a Chinese man who cooked at the Washington Casino and lived behind it in a little building.

The Chinese Restaurant was not the same as Alfred and Helen Wolff's Hillside Inn (once Metzger's) which started out serving Chinese food in the 1940s and had two Chinese Chefs.

Lisette Hensel (seated) in front of the Colonial in 1935. Photo courtesy of Helen Hensel Oset.

Christmas Card of Bradley's restaurant, signed, Florence and George Bradley. Card courtesy of Helen Hensel Oset.

Charles and Freida Guenther Flieger owned Twin Oak Cottage. Photo courtesy of the Town of Highland.

Chinese restaurant. Postcard courtesy of Kevin Marrinan.

Irwin Briggs often visited Garfield and Ella. Sometimes his family went with him. The Briggs Family Band: Irwin, Laura, Mildred, Mary, Myrtle, and Johnny with the trombone. Irwin's homemade "cello" is in the right hand corner. Photo courtesy of Mary Briggs Austin.

died a couple months after his father Samuel. Raymond was then a widower with six children: Doug, Donald, Christina, Marge, Evelyn, and Sherwood Hallock.

Raymond's sister Eunice Clark and her husband Ernest helped to raise Doug Hallock, along with their children: Stella, Orville, and Vernon Clark. Raymond and an elderly aunt raised his other children.

Maple Syrup time. Standing on left: Bessie Hill, her son Billy Lass. Cecelia Sullivan, the Algebra teacher in front of Billy. Joan Hill, the young girl in front. The other girls are Cecelia's sisters. Arthur Austin next to Alfred Hill on the right. Photo in Austin Family Collection.

February 1936
Sunday, February 2, Ella went to Highland Lake with Clinton to see her aunt Jennie Hull. Jim went to see Mort and Jennie Austin.

Wednesday Ella wrote, "Clinton went to town. Bill was here in the evening. Blizzards out west."

Thursday Clinton drove his aunt Jennie Hull to spend the afternoon with his mom, Ella.

Friday Clinton snow plowed for the County, widening the roads.

Sunday, February 16, Jim went to the Austin's for dinner.

Austin Smith stopped by with an old violin (he had gotten from Mr. MacIntyre) for Garfield to fix on Thursday.

Sunday, February 23, Dr. Gutfruend was called to check on Anna who was sick.

Friday, Mr. Briggs and the Austins were at the Leavenworth home. Mr. Briggs bought a cello for $11. Saturday was leap day. Mr. Briggs and his son John were at the Leavenworths all afternoon.

Maple Syrup Time
It was the season for maple syrup. Cecelia Sullivan boarded at Alfred and Bessie Hill's place. One year at sugaring time, Alfred, Bessie, their children Billy Lass and Joan Hill, and Arthur Austin went to the home of Cecelia, the algebra teacher. They feasted on maple syrup drizzled over snow.

March 1936
Sunday, March 1, Everett Kelley ate supper with the Leavenworths. Norman Wolff was in.

Mr. Briggs stopped by the Leavenworth's three afternoons that week. He bought a violin from Garfield for $6.

My dad Irwin Briggs had orchestras at all the churches. In Barryville I learned violin, two others did, too. When we gave a concert, Dad said we could play the song backwards and forwards. So we played it forwards and we turned our backs and played "backwards."—Mary B. Austin.

Saturday, March 14, Jim went to the Austin's.

The Leavenworths started working on the sap for maple syrup. They boiled 45-1/2 quart jars down to 1-1/2 quarts of syrup. Sunday they boiled the sap all day.

Bob and Herb Wolff, and the Leavenworth men went to the estate sale at Stege's. Charlie Foster was over for supper.

There was terrible flooding of the eastern rivers soon after the middle of March. Wednesday (18th) Clinton took Clara and Ella to see the flood at Barryville. Thursday the menfolk went to see the Delaware River in flood.

Saturday Jennie Austin visited with Ella in the afternoon.

Ell Austin's daughter-in-law Sadie Austin, in Pennsylvania, wrote to tell Ell how bad the flooding was. (Sadie's husband Henry was a half brother to Lillie.)

Sadie Austin, Honesdale, Pa., to Mr. J.E. Austin, Ossining, N.Y.
March 21, 1936
Dear Pop,

Your letter just rec'd. and we shure have had some excitement up here.

We had some flood. I had a cellar full of water and 16 inches of water. Water all over the first floor, but I moved everything upstairs but one rug in the kitchen, but the stove was on that so I didn't try to move that.

We have about two foot of water in the cellar yet and the river raised about 10 inches again, today, so I don't know what it will be by morning.

I am sick looking at mud and water. This is the second one

Barryville from across the Delaware River. The X marks where the Barryville parsonage was. Photo taken by Irwin Briggs courtesy of Mary Briggs Austin.

we have had. When the ice went out, we had 32 inches of water in the cellar then and I just got the worst of it cleaned up and now this mess again. They was about an inch-and-a-half of mud all over the floors.

We had to go up to Margo's [her daughter], but I am here and started a kitchen fire to try to dry out the place. But it is so damp I am going to stay at the Park Hotel tonight. We have a lot to be thankful for. There is so many more that is so much worse than we are. Hoping this finds you all o.k.

Love to all from all, Sadie

Monday, March 23, Garfield worked on the roof for Mort. Anna and Jim went to Theo Horton's.

Garfield worked for Mort on Wednesday.

Friday Jim, Anna, and Bill went to the high school play.

Saturday evening Jennie and Mort visited with the Leavenworths.

Sunday, March 29, Jim went to Austin's for awhile.

The last day of March Austin and Dorothy Smith visited with Ella and Garfield.

Bruno Hauptmann
"Bruno reprieved for 48 hours," Ella wrote on the last day of March. She was referring to Bruno Richard Hauptmann.

Bruno had been sentenced to death for the abduction and murder of the 20-month-old son of Charles and Anne Lindbergh. In actuality there was a delay, but he was executed four days later in the electric chair at the New Jersey State Prison.

April 1936
Wednesday, April 1, Austin and Dorothy Smith were at the Leavenworths for a lesson. Jim went to school. Garfield and Clinton cut logs for Clint's house.

Grandfather Garfield showed Dad (Clinton) a piece of his property with a lot of lumber and said, "There they are.

Laura Briggs with her violin. Mildred with her trumpet. Photo courtesy of Mary Briggs Austin.

Now go and cut them down."
—*Linda Leavenworth Bohs.*

It would take a year or two for the wood to dry and be ready for building a home.

Saturday Garfield and Clinton worked for Marcel Four. Anna and Bill went to the pictures. Jim went fishing and caught four trout.

Monday Jennie called on Ella.

Thursday, April 9, Garfield and Clinton were still working for Marcel Four. The heifer Garfield had bought from Hazens had her first calf.

Sunday, April 12, Bill and Clint cut logs for Clint's house. Garfield and Clara set out 75 raspberry bushes. Anna and Clara got their glasses from Monticello.

Monday Ella planted 107 strawberry plants. Garfield worked at Marcel Four's. Clinton burned brush on his property.

Wednesday Clara visited her uncle Mort and aunt Jennie Austin. Clara also planted flower seeds.

On Wednesday, Arthur Austin became a member of the New York State Employees' Retirement System. Perhaps this is when he started working for the Sullivan County Highway Department.

Friday Garfield and Ella took Truman Leavenworth (Garfield, Jennie, Charlotte, Martin, Anna, and Christina's brother) to the Callicoon Hospital.

Saturday Carl Wolff and his sons Bob and Herb were at the Leavenworths for the evening. Clinton and his aunt Jennie Austin went to Callicoon to see Truman Leavenworth.

Sunday, April 19, Emile Four set out small trees in the old Wait woods.

Aida Austin received a very interesting form letter from an unknown Eldred relative.

Jennie Austin beside her house with hollyhocks. Photo in the Austin Collection.

William Eldridge, Twin Falls, Idaho, to Aida Austin, Eldred
April 19, 1936
Dear Sir:
In order to obtain information of the family for my Eldred genealogy, I have been trying for some time to get into communication with descendants of the James Eldred who settled at Lumberland soon after 1815 and after whom his son, your Post Office was named.
He had eight children and it seems as if some of their descendants must surely be living somewhere in the vicinity. I will very much appreciate the favor if you will make inquiries and advise me of the results.
Yours very truly,
William Henry Eldridge

Monday and Tuesday Garfield worked on their grape arbor. Clara and Anna papered Anna's room.

Thursday Clinton took Anna to Hazen's after he came home from work.

Charlie Foster went home with Jim after school on Friday. Perry Foster, Charlie's father, skidded Clinton's logs and drew a half ton of hay from Avery's for Garfield. Saturday Perry finished the logs. Ed Toaspern visited Jim at the Leavenworth's for the afternoon. Clara went to Lizzie Wilson's.

Monday, April 27, Garfield worked at the Arlington for two days. Thursday Clara went with her aunt Jennie Austin to get shrubs. Jim as usual was stuck going to school.

May 1936
Saturday, May 2, Clinton went up to the Stege sale. Ella churned butter. (She made a total of 16-3/4 pounds of butter in May.) Clara set out plants her aunt Jennie Austin had given her.

At their third boarding house The Pines, Grandma had obtained and planted a few lady slippers and jack-in-the-pulpits under the pine trees which was their natural habitat and they were known not to survive under cultivation.
How she transported them from the woods and replanted them, I don't know. We were encouraged to look at them but NEVER to touch them under pain of I don't know what, but it would be dreadful, I was sure.—*Melva Austin Barney.*

Monday, May 4, Jim went to school. Clint worked. (He paid his parents $15 board.) Anna went to help in the Post Office.

Tuesday was a repeat of Monday except that Mr. Briggs was there for the evening.

Wednesday was a rerun for Clinton, Jim, and Anna. Garfield

worked seven hours for Emile Four. They took Truman home from the hospital.

Anna started working at the Post Office on Thursday. (Perhaps she had the job her cousin Art Austin left when he went to work for the County Highway Department.) Clara went to town and to the Styles'.

Garfield worked Thursday and Friday for Mr. Four.

Minnie Bosch Benedict died Friday night (and was buried on Monday).

Sunday, May 10, Clara went to Hazen's at eight o'clock.

Mort and Jennie were at Garfield and Ella's Friday evening. Clinton got a tractor from Ray Wells to gather the stumps on his property.

Saturday Garfield worked for Wait and Boyd. Anna went to Hazen's.

Thursday, May 21, Clara took some flower bulbs to Selma Dunlap. Selma was the wife of Charles Dunlap and mother of Carl. Her brother-in-law Harold Dunlap had or soon would have, a restaurant on the northeast corner of Eldred where William H. Wilson's store had once been.

Friday, May 22, Clara went to her aunt Lizzie's to buy eggs to hatch. Saturday Clara washed the water fountains and feeders to get ready for chicks.

The following Wednesday Clara went for another 53 eggs from Wilson's.

Clara went to the pictures with Lee Hansen (a boarder at the Leavenworths), perhaps for the first time on Thursday.

Since Clinton, Clara, and Anna, often boarded elsewhere, Garfield and Ella had rented out one of three bedrooms on the second floor. Martin Lee Hansen, who lived in Brooklyn and worked

Eldred and Highland Lake Boarding Houses, 1934–1936

Sunset Bar owned by Alfons and Johanna Theuer. Photo courtesy of Jeanie Staubes Turner.

Eldred
Foscola's
Attilio Foscola had a hunting lodge.

Highland Lake
Deer Head Lodge, K. Eggers
Hot and cold running water in every room. Boating, bathing, fishing, golf, dancing. Excellent meals. Booklet.

Highland Villa, M.J. Dennehy
Acc. 100. Running hot and cold water all rooms. All sports. $16.00 up.

Lake Shore Hotel, Chris E. Scott
Modern. Plentiful table. All sports. $16 to $18. Near churches.

Mountain Lake House, G. Staubes
Improvements. Boating, bathing, fishing. Booklet. On Lake.

Pinehurst Hotel, F. Sulzbach
All outdoor sports; modern; golf. Rate $16 up.

Bertram's Lodge
Art Bertram Sr. had emigrated from Oldenburg, Germany, to the U.S. around 1900. Arthur, his wife Clara, and their son Arthur Jr. lived in New Jersey in 1910. By 1920 Art Sr. was a manager of a grocery store. By 1935 Art Sr. bought a boarding house

Foscola's Hunting Lodge. Postcard courtesy of the Town of Highland.

on Highland Lake which became Bertram's Lodge. Bertram's had a reputation for quality food and accommodations. Around 1935, Art Jr. "Bucky" owned a bar/restaurant west and a bit north of the Lodge, on the other side of Highland Lake Road.

Sunset View House, Sunset Bar
The Sunset Bar and the Sunset View House were owned by Alfons and Johanna Theuer by the mid-1930s. The Sunset Bar was across the road and north of Sunset View House.

The Theuers—Alfons, his wife Johanna, and daughter Irene, had arrived in America from Germany on the *S.S. Cleveland*, in June 1926. They first lived in Brooklyn. Alfons was employed as a draftsman, in 1930.

Charlie Myers' Bar which he built after prohibition was over, opened by 1936. Richard Owen, bartender in the doorway. Photo courtesy of Timothy C. Rizzuto.

in the Eldred area for the Town, was their first renter. Lee rented a room, but did not eat there as a rule. He went home on the weekends.

On Thursday there were 32 baby chicks out of the first batch of eggs for Jim. Garfield worked for Wait and Boyd.

Friday Carl Wolff brought Jim a hen and nine ducks. Jim was sick with a sore throat. (He often had sore throats.)

Friday Clara worked at Abel Hazen's.

Clara was the only one in the Leavenworth family not home on Saturday. Garfield planted the garden and helped Perry plow. Garfield's shoes and Jim's sneaks arrived from Sears.

It had been the coldest month of May in years.

June 1936
Monday, June 1, Jennie Austin called in the evening.

On Tuesday Garfield bought 130 feet of one-inch mesh chicken wire from Wait and Boyd's.

Clara and Lee went to the pictures again.

Wednesday they put Jim's 32 chicks out doors for the first time. The last of Clinton's logs went to the mill.

Thursday Mort and Jennie called at the Leavenworth home.

Sunday Herbert Middaugh drew some lumber. A yard was built for Clara's chicks.

Mrs. J.Y. (Emily Christene Payne) Parker, 86, who had been sick for several months, died in June. Phoebe Owen in this next letter mentioned Emily Parker's death. Phoebe was not well either.

Phoebe Owen, Eldred, to the DeFeo Family, N.Y.C.
June 9, 1936
Dear Children,

Your welcome letter was received, but sorry Pearl that you have such a cold. Take care of yourself.

I came home on Saturday as planned; felt quite tired from my long ride. I stayed in bed till nearly noon each day.

I am living at Frances Knorr's [her niece]. I don't try to work. It is real nice up in the country, but not very warm. I am so thin, I don't feel the heat much. We go out for a little ride every night after supper, but haven't been to church yet. I still feel so weak

Phoebe Owen wrote to Fred and Pearl DeFeo. Photo courtesy of Pam Fischetti DeFeo.

in my knees and thigh. My hips and my stomach is no better. Sometimes I eat a little better than I did, but it don't take much for me.

Old Mrs. J. Parker is buried today. We didn't go to the funeral, but are going up to the cemetery tonight to see the flowers. I didn't get up Decoration Day, but I had Tina to plant a geranium in Pa's grave. Will try and walk over there tonight, but I can't walk much.

Chester was up to see me a few nights after I came home. Herbert had been past, but of course he never recognizes you unless you run right against him.

I will close with lots of love and trusting to hear from you soon and that your cold is all better. It is much worse to get a cold in summer than in winter and you can get pneumonia quick so get something and catch it.

Mother

Wednesday, June 10, Clara's 102 mixed chicks came. They had been shipped on the eighth from Buffalo.

Thursday Garfield started a larger coop for Jim's chicks. Two of Clara's chicks died.

Friday James found a baby deer and took it back to its mother.

It rained on Saturday when Mort Austin stopped by. They put Jim's 32 chicks in a brooder coop because of the cold rain. Carl Wolff and his sons were at Leavenworths in the evening.

Sunday, June 14, it continued to rain hard, so they put Jim's ducks on their screened front porch. Everett Kelley called. Clara and Viola Hazen were there for the afternoon.

Monday and Tuesday Garfield worked at Charlie Myers for eight and nine hours. Perhaps Garfield worked on the bar Charlie had built once Prohibition was over.

Tuesday they put Clara's 94 chicks in the brooder. It was exam time from Tuesday through Friday at school for Jim.

John Edward Hill, 1876–1936
Saturday was a very hot day. John Hill mowed the lawn of the Eldred Congregational Church.

John Hill drank a glass of ice cold well water and fell over with a heart attack. They carried him across the street to the corner garage. No doctor could be found and he died on the floor. He was well liked by everyone in town.
—Alan Gothard, grandson.

John Hill's children from his marriage with Esther Grinnell: Agnes Ernst, Gladys (Jake) Myers, Lena MacIntyre, Edna Hallock; Edgar, Alfred, and Alvin Hill; and Esther (Peggy) Hill from his second marriage to Harriet Classen Eldridge, who was now a widow for the second time.

Phoebe Owen, Eldred, to Pearl DeFeo, N.Y.C.
June 22, 1936
Dear Pearl,
Hope you are over your cold by this time. I am about as usual. Some days I feel better than others. Basil has this week off and is up here to put a concrete curb around our plot at the cemetery while he is here and get it fixed up for me.
The folks here are all well and Uncle Steve's folks [her sister Charlotte Myers' family] are good. Everybody is better than I am.
John Hill is buried tomorrow. He dropped dead in Boyd's garage. His family feels terrible.
Agnes [Ernst, John's

1936 World, National, and Local News

1936 World and National News
- *Gone with the Wind* by Margaret Mitchell published.
- Kodachrome—first color film made by Eastman Kodak.
- The first regular high-definition television service from the BBC.
- Stalin ordered "Great Purge" of "Old Bolsheviks" from the Communist Party of the Soviet Union 1936 to 1938; hundreds of thousands killed.
- Spanish Civil War: July 1936–April 1939.
- Mussolini aligned himself with Hitler.

March 1936
- German troops reoccupied the demilitarized Rhineland which violated Versailles Treaty.

May 1936
- Italy formally annexed Ethiopia. Emperor Haile Selassie left the country.

July 1936
- Stalin sent tanks, aircraft, and advisers to aid the Republicans who opposed Generalissimo Francisco Franco and his German and Italian allies.

August 1936
- Summer Olympic Games in Berlin. Jesse Owen, a black American, won four gold medals.

November 1936
- Franklin D. Roosevelt won a second presidential term.

December 1936
- King Edward VIII of England abdicated to marry American divorcee Wallis Simpson. His brother succeeded him and took the name George VI.

1936 Halfway Brook News
- After five years of service in the Merchant Marines, Ed Wilson returned to Tusten. He would have his own taxi business and at some point manage the Amoco Gas Station in Barryville for Art Rohman.

1936 Eldred Seniors
- Betty Boyd, Raymond Clouse, Helen Guenther, David Holden, Jack Kerr, Clareta Kuen, Carol McCann, Alvin Mitchell, John Purcell, Louis Wageman, Ian Warden, Samuel White.

1936 Births
- Marjorie Gladys Austin born to Raymond and Gladys Myers Austin.

1936 Deaths
- Emily C. Payne Parker, 1850–1936.
- Wilhelmina (Minnie) Bosch Benedict, 1876–1936.
- Francis Jackson Myers, 1919–1936.
- Frederick A. Bye, 1930–1936, son of Fred and Jeanette Bye died in March when a metal well top fell on his head.
- Mrs. Robert Greig died in October.
- Phoebe L. Middaugh Owen, 1870–1936.
- Ida M. Schwarz Hallock died.
- John Edward Hill, 1876–1936.
- Samuel Jesse Hallock, 1871–1936. Surviving relatives: his wife; seven sons: Oliver L., Merlin, Wilbur, Edgar, Raymond, Howard, and Elmer; and daughter Eunice Clark.
- Harry Dunlap, 1884–1936, Co D. 29th Inf.
- Kate Stege died in February.

Carl and Wilhelmina (Minnie) Bosch Benedict. Photo courtesy of Ken Bosch.

Edna Hill Hallock and Anna Sergeant Brague (Ort). Anna and Edna visited Ella on the same day. Photo courtesy Cynthia Leavenworth Bellinger.

Oliver L. and Edna Hill Hallock's children: Bob, Gene, and Hazel Hallock about 1933, in Matamoras, Pa. Photo courtesy of Carolyn Hallock Clark.

daughter] I guess is in bed over it.

I imagine Alice [Pearl's daughter] could get work at Warshauer's in Barryville if she wants to. Agnes Hill was to Warshauer's but left Saturday night.

I guess George Bradley has changed his mind about having Russell and Ina. Basil saw him Sunday and he said he was afraid he wouldn't work out. I think it would be just as well for Russell. I can't see where he would be better off to come here.

Hoping to hear from you soon and with lots of love,

I am as ever your loving mother.

Tuesday, June 23, the Leavenworth men went to John Hill's funeral.

Tuesday, June 30, Jim went over to Frank Bartle's for a while.

July 1936
Friday, July 3, Francis Myers, son of Norman and Bertha Eldred Myers, died. Francis was buried on Sunday. (The 1937 Yearbook would have a memorial to him, as that was the year he would have graduated.)

Tuesday, July 7, Anna Sergeant Brague visited her cousin Ella all day. Anna's husband Nathaniel Brague had died in 1935. Anna would later marry Charles Ort, son of Frank and Mary Ort. (Mary Ort was a midwife in town. She lived to be 104.)

Oliver L. and Edna Hill Hallock
Edna Hill Hallock (daughter of John Hill who had recently died) may have visited Ella at the same time as Anna Brague. There is a photo of both ladies in the Leavenworth collection.

Edna, also a descendant of Rev. Sergeant, lived in Matamoras, Pennsylvania, with her husband Oliver L. Hallock, and three cute children: Bob, Gene, and Hazel Hallock. Since Oliver worked for the A&P, in different locations, his family would also live in New York and New Jersey.

We met Oliver L. Hallock's grandfather Oliver Blizzard Hallock, in *The Mill on Halfway Brook*.

The Thursday after Anna's visit, it was 92 degrees in the shade. Friday was two degrees warmer. Oliver Dunlap called in the evening.

Sunday, July 12, Garfield finished working for Charlie Myers. His next job was working for Mr. Weber at Highland Lake, possibly on the Weber's Pine Beach Inn. Garfield completed that work on Monday, July 20.

Monday Jim went to town and to see his uncle Mort and aunt Jennie Austin. Mort worked too hard gardening and haying in the heat, and was sick on Friday. Garfield did the milking for Mort Saturday and Sunday. Mort was some better on Sunday.

Monday, July 27, Kate Love visited Ella for the afternoon. Garfield started cutting some more logs in the meadow. Jim had a letter from his cousin Marjorie Connor. Marjorie and her sister Marion often wrote Jim.

Friday, the last day of July, Kate Kuen and family called. Kate, was a daughter of Unita Sergeant Livingstone, Ella's aunt. Three of Kate's daughters are part of this story. Dot Kuen was the wife of Austin Smith; Clareta Kuen would marry Charles Sergeant; and Helen Kuen would marry his brother Grant Sergeant.

August 1936
Tuesday, August 4, Charlie Myers was at Garfield and Ella's for

dinner. Wednesday Ella finished her cut work for the Church Fair sponsored by the Ladies' Aide.

My dad Irwin Briggs remarked about Mort Austin after one of Methodist Church Bazaar Days in Eldred. The ladies were in the hot kitchen serving meals to the guests. The ladies would get frustrated with someone over something that had happened there. Mort had a knack or talent for cajoling them and joking with them and making them laugh. And things would carry on more smoothly.

One year, around the age of 11, I was at the annual Eldred Bazaar in an old fashioned white dress. I stood outside near Jennie Austin and she kind of patted me on the head. She said my name with her little laugh. Wouldn't she have been surprised to know that her son would marry me?—Mary Briggs Austin.

Tuesday, August 11, Charlie Sergeant was at Leavenworth's to practice piano chords.

Wednesday Bob Austin was there to play ball with his cousin Jim. (Bob must have been back from the C.C.C. Camp in California.)

Thursday Mort called in the afternoon. Ella had two bushels of apples (for $1.35) to can from Haas' Orchard in Pennsylvania. Friday Ella canned 20 quarts of applesauce.

Monday Garfield started cutting his oats and put Mort's in the barn. Thursday, August 20, Charlie Sergeant was at the Leavenworth's for supper. He was there in the evening when Mort and Jennie stopped by.

Friday Garfield got a permit and burned brush.

There were such terrible thunderstorms on Saturday and Sunday, that Ella sent to Montgomery Wards for lightning rods on Monday.

September 1936
Friday, September 4, Ella received a letter from her sister Hazel. It was Ella's birthday. Clara gave Ella a big birthday cake and $10 for her parents' 30th anniversary on Saturday, September 5. Earlier Clara had given Ella a beautiful cutwork tablecloth.

Wednesday it was time for Jim to once again start school.

Mort Austin had a knack for making the ladies at Church Bazaar days laugh. Photo in the Austin Collection.

Saturday, September 12, Ella made slip covers. Martin was there for dinner.

Thursday, September 17, Lottie Meyers gave Ella some cucumbers to make pickles.

1936–1937 Eldred School News

Howard K. Moore, the principal, had nine faculty. There were 175 students enrolled.

It was the first class for a while not to take an Easter trip to Washington D.C. or elsewhere.

Improvements: The physical education program was increased. It was the first year for achievement and intelligence tests. A room was remodeled for the newspaper office. A telephone was installed in the office. A secretary was hired for the Board and the Principal.

Several new steel filing cases were purchased. There was a new fire escape. Also green and gold fronts for the orchestra.

New courses: general science for grades seven and eight; general language, general mathematics, design I, economics, mechanical drawing 2A, and French III.

The girls wore white caps and gowns for commencement; the boys wore navy blue.

The Yearbook was named the *El Dorado*.

The boys won the Baseball League championship for the fourth consecutive time.

The dance orchestra was named the *Highland Serenaders*.

New Activities: Men's and ladies' nights in the gym. Science Club resumed as the Sir Humphrey Davy Club. Girl Scouts resumed.

Inter community men's softball teams: Barryville, Highland Lake, and Eldred.

First printed yearbook with engravings.

Lillie Calkin's mother, Emma Parmenter Austin was not feeling well in November. Photo courtesy of Katherine Calkin Traxler.

Friday Charlie Sergeant was at the Leavenworth's to practice piano.

Saturday Harry Dunlap died of heart failure. (Harry was an uncle to Harold Dunlap who owned the restaurant.)

Monday, September 21, Garfield started to work at Sand Beach. Jim and Frank Bartle went to the Leavenworth home at noon.

Harry Dunlap was buried on Tuesday. After work Charlie Sergeant stopped at Garfield's to practice. Ella made pickles.

Sunday, September 27, Clara was home for a while. Lee Hansen was there for supper for the first time. Tuesday Lee went home. ($2 was due for his board.)

October 1936

Friday, October 2, the Yankees and Giants played in the World Series. Yankees: 18, Giants: 4, in the second game.

Saturday Lee paid $4 which settled his bill. Garfield dug up potatoes.

Monday, Lee was at Garfield and Ella's for supper again.

Tuesday Mrs. Robert Greig Sr. was buried. Jim was home sick with the measles.

Anna worked at the Post Office for an hour or so, then quit working there for good.

Saturday Clara was home for the winter, so she was there when Lee Hansen had supper at the Leavenworth's on Monday and Tuesday. Tuesday Aunt Charlotte visited in the evening.

Sunday, October 18, the boys went after apples from John Dunlap. As did Garfield on Monday.

Garfield worked half days for Mort Austin on Wednesday and Thursday.

Saturday Clinton worked for the County. Jim went over to see his friend Frank Bartle.

Sunday, October 25, Garfield worked for John Dunlap. Clinton got an accordion. Tuesday through Friday Garfield worked for Mort.

The last day of October Hazel Connor and her family were in Highland Lake for the weekend. Ella went with them to see their stepmother Anna Sergeant.

November 1936

The Connor family went home on Sunday, November 1, the day Hazel turned 40. Clara went home with them for a week or so. Clinton and Jim went to Highland Lake and to Myers'.

Tuesday was election day and Franklin Delano Roosevelt was elected by a large majority.

Wednesday Anna canned the rest of the beef. Garfield made some cigars. (He grew tobacco.)

In Bethel Lillie wrote her father. The Austins (and the Leavenworths) had strong political views and the siblings were often divided as to if the Democrats or Republicans were the best choice.

We learn from Lillie's letter that Phoebe Owen died, that she had been very sick.

Lillie Calkin, Bethel, to Mr. J.E. Austin, Ossining, N.Y.
November 4, 1936
Dear Dad,

Well election's over. What a landslide! The people of the United States have certainly taken their stand on the New Deal, and now we of the minority can only take our medicine as gracefully as may be and hope that the majority are right. Perhaps things will turn out better than we expect.

Dorothy cast her first vote. I don't know about Dale, but the rest of us all voted a straight Republican ticket. That is the first time I ever voted a straight ticket, but as Al said, it seemed to be the only thing to do.

However, I'm not conceited enough to think my judgment is infallible, so I'll just hope everything will turn out all right. Can't do anything about it anyway, and the majority rules.

Mother hasn't been well. She had a bad attack of, I guess it was neuralgia. It settled in first one place and then another. It kept me pretty busy. She couldn't help herself much. I had to dress her. She is all right again now.

Murder, Inc.

Murder Incorporated (Murder, Inc.) was one of the names for the Brownsville Boys, an organized crime group in the 1930s–1940s that acted as the "enforcement arm" of the Jewish Mafia and later American Mafia in New York. Originally headed by Louis "Lepke" Buchalter, and later by Albert "The Mad Hatter" Anastasia, Murder, Inc. was responsible for between 400 and 1,000 contract killings, until the group was exposed in the early 1940s by informer and group member Abe "Kid Twist" Reles. In the trials that followed, many members were convicted and executed, and Abe Reles himself died after mysteriously falling out of a window. Thomas E. Dewey first came to prominence as a prosecutor of Murder, Inc. and other organized crime cases.—*wikipedia.org*.

Jay Lass—a deputy sheriff under Sheriff Harry Borden—was active in the arrest of various people who were involved in Murder, Inc. in 1936. Jay was married to Tillie Flynn, and they owned the last house on the right on Corkscrew Road. Later they lived in Middletown where John Conway, the Sullivan County Historian, met them when he was growing up.

It was just after 6 a.m. on a quiet Saturday in September 1936 and Dave Margolin, a young milkman from Hurleyville, was making deliveries.

As Margolin neared the main gate of one of his first stops, the secluded Paramount Manor Hotel just outside Loch Sheldrake, he came upon a stopped car blocking the long driveway. The driver's door was open.

He left his truck and approached the car. He noted it was a taxi, a dark-colored Lincoln sedan, New York license plate number 034-657. And then he saw something that would remain etched in his memory. A man lay face up in the driveway, his feet resting on the car's running board. Beneath his head, a dark pool of blood slowly soaked into the gravel.

Directly overhead, the hotel's sign spanned the driveway. It read, "Paramount Manor: Hotel of Happiness."

Margolin sprinted to the hotel and called Town of Fallsburg Constable William Kollander, who contacted state police Sgt. Thomas Mangan and Sullivan County Sheriff Harry Borden. Before long, half a dozen law enforcement officials had converged on the hotel.

The investigation begins

Troopers Joseph Miller and Richard Klausman and Deputy Sheriff Jay Lass cordoned off the crime scene while Mangan and Sullivan County Coroner Dr. Ralph S. Breakey examined the victim. He was quickly identified as 34-year-old Irving Ashkenas, a self-employed taxi driver who split his time between Brooklyn and Loch Sheldrake.

Police later learned that Ashkenas was an ex-con, convicted of manslaughter in connection with the death of Jacob Rothenberg in a 1930 garment strike riot and sentenced to 15 years in Sing Sing. He was on parole at the time of his death.

Breakey initially found five bullet wounds in the body. Four bullets, he determined, had been fired from

Jay Lass was a Sullivan County Deputy Sheriff. In this photo he is awaiting the uncovering of the grave of gangster Charles "Chink" Sherman in a barn in Hurleyville Sullivan County, in November of 1935. Photo courtesy of John Conway, Sullivan County Historian.

outside the car and one by someone alongside the driver in the front seat. All five shots had struck Ashkenas in the head or chest.—Excerpt from, John Conway, Murder, Inc. *or* The Milkman and Murder, Inc., *Times-Herald Record, September 26, 2003.*

Phoebe Middaugh Owen died about two weeks ago, cancer in the abdominal cavity and dropsy.

Burt parted with an abscessed tooth last Saturday. He has more work just now than he can handle, and help is hard to get and not worth much after you get it. He is building a barn for Henry Hadden whose barn burned in the middle of the day. Cause unknown. Burt has three other jobs on hand.

It has rained all day, but is not very cold. Burt is up to Dale's today. I've got to stop and do some school work. I'll see you some day this fall, if I can get away. I hope you all keep well. Regards to the ladies.

With love, Lillie

John Briggs often visited the Leavenworths with his father Irwin. Photo courtesy of Mary Briggs Austin.

Thursday, November 5, Garfield worked for Mort.

Saturday Jim went with Herbert Middaugh to Honesdale. Garfield worked for Mort some more.

Monday, November 9, Garfield, Anna, and Ella dressed and canned 17 chickens. Jennie Austin called in the afternoon.

Tuesday Ella baked pies and doughnuts.

Saturday, November 14, Hazel and her family drove Clara home.

Sunday the Connor family visited Anna Sergeant and her sister Jennie, then started for home. The old Wormuth house burned down at nine p.m.

Saturday Clinton went to a raffle and won a goose and a live little pig. On Sunday they took a pig pen up to the top of the hill at Garfield's.

Monday, November 23, Jim went to the high school play.

Wednesday, Garfield started working for Dr. George Mills.

Thursday John and Katherine Dunlap ate dinner with the Leavenworths.

Saturday Lee Hansen paid his board for the week.

Sunday Ed Toaspern was at the Leavenworths for the afternoon and evening.

After school on Monday (the last day of November), Jim went over to Frank Bartle's home.

December 1936

Wednesday, December 2, Mr. Briggs called on Garfield and Ella.

Thursday one ton of hay came; cost was $22.

Friday Lee Hansen finished working for the County and went home.

Tuesday, December 8, the Leavenworth children went to the Austin's in the evening.

Wednesday Bill and Garfield butchered a hog for Mort.

Bessie Hill told the story about Mort curing a ham. He built the fire and strung the ham over it. The only problem was that to hold up the ham, he used strong string or a rope and the fire burned the rope and the ham fell into the fire.

He said he cured the ham and roasted it beside and Jennie was not happy! "Takes a lot to please some people," he said.

Bessie Hill also "complained" that she never got the sweet potato pie that Jennie Austin had promised to make for her. She inferred that when Jennie set the pie on the window ledge to cool, her boys ate the pie.—Mary Briggs Austin.

Saturday Garfield worked for Dr. George Mills.

Jennie was at Ella's the afternoon of Friday, December 18.

Saturday Clinton helped Atwell Bradley saw wood.

Christmas Eve day, Clinton drove Bill Austin to Port Jervis to get Bill's tooth out.

Christmas was a clear, warm day. All the Leavenworths were

Irwin Briggs often visited at Garfield and Ella Leavenworth's home. Photo courtesy of Mary Briggs Austin.

home. Bill Meyers Jr. was down for supper and the evening. Charlie Sergeant called. "We had a very happy Christmas," Ella penned in her diary that night.

Saturday, December 26, Garfield worked for Dr. George Mills. The boys set traps. Bill and Anna went to the pictures in the evening. Wednesday Clinton caught a 26-inch mink.

As we read earlier in this chapter, Mort Austin seemed to be sick often. Mort was 71 at the start of 1937. He continued to be in poor health. Fortunately the Austins lived close to Jennie's brother Garfield who often helped out along with doing his own work and farming.

Garfield and Ella's family was growing. By 1939 they would have two sons-in-law, one daughter-in-law, and two grandsons. Garfield would be kept busy keeping everyones house in good repair.

Chapter 8
Prosperity Dampened
Life in Eldred, 1937–1939

After three years at the post office, I started to work in the office of the Sullivan County Highway Department. This marked the beginning of a more profitable era. In partnership with two of my brothers, I bought a car. The enjoyment of my prosperity was soon dampened by my father's death.—Arthur Austin.

Arthur Austin ready for work at the Sullivan County Highway Department. Photo in the Austin Collection.

Arthur Austin started work as a secretary in charge of checks and letters at the Sullivan County Highway Department, at least by 1937. He would work there for eleven years, counting the four years he served in World War II.

Art's brothers worked for the County Highway Department also. Bill worked on the road with pick and axe. Bob was a surveyor.

Art boarded or would board with Alfred and Bessie Hill whose home (on the east side of Eldred) was near where Highland Lake and Proctor Roads intersected.

The Austin brothers' cousins: Clara, Clinton, Anna, and Jim Leavenworth; and later Charlee Hirsch, lived on the west side of Eldred.

The Leavenworths, January 1937
Saturday, January 2, Ella bought six chairs from Rasmussen's for $10.50. (Rasmussen had a funeral home and a furniture store in Narrowsburg.)

Wednesday Clinton helped John Dunlap cut wood. Garfield worked for Dr. George Mills.

Thursday everyone was home. The men didn't work and there was no school due to an ice storm. Ella worked on her crazy quilt. Oliver Dunlap must have slid over that day when he visited Clinton.

Thursday, January 14, it rained part of the day, and night crawlers were out by the hundreds. Clinton drove his cousin Bill Austin to Monticello.

Friday afternoon Jennie Austin visited Ella. Clara and Ella were sewing quilts.

Saturday Clinton cut wood for his grandmother Anna Sergeant in Highland Lake. Garfield worked for George Mills again.

Sunday, January 17, Jim set traps. The following Saturday, he and Clinton got their fur money, $26.25.

Tuesday, January 26, Jennie called. Garfield worked eight hours for Dr. Mills.

February 1937
Monday, February 1, Anna visited the Meyers. Friday the Austins spent the evening at Garfield and Ella's. They stopped by a couple more times during the month. Ella finished piecing Clara's log

cabin quilt in February.

Garfield did a job for Emile Four one day. He repaired a guitar for Mr. Briggs (Irwin and Johnny stopped by to get it), and worked on a violin for Alexander Mills (a brother of Dr. George Mills).

Alex and George's grandfather had built the original Mills boarding house which Elizabeth Mills (their mother) still managed. Alex's wife Minnie was a daughter of Chris and Meta Meyer and had grown up in the Spring House in Barryville.

March 1937
Sunday, March 7, Alexander's wife Minnie called with their youngest daughter.

Monday Garfield went to Austin's for a while. Bob Austin visited Garfield Tuesday evening.

Thursday Alexander Mills picked up his violin. Friday Oliver Dunlap helped the men cut wood. Jim, of course, was at school. Clara, Anna, and Ella cleaned.

It snowed Saturday, but turned out to be nice enough for Jim to play baseball. Clinton cut wood for Oliver Dunlap. Selma Dunlap (wife of Oliver's cousin Charles) visited the Leavenworths for the afternoon. It was movie night for Anna and Bill.

Sunday, March 14, it started to snow about noon. The Kelley's house burned. Luella Kelley had passed away, but her son Everett lived there. His sister Raola and her husband Frank Daiber drove over to the Leavenworth's when they heard about the fire. Everett, Raola, and Frank stayed the night at Garfield and Ella's.

Monday it snowed about eight inches. Tuesday there was high wind and drifting snow, which continued into Wednesday. Raola, Frank, and Everett were still at the Leavenworths as they couldn't get home. Jim, though, was able to get to school.

Wednesday Everett sold a load of metal and iron that he had collected. Thursday it snowed again. Everett sorted his metal and iron collection.

Friday Clinton bought the Kelley place and property (seven acres) by Beaver Swamp from Everett and Raola for $300; and paid the taxes. Raola and Frank went home.

Clinton with the help of his family would build his home on the foundation of the former Kelley home. And in almost ten years, my parents would rent that home and my great-uncle Lon Austin would live with them.

The men worked at Kelley's on Saturday when it rained hard. Monday they were at Clinton's place again. Since Everett needed

Mr. Briggs and his son John were in to get the guitar Garfield repaired. Photo courtesy of Mary Briggs Austin.

a place to live after the fire, they also fixed up a hunter cabin on the property for Everett.

Wednesday and the following Sunday Garfield continued renovating Everett's cabin. On Monday, March 29, Everett moved into his new home. That evening Garfield worked at Ed Bosch's.

Tuesday the men helped Everett get settled in his place. Clara went to her aunt Lizzie Wilson's, perhaps to help her out with boarders. School teachers often boarded there. Anna went to a shower for Raymond Meyer, cousin of Bill Meyers Jr. Ed Toaspern spent the day at the Leavenworth home.

April 1937
Wednesday, the last day of March and Thursday, April 1, Garfield and Clinton worked at Ed Bosch's. Jim went to Toaspern's.

Saturday Garfield and Clinton continued construction work on Clinton's place. Jim caught seven trout. The Wolffs visited Garfield and Ella in the evening.

Lowell Thomas

Lowell Thomas became a broadcaster with the CBS radio network, in 1930. He delivered a nightly news and commentary program for two years. He switched to the NBC radio network but returned to CBS in 1947.

Mr. Thomas was not an employee of either NBC or CBS News. Before 1947 Lowell was employed by the broadcast's sponsor, Sunoco.

When he returned to CBS, Mr. Thomas established an independent company to produce the broadcast which he sold to CBS.

Mr. Thomas hosted the first-ever television-news broadcast in 1930 and the first regularly scheduled television news broadcast, which began February 21, 1940, on NBC.
—wikipedia.org.

Eldred Union Alumni in 1937

Class of 1929
Fred Fracke was an assistant superintendent of an apartment in New York.

Mary Kerr was married to Louis Eckhart, and had a Beauty Shop in Barryville. Klelah Kirby was a Post Office Assistant in Yulan.

Richard Palmer worked in the Office of the County Highway Department, Barryville.

Roger Sheen was a Station agent at Shohola. Donald Walter was a printer at Yulan. Marie Roberts was a teacher at Minisink Ford.

Forrest Wilson attended Law School in New York City.

Class of 1930
Arthur Austin worked at the Office of the County Highway Department, Barryville.

Class of 1931
Herman Fracke worked in a dye plant in Philadelphia. John Holbrook was at home in Cornwall, New York. Josephine Holbrook was Mrs. Russell Hulse, and lived in Cornwall, N.Y.

Gertrude Peirano was Mrs. Phillips and lived in Fosterdale.

Lillian Seitz was a nurse in a New York Hospital. Charles Sergeant worked at Love's sawmill in Eldred. Kenneth Sheen worked for a music company. Reginald Walter worked at Hillside, New York.

Class of 1932
Anna Leavenworth was at home in Eldred. Blanche Parker was a nurse in a hospital at Orangeburg, New Jersey. Roger Quick worked for the County.

Arthur Staubes worked at home in Highland Lake. Harry Sulzbach worked at Love's sawmill in Eldred.

Veronica Thiesen worked in New York City. Doris Vogt was a senior at Stroudsburg, S.T.C., Pennsylvania. William Warden worked with county surveyors.

Class of 1933
Robert Austin and Carl Vonderhorst worked with county surveyors. Clifford Crandall was the assistant manager of the A&P in Eldred.

Ernest Owen attended Buffalo State Teachers College. Marie Wait was a student at Hackensack New Jersey Business School.

Archie Warden worked in the statistical department of Luckenback Steamship Lines. John Zurowsky worked in New York City.

Class of 1934
Leslie Dunlap was an assistant manager of the A&P in Ellenville. Mildred Hill was Mrs. Lynn Myers and lived in Eldred.

Adolph Kalin worked in New York City.

Norman Myers and Warren Parker were at Fort Monmouth, Oceanport, New Jersey.

Mary Stanton was in Scarsdale, New York. Lucille Wait was a Junior at Oneonta Normal School.

Caroline Weber was a clerk in a real estate office in New Rochelle, New York.

Class of 1935
Blanche Bodin was at home in Yulan. Paul Bodin was a steward on the *Christobal* which sailed between New York and Panama.

Joe Clouse was at home in Barryville. Gordon Comstock was the Manager of the Amoco Gas Station in Barryville.

Annabelle Kalin worked in Sparrowbush. Lena Myers worked in Ridgewood, New Jersey.

Mary Myers was the secretary at Eldred High School. Eleanor Quick was at home in Barryville.

Rowland Ramsey and Walter Toaspern did post graduate at Eldred High School. Gwen Rohman was a sophomore at Bucknell University. Lillian Stanton worked at Kew Gardens, Long Island.

Clifford Sulzbach worked in New York City. Raymond Weber worked in a bank in New York City.

Troward Wells was a freshman at Lehigh University. Eleanor Williams was a Post Office assistant in Eldred.

Class of 1936
Betty Boyd was a student at Wyoming Seminary, Kingston, Pennsylvania.

Raymond Clouse was at home in Barryville. Helen Guenther was Mrs. J. Lieffert and lived in Yulan.

David Holden worked at the Offices of the American South-African Steamship Lines, New York City.

Jack Kerr, Ian Warden, and John Purcell took post graduate classes at Eldred High School.

Clareta Kuen was at home in Shohola, Pennsylvania. Carol McCann was a hat check girl at Savoy Plaza, New York City.

Alvin Perkins had a trucking business in Monticello, New York.

Louis Wagemann was at home in Barryville. Samuel White worked at home in Glen Spey.—*1937 Eldred Yearbook.*

Tuesday, April 13, Clara left to work for P. Hawker. Garfield completed the project for Ed Bosch on Thursday. Lee Hansen was at the Leavenworth's for supper. Friday afternoon Jennie Austin visited Ella. Carl Wolff was there in the evening.

Tuesday, April 20, Garfield had another job for George Mills. Clara was still at the Hawker's.

Selma Dunlap visited Ella the following Tuesday afternoon.

Jim played baseball quite a bit in the spring and summer of 1937. He was on the school baseball team and had practice Wednesday and Thursday after school.

May 1937
It was time to get ready for the

1937 baseball team. Front row: Bill Kinne, Jim Purcell (2nd base). Seated: Everett Frey (1st base), Thorne Sheen (outfielder), Ed Purcell (shortstop), Mike Aumick (2nd base), Captain Joe Foscola (outfield), Frank Hill (2nd base). Kneeling: John Vogt (catcher), Walter Campbell (outfield). Standing: Jim Leavenworth (pitcher), Jack Kerr (pitcher), Coach Titus, Millard Kinne (3rd base), Clifford Hulse (outfield and pitcher).

summer boarders. Wednesday, May 5, Anna went to Hazen's to clean house. Clara was still at Hawker's in Shohola.

Tuesday afternoon Jennie called on Ella. Wednesday Lee paid Ella his board money.

Thursday Ella was sick. Jennie Austin spent all Friday with her. Lee went home Saturday night and returned Sunday evening.

Sunday, Garfield "burned out" their chimney to clean it.

Monday Jim practiced baseball after school. He was playing ball when his aunt Jennie visited his mom in the afternoon.

Thursday Clara was home from the Hawker's.

Sunday, May 16, Clara and Lee went to the pictures for the first time. Anna worked at Hazen's. Clinton worked on his place.

Monday Orville Myers asked if Clara would work. (Most likely his wife Leversa "Lee" could use help with housework, as their daughter Patsy was six months old.) Jim had baseball practice.

Friday Clara took some flower bulbs to Selma Dunlap.

"Lost our cow. She broke her leg," wrote Ella on Saturday.

Friday, May 28, Clara worked at Hazen's. Later she and Lee went to the pictures again.

Saturday Anna and Bill went to the pictures. Clara worked at Hazen's. Lee went home to the city and returned Monday night.

June 1937

Wednesday, June 2, Lee and Clara went to the pictures.

Mort Austin was very sick again on Thursday. Garfield got four loads of hard wood from John Love.

Mort Austin Dies

Friday morning, June 4, my grandfather Mort Austin, 72, died about ten o'clock. Dr. Gutfruend recorded that Mort died of pneumonia.

Father was a God-fearing man; faithful to the church and Sunday School. His death brought forcefully to my mind the great comfort he had received from his God.

It influenced my life greatly because I realized that when death claims a loved one, the fact that he has lived close to God means more than all his worldly achievements.—Arthur Austin.

Saturday, June 5, Garfield and Ella went to the Austin home to comfort Jennie and her sons.

Sunday Anna Leavenworth (Garfield and Jennie Austin's sister) had dinner at Garfield's home.

Monday the funeral for my grandfather Mort Austin, was conducted by my maternal grandfather, Irwin Briggs.

Wednesday Jim went over to Frank Bartle's after school.

Tuesday, June 15, Jim started taking exams. Mr. Briggs called in the afternoon, perhaps to ask Garfield about playing at church, as Wednesday Garfield went to church to practice.

Back of the school in winter 1937. Photo courtesy of Christene Stevens Myers.

After a half day of classes on Friday, Jim was done with school until fall.

Sunday morning, June 20, Clinton started to work on his cellar. In the evening Garfield went to the practice at church.

It was the start of berry season which went through August. Saturday Lee and Jim picked six quarts of wild strawberries. Jennie visited Ella in the evening.

Anna worked at Hazen's for Clara on Sunday, June 27. Lee and Clara went to New York City for the day, perhaps for Clara to meet Lee's folks. They arrived back home about 9:20 p.m.

Monday Clinton and Jim worked on Clinton's cellar. Kate Love and Charlotte Leavenworth stopped by to say hello to Ella.

Tuesday Jim picked cherries at Hazen's. Wednesday Ella canned eight quarts of cherries and three jars of jam. Charlotte called. Bill and Anna went to the movies. Clara and Lee went out.

July 1937
Thursday, July 8, Anna and Jim picked berries at the old Leavenworth Echo Hill Farm.

Friday the tin roofing for Clinton's barn arrived. Garfield and Mr. Moore put the roofing on the following Tuesday.

Wednesday, July 14, Arthur Austin drove his cousin Anna to Hazen's to see Clara. The men continued to work on Clinton's house.

Thursday Jennie was at Ella's for the afternoon.

Saturday Ella bought a crate of raspberries from Wilson's for $6.40.

Sunday, July 18, Clinton and Ed Hill went fishing. Lee and Clara went to the movies.

Monday morning Lee left for New York City.

Grandpa Charles Mortimer Austin

Grandpa Austin was really esteemed by many people who told me over the years what a "good man" he was.

My grandpa Edwin Myers told me, with tears in his eyes, "I don't think that I could stand to see Mort dead. It would just be better if I didn't go to the funeral. I've never known a person that I respected more."

I remember a very gentle, quiet spoken man with a kind, comfortable smile and very blue eyes. I remember seeing fondness in his eyes and smile.

Although I couldn't have realized it then, I was receiving a "grandpa" smile that was just for me! As I am sure he would love to have turned on other grandchildren.

In the summer Grandpa brought vegetables from the garden to the house in some kind of baskets on each side on his farm horse. When the baskets were unloaded, Grandpa would spread a blanket on the horse for me to sit on and held on to me for a ride around the yard. Heaven!

Even when there was no produce to bring in, he would occasionally come to give me a ride. I have a snapshot in my mind of Grandpa, in his straw hat, leading the horse past a dining room window where I would watch for him; then run through the kitchen to go out for my ride.

Grandpa was another hard worker. It seems to me that he often went back out after supper. He sat with Uncle Bill, Uncle Bob, and Uncle Art to listen to the news with Lowell Thomas. The name of the sponsor fascinated me, "New Blue Sonoco," as did Lowell Thomas' voice. I'm not sure how much I really gleaned from the news, but I often sat on Grandpa's lap to listen.

I remember Grandpa reading the newspaper and some books, though I don't know what they were. This was probably evenings or "off season" for gardening and boarders and Sunday afternoons.

I don't think that I ever saw Grandpa in any but work clothes except

Mort Austin in his work clothes. Photo in the Austin Collection.

on Sunday for church. It seems that they never missed worship on Sunday and they didn't seem so busy as other days.

During the summer season they had to do meals for boarders and I'm sure there were necessary farm chores. I think that I remember Grandpa staying on at the church for a bit after services, but Grandma started right home. This made an impression because I would have liked to stay a while, too. But Grandma said we had to go right away. It may have been Grandpa's time to socialize and I think he was on a church board.

When the preacher Irwin Briggs went home later than usual, he said it was because he "thought those Austin boys were going to come to blows over politics."

"The Austin boys," meaning Grandpa Mort and Uncle Lon. Two milder men never existed. Seems that there was a side to them that I never saw.—Melva Austin Barney.

The Briggs pick blueberries. Third from left: Mary Briggs, Mr. Deats, Myrtle Briggs, Laura Briggs. Sitting down: Mildred and Johnny Briggs.

Eleanor Myers graduated in 1937. Photo courtesy of Timothy C. Rizzuto.

Once again it was time to preserve the summer produce. Tuesday July 27, Ella canned nine quarts of string beans.

Friday Anna, Jim, and Ella picked 21 quarts of blueberries, and canned 18 quarts. Saturday, the last day of July, Ella canned ten quarts of beans. Garfield helped cut hay on Clinton's place.

August 1937
Sunday, August 1, Kelley's barn was about full when the men finished haying.

Thursday Ella sent for kitchen ware for Anna. There would soon be a wedding.

Friday Jim went to town for 100# of sugar and two bushels of potatoes from Randolph's. Garfield finished his work at Mills'.

Tuesday, August 10, Ella canned 15 quarts of blackberries from John Dunlap. Martin Leavenworth was there for a visit.

Friday Jennie, Arthur, and Melva (Raymond and Gladys Austin's daughter) were at the Leavenworths for the evening. Daibers also called.

Wednesday, August 18, Anna and Ella canned 18 quarts of corn, made dill and treasure cucumbers, and also did some baking.

Thursday evening Jennie visited Garfield and Ella again.

Friday, August 27, Christina and Charlee Hirsch were down for dinner. Jennie Austin was at her sister Charlotte's when Ella stopped by for the evening.

Saturday Garfield gave music lessons to the Wolff boys. In the evening Christina and her family visited.

Monday and Tuesday Ella canned four bushels of peaches.

The Hirsch family—Anthony,

Wednesday Arthur Austin drove his cousin Anna to Hazen's. Photo in Austin Collection.

Mildred and Laura Briggs, 1937 graduates. Photo courtesy of Mary Briggs Austin.

Elsie Vonderhorst graduated in 1937. Photo courtesy of Timothy C. Rizzuto.

1937 World, National, and Local News

1937 World and National News
- Walt Disney's original, *Snow White and the Seven Dwarfs.*
- J.R.R. Tolkien's, *The Hobbit.*
- John Steinbeck's, *Of Mice and Men.*
- The 1937 World's Fair, Paris, France.
- The German dirigible airship Hindenburg exploded in the sky above Lakehurst, N.J., May 6. Fire consumed the 804-foot long ship within one minute; 36 people died.
- The Golden Gate Bridge opened to pedestrian and vehicle traffic.

May 1937
- King George VI of England crowned. Neville Chamberlain British prime minister.

June 1937
- Stalin's purges included some 35,000 officers from Red Army arrested, tortured, executed, or banished to Siberia.

July 1937
- Start of second Japan offensive against China. Prince Fujimaro Konoye announced that Japan had taken the first step towards a new order in Asia.

November 1937
- Hitler outlined his policy of gaining *Lebensraum* or Living space in Eastern Europe.

December 1937
- Japanese planes sank the Yangtze River gunboat *U.S.S. Panay*; two crew killed, 43 wounded. Japan apologized to the U.S. for its "unfortunate error." Japanese soldiers killed as many as 200,000 in the Chinese city of Nanking.

1937 Halfway Brook News

1937 Eldred Seniors
- Lester Aumick, Janith Boyd, Lulu Boyer, Cecilia Brennan, Laura Briggs, Mildred Briggs, Rita Cantwell, Stella Clark, Everett Frey, Ella Getz, Viola Guenther, Wallace MacKechnie, Helen Michell, Eleanor Myers, Virginia Scott, John Vogt, Elsie Vonderhorst.

1937 Moved
- The Hirsch family: Anthony Sr., Christine, Charlee, and Anthony Jr., moved to live near Cincinnati. Anthony Sr. was a bakery supply salesman and that was his territory.

1937 Births
- Kay Bosch born to Edward and Eleanor Schroeder Bosch.
- Edwin Mortimer born to Raymond and Gladys Austin December 10.
- Neal Burt Calkin born to Dale and Nellie Hill Calkin.
- William Owen born to Russell and Ina Owen.

1937 Marriages
- James Joseph Clark married Hope Tinn. James J. Clark was a son of George James and Mary Higgins Clark. The Clarks were descendants of George and Harriet Covert Clark.
- Rev. Briggs married Carl and Eleanor Vonderhorst at the Barryville Methodist Church.
- Anna Louise Leavenworth married William Meyers Jr.
- Clara Elizabeth Leavenworth married Martin Lee Hansen.
- Charlie Sergeant married Clareta Kuen.
- Elizabeth Watson, daughter of Leonard and Daisy Watson, married Maxwell Hart. (Leonard was an Eldred descendant.)

1937 Deaths
- Mary Fee Myers, wife of Martin D. Myers Sr., died in November.
- Alice Amelia Sergeant Hill, daughter of Alvah and Phebe Sergeant, died.
- Eliza Post Eldred, 1860–1937.
- Mort Austin, 1865–1937.
- Claude J. Angell, 1896–1937. Claude was a WWI veteran.

Ina Owen, wife of Russell Owen, with sons Barry (born 1931) and William (born 1937). Photo courtesy of Pam Fischetti DeFeo.

James Joseph Clark and Hope Tinn. Photo courtesy of James C. Clark.

- Margaret Emma Crawford Beufve, 1858–1937.
- Mrs. Harriet H. Rixton, 1873–1937, was the widow of Henry G. Rixton, and daughter of John C. and Matilda Wilson Metzger. Surviving relatives: daughter Mildred Consiglio; siblings Mrs. Henry Wolfe, and John and Fred Metzger; and grandson, Donald Consiglio. The funeral service was conducted by Rev. H.I. Briggs at the Barryville Methodist Church.

"Mr. Briggs and Alex Mills visited the Leavenworths." The Briggs Family: Irwin, Laura, Mildred, John, Myrtle, and Mary. Photo courtesy of Mary Briggs Austin.

Christina, and Charlee—may have left for Ohio, shortly after their Friday visit.

Around 1937 the Hirsch family moved to Ohio and lived near Cincinnati. Opa Anthony was a bakery supply salesman, and that's where his territory was. —Matt Schroedel.

September 1937
Wednesday, September 1, Ella canned eight quarts of sweet pickled apples. Unfortunately for him, Garfield had poison ivy.

Thursday Anna and Ella canned a few sweet apples and made peach jelly. Garfield visited Chester Middaugh.

Friday evening Anna and Bill went out. Clara and Lee stayed in. And Millard Hulse stopped by.

Bill and Anna Meyers' bungalow. Photo courtesy of Cynthia Leavenworth Bellinger.

Sunday afternoon, September 5, Roy Horton and Bill McBride stopped by the Leavenworth's.

Monday Garfield and Lee rode to Callicoon Center. Clinton and Jim worked on Clinton's place. Later Lee and Jim went to see a plane at the lake.

Wednesday Jim started back to school. Ella got some quilting frames and canned 28 quarts of beans. Thursday Garfield had his eyes tested.

Saturday Ella finished Anna's wedding quilt. Anna and Bill bought the ring and picked up the marriage license.

Monday, September 13, Garfield got his specs. Anna canned crab apples. Ella started Anna's second quilt.

Tuesday Garfield went to see his sister Jennie.

Saturday, September 18, Anna Leavenworth married William Meyers Jr. Anna's sister Clara and brother Clint stood up with them.

Anna and Bill were back at her parents' home on Sunday. They stayed there a couple nights until their bungalow on Airport Road was ready.

Tuesday Dorothy Wolff (Bill's sister) helped Anna clean and get set up in their new home. Jim was up to Anna's most of Wednesday.

Thursday Mr. Briggs and Alex Mills visited Garfield and Ella.

Sunday, Charlie Sergeant and Clareta Kuen were married in the Congregational Church.

Wednesday Anna, Ella, and Clara tied another quilt. Clara worked at Hazen's. Selma Dunlap visited Ella Thursday and Friday.

October 1937
Friday, October 1, Anna and Bill had supper with her parents.

Sunday evening Lee took Clara out. Bill and Anna called.

Thursday Anna cleaned Ella's upstairs for the Connor relatives to stay. Walter, Hazel, Marjorie and Marion Connor arrived on Saturday and left on Sunday.

Monday Garfield went down to the Austin's for a few minutes.

Mr. Briggs and Johnny called on Wednesday. Jim was home as it was Columbus Day. Clinton worked and went up to see Anna and Bill in the evening.

Saturday Claude Angell died. Jennie Austin was at Ella's for the day. In the evening the Wolffs were in for their lessons.

Wednesday, October 27, Jim went to school for a half day. Anna went to Claude Angell's funeral.

Thursday Jennie and her sister Charlotte went to the city. Jim was home Friday as there was a teachers' convention.

November 1937
Wednesday, November 3, Ed Toaspern spent the day with the Leavenworths. Garfield spent the evening with his brother Truman.

In November, Jennie Austin visited Raymond, Gladys, Melva, Joan, and Margie in Staten Island.

I remember Grandma's two-

week visit to our home at 6800 Hendrick Avenue in Staten Island when I was young.

Grandma taught me two songs: "You scream, I scream, we all scream for ice cream" (Grandma explained the play on words); and "Ha, ha, ha, happy are we, Anderson and Peterson and Peterson and me," which repeated.—Joan Austin Geier.

Mary Fee Myers Dies
Mary Fee Myers, 46, wife of Martin D. Myers Sr. died in November. Such a sad time for Martin Sr. and his children (ages 12–20): Mary, Martin Jr., Helen, and Tommy. Martin Myers Sr. was a first cousin to Jennie Austin and her Leavenworth siblings.

At the time of his mother's death, Martin Jr. worked at the Royal Scarlet. He used the money to help buy groceries.

December 1937
At the end of December Clara Leavenworth would marry Lee Hansen. Wednesday, December 1, Clara's dishes arrived.

Thursday Bill, Anna, and Jim went to Monticello to the pictures.

Jennie Austin was back from her visit with Raymond. She visited with Ella Friday afternoon.

December 11, 1937, Edwin Mortimer Austin was born to Raymond and Gladys Myers Austin. Edwin was named for his grandfathers—Edwin Myers and Mortimer Austin.

Tuesday, December 14, Mr. and Mrs. Briggs called. Ella sent a Christmas box to her sister Hazel. Jim went to school.

Saturday Clara and Lee picked up their marriage license. Lee bought a Ford.

Tuesday, December 21, Jennie Austin helped to tie a quilt for the Briggs. Anna and Bill ate supper at

Jennie Austin visited her grandchildren: Joan, Margie, and Melva Austin, in November 1937. Photo in Austin Collection.

her parents'. Anna was over again on Wednesday.

Thursday Ella went down to Jennie's for the evening.

Uncle Johnnie Von Blascom was very sick. Uncle John was not a relative, but a gentleman who boarded at Lottie Meyers' place. "Uncle John" became very close friends with the family and ended up staying with the Meyers who cared for him.

"All children home for dinner. Very nice Christmas for all," Ella wrote after her enjoyable Christmas Day.

Sunday, December 26, Clara and Lee were married. Garfield and Ella gave Clara and Anna a dinner together. Lee and Clara left for the city about two o'clock for a two-day honeymoon.

It's been some time since we have heard from Aida or Lon Austin. Lon updated his brother Ell in his end-of-December letter.

Lon Austin, Eldred, to Mr. J.E. Austin, Ossining, N.Y.
December 26, 1937
Dear Brother,

I am stopping with Mr. Carner for a while and I forgot your address. Consequently my Christmas Greeting is a little late, but they say better late than never. Mr. Carner fell and hurt himself, not badly.

The weather is fine. Aida and I are well, that is as well as can be expected for one of our tender years.

The M.E. Church had their Xmas Tree Program Thursday night; had a large attendance and a general good time.

Hope you are well. I wish you a Happy New Year. With love, Lon

Ell Austin had apparently sent his nephew Raymond a Christmas card.

Raymond Austin, Staten Island, to Mr. J.E. Austin, Ossining, N.Y.
December 29, 1937
Dear Uncle Ell,

We received your Christmas card, and were glad that you did not forget us, even though we did not get our cards out this year.

An addition to the family,

Edwin Mortimer by name, on December 11, disorganized our Christmas correspondence so that we gave up the idea of sending cards and are acknowledging those we received, with personal letters.

Gladys and the baby are getting along splendidly. He weighed 8 pounds and 6 ounces at birth and has gained 6 ounces.

The other children are very well, so, in spite of a little confusion, we came through Christmas in pretty good shape.

My father-in-law [Ed Myers] is spending a few weeks with us. Outside of being quite deaf, he is fairly well this winter, better than he has been the past four or five Winters. He gets around without any trouble and his only complaint is that he can't find enough to do down here.

He has been talking over old times around Eldred and it is quite interesting to listen to him. Last winter his memory seemed to be failing him and he often forgot half of what he wanted to tell. However, he has brightened up and now he is troubled very little by forgetfulness.

Ever since visiting you last summer, I have been going to write you a letter, but following our family tradition in letter writing, didn't get around to do it.

Mother spent about a week with us in November and Arthur was here one Sunday.

What do you think of the far eastern situation? It looks to me as though Japan intends to get us out of China if she can.

The children were a little disappointed not having a white Christmas, but that doesn't disappoint the grown ups much. The snow here doesn't stay white very long. The soot and smoke soon settles on it and turns it black, which is not very agreeable to look at.

I'll begin to work around to a close. Mr. Myers wants to be remembered to you.

Tell the ladies that I wish them a very happy new year and that I haven't forgotten their kind hospitality.

Gladys and the children send their love and best wishes for a happy New Year and I remain,
Affectionately your nephew,
Raymond Austin

1938
Jennie Austin, The Pines, Eldred, to Gladys Austin, Staten Island
Tuesday Eve. January 3, 1938
Dear Gladys,

I surely was glad to hear of Edwin Mortimer and that you are all well. I wonder if Jake [Raymond Myers' wife] brought Marjorie back yet? I understood she expected to last Sunday.

Am glad the children liked their things. When you was in the hospital, did Melva get the box of

Photo of adorable Margie Austin, daughter of Raymond and Gladys Austin, courtesy of Andy and Margie Austin Maglione.

cookies and an apron I sent her? If not it was insured and we might as well look after it.

Clara [Raymond's cousin] was married a week ago Sunday. Her husband seems very nice and he has some very nice people. They all came to pay their respects to Clara before the wedding. And they went to see his father and mother in Brooklyn after they were married.

I still have your Christmas present. You will get it before next Christmas.

The boys are still working, but Bob has been home for a few days. I wonder if your father is still down with you?

I am doing some embroidery work and want to make a quilt or two. I can't seem to find a pattern to make the dress I brought home to make over for Melva. All the patterns I run across have swing skirts and I am sure that is too narrow to make a full skirt. You remember it is a henna dress. I think you said Jake gave it to you.

I would like to come down later if only for a day or two. Don't think I can stand the round trip in one day.

Aunt Charlotte and I was talking perhaps early in the spring we would go down to see a Shakespearean play. If we went on a Friday, I might get over for Sunday or Saturday. It's just all talk so far.

I should write a couple more letters, but am going to bed instead. Love to you all, Mother

January 1938 at Leavenworths
In January Jennie often stopped by at her brother Garfield's place. Garfield sometimes went to Jennie's.

Towards the end of the month Clinton and Garfield cut wood at Proctor's. Clinton also cut wood for his grandmother Anna Hull Sergeant.

And January was the month that Clinton took Stella Clark out for the first time. He had seen Stella in town one time and told his brother Jim, "I am going to marry that girl."

February 1938
Saturday, February 5, Clinton visited Stella at her home.

Monday Clint worked on his cellar. Martin Leavenworth was at Garfield's house in the morning. Uncle John Von Blascom was very ill on Tuesday.

Terrible sadness at the Austin home in Staten Island on Thursday. Raymond and Gladys Austin's baby Edwin Mortimer Austin died. Such a heartbreaking time for Raymond, Gladys, Melva, Joan, and Margie.

Monday, February 14, Clinton worked on his place. Raymond and Gladys were at Garfield and Ella's for the evening.

A. Leavenworth, E. Islip, N.Y., to C.R. Austin family, Staten Island
February 14, 1938,
Dear Raymond and Gladys,
I am so sorry for you that I don't know how to express my grief. When the weather gets a little settled, try to bring the children and come over to see me.
With much sympathy,
Aunt Anna

Tuesday, February 15, Clint worked on his cellar. He went to Clarks a number of evenings. He was officially courting Stella Clark.

Wednesday Old Mr. Clark (Stella's grandfather John Henry Clark) was up to fix the saw for shingles.

Friday both Mr. Briggs and Walt Horton stopped by to talk to

1938 winter in Eldred. Photo courtesy Christene Stevens Myers.

Garfield at different times.

Saturday Clint worked on his place and went to see Stella in the evening. Anna and Bill stopped by her folks for a while, then they went to Bill's folks for supper.

March 1938
Jennie Austin, Eldred, to Melva Austin, Staten Island
Wed night. March 1, 1938
Dear Melva and all the rest of the Family,
We sure were glad to hear from you and to know you folks are well. I hear your grandfather is down with you.
We had a lunch down in the Church Hall today. They served salmon loaf, creamed potatoes, tomatoes, salad, and apple pudding.
Next time you come here, you will think you got in the wrong house for I am having the kitchen papered and painted and it is some job.
First the ceiling had to be washed and two coats of paint put on the ceiling and all the rest of the woodwork. Now they are ready for the paper which has not come yet, so they will begin to paint the room where you slept and paper it also.
I will try and send you some apples in a day or two and put in pieces of the wallpaper. I will
have two clean rooms. Tell your mother I will try and write to her soon.
Love to you all, Grandmother

Wednesday, March 2, the Meyers took "Uncle John" to the County Hospital. He died the next day.

Sunday, March 6, Stella joined Clint for supper at his folks' house for first time. Monday Lee and Garfield fixed Jennie's cupboard.

Tuesday Herbert Eldred, a relative of the Austin siblings, was buried in the Eldred Cemetery. Herbert Eldred, son of George W. Eldred, had died when he was hit by a truck, in Middletown where he had lived since 1921.

Wednesday Clint ate supper with the Clarks. Stella's brother Orville dined at the Leavenworth's. (Orville Clark would be a life-long friend of Jim.)

Monday, March 14, Clint got his loans. Frank Bartle was at the Leavenworth's for the evening.

Friday, Garfield started making window frames for Clint.

Saturday the men worked on Clint's cellar. They must have been digging it out to get ready to pour cement walls. Jennie Austin, Anna and Bill Meyers, and the Wolffs were at the Leavenworths for the evening. Jim's friend Frank Bartle had been there all day.

The Maier house on Crawford Road where Julius Maier lived. Photo courtesy of the Bosch Family.

Harvey and Emmy Marry

Sunday, March 20, Harvey Eldred and Emmy Draxler of Minisink Ford were married. Emmy was the daughter of Charles and Martha Draxler. Her sister Martha stood up with her. Her father Charles stood up with Harvey.

Harvey was another Eldred relative of the Austin siblings, though they may not have known each other. Harvey was the son of Lewis LaForde and Cora Sisson Eldred who had both died when Harvey was young.

Tuesday, March 22, Garfield and Orville put in forms for the walls of Clinton's cellar. Lee and Clinton drew sand. Clara and Ella cleaned house. Jim went to school.

Jennie Austin wrote the following letter on stationery with The Pines letterhead.

Jennie Austin, Eldred, to Mrs. Chas. R. Austin, Staten Island

March 22, 1938, Monday evening
Dear Gladys,

I did manage to send the apples I promised the children this morning. It is like summer today.

Yesterday they took John Love to the hospital. Three weeks ago he was taken down with pneumonia and from all accounts he has to have an operation like you had.

Annie Maier died with pneumonia. Julius had it, but has

Martha Draxler, Emmy Draxler and her husband Harvey Eldred on their wedding day. Photo courtesy of Martha Eldred Worzel.

recovered. "Uncle Johnny" died about three weeks ago. Everyone dies or is married up here this year.

Charlie Ort married Anna Brague. Lawrence Racine is married.

I am having my kitchen all cleaned up and it has had two coats of paint. The paper I sent for was sold out so am delayed at having the job finished. The room where you slept I have had a light paper put on and it looks very good.

I have been in about three weeks with a cold but last week ventured out. I don't know what in the world I would do if I got sick now, so have to be careful.

Nellie is going to help me again this summer. Perhaps after we get everything straightened out I can get away for a week or two. Anyway will live in hopes even if I die in despair. Nellie has been quite sick herself.

Dr. Gutfruend was in the Port Jervis hospital over a week. Little Frankie Clouse was operated on for mastoid this afternoon. Truman is under the weather again. This time jaundice.

If it don't clear up by Thursday, he is going up to the Callicoon hospital again.

I suppose you will be up at Easter time. I hear Melva is to come and I understood Joanie was to spend the week with Jake. Tell Raymond to be careful about catching cold this weather.

Love to all, Mother

Thursday, Garfield and Bill worked on forms for the basement of Clint's house.

Saturday Garfield worked some on Clint's window frames.

Sunday, March 27, Stella and her dad Ernest Clark visited Clint.

Wednesday Jim was home from school. Thursday Ernest Clark and Carl Wolff visited the Leavenworths for a while.

April 1938
Friday, April 1, Carl Wolff, Ernest Clark, Bill Sr., Bill Jr., Jim, Lee, Garfield, and Chester all helped Clint run cement for his cellar.

Saturday Garfield and Clinton cut shingles. Virginia McBride and Anna called; also Charlotte.

The following Friday, Anna stopped to see her folks, went to town, and then to see her aunt Jennie Austin.

Jennie Austin mentioned in her March letter that John Love had been sick for three weeks with pneumonia. John Love died two weeks later. Garfield and Clinton attended his funeral.

The next day Lee and Jim painted Garfield and Ella's house and oiled the shingles. Martin visited his brother Garfield for a while.

Sunday morning, April 24, Garfield, Ella, and all their family went to Clint's place when the men put up the rafters. Jim visited Frank Bartle in the afternoon.

Tuesday the newly married Mrs. Ort (Anna Sergeant Brague Ort) visited Ella for the day. Mrs. Schumacher was buried. She was 84 years old when she died.

Thursday the principal Mr. Moore stopped to talk to Jim (James) who had quit school.

When my 16th birthday came I quit school and worked here and there. I plowed gardens for people that spring and finally got a permanent job with Harry Wormuth in his sawmill. When the checks started coming, I started paying on the feed bill and then finished it off two years after when I was in the Air Corps.

I worked for Harry Wormuth about two years.—James Leavenworth.

Saturday a stone mason laid the brick for Clint's chimney.

May 1938
Saturday, May 7, Anna made Ella a Mother's Day cake.

Monday Jim plowed Chester Middaugh's garden. Tuesday Mr. Briggs called. Friday Jim plowed Everett's garden.

Jennie Austin's quip about everyone either dying or getting married, was again confirmed with the death of Abel Hazen.

Kate Parker

Kate Parker, daughter of Mary Murray Parker Schoonover died in 1938. Kate and her half sister Emma Waidler had helped raise their sister Laura Britt's daughters Ada and Kitty Britt, when Laura died young. Kate had continued to be a part of Ada Wood and Kitty James' families. Norma Wood James wrote a touching tribute to her great-aunt Kate.

Kate's outstanding needlework was her only source of income until she died. She never married; "never had her own home." This last she mentioned sadly to me alone in the kitchen a few weeks before she died.

She lived with us winters ever since I could remember and had spent every summer with her half sister Emma and her husband Will Waidler wherever they lived upstate, on whatever farm.

The words stuck in my throat. I wanted to, should have said, "What would we have done without you? But I could not speak. It was a devastating revelation for me, seeing myself as self-centered, just assuming that Aunt Kate knew she was loved, was needed, and had never had any dreams of her own, that she was satisfied with us all as her

Kate Parker. Photo courtesy of Richard James.

family and with sharing our dreams or their second-hand reflections.—Norma Wood James, great-niece.

Norman H. and Margaret Myers Sutherland on their wedding day, June 12, 1938. Alfred and Bessie Sutherland Lilley stood up with them. Bessie was Norman's oldest sister. Photo courtesy of Darlene Sutherland Haas.

Wednesday, May 18, Abel Hazen (husband of Viola Bradley) was buried.

Jennie visited Ella several times the last week of May.

June 1938
Wednesday, June 8, Garfield got a load of green hay from Jennie's. Jennie visited Ella Thursday.

Earl Wells. "Clinton went to see Earl Wells about a stove." Photo courtesy of Berniece Wells Haas.

Thursday, June 16, Anna and Bill got their electric ice box.

Sunday Clinton, Stella, and her grandmother Anna Hallock visited with the Leavenworths for awhile.

Garfield and Ella went to Bill and Anna's for Garfield's birthday. Anna gave her dad two jars of wild strawberry jam.

Sunday, June 26, Clint and Ella went up to his place. Then Clint went over to Earl Wells to see about a stove.

Earl Wells and his wife Ada's daughter Berniece was 10 in 1938. Berniece's future husband Harry Haas was 13.

Tuesday Clinton ran cement over his well. Wednesday Ella put a bed up for Jim in the small room on the first floor. She was freeing a room upstairs for Lee's parents who would be visiting for a week at the beginning of July.

Norman H. Sutherland Marries
The Sutherlands had settled in the area at least by 1826, though they hadn't all stayed there. (Their Drake relatives had settled in Mongaup pre-1800.)

In June 1938 Norman H. Sutherland married Margaret Myers in Shohola. Margaret was from New Jersey. Norman H. was the son of Norman W. and Barbara Bridge Sutherland.

Norman W. was a career railroad man. He worked as a trackman and brakeman on the Erie Railroad more than 50 years. Norman W.'s sister was Catherine, widow of William H. Horton.

Norman H. and his family would move to Barryville in the future. He would work for the Narrowsburg Lumber Company.

Charlie Pankow and Green Acres
There were new owners at Green Acres, originally Wilhelm Bosch's Lake House on Highland Lake.

Charles Pankow, his sister Agnes Schmid, and mother Agnes had been guests at the Lake House on Highland Lake for a couple years around 1935. They became interested in becoming innkeepers and rented the Lake House as innkeepers in 1936 and 1937.

The Haas Family. Sitting: Doris, Louise (mother), Richard Sr. (father), Donald. Standing: Marion, Richard Jr., Maurice, and Harry, future husband of Berniece Wells. Photo courtesy of Berniece Wells Haas.

1938 World, National, and Local News

1938 World and National News
- *Superman* first appeared in 1938.
- Thorton Wilder's, *Our Town*.
- Category 5 New England Hurricane. Property loss estimated at $306 million; 682–800 people killed.

February 1938
- British Secretary Anthony Eden resigned over Chamberlain's appeasement of Mussolini and Hitler.

March 1938
- Germans annexed Austria.

May 1938
- Naval Expansion Act approved; significant increase in strength of U.S. Navy; acquired 3,000 aircraft.

June 1938
- U.S. national minimum wage $0.25.

September 1938
- Germany's acquisition of Sudentland in Czechoslovakia, agreed to by Hitler, Prime Minister Chamberlain, French Premier Daladier, and Mussolini.

October 1938
- Orson Welles' *War of the Worlds* radio drama about a fake Martian invasion.

Dorothy Calkin married Raymond Hale. Photo courtesy of Katherine Calkin Traxler.

November 1938
- In Nazi Germany and Austria, in retaliation of a German diplomat assassinated in Paris, 91 Jews were murdered; 25,000 to 30,000 Jews were arrested and placed in concentration camps.

December 1938
- France and Germany signed a friendship agreement. By the end of 1938 there were approximately 60,000 inmates in the overcrowded Nazi concentration camps.

1938 Halfway Brook News
- Rowlee Schoonover retired as the chauffeur of Mrs. Douglas. Due to cataracts he couldn't drive safely. Rowlee's son William took over the chaueffeur job.

1938 Enlisted
- Whipple Bosch enlisted in the U.S. Army.

1938 Eldred Seniors
- Irene Barber, Olive Brower, Frank Hill, Martin D. Myers Jr., Christine Ott, Katherine Ott, Beatrice Parker, Edward Purcell.

1938 Births
- Edey LaBarr born to Jacob and Emily Harder LaBarr.
- Marnette Hart born to Maxwell and Elizabeth Watson Hart in Texas.
- Ed Wolff born to Albert and Ruth Foster Wolff.
- Kenneth Mills born to Jim and Sophia Mills.

1938 Weddings
- Dorothy Katherine Calkin, daughter of Burt and Lillie Austin Calkin, married Raymond Hale in October.
- Norma Beverly Wood, daughter of Arthur and Ada Britt Wood, married Edward Henry James.
- Harvey Eldred, son of Lewis Laforde and Cora Sisson Eldred, married Emmy Draxler, daughter of Charles and Martha Draxler.

Ed Wolff stands on large bluestone by his house. Photo courtesy of Ed Wolff.

- Norman H. Sutherland married Margaret Myers of Jersey City, N.J.
- Charlie Ort married Anna Sergeant Brague in March.
- Lawrence Racine was married.
- Clinton Leavenworth married Stella Adelaide Clark in October.

1938 Deaths
- Ida Belle Austin Brown, an Eldred-Austin cousin, died in January.
- Mrs. Schumacher died in 1938.
- Annie Maier died of pneumonia.
- John C. Love died.
- "Uncle" John Von Blascom died.
- Florence Middaugh, 1881–1938, died of bronchial pneumonia.
- Edwin M. Austin, infant son of Raymond and Gladys Austin, died.
- Kate Parker, daughter of Mary Murray Parker Schoonover, died.
- Herbert (Bert) Eldred, 1868–1938, was the son of George W. and Marietta West Eldred.
- Abel A. Hazen, 1860–1938, had operated Laurel Cottage for 47 years. He and his wife Viola Bradley celebrated their 50th wedding anniversary in 1937. Besides Mrs. Hazen, two children survived: Mabel Parker and J. Lewis Hazen.

Olympic House on Highland Lake was built by John and Rudolph Kistner. Photo courtesy of Jeanie Staubes Turner.

Highland Lake, 1938, Irene Theuer. Photo courtesy of Jeanie Staubes Turner.

In June 1938, Charlie Pankow purchased the Bosch Lake House from Ed and Eleanor Bosch. (Ed and Eleanor lived in the house Ed built in Eldred.)

At some point Lake House changed names to Green Acres. Eventually Green Acres would become Green Meadows.

Other Boarding Houses
Besides the usual boarding house and Green Acres' ads, there was information for several newer houses on Highland Lake: Emil Boch's Lakewood House; Art and Clara Bertram's Cottage, and the Kistner Brothers' Olympic House.

Irene Theuer's parents Alfons and Johanna ran Sunset Bar and Sunset View House.

West Shore Cottage on Washington Lake had changed ownership to Joseph Cantwell.

July 1938
Monday evening Bill Meyers Jr. drove Garfield and Ella to see fireworks. Lee, Clara, and his parents went to Callicoon.

Wednesday Ella canned six quarts of peas.

Saturday Clinton's gas range arrived. The freight was $2.89.

Sunday, July 10, Clara and Lee started keeping house in the Leavenworth's upstairs. The three bedrooms would be turned into an apartment with a living room, kitchen, and bedroom. They would share the downstairs bathroom.

Lee and Clara living upstairs meant that Jim's sleeping quarters would be the small room off his parents bedroom on the first floor.

Tuesday Clara and Lee's rug and house furnishings arrived. Wednesday Ella made curtains for Clara's closet and her cupboard.

Friday Jim started skidding logs for Harry Wormuth. Jim also helped Bill Meyers Sr. with haying.

Wednesday, July 20, Ella canned 30 quarts of peas.

Friday Garfield went up to see his sister Christina. Ella canned 42 quarts of cherries.

Sunday, July 24, there were

Garfield took their heifer to Julius Maier. Julius and his dog Nero. Photo courtesy of the Bosch Family.

Ed and Eleanor Schroeder Bosch enjoy a picnic in the woods with daughter Kay, and Grandpa William Schroeder. Photo courtesy of Ken Bosch.

Charlie Pankow and Green Acres

1930s Green Acres Dock. Green Acres (former Lake House) in the background on the left Photo courtesy of Diane Pankow.

Charlie Pankow, his mom Agnes Pankow, Henny and Agnes Schmid, around 1938. Photo courtesy of Diane Pankow.

1930s Henny and Agnes Schmid, Charlie Pankow. Photo courtesy of Diane Pankow.

Charles Pankow "Charlie" was born in Brooklyn in 1907 to Adolph and Agnes Ozanich Pankow who had emigrated from Germany. The family lived on Evergreen Avenue in the Williamsburg part of Brooklyn. Adolf worked as a *hod carrier* (a mason's assistant who carried hods of materials to the mason).

In 1923 Adolf made a second application for citizenship, accompanied by the required three letters from other citizens stating he had been back in the U.S. for a long period of time. Adolf and Agnes then opened a candy store on Evergreen Avenue.

In the 1930s Agnes Pankow was widowed and her daughter Agnes married Henry G. Schmid. Charlie, a foreman in a perfume factory, became responsible for the care of his mother.

Between 1930 and 1940, Charles Pankow, his sister Agnes Schmid, and mother Agnes, were guests at the Lake House on Highland Lake for about two years. They became interested in becoming innkeepers and rented the Lake House as the innkeepers. Two years later in 1938, they purchased the house for $7,500. (It was fully paid off in 1948.)

Charlie renamed the place Green Acres and it became a family endeavor. Charlie's sister Agnes Schmid and her husband Henry's sisters Catherine and Lillian, and a cousin Martha worked in the kitchen cooking; Charlie and Henry worked on renovations.

Henry Schmid worked for Commercial Union Insurance on Maiden Lane in Manhattan, and came up weekends. Henny was an accomplished self taught musician and entertained the guests with his ragtime piano skills, accordion, banjo or guitar. —*Diane Pankow.*

---

27 bridges that went out in the county because there had been so much rain and flooding.

Tuesday Ella canned 56 quarts of beans.

Friday Jim bought a harness and wagon. On Saturday he and Lee started haying at Ed Myers.

Sunday, the last day of July, Garfield shingled at Clint's all day.

August 1938
The first two days of August found Garfield and Jim haying at Ed Myers'. Sunday, August 7, Lee and Jim went down to Ed Myers. Clinton cut hay for himself.

Friday Garfield, Ella, Anna, and Clara pumped the well dry and cleaned it.

Sunday, August 14, Garfield and his sons ran cement for Clint's entrance.

Tuesday Jim was finished with his work for Harry for a week or so.

Wednesday Paul Knorr fixed the cellar button for the light. (The electric box had two buttons, one turned the light on; the other turned it off.)

Stella and Clinton Leavenworth on their wedding day. Photo courtesy of Linda Leavenworth Bohs, daughter.

Sunday, August 21, Christina and Charlee called. Jim picked and sold corn for $5.45. Clinton worked on his car. Garfield took their heifer to Julius Maier.

Tuesday Clinton and Stella were at his house for a while.

Wednesday the men went to a school meeting. Anna went to Dorothy Wolff's for the day. Ella canned her first two quarts of tomatoes of the year.

Thursday Clinton's doors and windows came from Jeffersonville. Friday the electrician wired Clint's house.

September 1938
Sunday evening, September 4, Stella's family: Ernest and Eunice Clark, Orville, and Vernon, visited the Leavenworths.

Garfield and Ella celebrated 32 years of marriage on Monday. Jim worked for Harry Wormuth again. Lee remodeled the hen coop for Clara.

Thursday Ella canned 20 quarts of tomatoes. Jim cut corn when he wasn't carrying water for Ella (to use in canning tomatoes). Jennie was there for the evening.

Friday Jim plowed for Chester Middaugh. Anna and Ella shelled and canned lima beans.

Saturday Jim and Chester dug potatoes and Jim plowed for Chester. Garfield worked on Clint's house. Clara, Anna, and Ella canned and cleaned.

Monday, September 12, Garfield took their large Jersey cow to Maier's. Clara gathered 2-1/2 bushels of their onions.

Clara and Ella canned pickles Tuesday. Clinton, Ernie Clark, and Garfield ran concrete for a coal bin for Clint.

Ella and Clara canned pears on Wednesday. Thursday they canned plums and made some jam for Clint. Charlie and Anna Ort stopped by in the evening.

The following Thursday (22) Jim and Garfield cleaned their chimney and cemented the roof.

Friday the men went up to tear down the barns on the old Leavenworth farm.

Sunday, September 25, Clinton and Stella ate supper at his parents' home.

Monday Clara tried to learn to drive Lee's car. Ella made sauerkraut on Tuesday.

Friday Anna and Ella canned 60 quarts of beets and carrots.

October 1938
Sunday, October 2, Jim and Garfield ran cement for the barn.

Monday Clint and Stella went to get their blood test for their marriage license.

Tuesday Stella and her mother Eunice were at Leavenworth's all day.

Jim worked for Harry on Saturday.

Clint's light fixtures arrived on Wednesday. Stella helped open them in the evening.

Thursday Jim took Ella to the Clark's for the day.

Saturday Jim worked at Harry Wormuth's. He also bought 100 pounds of sugar, 10 pounds of coffee, and 1 pail of honey.

Sunday, October 16, Garfield varnished three of Clint's floors. Bill, Anna, the Daibers, and Stella ate supper at the Leavenworth's.

Tuesday Clint moved his stove and fixtures up to his house. He and Stella went for their marriage license.

Wednesday Jim worked for Harry. Garfield went to Clint's, and to an evening school meeting.

Bill Meyers Jr. took the women in his life: his mother Lottie, sister Madelyn, wife Anna, and mother-in-law Ella, to Port Jervis on Saturday.

Clint Leavenworth was right. He did marry Stella Clark— October 22, 1938. They lived in the home which Clint had built. Clint (Goldie) worked in Liberty.

Dad [Clinton] worked for a foundry in Liberty when they were first married. I remember my Mom telling me that she didn't like people calling him "Goldie," but when he worked for the foundry, he used to duck the flying metals so fast that the guys named him "Rawhide." She thought Goldie sounded better than Rawhide, so she began calling him Goldie. That job also didn't work out and they came back. I always felt that they were such a very, very close family, that they got a little homesick.
—*Linda Leavenworth Bohs.*

Sunday, October 23, Orville and Vernon Clark spent the day with Jim.

The Ironic End of Kate Stege's Will

The Woman Who Talked to the Birds wanted to leave her estate for a game preserve, but now the $200,000 legacy must be given to her heirs.

Except for a bequest of $75,000 to Herbert Gordon, Mrs. Stege's unique will left her entire estate to the Conservation Society of New York City for the "protection, propagation, and preservation of animals, birds, and fowls."

When the personal property of the estate was sold at auction, it was discovered that in addition to the 35 Persian cats, there were 48 rabbits, 17 ducks, 4 goats, 22 pigs, 19 sheep, 4 lambs, 99 chickens, 4 bulls, 5 cows, a horse and countless pheasants, and wild turkeys which roamed around the place.

When no such organization as the Conservation Society of New York City was located, the State Conservation Department claimed the estate, only to have the surrogate's Court at Monticello refuse the will to probate, declare it invalid and order the entire estate divided up between Mrs. Stege's kinfolk. Then started the scramble of relatives to claim the fortune.

That meant that Mrs. Stege's one aim in life—to protect wild animals and birds—was impossible, for now the estate must be sold so that the heirs, a niece and seven grandnieces and grandnephews get their share.

Herbert Gordon, the step grandson, who worked and helped Mrs. Stege, gets nothing despite the fact that the nature-loving old woman left him a legacy in her will.

The latest step in the distribution of the music fortune made, came when Robert G. Rundle, a 50-year-old native of Eldred came out of Monticello courthouse richer by $25,000, or so it would appear.

Rundle won an award in that amount because he claimed that he had worked for Mrs. Stege as a game protector and caretaker for 24 years at an average weekly salary of $13.50, only because she had many times promised him that she would leave him $25,000 in her will.

But whether Rundle will ever live to see or actually hold that money in his hand is doubtful. Just as the entire purpose of Mrs. Stege in writing her will ironically seems to have gone wrong, so are Rundle's chances of getting his award most slim. For certainly the other heirs and the administratrix of the bird woman's estate will appeal from the jury verdict which granted the $25, 000 to Rundle, and, in addition, Rundle's doctor has told him that he is the victim of a serious ailment and that he may only live a few years during which his money will most likely still be tied up in court. He's been minus a job since Mrs. Stege's death and has been resting at home. He's wondering if, like the animals, he'll be out of luck, too.
—Sunday *Mirror Magazine* Section, February, 27, 1938, p. 2.

Monday Jennie Austin spent the day with Ella. Garfield worked upstairs on a kitchen for Clara.

Sunday, October 30, Jim ate supper at his sister Anna's.

Burt and Lillie Calkin had a new son-in-law. In October their daughter Dot married Raymond Hale. Ray and Dot had met roller skating. They lived in Port Jervis after they were married.

War of the Worlds
If anyone in the Town of Highland listened to CBS radio's Mercury Theater October 30, they heard an adaptation of H.G. Wells', *War of the Worlds,* read by Orson Welles.

The first two-thirds of the 60-minute broadcast were presented as a series of simulated news bulletins, which suggested to many listeners that an actual alien invasion by Martians was currently in progress. There were no commercial breaks when the Mercury Theatre was on the Air adding to the program's realism.—wikipedia.org.

November 1938
Thursday, November 3, both Clara and Clint received lamps as a wedding gift from their aunt Hazel Connor.

Saturday Florence Middaugh was very sick.

Sunday, November 6, Bill Austin stopped by his uncle Garfield's house possibly to ask for help shingling their house.

Newspaper article featured Orson Welles' reading of Welles' War of the Worlds *on Mercury Theater, at the end of October. Newspaper courtesy of Mary Briggs Austin.*

Tuesday Clara went down to Jennie Austin's for a while.

Friday and Saturday Garfield and Jim helped shingle the Austin home.

Saturday Florence Middaugh died at 5:30 p.m.

Monday Clara and Ella papered part of Clara's kitchen. Lee painted the ceiling.

Tuesday was the funeral service for Florence Middaugh. Clara and Ella finished papering Clara's kitchen.

Friday, November 18, Jim worked for Harry Wormuth.

Saturday Stella and Goldie were down for supper and the evening. Clara and Lee moved into their kitchen.

Tuesday, November 22, Garfield did some shingling for Harry Wormuth.

Wednesday Clara and Ella baked pies for Thanksgiving.

Thursday Anna and Bill ate Thanksgiving dinner with Garfield and Ella. On the second floor, Clara and Lee hosted the meal for Stella and Clinton in the Hansen's new kitchen.

Friday it snowed about 12 inches and drifted. No one stopped by the Leavenworth home.

Garfield and Lee got the heifers into the new barn they were building.

They put the cows and horses in the barn on Saturday. Jim shoveled snow. Garfield and Lee worked on the barn. Bill and Anna were there also. Goldie and Stella stopped by a short time.

December 1938
The following Saturday, December 3, Jim and Bill went hunting. Clara visited her aunt Charlotte and aunt Jennie.

Sunday Clinton shot a buck.

Friday, December 16, Jim was back working for Harry Wormuth.

Dottie Wait (Spider), Alex Wait, and Jim Wade in front of Wait and Boyd's garage, December 1938. Photo courtesy of Christene Stevens Myers.

Saturday Garfield and Ella drove to Goldie's home for the first time since he was married.

Goldie and Stella ate supper at his parents' on Sunday.

Monday, September 19, Ella received a package from her sister Hazel. Bill and Anna were there for supper. Friday Jim went up to Chester's for the evening. Most likely Chester was really missing his wife Florence.

Sunday, Christmas Day, there were some snow squalls in the afternoon. Perhaps that's the day a photo was taken of Dottie Wait (nicknamed Spider), her dad Alex Wait, and Jim Wade in front of the Wait and Boyd Garage.

The Leavenworth children were all in for Christmas dinner except Goldie and Stella. Lee's parents were also there. Supper included everyone except Anna and Bill who were probably at his parents.

Tuesday evening Chester stopped by. Thursday Jim skidded wood for Norm Myers part of the day. Friday the men drew two loads of hay from Ed Myers.

January 1939
Sunday, January 1, Anna and Bill were in. Jim was hunting.

Tuesday Jim worked for Harry. Clara went to the doctor's. Hmm.

Sunday, January 8, Charlie Sergeant bought the place his grandfather Edgar Sergeant had built.

Monday Garfield took the scaffolding off Jennie's house that they used when they were shingling the roof.

Thursday the men tore down two barns: one on Goldie's land and the other on the property Lee had bought between Goldie's and Echo Hill.

Saturday Lee, Clara, and Jim helped Stella celebrate her 19th birthday.

The following Saturday Lee worked for Harry. Clinton helped Herm Bosch with ice for two days.

Herman had a sawmill and dairy, as well as his ice business. Herman and Mary Bosch and their children: Herman Jr., Marjorie, and Bobby lived near the elderly Austin siblings, Aida and Lon. Herman and Mary were dear friends and good neighbors to Lon and Aida. We will hear more about them in the next three chapters.

February 1939
Sunday, February 5, Charles E. Sergeant was born to Charlie and Clareta Kuen Sergeant.

Monday Goldie worked for Mr. Tether cutting blocks of ice (icing) to put in the ice house.

Tuesday Anna and Bill became proud parents at 12:15 a.m.

James (Jimmy) Meyers weighed 6-pounds, 5-ounces. Wednesday Garfield and Ella went to see their first grandchild.

Thursday Jim Leavenworth visited his friend Orville Clark.

Friday Bill (the new father) asked his wife's sister Clara to help dress their new little one.

Saturday Frank Bartle enjoyed dinner with the Leavenworths. Goldie and Stella were in. Lee worked for Harry Wormuth.

Wednesday Anna was still in bed. Thursday and Friday Clara helped Anna. Thursday Lee worked on his place by Echo Hill, and at Harry's on Friday.

Sunday, February 19, when Garfield and Ella visited Alvah and Mary Sergeant, Garfield put Alvah's front room ceiling up. Lee and Clara visited Bill and Anna.

Monday, February 27, the meter man came—cost: $3.46.

March 1939
Wednesday, March 1, Lee and Jim worked on Lee's place. Clara went up to Anna's. Bill Meyers Jr. and Goldie started working for the County.

Thursday was the first time Anna and baby Jimmy visited his Leavenworth grandparents at their house.

Friday Lee and Clara worked on their land. Bill and Goldie worked for the County. Garfield and Jim painted Ella's kitchen.

Saturday the electric lines were down and the lights were out for 24 hours.

The next week on Thursday Lee and Jim went to Hawley. Lee had six teeth pulled.

Friday Jim went to the Clarks for the evening. Clara went to the doctor.

Tuesday, March 14, Garfield and Jim tore paper off the front room. Garfield painted the front

Herman Bosch's ice truck beside his home. Photo courtesy of Victoria Kohler.

Herman Bosch's Dairy Postcard captioned: Herman Bosch's Dairy Farm, Eldred, N.Y. Milk Cream Butter. EGGS POULTRY ICE. Photo courtesy of Victoria Kohler.

Herman Bosch's ice truck. Photo courtesy of Victoria Kohler.

Herman Bosch at work at his sawmill. Photo courtesy of Victoria Kohler.

The Connor Family, Walter, Hazel, Marion and Marjorie, on the steps of the Leavenworth home. Photo courtesy of Cynthia Leavenworth Bellinger.

room ceiling on Wednesday.

Sunday, March 19, Anna Hull Sergeant, Ella's stepmother died.

Monday Goldie and Stella took Jennie Hull (Anna Sergeant's sister) to Port Jervis (probably to the funeral home or to order flowers). Tuesday Walter and Hazel Connor arrived from Massachusetts. The two families went up to call on Goldie at his new house.

Wednesday Walter, Hazel, Garfield, and Ella went to Port Jervis in the morning. Anna Meyers left baby Jimmy with Clara while they went to the funeral for Anna Hull Sergeant. Anna and Bill stayed for supper. Hazel and Walter went home.

Anna Sergeant's death left her sister Jennie Hull by herself in the Sergeant home. Though Emile and Marcel Four owned the house, they allowed Jennie to continue living there. Jim Mills who lived nearby made sure that Jennie Hull was OK.

Friday afternoon Kate and Arthur Kuen, their daughter Clareta, and their new grandson Charlie E. Sergeant visited Garfield and Ella.

Friday the last day of the month was a busy one. Bob Austin called at Garfield and Ella's. Ed and Mabel Smith were there for the afternoon. Garfield worked for his sister Jennie Austin. Jennie's granddaughter Joan Austin was visiting. Joan ate supper at Garfield and Ella's. She told her grandmother that they had lizards to eat. (She meant gizzards.)

April 1939

The first week of April, Garfield helped his sister Jennie doing work that needed to be done on the house. Sunday, April 2, Garfield went to the Methodist Church.

Wednesday Anna and Jimmy Meyers were at her parents for the day. Garfield got a bushel of potatoes from Al Randolph's Royal Scarlet grocery store. (The store was in the former Von Ohlen location.)

Jennie and Joan Austin visited Ella for the afternoon.

Grandma Jennie Austin

In March of 1939, Joan Austin was at her grandmother Austin's at the time of her fifth birthday.

I stayed with Grandma Austin a couple weeks around the time of my fifth birthday. My parents weren't there.

The Minnie Ha Ha Cake was all the rage there in Eldred around 1939, and Grandma made it for my birthday. It had nuts, seeded raisins (which were sweet and sticky), and thick white icing. Grandma put a candle on the cake.

I didn't like the cake at all, and told Grandma, I think. A few years later, when I was older, I thought maybe I shouldn't have done that.

I felt there was a heaviness about Grandma. But she was very

Mabel Smith and her husband Ed stopped by the Leavenworths on a Friday afternoon. Photo courtesy of Cynthia Leavenworth Bellinger.

Joan Austin visited her grandmother Jennie Austin, on the right. The other lady is unknown. Photo in the Austin Collection.

1939 Halfway Brook News

New York Route 97 Dedicated
- In June 1911: State Legislature passed funding for Delaware River Highway, State Route 3A, to be built from Port Jervis to Hancock. August 1939: the highway was dedicated as Route 97.

James Eldred's 1830 House
- After living there a few years Grandpa James Eldred purchased land and built a frame house near the mill site. George Crandall owns the place now and he and his wife live there. The post office erected on the east side of the house and connected with it by a doorway leading into the sitting room was torn down when the Crandalls remodeled the house some years ago.—*Aida Austin, 1939 letter.*

1939 Eldred Seniors
- Franklin Bartle, Mary Jane Bartle, George Boyer, Walter Campbell, Dorothy Downey, Raymond Flynn, Charles Foster, Robert Haring, Gordon Hobbs, Arthur Hoehne, Clifford Hulse, Charles Kerr, Helen Kuen, Frank Michell, Clara O'Neill, John O'Neill, Jane Putnam, James Purcell, Thorne Sheen, Christene Stevens, Dorothy Wolff, Madeleine Ramsey.

1939 Births
- James Didrik Hansen born to Lee and Clara Leavenworth Hansen.
- James William Meyers born to William and Anna Leavenworth Meyers.
- About 1939 Frederick Bosch born to Ed and Eleanor Schroeder Bosch.
- Charles E. Sergeant born to Charlie and Clareta Kuen Sergeant.

1939 Marriages
- Elmer Hallock married Christina Ott.
- Edward Sulzbach married Margaret Olsen.
- Robert Nelson married Ruth Kerr.
- Harry Sulzbach married Dorothy Barker.

Highland Lake Double Wedding
Wednesday, June 28, at 10 a.m., a double wedding took place at St. Bernardine R.C. Church in Highland Lake. The two sons of Frances Sulzbach, Edward and Harry, were married to Margaret Mary Olsen of Astoria, Long Island, and Dorothy Mae Barker of Gloversville, N.Y., respectively.

Attendants were Miss Margaret Dolan and Christopher Scott Jr.; Hilda Proper, and Clifford Sulzbach.

The brides wore identical white lace and net gowns with long trains and hip length veils with orange blossoms. They carried bouquets of white roses and lilies of the valley.

Following the ceremony, a wedding breakfast was held at Scott's. Later the wedding reception was given at Sulzbach's Pinehurst Casino. One hundred and forty friends and relatives attended the reception.

Both couples will reside in Highland Lake where Harry and Edward manage the Pinehurst Casino for their mother, Mrs. Frances Sulzbach.

1939 Deaths
- Truman E. Leavenworth, 1878–1939.
- Abigail Wilson, 1881–1939.
- Mary Alice Whitney Kyte, 1858–1939, was the mother of Mary Wormuth and sister of Joseph Tether and Elizabeth Owen.
- Ann Eliza Gardner Cuddeback, 1844–1939, was born in Beaver Brook. She died in Huguenot, N.Y., in June 1939. Ann Eliza was the last child of James K. and Eliza Eldred Gardner to die. Ann Eliza was the widow of Louis Cuddeback. They were both buried in Cuddeback Cemetery, Cuddlebackville, N.Y.
- Stephen A. Myers, 1870–1939.
- Mrs. Ella Hulse died of a stroke.
- Anna L. Sergeant, 1868–1939, died at her home in Highland Lake, where she had lived for over 30 years. She was an invalid for the past 20 years. Mrs. Sergeant was the wife of the late Frank R. Sergeant. She is survived by one sister, Miss Jennie Hull of Highland Lake; two stepdaughters, Ella Leavenworth of Eldred, and Hazel Connor of East Hampton, Massachusetts. Services were held Wednesday afternoon at two o'clock. Rev. Bente of the Congregational Church, officiated. Interment was at Eldred.

Left: Mr. and Mrs. Harry Sulzbach; Right: Mr. and Mrs. Edward Sulzbach. Newspaper photo courtesy of Christene Stevens Myers.

---

loving and kind and paid me lots of attention.

She taught me how to make a cake—break an egg, and stir the batter, and how to make popcorn.

Grandma Austin had a room filled with material for rag rugs.

She had a scrapbook full of short animal stories for children that she had cut out of the newspaper for her children, probably. I sat on Grandma's lap while she read to me.

Grandma had dried apricots on a lower shelf and would ask if I would like one once in a while. Sometimes I helped myself. Then one day, the package wasn't there.

I think Grandma might have known what was going on.

Breakfast was oatmeal with heavy cream and canned peaches—really good. The milk came from Alfred and Bessie Hill. Also, eggs in egg cups for breakfast.

Grandma had a big wood stove. Her boys were really good about bringing in the wood for it and helping her out. They were polite and kind to each other.

Grandma had a local phone. But my parents didn't have a phone. When I was at Grandma's I was really homesick, but couldn't call home. Grandma held me and settled me down.

Grandma gave me a salt shaker and said it was real easy to catch a bird—just go sprinkle salt on a bird's tail. That kept me busy for a long time.—Joan Austin Geier.

Sunday, April 9, Lee and Jim went to the City for the day. Goldie drew his barn lumber with a horse.

Monday Jim put bird houses up for Garfield and Ella.

Wednesday Anna and Jimmy visited for the day. Jim went to the Clarks for Vernon's birthday.

Thursday Lee worked for Ray Wells. Austin and Dot Smith were at the Leavenworths for the evening. Lee was up North. (It probably was not the best timing for him to go North.)

Saturday Charlotte called at her brother Garfield's.

Thursday Clara was not feeling so good. Maybe that is because on Friday, April 21, James Didrik Hansen was born. Lee was still up North. Of course Anna and Bill and Stella and Goldie were over to see their new nephew.

Sunday, April 23, Clara and the baby were doing fine. Since both Leavenworth grandsons had the first name of their Leavenworth grandfather—James Garfield—the Hansen grandson was called Dick for his middle name, Didrik.

The Doctor called on Sunday. So did John and Katherine Dunlap and Alvah and Mary Sergeant.

Monday Anna was at her mom's all day. Lottie Meyers stopped by. Lee worked at the Lake skidding logs. Garfield worked with Tether. Jim started working on the Town roads.

Tuesday Jennie, Lottie, Anna, Jimmy, and Goldie were at the Leavenworth home. Lee plowed most of the garden.

Wednesday Carl Wolff gave Jim a cream separator.

Thursday James Didrik weighed six pounds and was 22 inches long.

Friday Garfield helped work on the Methodist Church cellar. Lee plowed on his land.

Saturday Anna and Jimmy were at her parents' all day. Bill came after work to take them home. Clara got up for an hour or so. Jim plowed the meadow. Clinton was also in.

May 1939
Monday, the first day of May was clear and lovely. All the Leavenworth children were in except Bill. Lee plowed for Bartles. Jim worked for the Town. Garfield built a fence.

Tuesday Mr. Briggs called. Lee started working for the County.

Saturday Mr. Briggs was at Leavenworth's again. Mr. Dunlap was there also. Stella and her mom Eunice Clark stopped by in the afternoon.

Thursday Lee worked for the County. Jennie and Lottie enjoyed dinner with Garfield and Ella. Jim worked for Mr. Dunlap Thursday and Friday.

Sunday afternoon, May 7, Ed and Mabel Smith, Charlie and Anna Ort were at Leavenworth's. The men drew hay from Charles West. The cost was $8 a ton.

Wednesday, May 17, Jim worked for Walter Tether.

Thursday Jim plowed for Goldie and Chester, and skidded for McBride.

The following Tuesday Jim plowed for the Orts and Groteclosses. He received $3 each.

The new A&P where Charlie MacIntyre would be manager. Photo courtesy of Christene Stevens Myers.

1939 World and National News

March 1939
- Hitler invaded remainder of Czechoslovakia; annexed a port city in Lithuania.
- Gen. Franco won Spanish Civil War with the help of Hitler.

April 1939
- Mussolini annexed Albania.
- New York World's Fair opened.

May 1939
- Rome-Berlin Axis created.

June 1939
- Baseball Hall of Fame opened in Cooperstown, N.Y.

August 1939
- Germany and Soviet Union signed a nonaggression pact. Germany to control Lithuania; and the U.S.S.R. Finland, Estonia, and Latvia.
- Soviet and Japanese troops clashed on Manchurian-Siberian border.
- Britain signed alliance with Poland.

September 1939
- Start of World War II in Europe. September 1, with no declaration of war, Germany invaded Poland; *Blitzkrieg* or lightning war.
- Chamberlain formed a war cabinet which included Winston Churchill.
- Children in London evacuated to areas free from air attack.
- German U-boat attacked Allied *S.S. Athenia*. 112 passengers and the crew perished. 1,418 saved.
- The United States declared its neutrality on September 5.
- Pres. Roosevelt hoped the country could stay out of the war.
- Four British Army divisions with 158,000 men, 25,000 vehicles crossed channel to France.
- Russia signed peace treaty with Japan.
- Soviet troops entered eastern Poland along the 800 mile border.
- Warsaw surrendered. Two days later, Germany and U.S.S.R. signed treaty regarding Poland's fate.

October 1939
- Over 40,000 Japanese troops died after an 11-day battle against the Chinese nationalists.
- President Roosevelt set up advisory committee to explore possible military uses after being alerted to the power of uranium.
- Appalling cruelties against the Polish by the Germans.
- German U-boat sank British battleship *Royal Oak*.
- Annihilation of Polish Jews started on October 26.

November 1939
- Japan established the New Order for East Asia to create peace in East Asia under the leadership of Japan.
- U.S. Neutrality Act repealed embargo on exporting arms to belligerent countries. Some 44,000,000 pounds of arms ordered by Britain and France; Between 300 and 400 aircraft were said to be waiting at American ports for Britain and France. Orders for at least 2,500 more, were held up.
- Gestapo ordered Warsaw's Jews to move into an area of the city designated as a ghetto; some 2 million Jews under Nazi rule.
- S.S. official Rinehart Heydrich outlined plans to clear Western Poland of Jews. Adolf Eichmann, former immigration officer, was put in charge of resettlement in the movement of the Jews to Poland.
- Japanese took the Chinese city, Nanning.
- Soviet troops and aircraft invaded Finland; a four-month War ensued.

December 1939
- British Royal Air Force dropped Ally bomb on German soil by accident.
- Russia bombed Helsinki.
- First Canadian troops landed in Britain; 7,400 men of the first division docked in Liverpool.
- Turkey earthquake; thousands die.
- Japan and China signed secret treaty.
- Hitler's new year talk: "We shall only talk of peace when we have won the war. The Jewish capitalistic world will not survive the 20th century."
- Congress of American States established a Neutral Zone 300 miles from the coast of the Americas.

Other 1939 News
- Nuclear fission discovered.
- *Batman* first appeared in 1939.
- Seven main concentration camps: Dachau (1933), Sachsenhausen (1936), Buchenwald (1937), Flossenbürg (1938), Neuengamme (1938), Mauthausen (1938), and the women's camp Ravensbrück (1939).—*holocaust-education.dk*.
- Countries in the Americas including Canada, Cuba, and the U.S. denied asylum to hundreds of Jewish German refugees on the *MS St. Louis* who were fleeing Germany. No country accepted the refugees and the ship returned to Germany with most of its passengers on board. Some committed suicide based on the prospect of returning to Nazi-run Germany.
- Mohandas Gandhi's peaceful resistance movement against the British colonial rule in India.
- Referendum in the Irish Free State in December 1937 on whether Ireland should continue to be a constitutional monarchy under King George VI or to become a republic results. Citizens voted in favour of a republic, ending the British sovereignty.

Saturday Jim finished planting most of garden, then started ripping down Garfield's old barn.

The New A&P

Around 1938 a new A&P had been built across from the Parker House. The original A&P had been in the Wilson building on the northwest corner of Eldred. In that location the meat market was next door to the A&P, but not connected. In the new store, the butcher shop was in the store.

The new A&P was built by Wait and Boyd on the lower end of their property and in line with the businesses that they had in the lower level of the garage.

Jim Wade had the barber shop there when I was really young and it was there for many, many years.—Christene Stevens Myers.

When I was in high school, Charlie MacIntyre was the manager and Clifford Crandall was the assistant manager. (Some time before World War II, Clifford left.) Jack Kerr worked there, too.

I (Bill Parker Jr.) was hired part time to work as a clerk while in high school. In those days you retrieved the groceries on the customer's list.

One of my jobs was to sort the 100-pound bag of potatoes into smaller peck bags, as customers bought potatoes by the peck.

Charlie taught me how to make the special knot at the top of the bag. It was a kind of hitch knot that farmers all used. My brother Howard was hired by Charlie to take the garbage from the A&P.—William H. Parker Jr.

Harold Dunlap ran Dunlap's restaurant with a soda fountain. It was in the same location that William H. Wilson's store had once been. Students crossed the street to eat there during the lunch hour.

June 1939

Thursday, June 1, Jennie Austin was at Ella's for the afternoon. Kate Love was there in the evening.

Sunday, June 4, Ray Wells drove his truck and tractor over for Jim to use.

Monday Garfield went to see George Mills. Jim seeded the meadow—the land behind Garfield's house, down the hill on a flat area.

The following Monday Jim helped draw hay for Averys with Ray Wells' truck.

Friday Clara, Anna, and Garfield went to Jennie Austin's for the day.

Monday, June 19, Clara visited her aunt Jennie Austin. Tuesday Ella and Jennie canned a crate of strawberries, $3.12 a crate.

Thursday, June 22, the A&P meat market opened across from the Parker Hotel.

Sunday Stella and Goldie ate supper with his folks. Bill and Anna stopped by.

Tuesday Jim and Bob Wolff cut hay with Carl's horse. Thursday night Jim took Carl Wolff's horse home.

There was a new boarding house on Washington Lake by summer 1939.

Maplecrest, Yulan, Reggie Walter

You may remember Cyrus and Ella Walter and their sons Donald and Reginald who were mentioned in two earlier chapters. Cyrus had purchased what was once Washington Lake House and quite a bit of acreage from Joseph Tether. By 1927 Cyrus had sold the Washington Lake House to Jacob Hensel, who had renamed it the Colonial.

Cyrus had died in a lumber accident eight years later. The Walters still owned some land near Washington Lake. Don and Reggie had continued farming. By 1939 Reggie had built Maplecrest next to Hensel's Colonial.

Before they were married, Joyce Walter, Reggie's wife, had worked at Sunset Cottage for Lewis and Elsie Hazen. Reggie fashioned their Maplecrest after the Hazen's house, but with no dormers. Don Walter offered boat rentals on Washington Lake at some point.

June 1939

Maplecrest Ad: *New house; hot and cold running water: handball court. Boating, bathing: $18 to 20. Barryville 2629, R. Walter.*

Baseball Hall of Fame

The second week of June, the Baseball Hall of Fame opened in

Jim Wade had a barber shop. Photo courtesy of Christene Stevens Myers.

Cooperstown, New York, home of one of baseball's founders, Abner Doubleday. The first class of inductees included Ty Cobb and Babe Ruth.

July 1939
Sunday, July 9, the Leavenworth crew went to Pond Eddy. They took Jimmy and Didrik's pictures.

Wednesday Jim helped Chester. Lee and Garfield went to Carl Wolff's in the evening.

Sunday, July 23, the men drew six tons of hay into the barn. Anna, Bill, and Jimmy were there in the evening.

Tuesday (and Saturday) Jim worked for Harry. Wednesday Jim and Chester finished haying on C. Love's place. It was free for the cutting.

Sunday, July 30, Garfield went over and staked out Grant Sergeant's cellar.

August 1939
Saturday, August 5, Anna and Jimmy were at her mom's all day.

Sunday Jennie visited Ella in the evening. Monday Clara and Ella repotted flowers all morning.

Sunday, August 13, Bill and Anna drove Mrs. Hazen to Ella's for a visit.

Wednesday Ella's two cousins Lillie Sergeant Brown and Anna Brague Ort called.

Friday Jim's sneakers he had ordered arrived.

Wednesday, August 23, Garfield and Chet Middaugh struck a good vein of water in a new well. Chet stayed for dinner with Garfield and Ella.

Thursday Jim's accordion arrived. It was the first item he had bought for himself.

The following Wednesday Mary Wormuth was in for a minute. She was Harry's wife and a granddaughter of Felix Kyte

Dunlap's Restaurant in Eldred, 1939. Photo courtesy of Kevin Marrinan.

Maplecrest built on Washington Lake. Postcard courtesy of Christene Stevens Myers.

View of the side of the Colonial which faced the water. Photo courtesy of Helen Hensel Oset.

Anna Meyers, Ella Leavenworth, Jimmy Meyers, Didrik Hansen, and Clara Hansen. Photo courtesy of Cynthia Leavenworth Bellinger.

Anna Meyers holding her son Jimmy. Photo courtesy of Cynthia Leavenworth Bellinger.

who had been the Congregational Pastor in the mid-1800s.

N.Y. 97 Officially Opened to Traffic
August 30, 1939, N.Y. Route 97 from Port Jervis to Hancock, was officially opened.

Several events were held to mark the road's opening, including a ribbon-cutting ceremony in Port Jervis featuring the mayors of Port Jervis and Hancock and a motorcade procession that traveled the length of the highway.

In all, it cost $4 million (equivalent to $66.8 million in 2012) to build N.Y. 97. The portion through the Hawk's Nest cost $2 million (equivalent to $33.4 million in 2012) to construct.
—wikipedia.org.

September 1939
Germany invaded Poland on Friday, September 1. The world would soon be at war.

"Fighting in Europe. Germans and Polish so far," Ella wrote on Saturday.

Sunday Clara and Ella took care of Jimmy so Anna and Bill could help Lottie Meyers with her boarding house.

Monday Lee and Garfield ran more cement in the barn.

Thursday the groceries were delivered from Al Randolph's Royal Scarlet.

Friday Ella wrote, "Babies both have teeth."

"War still on between Germany, England, etc.," Ella penned on Saturday.

In his Fireside Radio Chat Sunday, September 9, President Roosevelt said he fervently hoped the country could stay out of the war.

Wednesday, September 13, Jennie called. Garfield started cement for the new barn floor.

Friday afternoon Jennie was in to visit Ella again.

Saturday Jim worked. He paid

Mary Briggs was very ill in 1939. Photo courtesy of Mary Briggs Austin.

Mary Briggs, 14. Photo courtesy of Mary Briggs Austin.

his mom $5 board for two weeks.

"Cows in the new cement barn for first tonight. They are in out of the rain," Ella wrote on Tuesday, September 19.

Thursday and Friday Garfield worked down at the Methodist Church.

Sunday evening, September 24, Orville and Vernon Clark were in to see Jim. Monday Stella and her mother Eunice spent the day with Ella.

Thursday afternoon Jennie Austin, Anna, and Jimmy were in to see Ella.

Mary Briggs is Very Sick
When Mary Briggs was in ninth grade (1939–1940), she had quinsy sore throat and missed two months of school.

While I was sick, my brother Johnny would get assignments at school. The neighbor Mr. Sheen brought ice cream once-in-awhile. My mother took care of me day and night and collapsed on the floor.

I lost so much weight, I was like a pencil dressed up when I went back to school.—Mary Briggs Austin.

N.Y. Route 97 was officially completed from Port Jervis to Hancock on August 30, 1939. Hawk's Nest photo taken by Mr. Krause, courtesy of Kevin Marrinan.

October 1939
Sunday, October 8, Jim was at the Clark's for the day and Orville was at the Leavenworth's in the evening.

It was time for a new washer for Ella. Thursday after a couple loads of wash, the old washer went to pieces. Ella and Clara bought Kate Love's Maytag for $15. Clara bought Kate's new home sewing machine for $10.

Saturday Goldie moved most of his furniture from Kate Love's.

Tuesday, October 24, Clara and Lee took Anna a birthday cake. She turned 26 on Wednesday.

Friday was ladies' day out apparently. Anna, baby Jimmy (he had no choice), Clara, Lottie Meyers, Dorothy Wolff, and Ella went to Port Jervis for permanents.

Sunday, October 29, the men went to see about a bee tree. Orville and Jim went hunting.

Tuesday, the last day of October, Stella gave Ella a flower slip for planting.

November 1939
Wednesday, November 1, Clara and Ella washed feed bags. The feedbags came in prints and were used to make clothes or towels.

Sunday, November 5, Goldie moved the rest of his furniture.

Monday Paul Knorr fixed the washing machine.

Tuesday all the Leavenworths voted.

Sunday, November 12, Jim bought a new sink for his parents' kitchen. Garfield and Ella went up to see Goldie and Stella for the evening.

Tuesday afternoon Jennie visited Ella. Clara made sausage.

Saturday evening Jim went to Clark's. Orville went home with Jim and stayed overnight.

Garfield Leavenworth's new barn. "Cows in the new cement barn for first tonight. They are in out of the rain." Photo courtesy of Cynthia Leavenworth Bellinger.

Monday, November 20, Lee and Jim went to the movies at Monticello.

Thursday was Thanksgiving Day. The Leavenworths feasted on a goose dinner.

President Roosevelt had moved Thanksgiving to one week earlier than normal. The thinking was that it would help bolster retail sales. This was protested and after 1941, Thanksgiving took place on the fourth Thursday of November.

Thursday, the last day of the month, the Leavenworth family was together and celebrated a second Thanksgiving (on the original day) upstairs at Clara's.

December 1939

Saturday, December 2, Alex Mills called. Perhaps he had work for Garfield to do. Alex and his wife owned, or soon would own the Spring House in Barryville.

Tuesday Garfield finished working for the Mills.

Wednesday, December 6, Clara's Christmas gift order arrived and she and Ella wrapped the presents.

Thursday it was cloudy and rained at night. Jim worked. Lee and Clara went up to Bill's. The pigs arrived from Sears.

Monday, December 11, Jennie called at the Leavenworths.

Friday Anna and Jimmy were at her folks' in the evening while Bill went to see Earl Wells. Goldie and Stella were also there.

Sunday, December 17, Goldie, Jim, and Orville and Vernon Clark brought home Christmas trees.

Tuesday Ella sent a package to her sister Hazel, since the Connor family wouldn't be visiting for Christmas.

Ella started a crazy quilt for Clara on Wednesday.

Thursday evening Anna and Jimmy were at Ella's when Bill went to town. Madelyn Meyers went to the Christmas Party.

Saturday, December 23, the Leavenworth smoke house burned with about 200 pounds of pork in it.

Hazel, Walter, and family did visit for Christmas afterall.

Goldie and Stella took his cousins Marion and Marjorie Connor to see Pond Eddy's Christmas Tree.

It has been some time since we have heard from Lillie Calkin.

Lillie Calkin, Monticello, N.Y., to Mr. J.E. Austin, Ossining, N.Y.
December 23, 1939
Dear Dad,

London Children

In September 1939 children in London were evacuated to areas considered free from air attack. 1,500,000 evacuees (827,000 schoolchildren and their teachers; and 535,000 women expecting babies or with children under school age) were moved in three days.

Each child was labeled with name address and school number and carried a gas mask, night clothing, toothbrush, comb, soap and towel, spare underwear, handkerchief and overcoat if available. The children were left at railway stations and issued blank tickets with no destination given. The parents would be informed where they were as soon as possible. I can't imagine.—*World War II Day by Day*, p. 15.

The moving of the children to the country was the backdrop for one of C.S. Lewis' *Narnia* stories, which my dad Art Austin read to us.

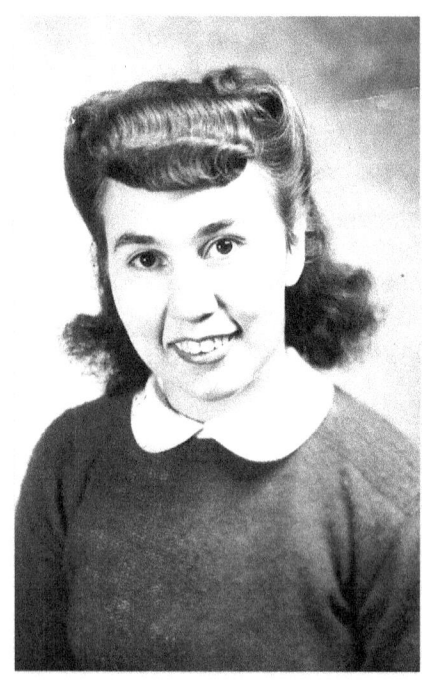
Madelyn Meyers joined the ladies when they went to get permanents at Port Jervis. Photo courtesy of Cynthia Leavenworth Bellinger.

Merry Christmas to you all. I sent a small package earlier in the week. Please use the money to get yourself something you really want or need. A larger package will follow next week with something you can all use.

*Love and Merry Xmas to all,
Lillie*

Garfield, Ella, their children (except Goldie and Stella) and the four Connors had a Christmas party on Christmas Eve (Sunday). It was the first time in 20 years that Ella and her sister had spent Christmas together.

Christmas Day the whole Leavenworth crew was there at some point. Anna and Bill, Clara and Lee were there for dinner. Goldie and Stella were in, too.

Hazel and her family left for their home in Massachusetts Tuesday morning.

Ella visited Goldie and Stella. Jim worked. The Leavenworth children all stopped by their parents' home at some point. Roy and Cappy Ott Horton were there for the evening.

Thursday, December 28, all Ella's children were in except Anna and Jimmy. Garfield stayed with his brother Truman who was ill and died later that day.

Garfield was up to the old Leavenworth place part of the day on Friday. Sunday, the last day of the year, there was a service for Truman in Port Jervis.

Ella and Garfield's Family, 1940
In 1940 Anna, Bill, and Jimmy Meyers lived in a little bungalow on Airport Road. They would soon buy a fixer upper house on the Eldred-Yulan Road.

The Hansen family who lived on the second floor of Garfield and Ella's home would live at the house Lee was building between

Spring House when owned by Mrs. Alex (Minnie Meyer) Mills. Postcard courtesy of Kevin Marrinan.

the old Leavenworth Echo Hill House and his brother-in-law Goldie's house. Goldie and Stella Leavenworth lived in their new home near beaver swamp. Jim Leavenworth lived with his parents Garfield and Ella.

Garfield would keep very busy with three houses: the Meyers' new fixer upper, Lee and Clara's house being built, and at times, remodeling his own place.

January 1940
Garfield and Ella Leavenworth started 1940 off with all of their family (minus Stella who perhaps

Anna and Bill Meyers standing on the porch of their second house on Eldred-Yulan Road 20 years after it was fixed up. Photo courtesy of Cynthia Leavenworth Bellinger.

was not feeling well) in at some point. Lee and Clara enjoyed a goose dinner with them. Grandson Jimmy and his dad Bill Meyers Jr. visited. Garfield's sister Anna Leavenworth called from East Islip.

Tuesday, January 2, Lee started digging the well for his and Clara's new home. While Lee worked on the well, Clara and Ella sometimes crocheted. Mid-month Garfield helped with digging Lee's well. Garfield also worked on his own well.

Wednesday, January 17, Lottie Meyers and Oliver Dunlap called on the Leavenworths. The next day Lee and Goldie did icing for Walter Tether. The following Tuesday Anna and Jimmy stopped by to see Ella, Clara, and Didrik. Lee and Garfield were still digging on the well.

Jim often visited the Clark brothers, Orville and Vernon. Sometimes they went ice fishing on nearby Montgomery Lake. Orville often stopped by to see Jim.

Saturday, January 27, the Leavenworth menfolk all helped to stone up Garfield's well.

Sunday Goldie and Lee drew

Charlotte Leavenworth's 1940 Class included children with familiar last names. 1st row: C. Wilson, W. McBride, C. Knorr, C. Marion, W. Williams, F. Clouse, P. Hallock, L. Lochner, H. Dunlap, F. Sullivan. 2nd row: E. Woodruff, D. Brodmerkel, G. Mills, R. Hill, E. Horton, D. Haas, Marilyn Horton, Madeline Horton, J. Woodruff, J. Hill, S. Myers, D. Mills, E. Clouse, C. Wilson, P. Hill. Back Row: Miss Leavenworth, F. Hallock. Photo courtesy of Cynthia Leavenworth Bellinger.

wood for Goldie's aunt Charlotte Leavenworth.

Mr. Briggs stopped by on Tuesday, the same day that Lee and Garfield each had five teeth pulled by a dentist in Hawley. Bill, Anna, baby Jimmy, and Ella went to Monticello. Goldie worked for Harry Wormuth.

February 1940
Thursday, February 1, Ella wrote, "Children in except Stella. Oliver Dunlap called." Friday Jim visited Roy Horton in the evening.

Monday, February 5, Garfield put his sister Charlotte's wood in for her.

Bill and Anna took Garfield to get the last of his teeth pulled on Wednesday. Bill and Anna each had a tooth filled. Lottie Meyers stopped by to see Ella for a second.

Friday the men stoned Garfield and Ella's well up to about five feet from the top.

Sunday, February 11, Garfield visited his sister Charlotte; Lee and Clara went up to their new place for a while.

Monday Lee, Charlie Sergeant, and Garfield finished stoning the Leavenworth well; Lee worked some on his place; Anna and baby Jimmy visited Ella all day; Goldie stopped in; Jim worked at Wormuth's; and Ella found out that George Crandall (Jennie Crandall's husband) was in the hospital. What a day!

Tuesday Garfield and Lee laid out Lee's cellar lines. Mary Sergeant was there all day. Lottie Meyers visited in the afternoon.

The blizzard on Valentine's Day (which would have been Sherman Leavenworth's 97th birthday) had started raging early the previous evening. Bill Meyers Sr. and Jr. plowed, which was awful difficult. The blowing and drifting continued into the next day.

Thursday while Lee plowed snow, Clara and Ella pieced quilts; Jim went to visit his sister Anna.

Jim took milk to his sister Anna and Clara on Friday. Ella continued to work on quilts.

Photo of Bradley's Restaurant and Bar with Ed Rider's 1933 Pontiac taken around 1940 by Mary Marrinan. Photo courtesy of Kevin Marrinan.

Jim visited Orville Clark on Orville's birthday, Sunday, the 18th.

Monday Lee left around 4 p.m. for New York City to visit his folks in Brooklyn. Carl Wolff visited the Leavenworths that evening.

Wednesday Garfield started helping Bill Jr. with his new home. It was quite the fixer upper.

Thursday when Garfield helped Bill with his house, Grant Sergeant helped Lee with his cellar. Friday Garfield and Jim helped Bill. Grant and Lee worked on Lee's cellar drain. This continued for some time. At times Jim helped Bill; other times he worked at Lee's.

Saturday while Grant and Jim helped Lee dig his cellar and Garfield helped Bill with his house, Lottie Meyers stopped by to see Ella.

Wednesday, February 28, Goldie, Stella, and Bill Meyers stopped by the Leavenworths. The feed came and the meter man stopped by to read the meter. Ella got a letter from Raola. Jim helped Lee. Garfield helped Bill.

The Leavenworths had a number of callers on leap day—Lottie Meyers, Katherine Clouse, and Dot and Austin Smith.

March 1940
Jim occasionally worked for Harry Wormuth in March, which claimed the worst ice storm in years on Sunday, March 3. Monday there were beautiful Northern Lights.

Friday Lee was still digging his cellar. Roy Horton and son Carl called. (Roy and his wife Cappy lived in the next house past Jennie Austin's, The Pines.)

Construction continued on the Hansen house; Lee was still digging out his cellar. Garfield alternated his help between Bill's remodeling and Lee's cellar.

Lottie Meyers and sometimes her daughter Madelyn stopped in for a visit with Ella. Or Jennie Austin and her granddaughter Joan might stop by to say hello to Ella. Saturday afternoon, March 9, all four ladies visited with Ella.

Sunday, March 17, Garfield and Lee worked about three hours on Lee's cellar. Tuesday, March 26, Howard Stevens stopped by the Leavenworth home. Wednesday Anna and Jimmy were at her parents' house all day. Jennie and Joan Austin stopped by.

April 1940
Apparently, working on two houses in the family was not enough to keep Garfield busy. On Monday, April 1 (a rather cruel joke), Goldie's roof heaved because of the ice, so Garfield helped his son. Two days later Goldie borrowed his parents' ladder as his roof was leaking.

Jim turned 18 on Tuesday. Jennie Austin was there all day. Lottie Meyers stopped by.

Friday Lee took the menfolk—Garfield, Goldie, and Jim—to Shohola to look over a stove.

The second week of April, Lee and Garfield helped Oliver Dunlap. Lottie and Madelyn called on Ella.

Saturday Ella wrote: "Our new Kalamazoo combination range came." Ella baked her first layer cake in the new stove on Sunday.

Monday, April 15, Lee and Garfield helped Oliver Dunlap. Garfield stopped in to see his sister Jennie who was sick. Tuesday Garfield and Lee finished working for Oliver Dunlap. Garfield went to see Jennie again on Wednesday.

Sunday, April 21, Dick Hansen turned a year old. Lottie took him a cute birthday cake on Monday.

Saturday, Anna, Bill, and Clara left their sons with Ella and Garfield, then went to Anna and Bill's place.

May 1940
Wednesday, May 1, Ella gave her information for the census to Jennie Crandall. Jim and Garfield plowed about half the garden with the new tractor. Anna and Jimmy visited Ella all day. Stella and Goldie were in for a bit. Bill Meyers was there for supper.

Sunday, May 12, Goldie brought home a pig, but the pig got out and Goldie couldn't find it. Garfield helped Bill Jr. sand the floors. Lee plowed his garden spot.

Wednesday Charlotte stopped by. Thursday the watch Ella had ordered from Montgomery Wards for Garfield arrived in the mail.

Friday, May 26, Goldie, Jim, Clara, and Dot Wolff helped Anna and Bill move into their house. The next day Garfield put up cupboard doors, etc. for them.

The Austins from Staten Island
In June of 1940 Raymond Austin moved his family to Eldred.

Ad for a Kalamazoo range, a few years after Ella got hers.

A group of visitors at the Glendella. Agnes Mary Lucke sitting on the grass on the far right. Photo courtesy of Mary Agnes Wilson Dorney.

My dad Raymond Austin thought with war looming we would be safer upstate.

There had already been some sabotage incidents around New York City (some more or less generally known) and a German sub actually arriving in Long Island Sound. Some officers had actually made their way into the city, attended a show and stopped a fishing boat on their way out and given them the ticket stubs! This was not generally known until after the war, but dad was in the Custom's service and it was known there right away.

So, we went to live in Eldred at my grandpa Edwin Myers' house. There we stayed through September 1942.—Melva Austin Barney.

Ed Wilson's Taxi Service
Ed Wilson managed the Amoco Gas Station in Barryville, but he also had a taxi service which was very helpful for summer guests as well as those who lived in town.

In the summer of 1940, Agnes Mary Lucke and her friends vacationed at the Glendella in Barryville.

The young ladies wanted to visit St. Joseph's Seminary in Callicoon, so they called for a Taxi—Ed Wilson's taxi.

Ed Wilson at the Amoco Station in 1941. Ed also ran a taxi service. Photo courtesy of Mary Agnes Wilson Dorney.

That fall letters from Barryville headed to Brooklyn where Agnes Mary Lucke lived and where she had grown up.

It was around the summer of 1940 that the Marrinan family from the Bronx started staying at the Colonial on Washington Lake for a few weeks every summer. Mary Marrinan took several photos in this book, including one of George Bradley's Restaurant and Bar *(see p. 202).*

I absolutely loved the summer at the Colonial. I made a lot of friends and kept in touch throughout the years and when I was old enough, I hunted with my friends. I loved how beautiful it was and it was always fun.
—Kevin Marrinan.

Kevin Marrinan would eventually own a home in Eldred and become good friends with Jim Leavenworth.

June 1940
Garfield and Ella spent Saturday, June 1, with Anna and Bill.

Jennie Austin went to the hospital where she would be for three months or so.

On Tuesday, June 4, Anna Ort spent the day with Ella and Garfield.

Wednesday, Ella went over to Anna's to help her clean. Garfield and Lee got their teeth. Sunday, Lottie Meyers and her daughters Dot Wolff and Madelyn stopped in for a bit.

Jennie Austin was operated on for goiter on Thursday, June 13. (Goiter is a form of hyperthyroidism. Jennie's was advanced and affected her heart.)

Mid-June, the cutting bar Jim had bought for his tractor was delivered. It cost $36.50.

Mid-June was also graduation

World and National News, January to July, 1940

1940 World and National News
- 1940 U.S. population: 132,164,569.
- Average cost of new car: $1,611; Gallon of gas: 18 cents.
- 82.8 percent of U.S. households owned a radio.
- 1# loaf of bread averaged 8 cents.
- Microwave, Jeep, and ballpoint pen invented in the 1940s.
- Walt Disney's animated *Pinocchio*.
- Alien Registration (Smith) Act.
- Oldsmobile first car maker to offer a fully automatic transmission.
- *Bugs Bunny; Tom and Jerry* cartoons.
- *Truth or Consequences*, NBC Radio.
- War in Europe began in earnest.
- Italy joined war with Germany. Conflict spread to North Africa.
- *Gone with the Wind* opened in Europe.
- The term RADAR was coined in 1940 by the U.S. Navy as an acronym for RAdio Detection And Ranging. Radar was secretly developed by several nations before and during World War II.—*wikipedia.org*.

January 1940
- Europe had a record snowfall.
- Exiled Polish government said Nazis killed 18,000 prominent Poles.
- Ida May Fuller first person to receive U.S. Social Security benefits.

February 1940
- Germany and the Soviet Union signed a trade agreement.
- Canadian forces arrived in England.
- Carbon-14 discovered.

March 1940
- The Conrad's newest ship *Queen Elizabeth* docked in New York City. Her sister ship the *Queen Mary* was already there. Both ships play a part in this story.
- Hitler and Mussolini met.

April 1940
- Germany invaded and occupied Denmark and Norway.

May 1940
- Germany invaded France, Belgium, and Netherlands.
- Churchill became British Prime Minister.
- Soviets won the war with Finland.
- Dutch Army surrendered.
- First McDonald's restaurant opened in San Bernardino, California.
- Roosevelt asked Congress to appropriate $1.18 billion for defense; to authorize production of 50,000 planes a year; to give a credit of $900 million; and to recommission 35 destroyers stored after WWI.
- Nazis conquered Brussels.
- British started rescue of British and French soldiers cut off by the German Army in Dunkirk, France, May 27–June 4.
- Belgian Army surrendered to Germany.
- Prototype of the F4U Corsair U.S. fighter made its first flight.

June 1940
- Germans crushed the French; Italy declared war on Britain and France.
- Dunkirk evacuation succeeded: 338,226 men saved; killed, wounded, or missing numbered 68,000; 222 naval vessels and 800 civilian crafts joined in the operation; 6 destroyers and 243 other ships were sunk.
- Japan advanced into the heart of China; within 400 miles of the Chinese Nationalist capital.
- June 14, Paris fell to Germany.
- Russian troops invaded Lithuania.
- The Sturgis Motorcycle Rally held for the first time in Sturgis, South Dakota.
- Britain's Churchill proclaimed the finest hour, his most famous wartime speech: "We shall fight on the beaches…We shall never surrender…Let us so bear ourselves that, if the British Empire and its Commonwealth last for a thousand years, men will still say, 'This was their finest hour.'"
- Roosevelt ordered export of surplus artillery and rifles to Britain.
- President Roosevelt signed Naval Expansion Act. It provided for an 11% increase in naval tonnage as well as an expansion of naval air capacity. Congress approved $4 billion to build a two-ocean Navy and procure 15,000 naval aircraft.
- Charles DeGaulle recognized as leader of France.
- Mussolini and Hitler met in Munich.
- The Republican Party nominated Wendell Willkie for president.
- The Red Army occupied part of Romania.

July 1940
- In North Africa Britain destroyed the French Navy. (After the fall of France and the armistice between France and Nazi, Operation Catapult was to take the French ships into British control or destroy them.)
- Start of Battle of Britain between the British Royal Air Force and the German Luftwaffe.
- Roosevelt barred export of war material to Japan. He signed a Navy bill which provided for construction of 45 more ships, with $550 million to finance them and other projects.
- The Democratic Party nominated Franklin D. Roosevelt for a third term as president.

—War related news mainly from *World War II Day by Day*, published by Dorling Kindersley Limited, 2004.

The Hirsch family moved back to Eldred and ran Echo Hill Farm House. Charlee Hirsch is on the porch. Photo is courtesy of Ric Schroedel.

time at Eldred Central. The class of 1940 included: Florine Burgess, Doris Doeller, Calvina Livingstone, Grace Kewley, Evelyn MacIntyre, Fred Meyer, Elsie Parker, Richard Putnam, Margaret Smith, Vera Vollmer, Clara Wolff, Ruth Worzel, and Frances Toaspern.

Late Monday, June 17, Christina Hirsch and her family arrived from Ohio where they had been living. Charlee had attended Glendale High School there. She would start at Eldred Central in the fall. This was probably when Anthony and Christina Hirsch started running Echo Hill as a boarding house. Charlee mainly waited tables and worked in the kitchen.

The Hirsches ran Echo Hill with the understanding that Christina's brother Martin Leavenworth would live there.

Cousin Art had Sunday dinner at our house each week. He would help me with algebra homework in the afternoon.—Charlee Hirsch Schrodel.

Friday Anthony Hirsch called on the Leavenworths. Lottie Meyers spent the day there.

Goldie and Stella were the proud parents of a son, Frederick Clinton Leavenworth born on June 25, 1940. Little Frederick,

Charlee Hirsch with a beloved cat Figaro, at the water pump. "Cousin Art had Sunday dinner at our house each week." Photo courtesy of Ric Schroedel.

two months premature, was born at Garfield and Ella's home. Anna and Bill visited for a short while.

Saturday, June 29, Ella went with Goldie to his house when he uncrated his new washer.

Freddie finally nursed for the first time. He wasn't getting enough milk and would not take a bottle.

Little Freddie had several bad spells. He seemed to be doing better, but he died on July 2. Clinton took him to Port Jervis to the funeral home. Another incredibly sad, sad time.

July 1940

Anna was at her parents' home helping out all day on Wednesday and Thursday. Stella's parents and grandmother Hallock visited her.

Saturday, Stella and Goldie went back to their own home.

Stella was still recovering on Thursday, July 19, when Goldie stopped in to see his parents.

Sunday, Ella stayed with Stella for the afternoon. That Friday Stella was able to visit Garfield and Ella at their home for the first time since the baby was born.

At the end of July the men cut hay. Lee went to Bethel. Goldie and Stella visited the Leavenworths for the day. Bill and Anna were there in the evening.

August 1940

In August Ella kept the sewing machine humming. She made four shorts for Lee; and five pairs of pillow cases for Anna to give for Christmas presents.

The next chapter continues 1940 in August, after first renewing our acquaintance with the somewhat unconventional Aida Austin and her brother Lon. Aida Austin's Diary will also help tell the story through the first part of 1943.

Chapter 9
Newspapers and Oatmeal
Lon and Aida Austin, 1940–1941

Aida: Save only the clippings that you want from newspapers.
Lon: Save the whole paper if you are interested.
(His house certainly attested to his following his belief.)
Aida: You should boil the water first when you make oatmeal.
Lon: You should mix the oatmeal in cold water, and then cook it.

Obviously with such diverse thinking, the elderly Austin siblings Lon and Aida couldn't live in the same house.

So Lon and Aida each lived in their own place next door to each other. The homes were on the original Austin property possibly bought around 1840. Lon lived in the house where he, Aida, and their siblings had grown up.

Though they couldn't possibly live in one house, they were very concerned and caring for one another. They were back and forth a dozen times a day to check on one another.

Lon was a lovely man. He looked very much like Grandpa Austin and treated me to the same smile, with the same very blue eyes, long after Grandpa was gone.

Uncle Lon lived in the smaller house (where the pictures of Uncle McKinley were taken). It was the older house and closer to the road. Aunt Aida lived in the larger house further back.—Melva Austin Barney.

Aida was a somewhat peppery, independent lady. Both she and Lon had strong opinions and tried to change things they thought were wrong.

Sometime around 1940 Aida researched the history of both her family and the Town of Highland (originally Lumberland). She hand copied excerpts of many land deeds, the oldest of which was from 1815.

Aida also continued to keep connected with her Eldred cousins (though by 1940, many had died) and the almost Austin cousins: Rowlee Schoonover and his sister Emma Waidler. Their half siblings: Laura Britt, George, and Kate Parker, whom Aida also called cousins, had died.

Aida discussed her research with Melva Austin, her great-niece. Melva at times helped Aida by carrying her groceries home. Melva would be tired out when she arrived at Aida's, but Aida was not. Aida made Melva hot chocolate. But first Aida had to chop some kindling wood so she could start the fire in the stove. As they drank hot chocolate, Aida talked to Melva

Mary Horton Bosch. Mary and her husband Herman were good neighbors, dear friends, and like family to Lon and Aida Austin. Photo courtesy of Victoria Kohler.

about the history she was finding and saving.

Sometimes Aida played recordings of Caruso for Melva, or played songs on the organ. (It was the organ she had mentioned in a letter as a possibility of selling so many years previous.)

I more and more realize that while we were socializing and she was telling me "stories," I was being taught.—Melva Austin Barney.

Aida entrusted Melva with her extensive assortment of photos, letters, and research, all of which has played a major part in this book series and was the basis for the story of the arrival of the James Eldred Family in, *The Mill on Halfway Brook*.

Eldred was called Halfway Brook Village when Lon and Aida were young. They continued to refer to Eldred as, "the Village."

In 1940 Aida, 79, Lon, 83, and their brother Ell, 85, were the last three living Austin siblings.

Lon and Aida walked the hilly, rough terrain from their place on Proctor Road to the Village and the A&P almost daily; sometimes twice a day—but at different times. From the A&P they often walked across the street to the Post Office in the Parker Hotel where Emily, Howard, and Christene (Teenie) Stevens lived. Emily was the Postmaster.

If the A&P did not have an item, Aida stopped at Andrew's (Andy and Marge Parker's Store) or Randolph's Royal Scarlet Store on her way home.

Andy and Marge Parker were Eldred fixtures for a number of years. They operated a magazine and newspaper shop and sold various and sundry other goods. Their store was located on the site of the former Von Ohlen empire. They shared the building that also housed Al Randolph's Royal Scarlet Grocery Store. Marge had a very friendly and outgoing nature.—Ken Bosch.

Andrew Parker's store was similar to a variety store. I bought Archie and Veronica *comic books there. My brother David bought baseball bubble gum cards. In the same building was the Royal Scarlet, a grocery store owned by Alex and Kathryn Myers Randolph. Each store had its own entry.*

Wait and Boyd's Garage was on Eldred's southwest corner. The A&P, south of Wait and Boyd's, but on the same side, had wooden floors. Next to the A&P was Jim Wade's Barber Shop.—Cynthia Leavenworth Bellinger.

My mother Emma Stevens had a table and chairs in the big lobby of the Post Office and there was always a morning gathering waiting for the mail. One day after Lon Austin was sitting

View to the left of Randolph's which Aida and Lon would pass each time they went to the A&P. Panoramic photo continued on opposite page.

Three unknown young folks in front of the homes where Aida (right) and her brother Lon Austin (left) lived. Photo in Austin Collection.

Al and Kay Randolph, and Marge Parker in front of Randolph's Royal Scarlet Grocery Store and Andrew Parker's Store. Photo courtesy of Victoria Kohler.

there, Mom looked out and saw what she thought was money, so checked and she was correct. She remembered exactly who was sitting there and Dad took the money to Lon.—Christene Stevens Myers.

The neighbors and townsfolk were very caring to Aida and Lon. Often a neighbor on the way to or from town would stop and give Aida or Lon a ride. Though Lon, at least, preferred to walk.

Herman, Mary, Herman Jr., Marjorie, and Bobby Bosch were very good neighbors and like family to Aida and Lon. Perhaps the fact that Herman Sr. had fought in the same places in France as their nephew McKinley Austin (who had died in France) made Herman like a son to them.

Aida's Diary of the early 1940s started around August of 1940 when Emma Waidler visited her brother Rowlee Schoonover (Uncle Dan to some in town).

Rowlee Schoonover
Rowlee Schoonover and his wife Emily Banner had moved back to Eldred around 1938. They lived in one of three bungalows on the northwest corner of Eldred, west of the Wilson building. Wait and Boyd had built the bungalows from the wood of Jackson Myers' old store, originally in that location. Rowlee's eyes had gotten so bad he had to retire from chauffeuring the widow of Dr. Douglas, in Tuxedo, New York.

Rowlee moved back to Eldred when he left Mrs. D. and opened a blacksmith shop. He closed the shop when he lost depth vision resulting from blindness in the one eye. They lived in the cottage across the street from the house he lived in until he was 12. He could see the foundation from the front stoop.—John D. Hull.

The Schoonovers were very good friends of my parents. In fact Uncle Dan had no transportation and when he was asked to do metal work on the new Barryville-Shohola Bridge, my dad took him to and from work every day. —Christene Stevens Myers.

In August Emma Waidler visited her brother Rowlee for

Andy and Marge Parker owners of Parker's which Aida called Andrew's. Photo courtesy of Victoria Kohler.

Emily and Howard Stevens who were so helpful to Aida and Lon Austin. Photo courtesy of Christene Stevens Myers.

Rowlee and Emily Banner Schoonover celebrated their 61st Wedding Anniversary in 1961. Photo courtesy of John D. Hull, great-grandson.

nine days. Emma lived in Cairo, New York. She often spent time with her nieces, Ada Britt Wood and Kitty Britt James and their families.

Aida Austin's Diary
Aida Austin's Diary written on the east side of Eldred joins the daily writing of Ella Sergeant Leavenworth on Eldred's west side to tell the story of the Town of Highland from August 1940 to early 1943. Some townsfolk are mentioned in both ladies' diaries.

August 1940
While Rowlee worked on the new Barryville-Shohola Bridge, Aida Austin had lunch with Rowlee's wife Emily, and his sister Emma.

Thursday Aida, Emily, Emma, and Mrs. Winter visited Mary Kyte Wormuth to look over old pictures of Eldred, and Lydd, England, where Mary's grandfather, Felix Kyte had been born in 1800.

Aida's nephew Bob Austin joined the Canadian Army the second week of August.

On the west side of Eldred, Everett Kelley was home from the County Farm (the poorly named home for elderly people).

Jennie Crawford Crandall
It's been some time since we have talked about Jennie Crandall who wrote such lively letters in *Echo Hill and Mountain Grove*. Jennie and Lillie Austin Calkin (Aida's niece) were lifelong friends.

In the middle of August, Jennie Crandall and Lillie visited Aida. Jennie lived in the house Aida Austin's grandfather James Eldred had built around 1830. That house had replaced the Eldred's original 1815 cabin by the sawmill.

Jennie and Lillie promised to show Aida a book they discovered in that 110-year-old house.

Aida and Lon Austin's sweet corn was ready to be picked on Tuesday, August 20. Aida went to tell Mae Parker, but Mae and her daughter Ruth had gone to Middletown. Only "the French woman and Mae's brother Will Hammond were there."

Mae Hammond Parker
Mae Hammond Parker managed the Hammond House on the northwest side of the Hartung and Highland Roads intersection. Quite possibly her brother Will Hammond helped run the House where he and Mae had most likely grown up. It was in operation at least by 1920. Mae's daughter Ruth also lived there. A French woman helped out. Mae's husband George may have worked elsewhere.

Friday Mae, Ruth, and the French woman stopped by Aida's to get corn. In the afternoon Aida went to the Village where she met Emily Schoonover at the A&P.

Aida stopped at Jennie Crandall's on the way home, but Jennie was not there. So Aida stopped at Elizabeth Wilson's. Elizabeth's daughter Georgia Styles was there and drove Aida home.

The Styles lived on the opposite side of Proctor Road, not far from Aida and Lon's houses. Georgia mentioned to Aida that

Main Street 1940. Rowlee and Emily Banner Schoonover lived to the west, behind the Wilson building on the northwest corner. Photo courtesy of Christene Stevens Myers.

Old Barryville-Shohola Bridge in distance. Dot in middle of photo shows where the Briggs lived. Photo by Irwin Briggs in the collection of Mary Briggs Austin.

Dr. Austin would be arriving on Tuesday. Dr. Austin was the brother of Henrietta Austin, wife of Walter Styles—until she ran off with a preacher. Aida and Lon rented from their cousin Dr. Austin, who owned the large property that once belonged to their father. Henry Austin had lost his land because of hard times financially.

Lon Austin saw the Briggs family at Chester Middaugh's clambake and cornroast.

Saturday the frost that killed the Leavenworth garden on the west side of Eldred, was probably not that good for Lon and Aida's garden on the east side, either.

Sunday, August 25, Rowlee was up to Aida's. He told her he would be working on the bridge for quite a long time.

Aida had a nice visit with John Dunlap on Monday when she took his milk can back to him. Chester Middaugh stopped by John's while Aida was there. (John and Katherine Dunlap were an older couple who lived on a back road near Highland Lake. We met them when they visited Garfield and Ella.)

Townsfolk in Aida Austin's Diary

Aida and Lon's Relatives
- Bill, Bob, Arthur Austin
- Raymond, Gladys, Melva, Joan Margie, Dawn Lee Austin
- Dr. Austin
- Lillie Austin Calkin
- Rowlee and Emily Schoonover
- Emma Schoonover Waidler

East Eldred and Highland Lake "Neighbors"
- Mae Parker and her daughter Ruth
- Harold Frint, married Ruth Parker
- Will Hammond, Mae's brother
- Walter and Georgia Styles
- Herman, Mary, Herman Jr., Margie, and Robbie/Bob Bosch
- Charles and Bertha Sullivan
- Alfred and Bessie Hill
- John and Katherine Dunlap
- Herbert Kinne
- Mrs. Winter
- Mrs. Bye
- Ernest Horton
- Pete Sullivan
- Hattie Schroeder
- Mabel Boyd Ryman

Central and West Eldred and other Neighbors
- Chester Middaugh
- Elizabeth Wilson
- Jennie Crandall
- Harry and Mary Kyte Wormuth
- Howard and Emily Stevens
- Teenie Stevens (Myers)
- Paul and Frances LaBarr Knorr
- Clarence Sergeant's wife Claudia
- Alvin and Harriet Hill
- Floyd Boyd
- Alex Wait
- Ed Myers
- Mrs. William Clouse
- Joseph and Florence Brague
- Anna Sergeant Brague Ort
- Mary Hulse Sergeant
- Nellie Crandall
- Mr. and Mrs. Briggs and John
- Walter Horton's wife, Cleta Myers
- Hazel LaBarr Angell
- Mrs. Sparks
- Delbert Rundle
- Mrs. Lewis

Spring House Garage and part of old bridge. Photo courtesy of Linda Guenther Anderson.

It was Friday before Dr. Austin arrived from New York City. He spent only a few minutes with Aida. Friday afternoon Bertha Sullivan called on Aida in the afternoon. Bertha ran a boarding house for summer boarders and fall hunters.

Saturday (when it rained very hard nearly all day) Dr. Lon Austin was at Aida's with Herman Bosch to see what needed to be done to the old Austin house. Dr. A. headed back to the city on Sunday.

On the west side of Eldred, Lee Hansen's new house had a cement foundation thanks to help from the Leavenworth men. In his spare time Garfield built a small stepladder for Ella. Ella often played with her grandsons Didrik Hansen and Jimmy Meyers so their mothers could wash and bake.

Jim Leavenworth worked a half day for Harry Wormuth the last week of August.

September 1940
Sunday evening, September 1, Charlie and Clareta Sergeant and their children visited Garfield and Ella.

Tuesday morning Aida met Jennie Crandall at the A&P in the Village.

Wednesday Ella cleaned all the rooms in her house. Anna took her a birthday cake. Stella and Goldie, and Orville Clark visited Ella Thursday—the same day Jim bought a rabbit dog from Roy Horton for $3.

Friday Lon Austin bought a half bushel of peaches.

Saturday was very rainy, as was Sunday. Aida was outside when Mae and Ruth stopped by and dropped off some papers for her. Lon was at church.

Aida picked up chips and pieces of wood on her property when the weather cleared on Monday, September 9.

Ever the free thinker and fascinating person, Aida spent the rainy Tuesday copying parts of the Scopes trial of July 21, 1925.

Thursday in west Eldred, Garfield worked a couple days at the Wormuth Mill for Jim who was sick. Stella and Goldie stopped in for the evening.

Aida was at the Village on Friday morning.

Friday afternoon Garfield's sister Anna Leavenworth stopped by to see him. Aunt Anna lived in East Islip and must have been staying with the Hirsch family at Echo Hill.

Saturday Howard Stevens took Aida some papers to read. (People saved papers for Aida.) Mae and Ruth visited a bit in the afternoon.

Monday, September, 16,

Chester Middaugh

Chester Middaugh was a great friend of my dad and helped him so much. My dad had a fear of chimney fires, so Chester helped him rebuild the Methodist Church chimney. Chester usually walked the four miles from Eldred to Barryville.

Every summer (as mentioned in Aida Austin's Diary) a group of folks would get together at Chester's house for a cornroast and clambake. Lon Austin and my family would go.

Chester had a bad stuttering speech, they told me, and swore alot until he was converted. Then he'd get himself calm and talk slow enough that he didn't stutter.

It seems Chester's wife Florence had wanted to go to church, but he wouldn't let her. Before she died she made Chester promise to go to church just one time. Chester decided to honor his wife's request the year a Mr. Melconian came for a revival at the Methodist Church.

Before leaving for the service, Chester set out his shot gun to use on himself when he got home. The first night Chester attended, he bolted out the back door before the service ended. But he didn't use his gun that night. Chester decided to go to the service a second night. Mr. Melconian told my Dad to close the service so he could talk to Chester before he could leave. Mr. Melconian and my dad talked to Chester and prayed with him and he became a Christian. Chester never had to use that gun after all.—*Mary Briggs Austin.*

Dynamite for blasting rock in Pond Eddy. The stone was used to build Route 97, which was completed in August 1939. Photos by Irwin Briggs in the collection of Mary Briggs Austin.

the Selective Training and Service Act of 1940, went into effect. It was the first peace time draft in U.S. history.

It was time for school. Lillie Calkin who taught at Yulan, stopped by to see her aunt Aida after school on Tuesday. Alfred Hill was drawing wood for Aida. Lillie promised Aida she would stop after school on Friday.

Ella Leavenworth's children were all grown, but the two youngest Briggs' children, Mary and John, were back in school. They both played in the band.

Anna Leavenworth visited with her sister-in-law Ella for the day on Thursday.

Thursday Aida was walking home from the A&P, when Mary Bosch "overtook me on the way back so I got a ride part way."

Lillie Calkin did visit Aida after school on Friday. She and Aida walked up past the north lot along the road where Lon had been cutting wood.

There was quite a hard shower Saturday afternoon, but it cleared before church time, though there was no church at night. (Aida didn't attend church, but she recorded when Lon went.)

Aida did her washing Monday, which was "pleasant all day."

It rained nearly all Wednesday. Aida visited Mae Parker in the afternoon. A young man Harold Frint boarded there, and was "keeping company" with Mae's daughter Ruth. The rain stopped just before Harold and Ruth took Aida home.

Thursday was clear and colder. Lon sawed wood. There was a heavy frost that night. Arthur Austin was out to church for the

1940 Halfway Brook News

Postcard of Reber's (once Clouse's) with the new bridge that was completed in 1941.

1940 Eckharts and Wilsons Move
- When the bridge was started in 1940, Eckharts and Wilsons in Barryville moved to a new location. Clouse's Casino remained and at some point became Reber's.

Route 97 Anniversary
- August 30; the one year celebration for the completion of Route 97.

1940 Entered the Service
- Bob Austin enlisted in the Canadian Army in August.

1940 Census Taker
- Jennie Crandall.

1940 Births
- Frederick Clinton Leavenworth (two months premature) born to Goldie and Stella Leavenworth.
- Earl Louis Lilley born to Emerson and Eleanor Ort Lilley.
- Dawn Lee Austin was born to Raymond and Gladys Austin.
- Wayne E. Hansen born to Lee and Clara Leavenworth Hansen.
- Mauna Lee Sergeant born to Charlie and Clareta Kuen Sergeant.
- Richard James born to Edward H. and Norma Wood James. Richard's cousin Gary Britt James born to Elwood and Ann Plachy James. Gary and Richard James are descendants of Laura Parker Britt.

1940 Marriages
- Ed Bornstein married Mary Oset in the early 1940s. His first wife had died some years before.
- Ed Wilson married Agnes Mary Lucke in Brooklyn.

1940 Deaths
- Frederick C. Leavenworth died July 2, at seven days old.
- Jennie Louisa Leavenworth Austin died in Eldred, November 6, 1940.
- Ella E. Breen Gardner, 1864–1940, was the mother of Edna Gardner.
- Charlotte E. Middaugh Myers, 1868–1940.
- Margaret C. Sergeant, 1872–1940.
- Fred Nitzsche died sometime in the 1940s.

special meetings on Thursday, but not on Friday, Lon told Aida.

Friday when Aida was at the A&P, she saw Emily Schoonover.

Saturday Stella, Goldie, and their new pup stopped in for a while at his parents'. Clara was there. The doctor had said it would be best if she stayed with Ella until her second child was born. Jim went to the movies.

Saturday the Methodists ended their special meetings. Arthur was there and drove Lon home after church.

October 1940
It was a nice, clear day when Dawn Lee Austin was born to Raymond and Gladys Austin. The new little Austin was named for the time she was born (Dawn) and Lee for her aunt Leversa (Lee) Myers.

Aida and Lon started October off by chopping wood. The next two days were rainy. Mae was at Aida's for an hour or so on Wednesday. Lon went down to the weekly church meeting. He was "not very much pleased with it."

When the weather cleared about noon on Thursday, Aida headed down to the A&P.

Friday Aida expected Lillie to visit, but she didn't.

Sunday, October 6, church was at the Methodists. (Apparently church alternated between the Methodist and Congregational Churches; Eldred or Barryville; morning or evening.)

Aida had a terrible cold for a few days, but she was much better on Tuesday. She stopped to give some pears to John and Katherine Dunlap on her way over to give pears to her friend Mae. Ruth Parker took Aida home.

Aida felt very tired on Wednesday, but Thursday she pulled beets, turnips, and carrots, and picked some cabbage. In the afternoon she went to the Village.

Friday Ella Leavenworth made five loaves of bread. Garfield, Orville Clark, Bill Ort Jr., and Lee's dad, worked on Lee's place for eight hours Saturday.

Tuesday, October 15, Alex Wait was at Aida's to see about getting a road through her two acres of land. Alex and Lon went up to look at the boundaries.

Sunday, October 20, John and Katherine Dunlap called on Garfield and Ella before they (the Dunlaps) went south for the winter. Mr. Wood the music teacher also stopped by.

Monday was very busy. Alex Wait was at Aida's in the morning to arrange about the road. Mr. Briggs was up to see Lon about going to a dinner Tuesday night at Port Jervis. Lon and Aida took in the turnips and carrots. Aida went to see Frances Knorr and Bessie Hill.

Tuesday Lon and Alex went to see about surveying the road through Aida's two acres. Floyd Boyd and young Twichell were also there. Lon went to the supper with Rev. Briggs that night.

Tuesday Anthony Hirsch (who ran Echo Hill Farm) went back to Ohio for four more weeks.

Wednesday Ella finished the pajamas and gowns she had been making. Wednesday morning Aida Austin walked to the A&P. Later, Arthur stopped in to see her and asked why Mr. Briggs wanted him.

Thursday Ruth Parker accompanied by her "gentleman friend Harold Frint," took some papers to Aida. Lon drew wood.

Friday Jim took his test for a car license at Monticello—which he received on Saturday.

Aida saw her cousin Elbert Clark on Saturday. Elbert, 73, had never married. He lived in Highland Lake with or near his youngest brother, Robert Clark, 64, and a widower.

Sunday, October 27, Anna Meyers, Dorothy Wolff, Madelyn Meyers, and Jim went to the World's Fair. Grandchildren Dick and Jimmy stayed with Garfield and Ella who, "sure enjoyed the

Margie Austin with her new sister Dawn Lee Austin. Photo courtesy of Melva Austin Barney.

Dawn Lee Austin was named for her aunt Lee Myers. Orville and Leversa (Lee) Myers. Photo courtesy of Pam Fischetti DeFeo.

two little fellows."

Jennie Austin had not been well for sometime. She was in the hospital at Middletown. Gladys Austin and her four daughters were staying at her father Edwin Myers' place. You may remember that Raymond had thought his family would be safer in Eldred, away from New York City.

Gladys Austin, Eldred, to Raymond Austin, Staten Island
October 29, 1940
Dearest Ray,

You will have received Arthur's letter before this reaches you so will know your mother's condition.

Arthur was in today on his way to Middletown. He said her left arm was paralyzed and that her mouth was drawn to one side, but the nurse told him this morning on the phone that she could move her fingers on that side now. It seems that it has affected her mind temporarily and she tries to get out of bed so they have to keep a nurse with her all the time. It's such a pity after all the boys have done and just when she seemed to be making good headway toward getting better.

Arthur is terribly broken up over it, but keeps himself well under control.

I can well imagine your feelings too, and believe me, dear, I'm thinking about you. Things have come fast and heavy for you in the last few years. [Mountain Grove had burned down, his father had died, and his baby son had died.]

Arthur will probably be going to Middletown every day while Jennie is in this condition, so if you wanted to see her when you come up Friday or Saturday, he could meet you there if you would let him know.

Front Left: Buddy Dunlap, H. Kuen, J. Lass, M. Lass, R. Worzel, Josette Marion, C. Myers, Mary Briggs, C. Ott, O. Worzel. Back: Mr. Cook, E. Worzel, John Briggs, M. Ort, J. Lovelace, W. Lass, R. Putnam. 1940 band photo courtesy of Linda Guenther Anderson.

I received your letter Monday. I still have the check, but will give it to Art tomorrow when he brings Melva's shoes, which he left in the shoemakers in Port Jervis today to be half soled.

I borrowed a dollar from Cliff [her brother] *so I could pay for the bread from the baker this week; so will give Art the $5 you owe him, plus whatever he paid for Melva's shoes. I'll still have a bit of change which will be all I'll need as payday is close at hand.*

Expect to do some house cleaning soon. Lee said she would give me a hand next week as she will have her cleaning finished.

The children are all well. Dawn Lee surely is a honey and except for a couple hour crying spell after supper each night, is very good. I wake her at 2 in the morning for feeding and except for that, she sleeps from 10 to 6 without a break. She's getting very cute looking, and she's growing like a weed.

Also bring the children's vaccination and inoculation certificates. They want them at school. Believe they are in the envelope marked Birth Certificates which I left in your drawer. Don't forget them.

Mary Briggs and her brother John Briggs with their dog Pal. The band got uniforms in 1940 or 1941. Photo courtesy of Mary Briggs Austin.

Look forward to seeing you this weekend. Lots of Love, Glad

The last day of October, Aida met Mrs. Winter in front of Dunlap's on her way to the A&P. Arthur was in front of the A&P with a telegram. His mother Jennie Austin had had a stroke. Her goiter was advanced and it had affected her heart.

November 1940
The next day, Friday, November 1, Arthur saw Lon in the Village, and told him his mother could not live.

Sunday Mae Parker and Harold Frint took papers to Aida.

Tuesday, November 5, was election day. Aida voted about nine o'clock. Lon had voted earlier.

On the west side of Eldred, Clara and Ella took Didrik with

Barryville-Shohola Bridge being built. Photo by Irwin Briggs in the collection of Mary Briggs Austin.

them when they went to vote.

A high cold wind blew through a partly cloudy sky on Wednesday, November 6. Lon brought home the newspaper with the headline: "Roosevelt Winner. Sweeps to victory in New York, Illinois…"

"Poor Aunt Jennie Austin died about noon today," wrote Ella on Wednesday, November 6.

It was a sad, sad time for Raymond, Bill, Art, and Bob. In three years time they had lost both parents. Jennie was 60 years old.

Art and Raymond had gone to see their mother on Wednesday. Raymond then went to the Shohola Depot to take the train to Staten Island where he lived. But Arthur, who had received a telegram that his mother had died, was able to telephone Raymond before he left Shohola.

Aida and Lon did not know of Jennie's death until the next day. Emma Stevens told Lon who told Aida that afternoon. Arthur also stopped in to tell his aunt and uncle that his mother had died.

Arthur told them that the funeral was to be at the church on Saturday about 2 or 2:30. The family was to meet at the house at 1:30. The body was at the undertakers, but was to be taken home that night.

On Friday afternoon Aida walked to the A&P. Mary Bosch drove Aida back home. Lon walked over to Bosch's to ask Mary for a ride to the funeral on Saturday, which of course she said she would do.

Saturday Garfield and the men worked on Lee's house in the morning, and went to Jennie Austin's funeral in the afternoon.

Mary Bosch drove Aida and Lon to the house about one o'clock. The family (Bob was serving in the Canadian Army) sat in the kitchen and the others were in the dining room. It was a large funeral and a great many flowers.

"The only service at the house was a short prayer by Mr. Briggs and there was no singing at the church," Aida wrote later that day.

Lillie was there. She came with Charlie Myers (Jennie's cousin) and his wife Elizabeth. Lillie had left her car at the Myers' place. Lillie went back with the Myers, but stopped at Aida's on her way home.

Saturday during the funeral, Lottie Meyers stayed with Ella. (Both Lottie and Ella had been good friends of Jennie Austin.) Stella and Goldie were in twice.

Thursday, November 14, Mae Parker stopped at Aida's to borrow a parasol. Mae was going to see lawyer Cuddeback in Port Jervis and put in a claim against George Parker's property. George had

Spring 1941 photo of Raymond and Gladys Austin's girls: Melva, Dawn Lee, Joan, and Margie. Melva: Something that has amused me about this picture, is that as the age line goes down, the degree of displeasure increases. I look happy, Joan looks not pleased, Margie looks about ready to cry and Dawn is in full bawl. It must have been an occasion when they were getting tired of it and with big sisterly compassion, I thought they were funny. Photo in the Austin Collection.

Jennie Leavenworth Austin, Mother, and Grandmother

I remember Grandma and Grandpa Austin very well. I had the opportunity of spending quite a bit of time with them and remember Grandma teaching me, Now I lay me down to sleep—and staying with me every night to say it with me.

We lived on Staten Island when I was a child, but we went to Eldred for every summer. We usually stayed at my maternal grandfather Edwin Myers' house on Barryville Road. But naturally I spent time with my Austin Grandparents, too.

There were other visits, too, when they were not so busy with boarders in winter or spring. Also, periods of time that I spent with her when Joan and Margie were born and we were there for some holidays.

Just before the U.S. entered World War II, we went to live in Eldred at Grandfather Myers' house. So of course I saw a great deal of Grandma and other Austin and Leavenworth relatives then.

Grandma was always busy. She did all the cooking for the boarding house, and of course, for her family. She also participated in the housekeeping although in the busy summer months she had assistance with the laundry.

A Mrs. Crandall had the washing machine going virtually all day. Grandpa kept a steady flow of vegetables from his garden, eggs, chickens, and fruit and berries in season. She did all the baking, usually, including the bread. She made gingerbread men on occasion and bread rolls or biscuits in interesting shapes.

In fall and winter Grandma did a lot of embroidery and piecing together for quilts. I was present for a couple of quilting bees. I was pretty impressed, still am when I think of it. I didn't think the results were particularly beautiful, but don't know why. My mother said that I shouldn't comment, because the purpose of them was to keep warm not to show. Grandma also made clothing and was always involved in Ladies' Aide projects.

Grandma Jennie Austin with her daughter Elizabeth and youngest son Bob. Photo in Austin Collection.

I may have left you with the impression that Grandma was a bustling person. She was not. She just seems to have constantly and methodically and calmly kept going. When she sat down to her sewing I felt that she had nothing else to do nor had she been doing anything else though I knew better.

Grandma liked to give her granddaughters dolls. She said she never had enough of them when she was a child and vowed any little girls who came her way would. And she made clothes for her granddaughters and the dolls.

As a grandma, she had many ways of keeping one happy on rainy or very cold days. One of my favorites was having her put a huge section of unused wall paper (plain side out) fastened to a section of the wall, providing a stack of old magazines, scissors, paste and crayons and letting you "have at it," letting me turn the room into any place I wanted it to be—shipboard or beach or jungle or movie making studio or ballroom are some I remember. I could move things around and use whatever I liked to build the scene. I'm sure I made some grand messes, but I thought she was truly intelligent to see what I was seeing.

And of course she heard prayers every night when I was there, and we went to Sunday School and Church and functions at the Church Hall.

When she thought I was getting out of hand (can't believe I really did but she sometimes saw it that way), she would say that Sally Spunk was there and I would have to sit on a chair until she went away.

When I was about three or four and couldn't get my way, I would say, "Then I will knock the house down." The usual adult reaction was, "Don't be silly," or some other comment that would leave me room for another argument or complaint. Her answer was, "Better be sure that you do it from the outside or it will fall on you and we wouldn't want you to get hurt."

Once when my father had told me to do or stop doing something and I stood my ground, he said if I didn't he would spank me. And I still didn't. So he reached over and smacked my fanny and grandma slapped his face. There was a second of stunned silence and I was sure I had won, but she apologized to him and scolded me for not obeying my father.—Melva Austin Barney.

Grandma was a great cook. She made delicious food and wonderful meals.—Joan Austin Geier.

I remember Grandma Austin sitting on the sun porch darning socks with her thick hair wrapped in a bun.

When she was in the hospital, Grandma Austin got a hairbrush and combed my hair.—Margie Austin Maglione.

The Herman Bosch homestead near where Lon and Aida Austin lived. Photo courtesy of Victoria Kohler.

been killed in an auto accident.

Friday Aida rode to the A&P with Mary Bosch. They had quite a long talk about Jennie's funeral.

Saturday was very cold all day but Lon sawed some wood in the afternoon. He went to the Methodist Church on Sunday morning.

Monday, November 18, was a miserable, cloudy day.

Tuesday was pleasant and Aida washed in the morning. Mrs. Winter and Clarence Sergeant's wife Claudia called on Aida in the afternoon when Lon was sawing wood. (Clarence was a relative of Ella Leavenworth.)

Wednesday morning Lon went to the Village. Aida went at noon and helped with the wood when she got back.

Lon was sick all Thursday, but well enough to go to the Friday prayer meeting; and to the Village Saturday morning. Aida carried wood on Saturday.

Sunday services on November 24, were at the Methodist Church in the evening.

Charlie and Anna Ort visited Garfield and Ella Sunday evening.

Monday Arthur visited his uncle Lon, and then his aunt Aida.

Later Aida walked up to visit Mary Bosch. Marjorie was home with a sore throat. Robbie Bosch came home from school before Aida left.

Tuesday, November 26, was very cold, but clear. Aida picked up wood near the north lot where the men had been sawing logs. In the morning she walked to the A&P.

December 1940
Monday was a cloudy day, but there was happiness in the Leavenworth household. Wayne Elliott Hansen, son of Lee and Clara Hansen, was born at 3:45 p.m. Stella helped Clara on Tuesday and then on Thursday when Wayne cried most of the night with colic. Anna helped on Friday.

Friday afternoon Aida hiked over to Mae's, and then trekked to the A&P for sugar. Arthur was at Aida's when she returned home.

Arthur visited his aunt Aida on a number of occasions. Sometimes she was very feisty and gave him a hard time which didn't make any sense to him. (Art had been Aida's favorite nephew after his brother McKinley died.)

Then Art discovered a pattern. If he sat in Lon's old Morris chair, Aida (thinking he must be Lon) would take to arguing with Art or demand he make pancakes for her. But if Arthur sat in one of the other chairs, everything was fine.

Wesley Morgan delivered a load of coal at Aida's on Saturday.

Sunday, December 8, Church was in the evening. Aida's part coal and part wood fire Sunday did not burn through the night. So Monday Aida used all coal.

Monday Jim Leavenworth quit working for Harry Wormuth.

Church picnic at High Point, 1939. Mrs. Winter is second from the right. The others are unknown. Aida often met Mrs. Winter who was very active in the town. When Mrs. Stege was alive, Mrs. Winter stayed with her and worked in the music business. Photo courtesy Christene Stevens Myers.

The other men continued to work on Lee's house.

Stella helped out with her new nephew Wayne on Tuesday. Goldie and Jim went up to the Stege property looking for work on both Tuesday and Wednesday. On Thursday they headed up to Narrowsburg.

Thursday Garfield, Lee, and Lee's dad worked on Lee's house. The doctor checked on Clara and Lee's new son, Wayne. Lee laid the brick for his chimney on Friday.

On Friday Herman Bosch and young Herman were at the Austins to see about hay. Saturday afternoon Herman Jr. and the boy who worked for them took up two truckloads of hay.

The church service was in the morning on Sunday, December 15. It rained all Monday. Aida let the fire out in the afternoon and built a new one.

Monday Jim started working for Mr. Walter Steiner, a farmer in Bethel.

When Aida went to the A&P on Tuesday, she met Rowlee's wife Emily, who said Rowlee was sick. Wednesday was very cold all day, but Lon headed off to the Village in the afternoon anyway.

Thursday afternoon Aida walked to Mae's, a little over a mile away. Friday, Aida walked almost a mile to the Village to see Walter Styles. She called on Emma who said Rowlee was better and had gone to work.

Friday Clara and Lee looked for light fixtures in Liberty. Ella and Garfield were at Goldie and Stella's until after 11 p.m.

Saturday morning Aida built a coal fire. She took a brisk walk to see the Bosches, but Mary and Marjorie had gone to Barryville.

So Aida went to see Walter Styles. She met Mary and Marjorie on their way home. They drove Aida back to her house.

There was no Church on Sunday, December 22. Aida started her fire Monday morning. The Methodists had their Christmas Tree Program that night.

Orville and Vernon Clark visited the Leavenworths for most of Monday. Jim went to get a Christmas tree.

> # World and National News, August–December 1940
>
> **August 1940**
> - British leased bases to U.S.
> - Italy ousted Britain from British Somaliland in Africa.
> - Exiled Leon Trotsky died.
>
> **September 1940**
> - U.S. prohibited sale of oil and scrap metal to Japan.
> - Japan entered Indochina.
> - Germany, Italy, and Japan declared war on any third party that joined the war against any one of them.
> - Selective Training Service Act: Sep. 16, 1940, all males 21–35 subject to induction.
> - 297,000 pounds of gunpowder blew up at the Hercules Munitions Plant in Succasunna-Kenvil, N.J.; 20 buildings leveled; 51 people died.—roxburynewjersey.com/hercules.htm.
> - Italian forces invaded Egypt.
> - London British cities blitzed; six bombs fell on Buckingham Palace.
> - French Jews faced harsh Nazi Laws.
>
> **October 1940**
> - Italy attacked Greece; didn't alert Hitler.
> - Chamberlain resigned; Churchill head of the Conservative Party.
> - Start of U.S. draft registration of some 16 million men.
> - German Army occupied Romania.
> - Pres. Roosevelt: "I shall say it again and again and again: your boys are not going to be sent into any foreign wars."
> - China forced Japan to withdraw troops.
>
> **November 1940**
> - Franklin Roosevelt, first person to win a third term as President.
> - Blizzard killed 144 in U.S. Midwest.
> - Disney's *Fantasia* box office failure.
>
> **December 1940**
> - The Chicago Bears defeated the Washington Redskins, 73–0 in the 1940 NFL Championship Game.
> - British defeated Italians in Egypt; took Italian bases in North Africa.
> - Charlie Chaplin starred in The Great Dictator.
> - London devastated by firebombs.
> - President Roosevelt (fireside chat):
>   1. "We must be the great arsenal of democracy," and give full aid to Britain.
>   2. "There is far less chance of the United States getting into war if we do all we can now to support the nations defending themselves against attack by the Axis than if we acquiesce in their defeat, submit tamely to an Axis victory, and wait our turn to be the object of attack in another war later on."
> - Films: *The Wizard of Oz*, Disney's *Pinocchio*, and Hollywood's *Sherlock Holmes*, with Basil Rathbone.

The Tuesday before Christmas, Aida rode up with Mr. Kinne to the A&P and Post Office where she saw Jennie Crandall and Mrs. Winter.

Tuesday Clara and Ella baked. On Christmas Day Ella, Garfield, and Jim went to Anna and Bill Meyers' for the day. Then Clara could use the kitchen to make

Mary Bosch with her children Bob and Marjorie. Photo courtesy of Victoria Kohler.

Christmas dinner for her family.

Aida and Lon had a busy Christmas Day. Will Hammond stopped on his way to Edith's for dinner, and gave Aida some papers. Rowlee was up about noon and brought a box of delicious homemade cookies for both Lon and Aida.

I would say the Edith that Bill Hammond visited was Edith Parker Pelton Besson. Edith's last husband was French. Edith (widow of Howard Pelton) and Louie were in the Post Office visiting Mom (Emily Stevens), who introduced them.—Christene Stevens Myers.

"Mr. Knorr came up a little after five with a Christmas dinner. I couldn't eat half of what they brought me. I have enough left for two dinners. I hope Lon don't try to eat all of his for I'm afraid he'll be sick if he does. Alfred Hill brought him up a little Christmas this afternoon," Aida noted on Christmas evening.

Aida cleaned her room and bedroom on a dark, rainy Thursday. Friday Lon put in the kitchen window pane and fixed the stove pipe upstairs for his sister.

Anthony Hirsch Sr. visited the Leavenworths Friday evening.

Opa's (my grandfather Anthony Hirsch) favorite dish was goulash and baked goods. He also baked which also makes sense since he was a baker by trade. Apparently he also hated clean pots and pans because he did his best to make them dirty.—Matt Schroedel (see p. 423).

It was rainy and dark again on Saturday. Aida started the fire in the morning, then did a little washing and ironing.

On Saturday Lee and Clara, Bill and Anna, and their sons went shopping in Liberty; Garfield worked on Lee's house; Goldie and Stella visited with her parents for a while; Jim worked.

Monday, December 30, the men helped move part of the Hansen's household goods to Lee and Clara's new home.

Tuesday was cold and cloudy. Lon bought grapes and grapefruit at the Village.

Ella Leavenworth summarized her year on Tuesday, the last day of the year. "Fairly good year for us. We had Clara and Dick since September with us and baby Wayne for a month."

1941
Ella, Anna, and Aida

Starting in 1941, a third diary contributes to the narrative. Some excerpts from Anna Leavenworth's Diary have been added to those of Aida Austin and Ella Leavenworth.

Anna Leavenworth had grown up in the Echo Hill Farm House. Long ago she had taught school in Yulan and then Eldred. Anna, 65, and her cat Jimmie Braddock lived in a quaint cottage she owned on Fern Ave., East Islip, New

Herman Bosch Jr. Young Herman and his dad helped out Aida and Lon Austin. Photo courtesy of Victoria Kohler.

Barryville-Shohola Bridge was under construction until October 1941. Photo courtesy of Ed Wolff.

York. Raymond Austin and his family in Staten Island often had Thanksgiving with Anna. Art and Bill Austin sometimes visited her.

Great-Aunt Anna's cat Jimmie Braddock was a most impressive, cat. I think he was the biggest, most battle-scarred cat I have ever seen. Yet with people, he was as purry and petable as you please.

We did not live very close to Aunt Anna. To get to her place we took a train or bus to the Staten Island Ferry; the subway to Pennsylvania Station; and train to E. Islip. It was an overnight stay if we were to spend any time with her.—Melva Austin Barney.

Great-Aunt Anna was a very hard worker. She had a lot of company (which she said she enjoyed) and always had some sweet cake, lemon pie, prune bread, or cookies to eat. Anna sewed quilts, hooked rugs, and made blankets for the British Relief.—Cynthia Leavenworth Bellinger.

At the beginning of 1941, the Barryville-Shohola Bridge was still being worked on. Sometime that year the new Eldred High School was started. Also that year Irwin Briggs' mother Indie Clark Briggs from Nebraska, visited the Briggs family in Barryville.

Goldie and Stella visited with her parents. Photo courtesy of Linda Leavenworth Bohs.

January 1941

January of 1941 was almost two degrees colder than normal in New York. But the month started off on a "lovely, clear and warm Wednesday," according to Ella Leavenworth. Her son Jim bought his first car for $25.

Clara, her sons, the senior Hansens, Anna, Bill, and Jimmy Meyers enjoyed another meal at Garfield and Ella's.

On the other side of Eldred, Aida Austin wrote that 1941 started off, "rather cold but pleasant all day. Arthur was up for a few minutes before dark." (Hopefully Art did not sit in his uncle Lon's chair when he visited.)

Thursday was pleasant, but quite cold. Aida walked the 1-1/2 mile round trip to the A&P, Harold's, and the Post Office and back. Mary Wormuth stopped in for a few minutes after paying Lon for the hay. It snowed about two inches before dark. It got so cold that Aida slept out in the sitting room near the wood stove.

There was no snow on Friday which was cloudy and cold. But at

Location for the new Eldred High School Building. Photo courtesy of Christene Stevens Myers.

least the temperature was warmer than Thursday. Warm enough that Aida could sleep in her own bed, though she still checked the fire several times in the night.

Friday Anna Meyers helped her sister Clara get set up in her new home. Garfield worked up there also.

Lon Austin went for bread and milk Friday and Saturday. It was so warm, Aida let the fire go out. She built a new fire Sunday morning, January 5, when the weather turned cold and it was windy all day. There was no church service in the morning.

Sunday was an exciting day for Clara Hansen and her family. They were able to completely move into their new home. Garfield and Ella took care of the three grandsons so Anna could help.

Monday it snowed. Garfield and Ella moved Jim's bed back upstairs.

Tuesday it snowed, but that didn't stop Lon Austin from going to the Village to get the *Daily News.* In the afternoon Teenie Stevens took some papers to Aida.

Monday and Tuesday Aida slept in her front room because it was so cold and windy. Wednesday was warmer and she was able to sleep in her own bed.

Thursday the weather was quite a little warmer. Ella went to Goldie and Stella's.

Friday was quite cold, but pleasant. Lon walked to the Village in the morning and Aida at noon.

Garfield worked on Lee's porch. Lee moved his hens to his new place. Clara and Anna and their families spent the evening at Garfield and Ella's. Stella and Goldie were in for a few minutes.

Saturday was colder, but sunny. Lee Hansen took his pigs up to their new home.

Saturday Lon was down to the Village. Sunday, January 12, it was quite cold but pleasant. (Church was in the morning, Aida noted.)

Sunday Garfield and Ella went

Irwin Briggs snaps the picture by remote. Irwin, John, with Pal, Indie Briggs (Irwin's mother), Mary, and Myrtle Briggs. Photo courtesy of Mary Briggs Austin.

Barryville, Yulan, Minisink Ford, Summer 1940–1941

Bornstein's Grand Vue. Postcard courtesy of Kevin Marrinan.

Colonial postcard taken around 1939, courtesy of Helen Hensel Oset.

Highland Hotel and Cottage postcard courtesy of the Town of Highland.

Washington Beach Hotel. Photo courtesy of Ivan J. and Jana Tether.

Burgess' Laurel Brook Cottage. Postcard courtesy of the Town of Highland.

A boat landing on Washington Lake. Photo courtesy of Kevin Marrinan.

Barryville

Glendella, E.H. Carroll
Modern house; water sports; $18–20.

Spring House, Chris and Meta Meyer
Laurel Brook Cottage, A.D. Burgess

Maple Grove Farm, Nitzsche & Frey
Overlooking Delaware. Pool, recreation hall, tennis, handball premises. Farm produce. $17–19.

Anna Toaspern Holden

Riverside Cottage, Warshauer

Tallwood Lodge, Hainzl

Woodland Cottages, Protz

Yulan

Bodine's Cottages, Mrs. B. Bodine
Running water all rooms. All outdoor sports. Boating, bathing, fishing free on private lake. Ping-pong, tennis. Near all churches. $18–20 weekly.

Colonial, Jack & Lisette Hensel
On lake. Boating, bathing, fishing; running water all rooms. Booklet. $18–20.

Highland Cottage, Edith Kalbfus

West's, Charles and Selma West

Laurel Cottage, Mrs. M. Parker
Inner spring mattresses. Own farm and dairy products. Acc. 50. Same family ownership since 1888.

Grand Vue, Bornstein

Kaese's, Albert and Ethel Kaese

Minisink Lodge, M.A. McCormack
On Washington Lake. Bathing, boating, good table. Booklet.

Park Hotel, Atwell Bradley

Sunset Cottage, Lewis Hazen
On lake. Boating, bathing, fishing, dancing, amuse., handball. Hot, cold water all rooms. $18–20.

The Maplecrest, Reginald Walter
On Lake. New House; hot, cold water, showers, innerspring mattresses; handball, ping-pong, boating, bathing. $18–20.

West Shore Cottages, J. Cantwell
On Washington Lake. $18 up. Acc. 100 Excellent meals. Modern. Showers. Hot, cold running water every room. Boating, bathing, handball, softball, badminton, table tennis. Near churches. Special June–Sept. rates.

Cold Spring Farm, Matilda Crandall

Carl and Anna Vonderhorst

Washington Beach Hotel, W. Tether

Minisink Ford

Gus and Frieda Dasener

York Lake Mountain House, Charles and Martha Draxler

Jim's first car parked in front of the Garfield Leavenworth home. Jim bought what appears to be a 1932 Ford, for $25 in 1941. Photo courtesy of Cynthia Leavenworth Bellinger.

to Goldie's. They stopped to see Clara in her new house.

The sun peeked through the clouds on a cold, windy Monday.

In East Islip Anna cleaned her basement in the morning "to be ready for Electric and Gas reader. Mrs. Bledsoe called in p.m."

Eldred was very cold with sunshine on Tuesday. Clara and her sons spent the warmer, but cloudy Wednesday at Ella's. Garfield and Jim drew six loads of oak slab wood from Steiner's.

In Islip Sunday, January 19, Mrs. Bledsoe called on Anna. Anna apparently wasn't going to the Islip Church any more.

Anna thought the minister "Dr. Ayer has a very unreasonable political attitude." But Mrs. Bledsoe didn't understand.

(Like Aida and Lon, Anna and her brother Garfield had very strong feelings about politics.)

Franklin D. Roosevelt was inaugurated on a sunny Monday. Anna listened to the President's inauguration address, and noted in her diary, "Have to feel a little sorry for Republicans."

In Eldred on Monday, Anna's nephew Jim Leavenworth worked for Mr. Steiner again.

Tuesday Aida Austin rode up to the A&P with Floyd Boyd and Alex Wait. About one o'clock, Lon went to Port Jervis with their nephew Bill Austin.

In Islip on Tuesday afternoon, Mrs. Lois Smith (a very pleasant lady who liked Jimmie B. the cat) came after two little rugs Anna had made.

On Wednesday in Eldred, Clara and Anna and their sons

Richard James, son of Ed and Norma Wood James, helps Emma Waidler—Norma's great aunt, and Rowlee's sister. Photo courtesy of Richard James.

visited with Ella. Clara hung out her wash. Bill, Goldie, and Lee, were in for a while.

On the east side of Eldred, Aida wrote Emma Waidler and sent the letter in the afternoon mail.

Thursday afternoon, even though the roads were icy, Aida went to Mae's, but Mae had gone to Port Jervis. Mrs. Bye, who was also at Mae's, accompanied Aida on the way to the Village.

Friday Aida bought butter on her daily outing to the store. It "commenced snowing about one o'clock," and continued to snow. The shovel plow went out about seven o'clock.

Saturday Lon shoveled a path from his house to Aida's kitchen door so she could get water; and a path from his porch to the road.

On the west side of Eldred Goldie and Stella were at his folks' house for dinner. Jim drove to Narrowsburg and visited the Clarks in the evening.

Sunday morning, January 26, Lon went to a special Methodist Church meeting with Alfred Hill. Alfred drove a group of folks to Barryville in his school bus. Lon told Aida there were four ministers there: a young minister with Mr. Briggs, Mr. Deats, and Mr. Dewey from Port Jervis.

Lon wasn't feeling well on Monday when he went to the Village to get bread. He was sick all day Tuesday. Aida tried to see Lon a couple times, but his door was locked.

"He seems pretty sick, but he wouldn't let me send for the doctor," Aida jotted in her diary.

Fortunately Lon was able to unlock the door. When Aida returned after a short visit with Mary Bosch, Aida was able to see her brother and build up the fire in the stove.

Eldred, Highland Lake, Summer 1940–1941

Sunset View, Theuer's Boarding House. Photo courtesy of Jeanie Staubes Turner.

Highland Lake Inn owned by the Asendorfs. Photo courtesy of Stuart and Geraldine Mills Russell.

Eldred
Avery's, Erwin and Norah Avery
Attilio and Angelina Foscola's
Pine Crest, Adelaide Strenglein
Straub's Hotel, Ida Straub

Highland Lake
Bertram Cottage, Art Bertram
$17 to 21

Arthur and Juliette Bertram's Restaurant

Highland Lake House, Jim Mills

Green Acres, Charles Pankow
Green Acres consists of the Main House, three Cottages and five Cabins in the rough. Excellent home cooking. Accommodations for 75. Churches conveniently located. Here you will find good swimming, two large floats, and an ample supply of boats. House dances and games are in a rustic barn, a stone's throw from the house. Other games you may enjoy besides softball are tennis, basketball, volley ball, ping-pong, croquet, horseshoes and shuffleboard. Horseback riding and golf nearby. There are 65 acres of woodland with shady lawns and pine groves and plenty of chairs and hammocks. Quiet country roads and wooded paths for hikers.

Deer Head Lodge, Eggers
New, modern, inexpensive. June and after Labor Day, $20. July to Labor Day, $21–25. On lake. Famous for fine food, boating, fishing, swimming, shuffleboard, handball, tennis, golf, horseback. Dancing. All conveniences. Near all churches.

Lake Shore Hotel, Chris E. Scott
$17 weekly and up.

Pinehurst, Frances Sulzbach
Highland Lake Inn, Belle Asendorf
Directly on Lake Highland Lake, N.Y. Swimming, canoeing, private tennis courts, badminton. Opposite golf course. Saddle horses. Best food. Dancing. Near churches. Acc. 150. Seasonal rates, $20–24.

Bertha Sullivan
Summer and hunting season lodgers.

Mills House, Agnes Mills
Hammond House, Mae Parker
Mountain Lake House, Staubes
Sunset View House, Theuers
Lake View, Charles Myers 🍂

Aida was at Lon's three times Tuesday night—9 p.m., midnight, and 3:30 a.m.—to fix the fire in Lon's stove.

Wednesday Lon was able to sit up, but looked very bad. Aida went to the A&P in the morning. It had snowed some and the wind had blown the paths full of snow. It became terribly cold, and Aida was glad not to have to go over to Lon's.

Wednesday in west Eldred, Clara and her sons visited with Ella all day. Garfield and Ella so enjoyed their grandsons. Ella's radio broke and Clara's husband Lee loaned them his small radio. Goldie took the broken radio to Millard Hulse to be fixed.

Wednesday in Islip, Anna worked on British Relief Blankets. She hoped to have six done for Thursday; and eventually 100.

Thursday the weather moderated some in Eldred. Aida shoveled out the paths in the afternoon. Lon must have felt better as he put up a small stove and Aida cleaned the chimney full of ashes and creosote. "I don't see how the fire burned at all. It has been smoking terribly for a week or two and kept getting worse."

January ended on a very cold day. Aida went to the A&P, the Post Office, and also Harold's.

Narrowsburg Lumber Company
Jim Leavenworth started driving a truck for Narrowsburg Lumber in Narrowsburg in February.

When I was 18, I then got a job for Narrowsburg Lumber

Lumber at Narrowsburg Lumber Company in Narrowsburg where Jim Leavenworth got a job. Photo courtesy of Howard Barnes.

Company and was there for two years. That was the best job I ever had and then the war came and I enlisted in the Air Corps for about 40 months.—James Leavenworth.

February 1941
In Eldred Aida shoveled the paths on Saturday, February 1. The snow had drifted them full. She checked to see if anyone had been around to Mrs. Schroeder's house.

Lon didn't feel well enough to go to the Village on Saturday, but was able to get to Sunday School Sunday morning and church at night. Arthur was at church and drove Lon home.

Monday afternoon Bob Austin visited his aunt Aida. He had arrived home Saturday morning for a two-week furlough. Bob had started from his camp in Canada on Friday. He had taken the train to Toronto, then to Buffalo, then to Scranton, then to Honesdale.

Someone had given him a ride to Narrowsburg. As he started to walk home, Bob met the game warden Mr. Hinkley, who drove him right to his house.

Monday in west Eldred, Garfield worked for Alvah Sergeant; Jim at Narrowsburg Lumber. Lee left for Maryland to see about work.

Tuesday was very cold. Lon went to see Harry Wormuth about getting wood, but decided to get coal. Young Hallock and another man stopped by Aida's with Watkins' goods.

Wednesday Lon shoveled out the lane so the truck could get in with the coal. Alfred Hill went through with a load of hay. Aida went to Andrew's and the A&P.

Thursday was cold and clear. It was raining Friday when Morgan delivered the coal to Aida's.

Saturday was very cold with the benefit of it also being icy. Lon slid to the Village, but Aida didn't go because it was so slippery.

Sunday, February 9, Lon preached for Mr. Briggs, as Mr. Briggs was sick. But Lon got sick in Sunday School.

Alfred, Bessie, and their children Billy and Joan took soup over to Lon. So did Alvin (Alfred's

Lumber stacked at Narrowsburg Lumber Company in Narrowsburg where Jim Leavenworth worked. Photo courtesy of Howard Barnes.

twin brother) and his wife Harriet. Arthur also checked on Lon.

Monday Aida was down to the A&P. Paul Knorr drove her home. Lon went up to see Bill and Arthur about having dinner at Aida's on Tuesday before Bob went to visit Raymond and his family in Staten Island. Lillie stopped by for a few minutes after school.

Monday was a sad day for the Leavenworths. Stella's grandmother Carrie Bogert Clark, died of a stroke.

Tuesday Aida had dinner ready but Bill and Bob didn't arrive until afterwards. Bill drove Bob to Shohola and dropped Aida off at the Post Office.

"Bob rather hated to go. He will stay with Raymond tomorrow and the next day take a bus from New York City to Scranton on his way back to camp. Has to be there Saturday 8 a.m.," Aida recorded.

Wednesday Aida went to her friend Mae's. Thursday Lon was to the Village. Aida read and slept pretty much all day.

Friday was cold and windy. Margie Bosch must have picked up some items for Lon and Aida as she stopped by to give them the cost of meat and other things.

Saturday afternoon Lon was once again at the Village. Margie Bosch took a piece of her birthday cake to Aida and Lon.

Saturday morning in East Islip was not a pleasant one. "Mrs. Cover here before breakfast in a terrible temper which I equaled before she left," Anna jotted down in her diary.

It was quite snowy in Eldred on Monday. Tuesday was terribly cold and windy. Aida was able to ride to the A&P with Mary Bosch.

Tuesday Anna in Islip received a nice letter from her nephew Bob Austin.

Wednesday was cold and windy

Some of the people who Lon may have met at the Methodist Church; many are mentioned in this book. Front row: Mary Briggs, Unknown, Gordon Knorr, Kay Randolph, Laura Briggs. Row 2: Paul Knorr, Frances Knorr holding Arlene Knorr, Mrs. Quick, Charlotte Middaugh Myers holding Marion Hulse, Minnie Nelson, Will Quick. Back row: Mildred Briggs, Hazel Angell, Mrs. Lottie Dewey and Mr. Dewey on either side of Pearl Owen Defeo, Stanley Myers, unknown, John Briggs, Alberta Myers, Unknown, Marie Hulse. Photo from two sources.

in Eldred. Jim Leavenworth was up to the Stege property.

Thursday Harold Frint braved the very cold, windy weather to ask how Lon was and give Aida some papers from Mae. Friday Arthur helped Alfred Hill draw two loads of hay from Ed Myers' to the small barn on Mort's place.

Friday and Saturday Jim went to Narrowsburg and to Anna's.

Marjorie Bosch with a cute dog and cat. Photo courtesy of Victoria Kohler.

Sunday morning, February 23, church was at the Methodist.

Aida didn't let the very cold Monday keep her from getting the oil she needed at the garage.

Tuesday was warmer and Aida let the fire go out in the night. It was very cold when she got up between six and seven.

Lon took his daily jaunt to the Village to get bread and butter on a terribly cold Wednesday. On a blustery, cold Friday afternoon (snow squalls) Aida went to Mary's and then rode to the A&P with Mrs. William Clouse.

March 1941

March 1 (Saturday) came in like a cold, blustery lion. Lon went up to Herman's in the morning to see about wood for the church. Then he was down to the Village.

Monday Aida went to the Village twice. She went back a second time to take Bertha Sullivan's apples to her. Mary Bosch drove by just as Aida passed Paul Knorr's place. So Aida went to Barryville with Mary.

Mary Horton Bosch in white shirt and black tie, and Tiny the cat. Photo courtesy of Victoria Kohler.

Tuesday Stella Leavenworth spent the day with Ella.

Tuesday it was too cold and windy for Aida to wash. Wednesday was still cold and windy. But the bright sunshine encouraged Aida to do some wash. Thursday morning Lon went to the Village for the mail. Aida had a letter from Emma Waidler, Rowlee's sister. Aida walked to the Village a little after noon for bread.

Friday afternoon Herman Bosch and his son Bob stopped by Aida's and trimmed an apple tree for her. Saturday, "it commenced snowing again."

On Saturday in Islip, Mr. Griffen shoveled Anna's walk. Sunday evening, March 9, Anna talked long distance to her sister Christina in Eldred.

The snow was quite deep Sunday morning in Eldred. Aida brushed out the paths before Lon went to Sunday School.

Lon was up to Mary Bosch's for milk on Monday, March 10. When he got back he went to the Village.

My Bosch grandparents were hardworking, very kind and generous people. In the photo albums you see Herman going fishing, etc. and Mary working out in the fields, plowing. Mary is frequently pictured wearing a man's black tie and white shirt. What a gal! In all the papers I have around here, it was she who took care of the business end of the farm. Not to say she was a workaholic as she was known for her many trips to Port Jervis, picnicking and photo ops on the Hawk's Nest. They had many pets: cats, dogs, goats, and horses. She loved music and reading.
—Victoria Kohler, granddaughter

Tuesday Aida walked to the A&P about noon. It snowed more that night, so on Wednesday Aida brushed out the paths again. Lon got his hair cut Thursday. He rode home with a fruit man and bought some apples from him.

Friday afternoon Dr. Austin, Herman and Robbie Bosch were at Lon's.

Ernest and Eunice Hallock Clark. Ernest was taken to the hospital in March. Photo courtesy of Vernon and Carolyn Hallock Clark.

Sunday morning, March 16, Dr. Austin was in to see Aida a few minutes. Lon had gone to church.

Sunday in west Eldred, Lee and Clara and their sons visited Garfield and Ella for the evening. Ernest Clark (Stella's father) was taken to the hospital.

Tuesday morning was very cold and windy. Aida went to the Village.

Aida thought, "Wednesday was the coldest and windiest day we have ever had."

Thursday was warmer. Aida met Rowlee near the Collin's place, and he gave her a ride to Mae's. Mae and Ruth were going to Port Jervis and took Aida with them, so Aida didn't get to the Village on Thursday. Lon went at noon on Friday for bread.

In west Eldred on Friday, Stella, Goldie, and Orville visited with Garfield and Ella.

Saturday Aida purchased oil on her daily trek to the Village.

Sunday morning, March 23, Lon went to Sunday School and Church. Arthur visited his aunt Aida for a few minutes in the afternoon.

Lon walked to the Village late Monday afternoon.

In west Eldred Garfield worked on Clara's porch. Anna Meyers called her dad twice. She had work that needed to be done at her house. So Tuesday Garfield worked on the Meyers' home.

Tuesday morning Aida went to the A&P. Herman Jr. trimmed the trees in the afternoon, but not on Wednesday when it was cold.

Wednesday in west Eldred, Anna and Clara and their little ones spent most of the day at their parents' home. Ed and Eleanor Bosch and their young children Kay and Fred visited Garfield and Ella for the evening. Ed must have been home from building bowling

Left: Kate Miller's cottage where Willie Bosch lived. Right: Charlie Bosch on the right, supervises the uprooting of a tree with his "tractor." Photos courtesy of Ken Bosch.

alleys on the east coast.

Thursday was much warmer. Herman Jr. trimmed the trees.

Friday in west Eldred Garfield helped a dog out of a trap at Anna's. Mary Sergeant spent the day with Ella.

Sunday, March 30, Bill Ort and Clifford Myers called on Garfield and Ella.

Sunday night Arthur went to church and drove Lon home afterwards. Monday Lon walked to the Village to get butter.

Monday Garfield worked for Ed Myers. Stella and Goldie visited with Ella. After work Jim went with Lee to the movies.

Charlie, Willie, and the Tractor

Ed Bosch's brother Charlie also worked on bowling alleys on the east coast. Charlie had a house and property off Bower Road.

Ed and Charlie undoubtedly knew Lon Austin as their brother Herman was Lon's neighbor. In a cartoon Charlie drew of Herman's sawmill he referred to a "Larn Austin" (*see Appendix, p. 410*).

Charlie's son Whipple (Henry) Bosch, entered the service in March 1941. Some time later Charlie wrote a letter to Whipple's brother Willie (Billy). Will usually stayed in Highland Lake at the cottage which had once belonged to his grandmother Kate Miller.

Charlie instructed Willie in tasks he wanted done so his place would be ready when he was in Highland Lake on weekends. The directions included feeding the deer at the Quinn Place, a small abandoned house near a quarry hole that held water and attracted deer.

The "tractor" was the remnant of an old truck with no hood and no bed.

Charlie Bosch, Flushing, L.I., to Willie Bosch, Highland Lake

Dear Little Willie,

Just to let you know that I will be up Friday nite about the same time. Keep honey at the Quinn Place. Also take some of the best apples, and put about a peach basket full (100) at the pond hole at the Quinn place. Scatter them all over. After they are about all gone, put about 30 or 40 apples there every time you go over.

Will, I am coming if Ed goes up. Have my mail from Eldred. Tell Charlie Myers I want a box of beer. Have it on hand in the ice box cold. Get the potatoes off the porch.

I want to see the plow and tractor (full of gas) at the bungalow when I come up.

Hope you are getting along fine. Write to Whipple:

Mary Bosch and her son Bob, looking cool. Photo courtesy of Victoria Kohler.

Henry M. Bosch, Co. C, 67th Regt., 2nd Armored Division, Med. Tanks, Fort Benning, Ga.
  Enough said, Great Stuff, Pop

April 1941
Anna in Islip had been doing relief work and straightening her attic. Tuesday, April 1, she sewed sheets and cleaned part of her cellar.

Tuesday morning in Eldred, Aida went to the Village; Garfield worked for Ed Myers. Jim worked half a day and then went to Bill Sullivan's funeral.

Wednesday Garfield worked for Ed Myers again. Anna and Jimmy were with Ella for the day. Bill, Lee, Goldie, and Stella were in later.

Wednesday afternoon Aida went over to Mae's, who had gone to Port Jervis, but Frank (Mac) O'Donnell was there. Mae's brother Will Hammond was sick.

Mac moved to Highland Lake in the early 1920s and worked at the Hammond boarding house.

As a young child I remember Mac best as occupying the first bar stool when you entered

Lillie Calkin, her husband Burt, and Burt's sister Hannah Calkin. Photo courtesy of Katherine Calkin Traxler.

Nellie Crandall dropped by to see Aida Austin. Photo courtesy of Christene Stevens Myers.

Mellan's tavern [owned by Bertrams in 1941]. Gregarious and friendly, he always greeted me with an enthusiastic and smiling "Great stuff, great stuff!!" I never knew where the phrase "great stuff" came from until later I found out it was one of my grandfather Charlie Bosch's trademark expressions; so Mac used it on me.—Ken Bosch.

Thursday morning Lon went to Mae's to see Will Hammond who was feeling better. In the afternoon Lon went to Monticello with Will Austin.

Friday Aida did her washing. Saturday she ironed. Lon went to the Village.

Sunday, April 6, was rainy and snowy, but clear in the afternoon.

Monday Lee took Garfield to see about work. Anna and Jimmy visited with Ella. Bill Meyers joined them for supper.

Tuesday morning Aida rode up to the A&P with Joseph and Florence Brague (Anna Ort's son).

In the afternoon she went over to Mae's. Herman and Robbie Bosch trimmed trees for her in the evening.

Wednesday morning Lon went to the Village. He and Aida picked up apple tree wood in the afternoon.

Thursday afternoon Aida went to the Village and then to see Anna Ort. Mary Sergeant was there. Aida was home when Nellie Crandall dropped by.

(You may remember that Nellie had been a very good friend of Jennie Austin. She had been a widow since 1925, when her husband Robert died. Her son Clifford was a good friend of Art Austin.)

Sunday, April 13, Garfield worked for Ed Myers. Clara, Dick, and baby Wayne were at Garfield and Ella's for supper.

Sunday Arthur drove Lon home from church and visited with his aunt Aida who had a terrible cold.

Monday morning Lon walked to the Village. Rowlee was up to Aida's for some watercress.

Tuesday afternoon Lon went to the Village for bread and butter.

Aida and Lon's niece Lillie wrote her dad Ell Austin and updated him on her family. Her daughter Dot was married to Ray Hale, and had been very ill.

Lillie Calkin, Bethel, to Mr. J.E. Austin, Ossining, N.Y.
April 15, 1941
Dear Dad,
 I've had a very strenuous spring. In March Dorothy had a recurrence of the peritonitis attack. I went down on Friday a.m. and came back the next Sunday. Mrs. Hale stayed with her until they came home. I went down each weekend for three weeks.

Emily and Howard Stevens were at Aida Austin's for watercress. Photo courtesy of Christene Stevens Myers.

Dorothy and Ray stayed with his folks until yesterday when they came home. Dorothy is pretty well now. She has gained fast this last week. Tomorrow she, Ray, and I are going to Binghamton where Ray is on the trail of a job. Burt has a small job in Liberty to start next week. If Ray doesn't get something in B., he will work with Burt. Everybody is well here now. Bobby, 6, and Neal, 4, are getting to be big boys (her grandsons).

June and George Crandall were here today.

I hope you keep well and that business picks up with you. It is lovely weather now. Our arboretus is budded.

With love, Lillie

In Islip on Wednesday, Anna wrote, "Not feeling too well today. Perhaps I worked too hard yesterday. News so bad from Greece and Belfast I can't listen to the radio."

In Eldred on Wednesday morning, Aida walked to the A&P. Her cold was much better, but she felt quite weak.

Wednesday Alfred Eldred called on Garfield and Ella Leavenworth. (Alfred, son of Herbert and Eliza Post Eldred, was a relative of the Austins.)

Thursday afternoon Mr. Briggs drove Lon to a Methodist supper in Port Jervis. Mrs. Briggs went with him for a ride and got some watercress.

Walter Horton's wife and their daughter stopped in at Aida's on their way from the Village.

Friday the Leavenworth menfolk worked. Ella spent the day with her daughter Anna. Lee was there for supper. Clara and the boys joined him. Jim and Lee plowed the garden. Buck McBride stopped by.

Friday in Islip, Anna cleaned the kitchen floor and baseboards. She finished the pillow cases for little pillows, and was very tired.

"Fires in Jersey but so far

A younger Bobby and Marjorie Bosch with one of their cows. Photo courtesy of Victoria Kohler.

Tuesday morning Aida went to the A&P and Post Office in the Parker House. Photo courtesy of Christene Stevens Myers.

none heard of on Long Island," Anna of Islip noted on Saturday.

Monday in west Eldred, Stella spent the day with Ella. Garfield worked. Jim was fighting fires. There were terrible fires in New Jersey, Pennsylvania, and New York.

Tuesday morning Aida went to the A&P and Post Office.

Wednesday Lon sawed a little short wood in the afternoon. Aida went up to Mary's to tell them their cows had come down. Aida rode back with Mary, Margie, and a friend of hers.

Thursday was very cold all day. In the morning Lon went to the Village. He rode part way there and back with Mary Bosch.

Friday in Islip, Anna completed four ambulance pillows.

Saturday was still cold in Eldred. Mr. Briggs stopped in to see Lon in the afternoon.

Wednesday morning Aida walked to the A&P. It was colder than Tuesday when she had gone to Mae's.

Aidaisms

My great-aunt Aida Austin was an unconventional lady. She had unique ways of expressing herself which could be called Aidaisms.

Aida handwrote all her research and letters. Letters she rewrote up to six times, and kept all the copies. Each version added a few new details, so it was necessary to save all the sheets in order to know the complete information and its nuances. Often information was written on whatever paper (scrap or new) was available.

Aidaisms (letter excerpts):
- Here I am at last. I'm afraid you will begin to think that I am very slow and have been very idle. I am slow but I have not been idle.
- Here I am at last. When I obtained your address, I planned to write to you just as soon as I had finished some work for my brother Eldred, which I thought would take only a few days…And I have worked steadily, excepting that once in a while I have taken just a few moments to berate Mr. Winston Churchill for keeping the world in such an uproar.
- I think I must be somewhat like a boy who a number of years ago worked for Mrs. Phillips of Black Lake. The first morning he went out to do the chores. He took a long time. So long that Mrs. Phillips became worried and went to see what had happened to him. When she reached the barn, she found him milking the cow, and he said to her, "Madam, I'm a very slow milker."
- I am not inferring that I am a slow milker, because I am not. When I was small and wanted to learn how to milk, my sisters said to me, "Don't you learn! If you do, you'll have to milk! So I followed their advice and never became a slow milker, but I will have to acknowledge I am a slow worker and seem to be getting slower and slower.
- It may be that the weather has been making me slower than usual. I can't say, for the weather don't stay in one place long enough for anyone to make a study of it. Sometimes, it comes flooding us with sunshine, and a few minutes later it has gone with the sun somewhere and is pelting us with snow and sleet. You would think such a freakish winter would be able to stop this war.

May 1941

Friday, May 2, there was quite a frost in the evening, but Aida didn't think it hurt the fruit. Emily and Howard Stevens were up for some watercress on Saturday evening just before dark.

Sunday morning, May 4, Lon took charge of the service because Mr. Briggs was at a conference.

Rowlee visited Aida about noon to give her book back and get some watercress. Arthur was there a few minutes in the afternoon. The Austin brothers had sold The Pines and wanted to store some items at Aida's.

Tuesday morning Aida walked to the A&P. Lon discussed storage options with Arthur. Tuesday Garfield went to a school meeting. Wednesday was warm and rainy. Thursday was clear and cooler.

Saturday afternoon Aida walked to the Eldred Cemetery and then over to see Emily Schoonover. Rowlee was working in his shop.

Sunday, May 11, it was cold all day. Edith Parker was up to Aida's in the morning for some watercress.

Bessie and Alfred took Lon and Arthur home after church. Late afternoon Arthur and Alfred drove some of the Austin belongings to Aida's, and put them in an upstairs room.

Tuesday morning Aida took her daily trek to the A&P.

At the Leavenworth home, a tricycle arrived for Garfield and Ella's grandson Dick.

Wednesday morning, Aida cleaned the windows and floor in the storage room for Arthur. In the afternoon she took Rowlee's wife Emily her paper and some watercress. When she got back, Aida walked over to Mae's.

Friday Ernest Horton (brother of Mary Bosch) stopped by in the afternoon and told Aida the funeral of Mrs. Jane Rundle would be in the Methodist Church on Saturday at two o'clock.

About one o'clock Saturday there was a thundershower. The funeral was quite large, but only six were there from Eldred: Mrs. William Parker, Mary Sergeant and her sister-in-law, Chester Middaugh, Lon, and Aida.

When Aida was walking home from the funeral, Pete Sullivan and his wife overtook her on the last hill. They stopped to speak to her, but Aida didn't recognize them until they told her who they were. Aida hadn't seen Pete since she taught at Wellstown when Pete was a little boy.

In East Islip Anna made a big blanket out of old coats.

In Eldred Monday, May 19, about noon, Aida rode to the A&P with the milkman. Arthur and Alfred Hill took some more things to be stored at Aida's in the evening; and another load on Friday. Bill Austin stayed at his house that night, but Arthur stayed at The Pines.

Saturday Aida went to the Village in the morning. Arthur was over with a mattress. The Austin brothers were all through cleaning out The Pines.

Saturday in west Eldred, Clara, Lee, and Dick went to get Dick a pair of shoes. They left Wayne with Garfield and Ella.

Sunday, May 25, Arthur stopped at Aida's for some books a little before 6 p.m. He said he would have to work every day that week.

Monday Anna left Jimmy with her mother Ella so she could help her mother-in-law Lottie wash.

Tuesday Ray Wells measured for a gas line for a stove for Garfield and Ella, which they got the next day. Ella baked with the gas and it worked just fine.

Wednesday and Thursday Aida cleaned house. Friday Mary Wormuth stopped in to see Aida. Her husband Harry went up on the hill to look after his lumber.

In Islip Anna started a letter to Aida Austin in Eldred. On Friday Anna walked up to the firehouse and saw the start of the Memorial Day parade.

Saturday night in Eldred, Jim took Clara, Dick, and Ella for a ride.

Fred and Kay Bosch, the cute children of Ed and Eleanor Bosch, pick potatoes. Photo courtesy of Ken Bosch.

In May George Andersen who rented two rooms from Charlie Bosch enlisted in the Army. Charlie referred to George in another letter to his son Willie.

Charlie Bosch, L.I., to Willie Bosch, Highland Lake
May or June 1941
Dear Billy,

Just these few lines to let you know that I will be up with Ed if he is working with me by Friday. Otherwise I will be up by Saturday night. Charlie (his son) and Uncle Menzo (his brother) said you were digging potatoes and had 17 bushel of 10 rows. That's right, take them out. Don't leave any squash go as I want those three big ones out near the woods by that spruce tree. Take it easy. Keep track of your time. 40 cents per hour; and get groceries when you need some. I'll sleep in the Bungalow when I come. I like to sleep there better than up at the big house. If Ralph (his brother) ain't working he can cut the field.

Tell Willie Brodmerkel I want that Tractor. But he will have to repair it and look it over. I'll have money for you when I come.

Also heard again from George Andersen. Keep my mail in one spot. Watch out for a special letter.

Today at two o'clock we started to build the first two alleys. We had lots of blocking up to do. 11 alleys on one floor and 11 downstairs. So far things went slow as we haven't only four men. But we will have the rest of the mechanics I think this week.

Ed I guess is working in Jersey. But he is sleeping upstairs now. I still have that sprained thumb getting no better. Take care of the cucumbers…Henry wants you to write: Pfc. Henry M. Bosch, Co. C. 67th Reg't., 2nd Armored Division, A.P.O. 252 Ragley, La.

Goodnite, Pop

Around 1945 Willie Bosch drives the "tractor" with the help of his son William. Photo courtesy of Ken Bosch.

Menzo Bosch with baskets of potatoes. Photo courtesy of Ken Bosch.

George Andersen enlisted in May 1941. He would write to Bill Austin during the war. Photo courtesy of Ken Bosch.

1941 Eldred Graduation in Sunshine Hall. Helen Myers is at the podium. Photo courtesy of Christene Stevens Myers.

June 1941

Sunday, June 1, Lon told Aida that Ruth and her fiance Harold Frint were at church in the morning.

Tuesday morning Aida was down to the A&P about eight. She talked a little while to Emma Stevens. Lon went to the Village before noon.

Tuesday evening on the west side, Clara, Dick, Lee, and the Clarks were at Garfield and Ella's for the evening.

Thursday Lon went to the Village about ten o'clock for bread. Arthur drove him down again about four to buy gasoline.

Garfield worked Thursday. Jim worked a half day. Lee took Ella and Garfield to get their glasses changed. Friday Jim worked a half day at Narrowsburg Lumber.

Sunday morning, June 8, Lon didn't go to Sunday School. Arthur stopped by to see if he was sick. In the evening Lon rode to the Methodist Church with Frances Knorr. Monday afternoon Mae rode to visit Aida with Mrs. Lewis. Lon went down to vote. Aida went down to the A&P after Lon was home and stopped at the Hall and voted.

Tuesday afternoon Lon sawed wood at Alfred Hill's.

Tuesday Clara and Lee went for Ella and Garfield's glasses.

When Aida visited Frances Knorr on Wednesday afternoon, Hazel Angell (Frances' sister) was there.

Thursday morning Aida rode to the Village with Herbert Kinne. She bought bread at the A&P and met Mrs. Winter in the Post Office.

June was graduation time for the Eldred Seniors. Helen Myers, daughter of Martin D. Myers Sr., gave the Valedictorian speech at the Graduation Ceremony in Sunshine Hall. Martin Sr. must

Frances LaBarr Knorr, wife of Paul Knorr. Photo courtesy of Pam Fischetti DeFeo.

have been so proud of her.

Sunday night, June 15, was Children's Day in the Methodist Church. Frances drove Lon home.

Tuesday morning Aida walked to the A&P. Lon went in the late afternoon. Southeast of Aida and Lon, some of the Leavenworth men started haying at Proctor's on Tuesday. Friday and Saturday the men continued haying. Jim went to the movies on Saturday.

Saturday Lillie Calkin and her daughter Dot Hale visited Aida for a few minutes in the afternoon. Lillie's school ended on Friday.

Lon went to Sunday Services at Highland Lake on Sunday morning, June 22. Arthur took him home. (This may be around the start of the Highland Lake Bible Conference.)

Sunday the Leavenworth crew celebrated Garfield's birthday, except Stella who was sick. The men were still haying.

Monday Jim Leavenworth used his own tractor for haying. Orville Clark helped. Garfield started work for the Lochners.

Tuesday the men hayed some, then Garfield went to Lochner's. Clara and her family visited Ella for the day and evening. The men continued haying through the following Monday.

1941 World and National News

1941
- NBC television launched.

January 1941
- 200 freighters (Liberty ships) to be built.
- Roosevelt's State of the Union message outlined the four essential freedoms: of speech, of worship, freedom from fear, and from want.
- Roosevelt's proposed budget: $17.5 billion; $10.8 billion for defense.
- January to May: Britain and Italy fought in Somaliland.

February 1941
- Rommel head of German Afrika Corps in Libya.

March 1941
- Lend-Lease approved—$7 billion in military credits for American manufactured war supplies to Great Britain and other Allies.

April 1941
- Japan and the Soviet Union signed a five-year neutrality agreement.
- Germany and Italy invaded Yugoslavia and Greece. Yugoslavia surrendered.

May 1941
- German U-boat sunk U.S. merchant ship in the Atlantic.
- Germans invaded Crete.
- British Navy sunk German *Bismarck*.
- Germany and Turkey signed friendship agreement.

June 1941
- Hitler invaded Russia with three German army groups and four air fleets. In six months, Red Army lost 4 to 5 million: 1.5 million killed; 3 million taken prisoner.
- German and Italian assets frozen in U.S.

July 1941
- Japanese assets frozen in Britain and U.S.
- U.S. naval forces occupied/defended Iceland.
- Stalin Commander-in-Chief.
- Congress asked to extend the draft period to 30 months.

August 1941
- Export of U.S. oil and aviation fuel forbidden except to the British Empire and Western Hemisphere countries. This hit Japan hard.
- 8-point Atlantic Charter of Churchill and Roosevelt to serve as blueprint for the postwar world.
- U.S. formally warned Japan to cease its aggression in Asia.

September 1941
- Japanese cabinet considered seizing Dutch East Indies' oil fields.
- U-boat attacked destroyer *U.S.S. Greer* off Iceland.
- Ted Williams batting average: .400.

October 1941
- Mount Rushmore carving finished after 14 years.
- Roosevelt rejected Japanese PM Konoye's summit conference request. Konoye resigned.
- German Army almost in Moscow.

November 1941
- A Lend-Lease pact approved for the U.S.S.R.—$1 billion loan.
- U.S. merchant ships could be armed when they entered war zones.
- The Japanese peace attempts rejected; Washington sent 10-point counterproposal.
- The Japanese did not respond. A Japanese carrier force: 6 aircraft carriers, 2 battleships, 9 destroyers, 3 submarines and tankers sailed from the Kurile Islands toward Hawaii. Their orders: to attack the U.S. Pacific Fleet at Pearl Harbor, Hawaii, if Japan did not reach an agreement with the U.S. by December 5.

December 1941
- Roosevelt made a final appeal to Emperor Hirohito for peace but received no reply.
- December 7: Japanese attacked U.S. fleet at Pearl Harbor, Hawaii, at 7:55 a.m. 9 U.S. fleet ships were sunk; 21 ships severely damaged. Death toll: 2,402; 1,282 wounded, including 68 civilians; 1,177 were from the *U.S.S. Arizona*.
- Roosevelt addressed Congress and described December 7 as a "date which will live in infamy."
- December 8: U.S. and Britain declared war on Japan. Japan invaded Thailand and Malaya; bombed Clark Field, the main U.S. airbase in Philippines.
- December 10: Japan invaded the Philippines.
- December 11: Germany and Italy declared war on U.S.
- U.S. declared war on Germany and Italy.
- British and U.S. Conference in Washington D.C. Defeat of Germany was top priority. U.S. Joint Chiefs of Staff established to direct the Allied war effort.
- Japan invaded Burma, British Borneo.
- Japan captured Wake Island and captured Hong Kong.
- Russian winter sets in; German forces halted in suburbs of Moscow.

S.S. Edwin Markham, *one of the early Liberty ships built by CalShip, was built in 111 days. Photo courtesy of Bill Ihlo.*

Wednesday morning Aida was at the Village and got some rhubarb from Frances.

Aida saw Alex Wait Thursday morning when she was at the A&P. She told him that Lon would like Alex to let Mr. Briggs know Lon wasn't going to the supper at Port Jervis that evening. Alfred Hill was up in the afternoon to get Lon's mowing machine.

Sunday, June 29, Arthur stopped at his aunt Aida's on his way to the Village. He wanted to let Lon know he would take him to church at Highland Lake. Art had heard from his brother Bob who was in Halifax. (Mabel Ryman drove Lon home after church.)

July 1941
Tuesday morning, July 1, Aida was down to the A&P. The last several days had been terribly hot. But the Leavenworth men were still haying. Garfield finished working at Lochner's before the hard thundershower in the afternoon.

The men finished haying at Proctor's on Tuesday.

It was also very hot weather in East Islip where Anna was busy getting ready for a trip with some friends. She would eventually visit her Myers relatives in the Binghamton, New York area.

In Eldred the Leavenworth men fixed Bill's mower on Thursday. It was ready to cut hay on Friday.

When Aida was at the A&P Thursday morning, she stopped to talk with Lizzie Wilson. On the way home she got some rhubarb from Frances.

On Friday Jim bought a cow from Norm Myers for $30. He continued to work for Narrowsburg Lumber Company. Jim also helped Bill Meyers Sr. with haying on Wednesday and Thursday.

William (Willie) Bosch and Florence Schmerfeld in the summer of 1941. Photo courtesy of Ken Bosch.

Thursday Ella and Garfield went to Clara's for dinner. Ella helped Clara with her wash. The whole crew went back to Garfield and Ella's in the evening.

Clara and her sons spent Friday with her parents. Jim and Garfield worked on the milk house. Doc Frier tested the cows.

Monday, July 14, Garfield and Jim were over at Bill's haying. Ella and Garfield went to Anna's Tuesday. The men were still haying. Jim was back in early evening to finish putting the hay in the barn.

Sunday, July 20, Jim mowed hay for his brother Goldie and raked hay at the Meyers'.

July was also a busy time for Lillie Calkin in Bethel.

Lillie Calkin, Bethel, to Mr. J.E. Austin, Ossining, N.Y.
July 22, 1941
Dear Dad,
I hope you are all well. I've been rather under the weather since about a week before school closed, but think I'll pull out of it now. First I had a nasty, grippy cold. Then within two weeks time, I had eight teeth out.

The combination of grippe and teeth has rather taken the starch out of me and I go to sleep about as soon as I sit down.

Dorothy and I have canned 39 qt. of raspberries, 7 pt. cherries, 2 pt. huckleberries, 12 qt. peas, and 4 jars of raspberry jam.

We have a very good garden, but so has nearly everyone this year. I never saw corn look better. We have sweet corn at least two feet higher than Burt's head. The only thing we lack is beets. The rabbits ate them.

Burt and Ray are working in Yulan now. They will probably be through in a day or so. I want to get down to see you before school starts. Love to all, Lillie

Wednesday Anna Leavenworth was in the Binghamton, New York area. She had dinner with her cousin Agnes Darling Curtiss and supper with her aunt Lottie Myers Darling, Agnes' mother. Lottie Darling, 83, was a sister to Anna's mother Maria Myers Leavenworth.

In Eldred on Monday and Tuesday Garfield worked for Beatrice McKeon. Ella reminisced about their wood porch swing her dad had "made 28 years ago."

Tuesday Anna found it very warm in East Islip when she arrived home. She rested some on Wednesday, did a small wash, baked a cake, and made a huckleberry pie. She also battled "quite some ants."

Thursday morning Aida saw Mrs. Sparks, Emma Stevens, Nellie Crandall, Mrs. Winter, and two boarders from Rothman's at the Eldred Post Office.

Green Acres, Highland Lake
In August of 1941 Florence

Herman and Mathilde's Woodland Cottages

Woodland Cottages on the Barryville-Yulan Mail Road was owned originally by Charles and Lottie Bradley Colville. Herman and Mathilde Protz had purchased the property by 1940.

The property may have originally been a farm with a main house, a nearby barn, and the very old Stern Cottage on the opposite side of the road.

My family went there first in 1947. A relative had recommended it to us as a well kept, well run family boarding house with excellent German-American style cuisine, activities for children, tennis, shuffleboard, and swimming in a pool filled with Artesian well water. The Woodland Cottage motto: You are a Stranger Here But Once."

When we arrived there were two attached buildings just behind the Main House and an adjacent tennis court, across the driveway. One was a three-story brick and tile-fronted edifice with guest rooms; the adjacent, a one-story stone cottage, also with guest rooms.

To the right of the stone house

Playing tennis at Woodland Cottages. Photo courtesy of Joan Polishook.

Joan's family stayed on the second floor of Stern Cottage. 1954 photo courtesy of Joan Polishook.

Herman and Mathilde Protz courtesy of Joan Polishook.

was a single row of clapboard rooms (something like an early motel). Each had its own bath, while most of the rooms in the three aforementioned buildings had shared baths on each floor. There was a laundry shed behind the stone house.

At first the Protzes lived in the lower portion of the brick and tile building. They eventually built The Pines where the barn might have been. It was a four-room guest house with a front porch set within the trees at the edge of a field. Much later, came the Recreation Hall near the handball and shuffleboard courts.

My family was assigned to the 100-year-old Stern Cottage. The two-story colonial was across the road from the handball court, and faced the swimming pool. On the ground floor there were three guest rooms. We stayed upstairs in two of the three attic guest rooms which shared a large full bathroom.

When the house was enlarged, the Protzes moved their living quarters to the back of the building. A garage was also added.

Next to the Stern Cottage was

"Max's Shack" named for a Max who had stayed there for several years. It was simply a room with a bed, dresser and curtained closet. Next to it was a flush toilet and shower, all on a concrete floor.

Beyond that was a newer one-family cottage labelled the Portman Cottage, for guests who had stayed there.

The fields and woods around were all a part of the property. Pines bordered the roadside. Many fruit trees had been planted.

Mathilde was a master gardener and she had many beautiful flower gardens, especially the large one at the roadside adjacent to the Stern Cottage.

In the early years they kept some cattle and chickens. There was plenty of room to go roaming and enjoy the country. The Protzes owned a parcel just down the road with a small pond on it. Early on they kept a row boat there for anyone who wanted to use it.

Helen and Alfred Wolff were very good friends of Herman and Mathilde Protz and were largely responsible for their coming to the area and buying their property that became Woodland Cottages on the Mail Rd., Barryville. Mathilde learned much of her cooking skills from Helen. All this I was told by Mathilde when I knew her in my early years.—Joan Polishook.

Woodland Cottages Main Building and Office. Photo courtesy of Joan Polishook.

Green Meadows—Matchmaker's Paradise

Green Meadows (first Bosch's Lake House, then Green Acres) was the most popular venue on Highland Lake for many years. Located on the swampy end of Highland Lake, Green Meadows did not even have a beach, just a boat house, a dock, and a submerged fenced plank platform for children to wade and swim.

Competing boarding houses may have had more luxurious accommodations and even a beach, but none could compete with the friendly, festive atmosphere and plentiful, delicious food that the Pankows provided. Charlie Pankow transformed Green Meadows into a thriving business for 25 years. He was a great entrepreneur who knew how to show his guests a good time.

At some point before the 1940s, a semi-circle of small cabins were constructed in the rear of the main houses, shaded by plentiful apple trees. The cabins were given colorful names, many named for well-known hotels: "The Waldorf," "The New Yorker," etc. Disney characters were painted on the cabins and even on the barn.

Every Saturday night there was a dance party in the barn, with much drinking and revelry. There was also a mid-week dance. Other nights featured movies, bingo games and other entertainment. In the early forties "mock weddings" of randomly selected singles were held, complete with costumes and a "preacher."

During the day, there were spirited games of bocce ball on the front lawn, lounging in the shade of the many trees, swimming and sunbathing at

Right: The bride Florence Schmerfeld (standing by one of Disney's Snow White dwarves) took part in a "Mock Wedding," one of the many fun social activities at Green Acres. A fellow guest was the groom in the "wedding" of August 1941. Photos courtesy of Ken Bosch.

1941, playing volleyball at Green Acres. Photo courtesy of Ken Bosch.

Florence Schmerfeld in 1941 at Green Acres. Photos courtesy of Ken Bosch.

Baseball. Photo courtesy of Diane Pankow.

Green Meadows—Matchmaker's Paradise (cont'd.)

the boat house, and driving to visit local attractions. There was a snack bar in the "barn" and outdoor speakers filled the air year after year with the memorable hit songs from the juke box.

The days were punctuated morning, noon and late afternoon by the welcome dinner bell, signifying the call to yet another delicious meal. In the evening boarders would stroll along the road and later congregate in the barn for a scheduled event or just to socialize.

In actuality, Green Meadows was a match-maker's paradise. Many couples met at Green Meadows and later married, including my mother and father. My mother, Florence Schmerfeld met my dad, Willie Bosch, while she was vacationing there in 1941 and they married the following year. His brothers Henry "Whipple" and Charlie both met their wives when they were guests at Green Meadows. Many waitresses, dishwashers, handymen and cleaners met friends and sweethearts while working summers at Green Meadows.
—Ken Bosch.

Green Acres Recreation Hall with Disney characters. Photo courtesy of Diane Pankow.

Dancing in the barn at Green Meadows. Photo courtesy of Diane Pankow.

Henny Schmid, on left playing accordion in the barn. Photo courtesy of Diane Pankow.

Agnes Pankow Schmid (left) and Martha, a kitchen helper for years, peel potatoes. Charlie Pankow in back, Agnes Pankow (sideview), mother of Agnes Schmid and Charlie. Photo courtesy of Diane Pankow.

Mini golf, shuffleboard, BBQ pit. Behind that the golf area became the horseshoe area. Photo courtesy of Diane Pankow.

Henny Schmid (husband of Charlie's sister Agnes) at the piano in the late 1950s. Photo courtesy of Diane Pankow.

Boating and swimming on Highland Lake at Green Meadows. Photo courtesy of Ken Bosch.

Schmerfeld and a group of her girlfriends were guests at Green Acres. Florence was a bookkeeper for an insurance firm on Wall Street.

Towards the end of her visit, she met Willie Bosch at a dance in the "Barn." She and Willie hit it off immediately and she arranged for a second week's vacation from work. Wedding bells were in Willie and Florence's future.

August 1941

It was still very hot in East Islip Friday, August 1, as Anna prepared for a trip to Eldred.

Monday morning, August 4, in Eldred, Aida couldn't find salt and saleratus (baking soda) at the A&P. She had to get them at Randolph's.

Anna Leavenworth

Monday Anna traveled from Islip to Eldred. "But Mr. N. came too early and I forgot to take my watch. Women always get the wrong end," she sputtered in her diary.

Anna stayed at her sister Christina's home which was the Echo Hill Farm House where they had grown up. Anna had been born in 1875 so she had known her Leavenworth grandparents, Sherman Buckley and Charlotte Ingram Leavenworth, and her grandmother Jane Ann Van Pelt Webb Myers.

Anna always rued the day she had been born with the long, graceful fingers of her French great-grandmother Elizabeth Lazerlier Van Pelt. Anna wanted the Dutch hands which she felt were good for working.

Tuesday Anna and her niece Charlee Hirsch began to weed the potatoes and corn. Anna often weeded during August, the month of "hot days and cold nights."

Lillie Austin Calkin, daughter of Ell and Emma Parmenter Austin, was busy canning in August. Photo courtesy of Katherine Calkin Traxler.

Tuesday Aida went to the A&P for sugar and milk. Wednesday she washed and got some wood.

Wednesday Anna Leavenworth went to the Church Fair and thought it "was poor and slow."

Thursday Aida ironed and went to the Village for bread. She canned some blackberries when she got home. Saturday morning Aida was back at the A&P.

Sunday, August 10, Lon went to the Methodist Church in the morning; in the evening he attended the Congregational.

Sunday the Austin brothers went to their aunt Christina's house to have dinner with their aunt Anna Leavenworth.

Tuesday afternoon Chester Middaugh was in to see Lon to tell him there was to be a clambake at Chester's place on Friday.

Wednesday Clara, Lee, and Dick went shopping. Little Wayne stayed with Garfield and Ella.

Thursday and Friday Jim worked for Narrowsburg Lumber.

Aunt Anna Leavenworth continued to weed at the old Leavenworth Farm.

Aida Austin continued her daily trek to the A&P. Friday morning Aida rode with Frances Knorr to get bread at the A&P. She met Jennie Crandall and Mary Bosch. Friday morning Lon went to the clambake at Chester Middaugh's about eleven. It began raining about noon and continued the rest of the day.

Sunday, August 17, the Austin brothers had dinner at their aunt Christina's and visited with their aunt Anna. Arthur drove his aunt Anna to visit his aunt Aida Austin.

"Peculiar views," my great-aunt Anna Leavenworth wrote about her conversation with my great-aunt Aida Austin.

Tuesday morning Aida rode to the A&P and back home with Howard and Teenie. Delbert Rundle was in the Post Office.

Lillie Calkin wrote her father on Tuesday.

Lillie Calkin, Bethel, to Mr. J.E. Austin, Ossining, N.Y.

August 19, 1941
Dear Dad,

I am sorry you are so poorly. I had expected to see you before this but Burt, Dot, and Ray are all up to Sidney. Burt and Ray are working on the housing project for workers in the Scintilla Magneto Factory which has recently been enlarged.

I can't leave mother for any length of time. She is well but I don't like to leave her alone over night.

I have canned 47 qts. of beans, 30 qt. of peas, 1 can each of shell beans and succotash and 3 cans mixed vegetables for vegetable soup. We have 40 qt. of peaches beside the raspberries. I have half-a-dozen cans of blackberries and huckleberries.

Our potatoes are the best we have had in years, nice and mealy like the ones you used to raise in Eldred.

1941 Halfway Brook News

Smoke pours from the windows of Rohman's Hotel in Shohola. Firemen from seven communities joined in the battle, April 25, 1941. Photos courtesy of Christene Stevens Myers.

1941 Rohman's Fire

The fire at Rohman's started in the barbershop owned by Chester Hulse and is thought to have been caused by the heat of the blowtorch painters were using. Up to $20,000 damage was estimated by Art Rohman.

The fire was contained, by means of a bucket brigade and a line from the booster tank of the Shohola fire truck while calls went out for mutual aid…Companies from Port Jervis, Milford, Hawley, Narrowsburg, Lava, and Matamoras responded. While the upper stories of the front and main portion of the building were gutted, the building was saved. It was soon repaired, but without the old cupola which once decorated the roof.—Fluhr, George J., Ibid., p. 5,6.

Margie Bosch graduated in 1941. Photo courtesy of Victoria Kohler.

1941 Bridge Opened
- October 7, 1941, the new Barryville-Shohola Bridge opened.

1941 Eldred Seniors
- Marjorie Bosch, Orville Clark, John Edwards, Ruth Edwards, Flora Foster, William Kalin, William Kinne, Helen Myers, Cynthia Ott, William Parker, Lewis Schmalzle, Betty Stanton, Mary Sulzbach, Virginia Tuthill, Donald Van Etten, Clara Vollmer, Ralph West, Carlton Woodruff.

1941 Enlisted in the Service
- Henry "Whipple" Bosch and George Andersen joined the Army; William H. Parker Jr. (17) entered the Navy.

1941 Marriages
- Elsie Parker married Ray Clouse.
- Clifford Crandall married Mary Myers.
- William Flieger (Sergeant-Livingstone descendant) married Lillian Piatt.
- Ed Wilson married Agnes Mary Lucke from Flatbush Brooklyn, N.Y. They then lived in Barryville.
- Marion Lass married Clinton Joseph Guenther.
- Royden Arthur Toaspern married Doris Boudman.

1941 Deaths
- Bill Sullivan, 33, died in March.
- Frank Austin, son of Ira and Minerva Austin, died in Illinois.
- Herman J. Rixton, 1862–1941.
- Carrie E. Bogert Clark, 1865–1941.
- Mary Nellie van Eastenbridge Bosch, 1861–1941, second wife of Wilhelm Bosch, was born in Netherlands and died in Highland Lake, New York. Mary Nellie van Eastenbridge and her second husband Wilhelm Bosch had one daughter, Christina Brodmerkel.
- Julius Maier, 1866–1941, served for years as the financial secretary for Sunshine Free Library in Eldred.
- Victor Ewart, a Leavenworth descendant, died.
- Jane Rundle died.

William and Lillian Piatt Flieger. Photo courtesy of Bill Flieger.

Clifford Crandall, his bride Mary Myers, Helen Myers, and Arthur Austin. Photo courtesy of Mary Briggs Austin.

Wedding photo of Clifford Crandall and Mary Myers. Helen Myers (sister to bride), Mary Myers (bride), Clifford Crandall (groom), Arthur Austin (best man). On steps, left to right: Lola Parker (Bill Parker's wife), Verna Eadie (Clifford's sister), Victoria Parker (Nellie's sister), and Nellie Crandall (Clifford's mother). Photo in Myers, Crandall, and Austin families' collections.

If frost holds off, I'll have lima beans, peppers, and tomatoes. I put up nine pints of corn last week. Bobby [her grandson] is staying with me for a couple of days. He starts school this fall. Hope you are all feeling better.

Love, Lillie

We'll visit the Scintilla Magneto Factory in Sidney, New York, in the next chapter. Ray and Dot Hale and several others from Eldred worked there at some point during the war.

Wednesday Anna left Eldred for her home in E. Islip.

Wednesday in Eldred Herman Bosch got some hay from the old Austin farm. Lon was at the Village about noon on Thursday. One of the men at the Rothman Place gave him a lift home. Herman was down for hay again.

Arthur drove Lon home from the prayer meeting Friday Evening.

Saturday Anna in Islip was very busy. She cleaned, sorted, and ironed; cut wood, weeded, and went to the vegetable market. Anna was so glad to be back in "mine own house."

In Eldred Monday morning, August 25, Mr. Bente stopped by Aida's to see if she knew anything about Mrs. Gray who joined the Congregational Church when it was first founded. Mr. Bente, the Congregational Pastor, was the husband of Belle Greig Grotecloss. He gave Aida the *Times*.

Arthur was in to see his aunt Aida in the afternoon. Aida also went to the A&P.

Monday it rained in Islip. Anna felt rather bad all Tuesday. But she managed to complete a rug and write to her nephew Bob Austin and mail it on Wednesday.

Wednesday in Eldred Garfield started remodeling their porch.

On the east side of Eldred, Mae called on Aida. After she went home, Aida called on Emily Schoonover. Emma Waidler was visiting her brother Rowlee again. Then Aida went to the A&P. As she started home, Gladys Austin overtook her at the Rothman house, and gave Aida a ride home.

Saturday afternoon Aida "was down to bid Emma Waidler good bye." Arthur stopped by after work. He had met the train for some of Gladys Austin's friends.

Charlie Bosch wrote more instructions to his son Willie (Billy) again in September.

Charlie Bosch, Flushing, LI, to Billy Bosch, Highland Lake
*September 1941
Dear Billy,
I am on the job at Mount Vernon—22 alleys. I have been working hard and still have that sprained thumb. It isn't any better. We work seven hours, five days per week. I'll be up with Ed next Friday about seven or eight o'clock.
You should cut that brush by the yellow pine by Herman's old place. But leave all nice trees and nice white birches stand. Also by the pines right near the two spruce trees over the fence is a few very small maples to leave standing. You can brush the road to the old barn both sides. Keep track of your time; you get 40 cents per hour.
If you want groceries, get them from Alex's Royal Scarlet Store. Bread also from Maney. Get what you need.
I am going to write to Willie Brodmerkel [his brother-in-law] to let you have the tractor and batteries. But he should take it down and first fix it up a little. We need that chain.
If you can get Herman's mow machine, then cut that garden or maybe young Herman can help for two hours, then you can rake it up and burn it. If so, we can plow it Saturday and Sunday.
Get more apples and put them on the Quinn Place. Maybe Ralph can help you.
Don't let any potatoes go or pumpkins. The cucumbers leave where they are. Hope you are getting along OK.
I'll write to Dunlap to leave you milk in the a.m. Hope you are in the little house. Take a day and clean up the things around there by the bungalow, 40 cents per hour. If you want something, write. Take it easy. Leave my mail on the table in the Bungalow.
Great Stuff, Pop*

Second Annual 97 Celebration
In September there was quite the second annual celebration of the completion of N.Y. Route 97.
Teenie Stevens competed in the *Old Fashioned Rider and Horse* event on Belle Greig Grotecloss Bente's horse, Rob Roy. Mr. Bente did not approve of women riding horses and didn't want his wife to ride, so Mrs. Bente had asked Teenie to ride and she took first place.

September 1941
Monday, September 1, was Labor Day. Art was at the old Austin farm for quite a while in the morning. (Maybe Art was talking some things over with his uncle Lon.)
Hattie Schroeder and her husband called on Aida in the afternoon.
On the west side of Eldred, Garfield worked on their porch floor. Tuesday Anna and Clara were with their mom for the day. They papered upstairs. And Garfield continued working on the porch floor. Tuesday morning Aida was once again at the A&P. In the afternoon her niece Lillie stopped by for a few minutes. Lillie had attended a teacher's meeting in the schoolhouse. She was going to "commence her school at Yulan" on Wednesday.
Wednesday Arthur was on his way home from work when he saw his uncle Lon who had just bought some ice cream at one of the grocery stores. Art drove his uncle home. Then the two of them went to Aida's, and all three (like true Austins) ate the ice cream.
Arthur and Aida talked a few minutes about an Algebra problem, then he went on home

N.Y. 97 Days, 1941

1941 Teenie and Mrs. Bente's horse, Rob Roy. Photo courtesy of Christene Stevens Myers.

Old Fashioned Rider and Horse
1st: E. Christene Stevens, 2nd: Ed Toaspern, 3rd: Peggy Gilmore.

Hay Ride
1st: Town of Lumberland, 2nd: Town of Neversink.

Draft Horses
1st: Narrowsburg Lumber Company.

Old Fashioned Rig
1st: H.C. Dewitt, Mrs. D. Merrill of Rowlands, 2nd: Mrs. H.E. Bente of Eldred.

Old Fashioned Dress
1st: Anna Oellrich, Narrowsburg, 2nd: Clara Wolff, Barryville, 3rd: Mrs. Robert Many, Grahamsville.

Dog Show
Farm dog: 1st: Mrs. R. Hoades, 2nd: Laverne Barnes; Bird dog: 1st: Eric Karg, 2nd: O.E. Vannatta; Hound dog: 1st: Ben Maas, 2nd: Mrs. Albrecht.

Horseshoe Pitching
Team: Tom O'Gara, Lake View Inn, Yulan; Lewis Schmalze, Shohola; Single: Tom O'Gara.

Square Dance Couple
1st: Mrs. Rose Downey, Glen Spey; Ed Smith, Barryville, 2nd: Mr. and Mrs. Wm. Bensett, Barryville.

Old Auto
1st: Walter Matter.—August 15, 1941, *Delaware Valley News.*

The Parker Family in the fall of 1941 at Lewis Hazen's boarding house: Standing, left to right: Lewis Hazen, Elsie Hazen, Jim Parker, Mabel Parker, Nell Crandall, Andy Parker, Marge Parker, Bill Parker Sr., Lola (Eleanora) Parker, Ray Clouse. Sitting: Viola Hazen, Marcella Hazen, Hazel Parker, Victoria Parker, Shirley Parker, Howard Parker, Elsie Parker Clouse. (William Parker Jr. was not in the photo since he was in the service.) Photo courtesy of William H. Parker Jr.

to Alfred and Bessie Hill's where he boarded, or soon would.

Thursday noon Aida was at the A&P. Lon asked his nephew Bill (who hadn't gone to work because it was so rainy) to give him a ride to Yulan.

Saturday morning in Eldred, Aida stopped at Lizzie Wilson's on her way to the A&P. Aida asked Mrs. Wilson to give Mr. Bente the paper Aida had about information on the Grays which Mr. Bente had requested. One of the boarders from the Rothman House accompanied Aida on her way home.

Dr. Austin was up to Elizabeth Wilson's in the afternoon, and to see Lon in the evening.

Sunday, September 7, Dr. Austin and Herman Bosch were in to see Aida after Lon went to church. In the afternoon Dr. Austin stopped at Aida's on his way to Port Jervis. It was settled that Lon and Aida could stay there another year. They rented from Dr. Austin.

Monday Lon ate dinner at the County House with a minister's organization. When he got back, Arthur drove him to Bill's and then back home.

It was terribly warm on Wednesday. Hopefully the butter Lon bought (along with some bread) at the A&P, did not melt on his way home.

On the west side of Eldred, it was canning time again for Ella. Thursday she canned 51 quarts of plums and 7 quarts of cauliflower. Garfield took some buttermilk to Doc Gutfruend. Friday and Saturday Garfield worked on the stables.

Mrs. Winter called on Aida Friday afternoon. Young Herman Bosch dropped by to get the mower.

Saturday morning Aida was down to the A&P. Her great-niece Melva stopped to see Aida in late afternoon. Herman and his son Robbie were cutting hay.

Sunday, September 14, Melva and one of Fred Morgan's girls visited Aida a little while after Sunday School at the Congregational Church where their mother went.

Monday morning Aida was once again at the Post Office and A&P. Later Ernest Horton stopped by her place to see if she and Lon had any pears.

Monday Garfield worked four hours for Beatrice McKeon.

Aunt Anna worked hard all Monday in Islip, canning most of the bushel of tomatoes she was given. She was delayed by the junk man wanting scrap metal.

In Eldred on Tuesday morning Lon went to Bessie's for milk. Aida washed on Tuesday. Arthur was over late afternoon for one of his books.

Clifford Marries Mary
Clifford Crandall married Mary Myers in September. My father Arthur Austin was the best man. Clifford was Art's good friend and Mary was Art's second cousin. After they were married Clifford and Mary lived with her father Martin D. Myers Sr. in Eldred, until 1947.

Tuesday, September 16, Arthur Austin was classed 1H by the Selective Service board.

Wednesday and Thursday Lon cut some wood in the woods.

Thursday morning Aida saw Mrs. Winter, Jennie Crandall, and Mrs. Lewis in the Post Office. After work, Arthur dropped off some papers for Lon.

"It is about eight o'clock now and the northern lights are flashing in the sky," Aida jotted in her diary that night.

Jim went to the movies with the Clark brothers on Friday. Buck McBride stopped by for green tomatoes and gave Ella a squash. W. Horton called.

Friday after the church prayer meeting, there was a rehearsal for Ruth Parker and Harold Frint's wedding which was the next day. Arthur drove Lon home after the meeting, then went back to lock the church after the wedding rehearsal.

Saturday Herman Jr. took a small load of wood over to the Austin siblings. Lon went down early in the evening to open the church for the wedding.

Saturday Garfield finished his work for Beatrice McKeon.

Frances Toaspern and cousin Albert Pegg in Maryland, fall 1941. Photo courtesy of Bill Ihlo.

Sunday, September 21, church was at the Methodist in the morning. Arthur was in the Village and gave Lon a lift home.

Monday Lon went to the A&P for bread. Tuesday Lon went to the Village to see Harry Wormuth about a load of wood for the church. Herman Jr. and a friend took a load of wood to the Austin's in the afternoon.

Tuesday in west Eldred Garfield worked on his daughter Clara's porch.

Thursday morning Aida went to Andrew's and the A&P. In the afternoon Mae Parker and the newlyweds, Ruth and Harold K. Frint, and his little girl, called on Aida.

Thursday on the west side of Eldred, Ella canned 23 quarts of sauerkraut. Norman Myers stopped by to say hello to Garfield.

Thursday night Harry Wormuth's mill burned.

Saturday Garfield started working at Buck McBride's.

Sunday, September 28, Elijah Moore from the Scout Camp visited with Garfield. Garfield also went up to Hirsch's for a while. Jim worked the next week for Paul Knorr.

Sunday Ernie Horton stopped by Aida's in the afternoon to see if Lon and Aida would go to the Republican caucus on Monday.

Sunday night Mr. Bente, his wife, and son (one of the Grotecloss brothers) went to the Methodist Church. Arthur drove Lon home. Lon Austin wrote a short note to his brother Ell.

Lon Austin, Eldred, to Mr. J.E. Austin, Ossining, N.Y.
Dear Brother,
Hope you are feeling well this fine weather. The bluebirds and robins have returned to their home in the north. It is very warm today. Hope it continues.
Best wishes, Lon

Frances Toaspern Visits Maryland
Frances Toaspern visited her aunt Julia Straub Pegg in Maryland in the fall of 1941. Julia (who at one time had helped run the Straub Hotel in Eldred) had married Albert Pegg who had a son Albert Jr. Mr. Pegg Sr. would soon be brought out of retirement to be the superintending engineer in charge of CalShip's Liberty Ship program in San Pedro, California. They would ultimately built 336 ships during the war (which would start before the year's end).

Frances' brother Ed would visit his aunt Julia and uncle Albert in California in 1945.

October 1941
Wednesday, October 1, Lon (84) received a birthday card from his brother Ell.

Thursday, October 2, one

Early 1950s view of Eldred Congregational Church and old School in the background. When Aida and Lon went to town, they would see these buildings on their left as they got close to Eldred's Four Corners. Photo courtesy of Christene Stevens Myers.

of the state police stopped in to see if Lon had seen anything of Harold Dunlap's adopted boy. "A lot of young fellows were riding horseback up our lane and down the field across the road. I think they must have been looking for Harold's boy," noted Aida.

Friday morning Aida was once again at the A&P. But they did not yet have the bread she wanted. Arthur and Lon had gone to Port Jervis in the morning. When they came back, Aida rode to the Village with Arthur for the bread. Art then drove Aida home.

Mae was over and told Aida that they found Harold's boy and he was with his aunt at Glen Spey. He had started out to find his father.

"Listened to exciting war news of ship sinking off Brazil," Aunt Anna of Islip wrote on Friday. On Saturday she worked hard until about 4 p.m. when several friends came with a cake to celebrate her 66th birthday a day early. They gave her some beautiful curtains.

Sunday, October 5, Anna heard Dr. Ayer preach. "Sorry he is so on side of traitors and Hitler. Most ministers seem to be on the side of tyrants anyhow," Anna wrote in her diary.

In Eldred Lon rode to church with Mildred Briggs on Sunday.

Monday Lon went to the A&P and the Post Office. He had a letter from Dr. Austin.

Monday evening Stella's Clark family were at the Leavenworths when the Yankees won the World Series. Perhaps they listened to the game on the radio.

Wednesday Rowlee stopped by Lon's to see about fixing the church door. Lon went down with him to the church. Rowlee also fixed the steps on the stoop at Aida's.

Aida was at the A&P and Post Office on Thursday.

Saturday was the Methodist Church Picnic. The group stayed in the Church Hall and didn't go to the lake as usual, because it was too windy.

Saturday evening Garfield and Ella had a houseful of folks: Anthony Hirsch and family; Clara, Lee, and their family; and Stella and Goldie. Jim was at Orville Clark's.

Sunday, October 12, in Islip, Anna knitted afghans for the British Belief.

Monday morning in Eldred, Lon went to the Post Office. Robbie Bosch and the Myers' boy who worked for them, took wood over to Lon's in the afternoon. Lon made some cider.

Ella bought 100 pounds of potatoes from the A&P on Monday.

Tuesday when Aida got back from the A&P, she helped Lon finish carrying in his wood. Lon made some more cider.

Thursday Lon went to both the A&P and Post Office. On Friday Lon went to Newburgh and then to Port Jervis with Mr. Briggs to meetings for Ministers and Laymen.

Saturday Lon took his almost daily jaunt to the A&P for bread. Arthur stopped at Aida's for one of his books.

Sunday morning, October 19, Garfield hung storm windows at Goldie's.

Tuesday Buck McBride and Beatrice McKeon stopped by the Leavenworths for a while.

On Tuesday in Islip, Anna chopped wood and worked on rugs. She was quite surprised to get a visit from Anthony Hirsch. "He seems to be in good health and stayed overnight," Anna wrote.

This may have been when Anthony started working in New York City during the week and staying at Anna's. He went home to Eldred on weekends.

Tuesday morning in Eldred, Aida was at the A&P. After school in the afternoon Melva visited her great-aunt Aida for a little while.

Wednesday Aida did her washing. Thursday four hunters Aida didn't know stopped by her place. They didn't stay very long as it began raining. It continued to rain off and on the rest of the day.

Saturday Jim and the Clark brothers went to the pictures. Anthony, Christina, and Charlee visited with Garfield and Ella for the evening. Ernest Clark (Stella's dad) was also there.

Monday morning, October 27, was rainy, but that did not stop Aida from taking her usual hike to the A&P. Arthur was at her place in the afternoon. It was the first day he had had off in two weeks. Arthur told Aida that his brother Bob was in the Anti-Aircraft Department, and expected to go overseas soon.

Tuesday it was clear, but very cold. Melva was at Aida's about noon to get something to wear to a masquerade party.

Wednesday afternoon in Islip, Anna ordered a Singer Sewing Machine. "I wish Charlee lived nearer," she lamented. It was delivered Friday morning. That night Jimmie Braddock her cat was in a terrible fight. Jimmie B. was appropriately named after the American boxer who had won the Heavyweight Title in 1935.

November 1941

It rained quite hard most of Saturday in Eldred. Herman Sr. and Jr. were down to see Lon in the evening. They asked about putting up signs forbidding hunting. Harry Wormuth was in to see Lon after the Bosches left.

Sunday, November 2, Garfield and Goldie went to the funeral of Elijah Moore, who they had worked for at the Scout Camp.

On Monday Garfield and Jim worked for Buck McBride.

Monday morning Aida went to Mary Bosch's to take back her bottles. Mary was not there. So Aida walked over a mile to Mae's and stayed for dinner. After dinner Aida walked to the A&P. She rode part way home with Mr. Kinne. She noticed signs had been put up on the road near her house.

Tuesday, election day, was rather ambivalent—partly clear and partly cloudy. Lon went to the Village about two o'clock, but came back without voting.

Howard Stevens stopped by between three and four to take Lon and Aida to vote. Howard also drove them back home.

Wednesday morning Aida, stopped at the A&P before going to the Post Office where she saw Howard. On her way

Melva Austin stopped by to see her great-aunt Aida Austin. Photo courtesy of Melva Austin Barney.

home Aida met Mrs. Winter by Harold Dunlap's. Lon went up to Wormuth's to order coal in the afternoon. He met Arthur in the Village and Arthur gave him a lift home.

Julius Maier, the last of the Maier family who lived on Crawford Road, died, and was buried Wednesday afternoon.

Wednesday Jim started working on the Stege place for Narrowsburg Lumber Company.

Friday was a pleasant day and Aida did her washing in the morning. Saturday morning she ironed. Mr. Briggs and his son John brought up some apples in the afternoon and made cider.

Arthur drove to New York City Friday night to see his good friend Clifford Crandall. He left for Eldred on Sunday.

On the west side of Eldred, Sunday afternoon, November 9, Stella stopped in to see Ella. Bill Austin was there for supper; and Anna, Bill, and Jimmy Meyers in the evening.

On Wednesday morning, a little bit after Aida's usual jaunt to the A&P, Lon went up to get

Margie Bosch's "very good" graduation photo courtesy of Victoria Kohler.

Mac Layden, Ed and Agnes Mary Lucke Wilson, Gertrude Lucke Keeley, Lawrence Keeley and Clement Lucke. Photo courtesy of Mary Agnes Wilson Dorney.

wood. John Dunlap gave Aida a ride home. Lon was already home when Aida arrived. He had ridden back with Alex Wait, who took him to the Dubois place to see how they were fixing the dam.

Thursday was cold all day. Lon didn't go to the woods.

Friday morning Lon went up to the woods again. Alex said some one had killed a deer by the dam Wednesday night—before deer season opened on Friday.

Mary Bosch stopped by for a little while and told Aida about Julius' death and funeral and his will.

Saturday morning Lon went to the Village. He was back a little while before the Myers' boy who worked for Bosches brought the load of wood Lon had cut.

Ed Wilson Marries Agnes Mary
Edward Wilson married Agnes Mary Lucke from Flatbush Brooklyn, New York, on November 15, 1941. After they were married Ed and Agnes Mary lived in Barryville. Ed had a taxi business and managed a gas station.

Sunday, November 16, Arthur was in the Village and gave Lon a ride home from church.

After shopping at the A&P Tuesday morning, Aida saw Mrs. Lewis in the Post Office. In the afternoon Mary Bosch stopped by Aida's to give her Margie's graduation picture which "was very good."

Wednesday Walter McBride stopped by Garfield and Ella's for the evening. Thursday Jim and Goldie went hunting in Delaware County.

Friday in Islip, Jimmie B. (the cat) had a major fight with a big white cat.

In Eldred Monday, November 24, Aida, in addition to her usual outing to the A&P, walked to the Eldred Cemetery. Mrs. Winter and Clarence Sergeant's wife stopped by Aida's for some pinecones and a short visit, in the afternoon.

Tuesday the West boy who worked for Harry Wormuth hauled a load of wood to Aida's in the morning and a load of coal about seven in the evening.

Wednesday was cold and windy, so Aida did not go anywhere. Thursday Aida went for bread and kerosene in the morning and for wood about noon. Lon kept busy writing his talk for the prayer meeting that night.

Jim and Orville went to the pictures in the evening. Orville and Vern were at Leavenworth's Friday evening.

Sunday, November 30, Arthur drove Lon home from Church. In the afternoon Art went to Aida's and left his *Sullivan County History* book with her. Art would continue to board with Alfred and Bessie Hill for the winter. (Most likely the history book was Quinlan's *History of Sullivan County*. Aida copied by hand a good deal of information from Quinlan's thick book.)

"War news is quite exciting," Anna of Islip wrote on Sunday, November 30. It was about to get too exciting.

December 1941
Monday morning, December 1, Aida went to the A&P. The weather was very cold and it felt like snow. Lon and Arthur went to church in Barryville.

Wednesday morning, on his day off, Arthur visited his aunt and uncle.

It was much colder on Friday when Jim started work again for Narrowsburg Lumber Company.

Sunday, December 7, Pearl Harbor was attacked.

"Anthony arrived about three p.m. War declared," recorded Anna

Mac O'Donnell and the Bachelors of Highland Lake

Aida mentioned Bill Hammond and Frank (Mac) O'Donnell in her early 1940s diary.

Billy Hammond's family had a boarding house in Highland Lake. During Prohibition Billy had a floating bar on Highland Lake called the Ark. In the early 1920s, Frank J. (Mac) O'Donnell left Brooklyn and took a job working at the Hammond boarding house for a summer. Mac spent the rest of his life in Highland Lake—except for being drafted into the Army during World War II.

Mac's duties included being a handyman, waiter, and piano player. He was known mainly as a painter and was very good at sign painting. He worked for a period of time for the Sullivan County Highway Department as a sign painter.

Mac was one of several memorable characters most of whom were bachelors that made up a part of the society in Highland Lake. Others included Billy Hammond, Herb Gordon, Abe Hulse, George Andersen, Russell Morgan, Jimmy Mills, and Charlie Ort.

They were all customers at my parent's [Mellan's] bar. My mother and father would always host a free Thanksgiving and Christmas Dinner as many no longer had any family in the area. I remember Mac getting very sad at Christmas time and trying to call either his niece or nephew on the telephone from my parent's bar. He would get upset when they would not have much to do with him. Otherwise he was always a good fun loving man who liked his beer.

I'm not sure how Mac survived in his little one-room home. But he always seemed to be happy and content. Mac always took time to talk to all the kids who grew up in the area.—Joe Mellan.

Charlie Bosch hired Mac occasionally to do odd jobs such as stenciling NO TRESPASSING signs, etc. It didn't hurt that Charlie usually had beer on hand.

Mac lived in a very small one-room cabin on the steep hill (appropriately named "Mac's Hill") at the south end of the Hartung Road. The cabin was covered on the three facing sides with the same light green asbestos shingles as the Highland Lake Fire House.

The interior had room for a bed, a small table and a gas heater. There was no cooking stove, no plumbing, no toilet facilities—there wasn't even an outhouse! These conditions provoked much humorous speculation as to how and where Mac took care of his biological necessities.

In 1930 Mac boarded at Billy Hammond's household, diagonally across Highland Lake Road from the end of the Hartung Road, a stone's throw from the eventual site of Mac's cabin.

Abe Hulse on the right with friend Joe Clark. Photo courtesy of Ken Bosch.

Mac was an accomplished piano player and sometimes, after sufficient libation, plied his skills to entertain the patrons at Mellan's. Mac gave piano lessons to the young Eddie Mellan. —Ken Bosch.

Mac's cabin, 2012. Photo courtesy of Ken Bosch.

of Islip on Monday. Tuesday Anna noted, "Radio humming all day. War declared on Japan. Worked on Christmas towels."

Tuesday morning in Eldred, Aida went to the A&P and then to see Ed Myers, where her Austin nieces stayed.

Wednesday in Islip Aunt Anna worked on guest towels for Christmas gifts. Anthony Hirsch stayed there during the week. Thursday Chef Anthony made a duck dinner for Anna's guests. "A good time," Anna jotted down in her diary.

Thursday Katherine Dunlap called on Ella on the west side of Eldred. Stella was in for a while. "Hitler and Italy declared war on the U.S.A.," Ella wrote that night. The Austin and Leavenworth aunts and uncles would be quite concerned during the next several

Barryville-Shohola Bridge was completed in fall 1941. Photo courtesy of Ed Wolff.

years as Art, Bill, and Bob Austin and Jim Leavenworth would eventually serve overseas.

Thursday afternoon Aida walked to Mae's. Mr. Frint drove Aida home. Sunday, December 14, Alfred Hill took Lon home after church and was up in the afternoon.

Anthony Hirsch was back at Anna's in Islip late on Monday. He left for Eldred early on Friday.

Friday was clear and rather warm in Eldred. Jim worked. Garfield was home. Lee, Goldie, and Stella were in.

With the U.S. now in a war, the townsfolk took turns watching

The Briggs dog Pal sits on a boat with the new bridge in the background. Photo courtesy of Mary Briggs Austin.

for planes at the golf course on what was once Dr. DeVenoge's property. Jim and Goldie watched for planes on Friday.

Sunday afternoon, December 21, Arthur was up to Aida's for his skates. The Methodist had their Christmas Tree in the evening.

Monday in Islip Aunt Anna worked on "Xmas cards of which there seems no end."

Tuesday morning Aida went to Mae's and the A&P. Martin Myers drove her home. At noon on Christmas Eve, Mae stopped by Aida's with some candy and cake.

Christmas Day was a beautiful day in East Islip. Anna went to a friend's for dinner. When they returned at 4 p.m. they found part of South Highway patrolled and guarded by anti-aircraft guns.

Christmas morning in Eldred, Arthur visited Aida for a little while. He went to Ed Myers' for dinner to be with his brother Raymond and his family. Late in the afternoon Emma Stevens and Teenie called on Lon and Aida. They had brought a basket of fruit for each of them.

Sunday, December 28, Arthur drove Lon home from church. Towards evening Arthur took over his trunk and other things. Perhaps he was getting ready to enlist, and stored his belongings with his Austin uncle and aunt.

Sunday night Garfield watched at the golf course.

Sunday in East Islip, Charlee and Anthony Hirsch arrived before Anna's supper was over. Monday Charlee made an apron with Anna's new machine. Anthony arrived late from his work, so Anna cooked supper.

Even though Monday morning in Eldred was very, very cold, Aida took her usual jaunt to the A&P. It was still cold on Tuesday when Margie Bosch took a bottle of milk to both Lon and Aida.

In Islip, Anna and her niece Charlee went to the Singer Machine Company and Charlee took lessons. Anna went to the eye doctor. Her eyes were not too good. She would gradually become blind. "Anthony did not come home so I had to cook supper Tuesday. I sure miss Anthony's cooking," Anna wrote wistfully on the last day of 1941.

Chapter 10
Human Nature Observed
World War II, 1942

At the time of Pearl Harbor, having no restraining ties and being prepared physically and, I supposed at the time, spiritually, I made preparations to join the Armed Forces.

The time spent in the army changed and shaped my life in many ways. While spending ten months in the states and three times as many in Africa and Italy, I had a great deal of time to observe human nature from many angles.—Arthur Austin.

Arthur Austin was with the 5th Army. Photo in the Austin Collection.

Arthur Austin, 28, still worked at the Sullivan County Highway Department when the new year began, but it would not be long until he joined the Army. Arthur boarded with Alfred and Bessie Hill, and their children Billy Lass and Joan Hill. The Hill family lived near the intersection of Highland Lake and Proctor Roads.

Art's brother Bob, in the Canadian Army, would enlist in the American Army in England.

Bill Austin also worked for the Sullivan County Highway Department. Bill, 39, would enlist in 1942, some time after Art.

The other Austin brother Raymond was a clerk for U.S. Customs for the U.S. Coast Guard in New York City. As mentioned in the last chapter, Raymond's wife Gladys and their four daughters lived in Eldred with Edwin Myers, Gladys' father, for safety reasons. Melva, though, would go to Staten Island for high school in the fall.

Since McKinley Austin had died in World War I and both their parents had died, there would be much concern for the three Austin brothers by the Leavenworth relatives: Garfield, Charlotte, Anna, and Christina Hirsch. And the Austins: Raymond, Gladys, their daughters; and, of course, Uncle Lon Austin and Aunt Aida Austin.

January 1942

"The Japanese took Manila," Art's aunt Ella Leavenworth wrote on Friday, January 2.

The warm start to January ended the third day with a storm. Art's cousin Charlee was with their aunt Anna Leavenworth in East Islip. Charlee's father Anthony Hirsch arrived at Anna's in the evening, but had left his car out in the snowstorm. It took Anthony and Charlee ten hours to drive home to Eldred where they spent the weekends.

Life in the Town of Highland seemed to stay the same. Jim Leavenworth and John Ort drew a load of hay from Proctor's on the 12th. Vernon and Orville Clark were at the Leavenworth's in the evening.

But there was a heightened sense of danger and the unknown. Highland townsfolk took different

Aida went to see Mary and Margie Bosch. Photo courtesy of Victoria Kohler.

shifts to watch for planes at the golf course on Lake DeVenoge. Garfield and Mr. Lochner watched on January 7; Garfield watched again six days later.

Mid-January the Leavenworth men drew two loads of hay with Norm Wolff's truck. Norm then ate dinner with the Leavenworths. Vernon and Orville Clark and Jim went to the movies.

Orville worked for Dr. George Mills on the Mills Farm. Vernon worked at Jim Mills' Highland Lake House near Highland Lake.

Between the two houses was the laundry area and summer kitchen. Our family, the Clarks, and the Hallocks were well known to each other. Stella, Vernon, and Christina Hallock all worked for my dad in the boarding house. Vernon was also my brother's best friend during high school years.
—*Geraldine Mills Russell.*

Besides washing all the dishes and pots and pans, I washed the front porch and a side porch every morning for the two years that I worked there.—*Vernon Clark.*

Lee Hansen started working on the new school which was being built. It would be completed by January 1943, or at least enough to have classes in it. Bill Meyers and Goldie worked on the new Barryville Bridge.

In Islip Anna Leavenworth sent a razor outfit to her nephew Bob Austin.

In Eldred Arthur Austin received a notice from the Selective Service Board that he was 1A.

At 9 a.m. Tuesday, January 19, Arthur stopped by Aunt Aida's place on his way to the city to enlist. His brother Bill took him to Port Jervis to meet the train. Uncle Lon Austin and Alfred Hill went along for the ride. Lon was back about 11 a.m.

It must have been very hard for Lon and Aida to see their nephew leave to enlist. Lon gave Art a New Testament with a short, loving note and two Bible verses.

"To Arthur, My dear nephew, May the Lord keep thee in all thy ways. Lovingly, Uncle Lon."

The following week was a busy one for Aida. Tuesday afternoon she went to the A&P and stopped at Mae's. On the way home she

Cornerstone for new school that was built on Route 55. Photo courtesy of Christene Stevens Myers.

Marion, Marie, and Raymond Hulse. Aida met Marie Hulse at the Post Office. Photo courtesy of Kathy Hulse Frisbie.

met Mary Bosch and Cleta Horton.

Wednesday Aida went to see Mary and Margie Bosch. Aida visited her Austin great-nieces at their grandfather Edwin Myers' house on Friday.

Saturday Melva Austin visited Aida. Bob Austin, in Scotland, had sent Aida a letter with a ring for his niece Melva. Lon walked to the Village three times that day.

It snowed from Sunday night, until Monday evening when it turned to rain.

Aida stopped to see Frances Knorr on the way back from the A&P on Tuesday. Paul Knorr drove Aida home.

Thursday, January 29, Aida met Marie Hulse at the Post Office. Aida saw Jennie Crandall at the A&P. Jennie's husband George drove Aida home.

Saturday, the last day of January, Anna (in E. Islip) woke up stiff with rheumatism. She had managed to fall off the last step of the stairs to the cellar, and was "crippled all day."

February 1942
Sunday (not surprisingly) Anna

Daylight Saving

On February 9, 1942, time once again jumped one hour ahead. A law in the U.S. had established daylight saving time to preserve daylight and provide for standard time during World War I, March 31, 1918. The new time was unpopular, lasting only seven months, and was repealed in 1919. Daylight Saving Time was then a local option until February 9, 1942, when President Roosevelt instituted Daylight Saving Time throughout the year—until September 30, 1945. Once again Daylight Saving Time became an option, until 1974.—*wikipedia.org.*

Postcard from Arthur Austin shows a company street scene, camp Upton, L.I. Co. G, 1222 Reception Center, Camp Upton, N.Y. Card courtesy of Mary Briggs Austin.

had a hard time getting out of bed. She was still stiff when Anthony Hirsch arrived about 6 p.m. on Monday. Anthony made her some noodle soup Tuesday.

Wednesday in Eldred, Garfield visited his sister Christina Hirsch.

Thursday Arthur Austin wrote his aunt and uncle from Camp Upton.

Arthur Austin, Camp Upton, N.Y., to Lon Austin, Eldred
February 4, 1942
Have been very lucky so far. Hope it continues. Expect to stay here about two more weeks. Art

Thursday evening Lon went to the prayer meeting at Floyd Boyd's.

Friday Alfred and Bessie Hill received a letter from Arthur.

Lon was sick with a sore throat on Saturday, so Aida went to the Village and picked up their mail from Arthur.

Daylight Saving Time began on a very cold Monday, February 9. Chester Middaugh stopped by Lon's with the church collection, as Lon (the treasurer) had been sick on Sunday.

Mary Bosch stopped by Aida's with some things of Annie Maier for her. Bill Austin arrived around 11 to take Lon to the store.

It was still cold on Tuesday. Lee Hansen helped Jim cut logs on the Stege Estate.

Wednesday was very cold. But around noon Aida trekked up to the A&P and then the Post Office to send Arthur a picture of Eldred. She stopped at Elizabeth Wilson's on her way home. It was even colder on Thursday.

The following Monday, February 16, was very icy. In the afternoon, Aida first went to Mae's, then to the Village to see Frances.

The news from Ella was that Orville Clark had the measles.

In E. Islip Anna went to First Aid Class Tuesday and Thursday.

Thursday in Eldred Aida got a ride to the A&P with Teenie and Jennie Crandall.

Monday, February 23, was windy, but not quite so cold as it had been on Sunday. Mary Bosch stopped by with milk for Lon.

Tuesday morning Aida went to the A&P. In the afternoon Mr. Frint brought over some books and papers. Norm Wolff and Garfield drew hay at Proctor's.

Anna in E. Islip was concerned when Anthony did not arrive as usual. He had had car trouble and arrived on Wednesday.

Highland Lake Spies?

Willie Bosch with fiancée Florence Schmerfeld at Niagara Falls, January 1942. Photo courtesy of Ken Bosch.

Many Town of Highland residents had German ancestry, but this is the only known story of someone being accused of being a spy.

Willie Bosch and fiancée Florence Schmerfeld traveled to Niagara Falls in January 1942 shortly after America's entry into World War II. Their German ancestry and each having a German-born parent, coupled with their presence at a sensitive border crossing, attracted the attention of F.B.I. border agents. The couple was detained for several hours and interviewed before they were released.—*Ken Bosch.*

The Briggs Family: John, Mildred, Myrtle, Laura, Mary, and Irwin. Photo courtesy of Mary Briggs Austin.

It was very windy in Eldred on Wednesday when Aida did the wash. She ironed on Thursday. Herman Jr. was in to see Lon for a few minutes.

"Naval battle raging off Java with Allies and Japanese," wrote Ella, February 27, 1942.

March 1942
March came in like a lamb, at least it did in East Islip.

In Eldred there was "a heavy fall of snow" Monday evening, March 2. Tuesday Jim and Garfield sat at the golf course from 1 to 7.

Forrest Wilson drove Aida to the A&P for some bread at noon on Wednesday.

Thursday morning Lon went to the Village. Later Herman Jr. dropped off two quarts of milk.

After teaching school on Friday, Lillie Calkin drove to her aunt Aida's for a visit. Lillie and her husband Burt had rented their farm in Bethel to a family from Denmark for a few years before the war.

Grandmother Lillie sent their friends generous gifts of items scarce in Denmark during the war. Her friends were obviously so appreciative.—Katherine Calkin Traxler.

When Lon went to the Post Office on Saturday, he found two letters from Arthur—one for him and one for Aida. That afternoon Margie Bosch took her typewriter to Aida's. She typed up some of the early history of Eldred that Aida had been collecting.

Goldie Leavenworth came down with the mumps on Monday, March 9.

Tuesday the snow in Eldred was almost entirely gone but it was very windy and cold. Around noon Aida went to the A&P. She rode part way home with Helen Boyd, her daughter, and Alex Wait's oldest girl.

It was a rather windy, cold Thursday morning when Aida did her washing. Bill came up with a letter from his brother Bob to Arthur which had been returned. It had been sent to Camp Upton, then Camp Lee, and then to Eldred. Aida wrote Arthur about the letter and mailed the homeless letter and hers to Camp Upton.

Ella Leavenworth also received a returned letter—one she had sent to Grant Sergeant.

That evening Mr. Briggs called for Lon and drove him to Mrs. Sullivan's to prayer meeting.

Friday after school, Melva rode her bicycle to her aunt Aida's and visited a little while.

Bill Austin visited Aida Saturday. He had a letter from Arthur in Camp Upton.

Monday, March 16, was rainy all day. Lon went to the Bosch's for milk in the morning and wrote to Arthur in the afternoon.

Tuesday, March 17, found Garfield and Jim sitting on observation at the golf course from 7 to 1.

Tuesday Aida met Rowlee and Jim Wade when she went to the A&P. Floyd Boyd gave her a ride home.

Aida went to Mae's Thursday afternoon, before going to the Village for bread. There was no cracked wheat in the A&P, so she had to go to Randolph's.

Arthur Austin arrived at Alfred and Bessie's home around 11 p.m., Saturday, March 21.

Jim Wade was just going to dinner when Aida Austin met him in the Village. Photo courtesy of Christene Stevens Myers.

1942 World and National

January 1942
- Japan took Manila.
- U.S. troops arrived in Europe.

February 1942
- Saturday, February 21, the S.S. *John C. Fremont*, first Liberty Ship of CalShip, was delivered to the U.S. Maritime Commission. (Albert Pegg, husband of Julia Straub, was the superintending engineer in charge of Calship's Liberty Ships.)

April 1942
- Hitler at peak of power in Europe.

June 1942
- U.S. carrier fleet defeated Japan's fleet in Battle of Midway.
- Rommel captured Tobruk, Libya, from the British.
- Eisenhower new U.S. Army Chief in Europe.

July 1942
- In Paris 9,000 French police arrested 14,000 of the registered Jews without a country. Some 6,000 were sent to Auschwitz.
- Japanese troops in New Guinea.
- Sixth year of China-Japan War.

August 1942
- Start of Battle of Guadalcanal.
- Japan set up airbase in New Guinea—the location Olliamus D. Smith (my future father-in-law) would be eventually.
- Churchill and Stalin met in Moscow.

- Lt. General Bernard Montgomery took command of the British 8th Army in North Africa.
- Germany attacked Stalingrad.

September 1942
- News leaked of the deportations, killings, gassing, and tortures suffered by large numbers of Jews, and others.
- U.S. aircraft carrier sunk by the Japanese in fight for Guadalcanal.

October 1942
- A second battle of El Alamein. The British under Montgomery forced Rommel to retreat.

November 1942
- The N. African campaign started. U.S. and British troops landed in French Morocco and Algeria.
- Germany and Italy occupied Vichy France.
- Nuclear bomb tested at Los Alamos, New Mexico.

December 1942
- Africa: Allied troops headed towards Tunis faced a monster new weapon: 56-ton-tiger tank mounting 88 mm guns.
- U.S. planes attacked Naples.
- Rommel forced to retreat in North Africa.

Produced or Written in 1942:
- *The Maltese Falcon*.
- *Arsenic and Old Lace*.
- Dmitri Shostakovich's *Leningrad* or *7th Symphony*.

Cover of the CD Cynthia Leavenworth Bellinger received from Maxim Shostakovich, son of Dmitri Shostakovich. Maxim's daughter Masha (Dmitri's granddaughter) was in Cynthia's kindergarten class. Maxim is the conductor shown on the cover.

S.S. John C. Fremont Liberty Ship built by CalShip. Photo courtesy of Bill Ihlo.

Sunday Art took Lon home after church and then visited with Aunt Aida for a few minutes. After dinner with his aunt Charlotte Leavenworth, Art left for camp.

On the west side of town, Jim and Garfield worked on a water trench from the well on Sunday. Garfield built a form for the water pump on Monday.

Aida went to the A&P at noon on Tuesday. Mr. Wade, the barber, was just going to dinner.

Mr. Frint left some papers for Aida on Wednesday.

Thursday Stella came down with the mumps. Her husband Goldie must have recovered enough that he could take care of her. Friday Goldie stopped by to see his parents for a few minutes. So did Lottie Meyers, Gladys Austin, and Clara Hansen and her sons.

The last Sunday in March the Leavenworth men ran cement for the well house.

It snowed all Sunday night.

Tallwood Lodge, Barryville

"Where the Catskills and Poconos meet the Delaware." The Gates of Tallwood Lodge are Open to Welcome You.

When Frank and Anna Hainzl bought Tallwood Lodge, there were two buildings—the main building or lodge and a Carriage House. Frank excavated an area near a stream which created a large pond. (It was deep enough that at a later time a diving board was put up.) The spillway off the pond made a small waterfall. Frank also built the Tallwood Casino—a bar with a dance floor.

Frank and Anna had a daughter Lillian. The family did everything, including cleaning. Lillian mowed lawns and made beds. At age 12 she worked the dining room, and when she was old enough, Lillian did the office work.

The stable, Carriage house, and Lodge. The spillway off the pond Frank dug. Photo courtesy of Lillian Hainzl Wolff.

Frank Hainzl's Tallwood Lodge, main house. Photo courtesy of Lillian Hainzl Wolff.

Tallwood Casino (a bar with a dance floor) on the left of the above photo, was built by Frank. Photo courtesy of Lillian Hainzl Wolff.

Frank and Anna Hainzl. Photo courtesy of Lillian Hainzl Wolff.

Playing golf at Tallwood. Photo and brochures courtesy of Lillian Hainzl Wolff.

Chapter 10: Human Nature Observed, 1942 • 257

Willie and Florence Schmerfeld Bosch on their honeymoon in Atlantic City, in April 1942. Photo courtesy of Ken Bosch.

Monday, Anna in E. Islip went over to the school "to cram for the first aid test tomorrow," which everyone passed.

Bill and Lon Austin went to Port Jervis Monday morning for a dental appointment and were back by noon. The snow was nearly all gone.

Tuesday morning, the last day of March, Aida went to the A&P. Mary Bosch gave her a ride part way there and part way back.

Tallwood Lodge
Frank Hainzl had sailed to the U.S. from Germany as a pastry chef on the *George Washington*. Eventually he and his wife Anna owned and ran the *Cafe Mozart Restaurant* on 86th Street in New York City. In the early 1940s Frank and Anna Hainzl bought Tallwood Lodge, a property with a carriage house and main building/lodge. It was a couple miles north of Barryville, near the junction of Hickok and Halfway Brooks. During the war Frank had a garden and raised a few hundred chickens.

April 1942
In April Willie Bosch married Florence Schmerfeld who he had met at Green Acres the previous summer. They went to Atlantic City on their honeymoon.

Wednesday, April 1, Ruth and Mr. Frint stopped by Aida's on their way to church with some papers, cake, and pie.

Lon went to the Village to get bread for Aida Thursday afternoon. Aida was at Lon's to get the bread when Emma Stevens stopped by.

On Friday, April 3, Lon sent Easter cards to his brother Ell and nephew Arthur.

Bill Austin went to Aida and Lon's early Monday afternoon to give them Arthur's new address.

Mr. Briggs was in to see Lon a while Wednesday afternoon.

On the opposite side of town, Garfield finished the trench into the cellar from the well. Thursday the men hooked up the sink and well.

Aida walked to the Village, the A&P, and the Post Office Thursday morning. She met Melva "just this side of Harold's," and saw Margie

Aida saw Nellie Crandall at the Post Office. Nellie (right) with her sister Victoria Parker. Photo courtesy of Emily Knecht Hallock.

Bosch and Charlie MacIntyre at the Post Office.

Saturday afternoon Bill stopped by to ask Lon to give Arthur's address to Mr. Briggs. (This may be how Mary Briggs got the address to write Arthur Austin.)

In 1942 when I was a junior in High School, I told my mother the girls were writing to soldiers in the

The Briggs Family were to be in Barryville another year. Back left: Myrtle, John, Irwin Briggs. Front row left: Laura, Mildred, Mary Briggs. Photo courtesy of Mary Briggs Austin.

Left photo, from left: Joe Meyer, Lena Bosch, Willie and Tina Brodmerkel, Florence Meyer, Johnny Meyer and Charlie Bosch.
Right photo: The Wicks brothers, sons of Ted and Tillie Bosch Wicks: Daniel, Doug, and Ted, in WWII. Photos courtesy of Ken Bosch.

army and asked who could I write.

My mother said I could write Arthur Austin. She probably thought he'd be safe for me to write to since his family were important people in our church.

I met Art the first time when I was 16. He, Bessie and Alfred Hill came to visit. Art played table tennis with me and wiped the dishes for me. He wasn't a special friend then though, just a family friend. (He was 28.)

I've no idea where I got the address, but I did write to him. And he wrote back!—Mary Briggs Austin.

The Leavenworth menfolk sat at the golf course from 6 to 12 on a sunny, Monday, April 13. The snow was nearly gone.

Lon ordered wood from Harry Wormuth. Then he went to Mary Bosch's for milk. In the afternoon Lon sawed some wood.

In East Islip Anna received a nice letter from her nephew Arthur who was at Camp Eustis.

Tuesday morning, April 14, was rather cold, but that didn't stop Aida from the usual trip to the A&P where she saw Mrs. Winter and Rowlee.

Wednesday was much warmer, and the snow was entirely gone. There was to be a blackout that night from 9:00 to 9:15, daylight saving time.

Garfield worked on the well. Goldie stopped in. Jim Leavenworth went up to his uncle Martin Leavenworth's that night.

That evening at the Methodist Prayer Meeting, Mr. Briggs read part of a letter which he had received from Arthur.

Thursday morning Aida went to the A&P for bread.

Anna L. in Islip sent a letter to her nephew Arthur Austin.

The following Wednesday there was a blackout from 9:00 to 9:45 p.m. daylight saving time.

At prayer meeting that night, Lon heard the good news that the Methodist Conference said Mr. Briggs would be staying another year. It must have been nine or after when Lon walked home, as he noticed they put out the lights at the Knorr's just as he passed by.

Thursday noon, April 23, Aida went to the Village to get bread and take Emily Schoonover's book back. She saw Emma Stevens, Nellie and Jennie Crandall when she stopped at the Post Office.

Aida washed a few items on Friday, a beautiful April day.

Jim Leavenworth got his Farm License (to take a tractor on the road) so he could go to his sister Anna's to hay.

Late Monday Emma and Teenie Stevens were up for some watercress at Aida's, but someone had taken most all of it.

In E. Islip Anna worked in her asparagus patch and also planted a small double row of carrots.

There was a letter from Arthur waiting for Aida at the Eldred Post Office on Tuesday. Aida rode part way down and most of the way back with Mary Bosch.

After dinner Wednesday Aida went to Mae's for papers. Mae and

Whipple Bosch wrote his brother Will in April. Photo courtesy of Ken Bosch.

the French woman were cleaning. Earlier Mr. Frint had taken Mae to the Hall to register for sugar. He also took Aida home.

There was another blackout from 9 to 10 p.m. on April 30.

The Bosch Family
Three sons of Wilhelm Bosch had served in World War I. A number of Bosch descendants would serve in World War II in some way.

Ralph Bosch, who had been in the first war, worked at the Wright Aeronautics Plant in Paterson, New Jersey.

Charlie Bosch Sr.'s youngest son Henry "Whipple" Bosch had enlisted in the Army in early 1941. Charlie Sr.'s son Charlie L. Bosch was the foreman of ship carpentry at the Ramberg Dry Dock and Repair at the Brooklyn Navy Yard. (His wife Karin was a relative of the Rambergs.) Charlie L.'s position allowed him to hire his uncle Menzo Bosch and his brother Willie Bosch for wartime work.

Ted and Tillie Bosch Wicks' sons, Ted Jr., Daniel, and Doug, were in the Army.

Florence van Eastenbridge Meyer was the daughter of Wilhelm Bosch's second wife Mary and her first husband. Joe and Florence Meyer's three sons—Raymond, John, and Fred—served in the war. Both the Meyer and Wicks families would lose one of their sons to the war.

Whipple Bosch (in B&C School in Georgia) wrote his brother Willie who had recently married. Sometime after this letter, Whipple married Elizabeth Gunstone. Whipple Bosch was with the 67th Armored Regiment of the 2nd Armored Division. A Staff Sargent, Whipple would serve in North Africa, Sicily, and in the European campaign.

Peggy Hill and her mother Harriet Eldridge Hill. Harriet's sons Charles and William Eldridge served in the war. Photo courtesy of Alan Gothard.

Tech. Henry (Whipple) Bosch, Ft. Bennin, Georgia, to Willie Bosch
April 1942
Willie,
By this time you will be able to answer this letter and tell me all about the wedding. I sure would have liked to have been there.

Well Willie, you beat me by a little bit, but you better take advantage of your lead, because it won't be long until I'm married, and I'm younger than you are.

I sure hope everything is going good with both of you and you find time to drop me a few lines in the near future. Your brother, Whipple. Great Stuff.

More Than One in the War
The Austin, Wicks, and Meyer families weren't the only Town of Highland families with more than one child who served in the war.

Harriet Hill had two sons from her first marriage: William and Charlie Eldridge; Eva Purcell's four sons: Ed, Jim, John, and Andy; Mary Oset Bornstein's sons: Chester, Joseph, Stanley, and Walter Oset; Isabelle Greig Grotecloss Bente's sons: Edward, Bennett, and Robert Grotecloss; and Richard and Louise Haas' sons: Maurice, Richard Jr., and Harry.

May 1942
Arthur Austin wrote letters to his uncle Lon and brother on May 3.

Arthur Austin, Fort Eustis, B'try D, 8th B, Va., to Lon Austin, Eldred
May 3, 1942
Dear Uncle,
Am a school boy again and every week day morning trudge off to school. So far the course has been easy, but I suppose it will get harder as we go along. We are supposed to have eight weeks of study, but sometimes they cut the course short. At any rate, school is sure to be easier than drilling, for the sun is beginning to beat down harder now. However, the

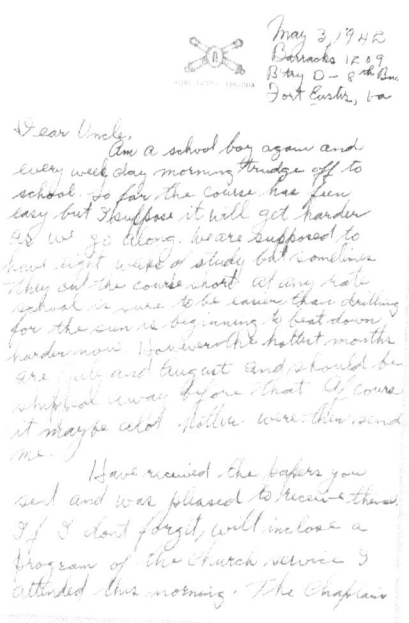
First page of Art's letter to Uncle Lon, May 3, 1942. Letter courtesy of Melva Austin Barney.

Anna Leavenworth registered for sugar rationing in E. Islip. Photo courtesy of Cynthia Leavenworth Bellinger.

hottest months are July and August and we should be shipped away before that. Of course, it may be a lot hotter where they send me.

Was pleased to receive the papers you sent. Will enclose a program of the church service I attended this morning. The chaplain is a Baptist and a very good speaker. As a rule he is the one that I go to hear—mainly because his services are at the most convenient hour of 10 a.m. If I attend the eleven o'clock service, it makes me hurry to get back to dinner in time and as a rule don't get up early enough to attend the nine o'clock service. Sunday is the only day we don't have to get up at 5:45 and I sure make the most of it.

Trust that you and Aunt Aida have both been well.

Sincerely, Art

Pvt. A. Austin, Fort Eustis, Va., to R. Austin, Staten Island, N.Y.
May 3, 1942
Dear Ray,

Well, I started to clerical school last Monday and so far have found it fairly easy. The Course is supposed to last eight weeks, but sometimes—when they need clerks—they cut the course short. If it wasn't for inspection Saturday morning, life would be very pleasant.

On Friday night, we really have to soldier. However the officer that inspects our rifles is a very nice fellow and overlooks quite a few things. Still at that, they should give us a break for the first few months for every time a fellow cleans his rifle there seems to be a new hole or crevice for dirt to collect.

The trouble is that we don't get much chance to clean our rifle while it is daylight on Friday afternoon and you undoubtedly know how different a rifle looks when you take it out in bright sunlight. As yet have run afoul of no army regulation and consequently, have received only my normal share of duties. Many of the fellows haven't been so fortunate, but their hard luck is gain for the rest of us.

While going to school they can only give us one guard or one KP—so, unless I do wrong (which is very easy to do) and get caught, should not get over worked in this respect.

There is some talk of cutting down our school hours and to give us 18 hours of drill a week. I would really prefer this myself. For if a fellow happens to get a

1942 Camp Shelby

Camp Shelby is located 12 miles from the city of Hattiesburg, Mississippi. It was built to accommodate 55,000 soldiers and is the second largest training camp. It cost more than $22 million.

Home of some 50,000 fighting men, Camp Shelby gets its name from a famed leader of men of Colonial days—Colonel Isaac Shelby.

It was created during World War I days.—*Camp Shelby Flyer, 1942.*

Bill Austin was stationed in Camp Shelby and sent his aunt Charlotte Leavenworth a postcard booklet of Camp Shelby photos.

Postcards of Camp Shelby in collection of Mary Briggs Austin.

rating, it can prove to be very embarrassing not knowing the fundamentals of soldiering.

Hoping you have all been well and to hear from you soon. Art

Rationing

Seventeen states in the U.S. began to ration fuel in May. A request had gone out shortly before that women should go without stockings in the summer so there would be enough for the winter.

At the beginning of May, Anna registered for sugar rationing at a school in E. Islip.

Granddaughter Lois Hansen Born

Garfield and Ella Leavenworth had a new granddaughter. Lois Olivia Hansen was born to Lee and Clara Hansen, Tuesday, May 5, at 3:30 a.m. Clara and Lois stayed at her folks' home almost two weeks.

Tuesday, May 6, Lon Austin walked to the A&P for bread. Wednesday noon Aida rode to the A&P with Mary Bosch. Lon had a letter from Arthur.

Right after dinner Wednesday, Aida went to see Mary Bosch. Margie had not gone to school that day as she was at the lake with her father Herman watching for airplanes. Aida then went to Mae's for papers. The apparently tireless Aida (80-1/2) walked to the Village to register for sugar.

Friday Aida rode with Paul Knorr to mail Arthur some papers. She was too late for the first mail. Aida rode to the A&P with some man from Glen Spey Saturday morning. But she forgot her sugar order and had to go back. The second time she had to walk. Aida walked part way back with Mrs. Winter. When Aida arrived home, she found some papers that Mae and Ruth had left.

In Islip on Sunday, Anna fell and hurt herself and her glasses

1942 Halfway Brook News

WWII Local Factory
- The old Redman's Hall was used as a factory during the war. Many local people worked there.

Promotion
- Fred Ihlo finished his officer training at Fort Knox and was made 2nd Lieutenant in November.

Walter C. Toaspern
- During WWII Walter C. Toaspern built roads in the Middle East and also set up his own company (Sullivan Highway Products) with sand and gravel, crushed stone, etc. at several places around the County.

1942 Eldred Seniors
- Edward Toaspern, Viola Hazen, Russell MacKechnie, Bernis Woodruff, Dorothy Wait, Andrew Purcell, Margaret Lloyd, Justin Kean, Veronica Clouse, Adga

Florence Schmerfeld Bosch, Willie Bosch, Charlie L. Bosch, William Schmerfeld (brother of the bride), and Herbie Bosch (Menzo's son). Photo courtesy of Ken Bosch.

Whipple and Elizabeth Gunstone Bosch. Photo courtesy of Ken Bosch.

Burgess, Edith Sjoquist, Maurice Haas, Edward Grotecloss, Lena White, Arthur Turner, Hazel Kuen, Carl Dunlap, Charlotte Hirsch.

1942 Births
- Lois Olivia Hansen born to Lee and Clara Leavenworth Hansen.
- Mary Agnes Wilson born to Ed and Agnes Mary Lucke Wilson.
- Linda Guenther born to Clinton J. and Marion Lass Guenther.
- Ron Flieger born to William and Lillian Piatt Flieger.

1942 Marriages
- William H. Bosch and Florence Schmerfeld married in April.
- Whipple Bosch married Elizabeth Gunstone in Georgia, in July.
- Martin David Myers Jr. married Christene Stevens in November.
- Alice DeFeo, daughter of Fred and Pearl Owen DeFeo, married Robert Riker in December, in N.Y.C.
- Dorothy Paton, daughter of Archie R. and Mabel Slagle Paton (an Eldred-Austin descendant), married Clarence Baker.

1942 Deaths
- Billings Kinne died.
- John Kerr, 1873–1942.
- Basil Owen, 1898–1942, died in a car accident, December 30.
- Alvin Hill (son of Thomas Hill Sr.) died in a hunting accident.

Clarence and Dorothy Paton Baker. Photo courtesy of Kathleen Baker Foster and Darren Foster.

Left: "We are all down on the bridge." Caption by Irwin Briggs who took the photos most likely during the May 1942 Flood. Right: Flooding in front of the Methodist Parsonage by the Delaware River. Photos courtesy of Mary Briggs Austin.

when she chased Jimmie (the cat) who had caught a yellow bird. She was glad she had extra glasses.

Bill Austin was at Aida and Lon Austin's in Eldred on Sunday and Monday. Bill would soon enlist in the Army.

Wednesday, May 13, Jim Leavenworth and Bill Meyers Sr. sat at the golf course from 6 to 12.

"Willie (Bill Austin) left for Camp," Aida wrote on Thursday. A third nephew in the war must have brought much angst to Aida and her brother Lon.

Bill Austin Enlists
Bill Austin, 39, enlisted for active service on May 14, at Fort Jay, New York. Bill, 5 feet 11 inches and 169 pounds, had worked in construction for the County.

Uncle Bill Austin was very strong, a legend. On one occasion a huge tree had been cut down, but the men couldn't move it from the road. So they said, "Go get the human crane." That was Uncle Bill. Bill was quiet, thoughtful—went and looked. He lifted the tree and rolled it out.—Melva Austin Barney.

Friday morning (the day after Bill left for camp) Aida went to the A&P for bread. She asked Alex Wait if he had heard from the Schoonovers. Rowlee was to have been operated on Monday.

Rowlee's daughter Mary Schoonover Osler was a nurse. She had married Dr. Jay Osler, a specialist in eyes, ears, and nose. Rowlee had very bad cataracts. Jay took care of one cataract before he left to serve in World War II.

By the time Jay returned from the War, Rowlee's other eye was beyond operable (state of medicine at the time).—John D. Hull.

G. Austin, Eldred, to C.R. Austin, U.S. Custom House, N.Y.C.
*Sunday Eve, May 1942
Dearest Ray,
Just a few lines as it's late and I'm plenty tired. It's been so hot all day. Melva went to see Doc today with another case of ivy poisoning. She has it on her chin, throat, chest and a bit on her arms and back. She hasn't been out in the fields or woods so don't know how she got it. He gave her some medicine to bathe in and a needle for immunizing. She has to take another needle tomorrow night. It's $2.00 a shot, but at least she won't suffer with itching all summer as she has other years. She was in misery all last night and today and shows fair chance of being tonight.
It's eleven o'clock now and she's walking the floor trying to control the urge to scratch it. Joan has just a touch of it also. I'm using Melva's medicine on her and it doesn't seem to be spreading much.
I shouldn't have told the children you might come up for Decoration Day. When I received your letter that you weren't*

1942 Flood Honesdale, Pa.

Six persons were reported missing and believed drowned today in one of a series of flash floods that swept through Eastern Pennsylvania, making hundreds homeless and paralyzing transportation over wide areas.

The Lackawaxen River, fed by recent rains, burst through the Seeleyville Dam three miles above this Northeastern Pennsylvania community and sent a wall of water six feet deep rushing through the streets just before daybreak.

Telephone company officials reported several houses were toppled over by the flood and it was believed those missing were trapped in their sleep. Communication with the town was difficult.

Residents reported "only four or five houses" remaining on Delaware Street in Honesdale where there had been 15.—Honesdale, Penn., May 23, www3.gendisasters.

Left: Irwin Briggs in front of the Methodist Parsonage by the Delaware River. Right: John the Barber's house during flooding. Photos by Irwin Briggs courtesy of Mary Briggs Austin.

coming you should have heard the howl that went up. Marjorie's eyes filled up with tears and she put her head down and began to cry. Joan cried and then got mad at the whole U.S. Government because you have to work and can't come up. Melva said, "Aw Gee," and then started to sputter. We had quite a commotion here for a little while.

They're all sort of figuring that you'll be up a week from Friday or Saturday night. They're planning picnics, walks, cake and cookie making and lots of activities that you're supposed to take part in.

Did I tell you that Melva received a letter from Bob? He's put in for a transfer to the U.S. Army. He sent us his picture taken while on leave I believe in Edinburgh. He seems pretty cheerful.

I heard from Arthur. Haven't even gotten a card from Bill, but will try and write to him soon anyhow. Wonder how long it would take a package to reach him if I sent it special delivery. Would send him some cookies if I thought he'd get them while they were still good.

We won't be down after school is out. I just can't afford to come.

Lots of love from all of us,
Gladys

Monday, May 18, Aida was disappointed she could not get her cracked wheat bread at the A&P. She stopped in at Andrew Parker's for a paper and saw Bertha Sullivan and her sister.

When Aida was at Randolph's on Tuesday, she and Marge Parker had a long talk about the war.

Thursday brought quite the thunderstorm and flood along the Delaware River. Anna in Islip was relieved to talk to her sister Christina in the evening and find out she was OK.

The paper on Saturday, May 23, reported terrible flooding in Honesdale, Pennsylvania, where Carl and Annie Walters and their son died in a flash flood. Annie Walters was a sister to both Bill Meyers Sr. and Joe Meyer.

On Saturday in Eldred, Aida went to the Village to mail a letter to Arthur and to find out what she could about her nephew Bill. Jim Wade said Bill was at Camp Upton.

Energetic Aida walked home and then back to the A&P for bread and sugar. Mrs. Morgan met Aida at the library. Charlie Dunlap came along and gave them a ride.

Monday, May 25, was pleasant all day—a change from the hard rain they had had for a few days.

There was no bread in either store on Tuesday because of the flooding on the Delaware River.

Wednesday morning Aida was once again at the A&P. But she had to get bread at Randolph's. Howard Stevens told Aida that he had a postcard from Rowlee saying he was getting along fine.

Wednesday Jim and Garfield sat at the Golf Course from 12 to 6.

Lon Austin stopped by the Post Office for the second mail. There was a card from his nephew Bill.

Charlotte Leavenworth had been to the Post Office earlier. She had received a postcard folder of Camp Shelby from Bill and had left Bill's address on a sheet of paper at the Post Office for Lon.

Bill was with the U.S. Army, Co. F, 338 Inf., Headquarters

Bill sent a collection of Camp Shelby cards to his aunt Charlotte Leavenworth. Photo taken by Mr. Mallison of Barryville, courtesy of Christene Stevens Myers.

Charlee Hirsch graduated in 1942. Photo courtesy of Ric Schroedel.

Walter Styles who was so instrumental in the creation of the library, was also at the Village. Photo courtesy of Christene Stevens Myers.

38 Division, at Camp Shelby, Hattiesburg, Mississippi.

Pvt. W. Austin, Camp Shelby, Miss., to Mr. A. Austin, Eldred
Have been down here since Tuesday. Bill

Poor Aida. She forgot Saturday was Decoration Day and that the A&P was closed. She wanted cracked wheat, but there was no cracked wheat at Randolph's (which must have been opened).

June 1942
Early Monday, June 1, Lon went to Bessie's for milk and butter. There was no bread at the A&P in the morning, so about noon Aida went to Randolph's for bread.

Aida met Paul Knorr by the barn on her way back. He told her there had been a big battle of airplanes in Europe.

On Tuesday afternoon Aida went to Mae's. Jennie (the French woman) was helping Ruth get ready to move to Port Jervis.

"Wednesday, June 3, The Japanese bombed Alaska," wrote Ella in her diary.

Wednesday Lon received a letter from Cpl. Arthur Austin, Battery C, 14 Battalion Building 1816, Fort Eustis, Virginia.

Friday Paul Knorr fixed Ella Leavenworth's washing machine.

Tuesday, June 9, Anna in Islip worked in her garden, cut grass with her mower, picked a quart of berries, and worked on a relief bed quilt. Anthony Hirsch was there. Wednesday Anna wrote Arthur Austin, then walked to the Post Office to mail the letter.

In Eldred Aida heard her first whippoorwill of the year. Wednesday morning was cool and nice, so Aida washed clothes. The afternoon was very warm. Lon was haying—just around in the yard. Lon told Aida that Alfred Hill had a card from Arthur who was in Massachusetts or Connecticut.

Anna in E. Islip hunted for some scrap rubber for defense on Sunday.

Monday, June 15, was quite cold in Eldred. Lon went to Port Jervis to a supper with Mr. Briggs, Mr. Kalbfus, and Mr. Deats.

Lon went to the Village on Tuesday and got Aida's bread. He had a letter from his nephew Bill.

Around dusk Edith (Sergeant) Timmerhoff and a friend took some papers to Aida.

When Aida went to the A&P on Thursday, she talked with Mary Sergeant. Mary had received three letters from her son Grant Sergeant (in the Army), all in the same mail.

Saturday was clear and sunny. Lon worked at getting in the hay.

Wait and Boyd hooked a new $8 gas tank on the range for Ella. Sunday she and Garfield went to daughter Anna's to celebrate Father's Day and an early birthday for Garfield.

Sunday morning, June 21, Sunday School and an extra service were at the Methodist Church. The high school baccalaureate sermon was at the Congregational Church in the evening.

Charlotte (Charlee) Hirsch
Anthony and Christina's daughter Charlotte Hirsch graduated from Eldred High School in 1942.

Charlotte joined us two years ago from Glendale High School, Ohio, and has ever since been "mowing us down" with four-

Kaiser's Cargo Planes

In July the industrialist Henry J. Kaiser promised the Senate committees that he would adapt the same techniques for building cargo planes as he had for manufacturing Liberty ships. "A ship can be a built in 80 hours using assembly line methods."—*WWII Day by Day, p. 320.*

syllable and five-dimensional words.

Why, just an ordinary dictionary editor to all of us would be a lexicographer to Charlotte. All this linguistic ability, however, has been very helpful to Charlotte for she's been an excellent English, French, and Latin student.—1942 Yearbook.

I think Mom [Charlee] went to work right away in Bridgeport, Connecticut, at a General Electric factory assembling electronic equipment, probably radios. She lived with Uncle Tony and Auntie Lil Hirsch during this time. —Matt Schroedel.

Monday, on his birthday, Garfield had a second birthday party. Clara brought a birthday cake for after supper that evening.

Tuesday Garfield worked eight hours on lockers for the Boy Scouts.

Tuesday on her way to the Village, Aida met Mrs. Winter in front of Mr. Geisler's house

(Geislers lived in what had been Aida's uncle C.C.P. Eldred's home. Mr. Geisler was County Superintendent and Arthur Austin had worked for him at the County.)

Walter Styles who worked at the library and was so instrumental in its creation, was also at the Village. Aida met Charlotte (Lottie) Leavenworth at the Post Office.

Thursday Frances Knorr drove Lon Austin, Mrs. Sparks, and Cleta Horton to the Asendorf Casino. Church Meetings were being held there that week. (Within the next couple years, this would be the location of the Highland Bible Conference.)

Friday, June 26, Goldie Leavenworth left for a defense job,

1942 Yearbook Dedication

1942 Dedication
Dedicated to the Alumni of our community who have unselfishly joined the colors to do their bit for Uncle Sam in the vast world conflict in which we are now involved. To the mothers and fathers of these men, be proud that you have raised sons who have the courage and nerve to fight for "life, liberty and the pursuit of happiness"—things we all hold so dear. To you men who are now a fighting part of the United States Army and Navy and who are risking your lives that we may be free, we are proud of you, and to you we say— God bless you and keep you and bring you home in safety to us soon.

Roll of Honor
- Lester Aumick, U.S. Navy, Hawaii
- Arthur Austin, Private, U.S. Army, Fort Eustis, Va.
- Robert Austin, Royal Canadian Army, Anti-Aircraft, England
- Franklin Bartle, 3rd Class Fire control man, U.S. Navy
- George Boyer, Corporal, U.S. Army, Calif.
- Walter Campbell, Private, U.S. Army
- Joseph Clouse, U.S. Naval Reserve, Rhode Island
- Charles Eldridge, Private, U.S. Army, Fort Bragg, N. Carolina
- Joseph Foscola, Private, U.S. Army, San Francisco
- Adolph Kalin, Private, U.S. Army, Camp Polk, La.
- Norm Myers, Staff Sergeant, Signal Corps, Port Monount, N.J.
- Harold Morgan, Machinist, U.S. Navy, Norfolk, Va.
- John O'Neil, Private, U.S. Army, Savannah, Georgia
- Warren Parker, Tech Sergeant, Signal Corps, Fort Monmouth, N.J.
- John Purcell, Private, U.S. Army, Fort Ethan Allen, Vt.
- James Smith
- Archie Von Ohlen, Private, U.S. Army, Calif.
- Archie Warden, Private, U.S. Army, Calif.
- Ian Warden, Private, U.S. Army, Hawaii
- Ray Weber, Army Air Corps
- Richard Palmer, U.S. Naval Reserve, Virginia

but was home on Saturday.

Saturday was a clear, lovely day. Jim put Lee Hansen's hay in. Clara rode the hay rake. Arthur Austin was home on leave and called on his uncle Garfield and aunt Ella.

Goldie was there until 11.

Arthur had arrived at Bessie's in the morning. He had started to walk from Port Jervis, but got a ride at Pond Eddy. Art had visited Aida in the afternoon.

On Sunday Arthur was at Aida's for a little while before noon. He had ridden up with one of the Steel boys and thought he would meet Lon on the way.

Sunday afternoon Corporal Arthur Austin went back to Camp Edwards in Massachusetts. He was with the 506th Coast Artillery Anti-Aircraft.

On her way to the A&P Monday morning, Aida saw Mary Bosch in front of Harold's.

Arthur Austin's cousin Jim Leavenworth, 20, registered for the draft June 30, 1942.

July 1942
Jim started haying at his sister Anna's Wednesday, July 1.

Thursday, July 2, Anthony Hirsch left Anna's home in E. Islip very discouraged about gas— either the cost or that it was hard to get. Anna worked on a rag rug

In her extended hand, Frances "holds" Emma Toaspern, mother of both Frances and Ed Toaspern. Photo courtesy of Bill Ihlo.

and polished silver. She had dyed the rags with onion skins and coffee grounds.

Thursday afternoon in Eldred, Edith Timmerhoff sent some papers to Aida with two children Aida didn't know.

Saturday morning Mr. Briggs and his son John picked a mess of sweet peas at Aida's place.

Bill Meyers and Jim L. were on watch at the Golf Course on Saturday. Everett Kelley visited the Leavenworths in the afternoon. Stella and Goldie went back to Poughkeepsie, New York.

July 4 was very quiet for Anna in Islip. But that didn't mean she did nothing all day. Besides baking biscuits, a pie, and a cake, she also cooked salmon and beans. In the afternoon she hunted for rubber and wood in the woods. She ended the day's entry with, "Tired."

Robert Austin in U.S. Army
Sunday, July 5, 1942, Bob Austin switched from the Canadian Armed Forces and enlisted in the U.S. Army in Thursley, England. (It took a while for this news to reach Eldred.)

In Eldred Bob's cousin Jim was still haying on his sister's property. Ken Crandall stopped by for the rest of the lockers Garfield had made for the Scout Camp.

Thursday morning Aida was once again at the Village for bread. In the afternoon Melva first rode her bike to Aida's and then pedaled over to the Leavenworths to see about getting the grass mowed at her grandfather Ed Myers' home.

Garfield and Jim finished haying on Friday. Goldie went back to Newburgh where he was working at the airport.

In Islip on Friday Anna was working outside when she saw the terrible sight of a plane going down over Carleton Ave. Anna was nervous (because of the plane crash) all the next day.

Monday, July 13, Aida arrived at the Eldred Post Office in time to send a letter to Arthur in the morning's mail.

Tuesday morning Aida met

Ruth Worzel. Mary Briggs took the train from Shohola to Pond Eddy to visit her friend Ruth Worzel. Photo courtesy of Ruth Worzel Myers.

Mrs. Winter at the A&P. She introduced Aida to Mrs. Geisler.

Aida did the wash Wednesday morning. She gave Arthur's new address to Mr. Briggs when he came by for some raspberries.

Thursday morning, July 16, Aida walked to the Village for bread. She met Jennie Crandall who told her that Ell Austin (Aida's brother) planned to be home in the summer.

Friday morning Mr. Briggs and his son John stopped by Austins to pick some raspberries.

In the summer of 1942 Mary Briggs took the train from Shohola

Ruth Worzel's parents: Herman and Blanche Worzel. Photos courtesy of Ruth Worzel Myers. Alfred Hill whose cows were in the Austin garden. Photo in 1944 yearbook. Ensign Edward Toaspern after he got his wings. Photo courtesy of Bill Ihlo.

Station to Pond Eddy to visit her good friend Ruth Worzel. She met Ruth's parents Herman and Blanche Quick Worzel; and Ruth's grandparents Napoleon and Frances White Quick.

Ed and Frances Toaspern
You may remember that Ed Toaspern and his sister Frances used to spend time with Jim Leavenworth when they were young as they were similar in age.

Ed and Frances were the children of Walt and Emma Straub Toaspern. Tuesday, July 21, Ed enlisted in the U.S. Naval Reserve Aviation Cadet Program at Squantum, Massachusetts. When he graduated, Ed was an Ensign and received his wings.

Frances lived in Brooklyn with friends of her parents and worked at a bank there during the war.

Tuesday morning, July 21, Lon went to the Village for bread. Aida was awakened by a car horn. Mr. Frint was letting her know with a honk (as he always did) that he had dropped off some papers for her.

When Aida went to the A&P on Wednesday morning to get sugar for canning, she saw her cousin Elbert Clark.

Thursday Aida rode to the A&P with Mary and Margie Bosch. Aida got the rest of her groceries.

Thursday Jim went back to Narrowsburg looking for a job. On Friday he took a new front door screen to his sister Clara. Garfield hung it on Saturday, while Ella canned 30 quarts of beans.

Monday, July 27 (between 2 and 3 a.m.), Alfred Hill's cows managed to get into the Austin garden. Aida woke up and called Lon. The two of them got the cows out of the garden. Lon went over to the Hill's, and woke up Alfred who took the cows home.

Ads from Brooklyn Daily Eagle Summer Resort and Travel Directory, 1942.

Tuesday there was a letter from Arthur waiting for Aida who stopped by the Post Office after her usual visit to the A&P.

August 1942
On Sunday morning, August 2, Harry Wormuth gave Lon a ride home from Sunday School.

Jennie Hull had dinner at Leavenworth's on Wednesday. Thursday Jim Leavenworth went to Newburgh and enlisted in the Army. It was the same location where his grandfather Sherman S. Leavenworth had enlisted for the Civil War.

Mr. Briggs was up to Aida's for blackberries on Thursday.

Saturday Jim went to get his papers signed. Goldie and Stella were in to see Garfield and Ella.

Saturday afternoon Harry Wormuth sent Fred Morgan to deliver the wood to the Austins. Mr. Frint left the papers while Fred was unloading the wood.

Tuesday after supper Clarence

Girls in the old gym create a V for victory, 1942. Photo courtesy of Christene Stevens Myers.

Sergeant took his wife and his sister Lillie to call on Aida Austin. Lillie went to school with Aida when she was 13 or 14 years old and they hadn't seen each other since.

Tuesday was a busy day at the Leavenworths. Jim worked and then went to the movies with Vernon and Orville Clark. Clara, Anna, and their families visited. Goldie was in for just a second. Cleta Horton was there in the evening.

It was partly cloudy on Wednesday. Ella cleaned upstairs and hung curtains. Garfield cut oats. Jim worked and later went swimming with Orville.

When Aida made her usual trip to the A&P about noon she met Emily Schoonover.

The U.S. Marines had taken the Guadalcanal Base in the battle of the same name in the Solomon Islands, on Friday, August 7. The Japanese fought back the next day and 1,000 Allied sailors were killed. The battle still raged a week later.

On Friday, August 14, Ella Leavenworth, very aware of the news wrote, "The battle still on at Solomon."

In Eldred on Saturday, Jim and Charlie Foster went swimming.

Tuesday afternoon Mr. Frint left some papers for Aida. There was also a cornroast at Chester Middaugh's, but Lon didn't go.

Wednesday in Islip Anthony Hirsch made a wonderful pot of soup for Anna and a friend.

In Eldred Aida Austin (81 in three months) picked berries and chopped kindling on Wednesday. Friday Aida went to the store in the afternoon and over to Rowlee's where she got the day's paper.

Orville Clark took Jim for his Army entrance exam on Friday. Jim was back the next day.

Lon preached on Sunday as Mr. Briggs had to be away. Monday morning Aida did her wash.

Anthony arrived in E. Islip early Monday evening and made

Melva's sisters Dawn Lee (above), Joan, and Margie stayed in Eldred. Photo courtesy of Andy and Margie Austin Maglione.

Anna and her friend a "fine pot roast dinner."

There was a total eclipse of the moon on Tuesday, August 25. Aida wrote her cousin Emma Waidler, sister of Rowlee Schoonover. She mailed the letter to Emma when she went to the A&P Wednesday morning.

Jim Leavenworth Leaves

Thursday when Jim Leavenworth left for camp, his sister Clara Hansen and her family were at the Leavenworth home. Always a hub of activity, Goldie and Stella and Jennie Hull dropped by in the evening.

Garfield had hurt his finger quite badly. But he still went to town on Saturday. A card from Jim was waiting for him at the Post Office. When Garfield picked up Jim's card at the Eldred Post Office, he may have seen Aida Austin who was there to send a postcard to Arthur Austin, her nephew (and also Garfield's). Aida also picked up her sugar ration for two months.

Sunday morning Lon said there were only four at the Methodist Sunday School.

Ella canned 28 quarts of peaches on Sunday.

Monday Garfield made what would become a very familiar trip to the Post Office. He was rewarded with a card and a letter from Jim.

On the east side of town Aida went to the Village for bread. Herman Bosch was haying.

The summer was coming to an end and soon school would start. The new school being built on Route 55 north of Eldred's Four Corners would be completed enough for students to attend in January.

Melva Austin went back to Staten Island for High School.

I went to Staten Island to start high school. My mother and sisters came back at the end of 1942. We continued going back for parts of summers, etc.
—Melva Austin Barney.

Joe and Mary Meet in New Jersey
It's been a while since we talked about Joe Mellan and his future wife Mary Paulik.

Joe and Mary's paths finally crossed again in 1942. Joe was home in Trenton on leave when Mary Paulik visited Anna Mellan, a life-long friend of Mary's mother. Joe and Mary, who had been first grade classmates in Romania, renewed their acquaintance. Love blossomed. They nurtured their relationship via regular correspondence.

Joe had been drafted into the Army Corps of Engineers which constructed roads, bridges, and other vital infrastructure.

He was not deployed overseas because he had fractured both elbows trying to secure a tarp over soldiers' knapsacks on the back of a truck. The driver, unaware of Joe, had lurched the truck forward.

Joe endured a long convalescence in military hospitals, being transferred from hospital to hospital. Mary's letters did not reach Joe, causing considerable anxiety.—Told to Ken Bosch by Mary Mellan.

September 1942
Herman Bosch continued to hay on Tuesday, the first day of September.

There was another letter from Jim for the Leavenworths on Tuesday, when Goldie, Stella, and Jennie Hull once again stopped in at Garfield and Ella's home.

Charlotte Leavenworth visited Aida for a little while Wednesday. Then the two of them headed off to the Village.

Thursday, September 3, Jim was stationed in Atlantic City, New Jersey.

Friday morning in Eldred Aida packed Arthur's books. Lon bought the bread and butter they needed.

Saturday Ella and Garfield happily read Jim's letter. Lee Hansen brought them a bushel of peaches—$2.

Bill Austin wrote to his aunt Christina Hirsch on Saturday. He was with Company F, 338 Infantry.

Pvt. W. Austin, Camp Shelby, Miss., to C. Hirsch, Eldred
September 5, 1942
Dear Aunt,
I hope you will excuse me for

Summer 1941: Emma Waidler, Ada Britt and her husband Arthur Wood, Ed James, husband of Norma Wood, holding their son Richard James. Robert Wood, son of Arthur and Ada, in front. Photo courtesy of Richard James.

Envelope with Victory stamp addressed to Aida Austin from her cousin Emma Waidler.

not answering your letter sooner. I am not much of a letter writer.

I had a letter from Uncle Garfield and he tells me that Jimmy has joined the Army. There can't be many young fellows around Eldred now.

Tell Aunt Charlotte I haven't forgot that I owe her a letter. I suppose she is pretty busy getting ready for school. Have they got the new building ready yet?

I had a letter from Aunt Anna some time ago. Also a couple bundles of magazines.

How was your garden this year? I suppose it is pretty near time for frost up there. How is Uncle Anthony and Charlee?

Write whenever you get time.
Your nephew, Bill

On Sunday, September 6, Orville Clark joined all Garfield and Ella's family (except Jim) for dinner. The men had cut wood during the day. Ella had canned 24 quarts of peaches.

Garfield worked six hours for Alvah Sergeant on Monday. Ella made three heavy shirts for her grandson Dick. Clara, Lee, Dick, and Wayne were in for a few minutes; Goldie for a second.

Monday morning Aida went for bread at Randolph's. In the

Martin D. Myers married Christene Stevens. Photo courtesy of Christene Stevens Myers.

afternoon Margie Bosch stopped by with a piece of lemon pie and a piece of apple pie for Aida, and the same for Lon.

Monday Emma Waidler attached a purple victory stamp to the envelope with the letter she wrote to Aida.

Mrs. W.J. Waidler, Cairo, N.Y., to Miss Aida Austin, Eldred,
September 7, 1942
Dear Cousin Aida,

What a pleasure it was to get a letter from you. And the "Good morning" poem is lovely. Why can not we have more of these beautiful sentiments. It does cheer us as we go down on the shady side.

I did come to almost breaking my neck, but my time has not come, yet. The dear Lord was watching over me and I am glad to say I am getting better, though I have to watch my step.

I'm expecting to go to Brooklyn to spend the winter with Laura's two girls. They are 55 and 52, so they are not girls any more, both grandmothers. But they want me to be with them and I'm glad to be with them.

I am hoping I can get out to Eldred before it gets too cold. I could not go this summer because I could not travel among so many people. How quickly the years roll around.

I did not get the stone for my father's grave [Perry Schoonover] last year, but hope to have it all done when I get up there.

Today is a perfect day. The mountains are lovely. I can sit in my window and look at them. It does not seem that the world is in such a commotion here. It is quiet and peaceful. I am glad that you did go to France.

Last night a friend and I went to see The Pied Piper. *If you have not read the book it is grand. I hardly ever go to the movies, but it was well worthwhile to see that. We saw a lot of France last night. Thank you so much for writing me. With love to you and Lon and hoping to see you later,*
Your cousin, Emma

Emma Waidler referred to her sister Laura's two girls: Ada Britt Wood and Kitty Britt James, whom she had helped raise. During the war Ada Britt's husband Arthur Wood worked at the New York Navy Yard. He had begun his Naval career in April of 1904 as an Apprentice Machinist. He eventually was promoted to Assistant to Civilian Head, Design Section Ordnance. Ed James, Norma Wood's husband was employed with Bendix (a defense related company), and had two children, so he was not drafted.

Back in Eldred letters arrived for Garfield and Ella from Jim on both Tuesday and Wednesday (September 9). Wednesday, Jennie Hull, Goldie and Stella, Clara and her children were all at the Leavenworths at some point.

When Aida returned from the A&P on Thursday morning, Lon gave her cousin Emma's letter.

Garfield picked up two postals from Jim on Thursday.

The Eldred Post Office was hopping on Saturday, September 12. Will Austin's letter to his aunt Charlotte (Lottie) Leavenworth said he was feeling good. This Lottie told Lon who was in the Village and had received a letter from Dr. Austin. Howard Stevens told Lon that Melva had received a letter from her uncle Bob which said he had been transferred to the American Army. Jim Leavenworth had a new address. He was at the Chanute Field, in Illinois.

Chanute Field
Jim Leavenworth was one of the thousands of airmen who received technical training at Chanute Field, some 130 miles south of Chicago. The field had been in existence since May of 1917. In March 1941 the Army Air Corps had instituted the Technical Training Command at the Chanute Field location.

Sunday in Eldred Jim's sister Anna Meyers drove Garfield and Ella to her house to spend the day.

Goldie was at his folks' home early Monday morning. Clara and her family were in for a while.

Martin Marries Emily Christene
There was a happy event in Eldred on September 13, 1942. Martin David Myers Jr. married Emily Christene Stevens. Martin

Chanute Field where Jim Leavenworth was trained as well as thousands of other airmen. Photo courtesy of Gisele Rouillon Leavenworth.

D. Myers Jr., son of Martin Sr., was a second cousin to Arthur Austin. Christene (Teenie) was the daughter of Howard and Emily Parker Stevens.

Scintilla Magneto, Sidney, N.Y.
After they married Martin and Teenie lived in Sidney, New York (until Martin was drafted, around April of 1943). They worked at Scintilla making airplane magnetos. Teenie worked at the Sidney Post Office.

There was a whole community in Sidney from the Town of Highland. Bob Wolff rode to work with Martin and Teenie. Teenie was friends with Eleanor Vonderhorst. Both Eleanor and her husband Carl were there, too.

You may remember that Lillie Calkin said her husband Burt and Dot's husband Raymond were working on a housing project for workers at the Scintilla Factory in 1941. Dot Hale and her husband Raymond also worked on the magnetos at the factory in Sidney.

When Garfield went to the Eldred Post Office on Monday, September 14, he was rewarded with letters from Jim.

Aida was out at the gate talking to Mrs. Morgan Tuesday morning when Lon returned from the Village with a letter from Arthur.

Wednesday Garfield cut brush and Ella waxed floors. Clara and her children were down for supper. Goldie and Stella stopped by later. They now had a photo of Jim looking handsome in his Army uniform. Two letters arrived from Jim on Wednesday which had to tide Garfield and Ella over until Saturday when there would be another one.

Saturday in E. Islip Anna worked on a blue rug with "proper rags" she had ransacked from the attic. "Heard some very foolish speeches about war," she remarked in her diary.

Monday morning, September 21, Aida was once again at the store and the Eldred Post Office. She had a letter from Melva.

There were two letters from Jim for Garfield on Monday and two more on Tuesday.

Tuesday, Anna walked to the E. Islip Post Office to mail her letter to Bill Austin. Anthony Hirsch did not arrive that evening. An alert interrupted the radio program *Can You Top This?* that Anna was listening to.

Wednesday morning Aida took her usual trek to the store and Post Office. Katherine Dunlap called on Aida in the afternoon and told her Clifford Myers was home, but still in plaster Paris.

Thursday Bessie told Aida that they had word from Arthur that he was to have three days off.

Jim Leavenworth looking handsome in his uniform. Photo courtesy of Gisele Rouillon Leavenworth.

And yet two more letters from Jim arrived on Thursday.

In Islip Anthony arrived before noon and said he was going to be moved to Buffalo. Anna spent Friday arranging scrap metal for the government drive.

Friday on the west side of Eldred, Garfield and Ella put the first coat of paint on Jim's room. They had no letter from him that day, but Ella commented, "the War sounds better."

Aida, on the east side of Eldred, went to the store in the afternoon. She and Mrs. Winter went to the church to see the list of the Town of Highland boys in the Army. Katherine Dunlap and Aida then went to the cemetery.

Arthur arrived at Ed Myers' at eight o'clock. He had ridden to Eldred with Roger Quick who had dropped Art off at Ed's.

Saturday afternoon Arthur stopped by Aida's for a few minutes. He had to go back on Sunday.

Goldie and Clara and her family were at their parents' home

Olliamus D. Smith would serve in the South Pacific at radar installations. Photo courtesy of Gary Smith.

on Saturday. Poor Garfield went to town twice, but there was no letter from Jim.

It rained Sunday morning and there were heavy showers in the afternoon, so there was no church service at night. Alfred and Bessie Hill took Arthur to the train at Middletown.

It was clearer and colder on Monday. Finally there were letters from Jim; two on Monday, one on Tuesday, and one on Wednesday, the last day of September.

Wednesday Anna and Jimmy visited her parents for the day. Jennie Hull was there for supper.

Olliamus Dean Smith

In September 1942 Olliamus Dean Smith, future father of Gary Dean Smith, left Oklahoma City for Camp Murphy, Florida, where he would train at a Radio Repairman's School for six months. O.D. (as he liked to be called) would serve in the South Pacific with the 5th Army Air Corps on radar installations.

October 1942

There was a letter from Jim Thursday, October 1, the day Ella finished papering Jim's room.

Friday Garfield went to town twice and retrieved one letter from Jim. Ella dug up the gladiolus and got them ready to store.

Sunday Garfield was over at Bill and Anna Meyers' for the day. He picked four bushels of corn and three pumpkins. Monday Garfield helped build stairs at Dixon's; Stella was at the Leavenworth's in the afternoon; Christina and Anthony were there for the evening; as was Everett.

In East Islip Anna gathered small scrap metal all morning, then took her collection and sorted it.

Anna worked on her blue rug; ironed several washings worth; and had a social cup of tea with Mrs. Bledsoe Tuesday. Anna had lots of mail, but bemoaned the fact that there was no word from Eldred.

The Leavenworths in Eldred received a letter from Jim on Tuesday—the same day the Cardinals won the World Series; a letter on Thursday; and one on Friday.

Friday Anna in Islip received a "cheerful letter at last from her sister Christina."

Saturday there were two more letters from Jim. Sunday Garfield went to the Hirsch's and Chet Middaugh's for spring water.

Sunday in E. Islip, Anna worked getting her attic ready for the Rock Wool (insulation installer) men. She started a letter to Christina.

Monday Anna worked on her rug. She started to work outside, but found her cats infested with wood ticks. So she stayed in and baked a pie and biscuit instead.

In Eldred Goldie, Stella, and Doug Hallock visited Garfield and Ella. They had another letter from Jim.

Melva Austin attended high school in Staten Island. She wrote her great-aunt Aida, and Aida wrote back.

Aida Austin, Eldred, to Melva Austin, Staten Island
October 12, 1942
Dear Melva,

I was pleased to receive your letter but very much surprised to learn that you had left the dear safe "Little Old Hometown" for the wilds of Staten Island.

Aren't you afraid you may wake up some morning and find (instead of the Star Spangled Banner) the banner of the Russians floating over you?

We will trust that this does not happen and that we all may still continue to sing:
When our land is illumined with
  Liberty's smile
If a foe from within strikes about
  other glory
Down down with the traitor that
  dares to defile
The flag of her stars and the page
  of her story
By the millions unchained who
  our birthright have gained
We will keep her bright blaze on
  for ever unstained
And the star spangled banner in
  triumph shall wave
While the land of the free is the
  home of the brave.

I am enclosing information I have with regard to the early history of Eldred. Am sorry I have not more ready for you. Aunt Aida

On Tuesday, October 13,

Garfield went to town and up to Hirsch's.

Anna walked to the village of E. Islip and mailed a Christmas box to her nephew Bob Austin; and worked on her rug.

The Leavenworths in Eldred had a letter from Jim on Thursday. Friday there was a letter from Jim and one from Grant Sergeant. Grant would be stationed in the South Pacific. Goldie and Stella stopped by. Saturday was a terribly rainy day. But that did not stop the letter from Jim with his first war pay of $20.

Clara and her boys walked down to her folks' house on Monday. Goldie left to look for work. Stella went to her grandma Hallock's house.

There was another letter from Jim on Monday.

Tuesday Aida went to the store in the morning. In the afternoon as she started to Bosch's to take back their milk bottles, Mary Bosch drove in to see her. Mae had asked Mary to check on Aida to see if she was sick. Aida had not taken the papers from the box that Mae had left a day or so before.

Lon went to the Post Office and came back with a letter from Melva for Aida.

There were two more letters from Jim on Wednesday when it was again rainy all day.

Thursday, October 22, Anna, her sister Clara, and their children were at their parents' house for the day. Ella thought Jim sounded "pretty homesick" in Thursday's letter.

Thursday Aida mailed Arthur a letter and bought some groceries.

Friday was another rainy day; and another letter from Jim.

Saturday, October 24, paint, roofing, etc. arrived from Narrowsburg Lumber Company; and a letter from Jim.

Grant Sergeant often wrote Ella and Garfield. He was stationed in the South Pacific. Photo courtesy of Sandy Sergeant McBride.

Saturday Lon Austin opened the Methodist Church for the funeral of Sadie Rundle. Aida was to the Village for bread and peppermint.

In Islip Anna finished her rug. But poor Jimmie the cat had a fight and got a tick in his eyelid. He was sick six days before the abscess broke at last.

Even though it was a very rainy Monday in Eldred, Aida Austin still went to the store. But they were out of bread. She met Norman Wolff in the store, then went to the Post Office and bought stamps.

Tuesday morning was cold, but pleasant. Aida was back at the store for bread. Lon was provoked at her for not going to the Post Office, too.

Thursday afternoon Aida went to see Mary Bosch who had been very sick Wednesday. Mary was all right. Aida visited Bessie Hill, then made the trek to the store and back home.

In Islip Anna's cat Jimmie was so bad on Thursday that she had the doctor (Dr. Fake) come over and take him to the small animal hospital at Bay Shore. Anna was happy to have a friend over for a fish fry dinner on Friday as she was feeling so bad about her cat.

Saturday, the last day of October, there were two letters from Jim.

As Aida started to the Village on Saturday, Lon gave her a letter from their brother Ell. Edith Timmerhoff was in the store when Aida arrived. The two ladies walked over to the front of the hill together. Later Mr. Briggs and Johnny were over to make cider.

November 1942

Monday afternoon, November 2, Aida went to the Village and bought sugar. Claudia Sergeant was in the store. There was no bread at that time, so Aida went back later. Lillie Austin Calkin stopped by just as Aida got home. Mr. Frint left papers on his way to work.

Garfield picked up two letters from Jim on Monday. That was the same day Jim's cousin Arthur Austin (now a clerk for a general officer) departed for overseas.

There was a letter from Jim on Tuesday.

It rained all morning in East Islip on Tuesday, but that did not stop Anna from voting. She also bought three pounds of sugar on her ticket, then walked home. (Her cat was much improved, but still in the hospital.)

Aida in Eldred wrote that she was busy with the wood and did not vote—rather a surprise as it seems she was quite vocal about politics.

Wednesday afternoon Aida met half of Eldred when she went to the Village. Jennie Crandall and Mrs. Winter were at the Post Office. James Clark, Bertha Sullivan, and Stella Boyd were in Andrew's. At Randolph's she met

Mrs. Sparks and Frances. Howard Stevens was in front of Sunshine Hall and drove Aida home.

Wednesday Garfield had their sugar cards replaced.

On an overcast Thursday in Islip, Anna, 67, cut some tough oak wood.

Thursday in Eldred was cold and clear when Aida, soon to be 81, worked in the wood.

At Randolph's Friday morning, Aida had to take rye bread. But Mr. Randolph said he would save her a cracked wheat on Saturday.

Howard Stevens was working by the library with Johnny Quick, when Aida walked home. Her niece Lillie visited about six o'clock and gave her a paper written by Aida's father William Henry Austin, with the birthdates of her family, and Aida's mother Mary Ann Eldred Austin's Bible.

Ella received a letter from Jim on Friday and wrote, "the War news sounds good."

On Saturday morning when Aida went for her cracked wheat bread at Randolph's, Howard Stevens was working at the library with the help of two men.

Thursday morning Aida took her usual jaunt to the Village to mail a letter to Melva and one to Mrs. Moore (the Austin researcher). But Aida was too late to mail the letters.

Thursday Bill Austin was home on furlough. He visited with his uncle Garfield and aunt Ella. Anna and Charlie Ort were there Friday evening.

In East Islip Anna's cat Jimmie was improving, but was still at the animal hospital. "He is quite an expensive cat," she noted in her diary. Anna continued to work on a rug and chop wood. On a very blustery Friday, the wind blew Anna's milk order away.

Bill Austin visited Garfield

Jimmy Meyers holding a puppy. Photo courtesy of Cynthia Leavenworth Bellinger.

and Ella again on the evening of Monday, November 16. They had received a letter from Jim that day. The following day a package arrived from Jim. Wednesday the Leavenworths received two letters and some snapshots from Jim.

Arthur Austin (with the 5th Army Anti-Aircraft Section) arrived at his destination—the European, African, and Middle East Theater—on November 19, 1942. He responded to a letter he had received from his uncle Lon.

Arthur Austin, Hq. & Hq. Co., 5th Army, to Lon Austin, Eldred
November, 1942
Dear Uncle,

Was pleased to receive your letter of 19 November and to learn that you and Aunt Aida have been well. Trust the winter has not dealt too severely with you since then.

The last few mornings a light skim of ice has frozen but a good stove in the tent keeps us comfortable. Up in the mountains the snow adds to the difficulties of life, however guess it can not be much worst than the rain and mud.

Glad to hear the fruit crop was plentiful this season and that you stored a good amount for the winter. Should help a lot to vary the store diet.

Well perhaps before too long the war will be over and things will return to normal; or let us hope a great deal better than ever before. Still I can't help but feel that it is a long ways in the future. Would not be much surprised but what this old world is in for a good deal more of turmoil than most people expect.

As you are undoubtedly reading in the papers we are going forward slowly at the present time. But we are all confident the pace will be speeded up in the future.

Trust that you and Aunt Aida are still in good health and to hear from you soon.

Your nephew, Arthur

Thanksgiving Day, 1942
In Islip Anna and her friends Esther and Sally had "a nice fat rooster" for Thanksgiving dinner. Jimmie the cat was finally home, but was still pretty sore.

Monday, November 30, was a cold, clear day in Eldred. Lon went to the A&P in the afternoon and brought Aida back her bread.

Ella sent "for a little Christmas for the babies from Jim" with the money Jim had sent her to buy gifts for his niece and nephews.

Goldie must have found work as he and Stella left for Connecticut at 7 a.m. on Thursday.

Late Friday Lon went to the Post Office and picked up a letter from Gladys for Aida. Aida went to the Village for bread.

Saturday Aida mailed a note to Gladys and was in time for the morning mail. Aida visited Mrs. Bye in the afternoon.

On the other side of town, Garfield and Anthony Hirsch

butchered a hog. Ella had a letter from Stella and Goldie, and one from Jim.

Aida went to the store Monday afternoon. She asked Mr. Styles about getting kerosene.

Garfield and John Dunlap butchered a cow on Monday. Garfield picked up a letter and check from Jim, and a letter from Stella when he went to town. Mary Ort, Anna and Charlie Ort, Clara, and the Clarks all visited with the Leavenworths at some point on Monday.

In E. Islip Anna was pretty happy with the insulation job on her house. "As I go to bed I find the house very warm."

Arthur Austin wrote to his aunt Christina Hirsch from somewhere on the North African Continent.

Art was with the Western task force, HQ & HQ Co. His address: A.P.O. #758. c/o Postmaster N.Y., N.Y. The letter was passed by U.S. Army Examiner: 04430.

Staff Sgt. Arthur Austin, to Mrs. Anthony Hirsch, Eldred
December 7, 1942
Dear folks,

Thought it about time that I wrote a line to let you all know that I arrived safely in north Africa and at the present time am quite comfortably situated. So far, while living conditions haven't been all that one could desire at times, the trip has been disgustingly uneventful. Still there is plenty of opportunity for the future I suppose.

It is a very interesting country and I hope to see a lot more of it. Many of the native Arabic inhabitants appear to be intelligent, but they certainly live in unbelievable filth and poverty.

The new section of many of the cities are very modern and it would be difficult to find more beautiful parks anywhere.

Next time I will write more but it has been so long since I have written anyone that I am going to use my spare time for the next few days just letting people know I am still alive. Art

S. Deyo and John J. Hull
Rowlee Schoonover's son-in-law S. Deyo Hull (husband of Justina) and grandson John J. Hull (Deyo and Justina's son) were both serving their country. You may remember from *Echo Hill and Mountain Grove* that Deyo Hull served on the *U.S.S. Arizona*. You can imagine the effect the sinking of the *Arizona* in the Pearl Harbor attack had on him.

Deyo, an employee of the New York Trust Company, took a leave of absence and enlisted in November for two years of service as Chief Storekeeper at the Navy Recruiting Station. Justina had a job with the Wright Aeronautical Corporation.

Deyo and Justina's son John J. Hull had enlisted in February and was training to be a yeoman at the Great Lakes Illinois Training Station, in Chicago.

Tuesday, December 8, Aida mailed a letter to Gladys Austin and went to see Alex Wait.

Wednesday Aida went to Bessie Hill's house, but Alfred told her Bessie had gone to Port Jervis. So Aida went to the store and then back home.

Norm Wolff delivered two tons of coal ($20.50) to the Leavenworths on December 10.

Friday Anna of East Islip worked on her new hollyhock rug and enjoyed the warmth of her new insulation. She had heard that there were shortages of both butter and meat in Islip.

Friday morning in Eldred,

John J. Hull and his father S. Deyo Hull both served in World War II. Newspaper article courtesy of John D. Hull.

Aida went for the mail and to see Alex. (Lon went down later.) Aida met Katherine Dunlap in front of Randolph's store. Katherine walked with Aida to where Proctor and Highland Lake Roads met.

Saturday Aida posted a letter to her nephew Bill in the morning mail; then went to see Alex. Alvin Hill was there. As she was leaving, she saw Floyd Boyd. Next she went to Randolph's. Aida walked part way home and Charlie MacIntyre gave her a ride the rest of the way.

There was Sunday School on Sunday morning, but no preaching. Mr. Briggs was sick.

On Monday morning Aida went to the Village for a gallon of kerosene. While there she met Alex Wait in front of Randolph's. Aida also saw Frank O'Donnell who was home on furlough. In the evening Aida and Lon went to the Hall to get blanks to fill out for kerosene. (Lon dropped the filled-in-sheets off at the Post Office on Tuesday.)

On Monday on the west side of Eldred, Garfield and Ella took care of Clara's little ones. Clara and Lee gave her parents a poinsettia. Anna and Charlie Ort called that day also.

Aida went to the Village for sugar on Wednesday afternoon. Kathryn Randolph was tending their store.

Jim Leavenworth had his tonsils removed at Christmas time. Photo courtesy of Cynthia Leavenworth Bellinger.

Wednesday evening Garfield and Ella took Everett Kelley to the nursing home in Liberty.

Thursday Ella received a letter from Jim and one from Stella. The Leavenworths made ice cream on Friday when Clara and her family were there for supper.

Anna in Islip sent Christmas cards to several soldiers on Friday.

Friday and Saturday Aida was to the Village—both the store and Post Office. She may have been in search for Alex who was in Shohola on Friday. Perhaps the search for Alex had to do with a land deed, as on Saturday she wrote, "Alex had the deed ready in the store."

The Methodists practiced for the Christmas Program both Sunday morning and night. Garfield went up to Hirsch's.

Tuesday, December 22, Aida signed the deed and gave it to Alex. She bought some groceries and Mr. Randolph drove her and the groceries home in his car.

Tuesday the Leavenworths got their Christmas tree. Charlie Sergeant and his son stopped in.

The Methodists had their Christmas Tree Program on Wednesday night.

Wednesday Garfield and Ella received a letter from Jim. Lee Hansen and his sons were there for a while. Stella and Goldie were there in the evening and stayed most of the day on Thursday, Christmas Eve.

Thursday morning Alex Wait gave Lon and Aida their oil coupons. Aida must not have been able to resist walking to the Village for bread at noon.

Christmas 1942
On Christmas Day Emma Stevens sent a box of fruit to Lon and one to Aida. Teenie Myers took Lon's to him and Martin Myers Jr. took a box to Aida.

The Leavenworth Christmas wasn't quite so quiet. Stella and Goldie, and Anna, Bill, and Jimmy Meyers were there for dinner. They went up to Clara's for supper. A letter from Jim told how he was supposed to come home for Christmas on leave, but had instead gotten sick with tonsillitis, and was in the hospital. He was to have his tonsils out. (Perhaps the answer to all the sore throats he had growing up.)

In East Islip, Anna had Christmas dinner with friends. Then Raymond Austin drove Anna to his home in Staten Island, and back again to her cottage.

On Saturday morning Alfred and Bessie Hill received a letter from Arthur in North Africa. Bessie's children Joan Hill and Bill Lass took Arthur's letter up to Aida for her to read.

Both Sunday School and Church were at the Methodist on Sunday morning.

Lee and Clara Hansen and their little ones had dinner with Garfield and Ella on Sunday.

Goldie and Stella left for Ansonia, Connecticut, where he worked in a steel factory. Perhaps Goldie worked at one of nearby Waterbury's brass factories which were kept busy for military needs during World War II. Working in this factory or one similar seems to have given Goldie an exemption from serving in the military.

Monday, December 28, Orville Clark, Stella's brother and Jim's best friend, enlisted.

Monday afternoon Aida started off to Randolph's and met John Horton just below Knorr's.

"It was terrible bad walking, but I got a ride almost all the way back," Aida mentioned in her dairy that evening.

And walking was even worse on Tuesday. But Lon was able to get a ride to the Village and back. Aida received a Christmas card from Nellie Kendall Barcaw, in California.

(Nellie was a granddaughter of C.C.P. and Effa Van Tuyl Eldred; and a cousin of Aida and Lon.)

Last Day of 1942
Thursday, the last day of the year, Lon went to the Village but forgot to send Bill a magazine. Aida was headed in that direction, so she mailed the magazine for him. Aida also picked up some turpentine at the garage.

The last day of the year in Islip, Anna Leavenworth walked to the Post Office and the store and found the meat cost very high.

Ella ended the year in her diary: "A very good year, but a sad one."

On the world front, the news on the last day of the year: Rommel was forced to retreat in North Africa; the Germans were doomed at Stalingrad. But this did not mean the end to the war was in sight, unfortunately.

Chapter 11
Correspondence
Letters and V-Mail, 1943–1944

While overseas, I corresponded casually with a girl from our community who was studying to be a nurse at the Methodist Hospital in Brooklyn.—Arthur Austin.

Mary Briggs at her high school graduation in June 1943. The new Barryville-Shohola Bridge is in the background. Photo courtesy of Mary Briggs Austin.

Arthur Austin and Mary Briggs had corresponded for close to a year in January of 1943. Mary would graduate in June of 1943 from Eldred High School. In the fall she would attend Methodist Hospital in Brooklyn for nurse's training. Their letters throughout the war continued to be casual, possibly because there was a twelve-year age difference.

Mary and Art wouldn't be the only ones to exchange letters. Post Offices would hum with neighbors and friends discussing the latest information they had received. War reports were given at the theater with the current movie. But that could never replace a message from someone you knew.

In January the new Eldred Central School building opened. The 1943 graduating class (which included Mary Briggs) was excited to spend at least one semester in the new school building. A number of the seniors enlisted in the Service before graduation.

January 1943
It was terribly cold all Saturday, the second day of the new year. That did not stop Aida from doing some wash in the afternoon.

On the west side of Eldred Garfield walked up the road to see his sister Christina on Sunday. Basil Owen's funeral was in the afternoon. (He had died in an accident December 30.) Rain turned to snow in the evening.

It continued to snow all day Monday. The blowing snow did not keep Aida from her usual visit to the Post Office and store.

Monday started very early and with great excitement for Garfield and Ella. Jim had arrived home about 3 a.m. for 10 days.

It was cold in East Islip also. So cold that Anna hung the clothes she washed in the attic to dry. She also did some major cooking—a pie, Scotch scones, and meat for her cat Jimmie.

Anna received a very welcome letter from her nephew Bob Austin Tuesday afternoon. Wednesday she went with a friend to Islip to pay her taxes and mail a package to her niece Charlee Hirsch.

Tuesday in Eldred Jim visited both his sisters, Clara Hansen and Anna Meyers.

Photo of the new Eldred Central School in the 1944 El Dorado school yearbook.

It was very cold Wednesday and Thursday. Jim and Garfield went to town. Clara and Anna and their children were at the Leavenworth home. Bill Meyers Sr. stopped by to see Jim.

Thursday afternoon (and again on Saturday) Aida bought oil and bread at the store.

Friday Jim took his nephew Dick to see the Clarks and his great-aunt Jennie Hull.

Jim's aunt Anna Leavenworth in Islip walked to the Post Office to mail an air letter to her nephew (and Jim's cousin) Arthur Austin. Saturday Anna "got a highly treasured pound of coffee."

Saturday in Eldred Jim went to town with Goldie and Stella. Goldie had a test to take.

Sunday, January 10, Aida helped Marjorie Bosch with her algebra. (It was possible to continue taking classes at Eldred after graduation. A number of graduates continued their studies, as had my dad Art Austin.)

Sunday the Leavenworth crew (minus Bill and Jimmy Meyers) were at Garfield and Ella's. Stella, Goldie, and Jim stayed overnight.

Monday evening Ken McBride called at the Leavenworths. Stella and Goldie were still there and left on Tuesday for Connecticut. Clara and her children visited and Jim went to town.

Aida Austin mailed the letters she had written to Mae Parker and Arthur early Tuesday morning, but not early enough as the mail had gone out. She also picked up some groceries.

Anna and Jimmy Meyers spent Wednesday at the Leavenworths. Jim went to town again. Charlie and Anna Ort and the Hansens stopped by the Leavenworths on Thursday.

Lon Austin went to the Village on Thursday and brought back a card from Bill (in Hattiesburg, Mississippi) for Aida.

Thursday in E. Islip Anna wrote to Bob Austin and Stella Leavenworth; and knitted on her afghan.

Friday Jim went back after his 10-day furlough. "Pray the dear Lord he isn't sent overseas and that the war will end soon," Ella wrote. Millions of mothers would have agreed.

Friday afternoon Aida met

Ken McBride visited Jim Leavenworth when he was home on furlough. Yearbook photo.

Lottie Leavenworth, Emma Toaspern, Frances Knorr, her daughter Arlene, and Norman Myers in the store when she was at the Village and Post Office. Frances gave Aida a ride home. Lon's letter from Arthur had been mailed December 7, 1942.

Ella received a letter from Jim and a card from Stella on Saturday.

Saturday afternoon in Islip, Anna gathered wood and burned the trash. Sunday she baked muffins, chocolate pie, and upside-down cake.

Monday in Eldred Ella received a letter from Jim.

Tuesday was very icy, but Aida wore old stockings over her shoes and went to the store and Post Office in the afternoon. She mailed a letter to Gladys Austin and picked up a letter for Lon from Bill. Wednesday was colder and more icy. Aida was glad that Lon "didn't dare go to the Village."

Garfield fixed the lights after the ice storm and they got a letter from Jim.

There was a letter from Melva waiting for Aida Friday afternoon. Saturday afternoon Aida went to both the store and Andrew's.

Sunday, January 24, was "just one dandy day" for Ella. Clara and her family were there for dinner. Anna was there for the afternoon. Goldie and Stella arrived around 10 p.m. to store his car at his parents'.

Monday Margie Bosch took some sauerkraut to Aida. She and her mother were going to Julius Maier's place.

Tuesday Stella and Goldie were back in Eldred because of the bad weather.

It was snowing Thursday when Marjorie Bosch stopped in with some milk for Lon and Aida. Aida had worked out an Algebra problem for Marjorie.

It continued to snow all day, but the Leavenworths still got a letter from Jim.

February 1943
Monday, February 1, Anna walked to the Islip Post Office, got her check, and went to the bank to pay the first installment for her new insulation. Tuesday she wrote to Charlee.

In Eldred on Wednesday Ella received her third letter of the month from Jim.

"February 4, Guadalcanal is finally in American hands. United States' first land victory over Japan," wrote Ella on Thursday.

On Friday there was a letter from Jim and one from Stella.

Friday Aida went for oleo—first to Randolph's and then to the A&P.

It was rainy and terribly icy Saturday when Aida went to Randolph's for bread. There was a letter from her brother Ell. In the afternoon Robbie Bosch was over.

Saturday Ella received "a lovely letter from Jim." Jim's cousin Bill Austin in Mississippi wrote his brother Raymond.

Pvt. W. Austin, Camp Shelby, Miss., to R. Austin, Staten Island
February 7, 1943
Dear Brother,

I received your letter in which you sent Art's letter. I also got a letter from Art, which I am enclosing. Have you heard from Bob? Aunt Anna's letter said that she had a letter from Bob written on 20th of December.

In your letter you said that you were sending a check to pay the taxes. Was the taxes just on the old place or was they on my place too? There should be three parcels of land to pay taxes on. One in Dad's name, one in Mother's and one in mine. Let me know the next time you write.

I am sending you a bond which I bought. I had it made out so you could cash it, too. Let me know if you get it OK.

Your brother, Bill

In Eldred Monday, February 8, was sunny and blustery; Tuesday was cold and icy. Wednesday morning Aida walked to Randolph's. In the afternoon she went to see Mary Bosch.

"He is sort of blue [sad]," wrote Ella after reading Jim's letter on Wednesday, February 17.

Thursday the snow was very deep and the weather cold. Katherine Dunlap was able to get to Aida's, even though the road through the lane was terrible.

Friday morning Katherine gave Aida a number of papers when she visited. In the afternoon Aida went to the A&P and Randolph's.

Saturday afternoon Aida went to Mary Bosch's. [Sadly, this is the end of Aida's Diary entries.]

Sunday was cold and snowy; Monday was warmer and the snow melted fast. In Islip Anna chopped kindling and sifted ashes. She listened to a rationing program and the President on the radio in the evening. There was quite a crowd at the school on Tuesday when Anna picked up her second ration book.

Ella and Garfield continued to get letters from Jim. Goldie wrote occasionally too.

The last day of the month Bill Austin wrote his aunt Charlotte.

Pvt. W. Austin, Camp Shelby, Miss., to C. Leavenworth, Eldred
February 28, 1943
Dear Aunt Charlotte,

I received your letter that said you had received the receipt for the Bond. I wish you would keep it for me.

We have had some chilly weather but not near as cold as you have had. It is a good thing it don't get very cold down here because we have been out in the field most of the time and there is lots of swamps to wade through.

I had a letter from Arthur dated 7 January. He was alright.

Tell Aunt Christina that I haven't forgot I owe her a letter.

Is Goldie and Stella still in Connecticut? I had a letter from them sometime ago which I haven't answered yet. I also owe Aunt Anna a letter.

I haven't saw Willie Eldridge yet. I did look up John Ort and Ray Wolfe. They are the only ones I haven't met down here from around Eldred.

Remember me to Uncle Anthony and Charlee. Write whenever you get time.

Your nephew, Bill

March 1943
Monday, March 1, Anna went to the Islip Post Office to send in her Federal Taxes. Tuesday she chopped some wood, and worked on a rug and an afghan. Jimmie Braddock (the cat) was sick again.

In Eldred on Tuesday, Earl Wells drew hay from Chester Middaugh's.

Wednesday Martin was in for milk from his brother Garfield.

Bill Austin standing with the group in the back, on the right. Photo in the Austin Collection.

Peggy Hill and her half brother Charlie Eldridge, Will's brother. Bill Austin had not seen "Willie Eldridge yet." Photo courtesy of Alan Gothard.

Ella sent two payments to Montgomery Ward.

In Islip Anna baked raisin bread, muffins, and white cake on Wednesday. Thursday she wrote her sister Charlotte. Anna also paid the balance on her taxes and wrote out checks for water, lights, and telephone.

Victoria Parker, Ruth Parker Frint, Nellie Crandall, in 1946. Vicky and Nellie's mother was the second wife of George Parker Sr., Ruth's grandfather. Photo courtesy of Emily Knecht Hallock.

In Eldred Aida received a letter from her friend Mae Parker who was staying with her daughter Ruth and her husband Harold Frint for the winter.

Mae Parker, Port Jervis, N.Y., to Aida Austin, Eldred
March 8, 1943
Dear Miss Austin,

I am hoping you are keeping warm. I was home one day last week for about an hour, but had to hurry back as Harold was working nights and he had to be at the factory at 4:30.

I hope Lon is well and that you are taking good care of Miss Austin and that you will be home in April and then we can talk.

I sent a Christmas card to Bill Austin at some camp in the south. I got the address from Frank O'Donnell who is still at Chicopee Fall, Mass.

I like living here in the winter better as one can get out once in a while. Write if you have a chance.

All send love. Sincerely your old school pupil, Mae

Monday, March 8, there were letters from Jim, Grant Sergeant, and Orville Clark for Ella.

Thursday Anna (in Islip) ironed all morning until a fuse blew out. Saturday she went to the village and used all her April stamps to buy meat for Jimmie B. She also bought raisins.

The next week when Anna cut a lot of wood and pruned the grape vine, she noticed that planes were "practicing over the woods."

In Eldred Tuesday, March 23, Ella had letters from Jim and Stella. Thursday Clara and Martin were in for milk. Friday Stella and Goldie visited. They were back for dinner on Saturday.

In Islip Anna, 67, raked leaves, burnt rubbish, cut much kindling, and did spade work both Saturday and Sunday. She groaned with her lame back. Monday morning Anna "embarked on a career of baking: mixed gingerbread, mince pie, prune bread, and tea biscuits."

Goldie and Stella left Eldred for Connecticut on Tuesday. And Ella received a letter from Jim.

April 1943
In April when Martin D. Myers Jr. entered the Navy, Teenie moved from Sidney, New York, back to Eldred to stay with her parents. She lived on the floor above the Post Office in the Parker Hotel.

Bob Wolff who had worked with Martin Jr. at the magneto plant in Sidney, joined the Army.

Anna walked to the Islip Post Office and picked up the package from her sister Christina on Thursday, April 1. Friday Anna bought several pounds of vegetables. She didn't need meat because Christina had sent a ham. Saturday Anna raked leaves, planted currant slips, and weeded strawberry beds. Her diary entry, "Tired tonight."

Anna's nephew Bill Austin in Company F, 338 Inf., Shreveport, Louisiana, wrote her sister (his aunt) Christina.

Pvt. W. Austin, Shreveport, La., to Mrs. Anthony Hirsch, Eldred
April 9,1943
Dear Aunt Christina,

I was glad to hear from you. As you can see by my address I left Shelby. We are somewhere in Louisiana. Just where I do not know but I think we are not very far from Texas. Leesville is near where we are camped.

We got down here Wednesday. How long we will stay I don't know. I think the maneuvers generally last about two months. We are living in tents and I guess

Bill Parker met Mary Whalen in spring 1943. Photo courtesy of William H. Parker Jr.

we won't see any barracks till after the maneuvers are over.

We don't suffer from the cold down here. It is getting quite hot. They say there are lots of snakes down here. I am not much afraid of them myself but some of the fellows worry quite a lot about them.

I guess it will be a month before it will be safe to plant up there. Remember me to Aunt Charlotte, Uncle Anthony, and Charlee. Your nephew Bill

Bill's brother Bob Austin arrived in Africa, Monday, April 12.

Wednesday Bill and Bob's uncle Garfield went to the Eldred Post Office twice. There was a letter from Jim and a package from Sears.

Sunday Jim arrived home at 4:30 a.m. and left 12 hours later at 4:30 p.m. Jim sent his mother a lovely Easter card which arrived on Friday.

William Meets Mary
Andy Parker's nephew Bill Parker Jr. was home on leave. Bill's future wife Mary Whalen, a graduate from Ithaca College, had started teaching Physical Education in Eldred in January, after Coach Werneke enlisted.

Martin entered the Navy in April 1943. Martin D. Myers Jr. and friend Bob Wolff, son of Carl and Freida Kloss Wolff. Photo courtesy of Christene Stevens Myers.

I was home from the service for five or six days and I just happened to be at Uncle Andy's store. Must have been April or May of 1943.

Mary Whalen came in the store and after she left, I said to my aunt Marge, "Who was that girl?" She said, "She's the new Physical Education teacher here, she just started."

So I had about five or six days home, and before I went back I asked her to go out. I didn't have a car then and there weren't many places to go. I had been in the Navy then for a couple years. You got used to taking girls out and tried to take them to a

Frances Toaspern when she worked in New York City in 1943. Photo courtesy of Bill Ihlo.

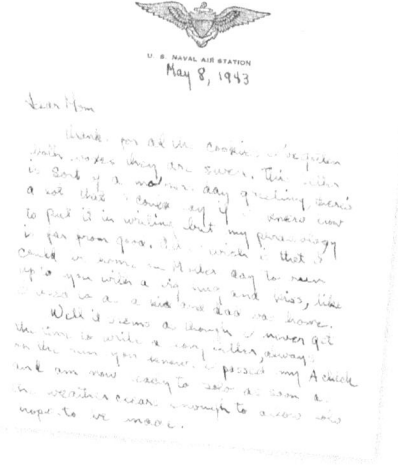

First page of Ed Toaspern's letter to his mother. Letter courtesy of Bill Ihlo.

halfway decent restaurant. There weren't many places in Eldred.

When I was home on leave I went to Rohman's Bar. There were two bartenders besides Art Rohman who stood at the left of bar and Art would say: "Give him what he wants and don't take money."—William H. Parker Jr.

William Parker wasn't the only serviceman Art Rohman gave a free drink. Stories indicate that Art was very generous to any serviceman who stopped by his place.

May 1943

Monday, May 3, Ella received a letter from both Goldie and Jim. Wednesday Garfield set out 33 raspberry plants.

Thursday Garfield covered the screens on the porch with copper wire. There were letters from Goldie and Jim again. Friday Garfield and Ella worked on the screens and painted the porch.

Saturday Ella planted one bushel of potatoes. Ella received another letter and a photo of Jim.

Ella wasn't the only Mother receiving much-looked-for mail. Jim's friend Ed Toaspern, training at the Naval Air Reserve Base (NARB) in Squantum, Massachusetts, wrote an endearing letter to his mom Emma Toaspern for Mother's Day.

Ed Toaspern, U.S. Navy, to Mrs. Emma Toaspern, Barryville

May 8, 1943
Dear Mom,

Thanks for all the cookies. I've gotten both boxes. They are swell. This letter is sort of a Mother's Day greeting. There's a lot that I could say if I knew how to put it in writing, but my phraseology is far from good. All I wish is that I could be home on Mother's Day to run up to you with a big hug and kiss, like I used to as a kid and dad was home.

Well it seems as though I never get the time to write a long letter, always on the run you know. I passed my A Check and am now ready to solo as soon as the weather clears enough to allow solo hops to be made.

Jim arrived here day before yesterday and is enjoying the place here. My liberties are all pretty good ones, so let me know as soon as dad gets home and I'll figure one out. Guess I'll have to close now as I'm in class and don't want to get caught. I'll write later. Love and Kisses, Ed

Walter, Emma, Ed, and Frances

Walter and Emma Toaspern's daughter Frances worked at a bank in Brooklyn in 1943. Frances stayed with family friends Al and Jane Smith who lived in Brooklyn, but had a summer place on Cemetery Hill in Barryville.

Frances' future husband Fred Ihlo lived nearby in Brooklyn.

Fred Ihlo at Camp Bowie, Texas, in 1943. Photo courtesy of his son Bill Ihlo.

He worked in a bank before he was drafted. By June 1943 Fred Ihlo was at Camp Bowie in Texas.

In Staten Island in May, Raymond Austin received a letter from a friend in England.

Burnham-on-Sea, Somerset, Eng., to R. Austin, Staten Island
May 22, 1943
Dear Mr. Austin,

I thought it nearly time to write to you again. I read about your rationing in a London paper and the restrictions on heating, gasoline, and food and drink. I read that many fish and poultry shops in New York had to close owing to being unable to make a profit at the prices fixed.

I was glad to read how successful the American troops are in the Aleutian Islands. They may be able to bomb Japan from there.

Here, the Americans have constructed airfields in different parts which will take their biggest bombers. We are now waiting for the next phase of the war after Tunisia. I hope you have heard from your brother and that he is

Jim Leavenworth, May 1943. Photo courtesy of Cynthia Leavenworth Bellinger.

well. I read the air offensive had saved thousands of lives in North Africa, and it may be the same when we get going in Europe.

The blasting of the three dams in Germany did great damage. We get raids here now and again, which keep us awake of a night, but don't do much damage. The big ports and cities get it the worst.

The Americans here are having a good time compared with those in Africa or the Pacific. Perhaps the U.S. will take over Australia after the war and admit it to the Union. Do you think so?

Mr. McCormack, the Chicago Publisher, proposes that all the British colonies be taken over by the U.S. He didn't mention Ireland. She will become a Republic I suppose. But I think that DeValera will do something after this war is over.

I hope you can manage to get enough to eat in spite of the restrictions. Feeding the devastated countries of Europe will be a problem after the war.

I suppose lil ole New York has not altered much. Quite a run on some of these war films I read.

The steamship companies have a long passenger list of those waiting to cross when the war is over. But I expect the Immigration authorities will put up the bars. You have enough racist troubles of your own, without introducing more from Europe. You cannot make an Irishman love an Englishman or a German either. But they all live under the Stars and Stripes. But a lot want to cross for business reasons.

I hope you and your family are keeping well, and enjoying some fine weekends.
Your Sincere Friend,
E.J. Davey

Thursday, May 27, Goldie and Stella were back in Eldred at his folks for a visit around 9:30.

"Heard first broadcast by Lowell Thomas from a helicopter," Ella jotted down on Friday.

Goldie and Stella went back to Connecticut on Monday.

June 1943
Mary Briggs graduated in June. The class of 1943 had started off with at least 30 students, but a number of them had entered the

Mary Briggs graduation photo courtesy of Mary Briggs Austin.

Chuck Myers photo after graduation and enlistment. Photo courtesy of Chuck Myers.

Charlee Hirsch. Photo courtesy of Ric Schroedel.

service before graduating. Many of those who graduated would soon be serving in one of the Armed Forces, or some other way.

Our class of 1943 was the first graduating class from the new school! It was during the war and Kate Strenglein and Chuck Myers were the main ones who helped put the yearbook together. I helped some, but I was in Barryville and couldn't help all that much. Others undoubtedly helped too. You couldn't get yearbooks published during that time, so we put it together and my dad (Irwin Briggs) knew where to send it to get it printed.

For the graduation ceremony the girls wore white robes and the boys royal blue robes. Someone got the idea of exchanging tassels. Our white ones were on the boys' blue caps and their blue ones on our white caps. The authorities did not look happy when we marched out on the stage for our graduation, and were quick to tell following graduates they were not to do that again!—Mary Briggs Austin.

Garfield worked two days for Belle Asendorf at the beginning of June. A card arrived from the War Department that said Jim had sailed on the *Queen Elizabeth*.

Sunday, June 6, in Islip, Anna canned rhubarb, did odd jobs around the house, and wrote to Bill Austin. Wednesday Anna walked to Islip in the rain to mail letters to Charlee.

In Eldred Garfield worked for Charlee's father Anthony all week. Arthur Austin with the 5th Army in Africa, wrote Charlee's mother, his aunt Christina.

Sgt. A. Austin, Hq. Co., 5th Army, to Mrs. C. Hirsch, Eldred
June 10, 1943
Dear folks,
    Returned a few weeks ago from a trip that covered about 3,000 miles for many of which I drove the jeep and of course was glad to find your letter at the orderly room when I returned.
    There was also one from Bill dated April 25. Apparently he expects to leave shortly. Received a letter from Raymond today saying that he had heard from Bob and that he was well. So far haven't received any word from him but I imagine I will soon.
    My traveling was stopped short by the end of the fighting in Africa. However saw some action for the last two days and have seen thousands of German prisoners [there were almost 250,000].
    There is some truly beautiful scenery here both inland and along the Mediterranean and was sorry there was not more time to enjoy it but of course had to keep moving most of the time.
    There are no regulations against sending newspaper clippings and would certainly like to receive any with Home information. Have been wondering what Cliff and Mary Crandall named their son.
    It will be nice if Charlee can get home once in a while with Mrs. Middaugh for I imagine you

Queen Elizabeth

After 1942 the *Queen Elizabeth* transported American troops to Europe from the North Atlantic. In November 1940 she had been fitted with anti-aircraft guns and her hull repainted black at Singapore's Naval Docks. Because of her high speed she could outrun hazards, mainly German U-boats, and travel by herself.
—wikipedia.org.
    Jim Leavenworth went overseas on the *Queen Elizabeth*.

Echo Hill Farm House where Anthony, Christina, and Charlee Hirsch lived. Photo courtesy of Ric Schroedel.

must miss her a great deal.

I suppose Aunt Charlotte is looking forward to vacation time. How big is the graduating class this year and where are they having their banquet?

Am enclosing a money order for $26.19, the amount of my insurance policy. I would appreciate it if you would get the bill from the post office when it arrives and for the money order with it. This is no time to let it lapse especially since we hope to play a more important part in future operations.

Meant to write long ago but have been quite busy and the hotter the weather gets the lazier I am. As I was not too ambitious to begin with hate to think what I will be before the summer is over.

Hope you are well and to hear from you soon. Arthur

Arthur Austin mentioned his friend Clifford's new little one. Clifford was home in June to visit his wife Mary and their son, Clifford David Crandall.

Late Saturday afternoon in Islip, Anna planted bush beans, cut grass, and picked strawberries.

Tuesday Ella and Garfield received their first letter (a V-mail) from Jim in England Tuesday. Jim, in the 520th Service Squad, had written on Monday.

Pfc. J. Leavenworth, N.Y., N.Y., to Mr. and Mrs. Leavenworth, Eldred
June 14, 1943
Dear Folks,

I surely hope that you take notice of my address, for I have moved again. It seems like a nice spot here and believe that I will like it.

How are things coming along back home? Suppose that Lee is still working for the railroad yet, and has Clinton been home

Victory Mail

V-mail correspondence was written on 7 by 9-1/8 inch letter sheets. The letter was censored, then photographed and transported as thumbnail-sized image in negative microfilm. At the letter's destination, the negative (microfilm) was blown up to 60% of the original size (4-1/4 inch by 5-3/16 inch) and printed.

A single sack of microfilmed copies (45 pounds) replaced 37 mail bags (2,575 pounds) which carried 150,000 one-page letters.

U.S. V-mail was based on the British airgraph. The airgraph was invented in the 1930s by the Eastman Kodak Company in conjunction with Imperial and Pan-American Airways to reduce the weight and bulk of mail carried by air.—*wikipedia.org.*

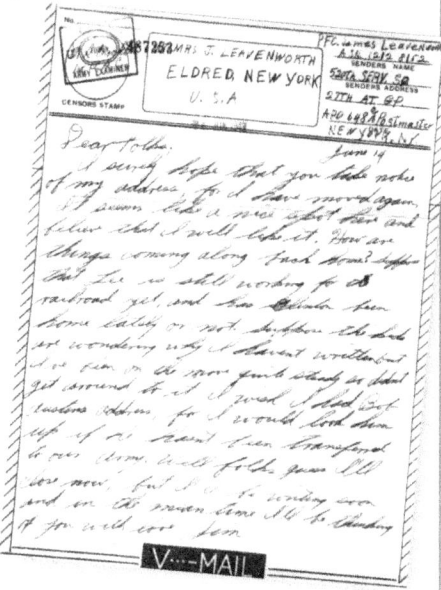

V-mail from Jim Leavenworth in England, June 14, 1943. V-mail courtesy of Cynthia Leavenworth Bellinger.

lately or not. Suppose the kids are wondering why I haven't written, but I've been on the move quite steady so didn't get around to it.

I wish I had Bob Austin's address for I would look him up if he hasn't been transferred to our army.

Well folks I'll be writing soon and in the mean time I'll be thinking of you with love. Jim

Jim's cousin Bill Austin was on his way to California. After training at Camp Shelby, in the swamps of Louisiana, the 85th Infantry Division, of which Bill Austin was a part, went to Camps Coxcomb and Pilot Knob at the Desert Training Area in California. Bill wrote a letter to his aunt Christina on his way to California.

(When Fred Ihlo trained at the

Fred Ihlo, front right, with his outfit in the Mojave Desert, California, where they trained. Photo courtesy of Bill Ihlo.

Desert Training Center a couple months earlier, Humphrey Bogart was filming his movie *Sahara* and used one of the 4th Armored battalions as extras.)

Pvt. W. Austin, L.A., Calif., to Mrs. Anthony Hirsch, Eldred
June 14, 1943
Dear Aunt Christina,

I am writing this letter on a train going west. Just now we are going through New Mexico. Where we are going I am not sure but I think somewhere in the southern part of California near the border of Arizona. I hear that we are going to get some training in desert warfare. However all this is just rumor and not official. I won't be able to mail this letter till we get to our destination so I will let you know at the end of it just where I am.

We left Merrysville, Louisiana, a few miles from the Texas line, at one o'clock Saturday noon. And we just got out of Texas this morning (Monday) so you see Texas is a pretty big state. Of course they don't make as good time as the railroads up north. It is only a single track and we have to wait for other trains to go by quite often, but still it is a long time to travel in one state by rail.

Raymond has a letter from Bob which was dated April 12. He was in Africa at the time. Bob said that he had a letter from Arthur but had not been able to get to see him until that date.

Tell Aunt Charlotte that I am going to answer her letter soon.

Is Goldie still working in Connecticut? I had a letter from him and intended to answer it but have lost his address. Could you kindly send me his address if you have it handy?

Calif., June 16, 1943: We arrived here last night. We are

Martin Myers holding his daughter Pat. Photo courtesy of the Clifford Crandall Family.

located in California about 12 miles from Arizona.

Remember me to Uncle Anthony, Aunt Charlotte, Charlee, and anybody else that might be interested in where I am or how I am getting along.

Your nephew, Bill

Thursday June 17, Ella received an air mail from Jim and a letter from Stella. Charlotte called her on Friday. Saturday there were letters from both Jim and Goldie.

Friday, June 25, Garfield finished haying at Hirsch's and started haying on his own meadow.

Saturday Goldie and Stella arrived back home for two weeks.

In Islip on Saturday, Anna wrote, "Watered all plants back of house and obtained seed potatoes late, but if Congress gets all its way, potatoes will be a dollar a piece."

Martin D. and Christene Myers
There was quite a bit of excitement for the Howard Stevens and the Martin Myers families in early July. Patricia Gail Myers was born to Martin and Christene Stevens Myers. Martin left Floyd Bennett Field in Brooklyn on a 24-hour pass and only had a couple hours with his new little one. Even though he was the father, Dr. George R. Mills (a family friend), made Martin keep visiting hour rules.

My dad served at Floyd Bennett Field in Brooklyn installing radar in planes. Radar was top secret stuff in those times, so the government did a security check on him in Eldred. His sister Mary Crandall was the school secretary, his mother-in-law Emily Stevens was the Postmaster. Either Dad or his dad (Martin D. Myers Sr.) was in the barber chair at Jim Wade's barber shop. I suppose they went to Wait & Boyd's, too.—Pat Myers Toaspern.

July 1943
Tuesday, July 6, Garfield built the porch on Goldie's house. Anna mailed her letter to Bill Austin at the Islip Post Office.

Friday Anthony Hirsch was at the Leavenworth's for a while.

Saturday Goldie and Stella (who had been home for two weeks) went back to Connecticut. You can be sure they were missed.

Saturday, July 24, Garfield worked for Hirsches. Anna in E. Islip battled Japanese and Mexican bean beetles during a hot, dry stretch of weather. Jim in England wrote his parents.

1943 Halfway Brook News

1943 School Opens
- The new Eldred Central School opened in January 1943.

1943 Enlisted
- Tom Myers enlisted in the Navy in July.

1943 Births
- Martha Eldred was born to Harvey and Emmy Draxler Eldred. Martha joined her brothers: Harvey Jr. and Charles. Harvey Sr., was a descendant of James Eldred's son Abraham Mulford Eldred.
- Martha Eldred's future husband William was born to Raymond and Emma Williams Worzel.
- Patricia Myers was born to Martin D. and Christene Stevens Myers.

Clifford Crandall Sr. holding his son Clifford Crandall. Photo courtesy of the Clifford Crandall Family.

- Pat Myers' future husband Dennis Toaspern was born to Royden and Doris Boudman Toaspern.
- Clifford D. Crandall was born to Clifford and Mary Crandall in April.
- Dorothy Knecht was born to "Red" and Margaret Harder Knecht.
- Richard Frank Bellinger, future husband of Cynthia Leavenworth, was born in July of 1943.
- William Bosch was born to Willie and Florence Schmerfeld Bosch.
- Beverly James was born to Edward and Norma Wood James at the Methodist Hospital in Brooklyn where Mary Briggs was training.
- Katherine Calkin born to Dale and Nellie Hill Calkin, two days after her great-grandfather Ell Austin died.

1943 Marriages
- Charles Kerr married Muriel Rennard in September.
- Walter (Bub) Toaspern married Doris Doeller.
- Will McBride and Viola Webber were married in April.

1943 Deaths
- Ralph Bosch died of a respiratory infection in 1943, in Paterson, New Jersey. He and his family had moved to New Jersey after the war started and Ralph worked at the Wright Aeronautics plant there.
- Sherman McBride Sr. died at home in Eldred, November 26, 1943.
- James Eldred Austin, 1855–1943.
- Perry Foster, 1868–1943.
- John Edwin Steel, 1865–1943.

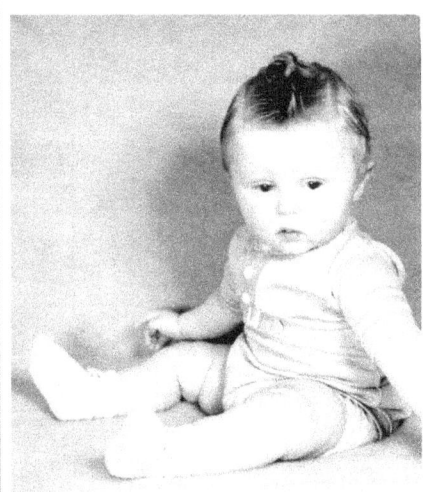

Richard Bellinger, future husband of Cynthia Leavenworth. Photo courtesy of Richard Bellinger.

Ralph Bosch. Photo courtesy of Ken Bosch.

J. Leavenworth, 520th Serv. Sq., to the Leavenworths, Eldred
July 26, 1943
Dear Mom and Dad,

It has been three days since I last wrote you. I had a fairly busy day yesterday as I spent the day in Glasgow. It sure is a big town and it wouldn't take much to lose me there. We did a little sightseeing in the early part of the afternoon. We bought ourselves a chicken dinner and it set us back a little better than $1 a piece.

Do you suppose that you folks could send me a little money as I am sort of running low. We were supposed to get paid last month but they got my records mixed up and I haven't been paid since last May. I should think that $20 would be enough. You can send it by money order as I can get them cashed over here. Please take care of this as soon as possible.

Have you heard any more about Frank Daiber and if so where is he stationed?

Which do you like best, Airmail or V-mail?

I had a letter from the Meyers family the other day. I bet that most of the folks back home

"American Cross Clubmobile somewhere in Great Britain. Just back from the Target. Passed by U.S. Army censor #21." Photo courtesy of Gisele Rouillon Leavenworth.

wonder why I don't write more often, but honestly there isn't a thing to write about. Everything that I would like to talk about is against Army regulations. I have been pretty lucky though as I have only had one letter sent back.

Well write soon as I like to hear from you.

With love, Jim

Jim serviced planes. He was in the 520th Service Squadron within the 807th Air Engineering. Once he worked on a plane that carried Dwight D. Eisenhower. Perhaps that was the plane General Eisenhower flew on to the Headquarters of Lt. General Mark Clark and the 5th Army in Italy where Arthur Austin, Jim's cousin, worked. Art on occasion saw General Eisenhower.

In Eldred on Monday, July 26, Walt McBride and Harry Strenglein were in to see the Leavenworths. Stella and Goldie arrived home on Tuesday.

Wednesday it was hot in Islip. It had been some time since Anna had heard any news from the Village of Eldred or her nephews who were away to the war.

Thursday, Anna heard President Roosevelt's speech at 1 a.m. Finally on Saturday Anna received some very welcomed letters from her sister Christina and nephew Arthur Austin.

August 1943

The summer was so dry in Islip that Anna irrigated her garden almost every day in August.

Stella and Goldie left Eldred on Sunday, August 1, to go back to Connecticut where he worked. They returned Monday. Tuesday they were up at their own house. Garfield worked for Walt McBride.

Arthur Austin continued to write letters to his aunts in Eldred, and of course Mary Briggs.

Arthur Austin, to Family in Eldred
August 10, 1943
Dear Folks:

Guess it's about time to drop a line to let you know that I am still leading a quiet life amidst all the excitement.

The news that the fight for Sicily is over, though taking somewhat longer than some of us had hoped at one time, was welcome.

Am anxious to hear from Bob. Once again his outfit has been in the thick of it. The few letters I have received from him have not contained much news. Apparently up to Sicily at least, he has come through untouched. Of course as he has been transferred several times, may not have been in the heaviest fighting.

It is hard to believe that summer is nearly over. I suppose the kids will be back to school again by the time this reaches you.

Well by this time next year,

1943 World and National News

January 1943
- Churchill and Roosevelt met at Casablanca, Morocco. Italian invasion to be first; then the second front in Europe.
- Tripoli (Libya) fell to Montgomery's Desert Army.
- Germans surrendered to U.S.S.R.

February 1943
- Gandhi fasted to gain his freedom.
- Fighting in Tunisia, N. Africa; Rommel head of German troops.

March 1943
- U.S. won Battle of Bismark Sea in South Pacific.

May 1943
- Central China attacked by Japan.
- Churchill and Roosevelt met in Washington to discuss strategy.
- Last German troops in N. Africa surrendered. Almost 250,000 became prisoners of war.

June 1943
- Leslie Howard shot down by the Germans. Leslie played Ashley Wilkes in *Gone with the Wind* and Professor Higgins in *Pygmalion*.

July 1943
- Allied air raid on Japan lasted for more than 12 hours.

August 1943
- Allies captured island of Sicily after five weeks of hard fighting.

1943 Casablanca meeting. Roosevelt with Major General George S. Patton Jr. Library of Congress P&P: LC-USZ62-105744; Lot 11568.

- Churchill and Roosevelt in Québec: atomic bomb collaboration agreement; pressed for a second front against Germany and France.

September 1943
- With Mussolini in jail, Italy signed armistice with Allies.
- Allies invasion of Italy launched; British and American forces landed north of Salerno and south of Naples.
- Germans occupied Rome; rescued Mussolini.
- Allied troops seized key New Guinea port.

October 1943
- Allied forces on way to Naples, Italy.

November 1943
- United Nations: 44 nations signed in for an organization which promised immediate relief to the populations of liberated countries.
- DeGaulle free French President.
- Italian stalemate. Monte Cassino near Gustav line held by the Axis.
- Allies launched new offensives in the Pacific. Third wave of U.S. landings in Solomon.
- Battle of Tarawa in Gilbert Islands. U.S. forces lost 1,000 lives taking islands due to miscalculations with maps and tides. U.S. Marines mown down by machine gun fire as they tried to wade ashore during an amphibious landing.
- Chiang Kai-Shek, Roosevelt, and Churchill planned the next moves in the Pacific war.
- Churchill, Roosevelt, and Stalin met in Tehran.

December 1943
- Enrico Fermi in Chicago made an atomic pile go critical producing energy and plutonium.
- Tito elected in Yugoslavia.
- Iran Summit committed Allies to a second front in France by the summer of 1944.
- Main invasion force landed on New Britain Island, New Guinea.
- Roosevelt appointed Eisenhower Supreme Allied Commander of the Allied Expeditionary Forces.

---

hope the time when we will all be returning will be in sight. Many think it will be over soon. But I am afraid it is the case of the wish being the father of the thought.

For myself, will be surprised if it takes less than a year and it can very easily take much longer. As long as I move every few months, don't believe the length of the war will bother me much.

The other day, two girls were walking ahead of me and just before they came to a couple soldiers sitting on a wall, they turned sharply. I called out to the boys, "Why scare the girls away?"

When I came alongside, was somewhat surprised to find they were both captains. Saluted and went on my way in a hurry. Every time I see the officers now, they start grinning, so guess they don't hold it against me. They have no reason to for that matter as I am sure their interest in the girls was not entirely military and possibly neither in the line of duty nor for the good of the service.

How are Mr. Myers and

Tom and Martin Myers Jr. Photo courtesy of Christene Stevens Myers.

Clifford? Has Clifford fully recovered or is he still partially crippled?

From all reports, Eldred must be pretty much deserted. Have met one of the boys from Eldred (Warren Parker) and received a letter from Dan West. Besides Jack Purcell is over here and I think several other fellows from our section.

Will write again in a few weeks.

Hope that you have all been well and to hear from you soon.

Art

August 13, 1943 envelope addressed to Miss Marry Briggs, Barryville, from S/Sgt. Arthur Austin, HQ& HQ. Co., 5th Army, N.Y., N.Y.

Art's second cousins Tom Myers and his brother Martin Myers Jr., both in the Navy, were home on leave in August.

Sunday, August 15, Everett Kelley called at the Leavenworth home.

Bob Austin, Battle of Messina

A week after Art's letter saying he was anxious to hear from his brother Bob, there was a major battle in Sicily which the Allies won, but which took a huge toll.

Bob Austin, a lineman, was one of the wounded in the Battle of Messina, Sicily.

Bob Austin transferred to the American Army just in time to take part in the first counter offensive of the war, long before the celebrated invasion of Normandy. He landed at Oran in the Sahara Desert, serving as a telephone lineman against the troops of Erwin Rommel, the Desert Fox, perhaps the greatest tactician in the German Army.

Telephone Linemen had one of the toughest and most dangerous jobs in the military. They had to crawl on their bellies (in Bob's case in Northern Africa, across the desert sands in 136 temperatures) with a roll of wire in their hands and their rifles slung on their backs (where they couldn't use them).

Linemen casualties were among the highest in any branch of the armed services. Bob survived intact only to have to take part in two more bloody invasions, one in Messina in Sicily where he was wounded.—Walter Geier.

Walter Geier was with the Marine Air Corps. He served as a meteorologist (Airology in the Marines) in the Pacific. He would

Ella received a snapshot of Jim Leavenworth. Photo courtesy of Cynthia Leavenworth Bellinger.

marry Bob Austin's niece Joan Austin and enjoy talking history with Bob for many years.

In Eldred Wednesday, August 25, Ella wrote, "Goldie got his notice to go for his physical tomorrow. Hope he doesn't have to go." Ella received a snapshot of Jim in a letter.

(Goldie seems to have gotten a deferment as he worked in a defense plant. Other reasons for deferment included someone who farmed, as well as those who couldn't see or hear well.)

Mary Briggs

Sometime in the fall of 1943, Mary Briggs started nurse's training at Brooklyn Methodist Hospital, in Brooklyn New York.

I was in the Cadet Nurse Corp. Our course at that time was three years for $300. They shortened it to two-and-a-half years and the

last six months we had the choice of going into a branch of the Service, the Indian Reservation, Public health, or stay at the hospital. I chose the hospital.
—Mary Briggs Austin.

September 1943
Friday, September 3, Garfield put cement block in for a heater in the bath. Anthony was in for a bit.

Sunday Skeet McBride and V. Sullivan called at the Leavenworths to get a guitar tuned.

Arthur Austin, Salerno, Italy
Arthur Austin, with the 5th U.S. Army, sailed on the Duchess of Bedford on September 9, 1943. They were a part of the assault waves of the landing at Salerno. The Duchess seems to have landed at Paestum south of Salerno.

The excitement started a few nights after the Paestum landing. I was comfortably relaxed in a bed in Baron Ricciardi's castle—the first bed I had seen in months on end. My but it was grand!

The Colonel winked when he gave me permission to guard the office that night, 'if I felt like it.' Without the proper authority, a foxhole, as usual, would have been my home. Of course, I felt like it—an understanding man, that Colonel.

Cadet Corps Nurse Mary Briggs. Photo courtesy of Mary Briggs Austin.

Near midnight, however, a messenger rushed through the room wildly proclaiming, "The Germans are coming! Burn all secret papers."

A groan from across the room proved that the Master Gunner, who was sharing the office defense with me, had heard the bad news. We hesitated a few moments. One who has not seen a bed in months, does not get up readily under any circumstances. But duty and self preservation demanded action.

We looked for clothing, secret office records, emergency chocolate rations; hunted for the absent Colonel's belongings to take along (might as well be captured as to leave them behind); searched all night long until daylight found us in a safe location.

Still, it was not a total loss. From that time on, everything missing on inspection days had been lost at the Baron's.
—Arthur Austin.

Finally the news that Robert Austin had been wounded was telegraphed to his brother Raymond Austin.

Shohola Penn, to Charles R. Austin, Stapleton, N.Y.
September 11, 1943
Regret to inform you your brother Private Robert C. Austin was slightly wounded in action on seventeenth August in the North Africa area. You will be advised as reports of condition are received.
The Adjutant General

George Andersen
George Andersen sent a V-mail to his friend Bill Austin on September 24. George had enlisted in the Army in May 1941.

George served in the Pacific all over the place, but most of the time in the Philippines. WWII was the one thing you could get him talking about—he would go on for hours with lots of gory stories like when his unit liberated Manila...or the Solomon Island natives who could tell by the scent 10 miles away if soldiers were Americans or Japanese. I think he regarded Whipple Bosch as his best friend."—George's stepson, David T. Fisher.

In the following letter George mentioned meeting Bill Austin at Freddie's Place (Straub's). Along with the Post Office, Straub's was a social center in Eldred.

Bill Austin (my uncle) would occasionally stop by Straub's for a beer. If folks got too loud, Uncle Bill would say, "Getting kind of noisy down there." And everyone would quiet down.

Pfc. Geo. W. Andersen, Hq., San Francisco, Calif., to Bill Austin
September 24, 1943
Hello Bill,
Was just thinking of some

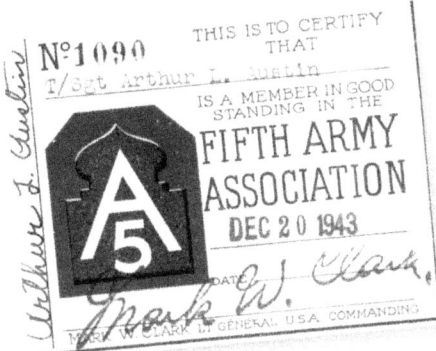

Arthur Austin's 5th Army Association Card. From the Austin Family Collection.

Jim Leavenworth with the 807 Air Engineering Squadron. Photo courtesy of Gisele Rouillon Leavenworth.

of my old friends and decided to write to you. I am ok so far and hope that this finds you the same. How is Art and Bob making out? Good I hope! I will be glad when us fellows can all meet again in Freddie's place and talk over the bar like we used to.

I wonder if Fred still has that round stove yet? If so, I'll bet it is going full blast now. Of course, I know he hasn't got many customers, but he will some day.

I never hear from Whipple at all. He is married now and must be writing to his wife only.

I know that this isn't much, Bill, but it is a letter anyhow. I would like to hear from you sometime in the near future.

As ever,
Pfc. Geo. W. Andersen

Sunday, September 26, Anthony Hirsch fixed the Leavenworth pump in Eldred. Jim was in England when he wrote the following letter home.

J. Leavenworth, 520th Serv. Sq., to the Leavenworths, Eldred
September 26, 1943
Dear Folks,

Today is a beautiful day and it also is my day off. I'm well and in perfect health. Sure hope you are the same. Have you got the new bath in yet? It sure will make a difference won't it.

Tell Goldie and Stella that I'll write soon. Tell Clara to write once in awhile too as her letters are always welcome. They no doubt are peeved because I don't write more often, but honestly there isn't much to write and besides one gets tired of writing.

The main ones I write to are you, Dorothy Wells, and Grace Kewley. Well folks so long.
With Love, Jim

Sept. 29, 1943
Dear Folks,

Things are going along good as usual and am enjoying my stay here fairly well.

Had a letter from Clara. She said that she was down and that Clareta came up with her kids. Bet that was a wild day wasn't it.

Well dad, how are things with you? Suppose you are still working up to Hirsch's. Is there much game this year? Sure would enjoy a couple days hunting.

Hope by now you have sold my car. I know I should have sold it before coming in the Army.

Well folks write soon. Until then, be good.
With love, Jim

October 1943
Bill Austin, in California wrote his aunt Christina Hirsch at the beginning of October.

Pvt. W. Austin, Co. F, 338 Inf., L.A., Calif., to C. Hirsch, Eldred
October 3, 1943
Dear Aunt Christina,

I received your letter a couple of days ago. I am always glad to hear from home. You said that Aunt Charlotte had some papers to send me. Tell her if she hasn't already sent them to hold them until she hears from me as I am expecting a new address before long. I will write her soon.

I had a letter from Raymond and he said that Dawn Lee was getting better but that she was still in the hospital.

Arthur was well the last he heard from him. Bob was slightly wounded in the campaign in Sicily. He was only in the hospital two days, so I guess he wasn't hurt very bad.

I suppose you are getting some cold weather by now. It is still hot out here in the daytime. It cools off at night and some nights I use both blankets.

I can't say for sure about a furlough, but I think I might get one within the next three months.

Give my regards to the family and write when you get time.
Your nephew,
Bill

Ella sent a box to Orville Clark. Photo courtesy of Vernon Clark.

Sunday, October 3, Ella sent a box to Orville Clark and Grant Sergeant. Anthony continued to work on the plumbing at the Leavenworth home.

In Islip Anna packed and sent Christmas boxes to her nephews Arthur Austin and Jim Leavenworth.

Tuesday Anna covered her "beloved peppers and tomatoes in the p.m.," because though it was a lovely day, it was cold. And in Eldred Anthony finished as much plumbing as he could for the Leavenworth's.

Thursday, October 7, Ella received a letter from Jim with $20. The same day Jim wrote a V-mail.

Pfc. J. Leavenworth, to Mr. & Mrs. J.G. Leavenworth, Eldred
October 7, 1943
Dear Mom and Dad,
Received your most welcome letter and enjoyed it very much. Hope you folks have been fine. As for myself things couldn't be any better.

Had another letter from Grant this week and he seems to be making out OK. How long has he been down there anyway?

Suppose Goldie and Lee are still up to Lordville. Does Mr. Meyers board with them or does he stay with another family? Take it easy and write. With Love, Jim

Saturday back in Eldred, Lee and Clara Hansen had a photo taken of their three children.

Anna in Islip cut her finger quite badly on Saturday. After she found a tick in her side on Sunday, Anna worked in the house. She was afraid of getting another tick. Anna didn't feel too well that week. She had a cold, a very sore finger, and a tick bite. She still did not feel well on Thursday, October

Bob Austin. Photo in Austin Collection.

14, when she wrote to Christina.

In Eldred, Garfield put the ceiling in the bathroom on Thursday.

Tuesday, October 19, Goldie and Stella left for Lordville where they would live for a while.

Tuesday in Islip Anna went to the school to get ration book 4. Saturday Anna wrote letters and then Christmas cards to soldiers from a list a friend gave her. Anna "rested as proper on Sunday."

The following Saturday in Eldred, Lee Hansen bought Jim's Chevy for $30.

Ella and Garfield had quite a crew stop by on Friday evening, October 29: Clara, Lee, Bill, Anna, Jimmy, Christina Hirsch, and Charlee. Two letters from Jim made for a perfect day.

Across the Atlantic Jim's cousin Bob Austin wrote to his brother Raymond.

Pvt. R.C. Austin, 7th Inf., to C.R. Austin, Staten Island, N.Y.
October 29, 1943
Dear Ray,
I have been receiving your letters quite regularly and sure appreciate your writing since it must be rather aggravating to write and receive no answer.

I have time to write more often but just can't think of much to say, but the same old thing. However, when I get back, I think I will be able to tell you something about what it is like over here.

I haven't heard from Arthur in a long time, but I think I owe him a letter. I got a letter from Aunt Anna a few weeks ago, but it was mailed to my old address and it took three months to get here.

I also received our election ballot and would like to have voted, but I didn't think they are kept secret. Anyhow, I have been away from home so long now that I don't know anything about local politics and might have voted the wrong way.

The weather over here is colder than it was last summer and it rains a little more often. We can keep quite comfortable here as we generally have our blankets. I don't think you have to worry about either Arthur or myself since I think we are both pretty safe. If you see Bill try and talk him into getting out of a line

Dick, Lois, and Wayne Hansen. Photo courtesy of Cynthia Leavenworth Bellinger.

Bill Austin. Photo in the Austin Collection.

outfit before he comes across.
 As Ever,
 Your brother Bob

November 1943
Bill Austin did get a furlough. Friday, November 5, Bill called at the Leavenworth home. Ella also received two letters from Jim.

In Islip, Anna worked on her rug and cut kindling. She received a letter from Jim Leavenworth; also a check from the L.I. Lighting Company with a refund for gas and electricity meters.

Saturday in Eldred Mr. Wait laid the small chimney for a bath heater at the Leavenworths.

Sunday Stella and Goldie, and Bill Austin had supper at the Leavenworth home.

Bill's brother Art wrote their brother Raymond in November.

Arthur Austin, to Mr. Charles R. Austin, Customhouse, N.Y., N.Y.
November 8, 1943
Dear Ray,
 Your letters have been coming through regularly and making fairly good time. Apparently mine haven't been so fast, as you hadn't heard from me as late as 20 October. I imagine you must have received at least one letter by now and hope you have also heard from Bob.
 If Bill is scheduled to go across, hope he manages to get his furlough in first. I imagine he must feel the cold in New York after spending the summer in the desert. I know I feel it much more than I used to.
 Am enclosing a picture of myself to show you how I looked when emerging from one of my recent homes here in Italy; also one of our Anti-Aircraft Section for you to keep until I return.
 The enclosed $20 money order is for Christmas presents for the children [Melva, Joan, Margie and Dawn Lee]. Have a few souvenirs that someday I may get the ambition to wrap up and mail. Hope that you have all kept well.
 Art

A week later Arthur Austin sent his brother Raymond and his family a special Christmas Card from the 5th Army in Italy.

In Eldred Ella made shirts for her grandsons on Wednesday, November 10. And quite exciting, their water system was filled and they now had bathroom facilities—no more outhouse!

Tuesday, November 16, Ensign Edward Toaspern reported to the Pensacola Naval Air Station for active duty. In about a year Ed would have a 27-day furlough to his home in Barryville. He would have an action-packed year.

In Islip on Tuesday Anna was surprised by a "pleasant call" from her nephew Bill Austin who let her know that his brothers Arthur and Bob were safe as of the previous two weeks.

Garfield and Ella were "especially glad" on November 25 when they "got a long awaited letter from Jim."

We haven't heard from Aida Austin for some time as there was no more record of her daily diary. Her nephew Bill (Will) Austin had apparently written his aunt Aida and sent her a photo. It arrived on Aida's 82nd birthday. Aida wrote to Bill the same day.

Aida Austin, Eldred, to Pfc. William Austin
November 28, 1943
Dear Will,

Lillie Austin Calkin's class in Yulan in the 1943–44 Eldred Yearbook. Front row: Gail Weber, Roger Weber, Robert Warden, Jeannette Weber, Dorothy Flieger, Arlene Wolff, Joan Hensel, Barbara Liefert, Georgia Anne Bradley. Back row: Mrs. Lydia Calkin, Arthur Flieger.

"Just a glad good morning," to tell you how glad I am.

Uncle Lon brought me your picture yesterday afternoon. Today is my birthday, so you see your picture came just in time for a birthday present. I wish I could get a picture like yours of Arthur and Rob. Do you suppose they could get their pictures where they are now? I will write to Arthur, but I don't know Rob's address.

That must have been a good place where your picture was taken, for it is the best picture I have seen of any of the boys who have sent their pictures home.

Uncle Lon has been very busy all this last week fixing the hen house, but he did not get the work on it finished and the weather has come off so cold. I don't know if he will be able to do anymore on it just now. He talks of getting a few chickens.

I had a card from Lillie [Calkin] yesterday saying Ell [Lillie's father, Aida's brother] is quite sick. He caught a heavy cold and has had an attack of pleurisy. The weather is so terribly changeable.

Hope you keep well and thank you very much for the picture.

Love, Aunt Aida

December 1943
Saturday, December 4, Walter Tether and his son Ivan visited Ella and Garfield. Ella made suits for Clara's two boys. In Islip Anna wrote Christmas cards to soldiers on Monday.

In Eldred Sunday, December 19, Ella wrote, "Dear little Wayne and Dick here yet as their dad is sick." And on Tuesday, "Dick and Wayne still here with us. I dread to have them go home."

As Aida mentioned in her letter, her brother Ell was quite sick. On December 23, 1943, James Eldred (Ell) Austin died. Only Aida and Lon Austin were left of a family of ten children.

James Eldred Austin Dies
My family knew James Eldred Austin as Uncle Ell. You may remember that his daughter Lillie Calkin taught school in Yulan. Lillie's children (Ell's grandchildren) were Dot Hale and Dale Calkin. At the time of his death Ell had two great-grandchildren, Bob and Neal Calkin. Their sister Kathy Calkin, Ell's third great-grandchild, was born at the end of the month. James Eldred Austin was buried in the Eldred Cemetery.

Christmas Time 1943
It's been a while since we talked about Harriet Hill. Harriet's sons Charlie and Bill Eldridge were in the Army. Charlie was home at Christmas time (before going overseas) and gave his sister Peggy "the best Christmas present" —a box of Baby Ruths.

Thursday, December 23, at the Leavenworth household, Ella got "a dandy letter from Jim" and one from her sister Hazel.

In Islip on Friday Anna had "a very welcome letter from Arthur. Bob and he were safe December 1."

In Eldred the Leavenworth Christmas Eve and Christmas guests were the same: Anna, Bill and Jimmy Meyers; Goldie and Stella; and Clara, Lois, Wayne, and Dick ("Bless him"). Unfortunately Goldie was sick, but he and Stella were still there for supper. Dick and Wayne went home with their mother.

In Islip Anna had Christmas dinner with a Mrs. O'Shea and enjoyed herself immensely.

Tuesday there was another

Christmas V-Mail and envelope from Arthur Austin to his brother Raymond's family. Card courtesy of Melva Austin Barney.

V-mail letter from Jim. And another one on Thursday when Charlie Foster was at the Leavenworths in the afternoon.

Wednesday, December 29, 1943, Bill Austin left with the 85th Division for North Africa and more training; Co. F, 338 Infantry, 60 MM Mortar, first Class; Messenger 675.

Friday, December 31, Mr. Briggs, Anthony Hirsch, Lee Hansen, and Goldie and Stella stopped by the Leavenworths.

Another year had ended and still the war was not over.

Wartime in France
Gisele Rouillon lived in Viroflay, a hamlet some 14 miles southwest of Paris.

When the Viroflay townsfolk heard the Nazis were coming

into Paris, Gisele and the others packed up what they could carry, took all the children, and walked to a safe town miles and miles away. When they got there, the Nazis were there, too. (Fortunately, the Nazis did not harm them.) So the group of French children and adults turned around and returned to Viroflay.

At nighttime Gisele could hear the Nazis and their *goose step march* on the cobblestones.

All their food was rationed and they had very little meat. They had a dark oil they poured on their potatoes while the Nazis used the butter to polish their boots.

During the war, Gisele was sent outside of town to get the ration of potatoes. Anyone caught out after curfew, would be taken by the Nazis and would never be seen again. (This did happen to a girl Gisele knew.)

One time the line for the potatoes was so long that Gisele didn't make curfew. On her way home, whenever a vehicle went by, she would dive into a ditch with her bike—just in case it was a Nazi jeep. Gisele did make it back safely, but everyone had feared the worst.

Windows had to be covered with blue paper so that the planes couldn't see the lights. Trains never completely stopped at the stations, but slowed down enough for a person to jump off. The younger folks sang on the trains to keep the older folks calm.

At school (war started around September 1939 when Gisele was 12) all the students had grey rectangular boxes that they wore as backpacks. Inside was a gas mask. Due to the shortage of food, each day they were given a cookie full of vitamins.

One day when the school children were home eating lunch,

Young Gisele Rouillon in France. Photo courtesy of Gisele Rouillon Leavenworth.

sirens went off (a warning to take cover). Bombs were dropping. On the way back to school Gisele and her friends saw arms and legs hanging in the trees. The Nazis had shot at Americans who were parachuting down. It was awful. The Nazis would not allow Gisele and her friends to leave flowers to honor the soldiers.

A young French girl was caught dating a Nazi soldier. They put her in the middle of the town square and shaved her head as a sign of embarrassment—similar to the *scarlet letter A* in Hawthorne's book.

January 1, 1944, Eldred and Islip
The first day of the 1944 New Year in Eldred (where Gisele would live in two years), Ella "got a nice air mail from Jim."

Ella continued to record the days she received letters from Jim. Sometimes she received up to four letters a day.

In Islip Anna started the "nice first day of the year" off by making tarts and gingerbread.

January 1, 1944, Brooklyn
Mary Briggs lived at the Nurse's Residence in Brooklyn where she continued her first year of nurse's training at the Brooklyn Methodist Hospital. Mary was also in the U.S. Cadet Nurses Corps.

The war of course affected those who lived in the U.S., though not in the same way as in Europe where it was up close and personal.

During World War II people collected items like tin cans and aluminum foil. They had to get ration cards for things like gasoline, sugar, stamps, meat, butter, etc. About everything was rationed including shoes and coffee. New tires could not be purchased.

Growing Victory Gardens were encouraged. People also saved the fat from foods in a canister. I didn't run into much rationing at school, though.

There were many shortages. One was nylon hose. Whenever we heard a shipment of nylons had come in, we'd rush out and stand in line at the store which had them. The line of people would stretch around a city block. I stood in line several times. Many of the patients gave us nylon hose as a thank-you gift when they left the hospital.—Mary B. Austin.

January 1, 1944, Italy
On January 1, 1944, in Italy, Arthur Austin, a Technical Sergeant at 5th Army's Headquarters in Italy, wrote to Mary Briggs.

T/Sgt. A. Austin, to M. Briggs, Methodist Hospital, Brooklyn
January 1, 1944
Dear Mary,
Well, here it is New Year's Day and I think it a good idea to catch up on my correspondence, otherwise the mailman will soon be passing me by.

Wonder Drug

During World War II penicillin made a major difference in the number of deaths and amputations caused by infected wounds. Alexander Fleming is credited for its accidental discovery in 1928.

In March of 1942 the first patient was treated for streptococcal septicemia with U.S.-made penicillin (using half of the total supply at that time) produced by Merck & Co. By June 1942 just enough U.S. penicillin was available to treat ten patients.

In July 1943 the War Production Board drew up a plan for the mass distribution of penicillin stocks to Allied troops fighting in Europe. The results of fermentation research on corn steep liquor at the Northern Regional Research Laboratory at Peoria, Illinois, allowed the U. S. to produce 2.3 million doses in time for the invasion of Normandy in the spring of 1944.—*wikipedia.org.*

Your very nice Christmas Card arrived shortly after Christmas and was glad to note the Bible reference. It is too bad that you were unable to be home for Christmas this year. (Or did things turn out better than you expected?) I can well imagine how much pleasure it would have given you to spend the holidays with your folks.

This makes my third Christmas overseas, but, as I haven't a real home to return to, it does not matter quite so much in my case—still, it would be nice to spend a Christmas with my friends back in Eldred or with my brother and his family on Staten Island.

Well, rotation seems to be moving right along, and perhaps sometime during the next year I will have an opportunity to spend at least a month in the states.

So they are really keeping you busy? That is supposed to be the best way to keep a person out of mischief. Is it true?

Heard from Reta Kalin awhile back and she said she had met you while staying in New York. Guess Reta really enjoyed herself in the city and is having it might easy going in school this year.

Received last years' El Dorado *[the Eldred Yearbook] about a month ago and of course was quick to note your picture among those of the Alumni in the service. Ella Getz's picture was also there and was surprised to learn a short while back that she is a nurse here in Italy. Have not had an opportunity to visit her yet, but hope to be able to do so before long.*

Oakie and John [Mary's brother] must undoubtedly have had a good time—who wouldn't meeting all those nurses (or rather nurses-to-be). Oakie is quite a handsome lad and might be just the one to take the place of — —.

Trust that even away from home you managed to have an enjoyable Christmas and New

Ella Getz was a nurse in Italy. Photo courtesy of Frank V Schwarz, son.

Mary Briggs, U.S. Cadet Nurses Corps. Photo courtesy of Mary Briggs Austin.

Year. Hope to hear from you again soon.

Sincerely, Art

By the way what is USNC— United States Candidate Nurses Corps, I betcha. [U.S. Cadet Nurses Corps.]

There were going to be some rough months ahead for Art and his brother Bob Austin who were both in Italy.

Their brother Bill would soon arrive in North Africa. His outfit would train first in the Atlas Mountains of Algeria; then at the Invasion Training Center on the coast of the Mediterranean Sea. Bill would eventually be in Italy.

Gustav Line, Italy, January 1944
January through May 1944 was the Battle for Cassino in the push to reach Rome.

The Germans had constructed the *Winter Line,* a series of defense lines south of Rome. The system was similar to the formidable Hindenburg Line in France in World War I.

The *Winter Line,* also called

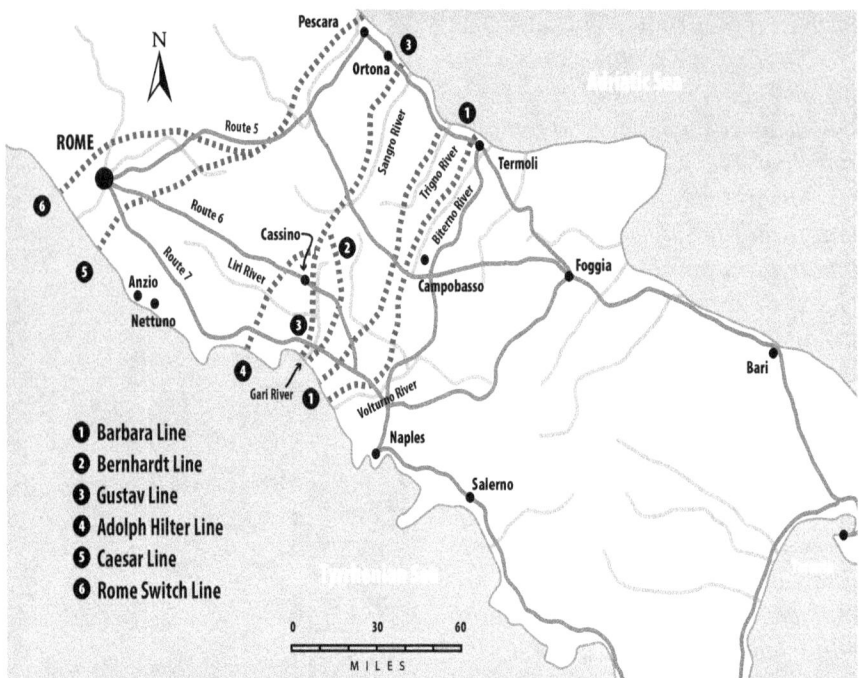

Map showing the Winter Line, including the major Gustav Line and Cassino where there was major fighting. Map: Gary Smith.

the *Gustav Line* (the major backbone of the *Winter Line*), was complete with gun pits, concrete bunkers, turreted machine-gun emplacements, and the usual barbed-wire and mine fields.

The *Gustav Line* (as did most of the lines) stretched northeast to southwest across Italy *(see map)*. Gustav crossed the main route north to Rome, near which was the town of Cassino. In the mountains behind Cassino sat Monte Cassino, an old abbey with its high elevation and view of any potential enemies.

The Allies fought through the Volturno, Barbara, and Bernhardt Lines and reached the *Gustav Line* by mid-January 1944.

The U.S. had a set back when they crossed the Gari River near Cassino. Both fronts became a stalemate after three attacks were made against the Gustav Line.

The scene was set for the four battles of Monte Cassino which would take place between January and May 1944.

New York, January 8, 1944
In Islip on a cold Saturday, January 8, Anna ironed a big ironing. Her friend Lucy stopped by and they made plans to go to Bay Shore for glasses for Anna.

Sunday Anna wrote a long letter to her nephew Bill Austin.

On Sunday in Eldred, Walt Horton Sr., Anthony Hirsch, and Roy Horton stopped by the Leavenworth home. Friday, Cliff Myers called. Ella's letter from Jim mentioned he was in Scotland and had visited the Scottish relatives of his friend Ian Warden.

Scotland photo from Jim Leavenworth, courtesy of Cynthia Leavenworth Bellinger.

Sunday, January 16, Islip was covered with snow and sleet. Anna stayed indoors and studied the Federal tax which she thought looked easier than at first.

Thursday in Eldred, Ella and Garfield's telephone was installed. "We feel nearer our neighbors now," Ella wrote. Perhaps Ella called a few folks to come for a visit, as Saturday Clara and her family and Stella and her brother Orville Clark (home on furlough), stopped by.

Sunday, January 23, Clara Hansen got a piano from Lottie Meyers. Madelyn Meyers was in to visit Ella for a few minutes.

Tuesday Garfield and Earl Wells drew hay—one load for the Leavenworths and one for Goldie.

Earl Wells' daughter Dorothy wrote Jim and sent him a photo in March. Earl's daughter Berniece's future husband Harry Haas served in the Navy.

Tuesday Anna walked to the Islip Post Office and sent off her Federal taxes.

Thursday Jimmie Braddock the cat was in the "doghouse" in a big way. He had gotten into the pantry and stolen two big pieces of liver and also some liverwurst. He was put on a milk diet for his thievery!

Anna Meyers in Eldred started a diary in January. On Thursday she wrote, "Roy Horton going into

Dorothy Wells wrote to Jim Leavenworth. "3/27/44, Good Luck, Jim, Dot." Photo courtesy of Cynthia Bellinger.

Frances and Ed Toaspern's cousin Albert Pegg Jr. is in the middle of the back row. Albert was a waist gunner killed on his 9th mission over Germany on March 23, 1945. Hard to imagine but there were nearly 1,000 B-17s sent out on this mission. Albert was with the 8th Air Force, 34th Bomb Group, and was based in Mendlesham, England. Photo and caption courtesy of Bill Ihlo.

Army in three weeks. Ray Hulse passed also. Alfred Hill deferred."

Friday Anna, Bill, and Jimmy Meyers; and Ella went to Honesdale. Anna and Ella had their eyes tested for glasses.

February 1944
Wednesday, February 2, Anna Leavenworth walked to the Islip Post Office and bank. She bought two bonds, one for her niece Charlee and one for herself. Then she went to a "brush party" with five others. Monday Anna worked on a relief afghan.

In Eldred on Tuesday, Garfield started to make a violin. Ella sold a pineapple tablecloth for $7. Mary Sergeant was there for the day.

Wednesday Jimmie B. in Islip was no longer on his milk regiment, or soon would be off, as Anna walked to Islip and bought a third bond, groceries, and liver for Jimmie.

It was clear and cold on Wednesday in Eldred when James K. Gardner died. (He was buried on Saturday.) James was a great-grandson of James Eldred, and the father of Edna Gardner.

On Valentine's Day Ella got a letter from Grant Sergeant. She forwarded that letter to Jim.

On Tuesday Anna was sewing up a storm in Islip. She finished a pillow, a cradle quilt, and knitted a block for a new afghan. She washed a few pieces and hung them to dry in the attic. Saturday, February 19, Lucy took Anna Leavenworth to Bayshore to get her glasses.

In Eldred Goldie got his induction papers on Saturday. Millard Hulse got his induction papers on Sunday.

On Thursday, January 24, Anna in Islip talked to her sister Christina in Eldred.

Monday the Leavenworths got two tons of coal from Mr. Wolff. It cost $23.90.

Crandall, Myers, Rizzuto
Sometime in February, Clifford Crandall was home on leave.

During the war Mary Crandall and their son Clifford lived at the home of Mary's father, Martin D. Myers Sr. Mary's brothers Tom and Martin Myers Jr. seem to have

Mary and Clifford Crandall and son Clifford. Photo courtesy of the Clifford Crandall Family.

Family of Martin D. Myers Sr.: Tom Myers, Mary Myers Crandall, Martin Sr., Helen Myers and Martin D. Myers Jr. Photo courtesy of Christene Stevens Myers.

been home at the same time. The photo of the Myers siblings with their dad included their sister Helen.

Martin Myers Sr.'s brother Charles still ran Lake View on Highland Lake. It would be for sale in a year. Charles and Elizabeth Myers' daughter Eleanor was or would soon be teaching in New Jersey. Sam Rizzuto, Eleanor's future husband was stationed at Camp Shanks, New York.

Sam Rizzuto had been in the National Guard for a time before he went into the C.C.C. around 1937. Even though Sam had lost an eye in an industrial accident while logging Cyprus trees in Louisiana, he was still drafted. Sam served in the medical corps, but probably because of his vision loss he was never sent overseas. He spent most of the war at Camp Shanks, escorting prisoners who came into Piermont Pier. At one point he received orders to head west. His unit got as far as Missoula, Montana, where they were put to work on the railroad for a time. Sam had experience as a heavy equipment operator.

Bob Austin Wounded Again
On February 29, 1944, Bob Austin was seriously wounded in Nettuno, Italy. It would be a bit before family and friends would hear the news.

Bob was patched up from his wound in Messina, Sicily, and "was up well enough to make the other in Nettuno, in southern Italy, where most of his right arm was shot away."—Walter Geier.

Eleanor Myers taught in New Jersey. Her future husband Sam Rizzuto was stationed at Camp Shanks, New York. Photo courtesy of Timothy C. Rizzuto.

Tom and Martin Myers Sr., Clifford Crandall. Photo courtesy of the Clifford Crandall Family.

March 1944

On Thursday, March 2, Anna in Islip received letters from her sister Christina and daughter Charlee; and a check.

In Eldred, Ella planned her garden and sent to Harris and Burpee's for seeds.

On Friday, March 3, Herman Bosch died of leukemia. He was a dear friend of Lon Austin. Garfield Leavenworth went to Herman's funeral on Monday. Earl Wells was there also.

On Tuesday Ella got a letter and a $25 money order from Jim.

Stella and Goldie were home for his blood test on Friday.

Saturday the Leavenworths paid their taxes: $18.17 county and $9.60 school.

Anna in Islip had been under the weather for quite a while with a cold. Wednesday she was feeling much better and went to the bank to get a stock certificate.

Unaware her nephew Bob was in the hospital, Anna wrote to him on Monday, March 20.

Monday, March 27, Ella in Eldred bought 200 pounds of Pillsbury flour for $10.00. Tuesday she made her granddaughter Lois a pinafore. Wednesday, Thursday, and Friday, Garfield worked a total of 16 hours for Walt McBride. Ella received a V-mail from Jim both Thursday and Friday.

April 1944

Saturday, April 1, Lee and the grandchildren were at the Leavenworths. Stella, Goldie, Mrs. Clark, and Doug Hallock were also in. There was a letter from Jim.

All of the Leavenworth children were in on Sunday, except of course Jim, who turned 22—in England.

In Islip on Sunday, Jimmie B. developed an abscess on his foot. Anna was tired from working so hard outside on Saturday. By Monday Anna had the energy to walk up to the bank and do some grocery shopping.

In Eldred Bill Meyers went to work for Walt Toaspern.

Art, Bob, and Bill Meet in Italy

Around the end of March, the Austin brothers were able to meet at the hospital where Bob was recuperating from his arm wound. Both Art (my father) and Bill wrote to their brother Raymond with the story of their meeting.

Arthur Austin, to Mr. Charles R. Austin, Customhouse, N.Y., N.Y.
April 4, 1944
Dear Ray,

Well at last I have some real news to tell. After all the failures in trying to contact Bob, I finally located not only Bob, but Bill as well. Managed to get a Jeep and then drove over and picked up Bill and we went down together to see Bob.

The three or four hours we had together passed rapidly, but for the time it seemed almost

Charlie, Eleanor, and Elizabeth Myers. Photo courtesy of Timothy C. Rizzuto.

like the old days when we used to gather around the stove at home.

Of course we all thought of you and that your presence would have made it a complete family reunion.

I know that we were all happy beyond measure at this unexpected meeting. Still there was a little sadness too, for, although we did not mention it, the chances of us ever all being together again before the end of the war (or ever for that matter) are extremely remote.

As you were in the last war, I know there isn't any use trying to soft soap you—guess we all have a good idea of an infantryman's chances and what must be expected. You can be sure though that we didn't waste anytime in sentiment, but enjoyed to the utmost the exchanging of experience.

Bob certainly has seen a lot of action and Bill undoubtedly will although I am still hoping that on account of his age, they may give him a break, in spite of being in

Herman Bosch

Herman Bosch with his son Bob around 1937. Photo courtesy of Victoria Kohler.

Herman Bosch, 1890–1944, passed away on Friday at his home at Eldred. He had been in ill health for about a year. He was a veteran of World War I. By trade he was an electric welder and was employed by the Sullivan County Highway Department.

Mr. Bosch was a son of William and Mary Maier Bosch, both deceased. He is survived by his wife Mary Horton Bosch; two sons Herman and Robert, and daughter Marjorie, all at home; brothers: Charles, Edward, and Menzo Bosch of Eldred; sisters: Lulu Lansmith, Little Neck, L.I.; Mrs. Matiltda Wicks of Corona, L.I., and Mrs. William Brodmerkel, of Eldred; also several nieces and nephews.

Funeral services were held at the Eldred Methodist Church at 2 p.m. following prayer services at his home, Monday afternoon. Rev. H.I. Briggs officiating the burial at the Eldred Cemetery. Delaware Valley Post No. 1020, American Legion, officiating at the grave.—*Newspaper article.*

good condition, 42 is far too old for a man in the infantry.

One of Bob's favorite souvenirs is a pay book with a piece of shrapnel embedded in it—just a minor close call that time.

Had dinner and supper with Bill, and his outfit certainly are fond of him. His Lieutenant, as well as many of the others, told me how well he was liked and how much they thought of him. He could have gotten off coming across, but he did not do it although he knows his chances of coming through safely are very slim. Foolish undoubtedly, but still a very good man for a brother. Art

Pfc. William Austin, Co. F, 338 Inf. A, to Mr. Charles R. Austin
April 6, 1944
Dear Brother,

Since I wrote you last, I have had a boat ride and am now somewhere in Italy.

A short time after I got here, I got in touch with Arthur through the Red Cross and talked to him over the telephone. He told me that Bob was in a hospital nearby. A couple days later he stopped in to see me and I got the afternoon off and we went to visit Bob.

I guess Bob's combat days are over as his right arm is in pretty bad shape. I am very much afraid that it will always be more or less crippled. He also has a touch of the yellow jaundice. He expects to be sent back to the states before long.

The war has sure left its mark on the country. Every meal there is always a bunch of children waiting along the mess lines for what the men have got left in their mess kits. Everywhere you see buildings that have been destroyed. I bet that generation of Italians have had enough of war.

Well, I will close now hoping that you and your family are well. Write when you get time.

Your brother, Bill

April 1944 in Eldred
In Eldred Earl Wells bought a cow from Goldie (the Austin brothers' cousin) for $90, on Sunday, April 9. Sherman McBride Jr. stopped by the Leavenworths for milk.

Wednesday Anna Meyers and her husband Bill Jr. went to the movies for the first time in six years.

Finally Raymond Austin received an official notice Bob had been wounded.

War Department, Washington, to Mr. Charles R. Austin
12 April 1944
Dear Mr. Austin:

It is with deep regret that I must confirm my recent telegram in which you were informed that your brother was wounded. As reports on our wounded are prepared under the adverse conditions of battle, they are of necessity brief and do not give the nature of the wound. It may be comforting to you to know that our soldiers are given the best possible medical care by some of this country's finest doctors who are assigned to the many excellent hospitals maintained at our overseas bases.

Theater Commanders submit periodic reports of progress on all hospitalized wounded, injured or seriously ill patients. Based on these reports, the War Department will keep you informed of his progress. In order that mail may reach him as soon as possible, you should use the following temporary address until he is released from the hospital or a change of address is furnished

1944 Halfway Brook News

New Owners of Spring House
- Alexander and Minnie Meyer Mills became the owners of Minnie's parents' Spring House Inn.

Highland Lake Bible Conference
- Formed by Merle Fuller in September, the Bible Conference would include the Myers' Lake View and Asendorf's Highland Lake Inn.

1944 Eldred Seniors
- Violet Markle, Eleanor Getz, Reta Kalin, Norma Wells, Betty Turner, Christina Hallock, Norma Ott, Edna Swartz, George Knight, Vernon Clark, Oakland Worzel, Kenneth Mills.

1944 Births
- Lois Kerr was born to Charles and Muriel Kerr.
- Ruth Ann Wilson was born to Ed and Agnes Mary Lucke Wilson.
- Clinton J. Guenther Jr. was born to Clinton J. and Marion Lass Guenther.

1944 Weddings
- John Ort married Ella Hulse.
- Robert Clinton Hallock, son of Edna May Hill and Oliver L. Hallock, married Doris Estler, in New Jersey.
- William Henry Parker Jr. married Mary Whalen in Canajoharie, N.Y.
- Ed Purcell married Gladys (Billie) Billings, July 1, 1944, at St. Ann's Church in Shohola. Ed served in the U.S. Air Force as a First Lieutenant and earned the Distinguished Flying Cross.
- Joe Mellan married Mary Paulik, in October, in Paterson, N.J.

1944 Commendation
- Arthur Wood, husband of Ada Britt, received a letter of recognition for 40 years of service at the Navy Yard from the Secretary of the Navy, James Forestal. Arthur would continue to serve until he retired in 1949.

1944 Wounded
- Bob Austin wounded in February.
- Bob Grotecloss seriously wounded.

1944 Deaths
- James K. Gardner, 1861–1944, was the son of Stephen St. John and Louisa McElroy Gardner. He was the father of Edna Gardner, and great-grandson of James Eldred.
- Elizabeth G. Mills, 1869–1944.
- Walter Oset died at the Battle of Normandy.
- Veronica Pope Clouse, 1882–1944.
- William Deats, 1879–1944.
- William G. Wilson, 1877–1944.
- Ezra McBride, 1896–1944.
- Herman Bosch, 1890–1944, good friend of Lon and Aida Austin, died of leukemia.
- Katherine Greening Kerr, 1873–1944, had 16 grandchildren.
- Daniel Wicks died in France. He was a Bosch descendant.
- Jennie Hull, sister of Anna Hull Sergeant, died in October.
- Edith Palmer Ewart, granddaughter of Sherman B. and Charlotte Ingram Leavenworth, died.

William H. Parker Jr. married Mary Whalen. Photo courtesy of William H. Parker Jr.

Robert C. Hallock and his future bride Doris Estler. Photo courtesy of Carolyn Hallock Clark, daughter.

---

you. It is requested that you inform all interested relatives and friends.

It is my earnest hope that news of his release from the hospital will soon be forthcoming.

Sincerely yours, Robert H. Dunlop, Acting Adjutant General

The news was quickly passed along to Bob's uncle Garfield and aunt Ella; aunts Charlotte, Christina (who wrote to Raymond right away), and Anna; and most likely Aida and Lon Austin.

C. Hirsch, Eldred, to Raymond and Gladys Austin, Staten Island

Archie and (Aunt) Minnie Sergeant Myers. Photo courtesy of Chuck Myers, son.

"Charles Myers is at Camp Shelby now." Photo courtesy of Chuck Myers.

Lt. Jim Purcell, "the pretty good pilot." Photo courtesy of Jim Purcell, son of Ed Purcell.

April 13, 1944
Dear Gladys and Raymond,

Have intended to write ever since we received your card and invitation to visit you. Aunt Charlotte is on her Easter vacation and Martin and I are pretty much alone, so now I'm going to get caught up on letters.

Orville Myers stopped in yesterday to tell me about the telegram that came about Bob. I hope you get word soon from him that it isn't so bad—it's almost too much to expect all three to come through safely, but we can hope. Arthur has been under the impression that Bob's outfit was having a tough time and hoped he would be sent home on a well earned furlough.

For the past few weeks I've intended writing all three boys—I write rather frequently to Bill and Art, but never have to Bob as he never has sent me any kind of correspondence, but I realize when he was growing up I was away and I really was a stranger to him and when Aunt Charlotte left she took all three addresses as she too had planned to write. We were sure Bob would be glad to receive a couple of unexpected letters, but now I don't know if I should write him or not—he probably will be moved far from his present or last address.

Bob Grotecloss also has been seriously wounded. I believe he is being sent home.

Charlee was home for Easter Sunday. Tony [her stepson] and Lily [Tony's wife] also Lily's mother and sister came.

I guess you know Clifford Myers is helping me this year. He is a good worker and just like one of the family to have around.

He hasn't been able to get six days in any week since he started. So much rain.

Isn't it nice that you got moved farther into the country before hot summer weather?

Will you have a little garden plot? It would be nice for the girls to work in to get a nice coat of tan. Your dad [Ed Myers] must like it where you are now Gladys, for he didn't usually make two trips in the winter, did he?

We were quite amused yesterday by a plane flying low and dipping, I suppose saluting. No one knew who it was then, but today we heard it was Jim Purcell of Barryville. I would call him "a pretty good pilot." Clifford thought it might be Ed Toaspern at the time, for he swooped low over him.

I guess you get most of Eldred news through Emma and Barryville news through Orville and his wife.

Charles Myers is at Camp Shelby now and Aunt Minnie [Chuck's mother] went to Binghamton on Monday to bring her Aunt Carrie Morre, a very old lady, home with her for the summer. Aunt Minnie was quite a sick person last winter and glad she is picking up so fast.

I often feel like calling you up to have a little visit. But I'd have to call after ten in the evening as our line is very busy up to that time and there wouldn't be much privacy. I wouldn't mind anyone

1944 World and National News

January 1944
- American Troops landed in New Guinea.
- Allied forces landed at Anzio, Italy. Battle: January 22–May 24, 1944.
- Jan. 30 to Feb. 23: U.S. captured the Marshall Islands from the Japanese.

February 1944
- February–May 18: Battle for Monte Cassino in Italy.

March 1944
- U.S. started bombing Berlin.
- Allied planes bombed Cassino, Italy.

April 1944
- The Red Army took Yalta.
- Hollandia in Dutch New Guinea was captured by the Allies.

May 1944
- Monte Cassino, Italy, finally fell.

June 1944
- June 4, 1944: U.S. troops entered Rome. Germans retreated into major defense lines.
- June 6, D-Day, Operation Overlord: American, British, Canadian forces invaded France at the beaches of Normandy; 180,000 Allied troops ashore. The Allied death toll was 2,500—1,000 at Omaha Beach.
- Battle of Philippine Sea.
- U.S. Army Air Force B-29s raided Japan.

July 1944
- Roosevelt ran for fourth term.
- Japanese Prime Minister Tojo resigned.
- Marines landed in Guam. Battle of Guam: July 21–Aug. 10.
- N. France Battle: July 25–Sep. 14.

August 1944
- Polish army tried to expel Germans. Up to 250,000 Polish civilians killed.
- Anne Frank, a 14-year-old Jewish girl in hiding with her family in Amsterdam since July 1942, was betrayed to the Gestapo.
- Men of Patton's 3rd Army raced towards the ports of Brittany.
- U.S. troops retook Guam.
- Romania surrendered to the Russians. Its oil fields Germany's only source of natural oil.
- August 25: Paris was liberated.

September 1944
- Brussels liberated.
- Northern Apennines: September 10, 1944–April 4, 1945.
- Finland and Bulgaria surrendered to the Russians.
- Roosevelt and Churchill in Québec; planned a strategy against Japan.
- Rhineland: September 15, 1944–March 21, 1945.

October 1944
- In Washington D.C. the Allies agreed to set up United Nations.
- Athens liberated.
- Rommel killed himself with poison.
- U.S. troops began invasion of Philippines by taking on Leyte Island. Gen. MacArthur waded ashore on Leyte saying, "I have returned."
- Battle of Leyte Gulf in Philippines: U.S. fleet defeated the Japanese. Japanese Navy began to use Kamikaze suicide pilots.

November 1944
- B-29 bombers begin to bomb Tokyo from bases in the Mariana Islands.
- President Roosevelt re-elected to fourth term.

December 1944
- December 16, 1944–January 25, 1945: Battle of the Bulge.
- December 22: Fierce fighting raged in the Battle of the Bulge. Several thousand lightly armed men of the 28th infantry and 10th and 101st U.S. Airborne Division were trapped in a network of roads and besieged by the Germans who surrounded the town of Bastogne. The Germans sent a courier with an ultimatum for the Americans to surrender, or be annihilated. The reply of General Anthony C. McAuliffe, acting commander of the 101st Airborne Division, was typed and delivered to the Germans.

To the German Commander. NUTS! The American Commander.

The 101st held off the Germans until the 4th Armored Division arrived on December 26. Fred Ihlo's 37th Tank Battalion (spearhead of the 4th Armored) was in the first group to relieve the 101st.

---

listening, but to have them ring in while talking about burns me up. I know who it was the last time you called us. Just a kid trying to get a number for someone else.

It's so cold and windy tonight. Hard to realize that it's near middle of April. Our coal is gone and when it's so windy, I'm afraid to open up drafts so the stoves aren't throwing off much heat.

Do you expect to come up to Eldred this summer? If you do, would love to have you and family up to spend the day with me. If I got to town oftener, I'd know more news to write, but I haven't even had a paper or mail for two days. If it's clear tomorrow, Clifford will bring mail on his way up.

Hope you are all well and that we hear encouraging news about Bob. With love to all,
Aunt Christina

Christina Hirsch mentioned her daughter Charlee who worked

American vehicles of the 5th Army pass the ancient Coliseum as they begin to occupy Rome, Italy. June 5, 1944. National Archives and Records Administration (111-SC-190312) courtesy of wwiiarchives.net.

for General Electric in Bridgeport.

Perhaps this is the time that Jim Purcell's brothers Ed and Andrew were also home on leave. Andy was on leave from San Antonio Aviation Cadet Center, Texas. Lt. James P. Purcell was on leave from the Pacific. Lt. Ed Purcell was home on a short leave from Langley Field, Virginia.

Ed Toaspern (the other possible pilot mentioned in Christina's letter) had been at San Diego Naval Air Station since March 20, 1944. In October Ed would be able to get a letter past the censors so his parents could learn about Ed's piloting adventures during 1944.

In Islip on Thursday, April 20, Anna cleaned part of her front room and chopped wood. She had a "very welcome letter" from Bill Austin explaining that his brother Bob's arm had been badly wounded.

On Friday Anna mailed letters to her three Austin nephews at the Islip Post Office. She also did her week's shopping.

Sunday Anna rested—if you call cooking a lamb stew dinner and writing a long letter to her nephew Arthur resting.

In Eldred on Tuesday, April 25, Lee Hansen went to Poughkeepsie to work for the De Laval Company (which made dairy and milking machines). Friday Ella fixed Madelyn Meyers' Scout dress.

Bob Austin Heads to the U.S.
The second day of May Bob Austin departed for the U.S., where his address was: England General Hospital, Atlantic City, New Jersey. It would be some time before Bob's arm healed and it would never be strong enough for work.

After twenty-two months in combat, Bob Austin finally got back to the States where he was awarded two purple hearts with three battle stars and honorably discharged with a total disability pension.

He lived the rest of his life extremely unpretentiously, to say the least, even managing to save a little each month from his meager pension.—Walter Geier.

May 1944 in New York
Monday, May 1, Martin was at his brother Garfield's for a while. Garfield and Ella's dog Old Bear was killed by a car on Wednesday. They buried Old Bear in the pasture below the house.

— DEDICATORY PROGRAM —

MARCH—"Old Glory" . . . . . Eldred Central School Band
INVOCATION . Father Adrian, Pastor Yulan Catholic Church
PLEDGE OF ALLEGIANCE TO THE FLAG
　　　　　　　　　　Led by Boy Scout William Lass
STAR SPANGLED BANNER (Sung by All)
　　　　　　　　　　Eldred Central School Band
UNVEILING OF ROLL OF HONOR, TOWN OF HIGHLAND
　Delaware Valley Post No. 1020, American Legion,
　Arthur N. Meyers of Narrowsburg in charge of Ceremonies
OUR PART AS CIVILIANS . . . . . Principal Karl D. Ebers
LINCOLN'S GETTYSBURG ADDRESS . . George Knight, Jr.
MUSIC—Intrepidant Overture . . Eldred Central School Band
ADDRESS . . . . Honorable Sydney F. Foster
AMERICA (Sung by All) . . . . . Eldred Central School Band
TAPS . . . . Henry Rave and John Briggs
RETREAT . . . . "　　"　　"　　"
TO THE COLORS . . . . "　　"　　"　　"
　　(Lowering of Flag by Legion)
BENEDICTION . . . . Rev. Irwin Briggs
　　　Pastor Barryville and Eldred Methodist Churches

May 30, 1944 Honor Roll Program for the Town of Highland. From the collection of Mary Briggs Austin.

Wednesday in Islip when the forsythia were in full bloom, Anna started some major spring cleaning. After two days in which she had washed all day, worked in her asparagus bed, ironed, and mowed the lawn, she concluded she had accomplished nothing. Anna continued her cleaning mode through Monday. Finally she was, "Tired at night."

In Eldred there was a $40 money order in the letter Ella received from Jim on Monday, May 8. Mary Sergeant and Myrtle Hill visited with Ella on Wednesday.

The second week of May in Islip, Anna was busy outdoors getting her lawn "under subjection."

Sunday, May 14, Bob Austin arrived in the U.S.

In Eldred Buck McBride plowed Lee Hansen's garden on Monday. Thursday Clara and Ella each sent $4 to the *Daily News* for a one-year subscription.

On Thursday in Islip Anna walked to the Islip Post Office and "mailed Army letters." The next week she transplanted sunflowers, zinnias, digitalis, and phlox.

In Eldred Thursday, May 25, Christina Hirsch gave her niece Anna some asparagus. Friday Anna's sister Clara went to Clara Wolff's for a permanent. Anna Ort stopped in to say hello to Ella.

Monday Mr. Lochner worked on the Leavenworth's plumbing for three days. Apparently Anthony had things wrong and it all had to be ripped out. The charge was $35.92.

Wednesday Lee Hansen left for Poughkeepsie. Goldie and Stella left for Lordville where Goldie worked for the railroad.

Wednesday evening there was a special program which honored those from the Town of Highland who were serving their country.

Smiling Italians approve the Allied entry into Rome. 5th Army. Rome area, Italy. 5 June 1944. National Archives and Records Administration, College Park, Maryland (111-SC-190313) courtesy of wwiiarchives.net.

Rome at last
The Gustav Line was finally broken. June 5, 1944, the U.S. troops entered Rome.

Lost in the Catacombs
Arthur Austin arrived in Rome with the 5th Army. He and his friend decided to visit the Catacombs. They managed to persuade the guard on duty to let them explore where the early Christians had hid.

There was no electricity in the area, so there was no lighting in the Catacombs. But Art's friend said not to worry as he had been a Boy Scout.

When they passed the same area more than once, Art decided he'd have to go with a better plan or they'd never get out. Since the men weren't supposed to have been allowed there, Art figured no one would look for them in that location. Art reached up over his head and found the electric wires that were used to light the place before the war. He hung on to and followed the wires, until finally they found their way out.

Battle of Normandy, June 6–30
Rome had fallen. It was time to free France in the Battle of Normandy (Operation Overlord) and not without a huge cost of lives. Mary Oset Bornstein would receive the grim news that her son Walter Oset was one of several thousand Allied troops who died in the landing on the beaches of Normandy. His body was never found.

June 1944, New York
The second week of June Garfield and his daughter Anna papered their bathroom and kitchen. Stella and Goldie were there one day. Goldie helped his dad put the ceiling on the north room. Stella and Goldie were home for good.

Anna of Islip picked eight quarts of strawberries and had shortcake for several of her

Crowds of French patriots line the Champs Élysées to view Allied tanks and half tracks pass through the Arc de Triomphe, after Paris was liberated on August 25, 1944. Photographer: Jack Downey; Library of Congress Prints and Photographs Division LC-DIG-fsac-1a55001.

friends the second week of June. Another day she cooked beef for a picnic dinner at Walken's, but did not enjoy the dinner because of the anti-Jewish opinions. Anna was still depressed about the comments the next day. She wrote to her nephews Bill and Arthur.

Thursday, June 15, Ella recorded the day's news, "Bombed Japan today. Stella, Goldie, Mrs. Clark and Doug Hallock in."

Task Force 58
Ensign Ed Toaspern reported to the Carrier Replacement Pool on Eniwetok Navy Base in the Marshall Islands on Tuesday, June 20. He awaited assignment to active duty with one of the Air Groups in Task Force 58. Task Force 58 was the main striking force of the U.S. Navy in the Pacific Ocean Theatre from January 1944 through the end of the war in August of 1945.

Elizabeth Mills Dies
In Highland Lake Mrs. George Mills died on Wednesday, June 21. Elizabeth Gillespie Mills had been an amazing woman. When her husband George Mills died in February of 1909, Elizabeth was left with six children ages 4 to 15 to raise by herself. Her children at the time of her death: Isabel Stalker, James Mills, Agnes Mills, Alexander Mills, Dr. George Ross Mills and Margaret (Peggy) Rasmussen.

July 1944
Saturday, July 1, in Islip, Anna talked to her nephew Bob Austin.

Sunday in Eldred Garfield was up to Lee Hansen's to help him with the dam at the beaver swamp. On Wednesday Garfield made a lawn chair for Ella.

Wednesday, July 12, was very hot in Islip. Anna bought a bushel of beans and stayed up until 11:30 p.m. canning. She received a letter from Bill Austin.

In Eldred Sunday, July 15, Stella and Goldie visited his parents. Goldie left for a week in Elmira.

Wednesday, July 19, Anna in Islip stayed up past midnight listening to the Democratic Convention.

In Eldred Mrs. Mary Ort was in the hospital on Friday.

Thursday, July 27, Ella got a letter from her sister Hazel and a snap (picture) in Jim's letter.

August 1944
Monday, August 7, Mr. Briggs and his son John visited Garfield and Ella. Iva Eldridge Foster also stopped by.

Sunday, August 13, Goldie and Stella stopped by his sister Anna's house for eggs. So did Buck McBride.

Wednesday Ella got a letter from Jim and one from her sister Hazel. Anna and Jimmy Meyers visited Ella the next day.

It was so very hot in Islip that Anna slept on the porch that night. The next day Anna made tomato lemon preserve and wrote to Bob Austin and Gladys Austin.

In the Pacific Ensign "Smiley" Toaspern reported for duty aboard the light aircraft carrier, *U.S.S. Cabot* on August 22, and participated in strikes on Palau and the Philippines.

Friday, August 25, was a cool, pleasant day in Islip. Anna dug up the ground to plant strawberries and irrigated. She baked bread and pie and received a "good letter from Bobby."

Liberation of Paris
"Paris free from Nazis," wrote Ella on Friday, August 25. And indeed that was the news. And super news it was.

Garfield and Ella's son Jim walked on the Champs-Élysées that very Friday, when American and Free French troops made a peaceful entrance.

Jim seems to have been stationed at Bourget Airport in France next. Within six months he would be transferred to the Villacoublay Air Base, in Villacoublay, France. There he would meet…but that is getting ahead of the story.

1944 Boarding Houses

Tallwood Lodge from the air. Photo courtesy of Lillian Hainzl Wolff.

Arial view of Green Acres. Photo courtesy of Diane Pankow.

Barryville

Laurel Brook Cottage, A.D. Burgess
Barryville 2372. Acc. 60. Modern impts. Handball, shuffleboard, recreation hall; swimming pool, table tennis, good food. Near churches.

Tallwood Lodge, Frank Hainzl Phone 2128. New modern house, 100 acres of pine woods, lake, all athletic sports. New innerspring mattresses. Near churches. Kitchen.

A wonderful vacation for short or extended holidays, offering every convenience and comfort, 1,500 feet above sea level, located within 92 miles of New York City, "Where the Catskills and Poconos meet the Delaware."

Here guests live in a picturesque setting amid the whispering pines and have a beautiful country estate for a playground. The climate is delightfully healthful and invigorating, offering relief to hay fever sufferers. Our rate schedule reflects the earnest efforts we have made to keep them as low as possible, consistent with our high standards of food and service.

The Hotel has five open fireplaces and automatic heat. Annex and Main House overlook the lake and trout stream; immaculately kept, cheerful rooms with private or conveniently located baths and showers; hot and cold running water in all rooms. Pure, crystal clear water from our artesian wells. A hearty welcome awaits you.
—Tallwood Flyer.

Yulan

Sunset Cottage
Tel. Barryville 2741; Modern house, located directly on Washington Lakefront. Hot and cold running water in every room, shower. Artesian well water. Boating, bathing, fishing, dancing, handball court and other amusements. Churches nearby. Rates $22 and $24 per week.

Colonial, Jack Hensel
On lake. Boating, bathing, fishing, running water all rooms.
Ph: Barryville 2622.

Washington Beach Hotel, W.T. Tether
Six furnished bungalows to rent.

The Maplecrest, Yulan, R. Walter
On lake. New house; hot, cold running water, showers. Innerspring mattresses. Handball, ping-pong, boating, bathing; apply for rates. Near Catholic Church. Ph: Barryville 2629.

Highland Lake

Deer Head Lodge, K. Eggers
New modern, inexpensive. July to Labor Day, $28 up. Famous for fine food. Boating, fishing, swimming, shuffleboard, handball, tennis, golf, horseback, dancing. All conveniences. Near all churches.

Washington Beach Hotel. Photo courtesy of Ivan J. and Jana Tether.

Jim Leavenworth at the Bourget Airfield in France. Photo courtesy of Gisele Rouillon Leavenworth.

Villacoublay Air Base
In June 1940 the Germans had seized Villacoublay Air Base, the French Air Force facility.

The Villacoublay Air Base was liberated by Allied ground forces August 27, 1944, and soon cleared of the mines on the base by the 818th Engineer Aviation Battalion, who also destroyed the Luftwaffe aircraft and filled in the bomb craters and cleared away the rubble on the runway. It was "A-42" by August 30. Almost immediately, the 48th Fighter Group moved into the repaired air base, flying P-47 Thunderbolts from August 29 until September 15, 1944…Villacoublay became a supply and maintenance base for combat aircraft.—wikipedia.org

Now the thrust of the war in Europe was of course the defeat of Germany. A number of Town of Highland people—including Clifford Crandall, Whipple Bosch, Russell MacKechnie, Fred DeFeo Jr., and Fred Ihlo, future husband of Frances Toaspern—would be involved in the next crucial battle in Europe.

Clifford Crandall was with the 100th Infantry Division which went into Europe through Marseilles, France, and Crailsheim, Germany. The 67th Regiment of the 2nd Armored Division (which Whipple Bosch was in) was or would soon be deployed. Fred DeFeo Jr. was with the 106th Infantry.

September 1944
Sunday, September 3, Ella sold $20 worth of crocheted pieces.

Monday was a very quiet Labor Day in Eldred. It was warm in Islip and Anna canned eggplant and made watermelon rind preserves. Tuesday she received a letter from her nephew Bill Austin.

Wednesday, September 13, 1944, in Mindanao, Philippines, Ed Toaspern was credited with two aerial victories.

Thursday there were cyclones all along the Eastern coast of the U.S. It grew to a tornado by 10 p.m. In Islip Anna heard the garage door blow open and had a sleepless night. In Eldred Ella's phone was dead all day.

Friday Anna wrote that the morning in Islip was "calm, but what destruction: electric off, trees down, garage door badly damaged, glass on one side gone, twigs and branches all over the ground."

Monday, September 18, in Eldred, Mr. Briggs called at the Leavenworth home. Tuesday the first issue of *Post* came. Ella also got a V-mail from Jim saying he had been moved. He was quite possibly in Villacoublay, France.

Anna in Islip wrote Bob Austin and Melva Austin on Tuesday. Mr. Carey was there and appraised the damage to her garage.

Ed Toaspern, Philippines
Thursday, September 21, 1944, in Luzon, Philippines, Ed Toaspern was credited with two aerial victories. He destroyed one plane on the ground and scored a direct bomb hit on a large building.

1944 Clifford Crandall in Germany. Photo courtesy of the Clifford Crandall Family.

Jim Leavenworth in France. Photo courtesy of Cynthia Leavenworth Bellinger.

No Letters from Jim

Garfield and Ella received no letters from Jim from September 26 through October 23. They were understandably very worried since Jim had been writing so often.

In October Ed Toaspern updated his folks as to what had happened that year.

Ed Toaspern, to Walt and Emma Straub Toaspern, Barryville
October 1944
Dear Folks,

For some time I have been trying to let you know the how and why of all my actions since leaving the states. Although none of this has any bad effects as to security, strict censorship would not allow it to go thru.

The place to start is at the beginning which brings me to Pearl Harbor. A very pleasant place indeed, very much like the states with every convenience and a few things that are rationed in the states.

I started flying F6Fs [Hellcats] as a replacement pilot and got in enough time including carrier qualification. After this the usual procedure is to be assigned to a Squadron and go aboard a carrier.

Instead of this, we flew to Majuro to ferry planes from there to Eniwetok [large coral atoll of 40 islands in the Pacific Ocean]. We stayed there from May 28 to June 20, and then were given orders to Eniwetok (Navy 3237). From here we were assigned to go aboard a small carrier which took replacement planes and pilots to where the fleet was in operation, which at that time happened to be Saipan. They needed planes, but no pilots, so we returned to Eniwetok and were put in the replacement pool there waiting for assignment to a carrier squadron.

Ed Toaspern, pilot from Barryville. Photo courtesy of Bill Ihlo.

We flew FM-2s (the old wildcat souped up) while waiting and I got into some trouble flathatting [buzzing people, buildings, etc. on the ground, well below safe levels and also at full speed] which almost cost me my wings. I finally got into a squadron (my first) about the middle of August and this has been the most enjoyable part of my whole tour of duty.

The squadron is VF-31 which at this writing I am still with.

September was quite a busy month and we were in the first strikes on Palau and the Philippines. I was very lucky and managed to shoot down four enemy planes for which I have been recommended for 2 DFCs [Distinguished Flying Cross].

Lt. J.G. Nooy (Connie) was my section leader, one of the finest pilots and an all round swell guy.

"Connie" has 15 planes to his credit, top man in the squadron and almost top man out here. I believe some pilot has around *19 or so, but he's from another carrier.*

Connie has been trying to drum some combat sense into my head and without his teaching I wouldn't have had nearly as good a chance. His personal interest and instruction helped me no end to overcome the inexperience which is prevalent with all new pilots.

The way things stand now, our squadron is in the process of being relieved to go back to the States. I have only had two months with the Squadron which is not enough time to go back with the Squadron; so I'll get off at Pearl Harbor and be sent to another squadron to get in the required four months combat time.

That brings things up to present and I hope it clarifies any doubts you may have had. As for mail, I realize that very often you will not hear from me for quite some time. This is due

Fred DeFeo Jr. Photo courtesy of Pam Fischetti DeFeo.

Fred and Pearl Owen DeFeo

Fred DeFeo Jr. wrote his parents, Fred and Pearl DeFeo, several letters. Fred and Pearl still lived in New York City. (You may remember that Pearl was the daughter of William and Phoebe Owen who had run Oakdene.) After the war my parents would visit them in New York City.

Cpl. F. DeFeo, 423 Inf., Camp Atterbury, Ind., to P. DeFeo, N.Y.

October 3, 1944
Dear Mom and Dad,

I received your package and also your letters. I hope you got the birthday card. If not, I want to wish you happy birthday anyway.

We still have been very busy and last night we had another inspection. We won't be here much longer, so keep your fingers crossed as I may get a chance to come home.

By the way, did you get any bonds lately? I started paying for them in August. I took a $25 allotment out this month so I guess you will get it next month.

Well, Mom, I guess by the

Fred and Pearl Owen DeFeo. Photo courtesy of Pam Fischetti DeFeo.

Alice DeFeo Riker, sister of Fred DeFeo Jr. Photo courtesy of Pam Fischetti DeFeo.

time you answer this I will be on my way, but you write anyway and they will forward it to me. Don't forget if anything happens I love you all and miss you.

I am as ever
Your Loving son, Fred

Fred may have had a chance to go home before he went overseas. There was a photo of Fred and one of his sister Alice Riker taken in a similar location.

October 1944

In Eldred Tuesday, October 3, Ella sent Christmas boxes to Orville Clark and Grant Sergeant.

In Islip on Tuesday Anna mailed a package overseas. She received a letter from Arthur.

In Eldred three tons of coal ($35.55) were delivered to Garfield and Ella's home on Wednesday.

Wednesday in the Pacific Ed Toaspern was rotated out of

---

to my being aboard ship where letters don't get mailed very often, so don't worry about that. Another thing is not to send any packages, because my address keeps changing so often that they will never reach me.

I imagine you are wondering how this letter is being mailed. Connie is taking it back to the states with him to mail it from there so it wouldn't have to go thru the censors. Incidentally, Connie lives out on Long Island only a short distance from where Aunt Rose stayed while out on the Island.

As soon as it is known, I will give you my new Squadron address and then I hope my mail catches up with me. I've had four letters since August 10th, so I figure there are some waiting.

Well, that amounts to about all I can think of for the present. I will continue to write whenever possible.

Love, Ed

Highland's WWII Service Roll

Barryville
- Wallace R. Austin, U.S. Army
- Emmet 'Steve' Barnes, U.S. Army
- Frank A. Bello, U.S. Army
- Clarence 'Sailor' Blaut, U.S. Army
- Clarence Bradley, U.S. Army
- Mary Briggs, Cadet Corps Nurse
- Adga D. Burgess, U.S. Army
- Charles W. Buser, U.S. Army
- Raymond A. Calkin Jr., U.S. Navy
- Joseph I. Clouse, U.S. Navy
- Raymond L. Clouse, U.S. Army
- Gordon Comstock, U.S. Army Air Forces
- Arthur 'Boo' Cordes, U.S. Army
- Lewis Eckhart, U.S. Army
- Peter C. Elvin, U.S. Army Air Forces
- John Fleiger, U.S. Army
- Everett C. Frey, U.S. Army Air Forces
- Elmer Getz, U.S. Army
- Clifford Hulse, U.S. Navy
- Kenneth F. Kelly, U.S. Army
- John 'Jack' Kerr, U.S. Navy
- William E. Koehler, U.S. Army
- Jay Lass, U.S. Army
- Sylvan S. Liebla, U.S. Navy
- John V. Liefert, U.S. Army
- Arthur W. Miller, U.S. Navy
- Frederick Miller, U.S. Army
- William B. Nieke, U.S. Army
- Maurice J. Nugent, U.S. Navy
- Robert E. O'Neill, U.S. Navy
- Richard Earl Palmer, U.S. Navy
- John H. Parker, U.S. Army
- Edmund Pepper, U.S. Army
- Thaddeus Z. Puchyr, U.S. Navy
- Andrew Purcell, U.S. Army Air Corps
- Edward Purcell, U.S. Army Air Forces
- James Purcell, U.S. Army Air Forces
- John Purcell, U.S. Army
- Richard 'Dick' Putnam, U.S. Army
- Thadeus 'Ted' Puycher, U.S. Navy
- Harvey G. Robinson, U.S. Army
- Lawrence H. Ross, U.S. Coast Guard
- John A. Rothacker, U.S. Army
- Charles Albert Sharkey, U.S. Navy
- James Smith, U.S. Navy

Lt. Ed Purcell. Photo courtesy of his son Jim Purcell.

Andy Purcell. Photo courtesy of Jim Purcell, son of Ed Purcell.

Ralph West. Photo courtesy of Lorraine West Daniels.

Chet Oset. Photo courtesy of Helen Hensel Oset.

Robert Wolff, April 1944. Photo Courtesy of Christene Stevens Myers.

Carl Dunlap. Photo courtesy of Carol Dunlap Brandau.

Sgt. Austin Decorated by Lt. Gen. Mark Clark

The Salerno Day Decoration ceremony which took place in the Tavernelle area, Italy, saw one of our county boys being decorated. The boy, M-Sgt, Arthur L. Austin of Eldred, N.Y., was presented with the Legion of Merit emblem by Lt. Gen. Mark W. Clark who is shown pinning the medal to Austin's tunic. Sgt. Austin is with the 5th Army Hqs. Photo and news article in the Austin Family Collection.

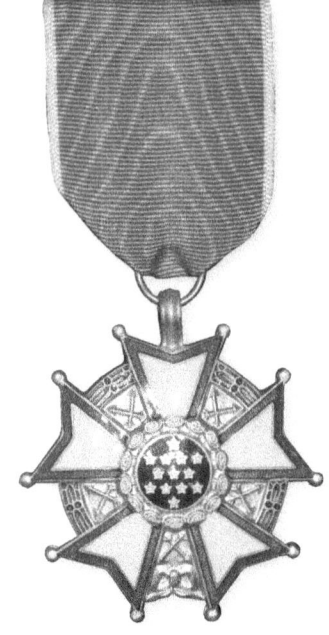

Arthur Austin's Legion of Merit Award courtesy of Mary Briggs Austin.

Arthur Austin received the Legion of Merit award at the Salerno Day Decoration Ceremony about a year after the Battle of Salerno. The Legion of Merit is the highest honor a non commissioned officer can achieve.

Presented to: Arthur L. Austin, Master Sergeant, Coast Artillery, Anti-Aircraft Section, Headquarters 5th Army, for exceptionally meritorious conduct in the performance of outstanding services.

As Chief Clerk, Operations, Anti-Aircraft Section, Headquarters 5th Army, from 1 February 1943 to 5 June 1944, Master Sergeant Austin's conduct and performance of duty have been exemplary and far above that expected of an enlisted man in a similar position. By his determined, tireless effort, initiative, deep interest, and desire to be of the greatest value to the service, he mastered every detail of the complicated operational function of the Anti-Aircraft Section.

He proved to be of inestimable value to the officers of the section in not only meticulously checking and rechecking every detail of maps, plans, and documents for all anti-aircraft operations, including the invasion of Italy, but throughout the entire period, he habitually, and as a matter of routine, carefully analyzed all papers for clarity of expression and meaning. Through his fine example and leadership he molded the enlisted men of his section into a smooth working team, and through his cheerful and cooperative attitude he gained the respect and cooperation of non commissioned officers of other sections in 5th Army Headquarters. Entered military service from Eldred, New York.

active duty, but kept in the Pacific theater.

Stella had a new phone on Tuesday, October 10. Ella received a package from Montgomery Ward and a letter from her sister Hazel.

The following Tuesday Arthur Austin received a Legion of Merit award from Lt. General Mark Clark at the Salerno Day Decoration Ceremony in Italy.

Jennie Hull's Death
Such a very sad time in Eldred for Ella Leavenworth. On Monday, October 16, Jim Mills and Mr. Wait were working on Jim's roof. Jim mentioned to Alex that he hadn't seen Jennie Hull (sister to Anna Hull Sergeant, Ella's stepmother) in a while.

Jim and Alex went to Jennie's place to check on her and found her dead on the kitchen floor.

On Tuesday Hazel (Ella's sister) and Walter Connor and their family arrived at 7 a.m. The whole family was there when their aunt Jennie was buried. Hazel and Walter left for their Massachusetts' home about 4:40 p.m.

Sunday, October 22, Stella, Goldie, and Vernon were at the Leavenworths. On Monday Clara

Highland's WWII Service Roll, cont'd.

Barryville cont'd.
- Rudolph H. Tessmer, U.S. Army
- Edward W. Toaspern, U.S. Navy
- Walter 'Bub' Toaspern, U.S. Navy
- John Traver, U.S. Navy
- Harry L. Tuthill, U.S. Army
- Theodore Vitanza, U.S. Navy
- John 'Ian' Warden, U.S. Army
- Calvina E. Weigele
- Charles Williams, U.S. Navy
- Francis Williams, U.S. Army
- John D. Williams, U.S. Army
- Robert C. Wolff, U.S. Army
- Irving Worzel, U.S. Merchant Marine

Yulan
- Paul Bodin, U.S. Army
- John Charles Cantwell, U.S. Navy
- Leonard Crandall, U.S. Army
- Kaska Kirby
- Klendin G. Kirby, U.S. Army
- Joseph McDonald, U.S. Navy
- Chester 'Chet' D. Oset, U.S. Navy
- Joseph Oset, U.S. Navy
- Stanley Oset, U.S. Navy
- Walter A. Oset, U.S. Navy
- Eugene Roberts, U.S. Army
- Carl Seitz, U.S. Navy
- Donald 'Sparky' Walter, U.S. Army
- Archie Warden, U.S. Army
- William J. Werneke, U.S. Army
- Daniel West
- Ralph West, U.S. Army
- Lawrence 'Larry' Wood, U.S. Army

Eldred
- Arthur Lawrence Austin, U.S. Army
- Robert Clinton Austin, U.S. Army
- William Sherman Austin, U.S. Army
- Ethel Barker, U.S. Marine Corps
- Franklin L. Bartle, U.S. Navy
- Orville Ernest Clark, U.S. Army
- Vernon Clark, U.S. Navy
- Clifford Crandall, U.S. Army
- Fred William DeFeo, U.S. Army
- Thomas Donaldson, U.S. Coast Guard
- Carl Dunlap, U.S. Army
- Charles Eldridge, U.S. Army

Raymond Hulse. Photo courtesy of his daughter Kathy Hulse Frisbie.

Franklin Bartle. Photo in the Leavenworth Collection.

Harry Haas. Photo courtesy of Berniece Wells Haas.

Mary Briggs, Cadet Corps Nurse. Photo courtesy of Mary Briggs Austin.

Howard Parker. Photo courtesy of William H. Parker Jr.

Vernon Clark. Photo courtesy of Vernon and Carolyn Hallock Clark.

and children were down for the day. Garfield was to town. You can imagine their concern when there was still no letter from Jim. He had last written the 24th of September.

But the next day, Tuesday, October 24, they received a letter Jim had written on September 4.

Thursday, October 26, Ed Toaspern was reassigned to VF-18 aboard the aircraft carrier, *U.S.S. Intrepid*.

November 1944

"F.D.R. in for four more years," wrote Ella on November 8, the day after the national election.

It has been quite some time since we have heard from Aida Austin. She wrote to her niece Melva Austin in November.

Aida Austin, Eldred, to Melva Austin, Staten Island
November 12, 1944
Dear Melva,

Quite a long time ago, I don't know just how long for I can't seem to keep track of the days and months anymore, when I was looking over some of my books and papers, I ran across a piece of poetry in an old scrapbook which I thought you would enjoy reading and have kept thinking I would copy it for you.

But the days slip by so quickly, I can't seem to accomplish only a small part of what I plan, so this morning I am letting my housework take care of itself while I write you a few lines and copy that piece of poetry for you.

Eldred went rather far afield election day, I think. But I see by the paper that we still have a Commander-in-Chief, so we need not be afraid of waking up some morning and finding the Rising Sun floating over us.

Tell mother, they plan to build a home on this place for orphans.

And tell her I will try to write to her some day this week and tell her about it. Love, Aunt Aida

From Highland Lake, Charlie Bosch wrote his son Willie.

Charlie Bosch, Highland Lake, to Willie Bosch, Queens, N.Y.
November 11, 1944

My road isn't plowed out yet. But the main road is. I'm home. Herman Jr. and Bobby were hunting with us. Herbie, Menzo, Herman, Bob, and myself. Might go out tomorrow if they come over. I have plenty of hulse [pun combining German word Holz *meaning wood and local Hulse family] and eats. It's just my dog Pippin and me here now. Hope you have a nice Thanksgiving Dinner. I'm invited to two places for dinner. Might go if not hunting. It took Herman and Bobbie two hours to get over here.*

Fred DeFeo Jr. in the center with two friends. Photo courtesy Pam Fischetti DeFeo.

Try and come up soon. No hunters here anymore. All went back with a long face.

Great Stuff. Pops

In Eldred Sunday, November 12, Lee Hansen gave Ella and Garfield a shepherd pup—perhaps it was their dog Judy.

Monday Fred DeFeo wrote his parents again.

Fred DeFeo Jr., to Mr. and Mrs. Fred DeFeo, N.Y.C., N.Y.
November 13, 1944
Dear Mom and Dad,

I am feeling fine and hope you are the same. I received a letter from you yesterday, the first one in a long time.

Enclosed you will find a money order for $100. Please take out the $40 you sent me and if you or dad need anything, well buy it with what's left over. If not, please start a joint bank account with what's left so we can both draw on it.

My allotment won't arrive until the beginning of December. I want you to take anything out you may need, and put the rest in the account. If you can convert the bonds into money, bank that also. I will try to send you a little each month. I would like a little money to look forward to when I get out of the Army as there is a couple of things I would like to do. I wish you would let me know if you get this letter with the money and understand what I have said.

Tell dad he better hurry up and get well because I can't be worrying about him, too.

Until next time,
All my love, Fred

Austins Visit Aunt Anna in Islip

Wednesday, November 15, Anna walked uptown to Islip and sent letters, a box, and Christmas cards

Highland's WWII, Service Roll, cont'd.

Eldred cont'd.

- William 'Bill' Eldridge, U.S. Army
- Joseph Foscola, Army
- Marcel C. Four, U.S. Army, 82nd Airborne
- Edgar F. Getz, U.S. Army Air Forces
- Anthony J. Goetke, U.S. Army
- Bennett Grotecloss, U.S. Merchant Marine
- Edward Greig Grotecloss, U.S. Army
- Robert Grotecloss, U.S. Army
- Harry G. Haas, U.S. Navy
- Maurice Haas, U.S. Army
- Richard Haas, U.S. Navy
- Eugene Hallock, U.S. Army Air Forces
- Robert C. Hallock, Eldred, U.S. Navy
- Frank Hill, U.S. Army
- Leroy 'Zip' Horton, U.S. Army
- Dewey Hulse, U.S. Army
- Raymond 'Ray' Hulse, U.S. Navy
- Thornton F. Jackson, U.S. Navy
- Fritz H. Kayser
- Helen C. Kuen, U.S. Army Nurse
- Arthur R. Lambert, U.S. Army
- James Leavenworth, U.S. Army Air Forces
- Evelyn MacIntyre
- William McBride, U.S. Army
- Harold Morgan, U.S. Navy
- Raymond Morgan, U.S. Army
- Charles 'Chuck' Myers, U.S. Army
- Martin D. Myers Jr., U.S. Navy
- Norman Myers, U.S. Army
- Thomas E. Myers, U.S. Navy
- James J. O'Connor, U.S. Marine Corps
- John Ort, U.S. Army
- Milton Davis Ort, U.S. Army
- William Ort Jr., U.S. Army
- Andrew Parker, U.S. Navy
- Howard Parker, U.S. Navy
- Warren Parker, U.S. Army
- William H. Parker, U.S. Navy
- Rowland 'Deac' Ramsey, U.S. Army
- Frederick W. Reuther, U.S. Army
- Burton Grant Sergeant, U.S. Army
- George L. Stolte, U.S. Army

Robert Hallock. Photo courtesy of Carolyn Hallock Clark.

Chuck Myers. Photo courtesy of Chuck Myers.

Helen Kuen. Photo courtesy of Sandy Sergeant McBride.

Clouse sons with their dad Herman Clouse. Photo courtesy of Veronica Clouse Rivera.

Fred DeFeo Jr. Photo courtesy Pam Fischetti DeFeo.

to Melva. The following Thursday she wrote to her sister Christina.

On Saturday, November 25, Anna (in Islip) got the bedrooms in "quite good order" for a visit from Gladys Austin and her three younger daughters, Joan, Margie, and Dawn Lee. Sunday Gladys, Joan, Margie, and Dawn Lee arrived on the 3:15 train, and enjoyed the turkey dinner their great-aunt Anna had cooked.

They left at noon on Monday when it was raining hard.

Great-Aunt Anna was a very kind, gentle woman, and she made magnificent Thanksgiving dinners. She had different games for us to play including Old Maid.—Joan Austin Geier.

And what is a nice visit without leaving something behind? On Tuesday Anna walked uptown to Islip and mailed Gladys' jacket and Joan's glasses to the Staten Island Austins.

Cpl. Nieke, 95th Inf. Division
Corporal William B. Nieke of

Glenn Miller Missing

As his band prepared to embark on a tour of Europe, Miller boarded a flight to Paris on December 15, 1944, to make preparatory arrangements for the rest of his group. Sadly, the transport on which Miller was a passenger disappeared over the English Channel and was never recovered. The disappearance of Miller's aircraft may have been caused by bad weather. However, records also suggest that bombs, jettisoned by Allied bombers returning from an aborted mission, may have inadvertently struck the plane.—*glennmiller.com/about/bio2.htm.*

Dawn Lee, Joan, and Margie Austin, 1944. Photo courtesy of Dawn Lee Austin Segarra.

Barryville was with the 95th Infantry in the 3rd Army under Lt. General Patton. Thanks to the "Iron Men of Metz," as the 95th Infantry Division was known, Metz in eastern France (about 100 miles south of Luxembourg, Belgium) was secured on November 22. Corporal Nieke would receive a commendation letter from Lt. Gen. Patton in April of 1945.

Ed Toaspern, Ace Status
Ed Toaspern, aboard the *U.S.S. Intrepid*, achieved Ace status on November 25, 1944, with his fifth aerial victory which he shot down over Nichols Field in the Philippines. The same day the *U.S.S. Intrepid* was hit by a Kamikaze (airstrike suicide attack by Japanese) pilot and badly damaged. Ed's flight log was burned up in the attack. The Intrepid was sent to California for repairs. Ed had a furlough from December 1944 to January 1945.

In Eldred on Thursday, November 30, Ella's phone had been out of order for nine days.

December 1944
Saturday, December 2, all the Leavenworth children (except of course Jim who Ella had not heard from all week) and grandchildren were in for supper. Orville Clark's girlfriend Mary Weisshaar visited that evening along with Goldie and Stella.

Tuesday, December 5, Garfield drew hay from the Wait barn.

Finally on Wednesday Ella got a letter from Jim and a bonus of a card from Arthur Austin.

Oh my, on Monday, Dick had the measles. Thursday Ella had "such dizzy spells all day. They sort of scare me."

Battle of the Bulge
Bill Eldridge was in one of the last trucks to escape the Germans at what came to be known as the Battle of the Bulge.

The battle raged in Europe from December 16, 1944 to January 25, 1945. Hitler launched an attack with over 200,000 troops in Ardennes, Belgium, a rugged, heavily forested area with poor roads. The Allied front (which stretched some 75 miles from southern Belgium into Luxembourg) held, but was pushed back in a broad semicircle or bulge (hence the name).

Fred Ihlo was HQ Company Commander of the 37th Tank Battalion, 4th Armored Division, spearhead of Patton's 3rd Army in Europe. They would be the first group to relieve the 101st caught in Germany's deadly trap.

*Patton's 3rd Army had to disengage from their winter battle in Alsace, make a 90 degree turn, and advance 120 miles to Bastogne during severe winter weather, including snow and ice. For these and subsequent actions, the 4th Armored would be awarded a Presidential Unit Citation in March 1945.
—Bill Ihlo.*

Highland's WWII Service Roll, cont'd.

Eldred cont'd.
- Frank Strenglein, U.S. Army
- Harry Strenglein, U.S. Army
- Clifford Sulzbach, U.S. Army Air Force
- Ernest Timerhoff, U.S. Army
- Archie Von Ohlen, U.S. Army
- Gordon 'Mick' White, U.S. Army
- Jack Williams, U.S. Army
- Forrest 'Pat' Wilson, U.S. Army
- Robert G. Wilson, U.S. Army Air Force
- Raymond Wolff, U.S. Navy
- Frank Yutz, U.S. Navy
- Paul G. Zimmermann, U.S. Navy

Highland Lake
- George Andersen, U.S. Army
- Henry Bosch, U.S. Army
- William Boyd, U.S. Merchant Marine
- Edward Brodmerkel, U.S. Army
- George Clouse, U.S. Army
- Herman Clouse, U.S. Army
- Ralph Clouse, Army
- Theodore Clouse, U.S. Army
- Barney Dankwardt, U.S. Army
- Eugene W. Gilmore Jr., U.S. Army
- Russell William MacKechnie
- John Meyer, U.S. Navy
- Joseph P. Meyer, U.S. Army
- Raymond C. Meyer, U.S. Army
- Fred Meyer, U.S. Army
- Frank 'Mac' O'Donnell, U.S. Army
- Art Staubes, Merchant Marine
- Al Whitney, U.S. Army

Minisink Ford
- Anthony J. Carmeci Sr., U.S. Army
- Cecil Vollmer, U.S. Army

Others
- Walter Campbell, U.S. Army
- Ella Getz served as a nurse in Italy
- Adolph Kalin, U.S. Army
- Henry H. Koch, U.S. Army
- William Turash, U.S. Army
- Robert Rauer, Johnstown, N.Y., stepfather of Richard Bellinger.
- *—Many names from wwiimemorial.com which had major contributions from Kevin Marrinan. Also see pp. 337, 458.*

Clifford Crandall. Photo courtesy of the Clifford Crandall Family.

Robert Rauer. Photo courtesy of Richard Bellinger.

Fred DeFeo Jr. and friend. Photo courtesy of Pam Fischetti DeFeo.

Jim Leavenworth. Photo courtesy of Gisele Rouillon Leavenworth.

Edward Toaspern on Furlough

Ensign Ed Toaspern recently reported back to San Francisco after spending a 27-day furlough at his home in Barryville. Before his furlough, Ensign Toaspern was on a tour of duty as pilot of a Navy fighter based on one of the Navy's big carriers in the Pacific.

Attached to Air Group 18 he flew a Grumman Hellcat and is credited with having knocked down five Japanese planes in addition to scoring nine bomb hits of Japanese shipping. Having seen action under enemy fire, Ed is now up for citation of the Distinguished Service Cross.

His squadron, officially known as the *Fighting 18* but referred unofficially as *Two-a-day 18*, shot down the amazingly large number of 172 enemy planes—an average of better than two a day.

In addition, Fighting 18 has destroyed over 200 planes on the ground, sunk one destroyer, beached another destroyer, knocked out 31 merchant ships, destroyed a great many ground installations and bombed and strafed many other Japanese warships including a large carrier and two big battleships.

His squadron leading ace is Lieutenant Cecil E. Harris who has shot down a total of 24 Japanese planes, to become the country's second highest scoring carrier pilot of planes shot down.—*News article* when Ed was home on leave December 1944 to January 1945.

Ed Toaspern on furlough at his parents' home in Barryville. Photo courtesy of Linda Guenther Anderson.

"They'll do it every time" by Jimmy Hatlo. Postcard sent to Bill Austin who was sick with yellow jaundice and in the hospital. Postcard courtesy of the Austin Family.

Christmas 1944

In Eldred on Sunday, Christmas Eve, Ella noted, "Children all in for Santa in the evening."

Christmas in Islip was rainy and warm. Anna had Christmas dinner at a Mrs. O'Shea's home. "Had a very pleasant time, but war puts a damper on everything."

In Eldred there was rain and sleet all day on Christmas, but that did not stop the Leavenworth children and grandchildren from joining their parents for dinner. They started a 1,000-piece jigsaw puzzle in the evening which was finished on Saturday.

Friday, December 29, was very cold and blustery in Islip. Anthony Hirsch arrived in the morning.

Bill Austin seems to have ended 1944 in the hospital with yellow jaundice.

Pfc. William Austin, Hospital, to Mrs. Anthony Hirsch, Eldred

December 29, 1944
Dear Aunt Christina,

I received the Christmas package from you and Aunt Charlotte for which I am very grateful. I also received one from the Ladies Aide Society. I wish you would tell them my thanks.

I have been in the hospital since 10 October with the yellow jaundice. I am still in bed with it but am feeling better than I did a while ago.

Remember me to Uncle Anthony and Charlee. Tell Aunt Charlotte that I haven't forgot that I owe her a letter.

Write when you get time.
Your nephew, Bill

The end of another year and still the war continued. The last pages of this chapter list those who served at some point in World War II from the Town of Highland. Some entered the War in 1945.

Chapter 12
"I Do."
Weddings, 1945–1946

After my discharge, I thought it would be a good idea to visit the hospital. My visits became so frequent that the people where I boarded used to sing for my benefit, a little ditty that starts like this: "Nursey, Nursey, please come quick."

As we were married a year or so later, this train of events certainly changed my life.—Arthur Austin.

After their wedding in Barryville, Art and Mary would honeymoon at Natural Bridge in Virginia. Photo courtesy of Mary Briggs Austin.

The featured wedding of this chapter is that of Arthur Austin and Mary Briggs, my parents. A number of weddings would take place before the marriage of Art and Mary in November 1946. After the ceremony, the new Mr. and Mrs. Arthur Austin would drive to Natural Bridge in Virginia for their honeymoon.

And the ghastly war continued into the new year. It was a very cold, hard winter in New York.

January 1945
In Islip on Tuesday, the second day of the new year, Anna worked on a relief work afghan, sewed on her machine, and cut out blue blocks for a cradle quilt.

Tuesday in Eldred Austin Smith was at the Leavenworths for a while. Friday evening he was back for a violin lesson.

Monday, January 8, Anna walked on the cold, slippery road to the Islip Post Office to post her tax letter. A neighbor shoveled the ice from her walk.

Tuesday Anna was cold when she wrote letters to soldiers, as a clinker caught in the furnace did not allow much heat.

Friday was stormy in Islip, but the snow was melting. A meeting was called at the school to try to get a vote for $8,000 more for land. "These politicians don't know a war is going on," quipped Anna.

Even though Anna received a letter from her sister Christina on Saturday, she felt miserable all Saturday. "I'm tired and disgusted with many things tonight."

Mid-January the cold continued in Islip. "Had to fight furnace for heat," wrote Anna.

In Eldred Tuesday, January 16, about 32 inches of snow fell. The week continued cold with blowing snow or snow squalls.

"Wonderful news of Nazi defeats in E. Germany," wrote Anna in Islip on Sunday, January 21. She continued to struggle with the furnace on Monday—trying to keep warm without burning too much coal. She made a prune bread for an excuse to have the oven heated. There had been no Dugan Bakery delivery. The Dugan's Bakery Truck arrived the

The big snow, February 1945. Eldred Four Corners looking south on Brook Road towards Barryville. Photo courtesy of Timothy C. Rizzuto.

next day. The driver had been sick during bad weather.

On Monday in Eldred Mrs. Ort Sr. was very ill. Ella got a V-mail from Jim. Wednesday, January 24, when it was snowing and blowing most of the day, Ella started a Lucky Star patterned tablecloth for Eleanor Bosch. One evening Austin Smith and his son Dale visited the Leavenworths.

Thursday it was 10 below zero in Eldred; and minus 26 at Highland Lake.

Lake View Cottage February 1945. Photo courtesy of Timothy C. Rizzuto.

Lake View, across the lake from Green Acres, 1945. Photo courtesy of Timothy C. Rizzuto.

The terrible cold and snowy winter weather was referred to in a letter of Charlie Bosch and later in a letter of my dad Arthur Austin. There were also a few 1945 winter photos: Charlie Myers' lovely Lake View and Cottage (which would soon be for sale); sisters Victoria Parker and Nellie Crandall; and cousins Alberta Brodmerkel and Margo Bosch.

Charlie Bosch (Grosspperino) was practically snowed in when he wrote his grandson Billy Bosch a lively letter at the end of January. "Little Billy" Bosch and his parents Willie and Florence lived in Ridgewood, Queens, in one of the downstairs apartments which Florence's parents William and Katherine Schmerfeld (grossfotter and grossmutter) owned.

Charlie Bosch, Highland Lake, to Willie Bosch, Queens, N.Y.
Sunday, January 28, 1945
Dear Little Billy, Mom, and Pop,
   Your long waited for letter received. Sure thought you had forgot your Grosspperino.
   You will have to talk to your other Grossfotter and Grossmutter to take you and Mom and Pop as you want to see Green Acres you heard so much about soon. Just now it's all snow at Green Acres and 27 to 25 below. You sure couldn't stand it as it is so cold.
   We have to stay in the house and keep the stove red hot. It's so cold the Rabvards [Billy's pronunciation of "rabbits"] won't come from under the porch. I feed them cabbage and frozen apples and rye bread. There are two Rabvards by your Hunkel Charles and Aunt Karina's door under the couch hiding. When I shoveled the snow off the porch they jumped off so quick they almost broke their tails off. Poor Rabvards.
   There's so much snow—4 feet in the woods, 30 inches on the fields. It's sure hard on the deer and the Mud Pond pickerel must be very near starved. Nobody is fishing there. I am now staying

1945 photo of Victoria Parker and her sister Nellie Crandall courtesy of Christene Stevens Myers. Photos of cousins Alberta Brodmerkel and Margo Bosch courtesy of Ken Bosch.

alone at the big house; just Pippin [his dog] and I. Of course I have plenty to eat and good firewood. I just stay inside and take it easy.

Suppose by now Santa Claus took the tree out. In the summer I will show you where those trees grow on the Quinn place in the swamp. I have enough wood in and by the house for a long time; enough groceries for six weeks or more. Have everything but bacon. I have pork chops, liverwurst, noodles, pancakes, and plenty of canned stuff in the cellar; and beans, cabbage, and carrots to make soup.

I'm not working at Aunt Mary's and Herman's anymore. I didn't feel so good, so went home for awhile. Hope for your nice letter soon and best wishes to your mom and pop and yourself.
Your Grandpopper
X X X
(Seven inches of snow last night.)

Battle of the Bulge Ends
The Town of Highland wasn't the only place experiencing a very cold winter. Europe had experienced an extreme winter which intensified the misery in the fighting at the Battle of the Bulge—perhaps the largest and bloodiest the Americans would fight. The battle which had started mid-December ended January 25.

Fred DeFeo Jr., son of Fred and Pearl Owen, fought in the Battle of the Bulge. As did Russell MacKechnie. Russell was in a support group for those at the battle front of the Battle of the Bulge. A shell exploded near him. Before he knew it he was at a first aid station where they took off his boots as he had shrapnel in his legs. He was flown to London (the first time he had ever flown). When he married, he still had shrapnel in one of his legs. Russ would earn a purple heart.

My dad Fred Ihlo was HQ company commander in the 37th

Lake View House for Sale

Lake View, Highland Lake, N.Y.
Fifty-five acres of ground, more or less, with riparian rights to middle of Lake.

Hotel contains 47 sleeping rooms all furnished, two parlors, large dining room, three kitchens, two large lavatories, Chef Gas Range in kitchen, large Frigidaire room.

Laundry complete with electric washer, ironer, and help lavatory. All kitchen utensils, china, silver, electric coffee urn, linens for both dining room and bedrooms complete. Shower room, separate heating device for same.

Office complete with two desks, safe, National Cash Register, two show cases for display of cigars, candy, etc.

Barn contains four help sleeping rooms overhead.

Grill room complete, ladies and gents lavatories and wash rooms, office; Grill kitchen fully equipped with all necessary utensils, Frigidaire, gas range, dishes and silverware complete.

A cottage containing eight rooms, two baths, hot and cold water, furnace in cellar, fully furnished, large porch. Artesian well 175 feet deep.

For sale, including everything with the exception of personal belongings. Price $30,000.00

Phone: Barryville 2708.

Jim with American military transport glider at Eiffel Tower. Photo courtesy of Gisele Rouillon Leavenworth.

Tank Battalion, 4th Armored Division, spearhead of Patton's 3rd Army in Europe. They were at the very front and did some unbelievable things. His Battalion Commander was Lt. Col. Creighton Abrams, later Army Chief of Staff and for whom the Abrams Tank was named.

I remember Dad telling a story about Col. Abrams who said that a real soldier's breakfast during the war was a black cigar and a glass of brandy—guess that would open your eyes in a hurry. Dad got a purple heart after being hit by shrapnel from a German 88 somewhere in France.—Bill Ihlo.

February 1945
Edward Toaspern, Fred Ihlo's

Near Villacoublay, France where Jim Leavenworth was stationed at the Air Base. Photo courtesy of Gisele Rouillon Leavenworth.

future brother-in-law, was appointed Lieutenant on February 1, 1945. Two weeks later he once again reported to VF-31 for a second tour of duty. Ed completed photo school at Barbours Point Naval Air Station, and became the photo officer on the *U.S.S. Belleau Wood*.

In Eldred on Monday, February 12, Ella was relieved to get a V-mail from Jim. She had not heard from him in two weeks. On Wednesday she received a letter from Jim with $50. And on Saturday she received the letter Jim had written on Wednesday.

(By February Jim was most likely stationed at the Villacoublay Air Base in France. He did some touring with friends.)

On Monday, February 19, Anna Leavenworth wrote many letters to soldiers and mailed them at the Islip Post Office.

On Friday Goldie, Stella, and Orville's girlfriend Mary called at the Leavenworth home. There was a snapshot of Jim in Ella's letter.

Milton Ort Dies
Tuesday, February 27, Pfc. Milton Ort, 413 Inf. 104 Inf. Div. died in battle. It would be a couple weeks before Milton's friends; parents William and Bertha LaBarr Ort; and siblings Eleanor Lilley, William, Florence, and John Ort, would hear about his death.

March 1945
Monday, March 5, Ella received two V-mails from Jim.

Sunday some city people (thanks to Madelyn Meyers) were over to buy some of Ella's crocheted pieces.

Ella heard about Milton Ort's death (though still not the actual date) on Wednesday, March 14. Jim sent $45 home. (He was working to pay off the chicken feed bill.)

Wednesday was a lovely day in Islip. Anna walked to the Post Office, bought war stamps, and wrote to Bob Austin at England General Hospital in Atlantic City, New Jersey. Bob received a letter from his brother Raymond.

R. Austin, Staten Island, to Pfc. R.C. Austin, Eng. Gen. Hospital
March 14, 1945
Dear brother Bob,

Just a card to let you know we are all OK and that we have heard from Bill and Art since you were here. Bill was out of the hospital and having some dental work done. Art thinks he may be home on furlough early this summer. Hope we see you soon. It must be pretty near time for your furlough to commence.

Hoping to see you soon.
Your brother, Ray

In Eldred on Thursday Garfield bought a calf from Herb Kinne for $5.

Sunday Grant Sergeant started on his way home from California.

Friday, March 23, Clara and Lee Hansen stayed over at the Scout Camp. Perhaps they helped out Goldie who had an appendix operation Sunday at the Callicoon Hospital.

The following Friday evening, Garfield, Bill, and Anna visited Goldie at the Callicoon Hospital. Saturday Ada Wells was operated on for her appendix.

April 1945
Sunday afternoon, April 1, Walter Tether and his son Ivan visited at the Leavenworth home.

Stella and Goldie stayed at his folks' home Tuesday night when he got out of the hospital. Stella's family were there for the evening.

Grant Sergeant was at the Leavenworths for supper on Saturday.

Some time in April, Jim Leavenworth met his future Bride.

Giselle Rouillon
Gisele Rouillon, a pretty young French woman, lived in Viroflay (southwest of Paris) and took the train back and forth to Paris where she worked as a secretary.

Villacoublay Air Base where Jim was stationed, was southeast of Viroflay—less than a three-mile

Grant Sergeant was at Leavenworths for supper on Saturday. Photo courtesy of Sandy Sergeant McBride.

Jim Leavenworth standing on one of the floors of the Eiffel Tower in France. Photo courtesy of Gisele Rouillon Leavenworth.

walk through the woods.

Gisele Rouillon stepped off the train at the Viroflay Station one day in April, and a tall, young American (Jim Leavenworth) asked her in broken French how to get to Paris.

Gisele smiled. It was a train station and there were signs all over. She figured he just wanted to strike up a conversation with her.

Jim was conveniently at the station many times from then on—just as Gisele returned from work. Jim and Gisele started dating. They went to the movies once or twice, and visited the nearby village. Other times they just walked and talked.

One time Jim and Gisele went to an open air market where there was a perfume stand. Jim bought a bottle of Channel No. 5 for his mother—a wonderful surprise present for Ella.

Jim sometimes walked Gisele to the house she lived in with Mama and Papa Cailloux, but he never went in.

Jim's cousin Arthur Austin in Italy wrote their aunt Christina Hirsch in April. Art also wrote his uncle Lon Austin.

M.Sgt. A. Austin, Hdq.Co., AA, N.Y., to Mrs. A. Hirsch, Eldred
April 8, 1945
Dear Aunt,

Was glad to receive your letter of March 11. Received a letter from Charlee the other day. Trust that by now Charlee has parted with her tonsils and is enjoying a rest.

At last I managed to see Bill for a few hours. He is out of the hospital but at present there is some doubt as to where he will be assigned. There is a good chance though that Bill will be classified as limited service because of his age and long sickness.

Bob expects to be discharged from the Army in a few months and is anxious to start working. I advised him to give thought to whatever educational possibilities the government is affording and

Milton Ort. Photo courtesy of Earl and Sharon Stewart Lilley.

Gisele Rouillon worked in Paris and lived in Viroflay, France. Photo courtesy of Gisele Rouillon Leavenworth.

if he does decide to get a job to consider the permanence of the work after the war ends.

Are you taking over Charlie Myers' original boarding house or the one across the way—the old Boyd place [Piermont] I believe—and which if I remember right he also has an interest? Certainly hope that you have a most successful season and that I am there to witness at least part of it.

The news has certainly been very encouraging lately and everyone has high hopes of ending this phase of the war in short order. Am afraid many people are losing sight of the Pacific. Quite a few of us will probably see service in that part of the world too. As long as they give me a chance to get home first I will not complain.

Hope that you are all well and to hear from you again soon. Art

M.Sgt. A. Austin, Hdq.Co., AA, N.Y., to Lon Austin, Eldred
*April 8, 1945
Dear Uncle Lon,
Was glad to hear from you and to learn how well you have come through the winter both physically and financially. It certainly must have been quite a storm. In a way am sorry to have missed it as 1945 has undoubtedly made history as far as Winters are concerned.*

Saw Bill a while ago and he is out of the hospital but is not sure where he will be assigned. I hope it will not be to an infantry outfit.

At last it really looks as though this war will end shortly. In any case I have good prospects of getting home this summer perhaps for longer than I expected.

However imagine most of us will see service in the Pacific before the war with Japan ends. The thought does not particularly disturb me. Have so far had an easy life in the army and so cannot complain if I see a few hardships before it is over.

Am interested in learning what is going to be done to the doctor's [Dr. Austin's] place by the new owners. I trust it will prove to be an asset to the community and will not disturb the woodchucks too much. Are you planning on a garden this year? I suppose the chucks will be very disappointed and probably hungry if you don't. [Uncle Lon had an ongoing battle with the woodchucks.]

Hope you and aunt Aida have kept well and to hear from you again soon. Your nephew, Art

Clifford Crandall's Birthday
When Clifford D. Crandall (son of Clifford and Mary Crandall) turned two in April, there was a grand birthday celebration with family including his cousin Pat and her parents Martin and Teenie. In one photo the house James Eldred built around 1830 can be seen in the background. (Sometime in the future Harry and Berniece Wells Haas would own the house.)

President Roosevelt Dies
Wednesday, April 11, was a nice day when Anna walked up to Islip to buy rug material. On Thursday she worked hard on a relief blanket and wrote in her diary: "News of President Roosevelt's death."

"President Roosevelt died at Warm Springs, Georgia, at four o'clock on Thursday, April 12," Ella recorded in her diary.

President Franklin Delano Roosevelt, 63, the only American president ever elected four times, died suddenly in Warm Springs, Georgia, in the afternoon while he was sitting for a portrait painting.

That evening Harry S. Truman, the Vice President, was sworn in as the 33rd President of the United States at the White House.

Robert Austin, Atlantic City, N.J., to Christina Hirsch, Eldred
*April 15, 1945
Dear Aunt Christina,
I received your letter sometime ago and would have answered before this but was operated on again much to my surprise. I was told last January that they were all through cutting [surgery on his arm]. I was going to ask for a furlough but when I was called in for my weekly interview they told me to get ready for an operation instead.*

It has been two weeks now and they are removing the stitches this Thursday. I am hoping that I can get up to see you before you start your spring house cleaning which I imagine will be a rather large job this year because you are taking over Charlie Myers' place. I think you will probably be kept busy all summer too, if the people come out to the country like they swarm down to Atlantic City.

Mary Crandall and son, Clifford. The James Eldred house built around 1830 is in the background. Photo courtesy of Christene Stevens Myers.

Left to right: Celia Myers (wife of Norm Myers) and son Jerry, Victoria Parker, Nellie Crandall, Jennie Crandall, Bertha Myers (Norm's mother) with Francis, Clifford and his mother Mary Crandall, Teenie and daughter Pat Myers. Photo taken by Mary Crandall's home courtesy of Christene Stevens Myers.

All the local papers claim that they are expecting to have their best season this year.

The weather has been real warm here lately. They had a very good Easter but I was unable to go out then so I could only watch the crowds on the boardwalk from the window.

I went to the ball game last Sunday and saw the Yankees play.

Things are quiet down here this week and all the theaters are closed because of the President's funeral.

Dr. Bente was in to see me the day before they operated. He also came in to see me once before when he was down here to see Bobby Grotecloss [Dr. Bente's stepson] right after he had been operated on.

I heard from Arthur a few days ago. He saw Bill just before he wrote and Bill is out of the hospital. Arthur is hoping he can get home this summer.

The way things are going I wouldn't be surprised if both of them would be back soon. They have both been over there a long time and should be the first to come back.

I haven't seen Raymond and Gladys lately but they write quite often. They got through the winter all right, but had their problems with the fuel shortage. Raymond is starting to work on his garden and I think gets a lot of pleasure from it since it is a change from office work. Am hoping this finds you all well.

As ever, Bob

Bob lived with Raymond and Gladys and their daughters on Staten Island, after he was discharged from the hospital.

Bob couldn't work, but he didn't waste his time. He read widely. He knew more about 18th and 19th century English literature than anyone I've ever met, including my college professors who taught the subject. He studied languages through books and recordings. He also was a scholar of World History.
—Walter Geier.

95th Infantry Commendation
In April Corporal William B. Nieke of Barryville received a letter from Lt. General G.S. Patton, Jr.

The letter—sent to the Commanding General of the 95th Infantry Division—commended the 95th Infantry for their achievement at Metz in late 1944.

Late April 1945 Islip and Eldred
On a sunny but cold Sunday, April 22, Anna of Islip cooked a beef

Adorable cousins Cliff Crandall and Pat Myers with Pat's father Martin Myers. Photo courtesy of the Clifford Crandall Family.

Lt. Gen. G.S. Patton Commends the 95th Infantry Division

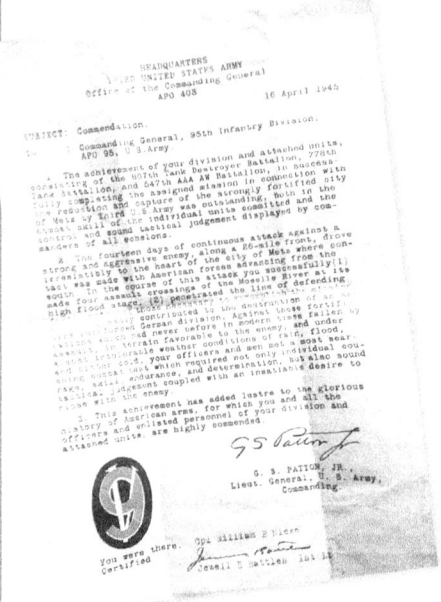

95th Infantry Patch and Patton letter courtesy of James Nieke.

G.S. Patton Jr., Hdqs., 3rd U.S. Army, to Commanding General, 95th Infantry Division
16 April 1945
1. The achievement of your division and attached units, consisting of the 607th Tank Destroyer Battalion, 778th Tank Battalion, and 547th AAA AW Battalion, in successfully completing the assigned mission in connection with the reduction and capture of the strongly fortified city of Metz by 3rd U.S. Army was outstanding, both in combat skill and sound tactical judgement displayed by commanders of all echelons.
2. The fourteen days of continuous attack against a strong and aggressive enemy, along a 26-mile front, drove irresistibly to the heart of the city of Metz where contact was made with American forces advancing from the south. In the course of this attack you successfully (1) made four assault crossings of the Moselle River at its high flood stage, (2) penetrated the line of defending forts, reducing those necessary to accomplish the mission and (3) greatly contributed to the destruction of an entire reinforced German division. Against these fortifications which had never before in modern times fallen by assault, in terrain favorable to the enemy, and under almost intolerable weather conditions of rain, flood, and bitter cold, your officers and men met a most searching combat test which required not only individual courage, skill, endurance, and determination, but also sound tactical judgement coupled with an insatiable desire to close with the enemy.
3. This achievement has added lustre to the glorious history of American arms, for which you and all the officers and enlisted personnel of your division and attached units, are highly commended.
  Lt. General, G.S. Patton, Jr.
  U.S. Army, Commanding

*You were there, Cpl. William B. Nieke
Certified: Jewell E. Battles, 1st Lt.*

pot roast. "Terrible pictures of German prison camps," she noted in her diary.

Monday Anna sent letters to her sister Christina and nephew Bill.

On Tuesday in Eldred, Ella received two V-mails and one air mail from Jim. Garfield started to make a desk for Stella.

May 1945
In Islip on Tuesday, May 1, Anna received a "good letter from Charlee."

Wednesday Anna walked to the bank, got fine fish at Bohack's, and bought regular sugar (which must last until September) at Nocars. Thursday there was "favorable news from Europe."

Saturday Grant Sergeant enjoyed dinner at Garfield and Ella's house.

Monday, May 7, Ella wrote, "Germany surrendered to the three powers unconditionally at 9:15 a.m. News band came at 2 minutes after 7 p.m. Victory in Europe or V.E. Day was proclaimed by Truman." Stella and Goldie, Christina, and Charlee all visited Garfield and Ella.

In Islip on Monday, Anna wrote, "Cold. Stood by radio to hear news that "did not become authoritative all day owing to the sneak Kennedy of the Associated Press."

She was relieved when she heard the news on Tuesday. "News of great surrender of Nazis to Western Allies. President Truman and Prime Minister Churchill on radio at 9 a.m. King George at 3 p.m. News of surrender to Russia late in afternoon. Relief!!"

V.E. Day was officially declared at 9 a.m. on Tuesday. Clara and her children were at Leavenworth's for the day. Stella and Goldie stopped by in the evening.

Sunday, May 13, Clara and her family ate dinner at her folks and then went home. Grant and Mary Sergeant stopped by. Great news for Grant. He had his discharge after five years in the Army. Garfield and Ella looked forward to their son Jim's return. But it would be a few more months.

Thursday, May 24, Ella received snapshots and a letter from Jim.

It was cold in Islip Saturday afternoon when Melva Austin visited her great-aunt Anna.

The last day of May, Anna sent letters off to Bob and Bill Austin.

Tom Myers with his sister Helen. Photo courtesy of the Clifford Crandall Family.

Martin and Tom Myers, and Richard Haas. Photo courtesy of Christene Stevens Myers.

Charlie Bosch

Charlie Bosch died of a heart attack on June 10, 1945, after a day's fishing at his beloved Mud Pond. He and son Willie had carried a row boat on the mile walk through the woods from his house on Bower Road to Mud Pond and back again at the end of the day. Charlie felt ill after dinner and he lay on his couch where he died.

Charlie commented that he could clearly hear his dog barking for the first time in years—he was almost totally deaf from proximity to artillery fire during his service in the U.S. Army around 1901.

Charlie was the third brother to die in as many years. Ralph died in 1943 and Herman in 1944.—Ken Bosch.

Charlie Bosch fishing on the bog at his beloved Mud Pond. Photo courtesy of Ken Bosch.

In May 1945 Tom Myers was home in Eldred. He was on leave while the *U.S.S. Wasp* was in for repairs. It had been bombed in the Pacific. Tom had lost all his belongings and gear, but fortunately he was on duty elsewhere on the ship.

June 1945
Friday, June 1, Ella received the Army magazine, *Yanks* from Jim.

Saturday, June 9, Alvah, Mary, and Grant Sergeant visited Garfield and Ella in the evening.

"Christianna Livingstone Flieger was buried today. Charlie Bosch Sr. died," Ella wrote in her diary on Sunday, June 10. Chris Flieger was a Sergeant cousin of Ella.

Tuesday, June 12, Garfield put siding on the garage. Clara, Lee, and their sons visited and stored some goods upstairs.

Judge Sweeny's house on Clark Road burned on Saturday.

Monday, June 18, 1945, Bill Austin arrived in the U.S.

Friday was a nice day in Islip, particularly in the afternoon. Anna wrote to Charlee and her aunt Lottie Darling.

Sunday was pretty warm in Islip, but that didn't stop Anna from mending a broken lawn mower with aluminum wire. It worked OK on a warm Monday when Anna mowed the grass.

Thursday, June 28, Goldie, Stella, and Tina Hallock were at the Leavenworths. Mary Crandall was there with her son Clifford.

It was very warm in Islip Saturday, when Bill Austin (officially a civilian for five days) stopped by his aunt Anna's cottage. They had a very pleasant visit. Bill had worn his winter uniform, and it continued to be warm on Sunday. Bill left at 1 p.m. Anna "felt sorry he was so warmly dressed. But he looks well and I was glad he came out."

July 1945
Monday, July 2, Garfield went to work for the Scouts for a few days.

Ella received a package from Jim.

Friday Tony Hirsch Jr. called Anna in Islip and announced the birth of his son. Martin called at the Leavenworths in Eldred with a nice bunch of asparagus on Friday. Saturday Bill Austin was in for a while.

The following Thursday Vernon Clark visited the Leavenworths. He had enlisted in March. Vernon would be a five-inch gun trainer on the *U.S.S. Franklin D. Roosevelt*.

The Briggs Family summer of 1945. Back: Irwin and John. Front: Mildred, Myrtle, Laura, and Mary. Photo courtesy of Mary Briggs Austin.

Arthur Austin departed for the U.S. on Friday, July 13.

Wednesday, July 18, Stella and Ella had a good visit. Thursday Ella received a letter from Jim which he had written July 11.

In Islip Sunday, July 22, Anna "enjoyed the *Tribune* after a long delivery strike."

Monday in Eldred Jim's sister Anna received a letter from Jim with snapshots. Tuesday, Garfield finished working at the Scouts.

Arthur Austin and his nieces. Melva holding Dawn Lee. Margie on the left; Joan on the right. Photo courtesy of Andy and Margie Austin Maglione.

Tuesday in Islip Anna's friend Mrs. Bledsoe helped her with Charlee's quilt. They had coffee, cake, and peaches—a nice time. Anna also had canned peaches.

In the Pacific on Tuesday, Edward Toaspern was credited with a direct bomb hit on the battleship ISE in Kure Harbor.

Arthur Austin arrived in the U.S. on Wednesday. He was officially a civilian four days later.

When he landed in the U.S. after the war, his duffle bag was not to be found. He lost all the mementos he had. All he had were some hankies that he gave to me. He didn't know if it was stolen or lost. He didn't even have all of his uniform! He had to borrow his brother Bill's hat and shirt to be in a wedding which required him to be in uniform.—Mary Briggs Austin.

Mary Briggs seems to have been in Barryville at least for a little while during the summer, perhaps for her brother John's graduation. There are photos of her with her family.

Bob, Art, and Bill Austin
Bob, Art, and Bill each visited their brother Raymond's when they arrived back in the states.

I remember each of our Austin uncles (Bob, Bill, and Art) showing up at our home on Staten Island after they were discharged from the service.

They came climbing up our hill at intervals, each one in uniform. It was so amazing and wonderful. They showed up at intervals without warning.

I think they had sailed into New York to be discharged, and then took the ferry and train out to our house.

My sister Dawn Lee was about five years old, and when she spotted the third uniform starting up the hill she ran into the house shouting, "There's another one coming, there's another one coming. I think it's an uncle."
—Joan Austin Geier.

And wasn't Anna Leavenworth "awfully glad to see her nephew Arthur Austin coming up the walk," on Monday, July 30. Art stayed overnight. Tuesday he went to Staten Island and visited his brother Raymond and his family.

August 1945
There were letters from Jim waiting for Garfield when he went to the Post Office on Friday.

In Islip on Tuesday, August 7, Anna's friend Mrs. Bledsoe helped her complete Charlee's quilt.

The War Ends; Victory over Japan
It was rumored that the Japanese were ready to surrender. Finally, on Tuesday, August 14, the surrender was finalized.

In Islip, Anna stayed near her radio most of Tuesday. In Eldred Ella wrote, "V.J. Day proclaimed by Truman. The Japanese surrendered unconditionally. News broadcast at 7:02 p.m."

1945 World and National News

- Future Presidents who served in WWII: John F. Kennedy, Dwight D. Eisenhower, Lyndon B. Johnson, Richard M. Nixon, Gerald R. Ford, James Carter Jr., George H.W. Bush.

January 1945
- Allied victory at Battle of the Bulge.

February 1945
- President Roosevelt, Prime Minister Churchill, and Premier Josef Stalin at Yalta Conference.
- 30,000 U.S. Marines landed on Iwo Jima.

March 1945
- Allied armies entered Germany and crossed the Rhine. Soviet forces within 100 miles of Berlin.

April 1945
- President Roosevelt died; succeeded by V.P. Harry S. Truman.
- Battle of Okinawa.
- United Nations Charter drafted in San Francisco. Agreed that major powers—U.S., Great Britain, U.S.S.R., France, and the Republic of China—would constitute the permanent members of the Security Council with veto power.
- Hitler married his mistress Eva Braun; the following day both committed suicide.
- Ernie Pyle, 44, American war correspondent killed by a Japanese sniper on island near Okinawa.

May 1945
- Germany surrendered to the Allies and was divided into four military occupation zones. Berlin was also divided into four zones.

July 1945
- Churchill, Truman, and Stalin met and demanded unconditional surrender from Japan. Churchill's government voted out of office before the end of the conference. Clement Attlee Prime Minister.
- The first atomic bomb exploded at Alamogordo, New Mexico.

August 1945
- The U.S. dropped an atomic bomb on Hiroshima; And a second bomb on Nagasaki three days later. Within four months, 150,000–245,000 died. (There is a wide range of estimates.)

September 1945
- Japanese surrendered aboard the battleship *U.S.S. Missouri* in Tokyo Bay. General Douglas A. MacArthur accepted on behalf of the Allies. U.S. forces occupied Japan, ruled by MacArthur for the next five years.

October 1945
- The United Nations charter ratified.

November 1945
- The trial of major German war criminals opened in Nuremberg.

December 1945
- War crimes trial began in Japan.

In the Pacific, the last day of the War, Ed Toaspern was credited with two aerial victories. Thirty-five minutes after Ed hit two Japanese Zeros (Zekes) over the coast of Japan on August 15, 1945, all planes were recalled. World War II was officially ended.

August 15 was celebrated as Victory over Japan or VJ Day—the day Japan surrendered and World War II ended. VJ Day applies to the day of the initial announcement of Japan's surrender on August 14, 1945 (as both Ella and Anna mentioned in their diaries) or to the afternoon of August 15, 1945, in Japan (because of time zone differences). It also applies to September 2, 1945, when the official document was signed ending World War II.

Thursday, August 16, was a warm day in Islip. "Peace holiday still on. Cupboard is getting bare and Jimmie is scolding," noted Anna.

In Eldred on Friday Ella received two letters from Jim.

Charles and Selma West
We first met the West family in *The Mill on Halfway Brook*. Marietta West had married George W. Eldred. When George died young, Marietta had married Sam Hoatson, father of Elizabeth Hoatson Clark Wilson. Marietta's brother Theodore West had run West Farm in Yulan for many years. Theodore's son Charles and his wife Selma ran the boarding house around 1930. Sometime around 1940 Charles and Selma West had some financial difficulties and had lost their West Farm. They moved to Passaic, New Jersey, where Charles worked at a garage and Selma volunteered in a hospital during the war. Two of their sons were in the war. Son Ralph wrote them from Guam.

Ralph West, Guam, to Charles and Selma West, Passaic, N.J.
August 16, 1945
Dear Folks,

I received your swell letter today. Gosh! it doesn't seem possible that this darn thing is all over but the shouting. Naturally don't have any idea as to how soon I will return, so can just keep hoping it won't be too long before I can be with you all again.

When we first received the news that Japan had surrendered with the condition, the roof was raised for a few minutes and then we settled down to waiting for the real thing to follow.

When the real thing came

On the top of this card was written "Pass north, south, east, or west; if you pass Maple Grove, you pass the best." Guests at Maple Grove Farm owned by the Charles and Gertrude Frey and Minnie Nitzsche, September 1945. Photo courtesy of Christopher Frey.

through we were just happy to think and talk about it quietly. The PX had beer on hand and sold it ration free the nite when we knew for sure it was over. Was over to the movie and saw the picture, Brewster's Millions.

Have been hearing on the radio of the celebrating in the states and take it they really raised the roof all nite? I received a letter from Dan (his brother). He said he was now 48th on the list and thought he would leave some time this month.

How is things at the garage Dad? Coming along okay now I hope. Well Moms that seems to be the news for this time so will say goodnite with my love to all. Write soon again Moms.

As always, Your loving Son and Brother, Ralph

Maple Grove Farm
Boarding houses had continued to have guests during the war, but now that it was ended, folks perhaps celebrated by vacationing.

A photo taken of guests at Maple Grove Farm in September was captioned: "Pass north, south, east, or west; if you pass Maple Grove, you pass the best." You may remember that two couples, Charles and Gertrude Frey and Fred and Minnie Nitzsche, ran Maple Grove Farm. Sometime in the 1940s Fred had died, but Minnie continued to help.

My grandparents, Charles and Gertrude Frey, had a full partner all the years they owned Maple Grove Farm on Corkscrew Road. Her name was Minnie Nitzsche and I always refer to her as my "bonus grandmother" because she treated the Frey boys as blood relatives. Her husband Fred was a partner as well, but he passed away long before I was born and, unfortunately, I know very little about him.

Like every boarding house owner/partner, Minnie worked long and hard all summer. She handled the laundry function as well as the bookkeeping and "marketing" for the boarding house. With several long term employees she managed to keep

1945 Seniors

John Briggs, Frances and Virginia McBride, Marion Doeller, Marion Haas, Mary Kean, Charles Kinne, William Lass, Meta Mills, Robert Sulzbach, Don Brinkerhoff, and Henry Rave.

1945 Meta Mills, daughter of Alexander and Minnie Meyer Mills.

1945 Bill Lass, son of Alfred and Bessie MacIntyre Lass Hill.

1945 Rita Cantwell, future wife of the "pretty good pilot" Jim Purcell.

1945 Virginia McBride, sister of Frances; daughter of Laura Avery McBride.

1945 John Briggs, brother of Mary, Laura, and Mildred; son of Irwin and Myrtle Briggs.

1945 Marion Doeller, daughter of the Doellers who ran Handsome Eddy.

Photos from the 1945 Yearbook.

1945 Halfway Brook News

1945 Marriages

- Fred Ihlo married Frances Toaspern at the Eldred Congregational Church.
- Lou Maudsley married Edith Rutlege in January.

Avery House Sold

- Avery House bought by Otto Schmidt.

Army Band

- After graduating John Briggs enlisted in the Army and played in the 2nd Inf. Division Band.

1945 Births

- Mary Maudsley born to Lou and Edith Maudsley in December.
- John Gilbert Clark was born to James Joseph and Hope Tinn Clark.

1945 Deaths

- Pfc. Raymond C. Meyer (son of Joseph and Florence Meyer) died in Epinal, France. He received a Bronze Star, Purple Heart. He fought with the U.S. Army, 255th Inf. Regiment, 63rd Infantry Division.
- Christianna Livingstone Flieger, 1893–1945.
- Charlie Bosch, 1882–1945.
- Milton Ort died in Germany.
- Emily A. Parmenter Austin, 1849–1945.
- Albert Pegg Jr., a waist gunner on a B-17, was shot down over Germany. Stepson of Albert and Julia Straub Pegg; cousin of Ed and Frances Toaspern.

John Briggs played in the Army Band. Photo courtesy of Mary Briggs Austin.

The Toaspern cousin, Albert Pegg Jr. Photo courtesy of Bill Ihlo.

Fred Ihlo with his bride Frances Toaspern. Photo courtesy of Bill Ihlo.

Albert Pegg Jr. died in March 1945. Photo courtesy of Bill Ihlo.

all the linens clean and ironed for all sixty guests despite having to rely on the sun and air to dry them. I will never understand how they managed that, but they did.—Christopher Frey.

Arthur Austin and Mary Briggs

When Arthur Austin returned to Eldred, he boarded at Bessie and Alfred Hill's home and worked for the Sullivan County Highway Department. On weekends Art visited his brother Raymond's family in Staten Island or his aunt Anna Leavenworth in Islip. Eventually, Art also visited a certain Barryville young lady who was taking nurse's training at Brooklyn Methodist Hospital.

Art and I continued on writing and finally he got out, as the war had ended. I had told him in a letter that when he came out maybe he could come and visit me. But he later told me that

Mary Briggs and Arthur Austin. Photo courtesy of Mary Briggs Austin.

he was afraid something would happen, so he went on back to Eldred.

When he went to church he told my dad (the minister then) that his little girl had been writing to him. This struck my dad as quite humorous and he laughed telling him I wasn't so little anymore! I was 20 at the time.

Being an honest person, Art decided that he should go once to see me since he'd promised he would. He stayed with his brother Raymond in Staten Island, and visited me in Brooklyn. Our first time out was to church in Brooklyn where I went to the Methodist School of Nursing.

We went out together several times, and then Art went back to Eldred to live and back to work.

When he went home, he said he hoped I'd write. I thought if I wrote to him first it would look like I was chasing him. The girls at the hospital talked me into writing to him. The least I could do was to thank him for the good times we had together, they said. That kept us going, as he probably wouldn't have ever written to me if I hadn't written to him.

We started going together in August 1945 and that Christmas, they kidded Art about having a "Mary" Christmas at a Church Christmas get together.—Mary Briggs Austin.

Several teachers also boarded at the Hill's house. Bessie Hill's niece Reta Kalin helped Bessie with the housework. When Reta made Art's bed for Bessie, she discovered Mary Briggs' picture on his dresser. For fun Reta put Mary's picture in the wastebasket and short sheeted Art's bed.

Neither Bessie nor Mary's parents had told anyone that Art and Mary were going together. Since Art and Mary dated in the Brooklyn area, no one in Eldred or Barryville knew they were going together until Art and Mary went to an Eldred High School concert together.

Irwin and Myrtle's Sabbatical
Mary Briggs' folks Irwin and Myrtle Briggs would leave for a year's sabbatical in six months or so. They would visit their family out west in Nebraska, Oregon, California, and Arizona. The night before they left Irwin and Myrtle

Irwin and Myrtle Briggs at the home of their friends Charles and Muriel Kerr. Irwin, Myrtle, Muriel Kerr holding daughter Lois, and Charlie Kerr. Photo courtesy of Mary Briggs Austin.

"Anna received a letter from Charlee at last." The Leavenworths loved cats. Photo courtesy of Ric Schroedel.

stayed at the home of their good friends Charles and Muriel Kerr.

Bradley/Avery Farm Sold
The original Isaac Bradley House had been run as a boarding house by Isaac's daughter Norah and her husband Ernie Avery for many years. It was sold in 1945.

Erwin and Norah Avery; Laura and her children: Virginia, Frances, and Kenneth McBride lived on the farm until 1945. The farm was then sold to Otto Schmidt and a partner. The Averys bought a cottage in Eldred and Laura married Jim Wade and bought a house near them. Frances married Otto Schmidt and left the area. Otto quickly sold the farm.—Bill Horton.

Otto Schmidt sold the house and farm to John and Celina Nikolaus who had a restaurant in New York City. We read more about them in the next chapter.

September 1945
Tuesday, September 4, was a nice day in Islip when Anna's nephew Arthur arrived. Art stayed overnight and left the next morning, perhaps to see pretty Mary Briggs.

Tuesday, September 6, Goldie and Stella moved to the Boy Scout Camp. They ate supper at his parents in Eldred.

On Friday, most of Anna's American Tea Company order arrived at her home in Islip. Sunday Anna talked on the phone to Arthur in Staten Island.

Monday, September 17, Anna received a letter from Charlee at last. She hadn't heard from Eldred in some time. On Friday Anna walked up to Islip where a card from Arthur was waiting for her.

Monday, September 24, in

Ed Toaspern with his aunt Julia Straub Pegg and uncle Bert Pegg, in California when he was on leave in November 1945. Photo courtesy of Bill Ihlo.

Eldred, there was a letter from Jim who was still in France. Garfield and Ella must have been wondering when their son would finally arrive home.

The following week Earl Wells' 50-pound-pig wandered into the Leavenworth yard during the night. It took three days to figure out who the pig belonged to.

October 1945
Thursday, October 4, Garfield went to town to get papers for Jim. Friday there was no letter from Jim. Garfield and Ella "hoped he was on his way home." Tuesday a package from Jim arrived.

"The Detroit Tigers won the World Series," Ella wrote on Wednesday, October 10, 1945. [It would be 1968 before the Tigers would win another Series.]

Finally on Friday, October 12, there was a letter from Jim that said he was on his way home.

The following Wednesday, Mary Sergeant, Mildred Myers, Stella, and Vernon all stopped in at Garfield and Ella's.

Jim had not yet left England on October 19.

There was still no word from Jim on Monday, October 22. "We are sure getting weary waiting," Ella commented in her diary.

Tuesday in Islip Anna took the train to Eldred. Anthony met her in Shohola.

There was a gentle rain on Wednesday, so Anna stayed in Anthony and Christina's house admiring the cats. Thursday evening Anthony took Anna down to see Garfield and Ella, who still had had no word from Jim.

Lt. Ed Toaspern was detached from VF-31 on Thursday and assigned to the Naval Air Station in Glenview, Illinois; and later to N.A.S. Corpus Christi, Texas for Flight Instructor School. Ed would soon be on leave and visit with his Uncle Bert and Aunt Julia Straub Pegg in California. They were most likely very happy to see him. Their stepson Albert (Ed's cousin) had died in the war earlier in the year.

Friday in Eldred Anna had an uneventful trip back to East Islip.

It was clear weather Saturday in Eldred when Stella and Goldie were at his folks for supper. Anna, Bill, and Jimmy were there for the evening. Garfield's sister Charlotte called that day also.

November 1945
Thursday, November 1, Ella washed 19 flour sacks—they came in different patterns. Ella made

Jim Leavenworth sailed home from England on the Queen Mary. Photo courtesy of Gisele Rouillon Leavenworth.

some of them into pillowcases; two became dish towels.

Friday Charlee Hirsch visited the Leavenworths.

Anna voted in Islip on November 6. Wednesday she chopped down a locust tree for kindling. Thursday was a beautiful, warm day. Anna chopped more kindling.

On Thursday in Eldred, Garfield put the two storm sashes on Jim's windows. Garfield and Ella were fixing up Jim's room, but there had been no word as to when Jim would arrive.

Finally at 7:30 a.m. Saturday, Jim called his parents on his way to Camp Dix. He had sailed back on the Queen Mary from England. Anna and Jimmy were there when he called, as they had come early to borrow some flour. Anna and Clara and their families were at Garfield and Ella's that evening.

Sunday, November 11, Jim called his folks from Camp Dix about 7 p.m.

Jim and Gisele
Jim had wanted to get married in France, but Gisele said no. She knew of girls who had married American soldiers and became pregnant. When the men returned to the states, they were never heard from again. Gisele told Jim that if he still wanted to marry her after he returned home, she would marry him.

Jim Arrives Home
It was the best of all news for Garfield, Ella, and their family. Around noon on Wednesday, November 14, Jim arrived home from the war for good.

Sergeant James Leavenworth had been overseas for 2-1/2 years. He received four battle stars for: Central Europe, Rhineland, North France, and Belgium.

Anna took her son Jimmy to see her brother after supper. Dick Hansen was still staying with his grandparents. Bill Meyers let Jim take his car for a few days.

On Thursday, November 15, Clara and her family were at her

Melva Austin called her great-aunt Anna Leavenworth to let her know her sisters and father arrived home safely. Photo courtesy of Cynthia Leavenworth Bellinger.

folks' home for dinner. In the evening her brother Jim went to the Clark's.

Friday in Eldred, Jim drove Anna and Jimmy Meyers and his nephew Dick Hansen to Middletown to shop. Stella and Goldie were at the Leavenworth home for supper and the evening. Clara and her family were over, too.

On Saturday, Jim was over to his sister Anna's for supper. Then he went to the Clark's for the evening.

In Islip Wednesday, November 21, Anna baked a cake and iced it for Thanksgiving. She had a nice Thanksgiving Dinner at her friend Esther's, and was home at 9:30.

In Eldred Bill and Anna Meyers hosted Thanksgiving at their home on Thursday. Bill and Jim went hunting.

Friday Garfield and Jim went hunting. Jim went to Alvah and Mary Sergeant's for supper.

Saturday, November 24, Anna in Islip called her sister Christina in Eldred.

On Tuesday Jim went with Goldie and Stella to the Boy Scout Camp and stayed several days.

East Islip had rain and wind all Thursday. Anna was getting ready for the Staten Island Austin family visit. "Cleaned the utility cupboard and stove. Good to expect company," she wrote in her diary. Friday morning had rain, snow, and wind in Islip. Anna worked "to get ready for the Staten Island folks tomorrow."

December 1945
Saturday, December 1, was a nice day in Islip. Anna was busy all day getting ready for Raymond, Joan, Margie, and Dawn Lee who arrived about 6 p.m.

Anna made pie and biscuits and enjoyed the visit. The four

Town of Highland Honor Roll

- Andersen, George
- Austin: Arthur L., Robert C., Wallace, William
- Balaban: Emil, William
- Bartle, Franklin
- Bodin, Paul
- Bosch, Henry (Whipple)
- Boyd, William
- Bradley, Clarence
- Briggs, Mary
- Burgess, Adga Jr.
- Campbell: Russell, Walter
- Cantwell, John C.
- Clark, Orville
- Clouse: George, Herman Jr., Joseph, Raymond, Theodore
- Cordes, Arthur
- Crandall: Clifford, Leonard
- Dankwardt, Barney
- Devlin, John W.
- Dunlap, Carl
- Duryea, Edward
- Eckhart, Lewis
- Ehrets, Warren
- Eldridge: Charles, William
- Fleiger, John
- Fream: Donald, Warren
- Frey, Everett
- Foscola, Joseph
- Geisler, Charles
- Grotecloss: Edward, Robert
- Haas: Harry, Maurice, Richard
- Hallock: Gene, Robert
- Hill, Frank
- Horton, LeRoy
- Hulse: Clifford, Dewey, James, Raymond
- Kalin: Adolph, Orville, William Jr.
- Kelly, Kenneth
- Kendrigan, Martin
- Kerr, John
- Kieferle, Forrest
- Kistner: John, Rudolph
- Koch, Henry Jr.
- Leavenworth, James
- Liebla: Orville, Sylvan, Ward
- Liefert, John
- McBride, William
- Meyer: Frederick, John C., Raymond
- Mohr, Frederick
- Morgan: Harold, Raymond
- Mueller, Ernest
- Myers: Charles, Martin Myers Jr., Norman H., Thomas
- Nieke, William
- O'Donnell, Frank
- Ort: John, Milton, William Jr.
- Oset: Chester, Joseph, Stanley, Walter
- Parker: Andrew, Harvey, Howard, John, Warren, William H. Jr.
- Polk, Jack
- Purcell: Andrew, Edward, James, John
- Putnam, Richard
- Puycher, Thaddeus
- Ramsey, Rowland
- Roberts, Eugene
- Seitz, Carl
- Sergeant, Grant
- Smith, James
- Staubes: Arthur, Charles E.
- Stevens: Charles, Harold
- Strenglein, Frank
- Sulzbach, Clifford
- Timmeroff Jr., Ernest
- Toaspern: Edward, Walter
- Traver, John
- Turash, William
- Van Etten, Donald
- Vollmer, Cecil
- Von Ohlen, Archie
- Vonderhorst, Charles
- Walter, Donald
- Warden: Archie, John (Ian) Jr.
- Weber, Arthur
- West: Daniel, Ralph
- Williams: Charles, Francis, Frederick, John
- Wilson, Forrest
- Wizlankus, Joseph
- Wood, Lawrence
- Woodruff, Carlton
- Wolff: Raymond, Robert
- Worzel, Irving
- Yutz, Frank

Town of Highland Honor Roll. Photo courtesy of Chuck Myers. See p. 458 for a later version of the list.

Note: The names come from several sources and are not all on the Memorial Board. Also see pp. 313, 315, 317, 319, 458.

Dick, Lois, and Wayne Hansen spent Christmas Eve and Day with their grandparents Garfield and Ella Leavenworth. Photos courtesy of Cynthia Leavenworth Bellinger.

Austins left at 11 a.m. Melva called Anna to let her know her family had arrived home.

Jim Leavenworth's Sawmill

Jim Leavenworth had not been sure what to do when he first got back to the states. But he decided to build a sawmill. Monday, December 3, Jim went over to see Perry Barnes Jr. and bought the mill machinery for his sawmill. (The mill mechanism takes the wood to the saw and the other parts of the rail system to discard the planks and the bark, etc.) Wednesday the men worked on Jim's mill site.

On Saturday, Anna, her son Jimmy, Clara, her three children, and Ella went to Port Jervis with Jim. Stella and Goldie were at the Leavenworths for supper.

On Monday, December 10, Jim and Ella went with Grant and Mary to Hawley, Pennsylvania. Jim also went with his dad to Beaver Brook.

Tuesday Jim and Garfield cut logs. They skidded logs on Wednesday and Thursday Jim.

In Islip on Thursday Anna walked to Zwisslers and bought enough meat to last Jimmie and herself a long time.

In Eldred on Friday, Jim worked on his truck. Saturday he brought home a Christmas tree. Mary, Alvah, Grant, and Clara and her family were at the Leavenworths for the evening. A Christmas ham of 12-1/2 pounds cost $4.75.

There was a major baking session going on in Islip at Anna Leavenworth's home. She made a pumpkin pie for Raymond Austin, chocolate cookies for Bob Austin, and cooked a roast pork for herself and her cat Jimmie B.

Tuesday in Eldred, Jim and Garfield cut logs on their property.

Tuesday was quite a decent day (at last) in Islip. Anna wrote Christmas cards and began a little hooked rug for Charlee.

Monday, Christmas Eve in Eldred, Clara, her family, and Anna and her family were at their parents' home for the tree. Grandsons Dick and Wayne stayed. Grant Sergeant was in for a while.

All the Leavenworth children were at their parents' place at some point on Christmas Day. Anna and family for dinner. Clara and family in the afternoon. Stella and Goldie for supper.

In Islip, Anna had an elegant dinner with her friend Mrs. O'Shea. She went home rather early as the radio forecast predicted bad weather which did not arrive until near midnight.

Not All Soldiers Home in 1945

The war was over, but not all service personnel had returned in 1945. In most cases it was just waiting for the soldiers to be processed to go home.

There was still much angst for Harriet Hill. Her son Charlie

Bill Meyers Sr. helped Jim Leavenworth set up his mill. Bill Sr., his wife Lottie Meyers, their granddaughter Eileen Wolff, and Eileen's cousins, Charles and Ed Wolff. Photo courtesy of Mary Ellen Busse Mackinder.

Orville Clark married Mary Weisshaar in January 1946. Photo courtesy of Vernon and Carolyn Hallock Clark.

1946 World and National News

- Benjamin Spock, *The Common Sense Book of Baby and Child Care*.
- United Nations General Assembly met in January in London. 51 nations were represented.
- 400,000 mine workers began to strike; other industries followed.
- The Basketball Association of America (later NBA) founded.
- Philippines gained independence from the U.S. in July.
- Microwave oven invented by American inventor Percy Spencer.
- Tupperware® sold in 1946.

Eldridge had seen such very heavy combat in Italy, that he was shell shocked and went missing.

Poor Harriet was worried to death and kept looking for the telegram man. The Red Cross did notify her that Charlie was found, so that brought Harriet some relief. It would be late 1946 before Charlie was able to return to the States.

January 1946
Tuesday, the second day of January, Chet Middaugh skidded logs for Jim.

Sunday Jim paid $15 to have the mill machinery he had bought from Perry Barnes Jr. in December, drawn to his mill property. It was set up near the road to the right of his dad Garfield's house. Bill Meyers Sr., Jim, and his dad Garfield, all worked to get the mill set up.

The following Sunday, Jim and his brother-in-law Bill Meyers Jr. helped Bill Sr. cut wood. Clara and her family ate supper with Garfield and Ella.

The last day of January, at three in the afternoon, Jim went to the Horton Memorial Hospital in Middletown. He was the best man when his good friend Orville Clark married Mary Weisshaar. The wedding was at the hospital because Mary's maid of honor was recuperating from an operation.

Aida Austin's good friend Mary Bosch died mid-January.

February 1946
In February the Leavenworths butchered a bull. Garfield cut up the beef and Ella canned 24 quarts of it.

The third week of February Garfield and Jim looked for pulleys, etc., for two days. Mid-week it snowed 12 to 16 inches. The last week of February, Jim took his mill pieces in to be welded. And Jimmy Meyers came down with scarlet fever.

It was March before Jim received the mill motor from Temple and Company. By Sunday, March 10, the men started sawing at Jim's new mill.

Jim also bought a horse from Chet Middaugh for $100. Carl Wolff shoed the horse.

During this time Jim and Gisele continued to correspond. And Ella wrote Gisele a welcoming letter.

Jim Leavenworth, Eldred, to Gisele Rouillon, Viroflay, France
Dear Gisele,

Our new home is a home of our own. It is what we both want. I have bought some furniture, but just the necessary. And you and I can get some extra furniture that we need when you arrive.

Our house is very large. My mother and father live downstairs and you and I will live upstairs.

We will have three nice rooms just for you and I and we can always share it should there be a

Mary Horton Bosch

Mary Horton Bosch, friend of Aida Austin. Photo courtesy of Victoria Kohler.

Mrs. Mary E. Bosch, widow of Herman Bosch, passed away Tuesday at her Eldred home. Mrs. Bosch was born in Eldred on March 7, 1900, the daughter of John and Elizabeth Stanton Horton. She is survived by two sons, Herman and Robert, and one daughter Marjorie, at home; two sisters Mrs. S.W. Mancy, of Port Jervis and Mrs. Herbert Bond, of Matamoras, Pa.; three brothers, Ernest, John H., and Walter D. Horton, all of Eldred; and several nieces and nephews.

Funeral services were held Friday, at 1:30 at the home and 2:00 at the Eldred Methodist Church. The Rev. H.I. Briggs officiated. Interment was in the Eldred Cemetery.—*Republican Watchman, January, 18, 1946.*

little gift from heaven.

Later I will build you a house with a white picket fence.

Here is a photo of our family.—Excerpt from Jim Leavenworth's letter.

Ella Leavenworth, Eldred, to Gisele Rouillon, Viroflay, France
March 14, 1946

Photo Jim sent Gisele of his family. 1. Mother (Ella), 2. Lois, my sister's girl, 3. Dad (Garfield), 4. Dick my sister's boy, 5. Lee, my brother-in-law, 6. Wayne his boy, 7. Jim, Anna's boy, 8. Anna, my sister, and X. Guess who? Photo courtesy of Gisele Rouillon Leavenworth.

Jim Leavenworth, his dad Garfield, and his brother Clinton (Goldie). Photo courtesy of Cynthia Leavenworth Bellinger.

Dear Gisele,

So glad to get your interesting and very welcome letter and will try and write you a few things about your soon-to-be relatives.

First Jimmy: When he first came home he was always saying, "Mom I sure wish Gisele was here."

Finally he decided to send you a card hoping you would answer. We are all very pleased the way things have turned out for you both and surely hope the laws will work fast so you can come to us all quickly.

Jimmy has his mill working and is sure one happy boy. Also, he sent for a few pieces of furniture for your home to be just what you will need to start housekeeping with. Then you can pick out what else you will want after you come.

It will be hard to come so far from your home, leaving your father and friends, but Jimmy surely loves you and the rest of us will try to make you happy for what Jimmy loves, I am very sure we can and will.

Today it is like Spring only a few patches of snow along the brook edges. Soon we'll start planting as we grow most all our vegetables and can them. So we have very little to buy.

When you come perhaps we can do this work together. I sure would like that.

Our two girls are married so they can not find much time to come and work with mother. One daughter Anna has a seven-year-old boy Jimmy. Daughter Clara has two boys, 7 and 5, and one girl 3 years.

Our eldest boy Goldie has no children. About stepmothers, I also had one. They are not very satisfactory toward stepdaughters. That I could never understand.

They tell me the bluebirds have come, but so far I have not seen one yet this Spring.

Gisele dear, think this will do for this letter. Please write again soon. Maybe we can get a little acquainted through exchanging letters. Hope to have you with us soon. Jimmy's mother and hope to be Gisele's soon.

Art and Mary

While Jim worked on his mill in Eldred and wrote to Gisele in France, Arthur Austin worked for the County Highway Department in Eldred during the week.

On weekends Art visited a certain nurse-to-be at the Methodist Hospital in Brooklyn.

Art stayed in Staten Island with his brother Raymond, his wife Gladys and their daughters: Melva, Joan, Margie, and Dawn Lee.

We went together my whole last year of Nurse's Training—going to the museums, parks, and restaurants in New York City.

Art came down weekends (not every one) and would go back on the last train there was that went to Port Jervis.

He said he wanted to go on the earlier train, but never did. He'd get home 4 a.m. and then up at 6 a.m. to go to work.

Art loved poetry and often quoted it. I asked him to write me a poem.
—Mary Briggs Austin.

1946 Halfway Brook News

Charles Schroeder married Norma Ott. Photo courtesy of Ken Bosch.

Art Staubes married Irene Theuer. The reception was at Bertram's Tavern. Photo courtesy of Jeanie Staubes Turner.

Fred Ihlo holding his daughter Barbara. Photo courtesy of Barabara Ihlo Sardone.

1946 Sold
- Howard and Emily Stevens sold the Parker House in 1946. They rented where they lived and the new owner made a couple of smaller apartments upstairs.
- John and Celina Nikolaus bought the Avery House from Otto Schmidt.

1946 Eldred Seniors
- Dorothy Dieckhoff, Edgar Getz, Katherine Hensel, Paul Kean, Betty MacIntyre, Anna Markle, Anna Rave, Ida Turner, Berniece Wells, George Wells, Herbert Wolff, Barbara Wickus.

1946 Moved
- Lou, Edith, and Mary Maudsley moved to Highland Lake to Dr. Mills' farm where Lou worked.

1946 Arrived from France
- Gisele Rouillon sailed from France to America on the *S.S. Nick Stoner*.
- Joseph and Juliette Lorphelin and their daughter Christiane arrived from France.

1946 Valor Award
- July 22, 1946, Cross of Military Valor awarded to Arthur Austin by the Italian Government (*see p. 407*).

1946 Reenlisted
- Harvey Parker enlisted again on December 18, 1946.

1946 Births
- Barbara Ihlo born to Fred and Frances Toaspern Ihlo.
- John Hallock born to Robert C. and Doris Estler Hallock.

1946 Weddings
- Orville Ernest Clark married Mary Weisshaar in January.
- Helen Zita Myers married Clifford M. Hulse in May.
- Charles (Chuck) Henry Myers married Ruth Worzel in June.

Cecil and Hazel Eldred's wedding. Front Row: Harvey Jr., Martha, Charles Eldred. Back Row: Eleanor Barnes, Cecil and Hazel Eldred, Harvey Eldred. Photo courtesy of Martha Eldred Worzel.

- Mildred Briggs married Laurence Lufburrow in July.
- Laura Briggs married Ervin Brink.
- James R. Leavenworth married Gisele Rouillon in August.
- John J. Hull married Josephine Lipinski, in Chicago, Illinois.
- Cecil L. Eldred married Hazel Crawford, a widow. Cecil was the brother of Harvey Eldred.
- Arthur L. Austin married Mary Rosamond Briggs in November.
- Art Staubes married Irene Theuer.
- Frank Bartle married Lee (Libra) Addabbo from Brooklyn.
- Charles Schroeder, son of William and Mary van Eastenbridge Schroeder, married Norma Ott, daughter of Charles and Christina Ott.

1946 Deaths
- Sophia S. Mills, 46, wife of Jim Mills and mother of Geraldine and Kenneth Mills, died.
- Mary Horton Bosch died in January.
- Sherman McBride Jr. died in April.
- Aida A. Austin died in April.
- Everett Kelley died in June.
- Harriet Classen Eldridge Hill died in July.

Art and Mary at Jack Dempsey's Restaurant. Photo courtesy of Mary Briggs Austin.

Poem for Mary
*Dearest Mary, You see
How eager I be
To please you and write,
By day or by night,
In prose or in poem,
At office or home.*

*Got home before four,
Slept an hour or more,
Rose unrefreshed,
Hurriedly dressed,
Time there was none;
My pail was not done.
Need must make haste;
No time to waste.*

*To work then I go;
Had I breakfast? No!
Much, much, too slow.
Sandwiches don't grow,
You make them you know.*

*I'll close as I start
And say from the Heart,
    Love, Art*

Besides meeting Mary on the weekends, Art took turns with his brother Bill staying nights with their aunt Aida who was ill. Bessie Hill also helped.

April 1946, Jim's Mill
In April Jim turned 24. The men cut and skidded the trees from Clarence Sergeant's to Jim's mill.

A few days after Jim's birthday, Ella was very sick with a ruptured hernia. She was taken to the hospital in Callicoon.

Jim took over the diary writing. Ella started doing better and had a number of visitors including of course her husband Garfield, Jim, Goldie and Stella, her son-in-law Lee, her sister Hazel Connor, and others.

There were a number of men who helped Jim at his mill. Dave Weber started working for Jim around mid-April.

Mid-April Sherman McBride Jr. was sick with gangrene in his leg. He died four days later.

Towards the end of April, Jim plowed the garden. He also hauled slab wood for Mr. Meyers.

Aida Austin Dies
Aida Austin, my great aunt, and the lady who preserved so much of the Austin information that is in this series of books, died at her home, Thursday evening, April 25, 1946. She was 84.

Aida was born in Eldred and lived there all her life. Though as the reader may know, she had spent much time in New York City when she was younger. Aida had also gone to College in Oswego and taught school. Lon Austin was the only one left of William Henry and Mary Ann Eldred Austin's ten children.

Lon wrote about Aida to a friend.

"The men cut and skidded the trees from Clarence Sergeant's to Jim's new mill." Jim Leavenworth's Mill. Photo courtesy of Cynthia Leavenworth Bellinger.

Yes, my sister was always ready to lend a helping hand to those who needed her help. She helped several to get their teacher's certificate and others on the road to knowledge.

One young lad was having a hard time with his studies and was only getting 40 and 45 credit marks. Someone told his mother how my sister helped them. His mother brought him during vacation for my sister to instruct him. The next summer he came and told her, "I am not getting 40 and 45 now. I am getting 85, 90, and up to 100 marks.—Lon Austin, about his sister Aida.

May 1946

Ella went home from the hospital Saturday, May 4. Four days later she was sick with giant hives. But by mid-May, Ella was able to write in her diary again.

Gisele Sails to the States

Jim sent Gisele some money to buy a ticket to sail to the U.S. Gisele would be leaving friends, family, the large city of Paris, and her country, knowing only textbook English. In France Gisele's coworkers got together to tell her good bye.

In Eldred Jim and his dad Garfield fixed the upstairs apartment for Jim and Gisele to live in.

Garfield built the sink and cupboards and worked on the rooms. Jim hooked the gas up to the kitchen stove. They painted and hung new fixtures.

Jim's sister Clara came down to help get things ready for Gisele who would be sailing from Le Harve on the *S.S. Nick Stoner*.

The *S.S. Nick Stoner* was a Liberty Ship—a cargo ship built during the war. There were ten passengers including Gisele on the ship. Gisele was the youngest at 19. The rest were either in their 30s, 40s, or 50s. One of the women befriended Gisele.

June 1946

The ship lines called Jim on Monday, June 3. A letter and a cable from Gisele arrived on Wednesday. Gisele was on board the *S.S. Nick Stoner* which was expected to dock in the U.S. on the Tuesday, June 18.

Friday, June 7, Everett Kelley died of a heart attack.

Monday, June 17, Jim's sister Clara cleaned up the apartment for the soon-to-be newlyweds.

But on Saturday, June 22, there was still no word as to when

Gisele Rouillon in Paris with her coworkers. Gisele is fourth from the left in the front row. Photo courtesy of Gisele Rouillon Leavenworth.

The S.S. Nick Stoner on which Gisele sailed to the U.S. They passed the Queen Mary on their way. Photo courtesy of Gisele Rouillon Leavenworth.

Chuck Myers married Ruth Worzel in June of 1946. Photo courtesy of Mary Briggs Austin.

the *S.S. Stoner* would arrive. That was because on June 15 Gisele was still at South Hampton, England. A propeller had broken on the ship, and it would be in dry dock two weeks for repairs. That information Jim received in a letter from Gisele which arrived on Monday, June 24, the day Jim helped his good friends Orville and Mary Clark move.

Art and Mary's good friends Charles H. Myers (son of Archie and Minnie Sergeant Myers) and Ruth Worzel (daughter of Herman and Blanche Quick Worzel) were married in June.

Jim Leavenworth was still waiting for the arrival of his bride Gisele at the end of June.

July 1946, Gisele in the U.S.
Finally, word arrived that the *S.S. Nick Stoner* would arrive on July 18, 1946. Jim and his sister Anna Meyers went to New York City to meet Gisele, and bring her back to Eldred. Such excitement!

A few days after Gisele arrived Ella made her a dress.

In the few weeks before they were married, Jim and Gisele went to the movies, picked huckleberries, went swimming, and spent time with relatives and friends Orville and Mary Clark.

Gisele even canned apples, swiss chard, peaches, and berries with Ella two weeks before the wedding. Stella must have visited at times as there is a photo of the three Leavenworth ladies, Gisele, Ella, and Stella which was most likely taken that summer.

August 1946, Jim Marries Gisele
On August 12, 1946, Jim and Gisele got their marriage license. The next day they were married in the Barryville Methodist Church by Rev. Beebout. Jim's good friends Orville and Mary Clark stood up with them.

The day after their wedding, Gisele and Jim went to their new home—the apartment that Jim and his dad had fixed up for them.

Gisele had been rather shocked at her first sight of the hamlet of Eldred, and the small

Gisele, Ella, and Stella Leavenworth. Photo courtesy of Cynthia Leavenworth Bellinger.

Mr. and Mrs. James Leavenworth on their wedding day. Photo courtesy of Gisele Rouillon Leavenworth.

dairy farm where she would live. What a change from the bustling city of Paris. Gisele had already done some canning with Ella before she was married. The rest of the summer Gisele worked alongside Ella and learned to make butter, can vegetables, dig up potatoes, and pluck a chicken. They canned two bushels of peaches, a half bushel of plums, beans, and carrots.

Sometimes Gisele rode with Jim when he delivered wood. Jim and Gisele spent time with their friends, Orville and Mary Clark; Frank Bartle and his girlfriend Lee (Libra); and Jim's sisters Clara and Anna.

Gisele was understandably very homesick at first. She and Jim's sister Anna often visited. It was very soothing to Gisele when Anna would brush her hair and just talk to her.

Boarding Houses 1946

Barryville

Delaware View Inn, Emil Poell
Ideal summer resort. 1,800 ft. high, overlooking Delaware River Valley. 36 airy outside rooms with running water. All outdoor sports, swimming pool, good German cooking.

Yulan

Laurel Cottage, Joseph Weber
On Washington Lake. New management. Private bathing beach. Hot and cold running water in all rooms; showers; innerspring mattresses. Acc. 50. Excellent food. Courteous service.

Colonial, Jack Hensel
On lake. Boating, bathing, fishing, running water all rooms. Booklet.

Yulan Hotel, Arthur Samyn
On Washington Lake. Modern Impts. boating, bathing, fishing, saddle horses, golf nearby $28 weekly up.

Twin Oaks, Flieger
On Washington Lake. Modern House. Private beach, boating, bathing, churches, casinos. Barryville 2745.

Eldred

Echo Hill House, Anthony Hirsch
In the foot of the Catskill Mountains. Private home remodeled to accommodate 25 guests. Walking distance of Washington Lake and Beach. Large, airy rooms. All innerspring mattresses. Good food. Resident baker and chef. $40 per week.

Highland Lake

Pine Hill Lodge, K. Lutz
Excellent food. Rooms with running water. Innerspring mattresses. Private beach. Boating, fishing, golfing, tennis, horses. Barryville 2180.

**Pinehurst on the Lake
Mrs. Robert Fierro**
Modern. Hot, cold running water every room. All sports. Bathing, boating, fishing. Excellent cuisine. Near churches. Booklet.

Lake Shore Hotel
Modern. Bathing, fishing, dancing, casino, bowling. Good home cooking. $27 to $30 per week

Deer Head Lodge, K. Eggers
New, modern. Fine food, boating, fishing, swimming, shuffleboard, handball, tennis, golf, horseback, dancing. All conveniences. May and June, $32. After July 1, $36 up.

Back road to Yulan during the 1940s. Photo courtesy of Betty Ann Mulvihill Doyle and Chris Doyle.

Yulan Hotel owned by Arthur Samyn. Postcard courtesy of Kevin Marrinan.

View of Washington Lake in the mid-1940s. Photo courtesy of Betty Ann Mulvihill Doyle and Chris Doyle.

Sunset View House owned by the Theuers. Photo courtesy of Jeanie Staubes Turner.

Alfons and Johanna Theuer owners of Sunset View House on Highland Lake. Photo courtesy of Jeanie Staubes Turner.

Joan Hill, Peggy Hill, and Margie Austin at a clambake in Port Jervis on the first day of September. Photo courtesy of Andy and Margie Austin Maglione.

Emery and Margaret Weber Getz, Edgar and Betty MacIntyre Getz, Charles and Lena Hill MacIntyre, in 1948. Charles and Lena MacIntyre adopted Peggy Hill. Photo courtesy of Alan Gothard.

When Mom (Gisele) came to America she was so lonely. Dad took her to town to meet another war bride. Bill Eldridge had married Jane Pochet who was from Belgium. Jane had been in town since May.

Jane and Bill Eldridge had an apartment over Pete Callahan's store. Mom said that she would go to town to see her practically every day. That made their days not so lonely. And they could converse in the same language.
—Cynthia Leavenworth Bellinger.

Charles and Lena Hill MacIntyre
Bill Eldridge's mother Harriet Hill (widow of John Hill) had died in July. Bill and his wife Jane were back from the war in May 1945, so Harriet had been able to see them before she passed away.

Harriet's daughter Peggy Hill was only 12 when her mother died. Her older half sisters took turns caring for her. Lena Hill MacIntyre was concerned that so many different homes left Peggy with no stability. So Lena and her husband Charlie MacIntyre adopted Peggy. Peggy had two new sisters (also her nieces): Evelyn and Betty MacIntyre.

In September Peggy went to a clambake in Port Jervis with her cousins Margie Austin and Joan Hill.

September 1946
Joseph and Juliette Lorphelin and their daughter Christiane, 18, from France, arrived in Eldred in September.

Juliette wanted to be with her sister Celina Nikolaus who had bought the old Avery/Bradley House.

Celina told Christiane, her niece, that there was another young French girl in town, and took Christiane to Garfield and Ella's to meet Gisele.

Ella called upstairs to Gisele to come down, and the two young women met.

We'll hear more about the Nikolaus Boarding House (renamed Deer Head Lodge) in 1947. But meanwhile Gisele had some friends she could talk to in French.

Mary Briggs Graduates
Mary Briggs graduated from Nurses Training in September.

Mary continued to work in October to make up for the days she missed when her tonsils were taken out (at the beginning of her classes). She also had to take the State Boards to officially be an R.N. (registered nurse).

Art Proposes to Mary
Arthur Austin gave Mary Briggs an engagement ring in September.

We were walking about his uncle Lon's property and Art asked me to marry him. I opened my mouth to say yes, and nothing came out. Finally, I said, "Sure."
—Mary Briggs Austin.

Art then wrote a letter to Mary's folks who were staying with Mary's grandmother Ida Crabtree in Oregon. The house Art mentioned was the one his cousin Goldie had built. Goldie and Stella lived at the Boy Scout Camp, so they rented out their home.

Arthur Austin, Eldred, to Rev. and Mrs. H.I. Briggs, Springfield, Ore.
September 17, 1946
Dear Mr. and Mrs. Briggs,
Mary and I are planning on being married the early part of November—after Mary takes her R.N. exams. We will probably be married by Rev. Beebout, our present minister.

We don't know yet where we will go for our honeymoon, but am afraid it won't be to the Yellowstone National Park; the old car would hardly stand the trip and I cannot see paying the price they are asking for a new one—would probably be money ahead though in the long run.

We have made arrangements to rent a six-room house about 1-1/2 miles out of Eldred on the back road to Yulan. It is a nice place, but am afraid Mary will be lonesome so far from town. She doesn't think so and would rather try it than to rent an apartment in Eldred.

Hope that when you return to the East you will pay us a long visit. It would please both of us very much.

My apologies for not writing sooner, but trust I am right in believing you will not disapprove and that our marriage will have your blessing. Mary will undoubtedly write you a fuller account.

Sincerely, Art

Before we were married, Art and I went to Port Jervis and bought linoleum for the kitchen and dining room, a rug for the living room, a gas stove, refrigerator, washing machine, living room and bedroom furniture; and a solid walnut dining room table, buffet, and chairs from a friend.—Mary Briggs Austin.

Uncle Lon Austin

There was a very special person Art had yet to tell about his marriage. Uncle Lon Austin had encouraged Art to get married so he would not be lonely.

Uncle Lon's very old house was drafty and not safe. Art was quite concerned about Lon living there alone in the winter. So the Sunday morning Art told Lon he was to be married, he also told his uncle that he could stay with them for the winter. "Is that so," Uncle Lon said.

"Want to go to church?" asked Art, who had often taken Uncle Lon to or from a church meeting.

"Yes, wait 'til I get ready." Lon got out of his chair, went to the basin of water, dipped his comb in the water and slicked back his hair. He was then ready to go to church.

Uncle Lon would stay with Art and Mary two winters. But as soon as spring came, he always went back to his old home in Eldred.

Charlie and Catherine

In the summer of 1946, Charlie Winter, fresh out of the Army, took the Erie Railroad to Port Jervis to enjoy a week in the mountains.

Charlie stayed at Alfons and Johanna Theuer's boarding house in Highland Lake. Charlie spent evenings at the Theuer's "Sunset Bar" just down the road from the boarding house.

Charlie played the piano in a rollicking style that encouraged good cheer, singing along and dancing. One evening, inspired by the good-time music, Mr. Theuer went across the road to his home to retrieve his violin. His daughter, Irene (later Staubes), brought along her accordion. Alfons and Irene joined Charlie for a jam session that entertained the assembled patrons until the wee hours of the morning.

Charlie expressed an interest in dating the waitress at the Sunset Bar, Margo Bosch. Margo responded by telling Charlie that she was already engaged to her husband-to-be, Fred Meyer. Margo told Charlie that, although she was unavailable, her sister-in-law, Florence Schmerfeld Bosch had a cute sister named Catherine.

Charlie approached Willie and Florence Bosch who were also at the Sunset Bar that evening and obtained Katherine's phone number. Charlie followed through when he returned home to Brooklyn. Charlie and Catherine married on September 14, 1947. They were married for over 63 years and had six children.

Charlie Winter hales from Bushwick in Brooklyn and is not related to the local Winter family.
—Ken Bosch.

Charlie and Catherine Schmerfeld Winter. Photo courtesy of Ken Bosch.

The After Affects of War

Harriet Hill's son Charlie Eldridge did not arrive back in the States until late 1946, and of course was devastated his mother had passed away. (Harriet had heard from the Red Cross that Charlie was OK before her death.) Perhaps the Army had held him longer because he had gone AWOL for a while after the horrid fighting in Italy.

Charlie was given a hard time and called a deserter when he returned. That along with not being able to see his mother before she died in July must have hurt terribly. The indescribable horrors of war had a huge affect

Goldie and Stella Leavenworth's home that Art and Mary lived in after they were married. Photo shows: Art, Mary, Charles Kerr holding Lois, Muriel Kerr, Myrtle Briggs, Pal the dog, and John Briggs. Photo courtesy of Mary Briggs Austin.

Art and Mary Briggs Austin on their wedding day in November, 1946. Photo courtesy of Mary Briggs Austin.

on many families long after the war. Charlie was fortunate to have met and married a fine young woman named Florence Bloom.

In a previous chapter it was mentioned that Joe Mellan spent a long convalescence in military hospitals. When he recovered, he spent the remainder of his enlistment as a medic/orderly caring for the physically and psychologically damaged soldiers returning from the war. Joe was discharged in 1946. Joe Mellan had married Mary Paulik in 1944 *(see Sidebars, pp. 303 and 363).*

October 1946
In October the Leavenworth men took up a bee tree. There were about 50 pounds of honey: 25 pounds for Garfield and Ella and 25 pounds for Clifford Myers.

The last Wednesday in October Gisele varnished furniture for Ella and scrubbed the floor which Ella waxed. The men cut and sawed logs.

In October Mary Briggs stayed a week with Edna Gardner while she studied (Art helped) for her State Boards—four days of tests to qualify for her nursing degree.

Edna Gardner was not related to Mary, but she was to Arthur Austin. It seemed to be important to Edna that Art was a relative. (Edna's father James K. Gardner and Art Austin were great-grandsons of James Eldred.)

Edna was a musician, music teacher, and the organist at the Methodist Church. As we shall see, she played for Mom and Dad's wedding. Edna later gave me a small bisque doll, which I consider a special treasure.

Mary stayed a few days with family friends Charlie and Muriel Kerr, before her wedding. Charles and Muriel were the only ones who knew Art and Mary's wedding date.

November 1946
Arthur Marries Mary
Saturday, November 2, 1946, Arthur L. Austin married Mary Rosamond Briggs at the Barryville Methodist Church. Rev. Beebout performed the ceremony.

My sister Laura made my dress. My corsage was white gardenias.

The organist Edna Gardner told us to wait outside the church vestibule doors and to come in when she played the Wedding March.

I waited for Here Comes the Bride, *but never heard it. Eventually Edna said, "Well where are they?" That was our cue to come in. The ceremony went fine and we were pronounce husband and wife, and off we went!*

During the ceremony (since no one knew our wedding date) two ladies were cleaning up after the lovely shower which had been given for us the night before. One lady, with a dust mop in her hand and a dust cap on her head, thought the Rev. Beebout was practicing his sermon. Another lady, trapped upstairs, congratulated us afterward.

No one knew when we were getting married because Art thought if we had a big wedding he'd be so nervous he wouldn't feel like he was married!

We went to Natural Bridge, Virginia for our Honeymoon trip. I'd told my girlfriends at the hospital that we'd be going to this cave and that cave and they thought they were quite clever when they said, "What does Art think he is—a cave man?"

When we came back Aunt Christina Leavenworth invited us to stay overnight as she knew everything wasn't in order in our house yet. Next day we went home—a short distance up the road from Echo Hill Farm.

Home was the lovely six-room, one-bath home from Art's cousin Goldie and his wife Stella, who were also our good friends. —Mary Briggs Austin.

Jimmy Meyers and Dick Hansen were both in their great-aunt Charlotte's 1946–47 first and second grade class. Front row: G. Nieke, B. Bertram, C. Flieger, H. Eldred, J. Henrickson, J. Traver, A. Draxler, M. Rudolph, C. Gentes, D. Grollimund, L. Hainzl, D. Reed, R. Kunkele, H. Wilson, R. Fierro. Second Row: D. Rundle, P. Sulzbach, C. Meyer, J. Beebout, J. Poth, L. Nieke, A. Reiser, D. Maney, J. Dede, N. Hill, H. Brown, W. Keller. Third Row: D. Hansen, P. Bertram, G. Horton, R. Mills, H. Kestler, E. Hill, C. Geiger, H. Stevens, Fred Bosch. Fourth Row: J. Barnes, F. Fracke, J. Hulse, P. Kestler, J. Meyers, R. Hill. Photo courtesy of Cynthia Leavenworth Bellinger.

During the next two years Art and Mary lived on the west side of Eldred. Mary sometimes worked at the hospital in Callicoon (an hour away). But often she helped people in the town that could use a nurse's help including Mr. Styles, and Elizabeth Hoatson Clark Wilson (Ella's aunt Lizzie), both of whom have been a part of this story.

Miss Leavenworth's 1946–1947 First and Second graders
Garfield and Ella's grandsons Jimmy Meyers and Dick Hansen were both in his sister (their great aunt) Charlotte Leavenworth's first/second grade class in the 1946–1947 school year. Their classmates included Lillian Hainzl, daughter of the owners of Tallwood Lodge and Fred Bosch, son of Ed and Eleanor Bosch.

November 1946
The Leavenworths were busy with Jim's sawmill all November.
Garfield and Earl Wells drew and skidded logs. Earl also delivered the lumber. As did Jim and Vern Clark who also sawed the logs at Jim's mill. Mid-November Earl and Frank Bartle cut logs at Schoverling's.

Fred Schoverling, owner of Hillcrest, died of a heart attack sometime in the late 1940s. Hillcrest was no longer operated as a boarding house.—Ken Bosch.

Frank Bartle, Garfield, and Earl continued to cut down trees. Vern Clark and Jim sawed and sometimes delivered the lumber.

While the men worked at the mill, Ella crocheted. One of her friends sold $11 of her crochet work. Gisele went with Mary Clark to Narrowsburg one day. Another day Jim and Gisele went to Port Jervis to shop.

Sometimes Jim took Gisele

Lumber outside Jim's Mill. Photo courtesy of Kevin Marrinan.

Ed Wilson's Atlantic Gas Station, 1946. The new Wilson home (rooftop can be seen) was moved so the pumps could be built. Photo courtesy of Mary Agnes Wilson Dorney.

December 1946

Monday December 2, Frank Bartle married Libra (Lee), an Italian girl from New York City.

The first part of December Mr. Howlett hooked up the sink for Ella; cost $9.55. Vernon worked with Jim in the mill.

Garfield and Earl put the stove pipe up and fixed the shed windows on the equipment shed. The hired men would stay there when they worked at Jim's mill.

Christmas 1946

As she usually did, Ella sent her sister Hazel Connor a Christmas package.

Four days before Christmas Jimmy Meyers had chicken pox.

Three days before Christmas Jim got a tree. Ella trimmed it.

Christmas Eve Garfield was sick. Jim, Gisele, and Ella went to Clara and Anna's to watch the children open their presents.

Christmas Day Jim and Gisele went to Clara's for dinner. Goldie and Stella went to his parents.

"Good Christmas except Dad sick," Ella wrote.

The last day of December, Jim and Gisele went to the movies.

and Ella when he delivered lumber. Towards the end of November Jim bought a tractor from Otto Schmidt at Avery's; Garfield bought a heater.

Ed Wilson's Garage

It's been some time since we talked about Ed and Agnes Mary Wilson who we first met when Agnes Mary called Ed's Taxi Service one summer when she was vacationing at Glendella.

In 1946 Ed and Agnes Mary had two adorable daughters, Mary Agnes and Ruth Ann. Ed's father Louis Wizlankas lived in Tusten, close enough for Ed and his family to visit often. Louis, a tailor and tinsmith, had first become acquainted with the area when he installed tin ceilings in Barryville and Tusten (including Barryville Congregational Church).

In 1946 Ed Wilson's Atlantic Gas Station was built in Barryville, on the corner created by Route 97 and Barryville-Yulan Road. The Wilsons also bought a house from Anthony Poth. Since the new house was located where the gas pumps would be, it was moved back so the gas station could be built.

A number of folks mentioned in *The Mill on Halfway Brook* had owned or had been part owners of the Wilson's new house as early as 1850. From May 1850 to April 1860, James K. Gardner, Chauncey Thomas, and Elias Calkin were owners. The house must have been passed along to James Gardner's wife Eliza; children Stephen St. John Gardner, Maria Calkin, Ann Cuddeback; and grandchildren James K. Gardner, Alonzo and Lillie Calkin.

Arthur C. Toaspern and Art Rohman owned the house from June 1930 to 1932; several other Rohmans had been joint owners.

"Four days before Christmas Jimmy Meyers had chicken pox." Photo courtesy of Cynthia Leavenworth Bellinger.

Ed Wilson, Ruth Ann, and Mary Agnes Wilson; and grandpa Louis Wizlankas (who installed tin ceilings). Photo courtesy of Mary Agnes Wilson Dorney.

Chapter 13
Old Home on the Hill
Farewell to Eldred, 1947–1950

Backward, turn backward, O Time, in your flight,
Make me a child again just for tonight.—Rock Me to Sleep,
by Elizabeth Allen, often quoted by Arthur Austin.

I am living with my nephew Arthur on the Kelley place. It is a new house with all the latest improvements but still it is not home...There comes an inner longing for the old home on the hill.—Lon Austin.

The years 1947–1950 would bring many changes in the lives of Art and Mary Austin. In this 1949 photo Art Austin holds their new little one, Louise. He quite likely quoted some poetry to her from his eclectic repertoire, perhaps, Rock Me to Sleep. *Photo courtesy of Mary Briggs Austin.*

I want to go back to the orchard.
The orchard that used to be mine.
The apples ripening and falling.
The air with their wine.
I want to run out through the pasture
And let down the dusty old bars.
I want to see her face there waiting
With eyes like the twin stars.
O nights ye are weary and dreary.
O days there is something you lack
To the farm in the valley,
I want to go back.

Lon Austin would turn 90 in September. He not only wished he could live in the home of his childhood that he loved, but to go back in time, when he quoted the wistful poem in a letter to a friend.

Lon had spent the winter with his nephew Arthur Austin and his wife Mary, who rented from Art's cousin Goldie Leavenworth. Perhaps you remember that Goldie had built his house on what was once the Kelley family's property.

January and February 1947
Goldie Leavenworth along with his dad Garfield, brother Jim, Vernon Clark, and Clifford Myers worked at Jim's sawmill in the month of January. Jim and Garfield delivered lumber. When he had some time off, Jim and Gisele might go fishing or to a movie with Mary and Orville Clark. Sometimes Art and Mary Austin stopped by to see his uncle Garfield and aunt Ella.

Jim delivered a couple loads of lumber in February. Gisele visited with Jane Eldridge several times.

March 1947
Uncle Lon, 89, the only child left of the ten children of Henry and Mary Ann Eldred Austin, wrote a nostalgic, eloquent letter to his friend Arthur (last name unknown). Lon wanted to go back to his old home, but he also looked forward to his final home.

Lon Austin, Eldred, to Friend Arthur
Dear Friend Arthur,
I started two or three times to answer your letter, but so far

In 1947 Irwin was transferred to pastor churches in South Dakota. Irwin and Myrtle spent four years at White River, two years at Timber Lake, then went to Hazel and Thomas, South Dakota. Photo courtesy of Mary Briggs Austin.

First page of Lon's letter to his friend Arthur. Letter courtesy of Melva Austin Barney.

haven't started as the weather is so beautiful, the air embracing and I am feeling much better than I did in the past, so I will try it again.

I got awfully tired moving and I caught a heavy cold which made me down and out. I am feeling OK now, except the weight of years. But I am looking forward to the day of my departure with great expectancy for all my toil and struggle, all my trials and temptations, all my loneliness of heart I leave them at death's portals and my soul will go sweeping through the gates into Paradise.

But do not misunderstand me. I do not expect to enter the city that hath foundations on my own goodness or my own merits, but I do expect to enter into the gates eternal through the merits of the crucified and the "power of an endless life."

What is death that we should shun it? Is it not the door that we enter into immortality? Who will regret having passed through it in the bloom of his manhood or even in youth's sweet prime.

True I am a member of a large family, fifth in line. I can not understand why I should stand in the center and see all the others fall around me like the sturdy oak deep rooted in the rocks and soil, behold all other trees uprooted by the storm. They tell me "time heals her ravages" but not all the up turned trees are re rooted again. The heart will bleed, but each wild throe, each parting link, one more call to the changeless land to which I go—I hope, I hope, I hope through all.

I have felt in other days, the blight of loneliness, but never felt its full weight until now.

I want the rose that the wind took yesterday, I want it more than this. It had no thorn, it was the sweetest rose that grew. I want the last night kiss.

I looked for you last summer, but looked in vain, but am glad to learn what was my loss was your gain. Was glad to learn that you were able to get out and see the beauties of the golden west. You infer that you had a good time, but was glad to get home. Home, sweet, home, there is no place like home.

I am living with my nephew Arthur on the Kelley place. It is a new house with all the latest improvements but still it is not home.

I lived on the old homestead (which is now Dr. Austin's place) for 30 years. It was my parents' home in the days of my childhood and there comes an inner longing for the old home on the hill.

You have a long way to go to catch up with my tender years. I held my own fairly good until I was about 80. Then I increased my momentum on the down grade and I am nearing the western sunset, the twilight deepens, Lord with me abide [reference to the hymn, Abide with Me]. The clouds hang low, deep dense and fog like.

I am feeling quite well. Got a new lease of life, a short one.

Not long ago, my nearest neighbors [Herman and Mary

Bosch] who were very kind to me, and it seemed almost like going home when I called upon them, both are gone. A little later my dear sister, the last nearest of kin passed on.

Just recently the last of my school mates of other days, days of long ago, crossed the bar. All my lovely companions are faded and gone and at times I feel as feel I must, that I am alone upon a great round world.

One soft sweet solemn thought
Comes to me o'er and o'er
I am nearer my Father's house today
Than ever I've been before.
Your friend, Lon

Irwin and Myrtle Briggs

Lon Austin was a lay preacher and sometimes had given the sermon at the Methodist Church for Irwin Briggs. Irwin and Myrtle Briggs, Mary Austin's folks, returned to Barryville in the spring of 1947. They had been traveling around the country visiting their relatives. They would soon leave for South Dakota where Irwin would pastor a Methodist Church.

Mary Austin, Nurse

Mary Austin was a registered nurse as of October 1946, and was able to put her nursing skills to good use in the area where she and Art lived. Mary helped at the Callicoon Hospital a couple times, but mostly she did private nursing.

April and May 1947

In April news at the Leavenworths: Jimmy Meyers had his tonsils out. The hired men started living in the shed by Jim's mill.

In May Dr. Crellin was killed in an auto accident at 2 a.m.

During May Jim and Gisele

1947 National & Halfway Brook News

Joe Livingston and his bride Evelyn MacIntyre. Photo courtesy of Alan Gothard.

1947 National News
- Chuck Yeager flew the Bell X-1 at Mach 1 at 45,000 feet, and became the first to break the sound barrier.
- The first *Howdy Doody* TV show.

1947 Eldred Seniors
- Edward Bisland, Yolanda Foscola, Evelyn Hallock, Helen Hensel, Henry Oset, Joyce Timmerhoff, Grace Brinkerhoff.

1947 Moved
- Lou, Edith, and Mary Maudsley moved to a second floor apartment in the old school.

1947 Births
- John D. Hull born to John J. and Josephine Lipinski Hull, in Guam.
- Christopher Frey born to Everett and Mary Ann Osborn Frey, in Brooklyn. The family would soon move to Barryville.
- Michael Hulse born to Clifford and Helen Zita Myers Hulse.

Helen Hensel. She would marry Chester Oset. Photo in 1947 Yearbook.

Sam and Eleanor Myers Rizzuto. Photo courtesy of their son Timothy C. Rizzuto.

- George Crandall born to Clifford and Mary Myers Crandall.

1947 Marriages
- Frederick Meyer married Margo Bosch.
- Joe Livingston married Evelyn MacIntyre.
- Sam Rizzuto married Eleanor Myers.
- Grant Sergeant married Helen Kuen.
- Ivan Tether married Helen Jayne.

1947 Deaths
- Doctor Crellin died in May.
- Charlotte Elizabeth (Lottie) Myers Darling, 1858–1947, was the daughter of Martin D. and Jane Ann Van Pelt Webb Myers.
- Clifford E. Myers, 1902–1947.
- John Henry Clark, 1867–1947, son of George Case and Mary Harding Brown Clark.
- Walter T. Tether, 1868–1947.
- Edward Smith, 1867–1947.
- Julius Maier, 1866–1947.
- Alice Spiers Sergeant, 1870–1947.
- Alexander Wait, 1883 to 1947.
- Herman L. Clouse, 1883–1947.

Alfred and Helen Wolff bought Hillside Inn (formerly Metzger's Bowling Alley and Dance Hall) and ran it as a restaurant. Postcard courtesy of Kevin Marrinan.

went fishing sometimes. Jim and Gisele took his sister Anna and her family, and his mother Ella to see Haas' apple blossoms at the orchard near Honesdale. The last Wednesday in May, George Bradley stopped by Garfield and Ella's.

Art and Mary Austin's Plans
With the GI bill paying tuition and books, Art, encouraged by Mary, decided to go to college. Since he had been out of high school 17 years, Art went to Eldred High School for math, science, and English books to study the year before he left Eldred to go to college in Houghton, New York.

New Boarding Houses Owners
The Boarding Houses in the area would continue almost 20 more years. Several boarding houses had new owners, and at least one of them changed names.

The Lorphelins ran what was first the Bradley House, then Averys. They changed the name to Deer View Lodge.

Joe and Mary Mellan bought Bertram's Tavern from Art (Bucky) and Julie Bertram. The Tavern became Mellan's Bar and Grill.

Bucky and Julie became managers of Bertram's Lodge after they bought it from his parents.

Deer View Lodge
John and Celina Nikolaus, owners of Deer View Lodge, also owned and ran Nikolaus' Steak House in Manhattan.

Celina's sister Juliette, her husband Joseph Lorphelin, and their daughter Christiane had arrived from France in fall 1946.

Since John and Celina were often in the city overseeing their restaurant, Joseph and Juliette managed Deer View Lodge.

Joseph and Juliette did not speak English, so their daughter Christiane, 18, greeted the guests, took reservations by phone, and picked up boarders at the Shohola Station.

If there were no rooms left for guests, they could board at other houses. But the guests would come back to Deer View Lodge for the meals because of the chef and the delicious entrees. (Some Boarding Houses did not serve meals.)

The chef from the Nikolaus' Steak House cooked at the boarding house during the summer months. Christiane asked him why he wanted to work at the boarding house seven days a week when he could be at the restaurant only five days a week. The chef said John Nikolaus had always been good to him and he wanted to return the favor by helping John out.

The chef wouldn't allow fans in the kitchen because he didn't want them to cool down the food. So in summer Joseph replaced the kitchen windows with screens so there could be some air exchange.

Each night Christiane typed up the menu for the next day and put them on the tables. The guests chose what they wanted from the menu.

Joseph Lorphelin had cows, chickens, and a large garden. So they had their own milk, butter, eggs, and vegetables.

They ordered baby chicks

Deer View Lodge was first owned by Isaac M. Bradley. Postcard courtesy of Christiane Lorphelin Stolte.

Deer View Lodge

Another view of Deer View Lodge courtesy of Christiane Lorphelin Stolte.

Deer View Lodge, in the heart of Sullivan County hills, is located less than 100 miles from New York City.

Bordering on Washington Lake with 1,000 acres of hunting grounds and a private lake, Deer View Lodge affords excellent fishing for bass, pickerel, and perch as well as boating, bathing, and picnic grounds.

This section of Sullivan County has the most beautiful scenic roads for the people who enjoy hiking. There is a nine-hole golf course a short distance from the lodge.

Our large, newly decorated and modern main house and private cottages can accommodate 60 people in 28 large, airy rooms.

The Kitchen (French cuisine) is under the personal supervision of Madame Juliette Lorphelin. All our eggs, poultry, and vegetables are supplied by our nearby farm and lakes. All pastries and cakes are baked in our own kitchen.

The Deer View Lodge has shady extensive lawns affording good ground for croquet, ping-pong, horseshoes, and badminton. Saddle horses are for hire.

1947 Deer View Lodge Menu which changed daily courtesy of Christiane Lorphelin Stolte.

to raise for eggs. When the tiny peeping balls of fluff arrived, Emma Stevens the Postmaster called and said, "Chicks are here."

The vegetables served depended on what was in season from the garden. Meat was ordered through the Nikolaus Restaurant in New York City.

Boarders were charged $8 per day for a room and three meals. If they stayed the week, it cost $45 for room and meals.

Hillside Inn

Near the Yulan's *Times Square* was what was long ago Metzger's Bowling Alley and Dance Hall. In 1947 Alfred and Helen Wolff bought the place and ran it as the restaurant, Hillside Inn.

Fred and Marion Hensel

Fred and Marion Hensel lived in nearby Yulan. Fred had been the Yulan Postmaster since 1938. In 1947 Fred and his wife Marion

Fred and Marion Hensel

Fred and Marion Hensel by Beaver Pond Dam in 1947. Photo courtesy of Dennis J. Carroll.

Dennis Carroll helping his uncle Fred Hensel raise the flag at what was once Yulan Cottage. Photo courtesy of Dennis J. Carroll.

It is almost fifty years since I last stayed in my aunt and uncle's house—long since sold when they moved back to New York City after Uncle Fred retired as the Postmaster of Yulan, New York…

Occasionally, I return for a day trip to envelop myself in the quiet and solitude of upstate New York and usually stop by the house in Yulan.

It originally was called Yulan Cottage, a boarding house owned and operated by the Hensel family, starting, I suspect, in the early part of the Twentieth Century. Back then and up to the early sixties, boarding houses like Twin Oaks, Sunset Cottage, The Colonial, and Maple Crest on Washington Lake, flourished. Boarders spent their two-week vacations—usually the same two weeks—there. They traveled on the Erie Railroad, which later merged with the Lackawanna. The trains, steam and later diesel, departed from Jersey City or Hoboken, up through New Jersey, New York State then at Port Jervis along the rim of Pennsylvania above the Delaware River to Shohola—I can still recall the smell of steam, smoke and cinders. Others took the Shortline Bus up from the Port Authority, and air horns echoed through the mountains, announcing two arrivals and two departures daily at the bus stop by the Post Office.

The house—located on what is now called Airport Road next to what used to be an Esso gas station, just down the hill from the Yulan Volunteer Fire Department—is an old Victorian, complete with wraparound porch. In the early days there was also a barn for the cows that grazed up on what became Bungalow Hill.

There were originally two entrances on either side of the house, one that led from across the lawn to the stoop at the front and the other at the top of the driveway that ran along the right side. A third was later added around the back with the addition of a bedroom, bathroom and kitchen after my aunt Marion and Uncle Fred married in the forties. By this time, they were out of the boarding house business and Yulan Cottage no longer existed.

A brick stoop stood by the entrance at the end of the driveway, which I suspected replaced a wooden one, like the one that remained at the front of the house. The door—the top part glass with a lace curtain behind it, opened with a skeleton key—led into the living room where the floors were wood partially covered with a large rug. It was furnished with an upholstered club chair made by my uncle along with the bookcases, coffee table and an end table, my uncle's Morris chair and a rocker for me where all three of us—"of an evening," as my aunt used to say—would read…

Through the living room was my bedroom. It had five large windows a big three pane bay in the front and two on the side. Bright light and the sensation of bare feet on a wooden floor on winter mornings are still vivid to me.

Upstairs there were three rooms, one of which my uncle used for his workshop. He bought me a tool set from the Sears and Roebuck Catalogue and taught me how to saw things safely, to hold a hammer properly and toe a nail, drill a pilot hole and how to sand and file. Our first joint project was a birdhouse.

Upstairs there was the attic, impossible to enter during the summer months but okay in winter with a coat. It was a full-sized attic that you could walk through completely. I remember looking up at the window at the roof peak from down on the lawn at an enormous hornet's nest that was always there and, explained away by my Uncle Fred: "don't bother the bees and they won't bother you."

Down in the full basement—a fieldstone wall structure as I recall—my aunt kept the jams and jellies that she canned…My uncle had an artesian well drilled; I seem to remember them striking water at about one hundred or so feet…—Excerpted from: Dennis J. Carroll, Remembering Yulan: A Spring Recollection, "Hancock Herald," March 23, 2011.

Hensel's Colonial

Left: Postcard of the Colonial in the 1950s. The lower left is a bungalow that was rented out to families usually for a week or so. The main building is on the top. To the right on the second floor was the owner's residence (Lisette Hensel). The kitchen and dishwashing room was below that. Right: The Colonial, 1942. Postcards courtesy of Helen Hensel Oset.

The L-shaped Colonial had three floors, with 26 rooms. Above the garage there were four rooms and then a bungalow (with three rooms) which large families would rent.

A huge open porch ran along the front of the building and at the end there was an enclosed porch.

The dining room was on the first floor in the long section of the *L*. There were also seven guest rooms with shared bathrooms and showers.

In the short part of the *L* was the kitchen, the dish washing area, the storage room with a walk-in fridge, and a sitting area.

Above the kitchen, on the second floor, were seven rooms (some were for the family to live in). On the second floor above the dining room were eight rooms with shared baths and showers.

The third floor had four rooms for the help (several to a room) and eight rooms for the guests.

In the 1960s a recreation room was built next to the garage for boarders to play cards. Movies were shown in the evenings.

Lisette Hensel served three meals a day; noon and supper meals were both big. She started preparing lunch right after breakfast was done; and after lunch, she started on supper.

Breakfast:
Homemade biscuits or rolls were served at breakfast. (There were no toasters in the early days.)
- Choice of cold cereal and a hot cereal which changed each day from oatmeal to cream of wheat.
- Beverages: juice, coffee, tea, or milk.
- The main breakfast meal would vary from eggs cooked in different ways, pancakes, bacon, sausage, etc.

The Noon Meal:
- Monday: Leg of lamb
- Tuesday: Roast Pork
- Wednesday: Chicken
- Thursday: Roast top sirloin of beef alternated with pot roast.
- Friday: Baked fish with homemade clam chowder.
- Saturday: Corned beef and cabbage alternated with large ham and boiled cabbage.
- Sunday: Turkey dinner. (Lisette wanted those who left at noon to have a good hearty meal before they headed home.)

The Evening Meal:
- Monday: Smoked pork tenderloin.
- Tuesday: Hungarian goulash on noodles.
- Wednesday: Pork chops.
- Thursday: Spaghetti and meatballs.
- Friday: Cold supper consisting of salads (macaroni, tuna, and cold cuts). If she didn't have tuna salad, she made fish cakes.
- Saturday: Steak and corn on the cob.
- Sunday: Lisette's famous German potato salad with sliced ham, tomatoes, and lettuce.

Lisette ordered meat from Trunz, a German meat market in Brooklyn, because they would cut the meat to her specifications.

Lisette's son in-law Chet Oset grilled the steaks every Saturday on the huge institutional sized stove. The burners had a large flat grill that would set down on top.

Helen's sister, Katherine and her husband Richard Haas were also there on Saturday night.

Every Saturday night the recreation hall showed movies.
—*Helen Hensel Oset.*

Around 1944: Yulan Times Square with the Post Office where Fred Hensel was Postmaster. Photo courtesy of Kevin Marrinan.

lived in the Yulan Cottage which his mother Katherine Hensel had once run as a boarding house. In the late 1940s and into the 1950s, Fred and Marion's nephew Dennis Carroll spent many happy hours with these loving folks.

At some point in time, Fred's brother Lou Hensel and his wife ran an "up-to-date" refreshment stand, which was next to the Yulan Post Office.

Hensel's Colonial
Fred and Marion's niece Helen Hensel graduated in June 1947. Helen had grown up in the Colonial, a boarding house on Washington Lake, which her parents Jacob and Lisette had operated since at least 1927.

You may remember that the Colonial was originally called Washington Lake House and built by Joseph Tether in the 1880s.

The boarding houses in the area helped each other out. There didn't seem to be any rivalry.

I remember how the boarding houses all worked together. If someone was short on something, they would borrow from each other. If one house ran out of rooms, other houses would put up the people for them.

Helen Hensel Oset would board people in her house in the 50s and 60s when her mom Lisette's Colonial, her mother in-law Mary Bornstein's Grand Vue, or Reggie Walter's Maplecrest were overbooked.—Cynthia Leavenworth Bellinger.

June Through August 1947
In June at the Leavenworths, Jim and Gisele went to the movies with either Mary and Orville Clark or Frank and Lee Bartle; and spent time with Bill and Jane Eldridge. Poor Lee and Clara. All three children had mumps. The last day of June, Jim and Gisele went swimming.

In July and August Clara and Lee looked for a farm near Delhi, New York. Sometimes their three children stayed with Garfield and Ella while they hunted for a place.

Haying season kept Jim busy.

In August Jim, Gisele, Anna, and Jimmy went to the circus. Jim and Gisele also went to see Bill and Jane Eldridge and their new baby girl. Walter, Hazel, and Marion Connor visited Garfield and Ella.

September 1947
Ed and Agnes Mary Wilson
In September Ed and Agnes Mary Wilson's daughter Kathy was born.

Ed kept busy with his Atlantic Station, his taxi service (which continued into the 1960s), and of course his adorable daughters— Mary Agnes, Ruth Ann, and Kathy.

Wilson's Taxi took folks to and from the Shohola Station to local boarding houses, camps, or other places they needed to be.

Ed Wilson also bowled in a league called *The Highlanders* at Rohman's Inn in Shohola during the 1940s and on into the 1950s.

People and Places Nearby
There were other cute children in the area. Ed Wolff (son of Albert and Ruth Foster Wolff) and his cousin Eileen Wolff (daughter of Norman and Dorothy Meyers Wolff) lived in Barryville near the Clouse Restaurant (Casino) which became Reber's.

Norman H. and Margaret Myers Sutherland and their children Barbara and Norman lived across the Delaware River in Shohola in 1947. (They would move to Barryville in nine years.) Barbara and Norman (Darlene wasn't born yet) liked to sit on the step of the Narrowsburg Lumber Company Truck their father drove.

Norman H. started working for the Narrowsburg Lumber Company in 1945 and would work for the company for 37 years.

Dennis Carroll with his aunt Marion Hensel on Bodine Lake. Photo courtesy of Dennis J. Carroll.

Colonial Memories

My first real job was working at the Colonial (sometimes called Lisette's) boarding house in Yulan. I waited tables and did chambermaid work during the summer months for several years. I have such fond memories of working there.

Lisette was a very special, wonderful lady. We all loved and respected her. She ran the Colonial as well as cooked fantastic meals for the boarding house guests by herself. She was never nervous or flustered even though she cooked three meals every day for many people—sometimes in very hot weather.

Everyone worked seven days a week, and it was hard work. Our day began early in the morning getting ready for breakfast and then serving it.

At 7 a.m. we were down in the dining room. We had set the table the night before. All meals were served family style. Every breakfast had a hot main course plus a choice of cold or hot cereal, juices, fruit and homemade biscuits.

After the guests had breakfast, we cleared the tables, swept the floor, and set up for lunch. Then all the help sat down together and had their breakfast.

The dishwasher then washed all the breakfast dishes by hand. We girls tended to the rooms—made up the beds or changed them if the occupants were leaving; and cleaned the bathrooms.

While we cleaned, Lisette prepared the noon meal, and the laundress washed and ironed.

The Laundry

The laundress' job was full time. There were no clothes dryers at the boarding house, so everything was hung outside. On days when it rained, towels were hung up above the garage to dry. The access to the attic was through a small passage way using a ladder to get to it. Helen and her sister would climb the ladder and hang up the towels.

Mangles (large machines for ironing damp sheets with heated rollers) were used to press the sheets and pillowcases.

Lunch

Lunch time was the next serving time and each day had its own special menu.

After lunch was served we cleared the tables, swept the floor and set up for supper. We then had our lunch. We sat around a huge table and talked about our plans for the remaining part of the day, when we were free to do as we wished.

We spent the afternoons swimming, water skiing, going into town, or hanging out on the porch. We enjoyed each other's company and we all got along well.

Evening Meal

Of course, there was no rest for Lisette as she began preparing the evening meal in the afternoon.

Suppertime came along and we again dressed in our white uniforms with white aprons and white shoes to serve the evening meal.

After supper, the tables were cleared, set up for the next morning's breakfast, and the floors swept and mopped. Then we all sat together—waitresses, dishwasher, kitchen help, Lisette and her family—and had our supper.

In the evening we all went our separate ways. Some of us went into town or home to see our families. Some of the older girls were dating and went out with their boyfriends. A group of us walked to the roller rink in town. On Saturday nights there was a sock hop at the rink.

Lisette treated us girls as if we were her own and watched over us. Our parents didn't have to worry that we were getting into trouble because Lisette would see that we didn't. We had a curfew in the evenings.

Some of the waitresses stayed at the boarding house and a few of the older girls drove home each evening. The first year I lived at home, but the following years I lived at the boarding house. I shared my room on the second floor with two other girls.

Many nice people came up from the city to stay at the Colonial and there were many fun times. I remember one family whose dad teased me by putting a trick spoon with a plastic fly on it by his plate. I was so embarrassed and apologized profusely until he started laughing.

That evening Lisette gave me a trick knife (that bent when used) to put by his plate. Lisette and all of us girls waited for him to use it. We laughed seeing the look on his face.—Cynthia Leavenworth Bellinger.

Good natured guest at the Colonial enjoys the joke played on him when his knife bent. Photo courtesy of Cynthia Leavenworth Bellinger standing beside the guest.

I worked along with Linda Guenther at the Colonial, in Yulan, during my high school years—late 50s. Lisette Hensel was the proprietor and she was a fabulous cook. We were waitresses and chambermaids in those days and had the most enjoyable summers working, swimming, and meeting new people...So many fond memories of the boarding house days indeed!
—Mary Agnes Wilson Dorney.

The Wilsons from left, Mary Agnes, Ed, Ruth Ann, and Kathy sitting on her mother Agnes Mary's lap at the Wilson Atlantic Station. Photo courtesy of Mary Agnes Wilson Dorney.

Ed Wolff and his cousin Eileen Wolff lived in Barryville near the Clouse Restaurant which became Reber's (in the background). 1944 photo courtesy of Ed Wolff.

Wilson's Taxi at Shohola Station around 1950. Photo courtesy of Mary Agnes Wilson Dorney.

Herbert and Lewis Eckhart

Herbert and Kathryn Eckhart's store and gas station on Route 97, was across from Ed Wilson's Atlantic Station.

Herbert's brother Lewis and his wife Mary lived on Barryville-Yulan Road, across the street from Ed's Station. Mary had a beautician shop in their home. Next door Lewis and Mary had a Luncheonette.

Clouses, Rebers, and the Riviera

You may remember there were two different Clouse Restaurants (called Casinos, but no gambling) in Barryville. One Clouse building became Reber's and was known for its German cuisine and Bavarian appearance. The Riviera Theater was or would be in the other Clouse Restaurant.

Joan Polishook's family vacationed in the area in the 1940s and 1950s, and Joan remembers the theater and Reber's.

While summering with my parents who boarded at Woodland Cottages up on Mail Road in the late 1940s and into the 1950s, I frequented the Riviera Theater known then as "Delaware Valley's Radio City." That came on the screen along with an advertisement for Shohola Feed and Grain, just before the start of the feature film.

The theater had a sloping wood floor and many times, someone would send an empty soda bottle rolling noisily down between the seats during the movie. It wasn't unusual for a skunk to wander through either!

One night a week was camp night and bus loads of campers with their counselors filled the house.

On another very crowded evening, one year, I sat on a folding chair in the doorway behind the last rows to see Gone With the Wind.

We were often driven to the theater, but on many occasions I walked the three miles along the partially paved Mail Road to the movies with my friends.

Barbara and Norman Sutherland sitting on the Narrowsburg Lumber Truck (1947 Ford) about 1949. Photo courtesy of their sister Darlene Sutherland Haas.

Herbert and Kathryn Eckhart

I often recall Eckhart's store with fond memories. As a child in the early 1960s, I visited this store just about every day. Along with it being a store/soda fountain, it was also Herbert and Kathryn Eckhart's home.

The first section of the store was a traditional store for that era. There were showcases, but on the top were candy bars, lifesavers, and gum among other things. There was also milk, bread and newspapers. Large grocery stores, which were few, were very rarely visited. The main grocery shopping was further down the road at Clouse's Store.

The second section of Eckhart's store was a long counter with stools to sit on and also small tables. There was a soda fountain where the best ice cream sundaes and sodas were created. Only Breyer's ice cream was used.

There also was a showcase where handmade items by Mrs. Eckhart were displayed. Winters in Barryville were long and cold. I can still see Mrs. Eckhart sitting in her rocking chair by the window crocheting or knitting items for that showcase. Barryville was a summer resort and those items were easily sold in the summer.

They sold postcards, souvenirs, and there was a penny scale. There also were racks of comic books and magazines.

The magazines that were not for "children" were hidden in the back of these racks. No matter how many warnings were given not to look at

Herbert and Kathryn Eckhart's Store. Postcard courtesy of Kevin Marrinan.

those magazines, every child's natural curiosity was drawn to that section. Some older kids were able to peek over the top to see if Mr. Eckhart was watching. When he felt that you were there too long, you would hear a slight cough telling you that he knew what you were trying to do. There would be some snickering and off the kids would go out the door, onto some other attraction, i.e. the "Back Road," the Cool Brook, or to Frank's Diner for some of their root beer served in frosty mugs.

Many days were spent by the soda fountain. While sipping a soda or eating a sundae I would sit and listen to Mr. Eckhart talk about the large white church up on the hill across from the store. As a curious child I would ask question after question. He would tell me how parishioners would tie their horses outside; how the church was built in 1835; and then a fire came in 1903 and it had to be rebuilt. It closed its doors in the 1950s.

Little did Mr. Eckhart know that the neighborhood kids would sneak up and go into the closed church. The pews were still there, the original Bible and hymnals. The pew seats were all red velvet. Today while enjoying genealogy, I wish I could remember all the history of the church and the town that was told over those sodas.

Herbert Eckhart was born in 1900 to Charles and Annie Beyer Eckhart and died in 1969 at the age of 68 years old after a two-car crash on Route 97 near Barryville, N.Y. His wife Kathryn died years later.
—Darlene Sutherland Haas.

Frank's Diner and Riviera Theater in the background. Postcard courtesy of Kevin Marrinan.

I also remember shopping in Barryville at Eckhart's store or Jensen's. There was the post office and the beauty parlor (Mary Eckhart was the hairdresser) as well.

Reber's was a great place. Hermann and Matilda Reber were the proprietors and the German-American cuisine was outstanding.

There was an organ that you could see from the bay window (facing the bridge road) and the music was very enjoyable. The Rebers soon built and operated a motel and lovely gift shop.—Joan Polishook.

Leavenworths, September 1947
Garfield and Ella's grandchildren—Dick, Wayne, and Lois Hansen; and Jimmy Meyers—were in school in September.

Jim Leavenworth started digging the cellar for the house with the white picket fence that he had promised Gisele.

He dug the cellar by hand with a pick and shovel. He hauled out the dirt with a horse pulling a stone sled. It took a while to save up for materials and to build it as he was working on other jobs.
—Cynthia Leavenworth Bellinger.

The Clouse building that became the Riviera Theater. Postcard courtesy of Kevin Marrinan.

Rohman Inn's Highlander Bowlers. Ed Wilson front row left. Back right: Richard Haas, then Reginald Walter. Photo courtesy of Mary Agnes Wilson Dorney.

Some years earlier, Edwin Van Schoick Myers with his granddaughter Melva. Photo courtesy of Joan Austin Geier.

Gisele and Ella canned. Jim continued to dig out the cellar, sometimes with help.

Alice Spiers Sergeant, second wife of Morgan Sergeant died of a stroke on September 4.

Jim and Gisele helped move a load of furniture to Clara and Lee Hansen's new place.

Towards the end of September Frank Bartle started working with Jim on lumber at Jim's mill. Gisele and Mary Austin visited some.

Clifford Myers Dies

Mid-September, Clifford Myers, 45, was found dead in the driveway of his home by Carl Vonderhorst of Barryville. His death was attributed to coronary thrombosis. Clifford had been receiving treatment for a heart ailment.

Clifford, a bachelor, lived alone on his farm. He farmed and at times worked on highway construction for the Sullivan County Department of Highways.

It's not hard to imagine how hard Clifford's death must have been on his family, especially his father Edwin Van Schoick Myers, 84. Edwin's mother had died when he was quite young. Two of his children died when they were infants.

Edwin's dear wife Mabel Owen had died in 1930, and his best friend Mort Austin had died in 1937. Edwin had two sons Raymond and Orville Myers, a daughter Gladys Austin, and several grandchildren to share his sorrow. Joan Austin wrote a poignant poem for her grandfather Edwin Myers.

Two Planks

Grandpa,
Your lap seemed safe.
Storms were calmer there.
Through sinking hollows
your blind eyes saw.
Your deaf ears heard
my silence.
Your heart,
under grey flannel,
labored against my cheek
and your hands,
where blood toiled
in teal cords,
smoothed my hair.

Old man,
awash in the long nights
I heard you pray.
You could not hear
your own voice
pleading through the dark.
Currents which sucked at me
were sweeping you.

When day came
I pressed like seaweed
to your shirt.
Rocking in your pipe's blue haze,
I anchored in the lightness
of your bones.
You and I were a small tough boat,
Two planks lashed in a
murderous sea.

Lon Austin Turns 90

Near the end of September Alfred and Bessie Hill joined Art and Mary to celebrate Lon's 90th birthday. Mary made the birthday cake. Lon grinned when he saw the candles in the shape of a 90.

Lon would soon be joining Art

Joe and Mary: Mellan's Bar and Grill

Joe and Mary Mellan purchased Bertram's Tavern in Highland Lake from Art "Bucky" and Julie Bertram in 1947.

After Joe Mellan was discharged in 1946, he found his return to civilian work difficult. Tasks such as shoveling would result in extreme pain in his damaged elbows. Joe would have to find a line of work that suited his physical limitations.

Mary's uncle Lotsey Toth, cognizant of Joe's physical work limitations, saw an opportunity for Joe in Bertram's Tavern in Highland Lake which was up for sale.

Joe and Mary followed up on Lotsey's tip and bought the tavern and surrounding property in 1947. (Art and Julie Bertram shortly thereafter assumed management of Bertram's Lodge from Art's parents, Arthur Sr. and Clara Bertram.) Joe and Mary embarked on what was to quickly become a thriving business.

Aside from running their bar and grill, Joe and Mary operated an ice cream/candy/souvenir/toy shop known as Mellan's Trading Post on a seasonal basis. They converted the rooms above the Trading Post and kitchen into a small family apartment where they lived until their log cabin style home was completed in early 1951.

Business boomed and the Mellans hired Herb Gordon, George Clouse, and others as extra bartenders to accommodate their growing public.

Mary introduced pizza to Highland Lake installing one of the first pizza ovens in the area.

Mellan's had a friendly, civil atmosphere. Many of the regulars were distinct characters and there was always good conversation and spirited repartee. Mellan's did not tolerate crude or over-the-top behavior. Mellan's Bar and Grill was the hub of Highland Lake social life for many years.

Joe and Mary donated land for the construction of the Highland Lake fire house in 1949, just across the parking lot from the bar.

Joe and Mary Mellan. Photo courtesy of the Mellan Family.

The community pitched in and assisted Charlie L. Bosch and other carpenters in its construction. A social room was constructed above the garage. The social room served as a meeting place for the Fire Department, but also was the venue for many social activities including dinners, parties, and meetings of other organizations.

Fire Department activity also brought a constant stream of business to Mellan's Bar and Grill. Joe served as Fire Chief and was active in the Fire Department for close to three decades.

Joe and Mary were always generous and civic-minded. Joe bought a tractor with a plow and for years he plowed snow from neighbors' driveways. Joe dug a boat canal and cleared snow from the Lake to allow area children to ice skate and play hockey.

His field and the surrounding woods were the gathering place for neighborhood children to play softball and football and to play "war" and "cowboys." Joe erected a basketball backboard on his parking lot.

Local residents facing financial difficulty often came to Joe as a lender of last resort. Joe and Mary helped their neighbors without blowing a loud horn before them—they did what needed to be done quietly and without fanfare.

Joe and Mary were benefactors to a community of single, aging men who lived alone in small cabins in the Highland Lake area. They provided food and transportation when one of their charges was ill and generally looked after their welfare.

Joe and Mary hosted free holiday dinners at the bar. Attendees included Mac O'Donnell, Herb Gordon, Abe Hulse, Billy Hammond, George Andersen, and others. Sometimes as many as twenty-five men attended.

As Mac's health began to fail, Joe and Mary Mellan saw to it that Mac was cared for, bringing him meals, driving him for medical care, etc. Mac died about 1970.—From interview of Mary Mellan by Ken Bosch.

This photo from the early 1950s, shows an ice fishing day at Mud Pond. It hung in Joe Mellan's bar as long as I can remember. Left to right: Harry Sulzbach, Charlie L. Bosch, Willie Bosch, Ed Grotecloss, Fred Fracke. Photo and comment courtesy of Ken Bosch.

Gladys and her daughter Joan Austin who wrote a special poem for her grandfather Myers. Photo courtesy of Joan Austin Geier.

and Mary to live at their place for a second winter.

One time Mary showed Lon how close Alaska was to Russia on a map. "Well Old Seward wasn't so wrong after all," remarked Lon. (Lon was 10 years old when Seward purchased Alaska from Russia for the United States.)

The Leavenworths, October 1947
In October Gisele visited with her friends Mary Clark, Mary Austin, Lee Bartle, and Jane Eldridge.

Garfield was operated on at the Callicoon Hospital (about an hour away) mid-October. Jim and Gisele visited him and sometimes took Ella, who was sure glad to see her daughter Clara and family when they visited.

Just when Garfield was better and Ella was understandably wishing they would send him home, Garfield caught a cold and was pretty sick again. But he recovered quickly and by the third of November, was back home.

Leavenworths, November 1947
The day after Garfield returned home, Dr. Petkus made two trips to the Leavenworth house. First to check on Garfield; and in the evening to check on Ella who was not feeling well. By the middle of November Garfield was feeling well and strong enough to carry in some wood.

Friday, November 21, Jim and Frank Bartle went to Monticello to file a partnership. They planned to build a spec house together.

Saturday Jim and Gisele went to Lee and Clara's in Hamden. They returned home on Sunday.

When I was a little boy and Aunt Gisele first came over, I thought she was the nicest person. When I visited her I didn't want to go home and asked Mom if Aunt Gisele could come home with us."—Wayne Hansen.

Goldie and Stella Leavenworth
Goldie and Stella lived at the Ten Mile River Boy Scout Camp. He was a caretaker of the Scout's Camp Manhattan on Crystal Lake.

Garfield and Ella visited Goldie and Stella at the Boy Scout Camp the end of November, and had a very nice time.

"It's a beautiful place. Large flocks of ducks," Ella observed. Stella's family stopped by in the evenings.

The last Friday in November there were, "Hundreds of ducks on the pond. Men hunting some.

"Saturday Garfield and I came home from Goldie's. I had a dandy visit," Ella commented in her diary.

December 1947
December was a busy month for Ella. She made seven aprons for Gisele and some pot holders for Christmas. She and Gisele made candy and cookies. The menfolk continued to work at the sawmill.

A few days before Christmas, Clara's husband Lee picked up Garfield and Ella in Eldred and drove them to Hamden to spend Christmas with the Hansens.

"We all had a nice Christmas. Clara had a dandy Christmas dinner," Ella wrote. The children came down with colds, but were better several days later. "We are still with Clara and family and having a grand time," Ella penned on the last day of December 1947.

1948
The year 1948 would bring about a major change for my parents Art and Mary Austin. And an end to my story of the Town of Highland. In September Art and his wife Mary would leave Eldred and move to Houghton, New York, where Art would attend Houghton College.

Leavenworths, January 1948
Bill, Anna, and Jimmy Meyers had New Year's supper at Jim and Gisele's Thursday, the start of the new year.

After a "dandy visit," Garfield and Ella went home on January 3. They were welcomed by Goldie, Stella, Anna and her family, and Judy, their dog. "Judy was sure glad to see us," Ella said on their return to Eldred.

Wednesday, January 14, Jim and Frank Bartle went fishing.

Ella started crocheting for Gisele. She also made Gisele some baby sheets in January.

February 1948
Mid-February Jim bought a refrigerator from his cousin Grant Sergeant for $25. Jim and Goldie moved the refrigerator to Jim and Gisele's second floor apartment. Jim and Gisele finished papering the baby's room.

Gisele and Mary Austin had gotten to be good friends and visited several times in the last part of February. In March Mary Austin (as both nurse and friend) went with Jim and Gisele to the

Green Acres/Green Meadows, late 1940s & 1950s

Green Meadows Sign on Hartung Road in front of Green Meadows. Photo courtesy of Diane Pankow.

In 1950 Charlie Pankow married Ann Hughes, a regional account manager for the Woolworth Company, who had been a guest in the Highland Lake area. At the time Ann, her sisters, brother, and mother Lillian Hughes lived in Brooklyn.

Ann had borrowed her older sister Mildred's name and working papers so she could get a job at Woolworth's before the legal age. The result was she was always known as Millie (except to her family) and Green Meadows became "Millie and Charlie's" place.

Charlie and Millie married in mid-September and there were still several guests left at Green Meadows. Millie was suddenly charged with the tasks of cooking, waitressing, and dish washing. She was used to eating out in New York City, and could "barely boil water." When she peeked out from the kitchen, she saw guests dropping her biscuits on the table to demonstrate their density.

Within a few winters Millie not only mastered the art of cooking and particularly baking, but became well known in the area for her meals and baked goods. Guests gained about 10 pounds on their week-long vacations, as food was served "family style" and offered in unlimited portions with everything being made from scratch.

On busy holiday weekends like the Fourth of July and Labor Day, many of the Green Meadows guests would have to sleep at some of the other boarding houses around the lake due to lack of rooms, but they ate at Green Meadows, requiring twice the amount of meals, which in turn, resulted in two seatings for meals. Guests were known to gather in the kitchen and help peel potatoes, crack eggs, and shuck corn. Most would come the same week or weeks every year. Some wives and children came for the whole summer and the husbands came up from New York City on weekends only.

During the winter, the Pankows would focus on renovating the cabins and rooms. The cabins were named after famous hotels of the era such as the Ritz, Astor, Manhattan, Carlton, Vanderbilt, Hilton, Edison, Plaza, Sheraton, New Yorker, Algonquin, Biltmore, Commodore, Madison, and the Roosevelt.

As opposed to the larger resorts in the Catskills, entertainment was mostly self-made, and included bingo, movies on the lawn, dancing and masquerade parties, outdoor barbecues, lawn races, horseshoes, ping-pong, badminton, shuffle board, miniature golf, baseball, swimming, bocci ball, etc.

Many local people worked at Green Meadows including: Florence Bosch, who was the head of housekeeping for years. Bill Schroeder delivered all the eggs and other provisions. Hank Schroeder was in charge of landscaping. A number of waiters and waitresses were also from the area and others lived on the premises for the summer.

Charlie had a corny sense of humor. To trick newcomers he put up a sign on a trail "To The Spring" which ended at a mattress spring in the woods. Signage on a little shed said "See the Monkey." When you opened the door, you were facing a mirror. A rock that looked like a baked potato would be in a bowl of baked potatoes for new guests. A tradition on Friday nights after the lawn games was for Millie to have made a meringue pie and one of the waiters would chase Charlie around until he got a pie in the face.
—Diane Pankow.

(See p. 412 for a few more photos of Green Meadows.)

Charlie Pankow and Ann Hughes, Agnes Schmid, their mother Agnes Pankow, the men are unknown, in the late 1940s. Photo courtesy of Diane Pankow.

Around 1960. Henny and Agnes Pankow Schmid front; back Lillian Hughes (Ann's mother); Charlie and Ann Pankow; a doctor who vacationed at Green Meadows. Photo courtesy of Diane Pankow.

Rose Nolan on left (cousin of Agnes and Charlie), Martha (kitchen helper), and Agnes Schmid peeling potatoes for guests. Photo courtesy of Diane Pankow.

Jim Leavenworth holds his daughter Cynthia. Photo courtesy of Cynthia Leavenworth Bellinger.

Callicoon Hospital to be with Gisele during labor. Mary was the first one to hold the new little Leavenworth.

March 1948
"A baby girl born to Jim and Gisele. Their first. 10 a.m. Cynthia Ella Jeanne," wrote a very delighted Grandmother Ella.

Gisele had not known what to do about Cynthia's middle name. She wanted to honor both her mother Jeanne Rouillon and Jim's mother Ella Leavenworth. Gisele had mentioned this to Arthur Austin who suggested using both Ella and Jeanne—Cynthia Ella Jeanne Leavenworth.

While Gisele was recuperating at the Callicoon Hospital, Jim, the proud, new father, visited every day. The proud Grandpa Garfield, and friends—Mary Clark and Art and Mary Austin—also visited Gisele and the new little one.

Jim's sister Anna went with him to Callicoon when he brought Gisele and baby Cynthia home.

"Gisele came home with the baby. It sure is cute. Mary and Arthur called. Anna, also Mary Sergeant here for the day," wrote a very proud Grandma Ella, when the new family arrived home.

Anna Meyers spent the next day with her new niece. As did Goldie and Stella, Mary Clark, and Mary Austin.

In March Mary Austin cared for Walter Styles, 85, who was quite ill. Walter Styles, who we first met in Sitka, Alaska, died in early April. His widow Georgia's mother, Elizabeth Hoatson Clark Wilson, was elderly and not well. Mary cared for her some also.

April and May 1948
Visitors at the Leavenworth home in April included Art and Mary Austin; and Frank and Lee Bartle.

In May Frank and Lee's son Howard was born. Soon Lee and Gisele were visiting each other with their new little ones.

Anna Meyers was excited to have a telephone installed.

At the end of May it was warm enough for Garfield to take the kitchen storm sash off. Jim shoed his horse.

June 1948
In June Gisele often pushed Cynthia in the baby carriage when she visited Anna Meyers, Jane Eldridge, and Mary Austin.

The last Saturday of the month, Ella watched her new granddaughter while Gisele went to Port Jervis with Mary and Art.

July and August 1948
Garfield made a crib for Cynthia in July. Gisele and Cynthia continued to visit Anna Meyers and Mary Austin.

The first week of August Frank Bartle and Jim bought a piece of land off Proctor Road. They planned to build a house on that piece of land to sell. (Orville and Mary Clark would live there while it was being built. Louis and Edith Maudsley would buy the house.)

The last week of August

Gisele Leavenworth holds her daughter Cynthia. Photo courtesy of Cynthia Leavenworth Bellinger.

Frank and Jim started a well on their new land and hit water.

During August Art and Mary's nieces, Joan, Margie, and Dawn Lee Austin spent some time with them.

Joan went to Eldred thinking her great-aunt Christina could use some help at the boarding house. Since Christina didn't need help, Joan stayed with Art and I, and we had lots of fun. Margie and Dawn Lee came for two weeks."
—Mary Briggs Austin.

Straubs and Toasperns
The Straubs and Toasperns have been a part of this story. In August the Straub siblings were together after their brother Fridolin Straub passed away. Emma Straub's husband Walter C. was a Toaspern.

The Toaspern family had been in the area some 30 years before the Straub family. There was also a photo of Meta Toaspern Lass with her sister Anna Toaspern Holden.

Albert Alonzo Austin Dies
When spring came, Uncle Lon had gone back to his house to live. It was quite hot on Sunday, August 29, but it did not stop Lon from

1949–1950 (and Beyond) Boarding Houses

Barryville

Riverside Cottage, L. Warshauer

Woodland Cottages, Protz
Crystal clear swimming pool. Tennis and handball courts. Nearby lakes and streams for fishing and boating. Golf links, movies within easy reach. Comfortable accommodations for 100—all with hot and cold water.

Maple Grove Farm, Nitzsche & Frey
Located on a bluff overlooking the Delaware River. High elevation. Accommodates 60 guests. Excellent table; all fresh farm products. Boating, fishing, movies, bowling, churches, all nearby. Swimming pool, recreation hall, tennis, handball courts, ping-pong, all on premises. All rooms have hot and cold running water. Reasonable rates.

Eldred

Orchard Terrace (Elizabeth Wilson's original home), Fritz and Ella Stickel
Beautiful location; quiet, high elevation. Modern, large rooms; private lake, bathing, boating, excellent home cooked meals. $35 weekly. $6 daily Tel. Barryville 2568.

Yulan

Yulan Hotel, Ann and Peter Bozza
Under new management, 1950.

Sunset Cottage, Lewis Hazen

West Shore Cottage and Minisink Lodge, Joseph H. Cantwell
On Washington Lake. 35th year. Own bathing beach. Acc. 200 Excellent meals. Hot and cold water all rooms. Showers, boating, bathing, shuffleboard, tennis, fishing, handball, softball, ping-pong. Near all churches. Tel. Barryville 2744.

Highland Hotel and Cottage Herman Umbreit
A country hotel with city comforts. All sports, private beach. Excellent cuisine. Cocktail bar.

The Maplecrest, R.C. Walter
Grand Vue Inn, Bornstein
Cottages with private baths, plus large porches. Tennis, ping-pong, shuffleboards, recreation room. For those who like to ride, play golf, swimming, etc., all are nearby. Spacious lawns among pine grove. We are known for our excellent home cooking and home baked pastries.

Highland Lake

Deer Head Lodge, K. Eggers

Green Meadows, Charlie Pankow

Singing Pines, Otto Seel

Pine Hill Lodge Rates, K. Lutz
$24 up. Near all churches. Booklet.

Highland Hotel and Cottage owned by Herman Umbreit by 1951. Photo courtesy of Cynthia Leavenworth Bellinger.

Andy Gugel feeding deer at his Gugel Game Farm. Photo courtesy of Christene Stevens Myers.

Ferncliff Lodge when Andy Gugel ran it as Gugel's Game Farm. Photo courtesy of Christene Stevens Myers.

Protz's Woodland Cottages. Postcard courtesy of the Town of Highland.

Pinehurst, Mrs. Freda Jung
Modern House. Hot and cold running water in every room. All sports, boating, swimming, fishing, bowling. Excellent cuisine. Near churches. Rates $35 up.

Meta Toaspern Lass and her sister Anna Toaspern Cordes Holden. Photo courtesy of Linda Guenther Anderson.

The Straubs August 1948, from left: Rose Straub Myers, Emma Straub Toaspern holding her granddaughter Barbara Ihlo, unknown, Ida Straub, Julia Straub and her husband Albert Pegg. Photo courtesy of Bill Ihlo.

Gladys Austin with her daughter Dawn Lee who spent a couple weeks with Art and Mary Austin. Photo courtesy of Dawn Lee Segarra.

walking to the Eldred Methodist Church. He collapsed half way up the hill to the church. Chester Middaugh carried Lon into the building beside the church. There Lon passed away.

I was so very weary
    Surely you cannot mourn
That I a little sooner
    Should lay my burden down.

Then weep not, weep not, darling
    God wipes away all tears,
'Tis only yet a little while
    Though you may call it
years.—Found in Lon's papers.

Albert Alonzo Austin died in Eldred at 11:15 a.m. on Sunday after a short illness. He became ill while on his way to attend the service in the Eldred Methodist Church and failed to rally.

Mr. Austin, who was one of the oldest and highly respected residents of the town of Highland, was born September 28, 1857, in Eldred, the son of William Henry Austin and Mary Ann Eldred Austin. The greater part of his life was spent in Eldred where he was engaged in farming. For many years he was a trustee and local preacher in the Eldred Methodist Church. Rev. John L. Beebout officiated at the service in the Eldred Methodist Church.—News article, September 1948.

Art's brother Raymond from Staten Island and their cousin Lillie Austin Calkin (Lon's niece) from Bethel were there for Lon's funeral.

(Lillie's son Dale and his wife Nellie had three children: Neal, Bob, and Kathy. Dale was a carpenter. Lillie's daughter Dot Hale lived in Sidney, New York, where she and her husband ran a magazine store.)

Raymond and his daughters went back to Staten Island.

Art and Mary Leave Eldred
After the funeral Art and Mary got ready to leave for Houghton College. Mary was so sick that her sister Mildred helped Art with the packing.

"Sunday, September 5, Art and Mary Austin left," wrote Ella.

When I got up in the morning of the day we moved to Houghton so Art could go to college, I went in the kitchen and decided to make Art a fine breakfast as I knew he needed a good breakfast.

When I was frying the bacon, the smell overcame me and I flew out the back door to get some fresh air! Art's brother Bill washed the kitchen floor for me.

Everyone but me knew why I was so sick. I was not able to do a thing. Charlie and Muriel Kerr drove the truck up to the College.
—Mary Briggs Austin.

Art, Mary, and Louise (the reason for Mary's morning sickness) would return to Eldred several times before their final move to Michigan.

Uncle Lon (Albert Alonzo) Austin

While time dimmed his eyes and weakened his knees, 90 years failed to tame Uncle Lon's independent spirit. During the last few years of his life, physical limitations did make it necessary for him to spend the winter months with a nephew.

However, with the first sign of spring, Uncle Lon was off to the old house on the hill where he had lived for many years. There among his pictures, with the old organ and older memories, he lived happily until the winds of December blowing through the rickety house proved too cold for his rheumatic bones.

The more it stormed and the more slippery the hills became, the more necessary it was that Uncle Lon go to the village to do his shopping. Why he never contracted pneumonia or broke some of his bones on the slippery roads is a mystery.

Probably the best explanation is that Uncle Lon led a charmed life. He could fall out of an apple tree or off a shed roof without injuring his aging bones. Even when he poured gasoline instead of kerosene on a fire, all that happened was a flame at the spout of the can which was easily extinguished.

Every spring, much to his disgust, the neighbors came running when he burned the grass off the meadow. The whole town prophesied that he would burn himself up some day. Their suggestions that greater precautions should be taken he disdained. He had burned the old north lot for thirty years and did not welcome any interferences now.

Although the woodchucks ate up much of his garden, Uncle Lon seemed to enjoy the constant warfare with them. While complaining bitterly about the 'chucks,' he never took any drastic action against them except one time when he plugged up the entrances to their homes with stones. After a few days the stones were removed because it did not seem right for him as a Christian to be starving animals to death.

During most of the last years of Uncle Lon's life, he was the janitor of the Methodist Church. This was a fortunate arrangement since no one else could heat the church to the right temperature. Every once-in-a-while, he would insist that the job be given to a younger man. But soon the new janitor, to Uncle Lon's way of thinking, was either roasting or freezing him to death, which made it necessary for him to resume his former duties.

Out of affection and respect for his advancing years, the church members tried to save him the walk home after services.

Uncle Lon used all the cunning accumulated in a long life time to avoid accepting this assistance. He would never come right out and refuse a ride, but would contrive to sneak off while those who had attended church were talking. Many times he would be well on his way home before anybody realized that he had left.

While the independent streak in Uncle Lon was strong, his faith was even stronger. His confidence in God never faltered. Whatever he considered the Lord's will he accepted without complaint. The last summer, however, he began to fret a little. His knees were aching more than usual, fall was coming on, and the time was drawing near when he would have to leave the old homestead for the winter. There did not seem to him to be much reason for remaining in a world from which all his brothers and sisters had departed. If the Lord did not have any further work for him to do, he would point out, it seemed about time for him to go to his heavenly home.

When, one Sunday morning, a few feet from the door of the church he had served so faithfully, his stout old heart beat its last, everyone considered that God had answered the longing of the old man's heart. Winter will no longer make it necessary for Uncle Lon to leave the surroundings that he loves.
—Arthur Austin.

Art and Mary lived in drab Army barracks affectionately called "Vetville" while at Houghton College. The rent was around $25 a month. While Art studied and went to classes in Houghton, everyday life continued on in the Village of Eldred.

The Royal Scarlet and Parker's stores were still on Eldred's northeast side near Straub's Hotel; Wait and Boyd's Garage was on the southwest corner; the A&P and the Post Office (in Parker's Hotel) were south of Eldred's Four Corners on opposite sides.

A band plays in front of Royal Scarlet and Parker's Store in Eldred. Photo courtesy of Christene Stevens Myers.

1948 Halfway Brook News

Four generations: Rowlee Schoonover in back. His daughter Justina Hull on the right; his grandson John J. Hull on the left; and John D. Hull, great-grandson of Rowlee in front. Photo courtesy of John D. Hull.

Four Generations
Rowlee and Emily Schoonover were visited by their great-grandson John D. Hull. John J. Hull, grandson, and daughter Justina Hull were also there.

1948 Eldred Central Seniors
Amy Wolff, Madelyn Meyers, Genevieve Schneider, Helen Rollenetz, Virginia Hill, Vivian Meiritz,

Madelyn Meyers, 1948 graduate from Eldred Central. Photo in 1948 Yearbook.

Edgar Getz married Betty MacIntyre. Photo courtesy of Alan Gothard.

Fred DeFeo Jr. married Pam Fischetti. Photo courtesy of Pam Fischetti DeFeo.

Harrison Bartle, Henry Oset, James Cannon, R. Hotzler, Gordon Worzel, Donald Haas, Richard Metzger.

1948 Births
- Cynthia Ella Jeanne Leavenworth born to Jim and Gisele Rouillon Leavenworth.
- Loretta Hull born to John J. and Josephine Lipinski Hull.
- Kathleen Wilson born to Ed and Agnes Mary Wilson.
- Howard Bartle born to Frank and Lee Bartle.
- Robert Myers born to Chuck and Ruth Worzel Myers.

1948 Marriages
- Fred DeFeo Jr. married Pam Fischetti.
- Chester Oset married Helen Hensel.
- Edgar Getz married Betty MacIntyre.
- Russell MacKechnie married Peggy Gilmore.

1948 Deaths
- Dr. Alonzo E. Austin, 1868–1948.
- Cora Hardcastle Eldred (descendant of James Eldred) died.
- Fridolin Straub, 1897–1948.
- Henry Von Ohlen, 1887–1948.
- Robert L. Clark, son of Irvin and Laura Austin Clark, died. He was survived by three nieces.
- Meda Breen Tether, 1870–1948.
- Daniel A. Gillespie, 81, Glen Spey Postmaster, died.
- Alonzo Calkin, descendant of James Eldred, died.
- Victoria Simpson Parker, 1870–1948.
- Walter B. Styles, 1862–1948.
- Elizabeth Hoatson Clark Wilson, 1872–1948.
- Albert Alonzo Austin, 1857–1948.
- Miss Nellie M. Austin, 80, was the daughter of Ira and Minerva Drake Austin. Survived by brother Ralph W. Austin and a sister Mabel Smith.
- Ida Emily Higginson Crabtree, mother of Myrtle Crabtree Briggs, died in Springfield, Oregon.

Jim Leavenworth and Frank Bartle continued working on their spec home (east of Eldred towards Glen Spey), as well as working several other jobs.

January–April 1949
On Tuesday, January 4, Anna Meyers took care of Cynthia while Jim and Gisele went to Clara's to get Garfield and Ella at the Hansen's. The foursome arrived back in Eldred at 6:15 p.m.

The next day Frank and Jim worked on their house. They finished the wiring a week later.

Ella bought a 50# bag of onions from Ort for $1.50.

The third week of January Garfield and Ella went to Hamden to stay with Clara and Lee's family to help out Clara who had heart trouble. They stayed from the end of January until mid-April when

1949 Halfway Brook News

- George Orwell published *Nineteen Eighty-Four* in 1949.

1949 Eldred Seniors
- Phyllis Hocker, Shirley Paulus, Mamie Turner, James Reiser, Barry Owen.

25th Anniversary
- Lewis and Elsie Hazen celebrated their 25th Wedding Anniversary.

1949 Births
- Louise Elizabeth born to Art and Mary Austin in Houghton, N.Y.
- Gary Dean Smith born to Olliamus D. and Wilna Smith, in California.
- Ken Bosch born to Willie and Florence Schmerfeld Bosch.
- Ivan J. Tether born to Ivan and Helen Jayne Tether.
- Amy Maudsley born to Lou and Edith Maudsley.
- William Ihlo born to Fred and Frances Toaspern Ihlo.
- Barbara Kate James born to Edward and Norma Beverly Wood James.
- Thomas Frey born to Everett and Mary Ann Osborn Frey.
- Kathleen Louise Baker born to Clarence and Dorothy Paton Baker (Eldred-Austin descendant).
- Elizabeth Ann Crandall born to Clifford and Mary Myers Crandall.

1949 Marriages
- Harry Haas married Berniece Wells.
- Ralph West married Sophie Zepka.
- Joseph Kohler married Marjorie Bosch at the St. Jacobi Church in Shohola.
- Marion Doeller married Rudolph Kistner, December 24.

1949 Deaths
- Ruth Foster Wolff died.
- John Wheeler Dunlap, 1870–1949.
- Emma Schoonover Waidler, 1879–1949. Burial was in Cairo Cemetery.
- James Eldred, son of George W. and Marietta West Eldred, died.
- Bill Meyers Sr. died in September.
- Norah A. Bradley Avery, 1875-1949.
- Celina Nikolaus died in December.
- Edith Toaspern Birr, 1872–1949.

Ivan, son of Ivan and Helen Jayne Tether. Photo courtesy of Ivan J. and Jana Tether.

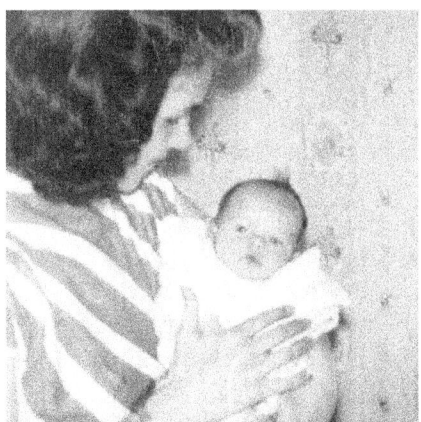

Dorothy Paton Baker and daughter Kathleen Louise Baker. Photo courtesy of Kathleen Baker Foster and Darren Foster.

Ken Bosch and his pet duck, Peedly. Photo courtesy of Ken Bosch.

Elsie and Lewis Hazen on their 25th wedding anniversary. Photo courtesy of Christene Stevens Myers.

Frances Ihlo holds her son Bill. Photo courtesy of Bill Ihlo.

Joseph Kohler and Marjorie Bosch. Photo courtesy of Victoria Kohler, daughter.

Gisele holding Cynthia. Wait and Boyd's Garage in the background. Photo courtesy of Gisele Rouillon Leavenworth.

Jim went to get them and brought them home.

Sunday, April 17, Jim drew gravel for the foundation of the house with the white picket fence that he had promised Gisele.

May–July 1949

In May Gisele cut her hand real bad. Garfield put in a bathroom window for Anna and Bill. Frank and Jim continued logging and working at Jim's mill. Floyd Boyd stopped by and asked if they could work on an addition to the A&P. Frank inquired as to the hourly wage.

"What do you want?"
"A dollar."
Mr. Boyd said, *"You have the job."*
Frank and Jim parked their logging truck and started digging on the 10- or 12-foot addition to the A&P.—David Leavenworth.

In Houghton, Louise Elizabeth Austin was born to Art and Mary Austin. She was the first of their four children.

The end of the month in the Town of Highland, was a very sad time for Albert Wolff and his sons Ed and Charles. Ruth Foster Wolff, wife and mother, died at the end of May. Ruth was a daughter of George and Jennie Hallock Foster.

In June Garfield started the forms for the cellar of Jim's new home. Gisele and Cynthia went to a baby shower for Helen Kuen Sergeant.

The third week of June was so hot on the second floor that Jim, Gisele, and Cynthia slept downstairs. In July Ella bought Cynthia an Amosandra doll. (Amosandra was the third child of Amos and Ruby in the February 20, 1949, *Amos and Andy* radio show.)

August–September 1949

The third week of August the men cut a few logs for Jim's house.

Sunday, September 4, Hazel Connor called to wish her sister Ella a Happy 60th Birthday. The third week of September Garfield and Jim framed Jim's house.

Bill Meyers Sr. died in September. Bill and his wife Lottie had been long time friends and neighbors of Garfield and Ella. The two families shared a grandson, Jimmy Meyers.

Monday, October 17, John Dunlap died. You may remember that John and his wife Katherine visited both Aida Austin and Garfield and Ella Leavenworth.

The last Saturday of October Jim started shingling his house. They put the gutters on in November.

In November Ella made Cynthia a dress and pajamas. Jim and Gisele went to the Morgan's to watch television for the first time.

December 1949

Such a sad time for Juliette Lorphelin who had sailed to the United States especially to be with her sister Celina. Celina died in December.

Garfield made Cynthia a table, chair, and doll crib for Christmas. The Leavenworths spent Christmas day at Anna and Bill Meyers'. Goldie and Stella were in for a while in the evening.

Cynthia with her Amosandra doll. Photo courtesy of Gisele Rouillon Leavenworth.

Louise Austin. Her dress, crocheted by Stella Leavenworth, was one of the gifts given to her by others including Gisele Leavenworth and Charlee Hirsch. Photo courtesy of Mary Briggs Austin.

1950 Halfway Brook News

John Hallock and his sister Carolyn Hallock. Photo courtesy of Carolyn Hallock Clark.

1950 Eldred Seniors
- Marguerite Bauer, Joyce Fisher, Dorothy Brodmerkel, Henrietta Reiser, Fred Weber, Joyce Murray, Geraldine Mills, Joan Brewster, Arlene Wolff, Henry Dieckhoff, Harry Hotzler, James Kalin, Francis Kean, Charles Paulus.

Hotel Fire
- Reber's Hotel burned in February.

1950 Weddings
- Charlie Pankow married Millie (Ann) Hughes in mid-September.
- Frank Colony Kyte married Rose Paden.

1950 Births
- Carolyn Ann Hallock born to Robert and Dorothy Estler Hallock.
- Josephine Hull born to John J. and Josephine Lipinski Hull.

1950 Deaths
- Kate McElroy Gardner, 1864–1950.
- Elizabeth Hardcastle Eldred (wife of James Eldred, son of George and Marietta West Eldred) died.
- Mabel Austin Smith, 1875-1950.
- Freida Josephine Meyer Guenther Bradley, 1888–1950. Freida's children at the time of her death: Clinton Guenther, Freida Flieger, Edith Humphries, Helen Leifert, and Violet Clancy; stepsons Clarence, George, and Clifford Bradley.
- Florence Bradley, 1911–1950, was survived by husband George H., daughters Georgia Anne and Maureen; mother Mrs. Nellie Poth and brother Anthony Poth of Yulan.
- Norman W. Sutherland was born in Mongaup in 1879. He died in Shohola, Pennsylvania, in 1950.
- *Ed Toaspern, 1924–1950, was instantly killed when his Aeronica Champion nose dived to the earth three miles north of Barryville near an old quarry. The inspection by the Civil Air Board Monday finds that the apparent cause of the accident was due to the pilot being unconscious at the time of the crash…Mr. Toaspern, the son of Walter C. and Emma Straub Toaspern, was a Navy flier during WWII, and was a lieutenant, junior grade, in the Naval Reserve… Surviving are his widow Barbara Wickus, parents Mr. and Mrs. Walter Toaspern, sister Mrs. Fred Ihlo of Barryville…—From* Delaware Valley News Times.

Charlie Pankow married Millie (Ann) Hughes. Photo courtesy of Diane Pankow.

Highland Lake children born 1947-1949. Left: Alan Schroeder, Judy Meyer (daughter of Fred and Margo Bosch Meyer), Ken Bosch, brother Bill behind him, Charles "Skip" Schroeder Jr., Charlie Winter Jr. (Alan and Skip, sons of Charlie and Norma Ott Schroeder.) Photo courtesy of Ken Bosch.

Freida Guenther Bradley with her children around 1940. Viola (Clancy), Edith (Humphries), Clinton Joseph Guenther, Freida Guenther Bradley, Freida (Flieger), Helen (Liefert). Photo courtesy of Linda Guenther Anderson.

Early view of Abel Myers' Orchard Terrace which became the school; and the Eldred Congregational Church. Photo courtesy of Chuck Myers.

January and February 1950
Ella started her last diary in January 1950. Jim and Gisele started both January and February by going to the movies. On Valentine's Day there was a foot or more of snow. February 22, Reber's Hotel burned early in the morning.

March and April 1950
In March it was once again time to think of planting. The seeds arrived from Harris the second week of March.

Aunt Anna Leavenworth in Islip called on Cynthia's second birthday.

Garfield finished planting his hot bed in April and Jim's ducks arrived.

May through August 1950
Jim took his radio to Millard Hulse to be fixed in May. Garfield started planting.

Aunt Anna Leavenworth was in Eldred near the end of May. (She stayed at least until December.) She visited with the Hirsches and some friends stopped by to see her. Aunt Anna and Gisele went to the Methodist Church Fair at the end of July. They also picked berries.

Jim started working for the County in the middle of August. Gisele and Cynthia went to the Congregational Church Fair.

September and October 1950
"Arthur Austin and family called," Ella wrote in September.

On September 6, when Clara and Lee were at Garfield and Ella's for the day, Art and Mary Austin and their daughter Louise visited. Jim Leavenworth was home as he had cut his leg (five stitches) in an encounter with a chain saw.

We drove from Houghton College and visited Uncle Garfield. They were out on the long porch. Louise was too shy to go to anyone but Aunt Anna. Anna took Louise's hand to show her a kitty, so Louise went with her great-aunt Anna Leavenworth.
—Mary Briggs Austin.

Farewell to Eldred
Art, Mary, and Louise visited with Alfred and Bessie Hill, then headed back to Houghton for Art's last year of college. The young Austin family would then move to Michigan.

"A good year 1950 for us all," wrote Ella at the end of the year.

And a good place to end *The Memoirs from Eldred, New York*.

The Boarding Houses in the Town would flourish and provide delightful memories for at least another ten years. Narrowsburg Lumber would soon have a new location by Stege's Lake. Flooding on the Delaware River would continue to be a problem.

Some of the townsfolk, including my uncle Bill Austin, and my Leavenworth and Myers relatives, continued to live in the Town of Highland. Others, like my parents Art and Mary Austin, moved to a different location to raise their family. The children raised elsewhere would perhaps be unaware (as was I) of the rich history of the area their ancestors had once settled.

They (like myself) would have no knowledge of the extensive forests and its many sawmills, the D&H Canal, the Roebling Bridge, the bluestone quarries, the hamlets that grew up near the Delaware River, and later its many Boarding Houses.

We would not be aware of the affect wars had on our ancestors. Or know the stories which would make a former era come to life.

To everything there is a season... And so a final farewell.

Long live the memory of the relatives, neighbors, and friends who long ago settled near Halfway Brook in what became the Town of Highland, New York.

Chapter 14
Epilogue
A Short Rest of the Story, 1950 and Beyond

*How dear to this heart are the scenes of my childhood,
When fond recollection presents them to view!
The orchard, the meadow, the deep-tangled wildwood,
And every loved spot which my infancy knew!
The wide-spreading pond, and the mill that stood by it,
The bridge, and the rock where the cataract fell,
The cot of my father, the dairy-house nigh it,
And e'en the rude bucket that hung in the well—
The old oaken bucket, the iron-bound bucket,
The moss-covered bucket which hung in the well.
—Samuel Woodworth,* The Old Oaken Bucket.

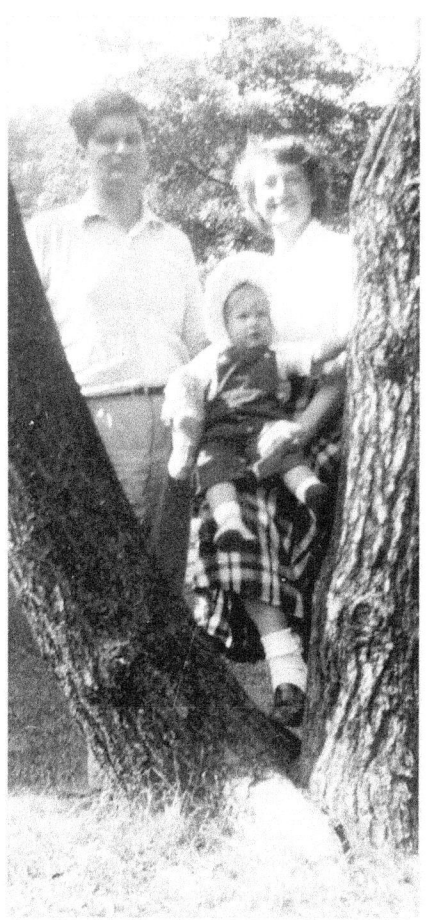

Art, Mary, and Louise Austin would move to Michigan. Photo courtesy of Mary Briggs Austin.

The Mill on Halfway Brook (the first of three in the *Memoirs from Eldred Series*) featured the arrival of my Hickok, Eldred, Austin, Leavenworth, and Myers relatives who settled near Halfway Brook. Halfway Brook flowed through the Town of Lumberland—later the Town of Highland with its five hamlets: Eldred, Highland Lake, Barryville, Minisink Ford, and Yulan.

Included in my continual pursuit for information, was the quest for several relatives who were unknown or last heard of around 1950. Happily they were found and shared photos and their family stories.

This chapter visits some of the descendants of the original settlers who were known in 1950; and a glimpse into the future of both my relatives and some of the townsfolk we have grown to love.

The Hickok Family
Asa and Esther Hinman Hickok and their family moved from Connecticut to what was then Lumberland in 1811. Only Justus Hickok and Hannah Eldred and their families stayed in Lumberland. There are known descendants of Justus and Mary Wells Hickok, though most of the family had moved from the area by 1920. The Hickok Brook in Eldred may be the only reminder that the Hickok family once lived in the Town of Lumberland.

James and Polly Mulford Eldred
At the end of 1815 James and Polly Mulford Eldred with their five children settled in a cabin near a sawmill close to Halfway Brook (which became the southeast corner of Eldred). Some of their descendants' surnames: Austin, Carmichael (there was another family not related), Gardner, Calkin, Mapes, Kendall, Barcaw, Young, Dunlap, Cuddeback, Paton, Baker, Foster, Webster, Watson, Myers, and Brown.

Most of the descendants of James Eldred who didn't live

Orvis Eldred, his son Richard O. Eldred. Lloyd Eldred on the right and Orvis Eldred were sons of John Franklin and Minnie Sears Eldred. Photo courtesy of Richard O. Eldred.

John J. Hull holding Marjorie Hull, Justina Schoonover Hull, Emily Banner and Rowlee Schoonover. In front, Loretta Ann (Lorry), Josephine (Jo), and John D. Hull. Photo courtesy of John D. Hull.

Rowlee, Jean Lack (granddaughter—daughter of John and Ethel Schoonover Lack), Justina Hull (daughter), and Emily Banner Schoonover. Photo courtesy of John D. Hull.

in Eldred or Barryville, settled originally in Pennsylvania, Orange County, New York, or in Iowa.

Grandson Lewis Carmichael and his wife Mary Bunce settled in Iowa. Their daughter Lina married Frank Watson. Frank and Lina's granddaughter Elizabeth Watson and her husband Maxwell Hart lived in Texas. Their daughter Marnette was 12, in 1950.

Richard O. Eldred, son of Orvis and Selma Myers Eldred, was 15. Richard's *The Eldred Family* would be printed in 1988.

In 1950 Harvey Eldred and his family may have been the only ones with the Eldred surname who lived in the Town of Highland. Harvey C. and Emma Draxler Eldred lived in Minisink Ford with their children: Harvey W., Charles C., and Martha Eldred. Sadly Harvey C. Eldred died at the age of 34, in 1952.

James and Hannah Hickok Eldred
James Eldred's first wife Polly Mulford died in 1825. James Eldred then married Hannah Hickock. Their daughter Mary Ann Eldred (my great-grandmother) married William Henry Austin.

Mary Ann Eldred's half sister Phebe Maria had married Augustus Austin, brother of William Henry Austin. So both Eldred-Austin families were descendants of James Eldred and Ralph and Fanny Knapp Austin.

The Austin Family
Ralph and Fanny Knapp Austin and their family had settled on what became Proctor Road by 1840. Augustus A. Austin had moved there some years earlier. (It is not known if Ralph Austin and Benjamin C. Austin, who also settled in the area, were related.)

Of Ralph and Fanny's nine children, five had descendants: Samuel Knapp Austin, Augustus Alonzo Austin, Clara Austin Teed, William Henry Austin, and Laura Austin Clark. By 1950 the main known information was about William Henry and Mary Ann Eldred Austin's descendants.

Ralph and Fanny's daughter Ann Mary Schoonover had died young. Her husband Perry had married Mary Murray Parker,

Alden Austin. His sister Mabel Austin Gibson with her son Robert Gibson. Alden and Mabel were grandchildren of Mortimer Bruce and Mary Millspaugh Austin, and descendants of Augustus and Phebe Maria Eldred Austin. Photos courtesy of Karen M. Gibson.

a widow with three children. Of those children and Perry and Mary Parker Schoonover's, only their son Rowlee was still living. Though not blood related, Aida Austin had called her uncle Perry's children, cousins. Rowlee and Emily Banner Schoonover continued to enjoy visits from children and grandchildren.

There may have been some descendants of Irvin and Laura Austin Clark in the area.

Of the Eldred-Austin Cousins (children of Augustus and Phebe Maria Eldred Austin) who spent much time together in both New York City and Eldred, and wrote lively letters (included in *The Mill on Halfway Brook*), some descendants of Mortimer Bruce Austin, Addie Austin Thompson, and Rand Austin Paton are known.

Mortimer Bruce and Mary Millspaugh Austin's son Charles Augustus Austin (first seen as a baby in Book 1) was the father of Alden Austin and Mabel Austin Gibson. Alden and Mabel lived into the 1980s.

There are several known descendants of Augustus Austin Thompson, son of Thomas J. and Addie Austin Thompson, who we read about in *Aida Austin's 1881 Diary*.

In 1950 Dorothy Paton Baker, granddaughter of Archie and Rand Austin Paton, and her husband Clarence Baker enjoyed their daughters, AnnMarie (Ree), 6, and Kathleen Louise Baker, 1. Dorothy's parents were Archie R. and Mabel Slagle Paton.

William Henry and Mary Ann
The most available information is on the descendants of Henry and Mary Ann Eldred Austin, my great-grandparents. Of Henry and Mary Ann's ten children, two married and had children: James

Elward Austin Thompson, Gertrude Cotton Thompson, with son Elbert Paul Thompson, Augustus A. Thompson (son of Thomas and Addie Austin Thompson), and daughter Gertrude Ruth Thompson. Photo courtesy of the Augustus A. Thompson Family.

Dorothy Paton, her husband Clarence Baker, Mabel Slagle Paton (mother of Dorothy, Archie C., and Marjorie), Archie C. Paton, and Marjorie Paton. Photo courtesy of Kathleen Baker Foster and Darren Foster.

Eldred (known as Uncle Ell to my family) and my grandfather Charles Mortimer (Mort) Austin.

Ell Austin had worked in Kansas and married the farmer's daughter, Emma Parmenter. Ell and Emma Austin's daughter Lillie was the favorite (and only) cousin of the Austin brothers, Raymond, Bill, Art, and Bob.

Lillie Austin had married Burt Calkin. Burt and Lillie had two

Lillie Austin Calkin, Grandmother

My grandmother Lillie Calkin is one of the women that I have most admired and loved in my life. I think of her often with gratitude and pride. After reading about the women in the Austin family, I understand her a little better.

Grandmother Lillie spent a lot of time with me when I was little. She was always a wonderful encourager of me, which is one of the reasons that I went to college and graduated.

Going to Grandma and Grandpa Calkin's house was always an adventure. Grandma started her week by baking bread and rolls—no Wonder bread at her house! I loved to help knead the dough and was always amazed how she would just throw the ingredients together—no measuring, just handfuls and pinches. At the end of the day the house was filled with the wonderful aroma of freshly baked bread.

I spent time in Grandma's garden. They had a large vegetable garden and a fabulous rose garden—her pride and joy. She would take me out in the fields behind her house to pick blueberries. We fed the birds suet which she hung out on her clothes line.

When I was quite young she taught me to look at the sun and find a big tree or some other landmark so that I could always find my way home.

She crocheted beautiful dresses for a small plastic doll (with little eyes that rolled) she kept for me at her house.

She took me to many historical places, and on my first train ride (about 90 miles away). I loved to go to the Presbyterian Church in Bethel with my Calkin grandparents.

Grandma taught school for many years. She was a great writer of letters and poetry; kept a journal on and off; and dabbled in writing and directing plays. She saved everything—her house could be called cluttered, and her attic was full of all kinds of treasures. She had more books than anyone I knew and I am sure she had read them all.

Lillie Austin Calkin. Photo courtesy of Katherine Calkin Traxler.

Grandma was very active in the Sullivan County Historical Society, the Garden Club, and did the New York Times crossword seven days a week. She loved pinochle and played Parcheesi and Chinese Checkers and lots of other games and cards with me.

When she had a chance Grandma would head to New England, Canada, or to see her daughter (my aunt) Dot. Sometimes after my grandfather Calkin died, Grandma would fail to let my father know that she was away. She was very independent!

Grandma loved to go with us on our Sunday outings. My dad had a boat and pulled us around so that we could water ski. Grandma would get in the front seat of the boat and ride up and down the lake with Dad. I never saw her in any kind of pants or sneakers—just one of her dresses and her everyday shoes.

Thanksgiving was always at Grandma's house. While everyone went hunting, she and I prepared the meal and set the table. I always got the story about the hungry children in China—part of the tradition.

Grandpa and Grandma Calkin had a farm that is now part of Bethel Woods Performing Arts Center—the site of the famous Woodstock Festival. The apple trees Dad planted when he was a boy are on the left of the main entrance.

Grandma Lillie died in 1965. At her wake at a funeral home in Damascus, Pennsylvania, a man and his wife came who no one knew. Grandmother had been his teacher many years ago and he felt that he had to come to pay his respects to her.

I was so moved to know my grandmother Lillie had touched his life in a very powerful way, but not surprised. She came from a line of strong women from the Austin family.
—Katherine Calkin Traxler.

Lillie Calkin's son Dale Calkin's Family in 1947: Nellie, Bob, Neal, Kathy, and Dale. Photo courtesy of Katherine Calkin Traxler.

 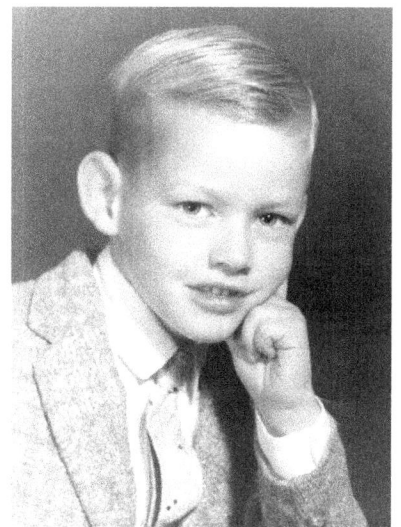 

Art and Mary Briggs Austin's children: Carol J., Charles A. (Chuck), and Mary Marie Austin. Photos courtesy of Mary Briggs Austin.

children: Dale and Dot. Dot and her husband Ray Hale lived in Sidney and ran a magazine store for many years. Dale spent most of his life working as a carpenter. He and his father Burt Calkin often worked together.

Dale and his wife Nellie Hill Calkin had three children: Robert (Bob), Neal, and Kathy.

Mort Austin's wife was Jennie Leavenworth. Two of their sons married: Raymond married Gladys Myers and Art married Mary Briggs. Mort and Jennie would have eight grandchildren.

We've met Raymond and Gladys Myers Austin's daughters: Melva, Joan, Margie, and Dawn Lee Austin. Art and Mary Briggs Austin had a daughter Louise, 1, in 1950. They would have three more children: Carol J., Charles Arthur (Chuck), and Mary Marie Austin.

Dot Calkin Hale and her brother Dale Calkin, grandchildren of Ell and Emily Parmenter Austin. Photo courtesy of Katherine Calkin Traxler.

Sherman Buckley and Charlotte Ingram Leavenworth

Jennie Leavenworth Austin's grandparents Sherman Buckley and Charlotte Ingram Leavenworth lived in Halfway Brook Village by 1835. Buckley and Charlotte had descendants from three children: Harriet Leavenworth Palmer, Sherman S. Leavenworth, and John Leavenworth.

Grandchildren of Harriet Palmer in 1950: Willard, Elliott, and Rolland Ewart, and their sister, Millie Pamela King (most lived in Detroit, Michigan).

John Leavenworth had married Amelia Bradley, the girl next door. (They later divorced.) Hazel Leavenworth Koenig (in Wisconsin) was the only one of their daughters still living.

Hazel Koenig's children in 1950: John, Gerald, and Marialyce Koenig. Hazel would celebrate her 100th birthday with children, grandchildren, and great-grandchildren; and live to be 102.

Sherman S. and Maria Myers Leavenworth Family

Sherman S. Leavenworth and his wife Maria Myers had stayed in Eldred and raised seven children. In 1950 Garfield, Charlotte, Anna, Christina Hirsch, and Martin were still living.

Some Descendants of Sherman Buckley and Charlotte Ingram Leavenworth

Hazel Leavenworth Koenig's 100th birthday party, March 17, 1996, in Kenosha, Wisconsin. All her children, grandchildren, and great-grandchildren (and spouses) are pictured. Top Row: Kathryn Kornkven Anderson holding Samuel Anderson, Eli Koenig, Doris Kestin Koenig, David Kornkven, Andrew Kornkven, Joseph Bowers, James Kornkven, Kristin Kornkven Berg, David Berg. Middle Row: Sarah Koenig holding Noah Koenig, Gerald Koenig, Hazel Koenig, Marialyce Koenig Kornkven, Ellen Kornkven Bowers. Bottom Row: Rachel Koenig, Lisa Hawker holding Isaiah Koenig, Jeanne Kornkven, Elliott Berg, Kenneth Anderson holding Joseph Anderson, Sarah Kornkven Bradley holding Ivy Berg, Brandon Counts, George Badecker holding Sarah Bowers. Photo courtesy of Marialyce Koenig Kornkven.

Hazel Koenig's first cousin Charlotte Leavenworth would have a special celebration in her honor for 50 years of teaching. Photo courtesy of Cynthia Leavenworth Bellinger.

Anna Leavenworth Meyers, Bill Meyers Jr., and Jimmy Meyers. Photo courtesy of Mary Ellen Busse Mackinder.

Edward and Charlee Hirsch Schroedel's sons: Tony, Matt, Ric, and in front Charles. Photo courtesy of Ric Schroedel.

Lee and Clara Leavenworth Hansen. Photo courtesy of Cynthia Leavenworth Bellinger.

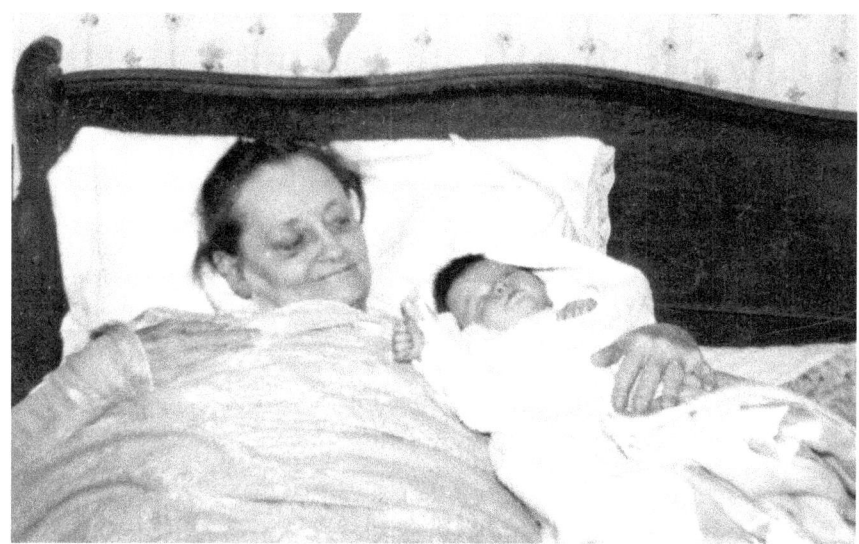

Left: Ella Sergeant Leavenworth holding Linda Leavenworth. Right: Linda Leavenworth. Photos courtesy of Linda Leavenworth Bohs.

Charlotte Leavenworth would teach first grade for ten more years. She would receive letters from then former President Eisenhower, President Kennedy, and then New York Governor Nelson Rockefeller, in honor of her 50 years of teaching.

Sherman and Maria had nine grandchildren who were living in 1950. The Austin brothers: Raymond, Bill, Art, and Bob Austin; Garfield and Ella's four children: Clara Hansen, Anna Meyers, Goldie and Jim Leavenworth; and Christina Hirsch's daughter Charlee. Charlee Hirsch would marry Ed Schroedel and they would have four sons: Ric, Tony, Matt, and Chuck.

Garfield and Ella Leavenworth
Garfield and Ella Sergeant Leavenworth would have eight grandchildren. We've met Lee and Clara Hansen's children: Dick, Wayne, and Lois; and Bill and Anna Meyers' son, Jimmy.

You may remember that Goldie and Stella Clark Leavenworth's son had died before he was a month old. Almost 12 years later Goldie and Stella's daughter Linda Louise Leavenworth was born.

Ella Leavenworth's health had been very poor for a couple years. Before Ella died she was able to have a photo taken with Goldie and Stella's newborn daughter Linda.

Jim and Gisele Leavenworth
Jim and Gisele Leavenworth had a daughter Cynthia in 1950. They would have two more children, David and Nancy. And Jim would complete the house with the picket fence that he had promised Gisele.

Chester Middaugh (whose family had long been in the area) continued to be a good friend of the Leavenworths.

I remember Chester very well. When I went to church I would see him pull the rope that rang the bell. I wondered how he was able to stay on the floor since he was a small person and the bell was so large. Dad said that Chester was a character before he got in the church.

Chester was born July 25, 1882, and had married Florence E. Hammond. He was a farmer and had worked for Proctor's.

Goldie Leavenworth with his daughter Linda. Photo courtesy of Linda Leavenworth Bohs.

Garfield and Ella Sergeant Leavenworth

Garfield Leavenworth with grandchildren Cynthia and David Leavenworth. Photo courtesy of Cynthia Leavenworth Bellinger.

Until I was three my family lived upstairs in my Leavenworth grandparents' home. I was able to spend a great deal of time with them.

Grandma Ella enjoyed doing jigsaw puzzles. I remember as a three-year-old watching her work on a puzzle. She would ask me to cross my arms Indian style so that I wouldn't be tempted to touch the pieces.

Grandma loved to crochet and do tatting. She crocheted doilies of all sizes and shapes. Many of her crocheted items were ordered by women in town and many were sold at the church sales.

Grandma, as did many homemakers back then, had a huge garden and put up lots of jars of canned goods each summer and fall. She canned all types of vegetables and bought crates of pineapples, cherries, and peaches to can and make jellies. She also canned chicken, beef, veal, and pork as there were no freezers back then. My dad said that finding a thousand jars in the cellar after her months of effort was not unusual.

Grandma Ella played the piano and gave piano lessons to many children in the town. My grandfather Garfield played the violin and also gave lessons.

Grandfather also made and repaired violins and cellos. He had begun to make a small violin for my little brother, but Grandpa died before he could finish it. I remember spending many hours watching him carefully chisel out the shape of a violin on the special frame work that he had built for this purpose.

Grandpa had a steamer in a work shop and would steam the wood with which he used to make the violins. He had a board equipped with pegs on which he would shape the wood that would be the sides of the violin and hold it in place with these pegs that he had made.

Grandpa was an excellent carpenter. He learned from my grandmother Ella's dad Frank Sergeant, who had a wonderful reputation as a builder and master of fine trim work.

My dad James Leavenworth continued the family name in carpentry. Now that my dad has passed on, my brother David carries on the business. A great many of the homes in the area have been built by one of these four men.

In later years Grandma Ella had diabetes. She also had a heart condition. As she grew older, the heart problems and diabetes took their toll on her.

Grandma died when I was three and after that we moved into our new home next door. I continued to visit my grandfather daily. After starting school, my weekends and vacations were spent going back and forth between my house and grandpa's.

I spent many fun days with my grandfather on the farm chasing piglets through the cornfield when they had gotten loose from their pen, stomping down silage in the silos, planting the garden, milking cows, squirting the milk in the mouths of the cats that were waiting patiently for a drink, herding up the cows for milking, and walking barefoot through the creek looking for pollywogs and pollywog eggs.

Grandpa taught me how to cut seed potatoes to plant in the garden. He helped me rescue a bird that was hurt and nurse it back to health.

I would help him write his Christmas cards and address the envelopes.

Every Sunday he would come over to our house and have Sunday dinner with us. When I was older, Grandpa started going over to my aunt Anna and uncle Bill's house for Sunday dinner. My brother and I would take turns going with him. We loved Aunt Anna's homemade bread with homemade jam and her little boiled onions in cream sauce.

Grandpa's favorite candies were Circus Peanuts—banana flavored marshmallow candies in the shape of a peanut. Whenever I have one, I think of him.—Cynthia Leavenworth Bellinger.

The Leavenworth grandchildren: Lois Hansen, Cynthia Leavenworth, Dick Hansen, Jimmy Meyers, and Wayne Hansen, fall 1948. Photo courtesy of Cynthia Leavenworth Bellinger.

Left photo: The house Jim built for Gisele. The white picket fence is behind Gisele, Cynthia, and David. Right photo from the left: Cynthia (dressed to be in a parade with her Girl Scout Troup), Gisele, Nancy, David (blowing bubble gum) and Chester Middaugh. Clara Leavenworth Hansen and daughter Lois in back. Photos courtesy Cynthia Leavenworth Bellinger.

Chester's house was at the base of the hill just below Echo Hill Farm House, on the same side of the road. It was set back in under tall pines.

Nellie seems to have been the horse Dad bought from Chester. Years later Dad gave Nellie back to Chester when she was an old horse and ready to retire from farm work. Chester took good care of Nellie and she lived out her life with Chet.

Nellie was the old horse that Chet let my brother David and I ride. He would walk behind us in his tall boots. She was a really smart horse. One time Nellie did not turn into our house like she should and headed towards the woods instead. Chester ran after her saying, "Whoa, Nellie, Whoa." Just as she got to the woods, she stopped, and Chester guided her back to our house.—Cynthia Leavenworth Bellinger.

Gisele Rouillon Leavenworth became a naturalized citizen on December 14, 1953. You may remember that in France Gisele Rouillon lived with Mama and Papa Cailloux after her mother and grandmother died. And that Gisele was very good friends with Marie Therese who also lived with the Cailloux.

In the 1970s Gisele flew back to France for the first time since 1946. She was able to meet with the children of Papa and Mama Cailloux: Mathilde Cailloux, and Pierre and his wife Suzanne, in the house where Gisele had grown up. Gisele stood in the same place at the Eiffel Tower as her husband Jim had in one of his photos from World War II.

Gisele also met with her friend Maria Therese in 1970. Gisele and Maria Therese have continued to meet through the years.

David and Nancy Leavenworth. Photos courtesy of Gisele Rouillon Leavenworth.

Tim C. Rizzuto, grandson of Charlie C. Myers. Photo courtesy of Timothy C. Rizzuto.

Jane Ann Myers Descendants

The children of Sherman S. and Maria Myers Leavenworth were related to Martin D. and Jane Ann Van Pelt Webb Myers who had moved near Hagan Pond (Highland Lake), not far from the Austin family in 1852. (Martin, Jane Ann's husband, had died young.) In 1950 the descendants of Jane Ann Van Pelt Webb Myers were children and grandchildren of Henry Webb (Jane's grandson from her first marriage); George W.T. and Martha Mills Myers: Charles C. Myers and Martin D. Myers Sr.; Sherman S. and Maria Myers Leavenworth: Jennie Austin, Christina Hirsch, Garfield Leavenworth, and Charlotte; and Charles and Charlotte (Lottie) Myers Darling: Agnes Curtis, Ida Whitmarsh, and Edith Sears.

Timothy C., Elizabeth, and Roberta Rizzuto are grandchildren of Charles C. Myers. Martin D. Myers Sr.'s grandchildren: Clifford D., George, Elizabeth, Helen, and Carol Crandall; Pat Myers Toaspern and Steven H. Myers; and Michael and Kevin Hulse.

Elizabeth Whitmarsh

Mary Ort, 100 years old. Photo courtesy of Christene Stevens Myers.

Schapals, granddaughter of Lottie Darling, would research the Van Pelt ancestors in the 1980s.

Mary Crandall Ort

This book would not be complete without mentioning Mary Crandall Ort who lived to be

Gisele Rouillon Leavenworth

Gisele with her life long friend Marie Therese Guerard. Photo courtesy of Gisele Rouillon Leavenworth.

Gisele standing in same place Jim stood at the Eiffel Tower. Photo courtesy of Gisele Rouillon Leavenworth.

Mathilde Cailloux, Gisele, Suzanne, wife of Pierre, and Pierre. Photo courtesy of Gisele Rouillon Leavenworth.

104 years old. Mary Ort was the mother of four sons: William, Frank, George, and Charles Ort. Mrs. Ort was a midwife and delivered many babies in the area.

Others in the Town of Highland
You may remember Jennie Crawford Crandall's lively, newsy letters in *Echo Hill and Mountain Grove*. George and Jennie Crandall's 50th wedding anniversary was celebrated by a number of folks who have been part of the story.

Several couples who have been a part of this story would celebrate 50 years of marriage: Earl and Ada Myers Wells; Martin D. and Christene Stevens Myers; Chuck and Ruth Worzel Myers (different Myers families); Jim and Gisele Rouillon Leavenworth; Oliver L. and Edna Hill Hallock; Charles and Martha Draxler; Ed and Helen Lass MacIntyre; and Norman H. and Margaret Myers Sutherland.

Return Visit to Highland Lake
Chapter 1 mentioned that Fred Schoverling had purchased Hillcrest from the Kosters in 1920, after Henry Koster was killed in an accident. Henry's wife and son Christian then moved. After Fred Schoverling died of a heart attack in the late 1940s, the Hillcrest was no longer operated as a boarding house.

Theodore and Ruth Rauscher purchased the 80-plus or minus acre property from Annette Shoverling in August 1964. The acreage was contiguous to the property of their daughter Linda and her husband Frederick Bosch, who inherited the land in 1994.

It is interesting to note that Linda Bosch was walking near the house during the summer of 1995, when a car stopped and an

George and Jennie Crandall's 50th Anniversary

George and Jenny Crandall's 50th anniversary celebration given at the Town Hall. People at the head table from left to right: Charlie Ort, Anna Sergeant Brague Ort, Emily Stevens, unknown, George and Jennie Crandall, Fred Lewis, Nell Crandall. Photo courtesy of Christene Stevens Myers.

Andy Parker, George Crandall, and Floyd Boyd at the anniversary party for George and Jennie Crandall. Photo courtesy of Christene Stevens Myers.

George and Jennie Crandall at their 50th wedding anniversary in 1956. Photo courtesy of Christene Stevens Myers.

More 50th Wedding Celebrations

Martin D. and Christene Stevens Myers at their 50th Anniversary. Photo courtesy of Christene Stevens Myers.

Jim and Gisele Rouillon Leavenworth at their 50th Anniversary. Photo courtesy of Gisele Rouillon Leavenworth.

Chuck and Ruth Worzel Myers at their 50th Anniversary. Photo courtesy of Chuck and Ruth Worzel Myers.

Oliver L. and Edna Hill Hallock celebrated 50 years of marriage. This photo was taken when they had been married 26 years. Photo courtesy of Carolyn Hallock Clark.

Earl and Ada Myers Wells celebrate their 50th Wedding anniversary. Photo courtesy of Berniece Wells Haas.

Ed and Helen Lass MacIntyre's 50th wedding Anniversary. Photo courtesy of Linda Guenther Anderson.

Norman H. and Margaret Myers Sutherland at their 50th wedding anniversary in 1988. Photo courtesy of Darlene Sutherland Haas.

Charles and Martha Draxler celebrate their 50th Wedding Anniversary. Photo courtesy of Martha Eldred Draxler.

The Narrowsburg Lumber Company would be built on Route 55. Jim Leavenworth would work there again. He said that working for the Narrowsburg Lumber Company was the best job he ever had. Photo courtesy of Howard Barnes.

old man and a very old man got out of the car. The very old man was the Koster's son Christian. He had wanted to see their old place again before he died.

Today, the first and second floors have been renovated and the old Hillcrest is rented as a large single family home. The old 1920 claw foot tub and toilet serve their original purpose in one of the two bathrooms.—Frederick Bosch.

Narrowsburg Lumber Company
The Narrowsburg Lumber Company was first started in 1927 in Narrowsburg. A Shohola branch was added in the 1930s. They opened a mill in Honesdale in the 1950s. In 1955 they bought Stege's property on Route 55 near Stege's Lake and put a mill there, though they had lumbered there in previous years.

Sawyers cut down trees in the winter time and sawed them into lumber in the summer because resin in the trees sawn in the winter turns blue and stains the

Mr. Ebers, Principal

Mr. Ebers was my principal all through my school years. He presented me with my Kindergarten diploma and was on stage when I received my high school diploma.

I always held Mr. Ebers in high esteem. All the students had a great respect for him.

Mr. Ebers would stand at the top of the school steps every morning and greet all the students as they came off the buses. At the end of the day, he would do the same thing. He would say "good night" to each of us as we headed to the buses.

I remember report cards were handed out by classroom teachers just before dismissal.

If your name wasn't called, you knew you had a failing or a borderline grade. The next morning he would call those who hadn't received their report card the day before into the office to collect it.

Mr. Ebers would remark on each subject. If you did well in some areas, he would acknowledge that. But he

Karl Ebers. Photo from the 1945 Yearbook.

would also let you know that he was disappointed in the lower grades. I think, at least in my case, that I was upset about disappointing him. He took an interest in all the students and made one feel that they mattered.
—Cynthia Leavenworth Bellinger.

1955 flooding in Eldred. Photo courtesy of Christene Stevens Myers.

1955 flooding in Eldred. Photo courtesy of Christene Stevens Myers.

1955 flooding. Photo courtesy of Christene Stevens Myers.

lumber. But in 1955 the year of the big "blow down" on the Stege property, they had to cut trees and saw all year round due to the high volume of trees which needed to be cleared.

Mr. Karl Ebers, Principal
Karl Ebers was thought of quite highly. He taught in Callicoon before becoming the principal of the Eldred Central School District from 1942 until 1971.

Emily Parker Stevens Retires as Postmaster, 1962
In the early 1930s Arthur Austin worked for Emily Stevens at the Eldred Post Office. Emma (as she was called) retired as Postmaster in 1962, and my dad wrote her a congratulatory letter.

Arthur Austin, Peach St., Wyandotte, Mich., to Emily Stevens, Eldred
4 Sept. 1962
Dear Emma,
Notice of your retirement brought to mind many memories of the earlier days that you served as Postmaster. It does not seem possible that so long a time has past since I worked for you. The experience of those interesting years has been of great value to me ever since.
I know that you have enjoyed serving the public as Postmaster, and am sure that you will enjoy the fruits of that service in the years to come. Best wishes for your future health and happiness.
Sincerely, Art Austin

1955 Flooding
In 1955 three Hurricanes hit the east coast of the U.S. There are photos of the damage Hurricane Diane caused along the Delaware River and in Eldred.

Hurricane Diane was the costliest Atlantic hurricane at the time. On August 17, Diane made landfall near Wilmington, North Carolina, weakened, then turned to the northeast where it dropped record rainfall across the northeastern United States. Diane produced heavy rainfall in eastern Pennsylvania, causing the worst floods on record, largely occurring in the Poconos and along the Delaware River.
—wikipedia.org.

I was very young, but I remember Dad and I walked to town for groceries because the little bridge over Blind Pond Brook just below our house was out. We had to climb over huge rocks and broken parts of the road. I thought it was exciting and an adventure.—Cynthia Leavenworth Bellinger.

Thanks to Original Contributors
A special thank you to my mom Mary Briggs Austin, my cousin Melva Austin Barney, and my second cousin Cynthia Leavenworth Bellinger for their original contribution of photos and information; and their continued help throughout the writing of all three *Memoirs from Eldred* books.

Appendix
Some old family photos were shared after the publication of *The Mill on Halfway Brook*. Those photographs are included in the Appendix which comes after the Bibliography. Photos from a number of the families who have been a part of the story have been interspersed with the Town of Highland Censuses at the end of the Appendix.

Letter Arthur Austin wrote Emma Stevens when she retired as Postmaster. Letter courtesy of Christene Stevens Myers.

Cynthia Leavenworth Bellinger. Photo: Brad Bellinger.

Melva Austin Barney. Photo courtesy of Tania Leigh Gaete.

Mary Briggs Austin. Photo: Gary Smith.

Bibliography

Family, Local Books, and Booklets

Austin, Arthur, *A Backward Look from the Halfway Mark*, College Paper, September 22, 1948

Eldred, Richard O.,
The Eldred Family: Elisha Eldred of Minisink, New York, and His Descendants, Baltimore: Gateway Press, Inc., 1988

Fluhr, George J.,
Rohman's Inn, Shohola Glen Hotel: Shohola, PA; 1849–1999, published: 1999

Johnston, John Willard,
Reminiscences, Town of Highland Cultural Resources Commission, 1987

Smith, Louise E.,
Aida Austin's 1881 Diary, Halfway Brook, 2010
Echo Hill and Mountain Grove, Halfway Brook, 2011
Grandma and Me, Austin-Smith Books, 2007
The Mill on Halfway Brook, Halfway Brook, 2010

Schwarz, Frank V, *History of the Eldred School District*, 2008

Whan, Clara Jean Briggs, *Briggs Heritage*, 1985

World War II References

World War II Day by Day, published by Dorling Kindersley Limited, 2004

Geoffrey C. Ward and Ken Burns,
The War an Intimate History, 1941 to 1945

The Library of Congress,
World War Two Companion

Keegan, John, general editor,
World War II, A Visual Encyclopedia

en.wikipedia.org/wiki/World_War_II
historynet.com/world-war-ii-anzio-operation.htm
history.army.mil/
wwiiarchives.net/
custermen.com

Timelines

en.wikipedia.org/wiki/1920s, 1930s, 1940s

World War II Day by Day, published by Dorling Kindersley Limited, 2004

Geoffrey C. Ward and Ken Burns,
The War an Intimate History, 1941 to 1945

Other Information Sources

A Century of Church Life: Centennial of the First Congregational Church of Eldred Celebrated, "The Tri-States Union," Vol. XLIX. No. 33. Port Jervis, N.Y., August 17, 1899

Historic Walking/Driving Tour of Barryville, New York, Highland Renaissance/Highland Pride, 2007

Barber, Gertrude A.,
Records of the First Congregational Church in the Town of Lumberland, Sullivan County, New York
Records of the Barryville Congregational Church, 1836 to 1927
Record of the Methodist Episcopal Church, Barryville, N.Y., 1931

Eldred Yearbooks, 1937–1950

Methodist Centennial and 150-Year booklets

Thompson, Barbara C.,
The Early History of Eldred Central School; Taken from Eldred Central School District attendance records, secondary schools reports, and the recollections of Dorothy Barker Sulzbach.

Werman, Edey, *Sullivan County Cemeteries*: usgwarchives.net/ny/sullivan/cemeteries/cemeterytoc.htm

Unpublished Diaries

Austin, Aida, 1940–1943 (Courtesy of Melva Austin Barney)
Leavenworth, Anna, 1941–1945 (Courtesy of Cynthia Leavenworth Bellinger)
Leavenworth, Ella Sergeant, 1931–1950 (Courtesy of Cynthia Leavenworth Bellinger)
Meyers, Anna, 1944–1950 (Courtesy of Cynthia Leavenworth Bellinger)

Website Sources of Interest

Books (old) on CD: betweenthelakes.com
Conway, John, *Retrospect:* sullivanretrospect.com
Encyclopedia online: wikipedia.org
Halfway Brook *Publishing*: halfwaybrook.com
Minisink Valley Historical Society: minisink.org
Old New York Newspapers: fultonhistory.com/Fulton.html
Proctor Family: sandpond.org
Shohola Area History: shohola.org
Town of Highland: townofhighlandny.com
Town of Lumberland: townoflumberland.org
Upper Delaware Scenic Byway: upperdelawarescenicbyway.org
World War II: wwiiarchives.net; wwiimemorial.com
Eldred Yearbooks online: ecs.schoolwires.com/page/336

Appendix

Charles Mortimer Austin Ancestors 392	The Briggs Family 415
Jennie Louisa Leavenworth Ancestors............... 393	Some James Eldred and Polly V. Mulford Descendants 416
Some Austin Descendants................................... 394	The Greig Mansion.. 417
Some Ralph and Fanny Knapp Austin Descendants 395	Some Asa and Esther Hinman Hickok Descendants 418
Some Old Austin Letters..................................... 396	Justus Hickok Family: Willard, Mary Ellen, and Dorothy 419
Augustus Austin Thompson 398	
Eldred-Austin Cousins in Eldred; Emma and Aida Austin............................... 399	Abby H. Smith Writes Cousin Emma Austin..... 420
Mabel Esther Austin Gibson, Grandmother....... 400	Some Leavenworth Descendants....................... 421
Dorothy Paton Baker... 401	Charlotte Leavenworth, Teacher........................ 422
Henry and Mary Ann Eldred Austin Family Gravestones..................................... 402	Anthony & Christina Leavenworth Hirsch 423
Excerpts from Lon Austin's Sermons 403	Anna L. Leavenworth's Autograph Book, 1930s 423
Aida Austin Memorabilia; Letter to Ell Austin, Grandpa..................................... 404	Jim Leavenworth Photos 424
Mort and Jennie Austin Memorabilia................. 405	Gisele Rouillon Leavenworth Photos................. 425
More Photos of Arthur Austin 406	Some Abel Sprague Myers Relatives 426
Arthur Austin, Yeoman and WWII Memorabilia. 407	Some Jane Ann Van Pelt Webb Myers Relatives 427
Charles Raymond and Gladys Myers Austin..................................... 408	Lazerlier, Van Pelt, Webb, and Myers Families 428
Raymond & Gladys, Art & Mary, and Bob Austin... 409	Some Rev. Isaac Sergeant Descendants 429
Charlie and Ed Bosch and the Folks They Knew................................. 410	Some Photos of Sergeant Descendants............. 430
Pepperoni Bluff and White Rabbit Thicket 411	Ed Walter Toaspern, 1924–1950 431
Bosch Lake House; Pankow Green Meadows 412	1920 Town of Highland Census with photos..... 432
Some Bradley Descendants 413	1925 Town of Highland Census with photos..... 443
	1930 Town of Highland Census with photos..... 447
Some Photos of Bradley Descendants............... 414	1940 Town of Highland Census with photos..... 457

Charles Mortimer Austin Ancestors

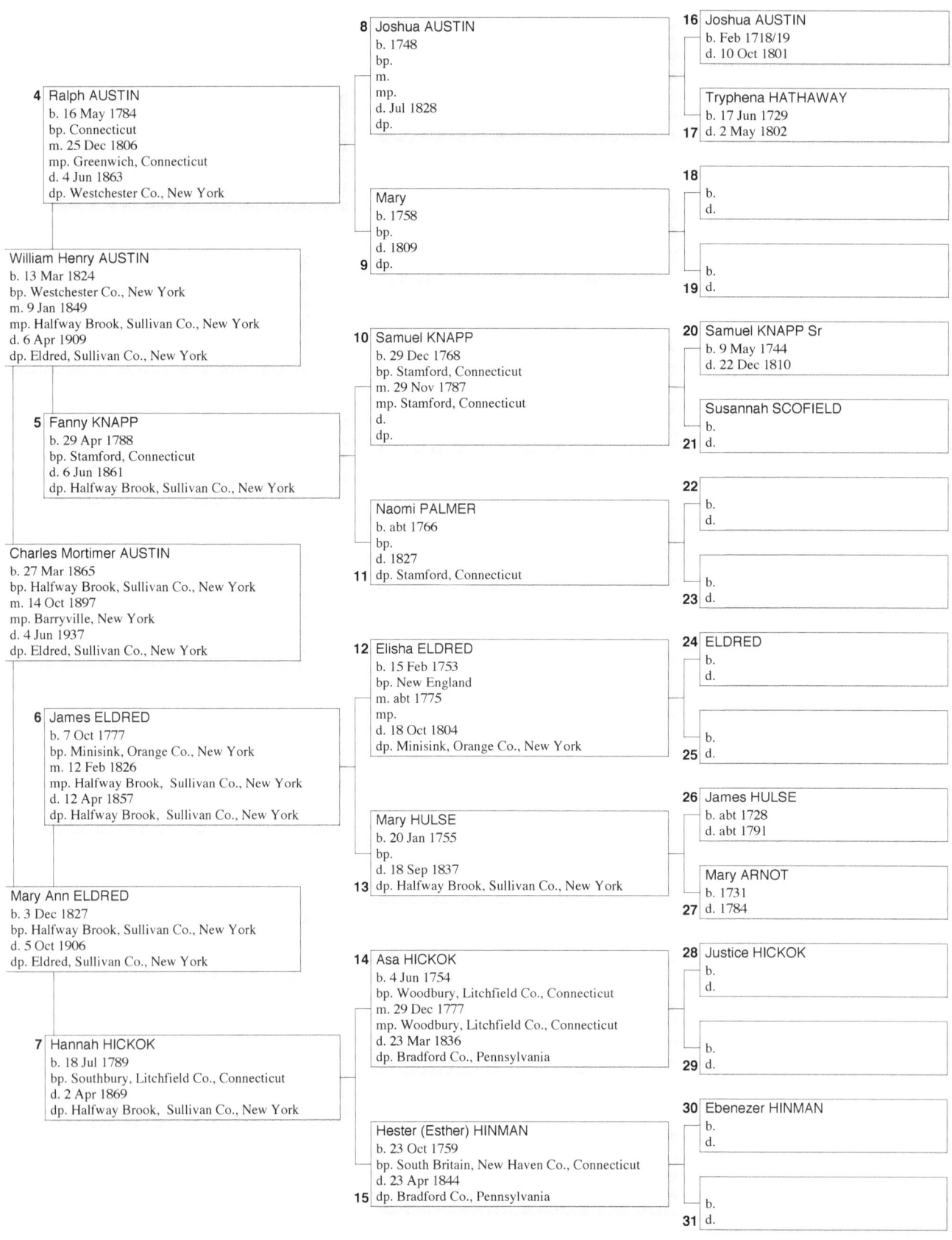

Jennie Louisa Leavenworth Ancestors

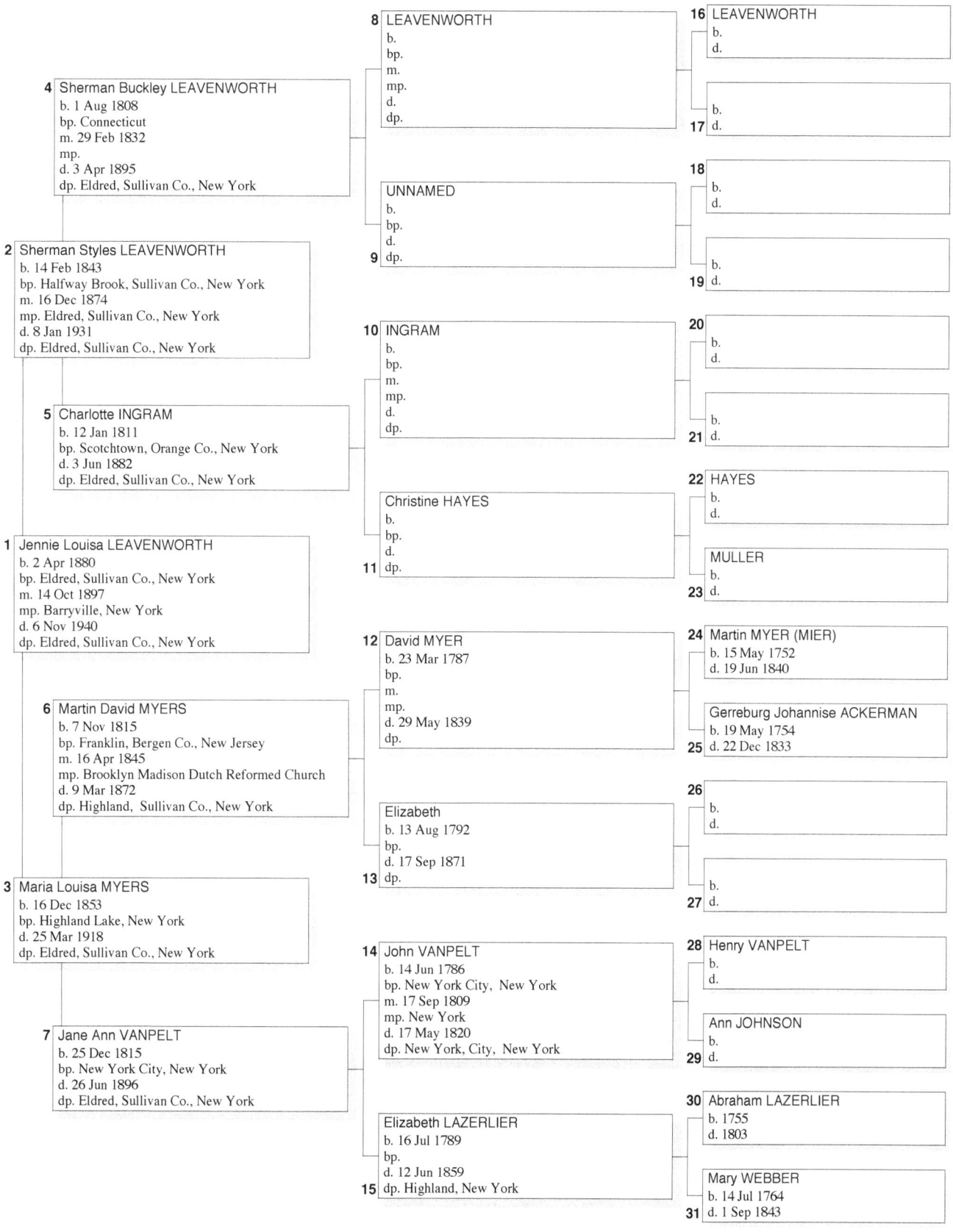

Some Austin Descendants

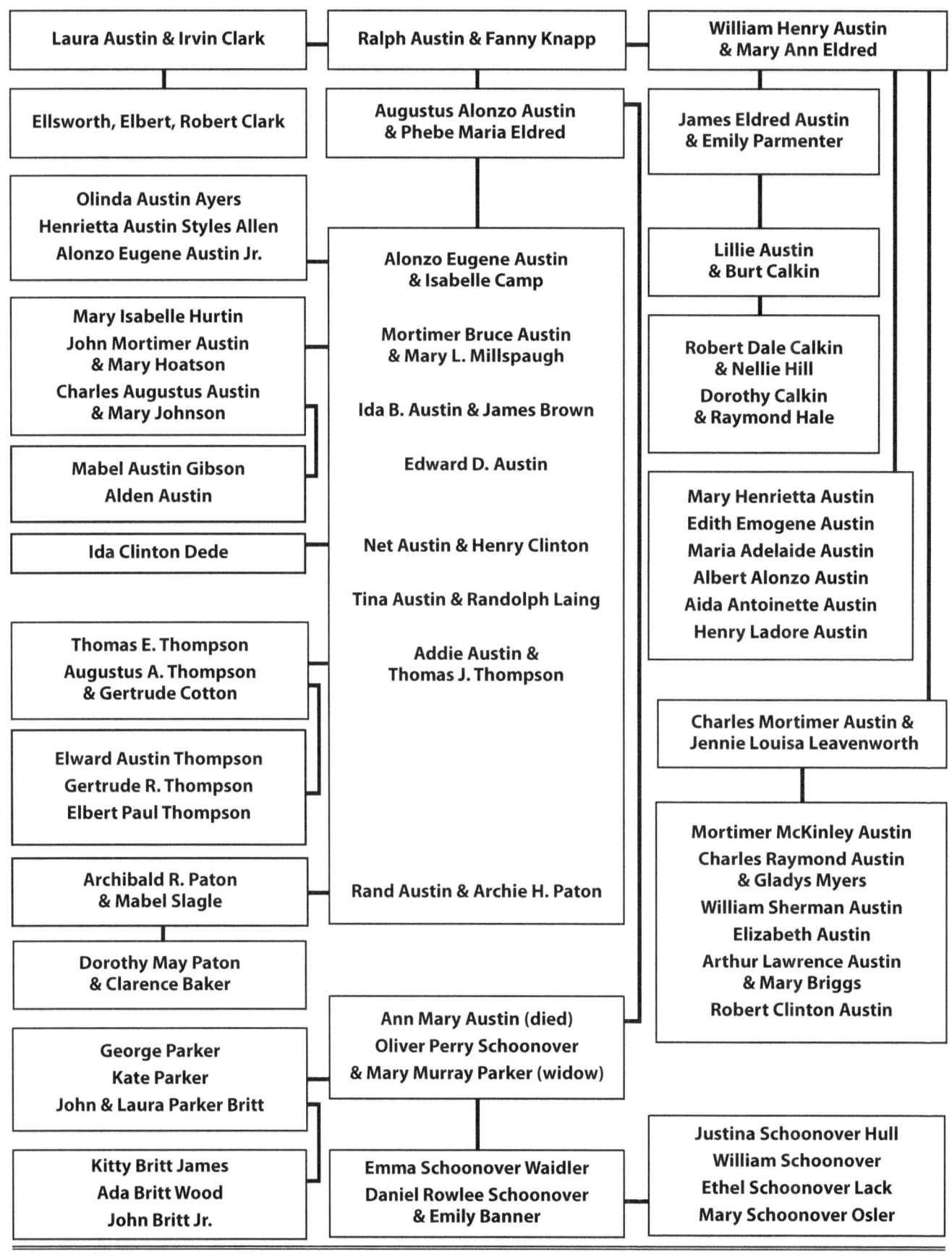

Some Ralph and Fanny Knapp Austin Descendants

Ann Mary Austin Schoonover, first wife of Perry Schoonover. Ralph Austin. James Austin, son of Ralph. Photos courtesy of Katherine Calkin Traxler. Dorothy and Archie C. Paton, grandchildren of Rand Austin Paton. Photo courtesy of Kathleen Baker Foster and Darren Foster.

Olinda Austin (Ayers) and Henrietta Austin (Styles/Allen). Photo courtesy of Katherine Calkin Traxler. Augustus A. and Gertrude Cotton Thompson. Addie Austin Thompson with grandson Elward Thompson and his mother Gertrude. Photos courtesy of the Augustus Austin Thompson Family.

Charles Augustus Austin. His daughter Mabel Austin. (Charles Augustus Austin was the son of Mortimer Bruce and Mary L. Millspaugh Austin.) Photos courtesy of Karen M. Gibson. Ida Belle Austin. Alonzo E. Austin Sr. Photos courtesy of the Augustus Austin Thompson Family.

Some Old Austin Letters

Hannah Hickok Eldred's letter to her granddaughter Emma Austin in New York City with her Eldred-Austin Cousins. Letter courtesy of Katherine Calkin Traxler.

The following letters were not included in *The Mill on Halfway Brook*. The letter from Hannah Hickok Eldred to her granddaughter Emma Austin (with her Eldred-Austin Cousins in New York City) was written at the end of a letter of Mary Ann Eldred Austin. For more on the Hickok Family, see pp. 418–420.

Hannah Hickok Eldred, Eldred, to Emma Austin, N.Y.C.
January 1864
Dear Granddaughter, I take a few moments this evening, altho I can barely see to write you, a few broken lines my dear Emma, to let you know how pleased and gratified I was with your kind letter and present…And now when you write again, I hope that will be soon. I would like to hear about your school…and what progress you are making.

What a great interest I took in your learning. I so often think of the pleasure I had when you was such a little girl, went with me to Sabbath school. You must read your Bible, not forget your prayers. Cannot write any more. You must give my love to them all and especially to your Uncle Augustus and Aunt Maria. Tell them I want to see them very much. From your loving grandmother, Hannah Eldred

Nettie Austin, N.Y.C, to Mary Ann Eldred Austin, Eldred
Wednesday, January 6, 1864
Dear Aunt Mary,

I received your letter some time ago, but have neglected to answer it. Little Ida has been very sick and we have had so much to do for the last two or three weeks that I could not get time to write.

I was down to Belle's all day yesterday and the day before to help take care of Mr. Camp. He is very sick with the typhoid fever. The doctors have very little hope of him. I am going down tonight to sit up with him.

Uncle James and Julia arrived here the day before New Years and were here to receive callers New Years Day. She seems like a very nice girl. Think we will like her very much.

I suppose you are all anxious to hear from Emma. She has had a cold in her head to keep company with the rest of us…I want to see you so bad. I have got so much to say to you, but have not got time to write. Enclosed I send you one of Father's and Mother's pictures which I think are very good.

With much love to you all,
Nettie

M.B. Austin, 121 Chambers St., N.Y.C., to Henry Austin, Eldred
August 22, 1866
Dear Uncle,

As I have nothing very urgent to do this morning, I thought I would write to you.

Uncle Perry was at our house not long since, and said that you was talking some of taking another Lumber job at Smith Mills. If you do try the lumber business again, you had ought to have it understood so that there will be no quibbling or misunderstanding when you come to make a settlement and not only that you should (must) be pretty well satisfied that you are going to make something for there is no use of your working yourself almost to death this winter and then when you come to settle in the spring find that you have made nothing and I should if I were you have it understood that if you were dissatisfied with the price they charge you for provisions, feed, etc., that you will be at liberty to make your purchases of supplies elsewhere and make them advance you the money as fast as you make it or may need it. If you should want any money to do business in that way, I will try and let you have it if you want and will purchase provisions etc., or ship them to you and you can pay me in the spring or when you settle.

If you don't take the job I think Lon would have you this winter to drive cart for him. He pays the man he has now $12 or $13 per week and I have no doubt he would give you $14 or $15. You could come here and go around with Father a week and then you would get along without much trouble. If you can do anything to make more money or that suits you better of course you will do so.

Has Thomas given you a deed for the place yet? If not, punch him up and don't be too easy with those you deal with. Make them toe the mark.

All the folks are well as usual. Addie and Emma are at Mount Kisco, Miranda and Belle intend to go to Barryville next week.

Hoping this will find you and Aunt Mary and little ones enjoying good health. I remain yours truly,
Mort B. Austin

M.B. Austin, 121 Chambers St., N.Y.C., to Henry Austin, Eldred
September 26, 1866
Dear Uncle,

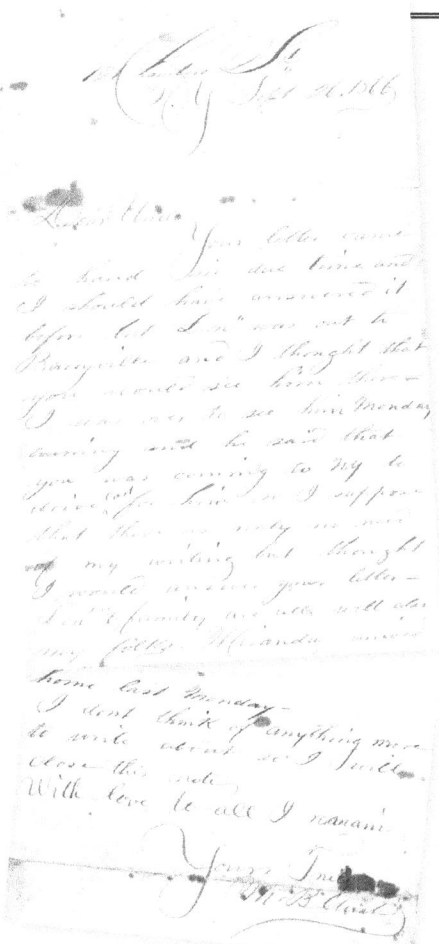

September 26, 1866 letter from M.B. Austin to his uncle Henry Austin. Letter courtesy of Katherine Calkin Traxler.

Your letter came to hand in due time and I should have answered it before but Lon was out to Barryville and I thought that you would see him there. I was over to see him Monday evening and he said that you was coming to N.Y. to drive cart for him so I suppose there is really no need of my writing but thought I would answer your letter.

Lon and family are all well, also my folks. Miranda arrived home last Monday. I will close this note. With love to all I remain
Yours Truly, M.B. Austin

M.B. Austin, N.Y.C., to Mary Ann Austin, Eldred
October 25, 1866
Dear Aunt,

Your letter came duly at hand and as you say that a letter from me at any time will be acceptable and as business is dull and having not much to do I thought that I might as well afflict you with a letter as any one else or at least an apology for one.

We are having beautiful weather here now and splendid moonlight nights.

I saw Lon [his brother] yesterday. His family are well he would like to have Uncle Henry come to N.Y. as soon as can possibly get away. The man he has driving for him is a miserable poor coot and can not be depended upon and does not take any care of his horse so that the sooner he gets rid of him the better.

Uncle James and wife are at our house and are both well.

I had a nice time [at a wedding]. Quite a number of my friends have departed this life of single blessedness the past few months. I think it more contagious than cholera and our board of health have done nothing to prevent its further spread although it's carried off more victims than any other disease and although any one would think to look at those that when first attracted with this (matrimonial) disease, that they were perfectly happy and contented to meet this fate. Well I think I have written about enough of this foolishness but you must excuse me for I did not know of anything else to write about unless it should be politics and that is a subject almost as bad as matrimony.

Give my love to Grandmother, the children and if acceptable reserve a share for yourself.
Yours Truly,
Mort

Augustus Austin Thompson

Augustus Austin Thompson. Photo courtesy of the Augustus Austin Thompson Family.

Augustus Austin Thompson, son of Thomas J. and Adelaide E. Austin Thompson, was named to honor his grandfather Augustus Austin, and in remembrance of his brother who had died at six months old.

Gus or Gussie was part of a lively multi-generational household of Austin and Thompson parents, grandparents, brothers, cousins, aunts and uncles. Portraits of Gussie from the 1880s portray a confident child comfortable in the urban environment in which he grew up. If we are to take as evidence the accounts included in some of the Austin "cousin letters," Gus as a child may have been a little too confident or even bratty. He would have grown up hearing tales, of his grandfather William "Corporal" Thompson and his popular (1830s–1850s) tavern "Madison Cottage," at the then terminus of the Fifth Avenue stage line.

Luckily, this city kid had ample exposure as Adelaide Austin's son to the country life offered by his extended Austin family in Eldred. The importance of this contact is reflected in Augustus' lifelong love of the natural world and push to rural retreats.

The child Gus became known as Austin as a young man. His parents saw that his schooling continued through college as a graduate of City College, then known as the Free Academy of the City of New York. Austin excelled in his studies with a particular love of literature. The engraved medal he won as a college prize for French in 1892, is still treasured by his grandson's family. After graduation, Austin became a New York City public school teacher, a position he held until his retirement years.

At some point in his college years, Austin Thompson became a Baptist and served as a Sunday School teacher for the older youth group in his church. One member of the youth group apparently stood out—Gertrude Cotton. The match was made, and they were married on July 7, 1898.

Austin taught at a school in Upper Manhattan. Their daughter Adelaide J. Thompson was born in July 1899. Austin and Gertrude's second residence was a house on Hawthorne Avenue in Yonkers. Both sets of parents would live there.

Austin's father Thomas and his sister (Austin's aunt) Polly ran a New Jersey summer boarding house often frequented by theater people escaping the City's summer heat. There Austin and Gertrude's young children—Adelaide (who died at age 6), Elward Austin, and Gertrude Ruth experienced all the outdoor country pleasures—including riding horseback, driving goat carts, and boating on the Navesink River.

After the deaths of his parents, Austin Thompson, at the suggestion of close friends, purchased a rustic summer cottage at Silver Bay on the western shore of Lake George in the Adirondack Mountains of northern New York. The cottage is still in the family.

The Thompson family, which now included Elbert Paul Thompson, started the summer by packing their huge steamer trunks and taking the night boat up the Hudson River to Albany, New York. From Albany they caught a train to Lake George Village at the end of the lake. A lake steamer at that dock took them to Silver Bay—the family's home for the entire summer.

As children married and moved out and Austin's teaching career wound down to a close, Austin turned with renewed spirit to his old loves of literature, religious and philosophical inquiry, and, with Gertrude, gardening and nature study—in both Yonkers and at Silver Bay. The couple also learned the joy of being grandparents (1930) and great-grandparents (1948).

Augustus Austin Thompson was remembered as a gentle, patient and scholarly man, warm and kind to those around him. Tall and thin with beautiful silky hair, A.A. Thompson (as he would sign) would encourage children to hike, to plant, to make things with their own hands and to read. He also advised them to brush their hair 100 strokes every night before bed!

After his sudden death in 1953 following surgery, his widow Gertrude carefully wrote down the comments of others on the character of Augustus Austin Thompson. Those impressions included ones that portray Austin as "a man of broad sympathies and tolerance, as well as keen judgement" and as "so full of ability and so warm with human interest and understanding—a choice friend."
—Elizabeth W. Thompson.

French medal awarded to Austin Thompson courtesy of the Augustus Austin Thompson Family.

Eldred-Austin Cousins in Eldred, Emma and Aida Austin

Eldred-Austin Cousins at the Austin Farm in Eldred. Photo courtesy of Mary Briggs Austin.

Edith Emogene Austin. Photo courtesy of Katherine Calkin Traxler.

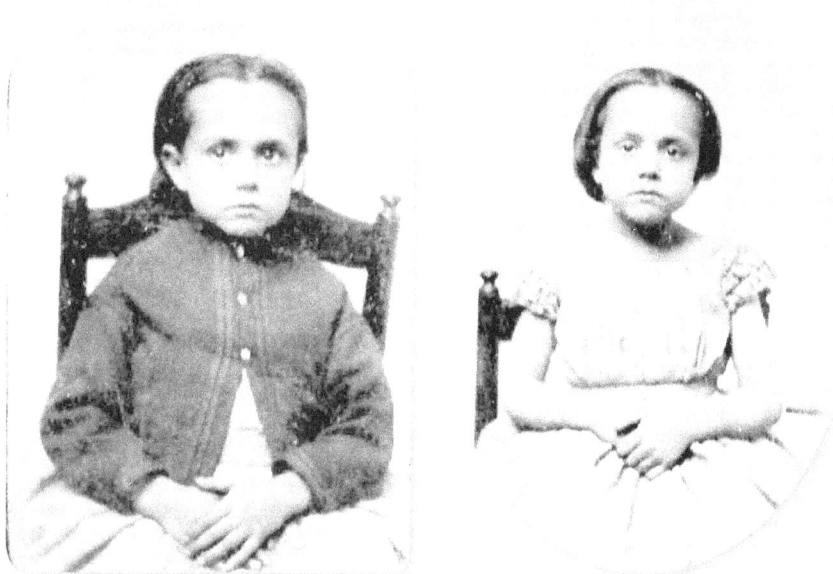

Photos of Aida Austin when younger courtesy of Katherine Calkin Traxler.

Aida Austin when she was young. Photo courtesy of Katherine Calkin Traxler.

Mabel Esther Austin Gibson, Grandmother

Mabel Austin, graduate from Cornell University, in 1929. Photo courtesy of Karen M. Gibson.

As a young child, I was lucky enough to live within walking distance of my grandmother, which was simply delightful. Her home was a wonderland to me and Grammy was the keeper of the keys to that wonderland.

Inside her house there was the cookie jar full of molasses cookies, the piano where Grammy played her favorite hymns and show tunes and I could sing along, the cards ready for playing Kings in the Corners, the table with the Scrabble board set up mid-game, the easel with her latest oil painting in progress, and small vases of sweet-smelling flowers tucked everywhere.

Outside was just as magical. The flower beds were in colorful bloom, the Norway maple trees spun their helicopter seeds, and the profusion of lilacs scented the air for weeks—there was never a better place to explore, to climb trees, to play hide and seek. And when we had time Grammy would take me on a nature walk down the back lane to the edge of the woods. She could tell me the name of every plant and point out every bird. Not only did she know the birds, but she could sing to the birds their own song and they would sing back! Talk about magical times!

Only recently have I begun to consider that Mabel was anything more than just my Grammy. As I comb through pictures and other memorabilia that she kept, I am learning how bold and adventurous she was as a young woman.

In a time when very few people attended college, and even fewer women, Mabel Esther Austin attended Cornell University from 1925-1929. Even more remarkable, she was one of only 16 women (out of a total class of 113) that graduated with a Bachelor's of Science degree from the College of Agriculture.

Upon graduation, Mabel applied for many teaching jobs, but as she told me more than once, schools wanted to hire science teachers that could double as coaches for the men's sports teams, not a young woman fresh out of college. And then the Great Depression hit.

Mabel married in 1930 and she and her husband later bought a farm in Stanley, New York. They had three children, of which my dad was the middle child and only son. From the mid-1940s until the late 1950s Mabel raised her children and operated the farm on her own, which must have taken immense strength and perseverance.

Music and art continued to be her passion; she sang in church and community choirs, played the piano, and took a mail-order art course to learn oil painting, for which she received several local awards over the years. In the 1960s and early 1970s Mabel worked as a substitute teacher in a nearby public school and as a dorm mother at William Smith College in Geneva, and Keuka College in Keuka Park, New York.

What I remember most about my grandmother was her passion for nature, art, poetry and music. Mabel loved being outdoors and loved to garden; she kept daily bird counts; she created her own greeting cards with sketches of nature scenes, birds and animals (rabbits, squirrels, deer and cats were her favorite subjects) on the cover and poems inside; she would spontaneously burst into song with a hymn or tune from a Broadway show; she had sparkling blue eyes and a smile that lit up a room.

She wasn't perfect by any stretch—she could hold a grudge and she would fret quite vocally if you did something she didn't think was right. She had the annoying habit of coming to visit but never staying long enough to even take her coat off—she always had to hurry back home. For all her imperfections, though, she was still a remarkable woman. And she passed along her love of nature to all five of her granddaughters—we are hikers, gardeners, scientists and farmers. Grammy would be proud!—Karen M. Gibson.

Mabel Austin Gibson in 1986. Photo courtesy of Karen M. Gibson, granddaughter.

Dorothy Paton Baker

Dorothy Paton Baker with daughter AnnMarie (Ree); and as a nurse during WWII. Photos courtesy of Kathleen Baker Foster and Darren Foster.

Dorothy Paton Baker, my mother, was my best friend. My earliest memory was that she was a very unique and attentive Mom. I will always remember the many dancing lessons, piano recitals, and all the hours of music lessons. When I was nine, my parents purchased an organ. That was the beginning of my love and appreciation for the relaxing and enjoyment we derived from having a little concert every night after my dad got home from work.

Mom was my biggest fan and staunch supporter. She was always there to give me her expert advice, whether it be my outfits for work or hair style. Mom was so excited and thrilled when I worked for a Supreme Court Justice in Albany. Once or twice a month, we would go shopping and she would help me pick out suits or outfits befitting a legal secretary to the Judge.

I always loved our nightly chats about how her day was and then all about mine.

When I married and moved from my hometown, the closeness never wavered. When we had our children, Mom insisted on coming up North and staying at our house to help us with the newborn. It meant so much to me to have her always by my side.

Mom always needed to please everyone and her biggest gift to not only me but to her family and friends, was the love and commitment when anyone asked her. I will always try follow the example Mom taught me and am thankful I was given the best Mother and friend for my lifetime. —Kathleen Baker Foster.

Grandmother (Nanny to her grandchildren) was a warm, wonderful, loving woman. She had had a stroke and suffered from high blood pressure, so she couldn't be too active with us kids. But she would take the time to sit with me for hours on end to help me with my reading. Nanny installed

Clarence and Dorothy Paton Baker on their wedding day. Photo courtesy of Kathleen Baker Foster and Darren Foster.

a love of reading, art, and culture. She was part of woman's group called the Shakespeare Society, a book club for Shakespeare plays and poems.

Nanny in her later years loved to paint. She and a neighbor lady painted for hours on end. After her death we each got at least one of her paintings. They were some of the most beautiful landscape seasonal pictures I'd ever seen. I guess she got her talents from her father Archie Paton. Even though Grandma didn't know much about her family history, she did give me the foundation and clues that would later help me in my research. I truly think of her often and still miss her.—Darren Foster.

Dorothy Paton Baker was the daughter of Archibald R. Paton and his second wife, Mabel Slagle. Halfway Brook readers may recall Archie R. Paton as "little Archie" in *Aida Austin's 1881 Diary*. Archie's parents were Archie and Rand Austin Paton.

Clarence Baker, a bio chemist, worked at the same hospital as Dorothy Paton Baker. Dot, as her friends called her, was a nurse in White Plains, New York, during the War. Clarence and Dot were introduced by his brother who also worked at the hospital.

Henry and Mary Ann Eldred Austin Family Gravestones

Entrance to Prairie Mound Cemetery in Kansas, where Edith Emogene Austin was buried. Photo: Gary Smith.

Edith Emogene Austin, the daughter of Henry and Mary Ann Eldred Austin, was my great-aunt. She had tuberculosis and went out to Solomon, Kansas, to live with her brothers, in hopes the drier weather would cure her. But she died there in Solomon in 1879. You can read about her in *The Mill on Halfway Brook*. In 1929 Ell Austin mentioned he purchased the plot Emma was buried in in Prairie Mound Cemetery, Solomon, Kansas *(see p. 82)*.

I had the opportunity in 2011 to stop in Solomon, Kansas, and visit Prairie Mound Cemetery where my great-aunt Emma Austin was buried. It was late in the afternoon, about 41 degrees, windy, and drizzly, when Gary and I drove into Prairie Mound Cemetery. The caretaker was just stopping by to close up the cemetery, but took the time to show us where the James (Ell) Austin and Parmenter plots were located. We located the Parmenter stones, but not Emma's.

Cousin Melva had said that when she was there 20 years earlier, there was a stone with the name Austin and another stone which she thought was Emma's (but the wind had pelted away the name) near the Austin plot.

In Echo Hill and Mountain Grove *are several letters William G. Sutherland wrote to Lon Austin.*

In William's letter of January 23, 1881, he mentioned that Arthur Sutherland's little girl had died. In a plot belonging to Arthur Sutherland, there was a memorial stone to one-year-old Gracie, daughter of Arthur and Annie Sutherland. There was also a plot with the name William Sutherland, but it is unknown if he was buried there.
—Louise Austin Smith.

Eldred Cemetery, Eldred, N.Y.
Henry and Mary Ann Eldred Austin's other children (except Henrietta) were buried in the old Eldred Cemetery, Eldred, New York. There is a headstone with the names: Dory (Henry L.), Maria, Ell (James E.), Aida, and Lon (Alonzo) Austin.

Plot map showing Arthur Sutherland, James Austin, Parmenter, and Wm. Sutherland Plots. Photo: Gary Smith.

Parmenter plot which was next to the James Austin plot, viewed from the back and side. Photo: Gary Smith.

Austin headstone in the Eldred Cemetery for siblings Henry Ladore, Maria A., James Eldred, Aida A., and Alonzo (Lon) Austin. Photo: Gary Smith.

Three of the Austin sibling stones that had each name. Photos courtesy of Cynthia Leavenworth Bellinger.

Excerpts from Lon Austin's Sermons

Afraid in the Storm

Our Lord upon a certain occasion, was so tired that he told his disciples to go board their ship and sail for the other side of Lake Galilee. He went down into the boat in hopes of getting a little rest in sleep.

The Father, who is ever mindful of the Son, beholds how tired and restless is his child. So he turns that little boat into a cradle, makes the waves its rocker and calls up the winds to sing the lullaby. (The more restless a child is, the harder the cradle is rocked; but Jesus sleeps as sweetly as the infant in its mother's arms.)

Oh how tired he must have been after his long walk and hard work. O sleep on thou Saviour of the world. But no, the mariners are awfully frightened. They do not hear the parental voice singing his weary one to rest. They mistake the lullaby, and think it is their funeral dirge.

Who would have thought that those old fisherman would have been so frightened, but they had been with Jesus and they saw their sinful nature and conscience makes cowards of us all.

"Carest thou not that we perish?" Oh the selfishness of that prayer. No thought of Christ to whom harm must first come.

"Peace be still." The waters calm. "Oh ye of little faith. Wherefore did ye doubt?"

Christ was not displeased because of the request, but it was the spirit of the prayer that grieved Him for it showed how little was their confidence.

Had they said, "Lord, help, we are in trouble," not a word of rebuke would have fallen from the lips of the weary Saviour.

"Call upon me in the day of trouble and I will deliver thee." Let us believe his Word and trust his grace.

Discords

I was thinking of the discords we make and it seems to me the most terrible ones are those which are produced by our actions being contrary to our words. We talk of being generous and kind, but a selfish desire comes in our way and forgetting what we have been saying, we stoop to gratify that desire and to shield ourselves we tell this falsehood so we think we are right. Judge not. Judge not.

No talk of rendering a good for evil, but another selfish desire must be gratified and again we stoop to treachery and this time we have an excuse. Someone has wronged us.

Now we talk of forgiveness. Our friend stumbles and makes a mistake. He is thoughtless and impulsive, but with all his thoughtlessness and impulsiveness, he is generous and kind and seeing his mistake, he comes to us frankly and asks us to forgive him.

And we with the profession of forgiveness still upon our lips, reach out and stab him. Oh these discords. Is it any wonder the world calls us hypocrites? Is it any wonder that souls seeking the light of Christ stagger back into the darkness and unbelief?

Pages in the New Testament that Lon Austin gave his nephew Arthur Austin, courtesy of Mary Briggs Austin.

Inscription on New Testament Lon Austin gave his nephew Arthur Austin. "To Arthur, My dear nephew, May the Lord keep thee in all thy ways. Lovingly, Uncle Lon.

Aida Austin Memorabilia

Excerpt from Aida Austin's 1942 "Diary," courtesy of Melva Austin Barney.

Card to unknown person that Aida wrote in 1937 courtesy of Katherine Calkin Traxler.

"Sometime when all life's lessons have been learned,
    And sun and stars forevermore have set,
The things which our weak judgments here have spurned
    The things o'er which we grieved with lashes wet
Will flash before us out of life's dark night,
    As stars shine most in deeper tints of blue;
And we shall see how all God's plans were right,
    And how what seemed reproof was love most true."
With love,
Aida A. Austin

Letter to Ell Austin, Grandpa

Ell Austin's Other Grandchildren

Ell Austin's grandchildren (children of Henry Austin, half brother of Lillie Austin Calkin) corresponded with Ell. Henry and Sadie LeRoy Austin's children: Ralph Austin; Mildred Austin Kiesel; Margo Austin Edsal; Myrtle Austin Hedden, Mabel Austin Inch; Alma Austin; and Hazel Austin Maver. Several of them lived in Pennsylvania.

Mrs. Charles Kiesel, 911 S. Maine Ave., Scranton, Pa., to Mr. J.E. Austin, Ossining, N.Y.
March 20, 1935
Dear Grandpa,

Just a line to ans. your card and letter I received at Xmas time and sure glad to hear from you. Have been going to answer it so many times, but I am so slow in writing anymore.

Hope this letter finds you in good health as it leaves us better now, but we were all sick. The children had the measles and I had the grippe I guess.

Ralph and Mabel's children also had the measles.

Mother [Sadie LeRoy Austin] was very low last week. I was up there from Thursday until Sunday night. She is under the Dr.'s care. We were all home Thursday night, but she is a lot better now. She is up at Margo's at present.

Dutch is at Margo's also helping them as he still is unemployed. He went to Harrisburg yesterday with a load of potatoes for Bob. The truck has gone again today, just past the house, but I guess Dutch didn't go today.

Well, how are you anyway, and all the rest of the folks. How is times down there? They're terrible up here, don't look as if it is going to be any better.

When I was up home, I seen the paper that you are in favor of the Bonus Bill. Do you think it will pass? I hope so as it would help us out a lot just now as Dutch was a vet.

Well, I guess I will have to close for this time and do my dinner dishes. Hoping to hear from you soon. When are you coming up to see us? Write me all the news. Will ring off for this time.

With love and kisses,
Mil [Mildred Austin Kiesel]

Mort and Jennie Austin Family Memorabilia

Mountain Grove House and the old Austin Barn. Photos courtesy of Mary Briggs Austin.

Gravestones for Mort and Jennie Leavenworth Austin in the Eldred Cemetery. Photos: Gary Smith.

In 1921, Raymond took spelling, shorthand, typewriting, dictations and transcriptions. He had 2-1/2 days of excused absence; and a 10 in both Deportment and Industry. Card courtesy of the Austin Family.

Poignant pose of Jennie Louisa Leavenworth Austin. Photo courtesy of Mary Briggs Austin.

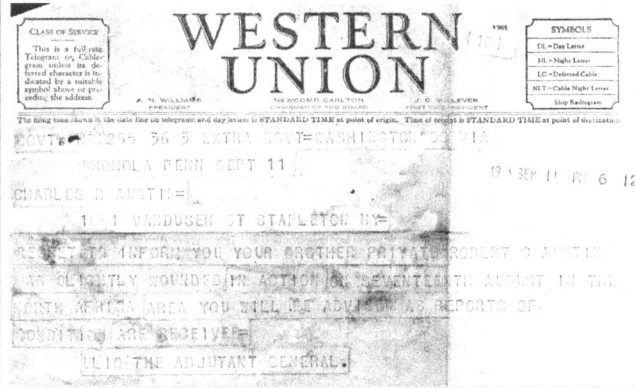

Western Union telegraph to Raymond Austin letting him know that his brother Bob had been slightly wounded in action in August. Copy in the Austin Collection.

Bob Austin on right with friends at Niagara Falls. Photo courtesy of Mary Briggs Austin.

More Photos of Arthur Austin

Art at graduation time, 1930. Photos courtesy of Mary Briggs Austin.

Art most likely photographed by Aida Austin. Photo in Austin Collection.

Arthur Austin as Uncle Dudley in a school play. Photos likely taken by Aida Austin courtesy of Mary Briggs Austin.

Arthur Austin, Yeoman and WWII Memorabilia

The USAT Chateau Thierry's itinerary, May 1932, courtesy of Mary Briggs Austin.

Sgt. Austin Decorated by Gen. Clark

The Salerno Day Decoration ceremony, which took place in the Tavernelle area, Italy, saw one of our county boys being decorated. The boy, M-Sgt. Arthur L. Austin of Eldred, N. Y., was presented with the Legion of Merit emblem by Lt. Gen. Mark W. Clark who is shown pinning the medal to Austin's tunic.

Sgt. Austin is with the Fifth Army Hqs.

Original Newspaper Article when Arthur Austin got his Legion of Merit, courtesy of Mary Briggs Austin.

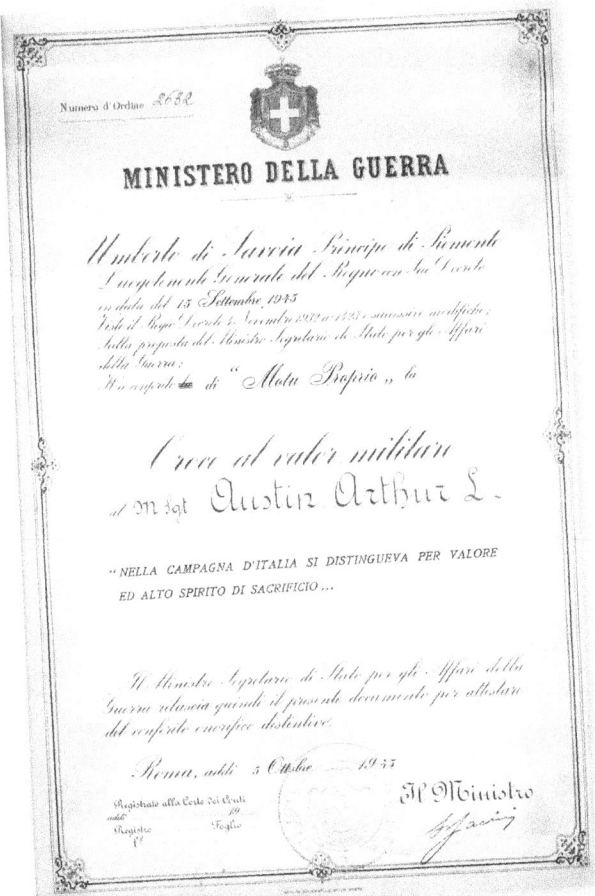

October 1945 Certificate from the Italian Government to Arthur Austin. Certificate courtesy of Mary Briggs Austin.

Barone Roberto Ricciardi's Card courtesy of Mary Briggs Austin.

1932 Pass for Arthur L. Austin, Steward's Yeoman aboard the U.S.S. Chateau Thierry. Pass courtesy of Mary Briggs Austin.

Postcard to Lon (A.A.) Austin from his nephew Arthur Austin in Camp Upton, February 1942. Card in Austin Collection.

Charles Raymond and Gladys Myers Austin

Gladys Austin. Photo courtesy of Andy and Margie Austin Maglione.

Raymond Austin. Photo courtesy of Andy and Margie Austin Maglione.

Raymond reading. Photo courtesy of Dawn Lee Austin Segarra.

Raymond and his daughter Dawn Lee in 1966. Photo courtesy of Dawn Lee Austin Segarra.

Raymond and Gladys Myers Austin celebrate their 50th Anniversary. Photo courtesy of Dawn Lee Austin Segarra.

Gladys and Raymond Austin. Photo courtesy of Joan Austin Geier.

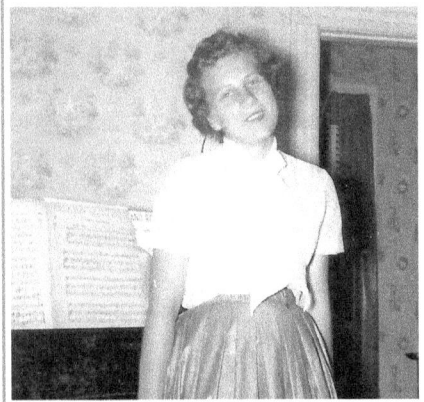

Margie Austin Maglione. Photo courtesy of Andy and Margie Austin Maglione.

Playing checkers was a very Austin thing to do and is mentioned in Aida Austin's 1881 Diary. Here Bob Austin plays checkers with Walter Geier, husband of Joan Austin Geier.

Raymond and Gladys Austin photo courtesy of Melva Austin Barney, daughter.

Raymond & Gladys; Art & Mary; and Bob Austin

Arthur Austin. Photo: Gary Smith.

Art and Mary Austin. Photo courtesy of Mary Briggs Austin.

Raymond and Gladys Austin; Mary and Arthur Austin. Photo courtesy of Joan Austin Geier.

Raymond, Art, and Bob Austin. Photo courtesy of Joan Austin Geier.

Bob Austin on the swings and walking along the ocean. Photos courtesy of Joan Austin Geier. Right photo: Mary M. Austin, Bob Austin, Joan Austin Geier; in back: Walter Geier and Chuck Austin. Photo courtesy of Mary Briggs Austin.

Charlie and Ed Bosch and the Folks They Knew

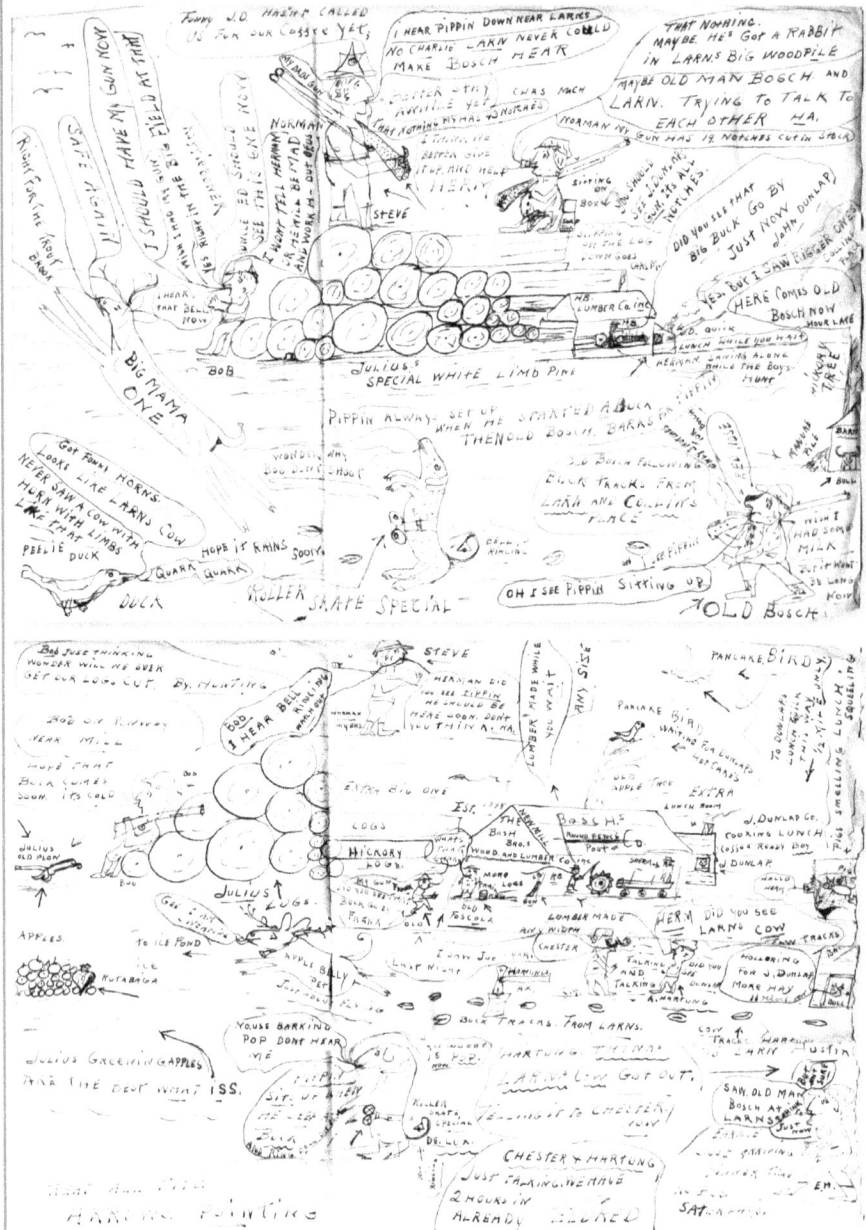

Charlie Bosch's cartoons about Herman Bosch's sawmill courtesy of Ken Bosch.

Charlie Bosch often included cartoons and doodles with his letters. These two cartoons deal with a day at Herman Bosch's sawmill where Charlie worked intermittently.

These stream-of-consciousness cartoons have at their theme the difficulties of Herman's getting and keeping help on the job with the overriding distractions of hunting season, not to mention the lure of breakfast, lunch and coffee at Dunlap's corner restaurant.

The names of many local people are referenced for inside jokes: Lon "Larn" Austin and his cow—Larn's cow is regularly confused with the elusive big buck "Apple Belly Pete" which Charlie Bosch was always tracking with his loyal dog Pippin (outfitted with roller skates on his belly and a bell to alert the hard-of-hearing Charlie); Bob Bosch waiting in vain at a deer stand; Julius Maier; Ernie Horton arriving for work at dinner time; Chester Middaugh and Art Hartung; Norm Myers; Frank Foscola, and others. While everyone is consumed by various diversions, Herman perseveres to keep the sawmill operating by himself.
—Ken Bosch.

People Ed Bosch Knew
Charlie's brother Ed Bosch wrote a list of people in several categories.

People who lived before Ed:
Wm. Wilson store, Dan Hallock, Charles Wilson, Gus Myers, Parker Bar room, Lewis French, Dunlap, Parson Edward Whitney, Jake Clouse, Mr. and Mrs. Beck, Hardcastles, Charlie Stage (farmer), Carmichaels, Sidwell Music, Kosters, Bischofs, Metzgers, Sergeants, Eldred House, Wallaces, Mills, Hartung shortcut, Waits, Boyds, George Myers, Hoatsons, Larn and Dory Austin, Quinns, McBrides, Dr. Austin, Sullivan Family.

In Eldred:
Abe Rundle, Abe Myers, Jack Myers, Warren Parker, Styles (missionary), Rev. Alonzo Eugene Austin (minister, Dr. Austin's father), Mort Austin, Sherm McBride, Greigs, Hipe Dailey, Racines, Bill Wait, Leavenworth (Civil War vet), Kelleys.

Road to Barryville
Ed Myers, Jim Morgan, Brower, Bert Kyte, Horton, Libly (Lillie?) Jake, Tom Collins, Quick store, Clouse carpenter, Harry Wormuth, Gardner, Bill Parker, Mr. and Mrs. Clark, Orts (old), John Love, Frank Mink?, Ed Kalbfus (Erie agent), Jim Clark (sawyer), Willard Wells, Ralph DeSilvey (drove team), Crawford (good worker), Jennie Crawford (teacher), John Hulse, veterinary?, Jim Hulse, Hoop splitter, Nelson Hulse, blacksmith.

My four doctors: Dr. Johnson, Dr. Smith, Dr. Crellin, Dr. Petkus.

Pepperoni Bluff and White Rabbit Thicket

Coonskin in the winter of 1962. Photo courtesy of Ken Bosch.

Wilderness Area by Bower Road

The Quinn Place mentioned in Chapter 9 was a hard scrabble farm down the first road off the Bower Road which ran past my grandfather Charlie Bosch's house (Coonskin).

My grandmother's family lived for a time on an abandoned farm off Bower Road known as the Quinn Place. My great-grandfather, Titus Leonhard Miller, had worked in Sullivan County in the late 1890s with his brothers Ben and Nick Muller as a stone mason, including a stint for Dr. DeVenoge. After a saloon venture in Hoboken, New Jersey failed, Leonhard, his wife Katherine Wiest Miller and children Lena and Ben moved into the Lake House at the behest of William Bosch.

After living with the Bosch's for a couple of months, the Millers moved into the Quinn Place. The small one story-house with sleeping lofts was situated on the flat top of a rocky ledge. Two or three decrepit outbuildings were built into the side of the small cliffs below the house. No one knew who owned it. All that remained when I was a child was a stone foundation, glass and pottery fragments, a lilac tree, some apple trees and an active spring below the road. The stone foundations of the outbuildings were intact. The house may have burned during a forest fire.

Today there are a number of archeological remnants of failed and abandoned farms scattered along the woodland roads, carrying the names of former owners such as the "McBride Place", the " Stolts Place" and others. Only stone walls, a rudimentary stone foundation or two, and some pieces of glass or rusty metal memorialize the years of wasted toil that were poured into these hardscrabble enterprises long since reclaimed by the forest. The names of these farms served only to denote a location in the woods.

My uncle Whipple Bosch drew a map in the early 1950s showing the roads that traversed the many miles of woods past my grandfather's house. For many years it hung in his hunting camp (which became "Coonskin" after my grandfather's house was sold). I found the names of the various features in the woodland to be particularly evocative—*Hoot Owl Swamp, Squirrel Swail, Bull Briars, Four Buck Gulch, Slaughter Pen, Red Ridge, Coonskin* (grandpa Charlie Bosch's house and immediate surroundings), *Dead Doe Pass, Big Bear Swamp,* and many other colorful names, including the mysterious *Morefedite (sic) Runway.* You can identify many of these features on Google Earth, although the old roads don't show up. The *Turnpike* was essentially an abandoned stretch of the old Newburgh-Cochecton Turnpike that ran through the unpopulated forest land. All the land on the map was wilderness at the time. Very few people in town were aware of these roads when I was growing up.

When Harvey Parker was stationed in Governor's Island in the late 1950s to the early 60s, he and his family spent weekends at Whipple's hunting camp between Bower Road and Lakeview Drive.

We explored the miles and miles of wilderness accessible by Bower Road and woodland paths known only to a select few. Parker went fishing at many of the isolated lakes, Mud Pond, Hull Pond, and Lebanon Lake. He used Whipple's Model A pickup to drive as far back as possible. The rest of the trip was carried out on foot following long-established trails.—*Ken Bosch.*

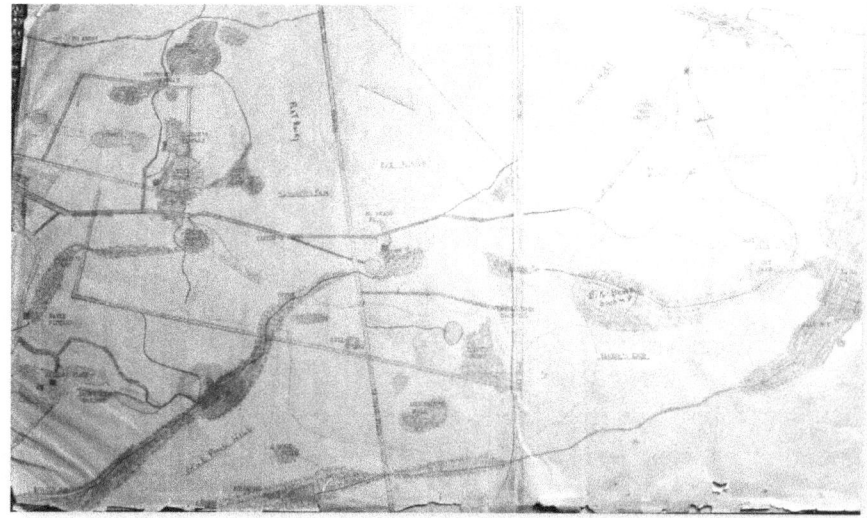

Area north and east of Highland Lake to Mud Pond, featuring Hoot Owl Swamp, Squirrel Swail, Bull Briars, Four Buck Gulch, Slaughter Pen, Red Ridge, Coonskin, Dead Doe Pass, Big Bear Swamp, Morefedite Runway. Map drawn by Whipple Bosch, courtesy of Ken Bosch.

Bosch Lake House; Pankow Green Meadows

Lake House Canal Wilhelm Bosch dug. Photo taken 1915–1917 courtesy of Ken Bosch.

Arial view of the main house at Green Meadows. Photo courtesy of Diane Pankow.

Lake House Canal as it was when it was Green Meadows in the 1940s–1950s. Photo courtesy of Diane Pankow.

Green Meadow's kitchen help. Photo courtesy of Diane Pankow.

2011 photo of the canal Wilhelm Bosch dug courtesy of Ken Bosch.

Green Meadows around 1960. Photo courtesy of Ken Bosch.

Some Bradley Descendants

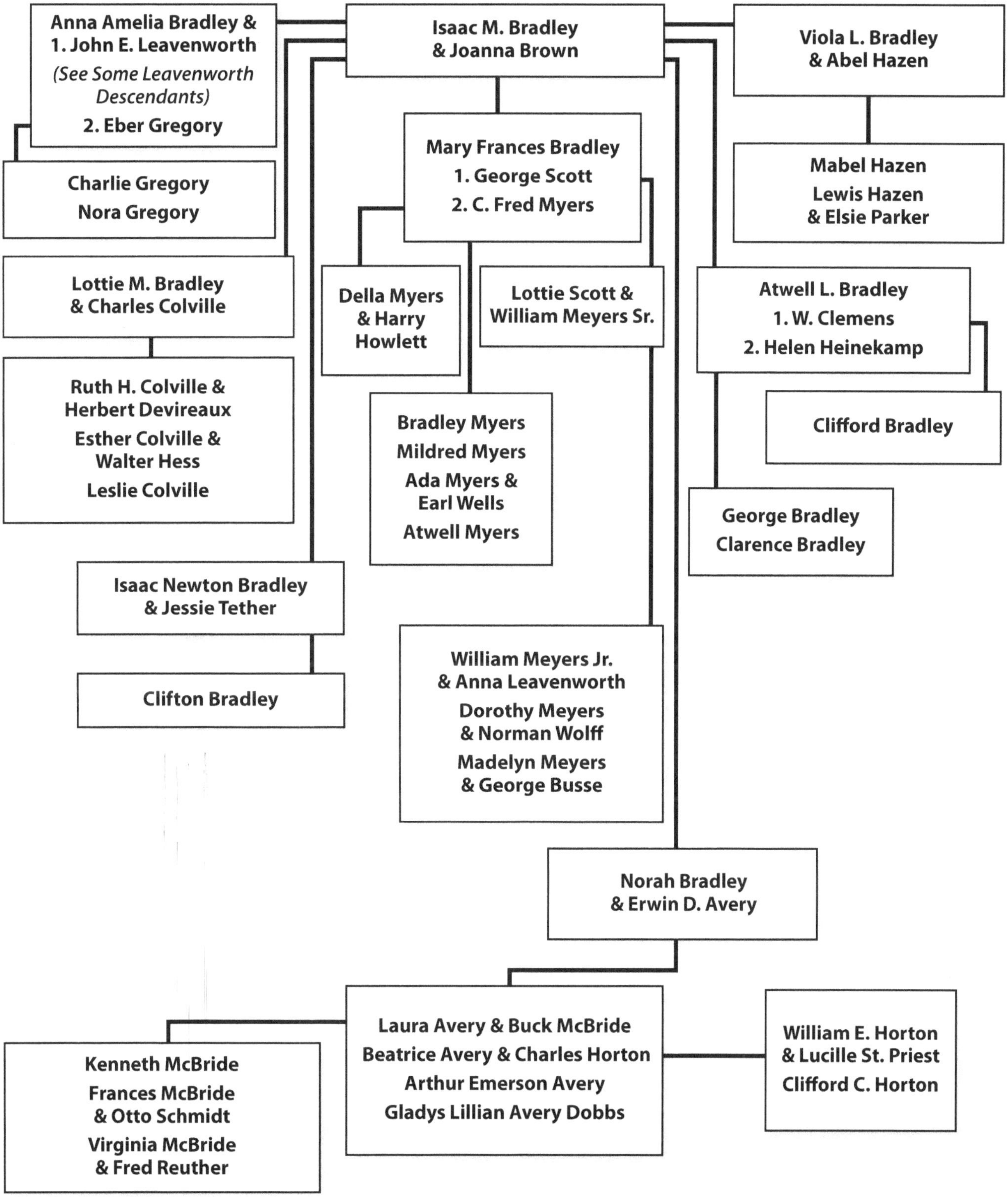

Isaac M. Bradley & Joanna Brown

Anna Amelia Bradley &
1. **John E. Leavenworth**
(See Some Leavenworth Descendants)
2. **Eber Gregory**

- Charlie Gregory
- Nora Gregory

Lottie M. Bradley & Charles Colville

- Ruth H. Colville & Herbert Devireaux
- Esther Colville & Walter Hess
- Leslie Colville

Isaac Newton Bradley & Jessie Tether

- Clifton Bradley

Mary Frances Bradley
1. George Scott
2. C. Fred Myers

- Della Myers & Harry Howlett
- Lottie Scott & William Meyers Sr.
- Bradley Myers
- Mildred Myers
- Ada Myers & Earl Wells
- Atwell Myers

William Meyers Jr. & Anna Leavenworth
- Dorothy Meyers & Norman Wolff
- Madelyn Meyers & George Busse

Viola L. Bradley & Abel Hazen

- Mabel Hazen
- Lewis Hazen & Elsie Parker

Atwell L. Bradley
1. W. Clemens
2. Helen Heinekamp

- Clifford Bradley
- George Bradley
- Clarence Bradley

Norah Bradley & Erwin D. Avery

- Laura Avery & Buck McBride
- Beatrice Avery & Charles Horton
- Arthur Emerson Avery
- Gladys Lillian Avery Dobbs

Kenneth McBride
Frances McBride & Otto Schmidt
Virginia McBride & Fred Reuther

William E. Horton & Lucille St. Priest
Clifford C. Horton

Some Photos of Bradley Descendants

Lottie Scott as a young girl. Photos courtesy of Mary Ellen Busse Mackinder.

Isaac M. and Joanna Brown Bradley. Photo courtesy of Mary Ellen Busse Mackinder.

Bill Meyers Sr. and his wife Lottie Scott, parents of Dorothy Wolff, Bill Jr., and Madelyn Busse. Photo courtesy of Ed Wolff.

Frances McBride, Laura McBride, Virginia McBride Reuther, Norah Avery, Erwin D. Avery. Photo courtesy of William E. Horton.

Four generations: Lottie Scott Meyers holding JoAnn Hallock, daughter of Don and Eileen Wolff Hallock; daughter Dorothy Meyers Wolff on right; on left granddaughter Eileen Wolff, wife of Don Hallock. Great-granddaughter Darlene Hallock on the right. Photo courtesy of Cynthia Leavenworth Bellinger.

Norman and Dorothy Meyers Wolff. Photo courtesy of Cynthia Leavenworth Bellinger.

Ken McBride, unknown, Erwin Avery, Norah Avery, Laura Avery McBride Wade and Jim Wade. Photo courtesy of William E. Horton.

Left: Lottie Meyers holding Granddaughter Mary Ellen Busse. Grandpa Busse is on the right. Photo courtesy of Cynthia Leavenworth Bellinger.

The Briggs Family

Irwin, John, Mildred, and Mary Briggs with the rabbits they raised.

Irwin holds Johnny, Ida Higginson Crabtree, Myrtle Crabtree Briggs, LeRoy Crabtree, Mary Crabtree. In front: Mildred, Laura, and Mary shielding her eyes from the sun. Photo courtesy of Mary Briggs Austin.

Myrtle and Irwin Briggs.

Top: Laura, baby Mary Rosamond, and Mildred Briggs. Center: Mary Briggs in carriage. Bottom: Laura, Irwin, Myrtle; front: Mildred, John, Mary Briggs.

Mary Briggs on parsonage lawn, graduation 1943.

John Briggs, 1945 graduation, with his Ford.

Mary, Laura, and Mildred Briggs.

John Briggs in 1945.

Photos courtesy of Mary Briggs Austin.

Some James Eldred and Polly V. Mulford Descendants

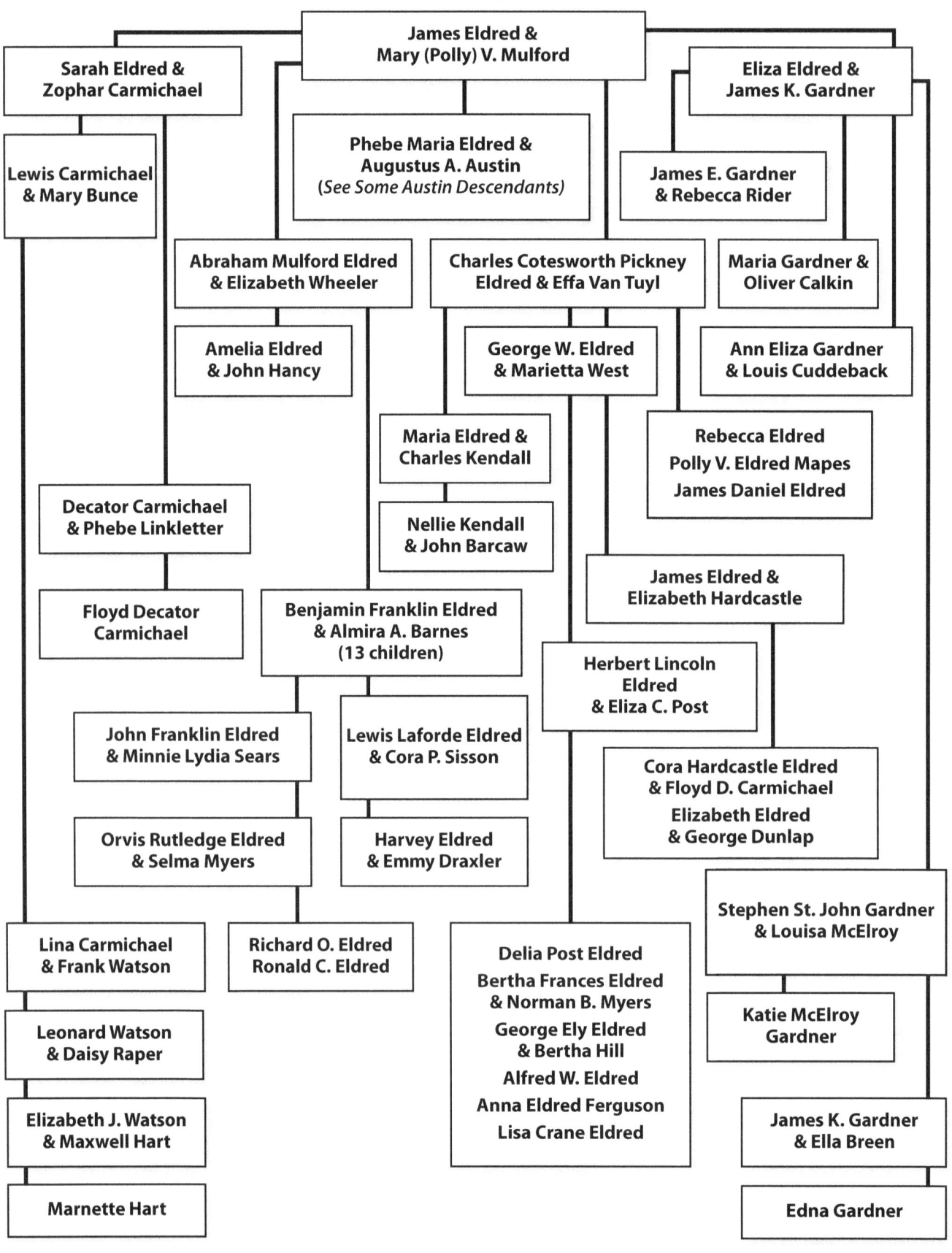

The Greig Mansion

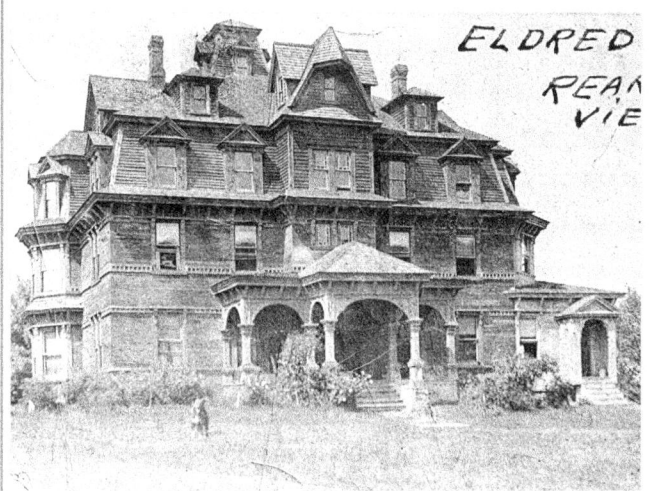

The Greig House photos courtesy of Ed Grotecloss III and Kevin Marrinan.

The Greig house was still standing when I was a youngster. Teenagers began to break in by the late 50s and smashed out windows, broke furniture, etc. Weather entering through the broken out windows and additional damages inflicted by subsequent legions of vandals resulted in the fire department burning the house down in the early 60s. It is difficult to find a trace of that magnificent structure today.

It was the autumn of 1957. I was in third grade and was allowed to stay after school to watch a high school football game. Against my mother's instructions I went off with Dave Strenglein and Walt Van Ness to see "Patter's Mansion" in the woods near the beginning of Stege Road.

What had been cleared fields in the circa 1900 photos, became a dense white pine forest in the intervening years. The road to the mansion was deeply rutted where wheels formerly had trodden. The ruts were deep enough to hold water. The center of the road and the shoulder were covered with thick tufts of tall grass.

We walked until we came to a clearing. There in the middle was a huge house, greyed from deteriorating white paint and weathering. There was a car port structure in front and steps leading to a large, well-weathered set of double doors. To our amazement, the front door was unlocked.

We entered into a foyer with a large chair with pegs for hanging coats. A pungent musty dusty smell filled our nostrils. A shabby, dusty oriental runner was on the floor. We entered the house proper and we were confronted by a large dark wooden staircase. Beautiful mahogany paneling lined the staircase walls. To left was small a bar, with actual bottles of liquor still there on the shelves which framed a mirror.

Everything was grey with dust and cobwebs. There was furniture in two parlors, on the right and left, ineffectually protected by moth-eaten dusty sheets.

We walked down a hallway to the left of the stairwell and came to a large kitchen. There was a gigantic black cast iron stove. There was a large pantry with mason jars of canned goods still there. There were plates left on the large table. Dried vegetables and pork chop bones on the plates were covered with dust. There were mouse tracks in the dust as well as droppings.

We were becoming increasingly frightened by this time as the sun was rapidly sinking. We investigated exiting via the back door of the kitchen, but the back porch had totally rotted off into a pile of grey soft boards seemingly bristled with rusty nails.

There was broken window glass and stones from the porch's foundation. All of this was about 10 feet below the door as the land in back of the house was lower than in front.

We exited the front door. We never went up the stairs. We hustled back the half mile or so back to the game which had just ended.

I remember going back to the mansion a couple of times during the next few years. There was a collapsing barn in the back, a completely rusted tractor with an equally rusted plow (or some such implement) still attached in the middle of the field. To the right of the mansion, there was a small house of newer construction with windows broken out and a large pine branch crushing part of the roof.

The mansion now had broken windows with smashed furniture and broken glass littering the ground. It had become a hazard. It was burned down sometime in the early 60s.

About 2005 I took a walk to where the mansion used to be. A forest of pine trees took the place of lawns and fields. After much searching, I located the remains of a stone foundation where the mansion used to stand. Very little else remained to validate my memory.—Ken Bosch.

Some Asa and Esther Hinman Hickok Descendants

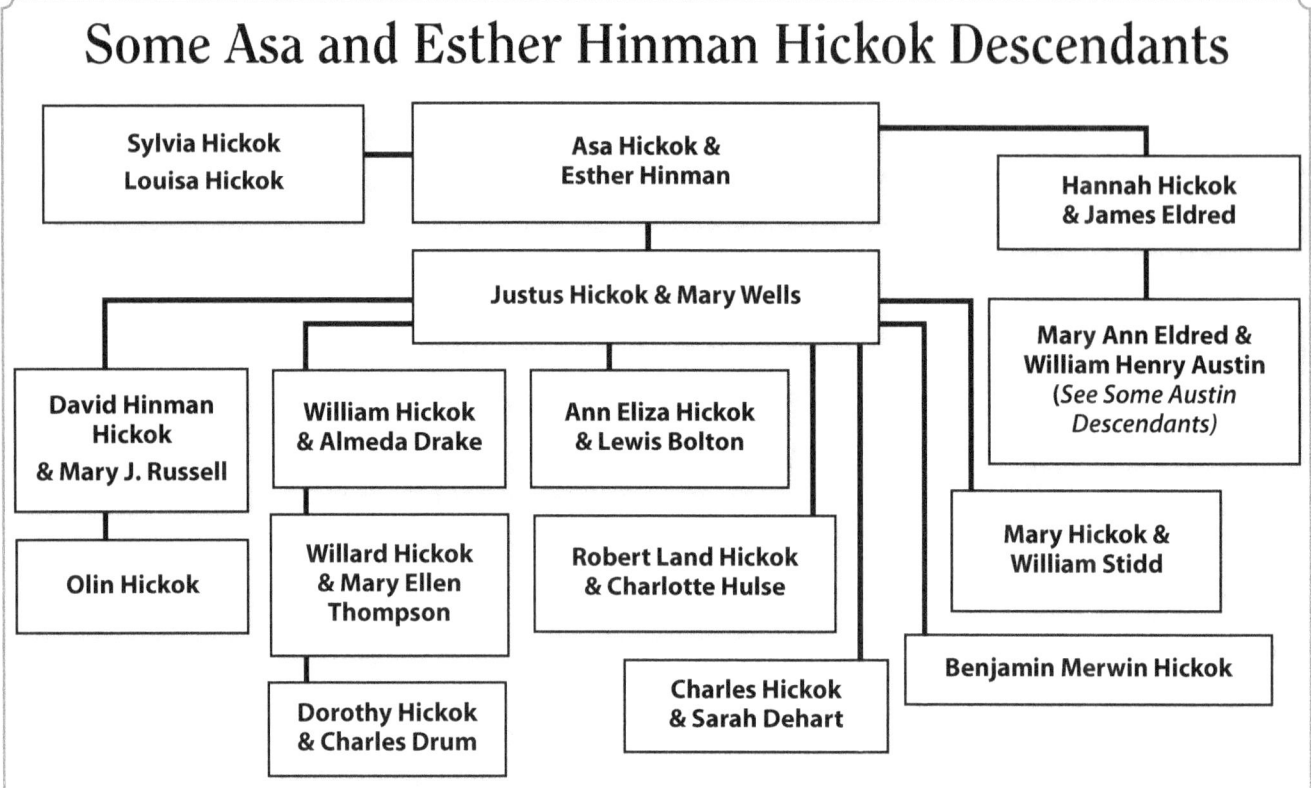

Amongst some Austin letters saved by Lillie Austin Calkin were some letters from an Abby Smith to my great-grandmother Mary Ann Eldred Austin.

In her letter of 1855 Abby Haddassah Smith of Glastonbury, Connecticut, mentioned several of her sisters' names.

Abby, Zephina, Cyrinthia, Laurilla, and Julia Smith were the daughters of Hannah Haddasseh Hickok and her husband Zephaniah Hollister Smith.

Hannah Haddassah Hickok Smith was a first cousin to my great-great-grandmother Hannah Hickok Eldred (*see p. 396 for a letter she wrote*) and her brother Justus Hickok who also lived in Eldred. In fact at least two of the Smith sisters visited Eldred. Justus Hickok was mentioned in the letters and Halfway Brook was mentioned at least once. And apparently Henry and Mary Ann Eldred Austin visited the sisters in Glastonbury.

The Zephiniah H. and Hannah H. Hickok Smith Family
The Zephaniah Smith daughters came from an accomplished and nonconformist family. Zephaniah Smith was a lawyer and former minister.

Their mother Hannah Hickok Smith was an amateur mathematician and poet.

Zephina was an inventor; Laurilla an artist; and Cyrinthia was a poet and horticulturist. Julia knew classical languages and even translated the Bible into English.

In 1872, Abby, 75, and her sister Julia, 80, lived in their family home, Kimberly Mansion, in Glastonbury, Connecticut. The town raised the taxes of the Smith sisters and two widows in Glastonbury, but not the taxes of any of the men.

Abby and Julia refused to pay their taxes until they were given representation. Abby took their concerns to the town council where she said:

The motto of our government is 'Proclaim liberty to all inhabitants of the land!' and here, where liberty is so highly extolled and glorified by every man in it, one-half of the inhabitants are not put under her laws, but are ruled over by the other half, who can take all they possess. How is Liberty pleased with such worship?

The town seized their beloved Alderney cows, auctioned them off and attempted to auction their farm as well.

The sisters were able to buy the cows back and fought the town in court, ultimately winning.

One of Abby Smith's letters is included on page 420. It was written in 1868 to my great-aunt Emma Austin, daughter of Henry and Mary Ann Eldred Austin.
—*Information from several sources including: ctmuseumquest.com, glasct.org, connecticuthistory.org.*

Justus Hickok Family: Willard, Mary Ellen, and Dorothy

Willard and Mary Ellen Thompson Hickok, parents of Dorothy Hickok Drum. Photo courtesy of Randy Drum Williamson.

Justus Hickok was a brother to Hannah Hickok Eldred. Justus and his wife Mary Wells Hickok were the grandparents of Willard Hickok.

Willard Hickok (born 1852) was the son of William and Almeda Drake Hickok. At the age of 12 Willard watched his father go off to war. Fortunately he watched him come back, too. In 1878 Willard married Mary Ellen Thompson. Mary's father Rufus Thompson and uncle Isaac, both part of the 120th N.Y. Inf. Regiment, were killed the same day at the battle of Gettysburg.

In 1880 Willard and Mary Hickok moved to Wilkes-Barre, Pennnsylvania where Willard was a freight agent for the Delaware and Hudson Railroad. Mary was a homemaker and active in their church. They raised and educated three children, Mary V., Clarence R. and Dorothy B. Hickok.

Dorothy B. Hickok, their third daughter, married Charles Drum. They were my grandparents.

Mamoo, as we called Dorothy, was a small, slender, reserved, and a well educated woman. After graduating with a Bachelor of Science degree from Syracuse University, she taught biology at Wilkes-Barre High School for several years.

Mamoo became a Navy wife when she married Charles H. Drum in June 1919; and a mother when son Burton arrived in 1923. Papoo (Charles) was stationed in the Philippines the last half of the 1920s. Dorothy was assigned to be Principal of the school on base for Navy dependents in several duty stations including Cuba. Returning to the States they settled in Washington D.C. and made Arlington their home. Papoo retired from the Navy in 1945 and the couple returned to his boyhood home, Gettysburg.

In Gettysburg Mamoo was active in local social clubs and was a Chapter Officer with the NSDAR, but their main job was to spoil their two granddaughters, in which they succeeded very well—providing them many memories of wonderful carefree summers in that magical little town. Every year after school was out, my folks would fly me, my sister, and Mike (the dog) to spend the summer with Mamoo and Papoo in Gettysburg, and I would adjust to being spoiled.

Papoo had bought Mamoo the largest house in Aspers, a small town north of Gettysburg. It was grand! The huge foyer was inlaid with beautiful Italian tile. It was there I had my Victorian doll house and my Roy Rogers/Dale Evans Double R Ranch 75-piece-play set. On the grounds was a 10-foot arbor filled with roses leading to a Koi pond inlaid with tile. One Easter the Gettysburg Country Club had an Easter Egg hunt for all the children. Guess who won? Papoo had to build a rabbit hutch for my new bunny and I got the first ride on the live elephant that was brought in to entertain the kids that day.

In 1956 my grandparents bought a small 29-acre farm about seven miles west of Gettysburg. Papoo's crop was Christmas trees. And that's where I learned to drive a small tractor. I was in heaven. They had a vegetable garden and I learned what fresh meant. Corn on the cob, asparagus, tomatoes, and the best cherry pie in the world.

Charles and Dorothy Hickok Drum on their wedding day. Photo courtesy of Randy Drum Williamson.

Willard and Mary Ellen Thompson Hickok, parents of Dorothy Hickok Drum. Photo courtesy of Randy Drum Williamson.

Papoo knew his Civil War history and he made the Gettysburg battle come alive. Every year he would take us to a different section and tell us what happened there. I wish I had been old enough to ask more questions.

Dorothy and Charles both passed away within months of each other in 1966. Mamoo and Papoo are still missed.—Randy Drum Williamson.

Abby H. Smith Writes Cousin Emma Austin

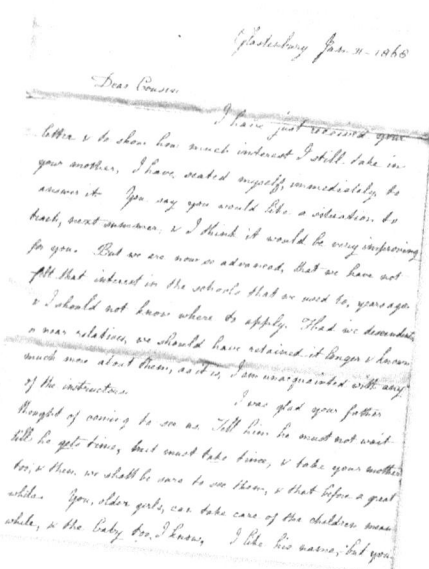

January 31, 1868 letter of Abby H. Smith to her cousin Emma Austin courtesy of Katherine Calkin Traxler.

Abby H. Smith wrote several letters to the Austin family who lived in Eldred. Mary Ann Eldred Austin's mother Hannah Hickok Eldred was a first cousin of Abby's mother Hannah Hickok Smith.

Glastonbury, Connecticut
January 31, 1868
Dear Cousin Emma,

I have just received your letter and to show how much interest I still take in your mother, I have seated myself, immediately to answer it. You say you would like a situation to teach, next summer and I think it would be very improving for you. But we are now so advanced, that we have not felt that interest in the schools that we used to years ago, and I should not know where to apply.

Had we descendants or near relatives, we should have retained it longer and known much more about them, as it is, I am unacquainted with any of the instructors. I was glad your father thought of coming to see us. Tell him he must not wait till he gets time, but he must take time and take your mother, too; and then we shall be sure to see them and that before a great while. You older girls can take care of the children meanwhile and the baby too…I like his name, but you don't tell us how old he is and whether he can run about and call your names.

I should like much to look in upon you and see all the children and among them your grandmother, perhaps, the most interesting to me, but since our last sister died, I have never expected to go so far from home as your house.

You do not tell us whether you have moved back to the old place. You say your grandmother is well this winter. You must give a great deal of love to her as well as to your father and mother. Our health has also been very good this winter and I think we have better help now living in the cottage that our sister Laurilla built for a tenant, than we have ever had before. They have been mostly Irish, but this is a colored family who came in July. We brought up the woman from 3 years old and she lived with us 18 years, so she seems like our family. She is now over 40. Her husband milks and does all the necessary work out of doors and she in the house whenever we want her. Tell your grandmother we often hear from Southbury, but she was so young when she left there, that she cannot know all the folks as we do. I would like to learn if your grandmother went to see Louisa, as she talked of doing when your mother wrote last, and how Louisa is doing. Tell your mother she must not give up writing. I want to know everything about her and your uncle Justus and family, too.

The weather has been cold with us in December; we have had some pleasant days this month…

Our rebel president still holds his seat, but I think the republicans will not keep theirs if they have not pluck enough to turn him out. I must close my letter tonight without filling the sheet, because the stage which takes our letters to the office comes too early in the morning to do it and if I miss it, it will lie over till Monday.

Yours with much affection,
Abby H. Smith

Some Leavenworth Descendants

- **Sherman Buckley Leavenworth & Charlotte Ingram**
  - **John Ellis Leavenworth & Amelia Bradley**
    - Florence Leavenworth
    - Ida May Leavenworth
    - Lottie Leavenworth & Len Andeway
    - **Hazel Leavenworth & Eugene C. Koenig**
      - John E. Koenig
      - Deloros Koenig
      - Gerald Koenig
      - Marialyce Koenig
  - **Harriet Elizabeth Leavenworth & Henry Palmer**
    - **Edith May Palmer & Albert Ewart**
      - Victor Ewart
      - Willard Ewart
      - Elliott Ewart
      - Millie (Pamela) Ewart
      - Rolland Ewart
  - **Sherman Stiles Leavenworth & Maria Louisa Myers**
    - Jennie Louisa Leavenworth & Charles Mortimer Austin *(See Some Austin Descendants)*
    - Anna Mae Leavenworth
    - Charlotte E. Leavenworth
    - Martin David Leavenworth
    - Truman Leavenworth
    - **Christina Hayes Leavenworth & Anthony Hirsch Sr.**
      - Charlee Hirsch & Ed Schroedel
    - **James Garfield Leavenworth & Ella Phoebe Sergeant**
      - Anna Louise Leavenworth & Bill Meyers Jr.
      - Sherman Clinton (Goldie) Leavenworth & Stella Clark
      - Clara Leavenworth & Lee Hansen
      - James R. Leavenworth & Gisele Rouillon

Sherman S. and Maria Myers Leavenworth stone. Martin D. and Truman Leavenworth were buried in the plot with their parents. Photos courtesy of Cynthia Leavenworth Bellinger.

Charlotte Leavenworth, Teacher

Charlotte Leavenworth at her Retirement Celebration. Photo courtesy of Cynthia Leavenworth Bellinger.

Letters from Nelson Rockefeller, Dwight Eisenhower, and The White House (President Kennedy) are courtesy of Cynthia Leavenworth Bellinger.

The 1944 Eldred Yearbook was dedicated to Charlotte Leavenworth.

Tribute to Charlotte Leavenworth in the 1961 yearbook.

APPENDIX • 423

Anthony & Christina Leavenworth Hirsch

Anthony Hirsch Sr. cooks up a storm. Photo courtesy of Ric Schroedel.

Anthony Hirsch Sr. in his younger days. Photos courtesy of Cynthia Leavenworth Bellinger and Ric Schroedel.

Christina and Tony Hirsch Jr. Photo in the Austin Collection.

Anna L. Leavenworth's Autograph Book, 1930s

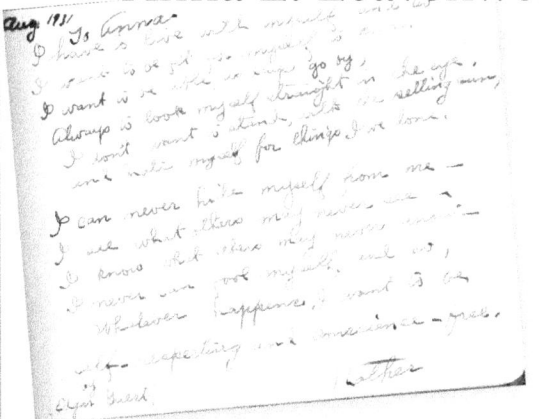

Ella Leavenworth's comment courtesy of Cynthia Leavenworth Bellinger.

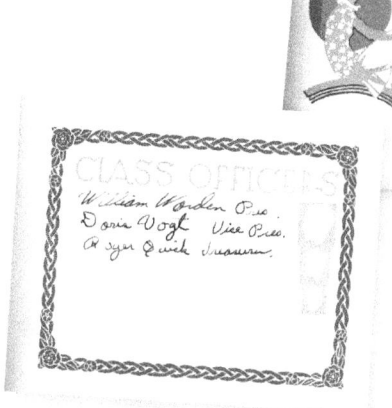

Helen Guenther, Katherine Love, and Viola Hazen signed Anna's Autograph Book courtesy of Cynthia Leavenworth Bellinger.

Jim Leavenworth Photos

Young Jim Leavenworth and his good friend Orville Clark. Orville Clark and his good friend Jim Leavenworth many years later. Jim and Gisele Leavenworth celebrate their 40th wedding anniversary. Photos courtesy of Gisele Rouillon Leavenworth.

Left: Jim Leavenworth in the snow. Middle: Jim Leavenworth with his daughters Nancy and Cynthia. Right: David Leavenworth in the snow. Jim Leavenworth's sawmill is in the background. Photos courtesy of Cynthia Leavenworth Bellinger.

Gisele Rouillon Leavenworth Photos

Gisele's father Cyrus Rouillon in France. Photo courtesy of Gisele Rouillon Leavenworth.

Standing: Cynthia Bellinger, Mary Briggs Austin, Gisele Rouillon Leavenworth. Sitting left: Joan Austin Geier, Melva Austin Barney. Photo courtesy of Cynthia Leavenworth Bellinger.

Mary Briggs Austin and Gisele Rouillon Leavenworth meet in 2008. Photo courtesy of Cynthia Leavenworth Bellinger.

Echo Hill in background and Charlotte's house in the early 1950s. Mrs. Spencer, Gisele, and Cynthia in the backyard of Mrs. Spencer's house, which was originally Lee and Clara Hansen's house.

Young Gisele Rouillon and Marie Therese, best of friends in France. Some years later Marie Therese Guerard and Gisele Leavenworth meet in France again. Photos courtesy of Gisele Rouillon Leavenworth.

Cynthia and David Leavenworth stand near the home with the white picket fence their father built. Photo courtesy of Cynthia Leavenworth Bellinger.

Mary Briggs Austin holds cute Cynthia Leavenworth in 1948. Photo courtesy of Gisele Rouillon Leavenworth.

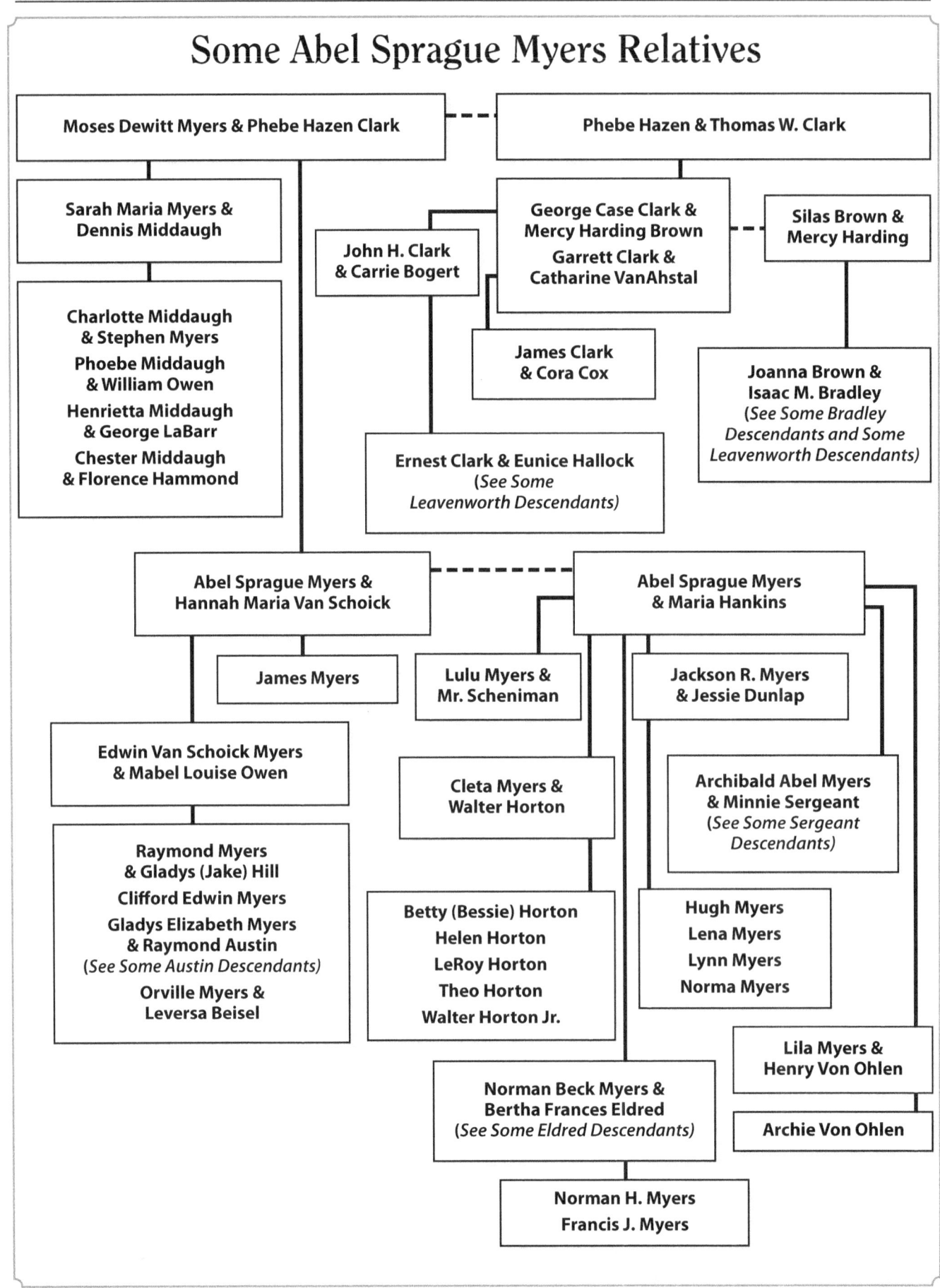

Some Jane Ann Van Pelt Webb Myers Relatives

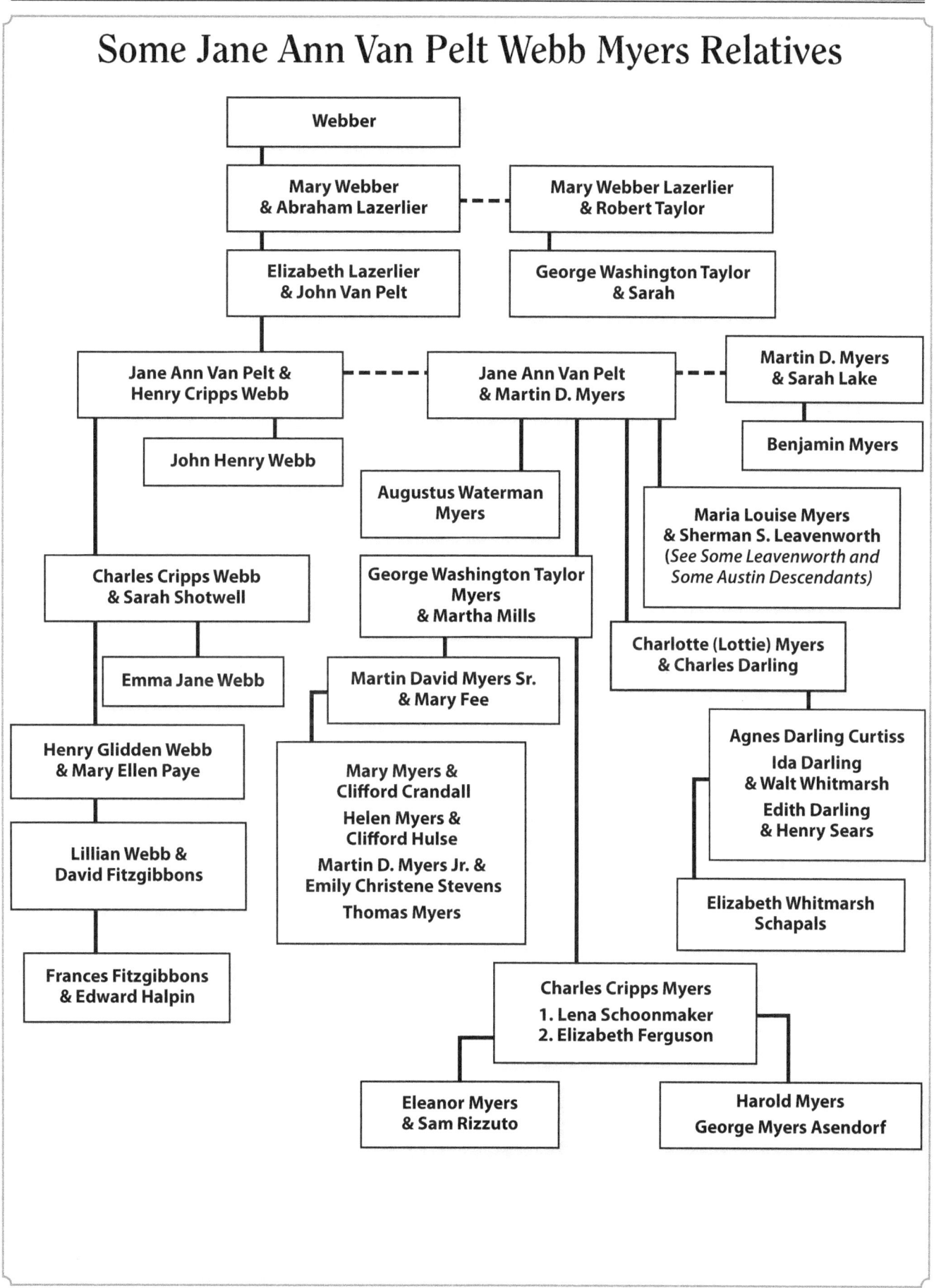

Lazerlier, Van Pelt, Webb, and Myers Families

The following information and letters were preserved and transcribed (fortunately) by Frances Fitzgibbons Halpin. They were shared by Magdala Trautsch Ray who received Frances' copies and original transcriptions of them. Frances Fitzgibbons Halpin was a great-great-granddaughter of Henry Cripps and Jane Ann Van Pelt Webb (Myers). Emma Jane Webb was a granddaughter of Jane Ann Van Pelt Webb Myers.

History of Family Written by Emma Jane Webb (circa 1940–1945), to Frances Fitzgibbons Halpin

(Note by Frances Fitzgibbons Halpin: "Watch for errors.") The information from two of Emma Jane Webb's letters have been combined.—Louise Smith.

A very wealthy family by the name of Webber came to America from Holland in either the 1600s or the 1700s. One of their descendants, a daughter, married a French man named Laziliere (a Huguenot). He died. She had a daughter by him (Elizabeth). After his death, she married an Englishman—Mr. Taylor. They had a son—George Washington Taylor—who founded the firm of Lord & Taylor.

The daughter by Mr. Laziliere (Elizabeth) married John Van Pelt from Holland. Their daughter was Jane Ann, who married Henry Cripps Webb, who was born in Tunbridge Wells, County Kent, England. Henry Cripps Webb and Jane Ann Van Pelt named their oldest son Charles Cripps Webb.

Henry Webb Cripps

Henry Webb Cripps, after losing his parents, was wanted by his family to buy a lieutenancy in the English Army, but he refused. A natural born sculptor, he wanted to become one, but it would be a disgrace to his family (Cripps), as they were not supposed to work. So he took his share of the money, changed his name to Henry Cripps Webb (his mother's maiden name) and came here, married Jane Ann Van Pelt and became an American…

He opened two stone yards here, one in Philadelphia, and one in New York City on Bank Street. One time while in Philadelphia, thousands of dollars worth of marble was broken up by men, whom he employed, and who were prisoners working in one section of the yard. In this way he was helping the U.S. promote a scheme the U.S. was trying. He lost a great deal of money, and became ill, and went home for a rest. While there he contracted pneumonia.

He and his wife—nee Jane Ann Van Pelt had two sons, Charles Cripps and John Henry. He refused to have his two boys brought up by the English so his wife brought them back. He died in March 1840. This is the life of my grandfather who was your great-great-grandfather. I have several papers, his marriage certificate and his burial record to prove all this.

Letter from Sarah Taylor to Jane Ann Van Pelt Myers

(Written on paper edged in black)
Carlton House May 10/54 [1854]

George W. Taylor. Photo courtesy of Magdala Trautsch Ray.

George W. Taylor family at their home in England. Photo courtesy of Magdala Trautsch Ray.

My Dear Jane Ann,

I dare say you have thought me very unkind in not answering your kind letter sooner but I will make no excuse for my negligence but trust to your kindness to excuse me. I should very much liked to have seen you and your dear little girl [Maria] and Georgy [George W.T. Myers] also, but as we take our departure for England on Saturday that is now impossible…My dear Jane Ann, Uncle George [Taylor] desired me to give his love to you, and to say he wished to make you and your children a small present, but he thought he could not do better than to send it to you in money and then you could buy anything you liked best.

Enclosed you will find an order on Lord and Taylor for 50 dollars. All you will have to do when you receive this is if Mr. Myers or any friend you can trust is coming to New York write a few lines and sign it, Jane Ann Myers to brother James and he will give them the money. Your mother is very well. I have seen her today. Uncle George saw Charles [Cripps Webb] on New Years day and he said he did not know him he had grown into such a fine young man. I suppose little Benny [Myers] is grown and a great big boy by this time. I often think of his round happy face…

Give our sincerest kind regards to Mr. Myers and with best love to yourself. Believe me I remain

Yours Affectionately,
Aunt Sarah [Taylor]

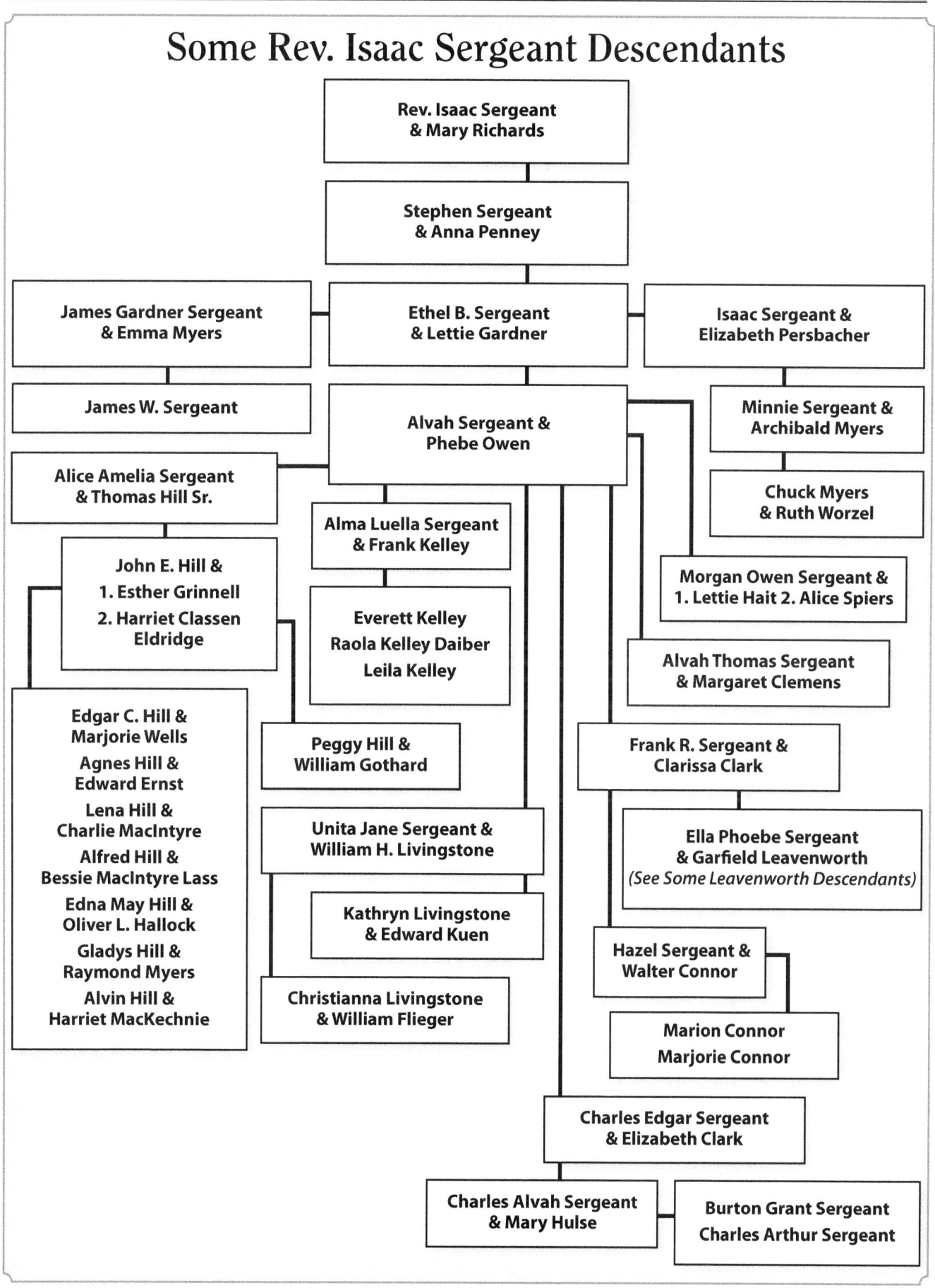

Some Photos of Sergeant Descendants

The Kelley family: Raola, Luella, Everett, Frank, Leila in front of her father, and two unknowns. Photo courtesy of Alan Gothard.

Thomas Hill Jr. and his brother John Edward Hill. Photo courtesy of Alan Gothard.

Alvah Thomas and Margaret Clemens Sergeant. Photo courtesy of Alan Gothard.

(Charles) Alvah Sergeant, husband of Mary Hulse. The photo, courtesy of Sandra Sergeant McBride, was taken in Lamoka, Pennsylvania, when Alvah was 18 years old.

William and Lillian Piat Flieger. Photo courtesy of Ron Flieger. William was the son of William and Christianna Livingstone Flieger.

Betty MacIntyre with her uncle Alvin Hill, a Sergeant descendant. Photo courtesy of Alan Gothard.

From right: Art, Mary, and Louise Austin visit with Sergeant descendant Alfred Hill and his wife Bessie MacIntyre Lass Hill. Photo in the Austin Collection.

Alfred and Bessie Hill's daughter Joan Hill holds Louise Austin. Photo courtesy of Mary Briggs Austin.

Pretty Peggy Hill (Gothard), daughter of John E. and Harriet Classen Eldridge Hill. Photo courtesy of Alan Gothard, son.

Ed Walter Toaspern, 1924–1950

The page above shows the four pilots of Division IV in Air Group 31—there were a total of 10 fighter crew divisions on the ship—U.S.S. Belleau Wood (CVL-24). On top: the main pilots in the division, George Shimek and Ed Toaspern; below are the wingmen, Tarabusi and Salminen. In the middle are the same four, from left to right: Salminen, Ed, Tarabusi, and Shimek. This page came from a book, Air Group 31, which included all 40 fighter pilots and 20 torpedo plane crews, and highlighted their tour of the Pacific. —Bill Ihlo.

Ed Toaspern added this note to a 1945 form letter from the U.S.S. Belleau: *This is strictly a ship's publication and can probably give you a lot of incidental dope that I would never write about—however, is [it] does not express my viewpoints or writing technique. The lurid description and self "back-patting" fails to impress me greatly.*

Ed and his VF 31 pilots in the U.S. Grant Hotel, San Diego, October 1945. Left: Jack Arnold, Frank Repp, H.H. Wicker, Bob Lewis, Jerry Wolf, George Shimek, Ed Toaspern, and a sailor related to one of the others. Photo courtesy of Bill Ihlo.

Ed Toaspern third from the left. Photo courtesy of Bill Ihlo.

Ed Toaspern holds Barbara Ihlo. His wife Barbara holds Bill Ihlo. Photo courtesy of Bill Ihlo.

1920 Census

Charles M. Colville was the enumerator of Highland Township

Crawford Road

Alvin Hill was a house carpenter. He and his wife Anna had a daughter Mildred.

Joel Crawford worked on the farm. His wife was Maud.

Joseph Maier, 85, and widowed, worked on his farm. His children Julius and Annie lived with him. Julius was a carpenter and did general work. Annie kept house.

Fred and Mary Frances Bradley Scott Myers ran a boarding house. Their daughter Ada was 19. Fred also farmed.

Nelson Hulse was a blacksmith with his own shop. He and his wife Ella had seven children: Bertha,

Westinghouse Light and Power Plant ad sold by Wait and Boyd, Eldred, N.Y. in Republican Watchman, 1923 or 1924.

housekeeper; Abram, farm worker; Ami, farm worker; Belle; Nelson, farm worker; Joseph; and Eliza.

Sherman McBride was a millright at his sawmill. He and his wife Eliza's children: Sherman, Emerson, Ezra, Walter, and Mabel.

Children of **Walter and Cleta Myers Horton**: Bessie, Helen, Walter, Leroy, and daughter Theo.

Board Road

Hiram Dailey, 71, a widower worked at a horse barn.

Elvina Crawford, a widow, was a dress maker. Elvina lived with her daughter Jennie and her husband **George Crandall**, a carpenter. George's parents: **David and Sarah Crandall** lived nearby.

James Morgan was a teamster on a dairy farm. He and his wife Sarah had two sons: Fred and Russell.

Children of **Samuel and Anna Hallock** (ages 2–20): Oliver, a truck driver; Wilber, a wood chopper; Raymond, Merlin, Howard, and Elmer. Their sister Eunice was married to **Ernest Clark**. Samuel Hallock was a teamster and lumbered woods.

Charles Ort lived with his parents **Frank and Mary Ort**. Frank was a shoemaker.

Emily Parker was a widow. Her daughter Emily Stevens (the Postmaster) and her husband **Howard Stevens**, herdsman at a dairy farm, lived with her at the Parker Hotel. **William H. Parker** was a carpenter. He and his wife Victoria's children: James Y. (herdsman on dairy farm), William, Elsie, and Andrew.

William Wait was a blacksmith. His wife was Carrie Wait 58.

Phebe Simpson Parker was 73.

Yulan-Mail Road

Frank Owen was a stone mason. He also had a boarding house. His wife was Katherine. Their children: Harold (stepson), Katherine, Franklin, Ernest, and Ella.

Children of **Charles and Selma West**: Theodore and Selma. Charles did general trucking. He would soon run his parents' West Farm.

Washington Lake Road

Children of **Henry and Matilda Wolff**: Alfred, and Amy. John Charles, 86, Matilda's father lived with them. Henry was an electrician for telephones.

Theodore and Phoebe West ran West farm. Theodore was listed as a farmer.

William and Phoebe Owen and son Russell lived in the lovely Oakdene boarding house. William, a mail carrier, died in 1920. Their older son Basil was not listed. Their daughter Pearl was married to **Fred DeFeo** and they had a daughter Alice.

Abel and Viola Hazen ran a boarding house. Their children: Lewis and Mabel.

Walter and Meda Tether and their son Ivan ran or soon would run Washington Beach House. Walter was listed as working on the farm. Two servants were listed as living

Left: James Y. Parker, born 1847. Right: William Parker, born 1872, and his son James Y. Parker. Photos courtesy of William H. Parker Jr.

with them (both worked on the farm): Thomas O'Grady, 76 and Raymond Beufve, 27.

Atwell and Helen Bradley had a boarding house. Clifford, 17, George, 12, and Clarence, 11, helped keep it a lively household. Sadly Helen died in 1920.

Alfred and Sophia Kaese ran a boarding house. Their children: Lola, Albert and Charles.

Erwin and Norah Bradley Avery were listed as farming. They ran the Bradley House. Their household: children Laura, Beatrice, Arthur, and Gladys; Norah's father Isaac Bradley, 82; and her uncle John Bradley, 66; and George, a servant.

Herman Bosch's ice house under construction. Photo courtesy of Victoria Kohler.

Beaver Brook Road

Sophia Petterson a widow lived with her daughter Anna, a dressmaker and brother-in-law, Frederick, 83. The Pettersons had a boarding house at one time.

Anna Johnson, a widow and her daughter Lillian lived next to Sophia and Anna and may have been relatives.

Household of **Lawrence and Matilda Crandall**: son Leonard, 2; father Milton, widowed; and sisters Bertha and Amy. The Crandall family ran Cold Spring Farm.

Edward and Georgianna Bornstein also had a boarding house.

Children of **John and Katie Weber**: John, Margarite, Rosa May, and Gertrude.

East Eldred Proctor Road

Walter Styles was a librarian. His wife was Georgia, 30. His parents: Charles H. Styles, 83 and Sarah, 81, lived with them.

Mort and Jennie Austin ran Mountain Grove House. Their children: Raymond, Bill, Elizabeth, Art, and Bob. Mort's brother Dory Austin lived with them.

Frank and Mabel LaBarr had four children: Marjory, Frances, Frank, and Ruth. Frank was a herdsman and dairy farmer.

Human Fly Arrested

George Gibson Polley was an American pioneer of (the then-unnamed act of) buildering, or climbing the walls of tall buildings, earning him the nickname "the human fly".

According to himself, he began his climbing career in 1910 when an owner of a clothing store promised him a suit if he would climb to the roof of the building. He succeeded. Over his career Polley climbed over 2,000 buildings. In 1920 he climbed the Woolworth building but was arrested, just when he reached the 30th floor and had 27 floors to go, for climbing without official permission. He also climbed 500 feet up the Custom House Tower in Boston. He would often spice up his performance by pretending to slip and fall from a windowsill to another.

George Polley died at the age of 29 due to a brain tumor.

—*wikipedia.org.*

Handsome Eddy Farm photo courtesy of Marion Doeller Kistner.

Lake Metaque, Lumberland. Photo courtesy of Ken Bosch.

Annie Rothman, 55, was single and had a boarding house near the Austins.

Children of **George and Jennie Foster**: Vivian, LeRoy, Ruth, George, Ada, twins: Edna and Edgar, Herbert, Daniel, Sidney, Earl, James, Ervin. George was a lumber teamster.

Daniel Hallock, 82, lived next to his sister Martha Hallock, 71.

Maggie Dunlap, 46, was a widow. Her sons: George, a herdsman for a dairy barn; and Harold. Harold would have the Dunlap restaurant in Eldred. **Charles and Selma Dunlap** had their own home.

Children of **Harry and Eveline Dunlap**: Gladys, Oliver, Lyle, Dorothy, Margaret, Isabel, and son Leslie. Harry Dunlap was a lumberer.

Children of **Nellie and Robert Crandall**: Verna, Stanley, and Clifford. Robert was a blacksmith at a dairy farm. **Bernard and Hilda Classen** were from Prussia. He was a carpenter.

The Austin friends **Thomas and Emma Collins** were listed as living on Proctor Road. Thomas died in 1920.

Children of **Herbert and Eliza Eldred**: George, 23, worked at a dairy barn; Alfred, 21, laborer; Annie, 18; and Lisa, 16. Herbert was a carpenter.

Children of **Norman and Bertha Myers**: Norman and Francis.

Children of **Jackson and Jessie Myers**: sons Hugh and Lynn, and daughters Norma and Lena. Louis Basque, a clerk at Jackson's general store, lived with them.

Children of **Fridolin and Juliana Straub**: Fridolin (Fred) Jr., Julia, Emma, Rosa, and Ida. The Straubs had a hotel and bar near Eldred's northeast corner.

William H. and Bertha Boyd Wilson's son Forrest was 9. William ran the general store on the northeast corner of Eldred.

Board Road

Daughters of **Willard and Minerva Wells**: Mabel, housekeeper; Marjory, waitress at boarding house; and Gladys, a housekeeper for a private family.

Ayers Road (in the census)

John Dunlap was a woodchopper at a lumber camp. His wife was Katharine.

Board Road

Peter Sullivan worked on the farm. His wife was Mary Sullivan. Their son Peter worked at an ice plant. **Charles and Bertha Sullivan**'s children: William, Ethel, Edna, and Victor.

Children of **William and Bertha Ort**: Eleanor, William, Florence, and John. William was a lumber teamster.

Edwin LaBarr worked at a sawmill. His widowed mother Caroline LaBarr lived with him and his wife Bessie.

Yulan-Barryville Mail Road

Household of **Ed and Catharine Schumacher**: stepsons, Charles and Arthur.

Unita Jane Livingstone was a widow. Her son Frank worked on a farm.

Dora Schumacher may have lived next to the Livingstones, but on Cochecton Road. Son

Henry, granddaughter Lillian Schumacher and Katie Glaab, a servant, lived in the same household.

Herman Barber worked on the farm. His wife was Isabel Barber.

John Warden and his wife had three sons.

Children of **Charles and Lottie Bradley Colville**: Ruth, Esther, and Les.

Fiddlers Elbow Road

Margaret Beufve was a widow. Her son Harold worked on the farm.

Frederick Heyen worked on a farm.

Rose McQuirk, a widow, ran a boarding house. Her sons John and William were farm workers.

Children of **John and Meta Lass**: John, 23, telegraph operator; Charles, a fireman for the railroad; Helen, a telephone operator; and Harry.

John and Edith Toaspern Birr had a boarding house. Their daughter Ida was a telephone operator.

Sons of **Arthur and Emma Toaspern**: Royden and Walter (Bub). Arthur was a Highway Superintendent.

River Road

George Beck, 49, worked on the highway.

John Campbell, 71, worked for the railroad. His wife was Emma.

Sons of **Charles and Jennie Traver**: John, 11, and Charles, 8.

Fred and Marjory Schwab must have been retired from their Handsome Eddy Farm Boarding House.

Fred Freeman was the Town of Highland Supervisor. His wife was Claudia Freeman.

Chris and Meta Meyer ran Spring House Inn. Their children: Anna, 29, housekeeper, John 26, chauffeur truck, Minnie, 19, waitress, boarding house, Chris, 18, book keeper.

Ella Watson, 65, lived with her brother George, 62, a truck driver and a peddler, and their ward John Humbart, 26.

James K. Gardner was a merchant at his General Store. He and his wife Ella had a daughter, Edna, 29, a music instructor. His sister **Kate McElroy Gardner**, 55, lived with them.

Yulan-Mail Road

Thomas and Myrtle LaBarr Hill had a young daughter Thelma.

Charles Mautz made periscopes. He and his wife Anna Mautz's household: stepson William was a 3rd officer on a sailing vessel; and mother-in-law Doris Nicolaus, 87, was a widow.

Thomas Hill Sr. worked on the farm as did his son William. Tom's wife was Alice Sergeant Hill.

Robert Litts, a student, lived with his Uncle **George and** Aunt **Alice Carner.**

Children of **Peter and Geraldine Devine**: Ada, Howard, William, Robert, and Elizabeth. Peter

Lass children, Charles, Helen, Harry, and Jay. Photo courtesy of Linda Guenther Anderson.

and daughter Ada were listed as cutters at the glass factory.

John Fleiger lived with his grandmother **Catharina Fleiger**.

August Wagermann was a cutter at the glass factory. He and his wife Margaret had a young son.

Max and Minnie Vonderhorst ran a boarding house. Their household: children Louise and Frederick; brother Eric and his wife and their sons: Karl and Walter.

Children of **Charles and Janette Kerr Wolff**: Carl, lumber foreman; Albert and Norman were cutters at the glass factory; and Anna.

River Road

Tracy Campbell did carpenter work for the bridge. He and his wife Minnie had a son Walter.

William Livingstone lumbered wood. His wife was Anna Livingstone.

Katie Durr, a widow, and her daughter Joanna rented their house.

Young Cyrus Rouillon (France) who would be the father of Gisele, the future Mrs. Jim Leavenworth. Photo courtesy of Gisele Rouillon Leavenworth.

Herman and Catharine Rixton were in their mid 50s. Herman was a salesman at the grocery store.

August Clouse, a carpenter (mentioned in *Echo Hill and Mountain Grove*), was a widower. He lived with his son Frederick. Fredrick and his wife Emma's sons: Joseph and Raymond.

Edmund Patterson was a pastor for the Congregational Church. His wife was Anna Patterson.

Emma Hankins, a widow, was a saleswoman at a confectionery store. She had two boarders: John Smith lumbered; John Fitzgerald drove a lumber truck.

Susan Gardner, 49, was a sales person at a grocery store.

Maria Calkins, 86, was a widow. She lived with her daughter Lillie, 58. Maria was a granddaughter of James and Polly Mulford Eldred.

William Vogt was a railroad carpenter. His wife was Margarite.

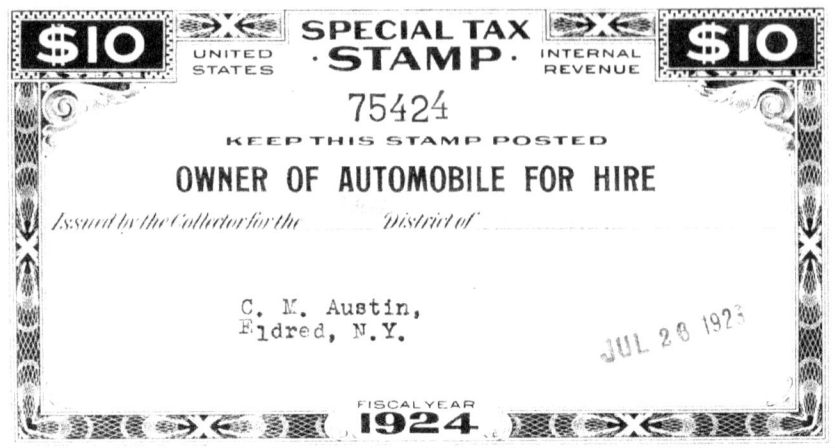

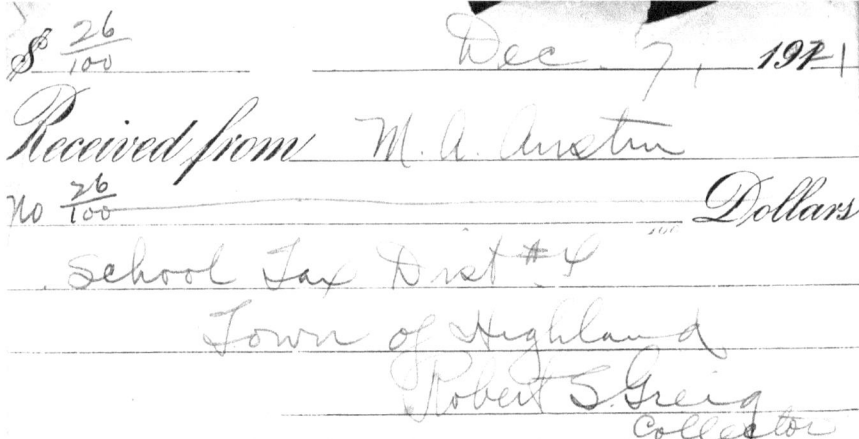

1921 School Tax and 1923 special tax stamp documents in Austin Collection.

Berm Bank Canal

Children of **Henry and Reka Dieckhoff**: Henry and Marie. Henry Sr. was a switchman for he railroad.

Howard Pelton was the foreman for the Glass Factory. His wife was Edith.

Albert Wilson was a foreman and lumbered woods. He and his wife had two daughters. Two employees: Edgar Mitchell and Frank Gillett, lived with them.

Household of **Mary Ann Nelson**: daughter Minnie Nelson, 46; William and Mary Nelson Deats; grandchildren: Mildred and

View of Edwin Myers property. Photo courtesy of Andy and Margie Austin Maglione.

Duane, Raymond, Willard and Maude Hulse around 1911. Melvin, Maude, Duane in front; Russell, Raymond, Ruth, and Willard L. Hulse around 1919. Photos courtesy of Kathy Hulse Frisbie.

William. Mr. Deats was an engineer.

Anna Breen, 73, a widow, lived with her brother Charles Campbell, a widower.

Canal Tow Path

Harriet Rixton was a mail clerk. Her daughter Mildred lived with her.

Children of **William and Mary Kerr**: Margaret, Jessie, Mary, Ruth, Helen, John.

Berm Bank Canal

Frank Wolff was a glass cutter at the glass factory. His wife was Mary Wolff.

Minerva Austin, 74, was a widow. Her household included: daughter Minnie Austin, **Ed and Mabel Austin Smith** and their son Austin, 9. Ed Smith worked at the glass factory.

John and Catherine Liebla had two daughters. John was a carpenter for bridgework.

Household of **Irving and Pearl Quick**: widowed father Menzo; grandmother Harriet Calkin, a widow; mother-in-law **Ella Ozenbaugh**, also a widow; and sister-in-law, Lillian Ozenbaugh. Irving was a salesman at a general store; his father Menzo was a retail merchant for a general store.

Children of **Ami and Anna Quick**: Harold, an office clerk for the Erie railroad, and Pauline.

Edward Shadler was a blacksmith with his own shop. His wife was Antonia.

Family of **Jacob and Hattie Liebla**: Lola, a waitress at a boarding house; George and Manning were cutters at the glass factory; and Orville, Dylvan, Ward, Madeline, Stanley, Helen, Elma. Jacob was an edger at a lumber mill.

Edward and Hazel Carroll had a young daughter. Ed was a superintendent at a lumber mill. But he would have a boarding house in the future.

Children of **Edward and Margaret Fish**: Margaret, Hilda, Clarissa, James, Robert. Edward was a sawyer at a lumber mill.

River Road

Robert Schoonmaker was a trainman for the railroad.

Frederick Simon was a druggist at a Pharmacy. His wife was Marie.

Otto Schmidt did manufacture embossing. He and his wife Aurelia had a daughter, Gladys.

Napoleon Campbell was a carpenter for the railroad. His wife was Sarah Campbell.

Harry Campbell was a carpenter.

Fred DeFeo Sr., husband of Pearl Owen. Photo courtesy of Pam Fischetti DeFeo.

He and his wife Mabel had a young son William.

Ernest Barnes was a carpenter for the railroad. He and his wife Agnes' children: Arthur, Edith, Allan, Lavonna, and Ernest.

Reuben Hessberger was a signal man for the railroad. His wife was Mabel.

Clarence Barber was a trackman for the railroad. His son Albert and mother-in-law **Louisa Ernst** (widow) lived with him.

Armanda and Martha Campbell were superintendents of summer resort. Their son was Earl. Ella Campbell, a widow, was a bridge keeper.

Greening Road

Margaret Greening, a widow, lived with her children Herbert and Joyce, and mother-in-law Elizabeth. Margaret was listed as farming.

George Vollmer worked on a farm. He and his wife Anna's children: Matthew, a carpenter for the railroad; and Charlotte.

Earl Palmer, 49, was a polisher at the glass factory. He and his wife Catherine's children: Kathryn, a telephone operator, and Richard.

Frederick Lewis, 39, was the superintendent of schools, and would be for many more years. His wife Mary, 27, was a teacher.

Stephen Shotwell did general work. His sister lived with him.

Willard Quick was a salesman for a general store. He and his wife Ethel had a daughter Olivia.

Board Road

Sons of **Ward and Gladys Brower**: John and Ward Jr. **Ernest McGinnis**, a farm laborer was listed as living with the family. Ward was a lawyer.

Children of **Duane and Maude Hulse**: Raymond, Willard, Russell, Ruth, and Melva. Duane, a blacksmith, had his own shop.

Edwin Myers was a truckman. He and his wife Mabel Owen's children: Raymond, Clifford was a cutter at the glass factory, Gladys, and Orville.

Charles MacKechnie lumbered wood. He and his wife Edith's children: Mildred and Harriet.

Children of **John and Esther Hill**: Agnes was a seamstress in an underwear factory; Edgar worked at a dairy; Gladys worked at a hat factory; and the younger children: Lena, Edna, and twins Alvin and Alfred. Granddaughter Gladys Ernst lived with them. John Hill was a machinist on a dairy farm.

Alvah and Margaret Sergeant had a daughter Elizabeth, 3.

From left: Minnie Meyer, Fred Dietz, Charlie and Jay Lass, Hannah, Caroline Quick, and Mrs. Rachel Sheen. Photo courtesy of Linda Guenther Anderson.

Yulan-Eldred Road

John C. Metzger was an internal revenue collector. His wife was Margaret. Their daughter Margaret worked at the Post Office.

Louis Acor, 85, was a widower. He lived with his daughter Lillian, a widow.

Children of **Henry and Blanche Bodine**: Paul 4-1/2; Blanche almost 3. They ran the Bodine Cottages.

Otto Geisler was a stone mason. His wife was Martha Geisler.

Robert Gainer was a general doctor. He and his wife Anna had a son Harold.

Myers Road

John Love had a sawmill. His wife was Katharine Love.

William Meyers was a lumberman. He and his wife Lottie Scott's children: William and Dorothy.

Chester Middaugh worked at a dairy farm. He and his wife Florence had a son Herbert.

Joseph Maier on right with young friend. Photo courtesy of Ken Bosch.

Sherman S. Leavenworth was a widower. His children who lived with him: Truman, lumber worker; and Charlotte, a teacher.

Everett Kelley lived with his parents, **Frank and Luella Sergeant Kelley**. Everett, 33, was an automobile machinist.

Archibald Myers was a carpenter. His wife was Minnie Sergeant.

Morgan Sergeant was a carpenter. His wife was Alice Spiers. Her sister Ellen Spiers, 60, lived with them.

Beaver Brook Road

Children of **Frank and Lena Ort**: John and Nona. Frank worked for a dairy farm.

Sons of **Alvah and Mary Sergeant**: Grant and Charles. Alvah was a wood chopper.

Children of **Warren** (a lumber teamster) **and Anna Parker**: Benjamin and Phillip worked on the dairy farm; George, Edna, Edith, Emeline, John, Blanche, Warren, and Harvey were too young to work.

Alice Dailey lived with her parents **Nathan and Ethel Dailey**. Nathan was a wood lumberer.

Webb and Ida LaBarr rented. Webb worked on a diary farm.

Harry Wormuth was a sawyer at his own lumber mill. His wife was Mary. Mary's mother **Mary Alice Whitney Kyte** lived with them.

Highland Lake Road

Emma Clouse was the widow of Jacob Clouse. Her sons Roy, a dairy farm carpenter; and Ralph, who worked at a dog kennel, lived with her.

Henry and Lila Myers Von Ohlen had a son Archie, 3. Henry was a salesman at his own general store.

Charles and Elizabeth Hoatson Clark Wilson had a house full: Arthur and his wife Abby, and son Robert; and Joseph and Julia

---

Sunshine Hall Free Library Building Campaign

Sunshine Hall Free Library
New Library Building Campaign
Building committee
F.R. Sergeant, J.G. Love, E.D. Avery, R.S. Greig, C.F. Scheniman, W.B. Styles
Campaign Committee
Dr. F.I. Smith, M.H. Roberts Jr., J.R. Myers, E.R. Kalbfus, J.H. Lass, L.D. Pine, Dr. A.E. Austin, F.D. Heyen, R.S. Greig

September 1, 1920
To contributors, Members and Friends of Sunshine Hall Free Library:

The Building Committee of Sunshine Hall Free Library is now erecting a new Library Building at Eldred under the direction of its trustees and councillors. The building will cost about $4,000; it will cost another thousand dollars to equip it and remodel the present building. This building will be devoted entirely to library work: the present building to community work and entertainment.

The history of Sunshine Hall Free Library is well known to most of you. It has developed from a modest beginning to a force for good. Its sphere of activity is continually broadening: it has developed a real live community spirit in our midst, it is a public educator that meets our needs from day to day. It serves Highland, Lumberland, and Shohola Townships and many villages in other towns. Today more than 9,000 books are on its shelves or awaiting shelf room. There are over 1100 members who read about 14,000 books yearly. The annual expenses of the Library are about $1500.00 which are met by your personal contributions and the splendid work of the Dramatic Club; whose members have done so much to promote the welfare of the Library. They were first to go on record in favor of a new library building; they also recommended that the present building be remodeled for community work. They went further; they pledged their support and volunteered their services in helping raise the money for such purposes.

The Trustees and Councillors finally took the necessary action based on their faith in you and the public. The increased advantages will afford a larger circulation and a better protection of the books.

We have borrowed $4,000 to insure the erection of the new building in order to provide the public and the library membership with more efficient service as soon as possible. We preferred to do this rather than to wait until the money had been pledged. Our sole purpose in public service on a larger scale due to the public's demand for such service as indicated by their generous support and use. We need $5,000 for its erection and equipment and the remodeling of the old building. We hope that this amount will be pledged during the drive September 6–13, 1920.

We ask your continued cooperation and support. Help as much as you can. Pledge as far as your means will permit for this worthy cause. It will come back to you three and four fold. If a pledge card is not enclosed with this letter, some member will call on you during Library Week.

We assure you of our appreciation of your contribution which we gratefully acknowledge.

Very respectfully, Frederick J. Lewis Campaign Manager

John Vogt Jr.'s German Hotel. Photo courtesy of Charles Paulus.

Shohola: Tuttle's General Store, at Twin Lakes and Woodtown Roads. Photo courtesy of Charles Paulus.

Photo of the Charles and Janette Kerr Wolff home from Ed Wolff.

Old photo of Parker Hotel courtesy of Alan Gothard.

John Horton around 1920. Photo courtesy of Victoria Kohler.

Cox; and Elizabeth's stepmother, Marietta West Eldred Hoatson, 76. Charles Wilson was a store keeper of a general store. Arthur worked at a grain company. He would have the A&P in the Wilson building on the northwest side of Eldred. Joseph Cox was a carpenter.

James and Cora Clark had grandson Alvin living with them on Highland Lake Road. James was an edger in a sawmill.

Lewis Blackman worked at a sawmill. He and his wife Mabel had two children.

Minnie Benedict, daughter of Wilhelm Bosch, does not seem to be listed in the 1920 Census. Photo courtesy of Ken Bosch.

Edgar Sergeant lumbered. His wife was Henrietta. Their daughter Edith, was a waitress.

Children of **Charles and Sara Scheniman**: Leida, William, and Alma.

Uncle **Lon Austin**, 61, was listed as a farmer; and Aunt **Aida Austin**, 56, was listed as a teacher.

Theodore and Thekla Kassner managed a hotel.

Children of **Herman and Veronica Clouse**: Ada, Gertrude, Herman, Helen, George, and Katharine.

William Hammond, his sister **Mae Parker** and her daughter Ruth lived at the Hammond Boarding House.

Clarence Sergeant was a wood lumberer. His wife was Claudia.

Bertha Winter was a widow.

Stephen A. and Charlotte Myers had a boarding house. Their children: Kathryn, Stanley, Marie.

Children of **Joseph and Florence van Eastenbridge Meyer**: Raymond, John, and Anna. Joseph worked on a farm.

James and Margaret Mills Boyd (perhaps retired from running a boarding house) had children at home: Mabel, Postmaster, George, carpenter, and Stella, assistant Postmaster.

Henry and Isabella Boyd Asendorf had a huge boarding house on Highland Lake. They had a son George.

Frank and Anna Hull Sergeant would soon live (for a short while) in what was once the Jane Ann Myers House. Anna's sister Jennie Hull lived with them. Frank was a millwright in a sawmill.

Henry and Elsie Graf had a young daughter, Bertha. They would have a boarding house in the future.

Charles and Selma Dunlap lived in the area.

Anton and Mary Rennenberg, and their son Anthony had a boarding house.

Peter and Mary Barth also had a boarding houses. As did **Catharine Loerch** and her daughter Matilda, both widows.

Robert Clark was a painter. His wife was Evelyn. His brother **Elbert Clark** was a stone mason.

Household of **Alexander and Ida Wait**: daughters Marie and Lucille; and his mother Mary Wait, a widow. Mary ran a boarding house. Alex was a carpenter.

Elizabeth Mills had been a widow for 11 years. She continued to run the Mills boarding house. Six children were still at home: Belle, a teacher; James, a chauffeur for the boarding house; Agnes, helped at the boarding house; Alexander, a carpenter; George (a future doctor), and Margaret.

Children of **Charles and Helen Bosch**: Charles, William, Henry (Whipple). Helen's mother Katherine Miller, a widow, lived with them.

Household of **Herman and Mary Horton Bosch**: son Herman; sister-in-law **Maude Kalin**; nephews: Robert, Eugene, Harold, and Kenneth Kalin; Mary's mother **Elizabeth Horton**; Mary's brother **John Horton**, who worked on a dairy farm. Herman Bosch was a plumber on a dairy farm.

Wilhelm and Mary Bosch still had a boarding House. Son Ralph and daughter Christina lived there, too. Ralph worked on a dairy farm.

Otto Hartung was a farmer. His wife was Amanda. Their daughter

Harvey and Beatrice Parker in 1924. Photo courtesy of Alice M. Aber.

Amanda lived with them.

Charles and Elizabeth Myers ran Lake View. Charles' son Harold was 13.

Daughters of **Martin D. and Mary Fee Myers**: Mary and Ethel. Martin was a chauffeur.

Augustus Myers, 63, had a servant, Rebecca Wasiddal, 63, who was a housekeeper.

Perry and Lucille Foster had a son Joseph.

Chester and Catharine Hulse had a son Millard. Chester was a barber with his own shop.

Floyd and Helen Boyd had a daughter, Elizabeth. Floyd was a carpenter.

North of Eldred

Kate Greig, 60, was a widow. Her son Robert was a civil engineer. Her daughter Isabel Kelso, 27, was a widow. Son Bennet Greig did general carpentry work. Sarah Greig, 87, was listed as a boarder, but was most likely a relative. Isabel would marry Edward Grotecloss Jr.

Julius Maier second from right. Photo courtesy of Victoria Kohler.

Partial Ira Austin house shown next to the Wolff house. Photo courtesy of Ed Wolff.

Robert and Thalia Day were caretakers for a private residence.

George and Elizabeth Beck ran Seven Oaks. George was a sculptor. **Edward and Katie Stege** lived on their property at Stege's Lake. Edward was a music printer.

Chris and Freida Koster had a boarding house.

1920 Lumberland

Agnes Wilson, a widow, was a teacher. So was her daughter Martha.

Addie Aumick was a widow. Her children: Charles, George, Nellie, Raymond, Cora Bowman and her daughter Laura.

Children of **Henry and Anna Thiele**: Della, Pauline, Eleanor, and Alvin, a weaver at mill. Henry was cigar maker.

Children of **Emery and Mamie Frey**: Ella, Paul, Henry, John.

Household of **Frank and Hannah Getz**: children Emery, Eugene, Amandus, Mary, Lavan, Katherine, and Ella; boarders: Wesley Miller and Elsworth Swartz.

Ida Kalin was a widow. Her children: Louise, Richard, Eva, and Herman.

Children of **Edward and Margaret Bisland**: Ethel and Edward.

Children of **Joseph and Augusta Schwarz**: son Francis, Louise, Ida, and Joseph. **Franz and Anna Schwarz**'s children: Victor, Walter, and Margarette.

Russell and Edith MacKechnie had a boarder, George Geary.

Children of **Leon D. and Anna Pine**: Hazel, Annie, and Louis.

Household of **George and Etta LaBarr**: daughters Hazel and Frances; boarders: Albert Cooper, James Goodrich, Charles Stratton.

Children of **Billings and Julia Kinne**: Herbert and Harriet.

Children of **James and Adaline MacIntyre** (at home): Edward, Charles, and Adelaide.

Children of **John and Katherine Kerr**: Cecelia, Katherine, Hazel, Adah, Christina, Helen, and John. Charlie was born in December.

Children of **Alfred and Katherine Van Tuyl**: Hazel, Laura, Harold, and Howard.

Agnes Schwab managed Handsome Eddy Farm.

Gladys Van Tuyl was a teacher.

1925 Census

Barryville

Christian and Meta Meyer ran Spring House. The **Doeller Family** ran Handsome Eddy.

Minerva Austin, widow of Ira, was 80. Her daughter Minnie lived with her.

James K. Gardner was a merchant. His wife Ella did house work. Edna, their daughter, was a music instructor. James' sister Katie Gardner, 61, lived with them.

Alice Hill's son William was a farmer. **Alvin Hill** was a carpenter. His wife was Anna and they had a daughter who was 9.

Thomas Hill, 44, was a mail carrier. He and his wife had a daughter Thelma and a son Frank.

Walter and Emma Straub Toaspern had two young children: Frances and Edward. Walter was listed as a lumber dealer. In the 1920s he was Town of Highland Highway Superintendent and also worked on construction projects upstate New York (Binghamton, Elmira, etc.).

The **Warshauers** ran Riverside Cottage.

Fred and Minnie Nitzsche and **Charles and Gertrude Frey** ran Maple Grove Farm.

Rose McQuirk had a boarding House.

Eldred

Sherman Leavenworth was 82. His children: Truman, Martin, and Charlotte, a school teacher, lived with him. Anna Leavenworth, daughter of Sherman may have lived in East Islip on Long Island in 1925.

Caroline Schoonmaker was 70.

John Love was a lumber dealer. His wife was Kathryn.

John Sparks was the Postmaster. His wife was Martha Sparks.

Ami and Violet Hulse had a daughter Ella, 1.

Robert Rundle was listed as a farm laborer. His wife was Jennie.

Truman Racine and his son Lawrence managed a garage near what was once the old James Eldred home.

Children of **Richard and Louise Haas**: Maurice, 1, and Harry, 12 days old.

Jim Wade was a barber. **George Steel** was a butcher.

Arthur and Abby Wilson had two young sons: Robert and Charles. Arthur ran a grocery store and would soon have an A&P.

Joseph and Julia Wilson Cox may have lived near or with Julia's (and Arthur's) stepmother Elizabeth Wilson. Joseph was a carpenter.

Phoebe Simpson was 78. Her son Samuel and his daughter Ruth, 7, Simpson were listed as living in her home.

Howard Stevens drove a taxi. He and his wife Emily had a cute little girl, Christene or Teenie as she would be called. Emily's mother, Emily C. Parker, 75, was listed as the head of the household. Tracey L. Myers, 30, Howard's cousin lived with them.

Emily C. Parker's son **William Parker** was a carpenter. William and his wife Victoria had sons James Y. and Andrew at home with them.

Floyd Boyd, 42, was a contractor and builder. He and his wife Helen's daughters: Betty and Janith.

Children of **Charles and Edith MacKechnie**: Mildred and Harriet.

Edwin V. Myers was a half brother of Archie Myers. Edwin was a truckman. He and his wife Mabel's children: Clifford, a telephone wire builder; Gladys, and Orville, a carpenter.

Raymond Myers, son of Edwin and Mabel Myers, worked on a farm. Raymond and his wife Gladys Hill Myers had a son John.

Martin D. Myers, the brother of Charles was a chauffeur for the Asendorf Highland Lake Inn. Martin and his wife Mary's children: Mary, Martin D. Jr., Helen, and Thomas. Their daughter Ethel had died young.

Children of **William H. and Eleanora Alston Parker**: Elsie, William H. Jr., and Howard Parker; and Stanley, Eleanora, and Doris Alston.

Fred DeFeo Jr. Photo courtesy of Pam Fischetti DeFeo.

Alvah Sergeant was a lumber laborer. He and his wife Mary had two sons in school: Grant and Charles.

Nellie Crandall, 47, was a recent widow. Her children: Henry, a chauffeur, and Verna; Stanley, and Clifford were in school.

Fred and Kathryn Fracke had two sons: Fred and Herman. Fred Sr. was the caretaker of an Estate.

Frank Ort was a mail carrier. He and his wife Lena had children: John and Nona.

William Greening was an iron maker. His wife was Bessie. Elizabeth Greening, 70, had two granddaughters, Margarete Pranana and Vivian Schaffer living with her.

Maria Myers, 73, was the widow of Abel Sprague Myers and listed in a house by herself. Her son Archie was a merchant. Charles (Chuck) Myers was born to **Archie and Minnie Sergeant Myers** in 1925.

Children of **Anna Parker** (ages 5–23): Phil, George, Edith, Emmaline, John, Blanche, Warren, Harvey, and Beatrice.

Erwin Avery, 47, ran the Bradley House. Erwin and Norah Bradley Avery's children at home: Beatrice, Arthur, and Gladys. Norah's father, **Isaac M. Bradley**, 88, and his brother **John Bradley**, 72, also lived with them.

Ezra McBride was trucking. He and his wife Laura Avery had a son Kenneth, six months old.

Children of **Jackson and Jessie Dunlap Myers**: sons Hugh and Lynn; daughters Norma and Lena.

Morgan Sergeant was a carpenter. His wife was Alice. Her sister Ellen lived with or near them.

Luella Kelley, a widow, lived with her son Everett, a farm laborer.

William Meyers and his wife Lottie Scott had two children: William Jr. and Dorothy.

Chester Middaugh worked on the farm. He and his wife Florence had a son Herbert.

Garfield Leavenworth was a carpenter. Garfield and Ella's children: Clara, Clinton, Anna, and Jim.

David Crandall was 74. His wife was Anna.

Webster LaBarr worked on a farm. His wife was Ida.

Bertha Wilson was a widow and a proprietor of her husband William's General Store. Forest (Pat) Wilson was 14 and in school.

Herman and Veronica Clouse, had or would soon have a boarding house. Their children: Ida, Gertrude, Laverne, Helen, George, Kathryn, Theo, and Veronica.

Edward and Katie Stege lived near Stege Lake.

Kate Greig and her son Robert (foreman of an Electric Plant) lived in the Greig Mansion.

Louis and Mabel Blackman had four children.

Emily Slonek, 83, and her daughter Stephanie were both from Austria and had become citizens in Jersey City. Dr. Joseph Gutfruend from Austria, lived or would live in the house that was once owned by the Sloneks.

Raymond Wells owned a garage, the last building on the right on the way to Barryville from Eldred.

Harry Dunlap, a widower, was a carpenter. His children: Oliver, Lyle, Leslie, and Isabelle.

John and Emily Morgan had two young children: Harold and Dorothy.

Mary Ort, 63, lived with her son, Charles, 28.

Clarence Sergeant, 39, was also a farm worker. His wife was Claudia.

Harry and Della Myers Howlett owned the first and second house on the left, near the start of Highland Lake Road. They boarded school teachers for many years. At that time the teachers had to live in the area. Harry was a plumber. Della was a teacher in New York City and was gone all week.

Children of **William and Bertha Ort**: Eleanor, William, Florence, John, and Milton.

Julia Straub, 54, had been a widow for five years. She ran Straub's Hotel.

Children of **Herman and Mary Horton Bosch**: Herman Jr., Marjorie, and Bob. Herman was listed as a plumber.

Anna Rothman, 53, ran her boarding house which was near the Austin's Mountain Grove.

Daughters of **George and Henrietta LaBarr**: Hazel and Frances.

Claude Angell, 28, was the proprietor of a casino.

Charles M. (Mort) Austin, 60, and his wife Jennie, 45, ran Mountain Grove boarding house. William was a farm laborer. Arthur and Robert were in school.

Dory Austin, 56, was a farm laborer. **Alonzo (Lon) Austin** was a farm laborer. **Aida** was a school teacher.

Emma Kelso Collins, 69, a widow, lived in the area.

Edgar Sergeant, 69, worked on a farm. His wife was Henrietta.

Walter Styles, 63, was the librarian. His wife Georgia, 36, was a school teacher.

Bernard and Hilda Classen from Germany were in their 60s. He was a carpenter. They both had become citizens.

Mae Parker, 46, and her daughter Ruth lived with Mae's brother William Hammond, 52.

George and Jenny Crawford Crandall were both 43. George was a carpenter.

Sons of **Emma Clouse**: Roy, 38, a carpenter; and Ralph, 22, a painter.

Harry Wormuth was a lumber dealer. His wife was Mary Kyte. Mary's mother **Mary A. Kyte** (widow of William) lived with them.

Charles and Selma Dunlap's son was six months old. Charles was a chauffeur. His mother Margaret Dunlap or Maggie, 50, lived next door with her son Harold, 22, a farm laborer. The other brother George must have been away from home.

Highland Lake

Daughters of **Alexander and Ida Wait**: Marie, Lucille, and Dorothy. Alexander was a carpenter. His mother **Mary Mills Wait**, 70, may still have run a boarding house.

Ray Ryman, 29, was an electrician.

James Boyd, 77, was a farm laborer. His wife Margaret was 72. Their daughter Mabel, 29 was Postmaster for Highland Lake. **George and Mildred Boyd** ran the Piermont Hotel of his parents.

Matilda Loerch, 42, continued to run Sunset View House.

Charles and Elizabeth Myers ran Lake View. His son Harold was in college. Their daughter Eleanor was 5.

Perry and Julia Foster had children: Joseph, Charles, and Flora.

Frederick Bye was the proprietor of a casino. He and his wife Janette had a daughter Alice, 5 months, who sadly died young.

Chris and Kathryn Scott ran Lakeshore House. Their children: Virginia and Chris. Chris Sr. was from Ireland.

Karl and Elsie Eggers ran Deer Head Lodge.

Mary and Peter Barth were proprietors of a casino.

Anton and Mary Rennenberg seem to be retired from running a boarding house. Their son Anthony was 20.

The Pinehurst was run by the Sulzbachs. **Harry and Frances Sulzbach**'s children (ages 1 to 10): Harry Jr., Clifford, Edward, and Mary. Harry Sr. was a printer.

Robert Clark (41, painter) and his brother **Elbert Clark** (58, farm laborer), cousins of Mort, Lon, and Aida Austin, lived in Highland Lake.

Mrs. Dennehy ran Highland Villa.

Hilko and Sadie Turash from Austria had two children. Hilko was a chef.

William and Anna Balabau from Austria ran a boarding house.

Albert Bye, 58, was a horse trainer from England.

Erwin and Edwin Kuck seem to be brothers who were both musicians.

Henry and Belle Asendorf were proprietors of the Highland Lake Inn. George Myers Asendorf was 11 and in school.

Margaret Noble ran a Boarding House.

Henry and Elsie Graf ran Pine Grove House. Their daughter Bertha was 8.

Frank and Anna Hull Sergeant lived near Highland Lake. Frank was a lumber dealer. Anna's sister Jennie Hull lived with them.

Sidney Johnston was the proprietor of a Road House. As was Rudolph Schroder.

Charles Reid was a musician.

Elizabeth Mills, 62, was still running the Mills House. Belle Mills, 30, was a school teacher. Agnes Mills, 27, helped out with boarders. George and Margaret Mills were at college. George Mills would be a doctor.

James and Sophie Mills ran what was once the Jane Ann Myers boarding House.

Children of **Joseph and Florence Meyer**: Raymond, John, and Frederick.

Wilhelm and Mary Bosch and daughter Christina lived in the house Wilhelm's son Ed built for them on Hartung Road. **Ed Bosch** and Mary's son, **John van Eastenbridge** (29), a chauffeur, also lived there. **Ralph and Paula Schreib Bosch** and son George lived adjacent to the Lake House.

Fred and Annette Schoverling ran Hillcrest Boarding House on Stege Road. They had purchased the house on some 80+ acres from the Kosters, in 1920.

Otto and Marie Schreib possibly ran the Bosch Lake House. **Carl and Minnie Bosch Benedict** and their grandchildren: Christena and Kathryn, seem to live next to the Schreibs.

Joseph Stolt had a boarding house. His wife was Sadie.

Charlie Bosch, 44, worked on the farm. His sons: Charles Jr. was a chauffeur; William and Henry (Whipple) were in school.

Albert Schoverling ran the Adelaide boarding house which seems to be on the corner of Hartung and Stege Roads. The boarding house had first belonged to Herman Bosch, who had it built in 1920.

James Clark, 59, was a farm laborer. His wife was Cora.

Yulan

Henry Bodine, 66, and his wife Blanche, 47, ran Bodine's on Bodine Lake. Their children: Paul, 9, and Blanche, 8.

Ed and Georgianna Bornstein ran Grand Vue.

Atwell Bradley ran Park Hotel. He married **Freida Meyer Guenther** in December. Freida's children: Edith, Clinton, Helen, and Viola Guenther. George, and Clarence, were Atwell's sons from his second marriage.

George Cantwell, 34, was a chauffeur. His mother, Margarite Cantwell had run Westshore Cottage since at least 1924.

M.A. McCormick ran Minisink Lodge.

Lottie Colville, a widow, seems to have continued running Woodland Cottage. She was listed as farming. Her children: Esther, 19, and Les, 16. Ruth was married.

Abel Hazen was 65, and listed as a farmer. He and his wife Viola ran Laurel Cottage, also known as Hazens. Their daughter Mabel, 29, helped at the boarding house. Son Louis, 21, was a chauffeur. Louis and his wife Elsie had a daughter Viola, 100 days old.

Phoebe Owen, a widow of five years, ran Oakdene. Her son Basil was a carpenter. Son Russell was 20. Daughter **Pearl DeFeo** and her family lived in New York City.

Walter and Meda Tether ran Washington Beach House.

Cyrus Walter, 56 and wife Ella had sons Donald and Reginald. Cyrus was listed as being a lumberman. He owned what was once the Tether Washington Lake House and quite a bit of property.

Helen Hughes and **Clara Hughes Davies** ran Nancy Lee, the former Washington Lake House.

Edith Kalbfus, 41, was the proprietor of Highland Hotel.

The Kaeses still ran their Lake View Farm House.

Louise Vonderhorst, a widow, had a boarding house. Her children: Carl, 10, Walter, 7, Elsie, 5.

Minisink Ford

Children of **Charles and Martha Draxler**: John, Charles Jr., Emmy, Elsa, and Martha.

Arthur and Eleanor Eldred Barnes also lived in Minisink Ford.

1930 Census

Daughters of **Frederick and Julia Heyen**: Marion and Betty. Fred was a truck farmer.

Meta Lass, 51, was widowed, as was her daughter-in-law Veronica, 26, a telephone operator. **Veronica Lass**' children: Marion, Jean, Meta, and Charles.

Jay and Matilda Lass had been married two years. He was a clerk for the railroad.

Children of **Charles and Gertrude Frey**: Everett and Norma. Charles and Gertrude Frey and **Frederick and Minnie Nitzsche** ran Maple Grove Farm.

George Beck, 59, worked on the road.

Emma Campbell, 76, was a widow. Tracy Campbell, 50, was a butcher at the meat market.

Louis and Mildred Warshauer were proprietors of Riverside Cottage. Their children: William and Muriel; Ruth Foster, 22, was listed as a servant.

Henry Mallison was a photographer. His wife was Catherine.

Sons of **Eva Purcell**: John, Edward, James, and Andrew.

Ellsworth Swartz, widower, worked on the road; His daughters: Edna and Jean Swartz.

George and Johanna Beodeker owned their house. He was a house painter.

Christian and Meta Meyer owned Spring House. Children: Anna helped at their boarding house; John was proprietor of the Spring House auto repair shop; Christian was an auto mechanic.

Margaret Beufve, 71, was a widow. Her son Raymond, 38, was a laborer.

Alvin Schoner, 55, widowed, was a butcher.

Ella Watson, 74, owned her house and was a nurse. Her brother George Watson, 72, was a merchant. Lodgers: Emma Lang, 65, widow, housekeeper; John Humbert, 41, single; and William Humbert, 71, widower. The Watson family had been in that location for a very long time. They lived next to the James K. Gardner family.

James K. Gardner, 68, was a merchant at his general store. His wife Ella was 65. Their daughter Edna, 39, was a music teacher. His sister Kate McElroy Gardner, 66 lived with them.

Herman and Catherine Rixton owned their home. He was a real estate broker and she was a telephone exchange operator.

J. Edwin and Anna Steel owned their home. Boarders: Henrietta Gottsch, 56, **Joseph W. Rixton**, 57, widower.

Mary Hankins was the proprietor of a boarding house. John Smith, a lumber foreman, was a boarder.

Henry and Reka Dieckhoff owned their home. He worked on the road. Daughter Marie Schrefer and her son Frederick Schrefer, lived with them.

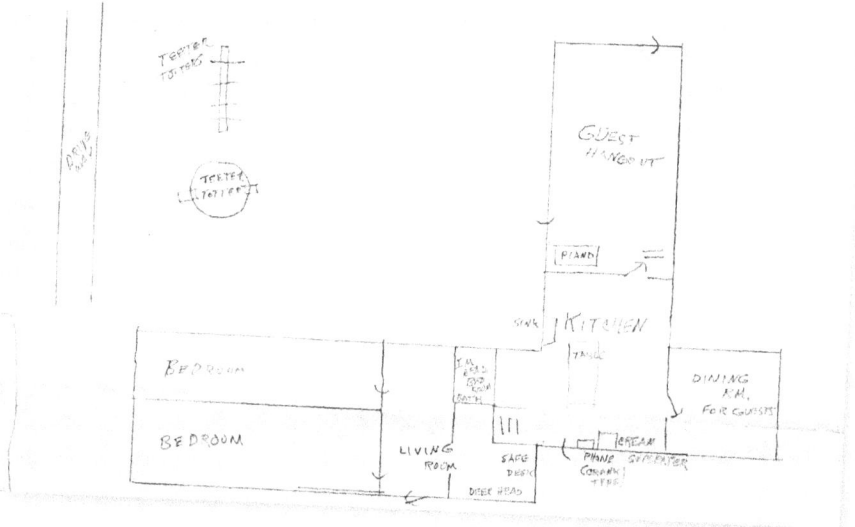

Bradley/Avery House. To me, the farm was a fascinating place. In back of the house were large swings, up and down teeter-totters and teeter-totters that go round and round. A wood house and an ice house. We would chase the cows home to the barn in the evening. The brook was dammed up and made a small pond. Back in the woods was another brook where Grandad Avery and Kenny built another dam in the early forties. That winter the ice took the dam out. Floor plan of the Bradley Avery House and comment courtesy of William E. Horton.

Yulan's Four Corners courtesy of Kevin Marrinan. Fritz Suessman's Shohola Meat Market in 1935. Photo courtesy of Charles Paulus.

Millard and Ethel Quick owned their home. He worked at a nursery. Their daughter Olivia was a clerk at a dry goods store.

Charles Campbell, 75, a widower, worked on the road. His daughter Anna Phelps, also a widow, and her very young children: Catherine and Charles Phelps, lived with him.

William and Mary Bridge owned their home. They had been married 62 years. Their daughter **Ida Calkin**, a widow (since 1906), lived with them.

Fred and Emma Clouse were the proprietors of an ice cream parlor. Their sons: Joseph, 11, Raymond, 10.

Edward MacIntyre worked on the road. His wife was Helen.

Herbert Eckhart was a merchant at a general store. His wife was Kathryn.

Louise Hill owned her home. She was 75 and widowed. Matt O. Callahan, 47, worked on a truck farm and lodged there.

Children of **Frank and Gracie Williams**: Nettie and sons Francis, John, and Charles. Frank worked on the road.

Ami and Anna Quick owned their home. He was a rural postmaster. Their daughter Pauline was a stenographer.

Frank and Mary Wolff were both 38. He was a chauffeur for a truck farm. Their children: Dorothy and Raymond.

Albert and Anna Eckhart had been married four years. He was a stone mason.

Chester and Catherine Hulse had been married 24 years. He was a barber. Their sons: Millard, 21, worked on the road; Clifford, 9.

Minerva Austin, 84, was the widow of Ira. She owned her home. Her household: Minnie Austin, 60; **Edward and Mabel Austin Smith**, and son Austin Smith, 19. Ed was caretaker of, a private estate; Austin was a silk weaver at the silk mill.

Agnes Schwab, 55, single, was a house worker at a boarding house, most likely Handsome Eddy.

Charles Wolff, 71, and a widower, was a truck farmer. His children lived with him: Albert, 31, and single, worked on the road. Norman Wolff, 30, and single, was an automobile mechanic. Anna Wolff, 23, and single, was a telephone operator.

John Quick was a gardener for a private estate. His wife was Bertha. Their sons: John Jr. and Roger. Grandfather **Hugh, 85, Quick** lived with them.

William and Mary Kerr owned their home. He worked on the road. Their children: Margaret was married; Jessie worked for the post office; Mary, Ruth, Helen, and Jack.

Edward and Hazel Carroll were proprietors of Glendella.

Stephen Shotwell, 66, worked on the road.

Frederick and Mary Lewis owned their home ($9,000). He was District School Superintendent and Mary was a teacher. **Susan Gardner**, 60, had run a store in Barryville at one time. **Charles Griffin**, 60, widowed, was a merchant of general store.

Walter and Meda Tether owned their home and were proprietors of Washington Beach Hotel. Their son Ivan, 23, was a chauffeur for the boarding house.

Thomas and Myrtle Hill owned their home. He was a rural mail carrier. Their children: Thelma and Frank.

Irving and Pearl Quick owned their home. Their household: Pearl's sister Lillian Ozenbaugh, a servant for a private family; her mother **Ella Ozenbaugh**, widowed, and grandmother, **Harriet Calkins**, 97, was a widow.

Earl and Catherine Palmer owned their home. He was caretaker of the state bridge. Son Richard was 19.

Margaret Greening, a widow, owned her home. Others in her home: John and Joyce; nephew John H. Fleiger; mother **Catherine Fleiger**, 79, widow; and boarder Lee O'Neill, a worker in the lumber camp.

Charles and Margaret Osterhout were caretakers at a boys' camp. **James Osborne**, 70, widower, was a caretaker at a boys camp.

John and Edith Toaspern Birr owned their house. He was a carpenter, originally from France.

Jane Livingstone, 78, widowed, owned her home. Her son Frank Livingstone, 48, worked at odd jobs.

Harold and Loretta Beufve owned their home. He was a truck farmer.

Children of **Lottie Colville**: Esther and son Leslie. Daughter Ruth and her husband **Herbert Devireaux** lived in Shohola, Pennsylvania.

Carl Mohr, a widower, had a son Fred Mohr, 12. His father-in-law Bathasar Mora, 78, also a widower, lived with them.

Charles Blaut owned his place. He was a truck farmer.

Alice Hill, 72, a widow, owned her home. Son William Hill worked on the road.

George Carner and his wife Alice owned their home. He was a farmer for a truck farm.

August and Margaret Wagermann owned their place. He was a clerk in a feed store. Their son Louis was 13.

Hattie Austin Liebla owned her home. She was 54 and a widow. Her sons: Orville and Stanley worked at odd jobs.

Arthur and Emma Toaspern owned their home. Royden, 18, was an assistant for the road construction. Walter (Bub) was 12.

Walter and Emma Straub Toaspern owned their place. Their children: Frances and Edward.

John and Jennie Warden owned their home. He was a carpenter for the bridge. Their children: William, Archibald, and John Jr.

Charles Flieger and his wife Frieda owned their home. He also worked on the bridge. Arthur Flieger was seven months old.

Edwin Myers owned his home. His wife Mabel died in 1930. Sons: Clifford worked at odd jobs, and Orville was a time keeper for road construction.

Raymond and Marion Wells owned their place. He was proprietor of a garage.

Martin D. and Mary Myers owned their place. He was a chauffeur for the Asendorf Highland Lake Inn. Their children: Mary, Martin D. Jr., Helen, and Thomas.

John and Hattie Hill owned their home. He was a janitor at the high school. This was a second marriage for both of them. Harriet's children from her first marriage: Benjamin, Hilda, Iva, Charlie, and William Eldridge.

James and Sarah Morgan owned their home. He worked in road construction. Son Russell, 24, worked at odd jobs.

Fred and Charlotte Morgan owned their home. He worked at odd jobs. Their children: Fred Jr. and Evelyn.

George and Jennie Crandall, 47, owned their home.

Jim and Cora Clark owned their home. He worked at a lumber camp.

Truman Racine, 78, widowed, was the proprietor of a garage, as was his son Lawrence.

Stephen A. Myers and his son Stanley had a garage. Stephen's wife was Charlotte Myers. Their daughter was **Marie Hulse**.

William and Eva Kalin owned their home. He worked at odd jobs. Their children: Adolph, Annabella, Orville, William, Doris, and Vernon.

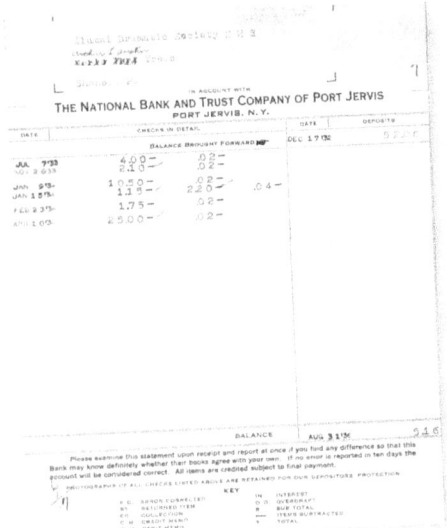

1932 Alumni Dramatic Society of Eldred's bank statement. Arthur Austin was treasurer. Statement courtesy of Mary Briggs Austin.

Howard Stevens was the Superintendent of Highways. Howard, his wife Emily, their daughter Teenie, Emily's mother **Emily Parker**, 79, a widow, and Howard's cousin **Tracey Myers**, 34, house painter, lived at the Parker Hotel.

Ray and Mabel Boyd Ryman owned their home. He was an electrical salesman. **James, 83, Margaret, 76, Boyd** were her parents.

Charles and Lena MacIntyre owned their home. He managed a grocery store. Their daughters: Evelyn and Elizabeth. **Alfred Hill**, a garage chauffeur, boarded with them. Alfred married **Bessie MacIntyre Lass**, a widow with a son Billy Lass, in June.

John Sparks and wife Martha owned their home. He was Eldred's Postmaster and she was an assistant Postmaster.

Children of **Floyd and Helen Kalbfus Boyd**: Elizabeth, Janith, and Floyd Jr. Floyd was a proprietor of a garage with his cousin Alexander Wait.

Alexander and Ida Wait's family: children—Marie, Lucille, Dorothy; and his mother Mary Wait.

Harry Siegel was the proprietor of a general store. Harry and his wife Anna's children: Rita, Arnold, and Martin.

Fred Straub was the proprietor of the Straub Hotel, after his mother died. Fred's sisters: Julia, Rosa, and Ida.

Henry and Lila Myers Von Ohlen had a son Archibald. Henry was the proprietor of Von Ohlen's general store.

Walter and Georgia Styles lived across from Mountain Grove House. Walter, 67, was a librarian. Georgia was a teacher.

Harry and Della Myers Howlett had been married 20 years. Teachers boarded at their house.

Children of **William and Eleanora Parker**: Elsie, William H., Howard, Hazel, and Shirley. William Sr. was a house carpenter.

Clarence Sergeant was a chauffeur with road work. His wife was Claudia McBride Sergeant.

Bertha Winter, a widow, designed ladies wear.

Family of **Gibson and Ethel Barrow**: children—Lillian and Gibson Jr.; and her mother Sarah Baker, 70, a widow. Gibson was a bartender on a steamship.

William and Victoria Simpson Parker's son Andrew was 24. William was a house carpenter.

William and Maude Clouse were proprietors of a laundry.

Guido Bischof, 54, ran Ferncliff Lodge.

Ernest and Edith Timmerhoff owned their home. He worked at odd jobs. Their children: Beatrice, Ernest, and Pauline.

Herman and Veronica Clouse ran a boarding house. Their children: Ida, Gertrude, Herman, Helen, George, Katherine, Theodore, Veronica, and Girard.

William Hammond, 57, worked at odd jobs and lived at the Hammond Boarding House, as did his sister **Mae Parker**, 52, her daughter Ruth Parker, 21, and boarder **Frank J. O'Donnell**, who did road construction.

James and Sophia Mills were proprietors of a Boarding House. Their son Kenneth was 2.

Frank and Anna Hull Sergeant lived near Highland Lake. Frank was a house carpenter. Anna's sister **Jennie Hull**, 56, lived with them.

Henry and Elsie Graf were proprietors of Pine Grove House. They had a daughter Bertha.

George Keil was a butcher at a butcher shop.

Harry and Frances Sulzbach ran Pinehurst. Their children: Harry, Clifford, Edward, Mary, Robert, and Frances.

Anton, 68, and Mary, 60, **Rennenberg** owned their home. Their family included son Anthony and Mary's mother Anna Schragen, 84, a widow.

Gustave and Hattie Staubes ran Mountain Lake House. Their son Arthur and Hattie's mother Matilda Braunschweig, 65, lived with them.

Albert Bye, 61, was a horse breeder.

Karl and Elsie Eggers ran Deer Head Lodge.

Frederick Bye was a house carpenter. His wife was Jeanette.

Children of **Perry and Juliet Foster**: Joseph, Charles, and Flora. Perry was a truck farmer.

Emerson McBride was a chauffeur for the lumber company. His wife was Julia McBride. **Delbert Rundle**, Julia's brother, worked at odd jobs.

Carl Wolff was a truck farmer. Children of **Carl and Frieda Wolff**: Clara, Robert, and Herbert.

Children of **Carl and Borghild Seitz**: Lillian, and Carl. Carl Sr. was a truck farmer.

Nathaniel and Anna Sergeant Brague lived next to their son Joseph Brague and his wife Alice. Joseph worked on road construction.

Charles and Elizabeth Myers ran Lake View. Their daughter Eleanor was 9.

Elizabeth Mills, 61, widow, ran the Mills House. Her daughters: Agnes and Margaret.

Alexander and Minnie Meyer Mills had a daughter Meta. Alexander was a house carpenter.

Charles W. Bosch did odd jobs. **Ralph and Paula Bosch**'s children: George and Marie. Ralph was a truck farmer.

Wilhelm and Mary Bosch were retired. **Carl and Minnie Bosch Benedict** ran a chicken farm. Their granddaughters: Anna and Gertrude lived with them.

Amanda Hartung had a boarder, Arthur, who did odd jobs.

Robert Clark, a painter, was a widower.

Edward, 69, and Katie, 54, Stege had been married for 15 years. **Robert Day**, 74, a servant, was listed as a stationary engineer.

Fred and Annette Schoverling ran Hillside Cottage.

Children of **Joseph and Florence Meyer**: Raymond, John, Fred, and Florence.

Children of **Abe and Catherine Hulse**: Stewart, Douglas. Abe worked at odd jobs.

Elizabeth Wilson, 57, widow ran the boarding house behind the Wilson building on the northwest corner of Eldred. **James Wade**, a barber, boarded there.

William and Mary Cox were both 65. Their son Herman worked at a lumber camp.

Archie and Minnie Myers' son was Charles (Chuck). Archie was a butcher at a butcher shop.

Kate Greig, 72, was a widow. Jennie Wells was her housekeeper.

Children of **William and Bertha Ort**: Eleanor, William, Florence, John, and Milton.

Charles and Bertha Sullivan owned their home. He was a house mason. Their children: William, Charles, and Eva. Boarder Laurence Beam, 25, from North Carolina, was a lumberer.

Children of **Duane and Maude Hulse**: Raymond, an automobile mechanic, and his wife Marie; William, house carpenter; Russell, house carpenter; Ruth, Melvin, Harold, Elmer, and Lillian. Duane worked in the lumbering industry.

Willard Wells, 77, widower, lumbered trees. His daughter Mabel lived with him.

Mary Sullivan's granddaughter Lulu lived with her.

Robert and Jennie Rundle owned their home. He was a truck farmer.

Ernest and Georgiana Horton had a daughter Emeline, 2. He was a truck farmer.

Ami Hulse worked at a lumber camp. His wife was Violet. They had two daughters, Gladys and Ella.

Amelia Darling, a widow, taught school. Her mother Emily Reich, also a widow, most likely watched Elliott, 2.

Sons of **Emma Clouse**: Roy, 43, a carpenter, and Ralph, 28, a painter.

Nellie Crandall did housework for a private family. Her son Clifford was still at home.

1939 Shohola Students grades 1 through 4: Front row left: Donald Knealing, Albert Schields, Arthur Eime, William Hencken, Nicholas Eggenberger. Second row: Edna Meisner, Roger Hess, Margaret Prigge, Harriet Hencken, Robert Brennan, Clara McKean, Harvey McKean, Gibson McKeon. Third row: Jessie McKean, Doris Brennan, Fred Ficken, Hugh McKean, Inez Hocker, Donald Paulus, Marjorie Hess, Dorothy Rocksandich, Rene Wendt, Caroline Schields, Phyllis Hocker. Fourth Row Joe Jacobus, teacher Dorothy Krause, Charles Paulus. Photo courtesy of Charles Paulus.

Walter and Esther Colville Hess

We lived in a seven-room, two-story house with a basement. My parents Walter and Esther Hess bought the plans from Sears Roebuck. My father owned 295-1/4 acres of land which was given to him when he was 20 by his parents. They didn't want him to go to war in 1918, so they gave him the farm. My parents were married in 1931 and built the house that summer. The lumber was cut off the property. They owned a sawmill where the logs were cut. The lumber was dried and planed in the planer my uncle owned. My father, uncle, and a friend built the house.

The electric available was a few miles down the road. In order to get it, the electric company would provide one pole and my father would have to pay for the others needed. So we had our own electricity provided by batteries.

We had a hand dug well which provided water for bath and running water in the house. It was probably the only house in the area that had electric or indoor plumbing. I didn't realize we had things other people didn't have when I was a child, so I never thought we were "special."

My parents were hard workers and got most of their food from the farm. They raised pigs, beef cattle, and a couple of milk cows, plus chickens and sometimes ducks. My father worked part time on local roads doing labor work or driving truck (which he owned). We didn't have much money, but we had material things.

They had a garden and my mother canned or pickled the produce. We had no refrigerator until I was about 12 years old. The house had a built in "dumb waiter" in the cellar way. It was used to keep things cool. We had an ice box in the cellar and in the summer we bought blocks of ice to put in it to keep food cool.

I went to the local Shohola Elementary School for grades one to eight; and attended the Milford High School, grades nine to twelve. I rode the school bus to both schools, being picked up at the house. The High School was about 20 miles away and it was an hour ride each morning and evening.—Marjorie Hess Worzel.

John Clark was a sawyer at a lumber mill. His wife was Carrie Clark.

Henry Bodine and his wife Blanche were proprietors of Bodine Cottages. Their children: Paul and Blanche.

Louis Acor, 94, lived with his daughter **Lillian Stidd** who ran a boarding house on Montgomery Lake.

Children of **John and Emily Morgan**: Harold, 8, Dorothy, 6, James, 2. He lumbered.

Charles and Selma Dunlap's son Carl was 5. His mother Margaret Dunlap, 57, a widow, lived with them. Charles was a house carpenter.

Children of **Sherman and Eliza McBride**: Sherman, Ezra, and Walter did road construction. Grandson William lived with them.

John Dunlap was a teamster for a lumber camp. His wife was Catherine Dunlap.

1938 newspaper ad.

Harry Wormuth was a sawyer at his lumber mill. His wife was **Mary Kyte Wormuth**. Mary's mother, **Mary A. Kyte**, 71, a widow, lived with them.

Alvin and Harriet Hill owned their home. He was an automobile mechanic.

Harry Dunlap, 45, a widower, was a house carpenter. His children: Isabelle, 15, Leslie, son, 13.

John Horton, 39, single, was a truck farmer. His sister **Mabel Wormuth**, 41, widow, was a house worker for a private family. Her daughter Dolores Wormuth and a nephew Kenneth Kalin also lived in the home.

Lon Austin was 72. His sister **Aida Austin**, 68, was listed as a teacher.

Otto and Hattie Schroeder owned their home.

Anna Rothman, 56, widow, still ran her boarding house which was near the Austin's.

Paul Knorr was an electrician. He and his wife Frances lived with her mother, **Henrietta LaBarr**, 57, a widow.

Claude Angell was an automobile salesman. His wife was Hazel, Frances Knorr's sister.

Charles (Mort), 65, **and Jennie Austin**, 50, ran Mountain Grove House. Their sons: William, 27, Arthur, 17, and Robert, 14.

Elbert Clark, 63, (Mort's cousin) was a house mason.

Children of **Walter and Cleta Horton**: son Walter Jr. and daughter Theo; and Cleta's mother **Maria Myers**. Walter was a lumber teamster.

John and Catherine Love. He was a lumbering proprietor.

Children of **William and Lottie Meyers**: William Jr. (who worked in road construction) and Dorothy. William Sr. was a truck farmer.

Chester and Florence Middaugh owned their home. He worked on a farm. Son Herbert, 20, worked at the golf course.

Sherman Leavenworth, 87, lived at Echo Hill with his children: Truman, 52, lumber teamster; Martin, 44, and Charlotte, 42, teacher.

Luella Kelley, a widow, owned her home.

Ed Crail, 50, worked at odd jobs.

Morgan Sergeant was a house carpenter. His wife Alice's sister Helen Spiers, lived with them.

Jessie Dunlap Myers' family: sons Hugh, chauffeur for road construction and Lynn, auto mechanic; daughters, Lena Myers and Norma Weintz.

Laura McBride, 24, and her children: Ken, 5, Virginia, 3, Frances, 2, seem to be at the Avery house. **Erwin and Norah Avery** ran the Bradley House. Their daughter Gladys, 18, and her father **Isaac M. Bradley**, 93, lived there.

Children of **Garfield and Ella Leavenworth**: Clara, Clinton, Anna, and Jim. Garfield was a house carpenter.

N.Y. Route 97

The Delaware River corridor had been linked by a road along the cliffs overlooking the river since at least 1851. When the plans for a new highway through the corridor were initially drawn up, it was to bypass what became the Hawk's Nest, in favor of a shoreline route. However, the Erie Railroad refused to sell the necessary right-of-way, forcing the state to construct the improved road along the cliffside instead.

In 1911, the New York State Legislature created Route 3A, an unsigned legislative route extending from the Pennsylvania state line at Port Jervis to Route 4 (later N.Y. 17) in Hancock along the Delaware River. Very little of this highway actually existed in reality; by 1920, only 3.69 miles of the 62.27-mile long route had been built.

In the 1930 renumbering of state highways in New York, the segment of former Route 3A from Port Jervis to Callicoon was designated as N.Y. 97, even though two sections of the route—between N.Y. 42 at Sparrow Bush and Mongaup and from Pond Eddy to near the hamlet of Tusten—were still incomplete.

The remainder of old Route 3A north of Callicoon, which was fully constructed by 1930, became part of N.Y. 17B. In 1932, then-Governor Franklin D. Roosevelt signed legislation designating N.Y. 97 as the "Upper Delaware Scenic Byway." —*wikipedia.org.*

Dr. Joseph Gutfruend, 63, was from Poland. His granddaughter **Shirley Sanders**, 10, lived with him.

Margaret Hellman, 53, widow, ran a boarding house that would later be called, The Pines. Eleanora Alston Parker had run it in the early 1920s.

Ella Hulse was a widow. Her children: Bertha Hulse and Dewey, 30, an auto mechanic.

Children of **Richard and Louise Haas**: Maurice, Harry, Richard, Marian, and Donald. Richard Sr. was a chauffeur for road construction.

William and Bessie Greening owned their home. He was an electrical lineman. Their son William was a year old.

Sons of **Alvah and Mary Sergeant**: Burton (who worked with bridge construction) and Charles. Alvah lumbered.

Yulan

Kathryn Hensel, 64, a widow, lived at Yulan Cottage. Her son Frederick Hensel, 38, single, managed the Yulan Cottage boarding house.

Margaret Cantwell, 62, a widow, was the proprietor of West Shore Lodge. Her son George, 40, was the chauffeur for the boarding house.

Atwell and Frieda Bradley ran Park Hotel. Clarence Bradley was 20. Frieda's children: Edith Guenther was a commercial stenographer; Clinton Guenther, Helen Guenther, and Viola Guenther.

Albert Kaese, 23, managed the Kaese boarding house. Albert's wife was Ethel. His brother Charles was a painter; his sister was Lola, and his mother Sophie Kaese, 53, was a widow.

Herman Barber, 76, was a truck farmer. His wife was Isabel.

William Holden drilled artesian wells. His wife **Anna Toaspern Cordes** was the proprietor of a boarding house. There were a number of people at their home: son David Holden; Elmer Meyers, boarder, a teacher; Margaret Cordes, phone operator; and Bertha Cordes, a secretary for a steamship company.

Pete and Anna Callahan, 29, had been married one year. He was a chauffeur for a taxi company; she was a commercial bookkeeper.

Henry Wolff was an electrician for the phone company. His wife was Matilda Wolff. Their son Alfred and his wife Helen lived with them. Alfred was a Lineman for the phone company.

Theodore West was 84. **Charles and Selma West** managed the West boarding house. Charles and Selma's children: Theodore, Selma, Daniel, Ralph, and Paul. Selma's mother, Selma Werner, 67, was a widow.

Russell and Ina Owen had been married one year. He was a rural mail carrier. **Phoebe Owen**, 60, widow, may still have run Oakdene as a boarding house.

Abel and Viola Hazen ran Laurel Cottage. **Lewis and Elsie Hazen** ran their new boarding house, Sunset Cottage. Their daughters: Viola and Marcella.

Jacob and Lisette Hensel were the proprietors of the Colonial boarding house. Their children: Katherine and Helen.

John Metzger was an income tax consultant. His wife was Caroline.

Edward Schumacher was a truck farmer. His wife was Catharine.

Herman Bosch was listed as a plumber, though he also had a dairy and an ice business. Herman and Mary Bosch's children: Herman, Marjorie, and Robert.

Children of **William and Clara Ramsey**: Rowland and Madeline. He was superintendent of the Country Club.

Charles and Lillian Greer had been married one year.

Edward and Georgianna Bornstein were the proprietors of Grand Vue. Harry Baker, 35, was listed as their servant.

Children of **Carl and Henrietta Carlson**: Dorothy, Ruth, Kent, and Donald.

Lawrence Crandall was a house carpenter. He and his wife Matilda's son Leonard was 13.

Ken and Emma Crandall had been married three years. He was a house carpenter. Their son Douglas was six months old.

John Weber was a house carpenter. His wife was Katie Weber. Their daughter Gertrude was 17.

John H. and Eva Weber had been married six years. Their children: Virginia and David.

Charles and Caroline Kirby's daughter Klelah was 17.

Kaska Kirby was a silk weaver at a silk mill. He and his wife Dorothy had a son Klendin, 11 months old.

John Cook, 47, single, was the caretaker of a private estate.

Frank and Katherine Owen may have still run a boarding house. He was a merchant at a general store. Their children: Katherine, a nurse at a clinic; Franklin, a chauffeur for groceries; Ernest, and Ella. Frank Ehret, 72, a widower, boarded with them.

Sons of **Cyrus and Ella Walter**: Donald, a radio electrician, and Reginald.

Children of **Henry and Edith Koch**: Henry Jr. and Betsy.

Napoleon Campbell's wife was Sarah. He was 68. **Harry Campbell** was a carpenter for the steam railroad. His wife was Mabel. Their children: William worked for the steam railroad, Walter, and Russell.

Margaret Hessberger was a widow. Her daughter Louise Nifenecker was a seamstress for a private family. Louise's husband **Camille Nifenecker** was a signal man for the steam railroad.

Henry Rupp was a time keeper for the steam railroad. His wife was Minnie. Their family: Catherine Smith, Carol Rupp, and George and Henry Rupp; grandchildren: Catherine E. Smith and Joseph Smith; and boarder Frank Kriebich who worked for the steam railroad.

Clarence Barber, a widower, worked for the steam railroad. His mother-in-law Louise Ernest, 63, was also widowed.

Charles and Martha Draxler ran York Lake Mountain House in Minisink Ford. He was a carpenter for the steam railroad. Their children: Carl Draxler, a truck farmer, Emmy Draxler, a housekeeper for a private family, Elsa, a cook for a private family, and Martha.

Anna Parker, 48, a widow, worked for a private family. Her children: Blanche, Warren Jr., Harvey, and Beatrice. **William Angerman**, son-in-law, 30, was widowed.

1941 Parkers Glen Geyser

April 1941 geyser in Parkers Glen. Photo courtesy Christene Stevens Myers.

The Parkers Glen geyser shown above was created when the railroad water tower was built to supply water to the steam locomotives. Today only the concrete base of the water tower still exists. There are many postcard pictures dating from about 1900. It was a tourist attraction, noted by everyone who rode on the railroad. It was formed when a strainer was put at the junction of Walker Lake Creek and Twin Lakes Creek, and a pipe was run to fill the water tower. Water pressure created much overflow and the pipe was run under the tracks creating the fountain on the river side. (I believe it was as high as sixty feet and it was frozen in winter.) It existed from some time in the 1800s to 1955 when Hurricane Diane destroyed it.
—*George J. Fluhr.*

Julius Maier was listed as a truck farmer. His sister **Annie Maier** was 60.

Children of **Earl and Ada Wells**: Dorothy, Norma, Berniece, and George.

Alvin Hill was a house carpenter. He and his wife Anna Crawford Hill had a daughter Mildred. Anna's mother **Henrietta Crawford Sergeant** (a second time widow) lived with them.

Mary Agnes, Ruth Ann, and Kathy Wilson. Photo courtesy of Mary Agnes Wilson Dorney.

Margie Austin with her uncle Raymond Myers at the clambake in September 1946. Photo courtesy of Andy and Margie Austin Maglione.

James Parker was a house carpenter. His wife was **Mabel Hazen**.

Edith Kalbfus was the proprietor of Highland Hotel and Cottage. Conrad Keller, 19, was the boarding house chauffeur.

William Nieke was a clerk at an enamel manufacturer. He and his wife Barbara Nieke's sons: George and William.

Norman and Bertha Myers worked at the Country Club. He was a caretaker and she was a cook. Their sons: Norman and Francis.

Emmet Barnes was a house carpenter. He and his wife Agnes' children: Allen, did road construction, Lavona, and Emmet Jr. John Christian, who worked for the steam railroad, was a boarder.

Carl and Anna Vonderhorst ran a boarding house. Son Carl, a truck farmer, and grandson Carl Vonderhorst, 14, were listed as living with them.

Henry Schumacher was a truck farmer. His wife was Kate.

Ralph Stanley was the high school principal.

Fred and Charlotte Williams had a son Jack. Fred was a chauffeur with the cab service.

Lumberland 1930
Route 3A State Highway

Russell MacKechnie was an automobile mechanic. His wife Edith was a store manager. Their children: Mabel and Russell. J.R. Stanton, a teacher, boarded with them.

Mary Portz, 53, a widow, managed a boarding house.

Hollow Road

Napoleon B. Quick was a house carpenter. He and his wife Fannie's sons: Ralph, an auto mechanic and Horton, a truck driver. Their daughter Blanche was married to **Herman Worzel** who worked for the Erie Railroad. Herman and Blanche's children: Ruth, Herman, and Gordon Worzel.

Sons of **Samuel and Anna Hallock** (at home): Edgar and Charles (who worked on the highway), and Elmer.

Arthur W. Gieselman was a carpenter contractor.

Katherine Bridge, 52, a widow, managed a boarding house.

Pond Eddy, New York

Ernest Clark worked at a stone quarry. He and his wife Eunice's children: Stella, Orville, and Vernon Clark.

Children of **Raymond and Mary Hallock**: Sherwood, Christina, and Evelyn.

John W. and Ida Johnson's son William, 31, was a signal man for the railroad.

Walter D. LaValle was a merchant for a grocery store. His wife was Edythe.

Claude Maxwell, 45, was the president of a bluestone company. His brother Harry was a grocery store salesman.

Louisa Worzel was widowed. Her sons: Oscar, a railroad track foreman, and Raymond, a railroad track worker, lived with her.

Alice McCaffrey managed a boarding house. Her son William was a college student. William Blakney was a lodger.

Frederick A. and Gertrude Doeller managed Handsome Eddy Farm. Their daughters: Doris and Marion. **A. Fisher**, the chef, co-owned Handsome Eddy Boarding House.

Alfred Van Tuyl, 58, was widowed. He worked on the farm. His children: Hazel, Laura, and twins, Howard and Harold.

John Twichell, 68, farmed. His wife was Edith. Their daughter Ada lived with them.

John H. Kerr farmed. He and his wife Katherine's children: Katherine E., telephone operator, Ada, John A., highway worker; Christina, Helen, and Charles were in school.

Hillside Road

James MacIntyre, 82, was a harness maker. His wife was Adeline. Their children: **Bessie Lass**, widow, and her son, William Lass; **Herman and Adelaide Kalin** and their daughter Reta. Herman Kalin was the highway superintendent.

Fred Fracke was the Superintendent of Brookwood House. He and his wife Katherine's sons: Frederick C. and Herman.

Billings Kinne, 65, was the caretaker of a private estate. His wife was Julia. Their daughter Harriet was a teacher.

Herbert Kinne was a farmer for a private estate. His wife was Mildred. They had a son Charles. Charles Murray lodged with them and worked on the private estate.

Emery Frey worked on the highway. He and his wife Mamie had seven children who worked at various jobs: home nurse, car mechanic, dairyman, truck driver.

Mildred Briggs with some bunnies and their dog Pal. Old Barryville-Shohola Bridge in background. Photo courtesy of Mary Briggs Austin.

Pond Eddy and Glen Spey Rd.

Andrew Paye, 60, was State Superintendent of Highways. His wife was Harriet.

Glen Spey, New York

Grace Ewing, 79, was a widow. Her son George was an executive. George and his wife Myra's sons: George R.M. Jr. and Alexander. Servants: Hannah Fahey, Mary Clarkin, Katherine Breslin, and Millard King.

Homer Osterhoudt was superintendent of a girls' camp. His wife was Elva. John Ryan, a teacher, boarded with them.

Edward Bisland, 58, was Game Protector for New York State. His wife was Margaret. Their daughter Ethel taught high school. Their son Edward Jr. was a college student.

Augusta Schwarz, 60, was a widow.

Frank Getz was 71. His wife was Hannah. Their children: Eugene drove a tractor for the county highway; Amandus was a driller for the county highway; daughter-in-law Dorothy was a weaver at the silk mill; daughter Mary was a stenographer; Katherine, Ella, and Elmer were in school.

Daniel Gillespie, 62, was the Town of Lumberland Postmaster. His wife was Nettie.

William Sharpe, 51, was clerk for the Town of Lumberland.

Walter Schwarz, 31, managed a boarding house. His mother Anna Marie, 63, was a widow.

Ida Kalin, 55, was a widow.

Draketown Road

Agnes Wilson, 65, was a widow. Her daughter Martha taught school.

1940 Census

Village of Eldred

Daniel Rowlee and Emily Schoonover rented a bungalow for $20 a month. He was a retired private chauffeur.

Harry Wormuth was a lumberman. His wife was **Mary Kyte**.

Nellie Crandall was a widow. Her son Clifford was a grocery clerk/assistant manager for the A&P store.

John H. Clark was 72. His wife Carrie was 74.

Dr. Joseph Gutfruend, 75, from Austria owned his house. Anna Scotti, 43, a widow, was his housekeeper.

Fire practice drill at what was once the Straub Hotel. Photos courtesy of Christene Stevens Myers.

Eldred Parade. Cynthia Leavenworth in the middle by the X. Photo courtesy of Cynthia Leavenworth Bellinger.

License of Ed Wilson in 1943. Also his Atlantic Service Station business card courtesy of Mary Agnes Wilson Dorney.

Alvin Hill worked for the county roads. He and his wife Harriet had a son Ronald.

Alexander Randolph and his wife Kathryn ran Royal Scarlet Store.

Charles MacIntyre managed the A&P. He and his wife Lena's daughters: Evelyn and Elizabeth.

J. Wesley Morgan was a lumber and coal dealer. His brother Russell Morgan worked in construction.

Harold Dunlap was the manager of a restaurant which he owned. His wife Anna was a waitress. They had a foster son, Richard. Lyle Dunlap was a truck driver. In 1935 he lived in Brooklyn. His wife was Florence; sons: Robert and Phillip.

Lillian Stidd was 65.

Walter Styles, 77, was the town clerk and town librarian. His wife Georgia, 50, taught school.

Lodgers: **James Wade** ran his own barber shop; **Mac O'Donnell** was a painter.

Herman Cox and his father William rented at $5 a month.

Andrew and Margie Parker ran Parker's general store. His mother **Victoria Simpson Parker** was widowed.

Abraham Hulse, 50, worked on a farm. His brother Dewey was a general laborer in wood.

Town of Highland Honor Roll, later version with a few more names. Photo courtesy of Christene Stevens Myers. (See p. 337 for earlier version.)

William and Eleanora Alston Parker had four children: William, Howard, Hazel, and Shirley. William was a painter and seeking work in March.

William Steele taught at Eldred Central School. His wife was Nellie.

Fred and Charlotte Morgan's children: Raymond and Evelyn.

Lawrence Racine did road work.

Hattie Hill was widowed and a school janitor. Her children at home: sons Charles and William Eldridge; and daughter Esther (Peggy) Hill.

Raymond Wells was the proprietor of a garage. His wife was Marion Wells.

Archie Myers worked on the bridge with the County. He and his wife Minnie had a son Charles, 14. **Emmett Pyle**, the P.E. teacher lodged with them. Emmet made $1440 per year.

Vera Terpening, also a teacher at Eldred Central, lodged with **Edgar and Marjorie Hill** and their daughter Virginia. Edgar was a machinist with the County Highway Department.

Raymond and Marie Hulse's daughter Marion was 5. Raymond was a carpenter.

Stanley Myers was an auto mechanic. His wife Alberta was a beautician and had a beauty shop in her home. His mother **Charlotte Middaugh Myers**, a widow, lived with them. Anna Banks, 18, was a helper.

Ed Bosch, 48, was a successful carpenter for bowling alleys. He and his wife Eleanor had a daughter Kathryn and son Frederick.

Henry Von Ohlen rented for $15/month. He was a real estate broker. He and his wife Lila had a son Archie, a painter with the County Highway Construction.

Ernest Clark was a watchman for the County Highway Construction. He and his wife Eunice had two sons: Orville, 17, general helper at a boarding house, and Vernon, 12. Their nephew **Douglas Hallock**, 4, lived with them (since 1936 when his mother died a few months after he was born).

Fritz and Ella Stickle owned the house of Elizabeth Wilson on the northwest corner of Eldred. They called it Orchard Terrace.

Stella Van Etten was a waitress at a boarding house. Her son Donald, was 16.

Mary Ort, 80, was a widow who lived with her son William, a carpenter.

Charles Ort worked for the County Highway Maintenance. His wife was Anna Sergeant Brague.

Alfred Hill owned his home. He was a school bus driver. He and his wife Bessie kept boarders in their home. Bessie's son William Lass was 12. Alfred and Bessie's daughter Joan was 6. Bessie's mother **Adeline MacIntyre**, 73, lived with them. They had two lodgers: **Helen Williams and Cecelia Sullivan**, both teachers at Eldred Central High—40 weeks of work for a salary of $1200.

Joseph Hulse and his wife rented. Joseph worked at Brookwood Camp.

Harry Howlett was a painter. His wife Della had boarders: Lucille Stalker and Matilda Bower, both teachers at Eldred Central—40 weeks/$1300 salary.

Charles Geisler, a widower, was a professional engineer. His salary, $2,346 a year.

Martin D. Myers Sr. was a garage attendant. His daughter Mary Myers was Eldred Central's secretary. His son Martin Myers Jr. worked at Royal Scarlet. His daughter Helen and son Thomas were still in school.

Fred Straub lived at the Straub Hotel and Bar which his sister Ida Straub, 34, managed.

Hugh Myers and his wife Rosa Straub had a son Jackson and daughter Shirley.

Martha Sparks, 68, was a widow and rented.

Forrest Wilson was a lawyer. His mother Bertha Wilson, 63, was a widow.

Ralph Hessberger, the butcher, owned his own meat market. He and his wife Gertrude had a daughter Marion, 3. Clark LaRue, a butcher, lodged with them.

Alexander and Ida Wait lived above the Wait and Boyd garage. Daughter Marie worked at the Eldred Post Office for $420 a year. Daughter Lucille taught at Harper School in Endwell, New York. Daughter Dorothy (Spider) was still in school. Clara Saggel, sister-in-law lived with them.

Ed Wilson's Atlantic Station. Photo courtesy of Mary Agnes Wilson Dorney.

Floyd Boyd was a carpenter. He and his wife Helen had two daughters: Elizabeth and Janith, both waitresses at a boarding house (8 weeks for around $180).

Frederick J. Lewis was still the District Superintendent of Schools. His salary was $3,000. His wife was Mary Lewis.

Lynn Myers was a road grader operator—40 weeks $720. His wife was Mildred Myers.

Frederick Williams was a painter for the County Highway Department. His wife was a dressmaker. They had two sons, Fred and William.

Howard and Emily Stevens owned their home. He was the Town Superintendent of Highways. Emily was the Postmaster. Their daughter Christene was 19. His nephew Tracey Myers was a painter for the County Highway Department.

Jennie Austin's three sons worked for the County Highway Department: William, 37, was a road worker—32 weeks/$750; Arthur, 27, clerical work—52 weeks/$1254; Robert, 24, assistant surveyor—32 weeks/$600.

George Crandall was a carpenter and painter. He and his wife **Jennie Crawford** were 57.

Eldred-Glen Spey Road

Oren Spangenberg was the manager of a gas station—52 weeks for $1612. He and his wife Lucy had a son, 7. Orin's brother Earl, who did landscaping and gardening, lived with them.

Walter Horton was a lumberman. He cut and skidded logs—40 weeks/$1120. His wife was Alice and they had a daughter, Lila.

John Horton did road work for the WPA project. His wife was Emma. Stepson Everett Stevens and step granddaughter Helen Stevens, 1, lived with them.

Merlin Hallock also did road work for the WPA project—$560 for 35 weeks. His wife Mabel was a laundress. Their children: Florence and Percy.

Herman Bosch, 50, was a welder for the County Highway Department—$1360 for 46 weeks. He and his wife **Mary Horton**, 40, had a son Herman, 21, a wood cutter who sold wood and ice; a daughter Marjorie, 16; and a son Robert, 15.

Aida Austin, 78, a former teacher, and her brother **Alonzo Austin**, 81, rented from their cousin who owned the Austin land on Proctor Road.

Paul Knorr, an electrician, and his wife Frances had two children: Gordon and Arlene. Paul's brother Clair, a handy man, lived with them.

Barryville-Eldred Road

Frederick Fracke worked for the Town Highway Department—$300 for 20 weeks. He and his wife Catherine were both from Germany.

Arthur C. Toaspern, 54, was the road supervisor for the Department of Highways—$3,000 for 52 weeks. He and his wife Emma's sons: Royden, 28, assistant engineer for road construction—$1,500 for 48 weeks; and Walter, 22, salesman for road machinery—$1193 for 50 weeks.

Walter Toaspern, construction foreman for the County Highway Department, earned $2,000 for 50 weeks. He and his wife Emma's children, Frances and Edward, were both in high school.

Edwin V. Myers, 77, was widowed. His son Clifford, 38, lived with him and worked for the County Highway Department.

Charles MacKechnie, 62, worked for the County Highway

Department. His wife Edith, 61, kept boarders: Merrill Cook, music teacher, and Howard B. Bretsch, social studies teacher; both worked at Eldred Central—40 weeks for $1,800.

Barryville

Stanley Libela, 31, and his brother Ward were general laborers.

Thomas F. Hill was a mail carrier—52 weeks for $840. His wife was Myrtle. Their son Frank worked at the theater in Barryville.

Irving Quick was a house painter—12 weeks for $475. Irving's wife Pearl was 56. Pearl's sister **Lillian Ozenbaugh** lived with them.

Austin Smith drove a tow truck for the county—28 weeks for $500. Austin's wife Dorothy was a nurse—17 weeks for $800. Dorothy's sister **Helen Kuen** was a waitress at a restaurant— 4 weeks/$250.

Chester Hulse (Rowlee Schoonover's friend) was a barber at a Hotel in Pennsylvania. His wife was Catherine. Their son Clifford worked as a grocery clerk at the A&P store at 9 weeks/$150. (Clifford would marry Helen Myers.)

Millard Hulse was a truck driver for the County—30 weeks for $810. His wife was Kathryn and they had a son Millard.

Louis Wilson rented. He was an automobile mechanic—20 weeks for $134. His wife Dorothy was a nurse.

Advertisements in 1942 Yearbook.

Albert and Anna Eckhart also rented. Albert worked at a bar and grill restaurant.

Ed and Mabel Smith owned their home. He worked for the town highway—30 weeks for $325. Mabel's sister **Nellie Austin**, 72, and brother **Ralph W. Austin**, 58, a mining engineer inspector for the WPA (10 weeks/$800) and **Wallace Austin**, 25, an electrician, lived with them.

Eleanora Alston Parker. Photo courtesy of William H. Parker Jr., her son.

Jennie Crawford Crandall and Anna Crawford Hill (mother of Mildred Myers). Photo courtesy of Christene Stevens Myers.

Albert Wolff was a crusher operator for the County Highway Department—32 weeks for $1100. He and his wife Ruth had two young sons, Charles and Edward.

Norman Wolff a school bus driver, also worked for the highway department. He and his wife Dorothy Meyers had a daughter Eileen, 4.

Jane Putnam (daughter of **Edward and Blanch Putnam**) worked at Clouse's Hotel—20 weeks for $250. She had a brother Richard, 17.

William and Mary Kerr owned their home. William was a road foreman for the County Highway Department—28 weeks for $650. Their son John (Jack) was a clerk at the A&P. Their daughter Ruth's husband, **Robert Nelson** worked in New York City as an iron worker.

Frank and Gussie Williams had two sons: John and Charles. Frank was a road foreman for the county highway department—32 weeks for $1,000.

Fred and Emma Clouse owned their home. They owned the bar and grille restaurant and their sons, Joseph and Raymond worked there.

Herbert and Kathryn Eckhart had two young sons: Ronald and Gary. Herbert ran his own store.

Gordon Comstock was a gas station dealer. He and his wife Matilda had a son Gordon, 11 months.

Oscar Worzel was a foreman on the Erie Railroad—52 weeks at $1800. His mother Louisa, a widow, lived with him.

Lewis Eckhart's wife Mary was a hair dresser.

Eva Purcell was the Postmaster for Barryville—52 weeks for $1200. Her sons: John, assistant Postmaster, Barryville—52 weeks for $588; Edward, a clerk in the Yulan Post Office—10 weeks for $100; James and Andrew were still in school.

Edward MacIntyre and his wife Helen owned their home. He was a road foreman for the County Highway—52 weeks/$1,000.

Christian and Delores Meyer owned their residence. He was an automobile mechanic—52 weeks for $1,000. They had two young daughters, Judith Ruth and Carol Jane.

Carl and Naomi Daub owned their home. Carl was a yardmaster at a lumber company—50 weeks and $1200. Their children: Alice Marie and Carl William.

Charles and Jennie Traver owned their home. He was retired.

Henry and Catherine Mallison owned their home. He was a photographer.

Mary Bridge, 87, and her daughter Ida, 56, were both widowed, but owned their home.

Minnie Nelson, 66, lived with her widowed brother-in-law, **William Deats**, 70, a mechanical engineer/inventor.

Frank and Mary Wolff owned their house. He was a maintenance man for the Highway Department—26 weeks for $468. Their daughter Dorothy was a waitress at a boarding house; and son Raymond was a handy man at a boarding house.

George and Johanna Brodeker owned their house. He was a house painter and Johanna had a tea room in her house.

John Traver and his wife owned their home. He had a barber shop. They had a daughter Joan Marie.

Dorothy Sulzbach, 1947 Eldred Yearbook.

Mary Briggs and her friend Kate Strenglein in 1943 Yearbook.

James E. Smith was a salesman for the American Oil Company—$2,800 for the year. His wife's name was Eda.

Katherine Durr, 71, was widowed. Her granddaughters Edna and Jane Swartz lived with her and her widowed son-in-law, Elsworth, a general laborer.

Chris, 75, and Meta, 74, Meyer still ran Spring House for summer boarders (27 weeks). Their daughter Anna and son John, a garage owner, lived with them.

James K. Gardner, 78, a widower, had a general store in Shohola, Pennsylvania. His sister **Kate McElroy Gardner**, 76, and his daughter Edna, 49, a music teacher, lived with him.

Walter and Meda Tether owned their house. Their son Ivan helped with their Washington Beach Hotel.

Herman Rixton, 77, and his wife, 75, owned their home.

Edwin and Anna Steele had boarders in their home: Bernadine Reuter, 72, and widowed; Etta Gottson, 66; and Thelma Wynkoot, 27, Barryville teacher.

Elias and Rachel Sheen owned their house. Elias was a station agent for the Erie Railroad at $1,900 per year. Their son Thorne also worked for the Erie Railroad.

The Briggs family lived in the Barryville Methodist Parsonage. Irwin's salary was $1,400 for the year. He and his wife Myrtle's children: Laura, Mildred, Mary, and John.

William Quick and his wife rented their home. His sister Eva lived with them.

William and Anna Vogt owned their home. He worked at the theater. Anna was a teacher—$1,700 for 40 weeks.

Ralph and Fanny Livingstone owned their home. He worked on county roads—34 weeks at $652. Fanny did housework for a private family. Their daughter was 17. Fanny's mother Mrs. Holmes, a widow, lived with them.

Annie Philips was a nurse taking care of people in her home—$850 for 52 weeks. Her sister Emma Barber, 80, lived with her. John Hermbert, 50, was a boarder.

Walter and Katherine Campbell owned their own home. He was a fruit peddler.

Barryville to Yulan Road

Joseph and Blanche Rudolph owned their own home. He was a plumber. Their nephew John Cantwell, 16, an apprentice plumber, lived with them.

Harold and Laurette Beufve owned their own home. He was a building carpenter—20 weeks, $500. Laurette's mother Elizabeth Penney lived with them.

William and Anna Toaspern Cordes Holden owned their own home. Bill was a well driller. Anna ran the boarding house. Their son David was also a well driller.

Otto and Bertha Feigenhiemer owned their home. He was a chef. They had a young daughter Nancy.

Marion Hensel, wife of Fred Hensel, by Beaver Brook. Photo courtesy of Dennis J. Carroll.

Ed and Helen Lass MacIntyre's 50th wedding Anniversary. Ed's aunt Mary Kerr joined them. Photo courtesy of Linda Guenther Anderson.

William and Barry Owen. Photo courtesy of Pam DeFeo Fischetti.

Agnes Mary and Ed Wilson. Photo courtesy of Mary Agnes Wilson Dorney.

Mildred and Laura Briggs sit on the little dam on Haflway Brook almost across from the Library, near Charlie Geisler's. Photo courtesy of Mary Briggs Austin.

Raymond Beufve lived with his sister Edna Miller. Edna kept summer lodgers. Raymond was a handy man, gardening and painting—26 weeks for $468.

John B. and Edith Toaspern Birr owned their home. John was a carpenter.

William and Anita Barber owned their home. William was a machine operator for the Highway Department—24 weeks at $600.

Peter and Anna Callahan owned their home. Pete was Supervisor of the Town of Highland—52 weeks/$2200. Anna had roomers in their home. [He would have Callahan appliance store.]

John and Janet Warden owned their home. He worked for the County Highway. Their sons: Archie worked at a diner; Ian was a mechanic helper for the County Highway; William was an inspector for the County Highway Department. William and his wife Catherine had a son, Robert, 4.

Charles and Edith Kaese owned their home. He was a laborer; she ran their boarding house.

Yulan

Fred Covert did road maintenance work. His wife Anna Covert was the school janitor for Yulan—40 weeks for $100. Charles Greer, 59, was a mail carrier for the Yulan/Barryville route—40 weeks for $100.

Ed and Mary Oset Bornstein ran Grand Vue. Mary's son **Joseph Oset** was with the Hawaiian Aviation Corps.

Carl and Anna Vonderhorst had a boarding house. Their son Charles, 37, was the chef.

Edward Schumacher and his wife owned their home. He worked on the road—$180 for 12 weeks. She hosted summer boarders.

Henry and Matilda Wolff owned their home. He ran road rollers for the County Highway—28 weeks for $737.

Fred Hensel was the Yulan Postmaster—$1027 per year. His mother Katherine, 74, was a widow.

Ludwig and Helen Hensel owned their home. He owned his own garage and they had a daughter, Joan.

George Bradley ran a bar and restaurant which he owned. He and his wife Florence had a daughter Georgia Anne. Living with the family: Florence's mother **Nellie Poth**; brother Anthony, his wife Elsie, and their daughters: Florence and Jeannine.

John Metzger and his wife Caroline owned their home. He was 78 and an income tax advisor.

Blanche Bodine, a widow owned her boarding house. Her son Paul helped run Bodine Cottage.

Charles and Caroline Kirby owned their home. Their daughter Kelay was attendance supervisor for Eldred Central. They had two grandchildren, Klendin and Kleona.

John H. and Eva Weber owned their home. He was a laborer and earned $488 in 21 weeks. Eva was a laundress for Eldred Laundry—$150 for 15 weeks. Their children: Virginia, David, Fred, Jeanette, Roger, and Gail.

Eugene Roberts was an assistant camp engineer for the Boy Scouts—52 weeks $780. His wife **Gertrude Roberts** drove the Eldred school bus. Gertrude's mother, Katie, 68, a widow, lived with them.

Matilda Crandall, 57, a widow, ran her own boarding house. Her son Leonard was a farmer. His wife Katherine taught at

Eldred Central. Arthur and Clara Mather were hired hands. **Milton Crandall**, 86, was widowed.

Yulan-Eldred Rd.

William Kalin and his wife Eva owned their home. He was a building carpenter—32 weeks/$1020. Eva did laundry at home. Their children: Orval, William, Doris, Vernon, Loritha, Vincent, and Shelby Jean. John King, a brick layer, was a boarder.

Percy and Emily Bartle owned their home. In 1935 they lived in Hornell, New York. Percy was a brick layer. Their children: Franklin, Mary Jane, and Harrison, 8.

Walter Horton was a teamster doing lumbering. His wife was **Cleta Myers**.

Sherman McBride, 73, ran the road roller on town roads—$369 for 16 weeks. His wife Eliza was 76; their adult sons at home: Sherman, Ezra, and Walter.

Charles and Selma Dunlap owned their home. Charles was a milkman. They had a son Carl.

Oliver and Margaret Dunlap rented their home. He was a carpenter at the World's Fair—36 weeks, $2196.

Richard and Louise Haas owned their home. He was a truck driver for the County Highway Department. Their children: Maurice, Harry, Richard, Marion, Donald, and Doris.

Emerson and Julia McBride owned their home. He worked on the town road—27 weeks/$560. They had a son Walter. Julia's

Henry Von Ohlen
REAL ESTATE BROKER

Eldred, New York

Telephone: Barryville 2564

FORREST W. WILSON
Eldred, N. Y.
Attorney-at-Law
Notary   Realty
Tel.: Barryville 2542

1941 ads.

father Robert Rundle, 59, lived with them.

William and Anna Meyers' son Jimmy was 1. William was a shovel operator for the County Highway Department—$1,200 for 32 weeks.

Louis and Florence Batonick rented their home. He was a construction engineer; she was born in Poland and had a year of college. They lived in New York City in 1935.

Willie Bosch in 1969. Photo courtesy of Ken Bosch, his son.

Fred and Gertrude Lochner owned their home. They lived in Bellaire, N.Y., in 1935. He was an automobile mechanic for auto fleets—$1980 for 35 weeks. Their children: Fred, LeRoy, George, and David. Gertrude's mother Ida Koop lived with them.

Town of Lumberland Town Hall. Photo: Gary Smith.

Plaque in memory of Chester Middaugh, for loving and devoted service to the Eldred United Methodist Church as Church Custodian and Bell Ringer from 1940–1968. Photo courtesy of Cynthia Leavenworth Bellinger.

Barryville Backroad/Crawford

William Angerman and his wife Anna owned their home. He worked for the County Highway Department at $527 for 28 weeks. Stepdaughter **Beatrice Parker** was a waitress at a boarding house—$56/9 weeks.

Julius Maier, 74, was a carpenter. **Earl and Ada Wells** owned their home. Earl was a well driller. Their children: Dorothy, Norma, Berniece, George, and Wayne. Harold MacIntyre, 36, was a well driller and boarded with the family.

Eldred

Charles and Christina Ott rented. He was an automobile mechanic—40 weeks/$480. Children: Cynthia and Norma.

Charles Smith, 69 was a widower.

Alvin and Anna Hill owned their home. He was a carpenter—17 weeks for $489.

Henry Rave was a WPA worker on road projects—37 weeks/$444. He and his wife Margaret's children: Henry Jr., William, and Anna Marie. Margaret's father Carl Mohr lived with them.

Norman Myers was a caretaker for Highland Field and Stream Game Preserve—$900 for 52 weeks. His wife was Bertha. Their son Norman Jr. ran an automotive garage.

Eldred Club Road/Clark Road

Alvah and Mary Sergeant owned their home. Alvah and their son **Grant Sergeant** did construction work.

Adelaide Strenglein owned her home. She was a widow and ran a boarding house. Her children: Frank did road work for the county; and Harry and Kate went to school.

Webster and Ida LaBarr owned their home. He was a log cutter—40 weeks for $768.

LeRoy Horton worked at a sawmill—26 weeks for $312. He and his wife Katherine (Cappy Ott) had a son Carl, 1.

Highland Lake-Eldred

Bertha Winter, 66, a widow, designed women's apparel.

Clarence and Claudia Sergeant owned their home. He was a truck driver for the Town Highway.

Charles and Clareta Sergeant owned their home. Their son Charles E. Jr. was 1.

William Clouse and his wife Maud owned their home. They ran a laundry.

Guido and Hedwig Bischof seem to still be running Ferncliff Lodge. Their daughter was Leona.

Ernest and Edith Sergeant Timmerhoff owned their home. He was a painter on the county bridge—34 weeks/$750. She did laundry—9 weeks/$98. Their daughter Beatrice worked at a boarding house—12 weeks/$50; son Charles was a caddie on a golf course—12 weeks/$50; Joyce and Anne were too young to work.

Laurence Westerfield, 70, was a shoe salesman. His wife Edith was 60.

Herman and Veronica Clouse owned their house. He worked on the town road—47 weeks/$306. Children: Theodore did farm work; and Veronica.

Mae Parker still ran a boarding house. Her daughter Ruth Parker and brother **William Hammond** (road worker) lived there.

Jennie Hull, 68, single, was a bookkeeper. Louise Parker, 69, widowed was a visitor.

James and Sophia Mills ran a boarding house. Their children: Kenneth and Geraldine.

Arthur and Julietta Bertram ran Bertram's Tavern.

Frances Sulzbach was a widow. She managed her boarding house. Son Christopher assisted and was also the Bartender. Frances' other children: Mary, Robert, Frances, and Harry, who worked for the County Highway—24 weeks, $432. Fred Murphy, friend, 25, was a bar tender in the summer.

Arthur (Sr.) and Clara Bertram owned Bertram's Lodge.

Gustave and Hattie Staubes ran Mountain Lake House. He also worked on the town road—16 weeks/$224. Son Arthur was a painter. Hattie's mother **Matilda Braunschweig** lived with them.

Frederick and Jeanette Bye owned their house. He was Chief Clerk for the County Highway Department—$1800/year. She was the Highland Lake Postmaster—$600 per year.

Albert Bye, 70 (from England) owned his home.

Anton and Mary Rennenberg were retired from running a Hotel. Their son Anthony was an auto mechanic with his own business. Mary's sister Gertrude Fuchrer, widow, seemed to live with them.

Karl and Elsie Eggers ran a boarding house. Hamiak Mozurkinch, 26, was their servant.

Eldred, Highland Lake

Charles and Elizabeth Myers had the huge boarding house on Highland Lake. Their daughter Eleanor had completed a year of college.

Ray and Mabel Boyd Ryman owned their home. He was an electrician. Their nephew Arthur, 20, was an electrical helper—$300 for 26 weeks.

Alexander and Minnie Mills owned their home. Alexander farmed—50 weeks/$1,000. Their children: Meta, Dorothy Ann, and Ross. **Agnes Mills** managed the Mills farm and boarding house—50 weeks/$500. Her mother Elizabeth, 70, a widow lived with her.

Charles and Hilda Wilson's children: Charles Jr. and Carol.

Herbert Bente, a non-denominational clergyman made $1,000 a year. He was married to **Isabel Greig Kelso Grotecloss**. Isabel ran an academy. Her sons: Edward G., Robert, Bennet lived with them.

Perry and Juliette Foster's children: Charles, a helper in the laundry; Flora, worked at boarding houses.

Leslie Gordon rented. He was in the music publishing business. His brother Herbert lived there, too.

Highland Lake Back Road

Joseph and Florence Meyer owned their home. He was a general laborer—26 weeks, $360. Their children: Raymond was widowed and did general farm work; John was a chauffeur; Fred and Florence. **Harvey Parker**, delivery truck driver, and his wife Obal, a glass cutter, were lodgers.

Charles Bosch owned his home. He was a carpenter for a bowling alley; 9 weeks/$500.

William and Christina Brodmerkel had two daughters: Dorothy and Alberta. He was an automobile mechanic.

Oakland (Oakie) Worzel, brother of Ruth Worzel. 1944 Yearbook photo.

Reta Kalin, good friend of Mary Briggs. 1944 Yearbook photo.

Verna Eadie (Clifford Crandall's sister) holding her nephew Clifford Crandall. Photo courtesy of the Clifford Crandall Family.

Aerial view of Washington Lake. Photo courtesy of Kevin Marrinan.

1946 Class of first and second graders. Front Row: Charlotte Gentes, Rose Kunkeli, Lorriane Nieke, Jeannette Russo, Joy Dailey, Janet Hulse, Barbara Liefert, Helen Stevens Gloria Horton, Alma Reiser, Doris Maney, Dane Reed. Second row: Carl Horton, Edwin Martin, Paul Bertram, Ernest Hill, Charles Reiser, Ernest Van Tuyl, William Turner, Ross Mills. Back row: Frederick Hiegl, John Barnes, Ronald Hill, Peter Kestler, Donald Rupp, Carl Daub, Harry Kestler, Frederick Bosch, Miss Leavenworth, Teacher.

Charles Pankow owned the old Bosch boarding house. In 1935 he lived in Queens, as did his mother Agnes Pankow, a widow. She lived in Highland Lake in 1940.

Arthur Hartung, 50, single, did road work for the WPA—26 weeks/$390.

Ralph and Paula Bosch's children: George, Marie, Edward, Harold, and Ronald. Ralph farmed and gardened.

Robert Clark, 64, was a widower. He earned $520 for 26 weeks. His brother **Elbert Clark** was 73. (They were cousins of Lon, Aida, and Ell Austin.)

John and Katherine Dunlap rented for $16 per month. John farmed and earned $360 for the year.

John and Evelyn Meiritz owned their home. He was a carpenter on the county bridge—35 weeks/$1050. Their two daughters: Evelyn Vivian and Joan Ann.

Edward and Flossie Brague owned their home. Ed was a truck driver for the County Highway—35 weeks, $800.

Bertha Ort owned her home. Her son William Jr. worked for the WPA, building the bridge—28 weeks/$431. Her daughter Florence Ort did general house work for boarding houses—$7 per week. Son John worked as a builder—34 weeks/$652. Son Milton was 17.

Edwin and Elsie LaBarr owned their home. Ed worked for the WPA building roads—25 weeks/$411.

Wellstown Road

Charles and Bertha Sullivan owned their home. He worked on the Town Highway. Bertha had summer and hunting season lodgers in their home. Ebba, their daughter, washed the dishes; Frederick was 9. **Ami Hulse**, 37, was a boarder. He drilled wells—30 weeks/$540.

William Sullivan rented. He was an ice delivery man—8 weeks/$144.

Ernest and Bessie Rollenetz owned their home. Ernest worked on a WPA project—26 weeks/$625. Bessie did general house work at a boarding house. Their daughter Helen was 5. Her daughter Betty Parker did housework for a private family—51 weeks/$300.

Jim and Cora Clark rented for $15 a month. He was the caretaker for the Excelsior Hunting Club—51 weeks/$300.

Chester and Gladys Kewley owned their home. He was a carpenter. They had a daughter Grace.

Willard Wells, 87, a widower rented. He was a lumberman. His daughter Mabel lived with him.

Attilio and Angelina Foscolo owned their home. The family had been in the same house in 1935. He had a lumber business. They also had boarders. Their children: Joseph and Yolanda.

Ernest and Georgia Horton rented at $5 per month. He worked on a WPA road project—19 weeks/285. Their children: Emaline, Ken, Madeline, Elizabeth, and Gloria.

Robert and Jane Rundle owned their home. Jane was a laundress at home. Grandchildren: Ella, Gladys, and Janet Hulse lived with them.

West Eldred

Garfield and Ella Leavenworth owned their home. He was a carpenter—10 weeks/$250. Their son James worked at a lumber mill—12 weeks/$192. **Lee and Clara Hansen** rented from her parents. He was a driller for the County Highway—28 weeks/$600. They had a young son James Didrik.

William Meyers Sr. and his wife Lottie owned their home. Bill did road work for the county—24 weeks/$453. Lottie had summer boarders. Their daughter Madelyn was 9.

Erwin and Norah Avery owned their house. Erwin farmed and cared for boarders. Their daughter **Laura McBride** (divorced) lived with them along with her children: Ken, Virginia, and Frances. Harry Frierwuth was a lodger. He worked on the farm—$120 for 40 weeks.

Charlotte Leavenworth, the primary teacher in Eldred, owned her home. She received $1,890 for 40 weeks of teaching. Her brother Martin, 54, lived with her.

Everett Kelley owned his home.

Chester Middaugh owned his home. He was 47 and widowed. He did general road work.

Clinton and Stella Leavenworth owned their home. He drove the tractor for the County Highway Department—32 weeks/$900.

Morgan and Alice Sergeant owned their home. He was a caretaker. She was a teacher.

Eldred Yulan Road

Albert and Ethel Kaese owned their boarding house. Lola his sister must have helped out with their summer boarders.

Margaret Cantwell, 73, widowed lived with her son **George**, a painter for the county highway department—35 weeks/$851.

Atwell and Frieda Bradley had a boarding business opened 26 weeks. Clinton Guenther, Frieda's son, worked for the County Highway Department.

Charles and Freida Flieger owned a boarding house. He worked as a truck driver for the county highway department—50 weeks/$1350. Their children: Arthur, 10, Catherine Josephine, 9, Dorothy Edith, 6, Charles, 4 months.

Joseph and Catherine Cantwell ran West Shore Lodge. Their children: James and Rita. Robert Gallaway was an employee/handyman—$350 for 40 weeks.

James and Mabel Parker ran Laurel Cottage. James was a carpenter on the county bridge—33 weeks/$1500. **Viola Hazen**, 76, had a lease for life.

Edith Kalbfus ran a boarding house. Her daughter **Vouletti McCann** was a hostess at the boarding house. Christopher McCann, Vouletti's son, was 7. Ross Littleton worked there.

Yulan-Barryville Road

Edward Duryea and his wife Dorothy owned their home.

Lewis and Elsie Parker Hazen ran Sunset Cottage. Their daughters: Marcella and Viola.

Reginald and Joyce Walter ran Maplecrest. They had summer boarders for 26 weeks.

1948 Eldred Class trip to Washington D.C. in 1948 Eldred Yearbook.

Ella Walter owned her home. She was 61 and widowed. She had summer boarders for 12 weeks. Her son Donald farmed.

Margaret Greening owned her home and kept summer boarders.

Jacob and Lisette Hensel ran the Colonial. Their daughters: Katherine and Helen.

Ina Owen had sons Barry and William Owen.

Charles and Selma West's children: Selma, Daniel, Ralph, Paul, and Frank. Charles drove a truck for the town and did roadwork—16 weeks/$160.

Yulan-Barryville Mail Road

John Ridley, 70, a widower was the caretaker of Wolff Lake Club. **Katie Schumacher**, 65, a widow, farmed.

Herman and Mathilde Protz ran Woodland Cottages.

Charles Blaut owned his home. He did road work for the WPA—15 weeks/$235.

Bill and Hilda Hill owned their home. He worked on the road—27 weeks/$423. Their children: Ruth, Alice, Hazel, Ernest.

George Carner, 78, widowed, was a grocer.

August and Margaret Wagermann owned their home. He worked for the highway department—34 weeks/$360. Son Louis worked road construction—12 weeks/$200.

William and Mary Wolff owned their home. He did county road maintenance—25 weeks/$400.

Alfred and Helene Wolff owned their home. He was a storeroom clerk for the County Highway Department—51 weeks/$1123. Their daughters: Amy and Arlene.

Emil and Irmgard Poel owned their home. In 1935 they lived in Brooklyn. Emil was a salesman for a brewery—52 weeks/$900. His wife had summer boarders.

Carl and Frieda Wolff owned their home. Carl worked for the County Highway Department. Their children: Clara, Robert, Herbert.

Yulan-Barryville Road

Julia Heyen, 50, a widow, owned her home. Her daughters: Marion and Betty.

Max and Anna Weltner owned their house, the same one they had in 1935.

Karl Angerstein, 59, a widower owned a boarding house valued at $40,000. Gustav Johnston was the hired hand.

Charles and Gertrude Frey ran Maple Grove Farm for 26 weeks of the year. Son Everett did roadwork for the WPA—7 weeks/$117.

Fred Nitzsche and his wife Minnie co-ran Maple Grove Boarding House with the Freys.

Meta Lass, 62, owned her home. Her family: Veronica, daughter-in-law, widowed; grandchildren: Marion, Jean, Meta, and Charles Lass.

Ed and Hazel Carroll ran Glendella. In their household: Hazel's mother, Irene Kahn, 78, widow; Harriett Mattingly, sister-in-law (worked in boarding house); and Reta niece, 14.

Barryville-Minisink Road

George Wendt and his wife Anna rented. He worked at the Erie Railroad—52 weeks/$1344. Their children: William, Richard, and Inez.

Adga and Theresa Burgess ran a boarding house. Their children: Florence and Adga Jr.

George and Leona Nieke's children: Gloria and Lorraine.

George was a track hand with the Erie Canal.

Barbara Nieke owned her home. Her son William worked for the Erie Railroad. Her sister Laura Knapp lived with them.

Gus Dasener and his wife Frieda ran a boarding house.

Mimie Rupp, 63, widowed, ran her own boarding house. Son George, was a truck driver for the town highway—24 weeks/$400. Daughter Caroline worked at a boarding house—16 weeks/$170.

William Brower and his wife Jennie rented for $10 a month. He was the toll gate keeper at the federal bridge—$960 per year. Their son William Jr. was 15.

Walter and Barbara Kramer ran a boarding house.

Barryville Monument Roads and York Lake

Ruben and Mabel Hessberger owned their home. He worked the signals for the Erie Railroad—$1,809 a year.

Ervin and Dorothy Worzel rented for $10 a month. He was a section foreman for the Erie Railroad—$1802 a year. Their children: Ervin, Robert, Arthur, Dorothy, Estelle, Kenneth, and Bruce.

Camille and Louise Nifenocker owned their home. He was a signal helper for the Erie Railroad. Louise's mother Margaret Hessberger, 77, lived with them.

Emmet Barnes Sr., 71, was a carpenter tool handle maker. His wife Agnes was 60.

Carl and Hilda Draxler owned their home. He worked for the Erie Railroad—26 weeks/$700. Their children: Carl Jr. and Hilda.

Emmet and Christena Barnes owned their home. He worked for the Erie Railroad—28 weeks/$520. They had a son John, 2.

Matthew and Hazel Vollmer owned their home. He was a carpenter and a foreman for the Erie Railroad—$2191 a year. Their children: Vera, Clara, Cecil, and Paul.

Charles and Martha Draxler owned a boarding house. Charles was a carpenter for the Erie Railroad—$800 for 40 weeks. Their daughter Martha was 23.

Harvey and Emmy Eldred had a son Harvey Jr., 1. Harvey Sr. worked for the Erie Railroad—$353 for 26 weeks.

Albert Barber worked for the Erie Railroad—$650 for 30 weeks.

Allen and Elsa Barnes owned their home. He was a laborer—16 weeks/$320.

Arthur and Eleanor Barnes owned their home. He did road work for the WPA, 20 weeks/$300.

Adolf and Dora Ahmen owned their home.

Henry and Edith Koch owned their home. He was a school bus driver for Eldred Central School—40 weeks/$850. Their children were Henry and Betsy Koch.

Louis and Mildred Warshauer ran a boarding house. Their children: William Louis and Muriel Warshauer.

Henry Dieckhoff Jr., was an engineer for the Erie Railroad.

Yulan Road

George Maunz, 60, was a salesman for florist supplies. His wife was Maude.

Lumberland

Joseph MacKechnie worked at a boys' camp.

In 1946 Irene and Art Staubes held their wedding reception at Bertram's Tavern (bought by Joe and Mary Mellan in 1947). Seated at bottom left, Julie and Art "Bucky" Bertram. Seated at the very end of that row is Gustave Staubes. Standing in the upper right corner are Alfons and Johanna Theuer. Photo courtesy of Jeanie Staubes Turner.

Sunset Tavern with unknown person. Photo courtesy of Jeanie Staubes Turner.

Daniel Gillespie, 72, was a merchant for a grocery store. Mary Stanton was assistant Postmaster.

George and Myra Ewing's sons: George R.M. Jr. and Alexander.

Russell S. MacKechnie was a caretaker for a private estate. His wife was Edith. Son Russell W. was 15.

Amandus Getz was a building carpenter. He and his wife Dorothy had a daughter Jane, 3.

Emery and Margaret Getz's children: Eleanore, Edgar, and Isabel. He was road Superintendent for the Town Highway.

Louise Weber's household: **Raymond Hallock**, nephew, 35, widower, worked on the town highways; and Raymond's children: Sherwood, Christine, Evelyn, Donald and Marjorie Hallock.

Emery and Mamie Frey owned their home. He was a janitor for a private school. Their children: Paul, John, Lester, and Lillian.

Billings Kinne was the Superintendent for a Private Estate. His wife was Julia.

Herbert Kinne was caretaker for a Private Estate. His wife was Mildred. Their son Charles was 12.

Hillside

Herman and Adelaide Kalin's household: children Reta and James; Herman's mother Ida, 67, widow. Herman was a mill hand at a sawmill.

John and Angie Van Tuyl (71, 70); daughter, **Gladys** and her husband Charles Murray and their daughter, Joyce Murray, 6. John was a farmer. Gladys was a school teacher—$1100 for 40 weeks. Charles worked on the farm.

Fred and Gertrude Doeller's daughters: Doris and Marion. Fred farmed and ran the Handsome Eddy Farm along with **Albert Fischer**, the chef.

John and Katherine Kerr were both 67. Their son Charles was 19.

Agnes Wilson, once a teacher in Eldred, was 74.

Samuel and Helen Wilson rented for $15. Eugene, 6, Jacob Wilson, 65, widowed. Samuel was an attendant at a filling station.

George and Clara Osterhout's son George, 25, worked in construction. George Sr. drove the school bus—$1,360 for 40 weeks.

Herman and Blanche Worzel's family: Ruth, 15, Herman 12, Gordon, 10, and Virginia, 5. Herman Sr. was a section foreman for the railroad.

Fannie Quick, 61, was a widow. Her son Ralph worked on Town roads.

Anna Hallock, 63, was a widow. Her household: Charles worked on the highways; Elmer and his wife Christine. Elmer was a truck operator on Town roads.

John W. Johnson was 72. His wife Ida was 71.

Walter and Edythe LaValle had a son Clayton, 2. Edythe's brother Harry Maxwell lived with them. Walter and Harry were clerks in retail grocery store.

Raymond and Emma Worzel's children: Shirley, Beatrice, and Francis. Raymond was a trackman on the railroad.

George and Helen Knight owned their home. Their children: Ross, George Jr. and James. George Sr. worked on Town roads. 🌿

Fred and Pearl Owen DeFeo. Photo courtesy of Pam Fischetti DeFeo.

Index

2nd Armored Div., 230, 233, 310
3M Company, 137
3rd U.S. Army, 305, 318, 324, 328
95th Infantry, 318, 327, 328
4th Armored Div., 305, 318, 324
5th Army, 251, 272, 274, 284, 288, 290, 291, 294, 296, 306, 307, 314
8th Air Force, 299
18th Amendment, 15, 65
19th Amendment, 15
21st Ammendment, 137
28th Infantry, 305
37th Tank Battalion, 305, 318, 323
67th Armored Regiment, 259, 310
82nd Airborne, 317
85th Infantry Division, 285, 295
100th Infantry Division, 310
101st U.S. Airborne, 305
106th Infantry, 310
807 Air Engineering, 288, 292
818 Engineer Aviation Battalion, 310
1929 Depression, 83, 84, 106, 109
1930 U.S. Census, 109

A

Abele, Mary Purcell, V
Aber, Alice M., V
Abrams, Lt. Col. Creighton, 324
Acor, Louis, 93, 438, 452
Adelaide, 17, 38, 41, 93, 106, 446
Ahmen, Adolf and Dora, 471
Aidaisms, 232
Air Group, 18, 320
Alaska, 264, 364
Albania, 195
Albrecht, Mrs., 243
Algeria, Atlas Mountains, 297
Allen, Henrietta Austin Styles, 211, 394, 395
Allies, 31, 235, 254, 289, 290, 298, 305, 328, 331
American Cross Clubmobile, 288
American South-African Steamship Lines, 173
Amoco Gas Station, 165, 173, 204
Andersen, George, 153, 154, 233, 241, 249, 291, 292, 319, 337, 363
Anderson
    Andy, 85
    Joseph, 380
    Kathryn Kornkven, 380
    Linda Guenther V, 8, 215, 261, 359, 386, 438
    Samuel, 380
Andeway, Charlotte (Lottie) Leavenworth, 18, 34, 51, 118, 145, 421
Angell
    Claude, 28, 61, 77, 81, 86, 113, 122, 126, 128, 177, 178, 445, 453
    Hazel Labarr, 28, 77, 152, 211, 227, 234
Angerman, William, 455, 466
Angerstein, Karl, 470
A&P
    1938, 194, 196, 208, 369
    Art Wilson's, 14, 107, 130, 151
Arbuckle, Fatty, 15
Arlin, Harold, 31
Arlington, 39, 41, 162, 419
Armstrong, Louis, 15
Asendorf
    Belle Boyd, 19, 104, 225, 284
    George Myers, 19, 104, 427
    Henry, 11, 18, 19, 36, 39, 93, 100, 104, 129, 145, 147, 152
    Henry and Belle Boyd, 446
Asendorf Casino, 265
Ashkenas, Irving, 169
Astor, Mary, 15
Atlantic Charter, 235
Atlantic Station, 358, 360, 460
atomic bomb, 289, 331
Attlee, Clement, 331
Aumick
    Addie, 442
    Lester, 265
    Mike, 174
Auschwitz, 255
Austin
    Aida, IV, 3, 17-9, 23-4, 27, 32-4, 62, 66, 70, 76, 79, 81, 83, 86, 122, 138, 139, 152, 162, 179, 190, 193, 206-216, 218-22, 224-8, 230-4, 236, 240, 242-255, 257-280, 294-5, 303, 316, 326, 339, 341-3, 372, 377, 390, 391, 394, 399, 401-2, 404, 406, 408, 440, 445, 453, 460
    Albert Alonzo (Lon), 2, 17-8, 20, 23, 27, 32-3, 52, 57, 64, 70-1, 75-6, 81, 82, 108, 138-9, 146, 172, 175, 179, 207-14, 216, 218-20, 222, 224-30, 232, 234, 236, 242-8, 250-5, 257, 259, 261-5, 267-8, 270, 273-8, 295, 301, 303, 325-6, 342, 343, 347, 351, 353, 362, 366, 368-70, 391, 394, 402, 403, 410, 440, 445, 453, 460
    Alden, 18, 145, 376, 377, 394
    Alma, 404
    Alonzo E. (Dr.), 18, 32, 52, 211-2, 228, 244, 246, 270, 326, 352, 370, 394, 410
    Alonzo E. (Rev.), 18, 394-5, 410
    Art and Mary Briggs, 172, 321, 334, 340, 342, 344, 347-9, 351, 354, 362, 364, 366, 368, 369, 371-2, 374-5, 379, 394, 409, 430
    Arthur, 1-3, 20, 21, 39, 45, 48, 51-2, 54, 60-2, 64, 66, 79, 83, 107, 108, 111, 113, 118, 122, 123, 138, 143-4, 150-1, 154, 160, 162-3, 171, 173-6, 200, 206, 211, 213-4, 216, 218, 221, 227, 229-30, 232-4, 236, 242-8, 250-4, 257-61, 263-5, 268-9, 271-8, 284-5, 288, 290-1, 293-6, 301-2, 304, 307, 314-5, 318, 322, 325-7, 330, 333, 335, 337, 341, 346, 353, 366, 377, 381, 388-9, 391, 403, 406-7, 450
    Augustus/Phebe Maria Eldred, 18, 376-7, 394, 416
    Beatrice (Gertie) Horton, 145
    Benjamin C., 376
    Carol J., V, 379
    Charles Arthur, V, 379, 409
    Charles Augustus, 18, 377, 394, 395
    Charles Mortimer (Mort), X, XI, 2, 11, 14, 16-8, 20-5, 27, 35, 39, 42, 47, 54, 57-60, 64,

66, 69–70, 72, 78–81, 107, 113, 126, 134, 139, 146, 148, 150–1, 154, 156–7, 161–4, 166–8, 170, 174–5, 177, 179, 217, 362, 377, 379, 391–2, 394, 405, 410, 421, 433, 445, 453
Charles Raymond, 20, 26, 45, 47, 48–9, 51, 54, 60, 62–4, 68, 70, 72–3, 79, 107–8, 111, 113, 134, 138, 145, 148, 178–81, 185, 203–4, 213–16, 251, 260, 262, 276, 279, 283, 291, 293–4, 301–4, 324, 327, 334, 338, 340, 368, 377, 379, 381, 394, 405, 408–9, 426
Charles Raymond family, 181, 211, 227, 250, 333, 336
Dory (Henry Ladore), 18, 20, 23, 60, 61, 66, 69, 81, 394, 402, 410, 433, 445
Edward, 394
Edwin M., 177, 179–81, 185
Elizabeth, 1, 2, 20–2, 25, 49, 217, 394
Emily Parmenter, 23, 40, 45, 168, 240, 333, 377, 379, 394
Emma (Edith Emogene), 23, 81–2, 394, 396, 399, 402
Fanny Knapp, 146
Frank, 127, 241
Gladys Myers, 26, 37, 45, 54, 60, 63, 68, 71, 73, 78–9, 108, 111, 138, 145, 150, 165, 176–82, 185, 213–6, 242, 251, 255, 262, 274–5, 278, 303–4, 308, 318, 327, 340, 362, 364, 368, 379, 391, 408–9, 426
Henry and Sadie LeRoy, 404
Henry (Emily's son), 23
Ira and Minerva Drake, 241, 370
Ira Austin, 6, 7, 25, 121–2, 127
James, 395
James and Julia, 396–7
James Eldred (Ell), 18, 20, 23, 24, 28, 30, 39–40, 42, 44, 45–50, 53–4, 56, 58–9, 64, 66, 69, 76, 79, 81–4, 109, 110, 135, 141–2, 146, 148, 151–2, 161, 168, 179, 200, 208, 230, 236, 240, 245, 257, 266, 273, 279, 287, 295, 377, 379, 391, 394, 402, 404
Jennie Leavenworth, X, XI, 2, 10, 14, 17–8, 20–22, 24, 25–7, 36–7, 39, 43–4, 47–9, 51, 54, 56, 60–1, 65, 66, 68, 72, 79, 107, 110, 113, 116, 120, 122, 128, 133–5, 138–9, 150–1, 154–6, 158, 160–4, 166–7, 170–1, 173, 174–6, 178, 179–84, 188–90, 192–4, 196–9, 203–4, 213, 215–7, 379, 384, 391, 393–4, 405, 421, 433, 453, 460
John Mortimer, 18, 394
Maria, 81, 394, 402
Martin van Buren, 25
Mary Ann Eldred, 56, 397
Mary Briggs, IV, V, 52–3, 86, 138–41, 143, 167, 198–9, 215, 222, 227, 258, 266, 277, 283–4, 288, 290–1, 296–7, 313, 315, 330, 334, 337, 340–2, 346, 353, 389, 425, 462
Mary Henrietta, 394
Mary Hoatson, 18, 25, 394
Mary Johnson, 18, 394
Mary Marie, V, 379, 409
Mary Millspaugh, 18, 376, 377, 394–5
Minerva Drake, 6, 7, 126–7, 437, 443, 448
Minnie Austin, 6, 7
Mortimer Bruce, 18, 376–7, 394–7
Mortimer McKinley, 9, 20–1, 24–5, 32–4, 42, 48–9, 62, 99, 207, 209, 218, 251, 394
Moses, 78
Nellie, 127, 143, 370, 461
Ralph and Fanny Knapp, 18, 20, 376, 391, 394–5
Ralph (s/o Henry and Sadie), 404
Ralph Waldo, 127, 370, 461
Robert (Bob), 1–2, 20, 39, 45–8, 51, 55, 60, 64, 66, 68, 108, 111, 113, 118, 148, 150, 167, 171–3, 180, 192, 210–1, 213, 216–7, 226–7, 236, 242, 247, 250, 252, 254, 265–6, 270, 273, 277–8, 281, 285, 290–1, 293, 297, 300–4, 306–8, 310, 315, 324, 326–8, 330, 337, 338, 377, 381, 391, 394, 405, 408–9
Sadie, 161
Samuel Knapp, 376
Stephen, 78
Wallace, 313, 337
William (Bill), 20, 27, 47–8, 51, 60, 76, 108, 111, 113, 144, 154, 170–1, 189, 211, 216, 224, 227, 230, 232, 247, 251–4, 257, 260, 262–4, 269, 270–1, 274–6, 278, 279–80, 284–6, 291, 292–5, 298, 301–2, 304, 306, 308, 310, 315, 320, 325–6, 328–30, 337, 368, 374, 377, 381, 394
William H. and Mary Ann Eldred, 18, 274, 342, 351, 368, 376–7, 394, 396, 402, 418
Austria, 145, 185, 444, 445, 457
Avery
   Arthur, 34, 35, 98, 119–20, 127, 413
   Arthur Jr., 127
   Avery Family, 35, 38, 50
   Erwin, 11, 41, 83, 93, 98, 120, 125, 136, 148, 439
   Erwin/Norah Bradley, 10, 30, 113, 116, 119, 225, 335, 413–4, 433, 444, 453, 469
   Marian Ayers, 119–20, 127
   Norah Bradley, 32, 34, 136, 371
Axis, 195, 219, 289
Ayer, Dr., 224, 246
Ayers, Olinda Austin, 394, 395

B

B-17, 333
B-29, 305
Badecker, George, 380
Baker
   AnnMarie (Ree), 401
   Clarence and Dorothy Paton, 261, 371, 377, 394, 401
   Dorothy Paton, 18, 391, 395
Baker's Business School, 108
Balaban, Emil; William, 337
Balabau, William and Anna, 445

Balmer, Rev., 22
Bank, J.P. Morgan, 15
Baque, Mr., 60–1, 64
Barber
    Clarence, 438, 455
    Herman and Isabel, 435, 454
    Irene, 185
    William and Anita, 464
Barcaw, Nellie Kendall, 276, 416
Barker, Ethel, 315
Barnes
    Allen and Elsa, 471
    Arthur and Eleanor Eldred, 447, 471
    Eleanor Eldred, 78, 98, 341
    Emmet, 313, 456
    Emmet and Christena, 471
    E.O., 68
    Ernest Barnes, 438
    J., 349
    Joe, 132
    Laverne, 243
    Perry Jr., 338, 339
Barney, Melva Austin, IV, V, 79, 108, 110–1, 122, 135, 138, 150, 162, 178–9, 181, 183, 207–8, 216–7, 221, 244, 247, 251, 252, 254, 257, 262–3, 266, 268, 270–2, 310, 316, 328, 330, 340, 362, 379, 389, 425
Barrow, Gibson and Ethel, 450
Barrymore, Ethel, John, Lionel, 15
Barryville Glass Factory, 4, 5, 14
Barryville-Shohola Bridge, 6, 209–11, 216, 221, 241, 250, 277
Barth
    Mrs., 33, 34
    Peter and Mary, 441, 445
    Peter, 37, 41
Bartle
    Franklin, 113, 166, 168, 170, 174, 181, 183, 191, 193, 265, 315, 337, 341, 344, 349, 350, 362, 364, 366, 370, 372
    Harrison, 370
    Howard, 366
    Lee (Libra) Addabbo, 341, 350, 364, 366, 370
    Mary Jane, 193
    Percy and Emily, 465

Bartok, Bela Bartok, 15
Baseball, 29, 31
    1925, 55
    Barryville Braves, 9, 147
    Detroit Tigers, 156, 335
    Hall of Fame, 195–7
    Pirates/Phillies, 31
    Red Sox, 124
    World Series, 134, 156, 168, 246, 272, 335
    Yankees, 168, 246, 327
    Yankee Stadium, 31
Batonick, Louis and Florence, 465
Battles
    Cassino, 297, 305
    Bismark Sea, 289
    Guadalcanal, 255, 268, 279
    Leyte Gulf, 305
    Midway, 255
    Normandy, 303, 307
    Okinawa, 331
    Philippine Sea, 305
    Tarawa, 289
    The Bulge, 305, 318, 323, 331
    The Rhineland, 165, 305, 336
Bauer
    Emma, 146
    Marguerite, 373
Baumgartner, William, 21, 22
Beaver Brook Road, 92, 433, 439
Beck
    Elizabeth, 11, 99
    George and Elizabeth, 410, 442
    George Jr., 447
Becker's Woods, 98, 151
Beebout, Rev. John, 344, 346, 348–9, 368
Belgium
    Ardennes, 318
    Brussels, 205, 305
Bellinger
    Brad, V
    Cynthia Leavenworth, IV, V, 208, 366, 370, 372, 381–3, 389, 424, 425
    Richard, V, 287
Bello, Frank 313
Bendix, 270
Benedict
    Carl, 37, 41, 104, 165, 451
    Wilhelmina (Minnie) Bosch, 37, 104, 109, 153, 163, 165, 242, 243, 245, 440, 446, 451
Bennett
    Betty (Bessie) Horton, 60
    Floyd, 57
    Rev. John, 36, 55, 60
Bensett, Mr. and Mrs. Wm., 243
Bente
    Dr. Herbert, 193, 242, 243, 244–5, 327, 467
    Isabel Greig Kelso Grotecloss, 16, 29, 56, 99, 134, 243, 259, 467
Beodeker, George and Johanna, 447
Berg, David, Elliott, Ivy, and Kristin Kornkven, 380
Berlin, Irving, 15
Bertram
    Arthur Jr. and Julietta, 225, 354, 363, 466, 471
    Arthur Jr. (Bucky), 163
    Arthur and Clara, 163, 186, 363, 467
    Art Sr., 225
    B. and P., 349
Bertram's Cottage/Lodge, 102, 163, 186, 225, 354, 363, 467
Bertram's Tavern, 341, 354, 363, 466, 471
Besson
    Edith Parker Pelton, 220
    Louie, 220
Beufve
    Harold and Laurette, 463
    Harold, 117
    Margaret Crawford, 177, 435, 447
    Raymond, 433, 464
Birdseye, Clarence, 31, 109
Birr
    Edith Toaspern, 8, 371, 435, 464
    John, 8, 464
Bischof/Bischof's
    Guido/Bischof's, 15, 99, 101, 133, 410, 450
    Guido and Hedwig, 466
Bisland
    Edward and Margaret, 442
    Edward, 353, 457
Bismarck (ship), 235
Black, Harold, 55
Black Lake Brook, 53

Blackman, Louis and Mabel, 440, 444
Blaut
    Charles, 449, 470
    Clarence, 313
Blauvelt, Mrs., 19
Bledsoe, Mrs., 224, 272, 330
Blue Ribbon Restaurant, 159
Bluff, 7, 8, 87, 89, 139
Boarding House Ads, 11, 41, 93, 95, 100, 129, 159, 163, 223, 225, 367
Boch, Emil, 186
Bodin(e)
    Blanche, 173, 464
    Henry and Blanche, 8, 11, 93, 438, 452
    Henry, 93, 95, 159, 446
    Justin, 8, 93
    Paul, 157, 173, 315, 337
Bodine Lake, 2, 8, 92, 93, 95, 159, 358, 446
Bodine's Cottages (Little Pond), 8, 11, 93, 95, 129, 159, 223, 438, 446
Bogart, Humphrey, 286
Bogert
    Amanda Hogencamp, 43, 63
    Edgar, Irving, Isaac, John, 43
Bohr, Niels, 15
Bohs
    Linda Leavenworth, 52, 142, 162, 381
    Norman and Linda Leavenworth, V
Borden, Sheriff Harry, 169
Borneo, 235
Bornstein, 11, 93, 367, 433, 446
    Ed and Georgiana, 93, 454
    Edward, 93, 213, 464
    Mary Oset, 93, 213, 259, 307, 358, 464
Bosch
    Charles Sr. and Helen, 441
    Charles L., 58, 137, 153, 233, 239, 259, 261, 363
    Charlie Sr., 18, 37, 58, 65, 85, 104, 109, 137, 153–4, 229, 233, 242, 258–9, 302, 316, 322, 329, 333, 410–1, 451, 466–7
    Ed and Eleanor Schroeder, 153, 157, 177, 186, 228, 233, 349
    Edward, 17, 43, 65, 85, 104, 106, 109, 113, 172–3, 193, 229, 302, 391, 410, 446, 459
    Eleanor Schroeder, 193, 322
    Elizabeth Gunstone, 259, 261
    Florence Schmerfeld, 236, 238–40, 253, 257, 261, 287, 322, 347, 365, 371
    Fred, 106, 193, 228, 233, 349, 387, 468
    Frederick and Linda, 385
    Herb, 58, 261
    Herman and Mary Horton, IV, 441, 445, 454, 460
    Herman Jr., 3, 17, 70–1, 114, 121, 125, 190, 209, 211, 219, 220, 228–9, 243, 245, 247, 254, 302, 316, 339, 445
    Herman Sr., 17, 32, 70–1, 109, 112–3, 115, 153, 191, 209, 212, 218–9, 228, 230, 242, 244, 247, 268–9, 301–3, 410
    Herman Sr. family, 211
    Karin Nielsen, 137, 153, 259, 322
    Kay, 177, 186, 228, 233
    Ken, IV, V, 371, 373, 417
    Lena Miller, 58, 63, 106, 258
    Mary Horton, 3, 17, 32, 70, 76, 78, 132, 190, 207, 209, 213, 218–20, 224, 227–9, 231, 247–8, 252–3, 257–8, 261, 267, 273, 279, 302, 339, 341
    Mary Maier, 13, 108–9, 302
    Mary van Eastenbridge, 17–8, 104, 106, 109, 153, 241, 259
    Menzo, 37, 58, 63, 106, 109, 153, 233, 259, 261, 302, 316, 437
    Ralph, 109, 153, 243, 259, 287
    Ralph and Paula Schreib, 18, 29, 104, 446, 451, 468
    Robert, 76, 113, 125, 190, 209, 211, 218, 220, 228–9, 230–1, 244, 246, 279, 302, 339, 410
    Whipple (Henry), 106, 185, 229, 233, 239, 241, 258–9, 261, 291–2, 310, 319, 337, 411, 441, 446
    Wilhelm, 11, 13, 17, 104, 108, 109, 184, 241, 259, 302, 411, 412, 440
    Wilhelm and Mary van Eastenbridge, 441, 446, 451
    William Jr., 287, 322, 373
    William (Willie), 58, 229, 233, 236, 239–40, 243, 253, 257, 259, 261, 287, 316, 322, 329, 347, 363, 371, 465
Bosch's Dairy, 191
Bosch's Pond, 17, 70, 98, 128, 136, 137
Boulder/Hoover Dam, 77
Bow, Clara, 124
Bower Road, 18, 104, 106, 154, 229, 329, 411
Bowers, Ellen, Joseph, Sarah, 380
Bower's Lumber Co., 63
Boyd
    Betty, 118, 173
    Floyd and Helen Kalbfus, 441, 450, 460
    Floyd Boyd, 211, 214, 224, 253, 254, 275, 372, 385, 443
    George, 93, 100, 104
    Helen Kalbfus, 254
    James, 78, 156, 157, 441, 445, 450
    Margaret Mills, 441, 445, 450
    William, 118, 319, 337
Boyer
    George, 193, 265
    Lulu, 177
Bozza, Ann and Peter, 367
Braddock, James J., 154
Bradley
    Atwell, 9–11, 32, 35, 38, 41, 51, 55–6, 93–6, 116, 129, 159, 170, 223, 413, 446
    Atwell and Frieda Guenther, 454, 469
    Atwell and Helen, 433
    Clarence, 10, 32, 55, 96, 313, 337, 373, 413, 454
    Clifford, 10, 55, 96, 373, 413
    Clifton, 413
    Florence, 159, 373
    Frieda Meyer Guenther, 22, 25, 55–6, 96, 373, 446
    George, 10, 55, 96, 159, 166, 204, 354, 373, 413, 464
    Georgia Anne, 294, 373
    Helen, 9, 10, 56, 413

Isaac M., 10, 13, 18, 32, 34–5, 37, 50–1, 98, 113, 116–8, 354, 413–4, 426, 453
Isaac N., 10, 32, 116, 119, 413
Jessie Tether, 10, 32, 34, 79, 83, 109, 119, 413
Joanna Brown, 10, 413–4, 426
John P., 109
Maureen, 373
Sarah Kornkven, 380
Wilhelmina Clemens, 413
Bradley/Avery House, 10–1, 30, 34–5, 38, 41, 50–1, 93, 98, 114, 116–9, 128, 130, 131, 134–6, 143–4, 151, 154, 162, 196, 225, 333, 335, 341, 346, 350, 354, 433–4, 447, 453
Bradley's Restaurant, 159, 202, 204
Brague
    Edward and Flossie, 468
    Joseph and Florence, 211, 230
    Nathaniel, 157, 166
    Nathaniel and Anna Sergeant, 451
Brandau, Carol Dunlap, V
Braun, Eva, 331
Breakey, Ralph S., 169
Breen, Anna, 437
Brett, Adelaide Parker, 109
Bridge
    Katherine, 456
    William and Mary, 448
Briggs
    Briggs family, 30, 52–3, 84, 138–40, 142, 160, 178, 211, 221, 254, 257, 330, 391, 415, 463
    Clinton Lane, 83
    H.I. (Irwin), 7, 9, 20, 25, 30, 52–3, 55, 75, 83–4, 138, 139–0, 142, 145, 160–2, 167, 170, 172, 174–5, 177–9, 181, 183, 194, 202, 211, 213–4, 216, 221, 222, 224, 226, 231–2, 236, 246–7, 254, 257, 258, 262–4, 266, 267–8, 273, 275, 284, 295, 302, 308, 310, 330, 332, 334, 339, 346, 352–3, 415, 463
    Indie Clark, 221–2
    John, 75, 86, 139–40, 143, 148, 160, 170, 172, 178, 211, 215, 222, 227, 247, 266, 332–3, 348, 415
    Myrtle Crabtree, 9, 20, 25, 52, 53, 75, 84, 139, 140, 142, 179, 211, 222, 231, 334, 346, 348, 352–3, 370
    Robert, 84
Brink
    Ervin, 341
    Laura Briggs, 139–40, 161, 176, 177, 227, 341, 349, 464
Brinkerhoff
    Don, 332
    Grace, 353
British 8th Army, 255
British Broadcasting Co. (BBC), 31, 165
British Relief, 221, 225
Britt
    John and Laura Parker, 394
    John, 19
    John Jr., 394
    Laura Parker, 19, 149, 183, 207, 213
Britton, Jack, 124
Brodeker, George and Johanna, 462
Brodmerkel
    Alberta, 322, 323
    D., 202
    Edward, 319
    Tina Bosch, 18, 83, 106, 109, 117, 145, 153, 241, 258, 302
    William, 83, 117, 145, 153, 233, 243, 258
    William and Tina Bosch, 467
Bronx Home News, 74
Brookside Farm, 41, 93, 97
Brookwood, 43, 457, 459
Brower
    Olive, 185
    Ward and Gladys, 438
    William and Jennie, 471
Brown
    H., 349
    Ida Belle Austin, 185, 395
    James and Ida Belle Austin, 394
    Lillie Sergeant, 197
    Silas and Mercy Harding, 426
Bucknell University, 173
Bulgaria, 305
Burgess
    Adga, 223, 261, 309, 313
    Adga and Theresa, 470
    Adga Jr., 337
    Florine, 206
Burma, 235
Burma Shave, 54
Burns, Theresa, 36, 38
Buser, Charles, 313
Bush, George H.W., 331
Busse
    George, 413
    Madelyn Meyers, 82, 113, 114, 126, 144, 150, 188, 200, 203, 204, 214, 298, 306, 324, 370, 413, 414, 469
Bye
    Albert, 445, 451, 467
    Alice, 77
    Frederick A., (son), 165
    Frederick and Jeanette, 467
    Fred Sr., 77, 117, 165, 445, 451
    Jeanette, 77, 165, 211, 224, 274
Byrd, Richard E. Jr., 57, 77

C

Cafe Mozart Restaurant, 257
Cailloux
    Mathilde, 136, 383, 384
    Mr. and Mrs. Cailloux, 136, 325, 383
    Pierre, 136
    Pierre and Suzanne, 383, 384
California
    Berkeley, 31
    Desert Training, 285, 286
    Los Angeles, 42
    Mojave Desert, 285
    San Diego NAS, 306
    San Francisco, 42, 150, 265, 291, 331
Calkin/Calkins
    Alonzo, 350, 370
    Burt, 23, 42, 44–5, 49, 50, 53, 141, 169, 177, 185, 189, 230, 236, 271, 377, 378–9, 394
    Dale, 23, 40, 44–5, 53, 84, 141, 145, 157, 295
    Dale and Nellie Hill, 287, 368, 378–9, 394
    Elias, 350
    Hannah, 40, 46, 230
    Harriet, 449

Ida Bridge, 448, 462
Lillie Austin, 23, 28, 39–40, 42, 44–50, 53–6, 59, 64, 69, 82, 141–2, 145, 168, 185, 189, 200, 210–1, 213, 216, 227, 230, 234, 236, 240, 243, 254, 271, 273, 294–5, 350, 368, 377–8, 394, 404, 418
Maria Gardner, 18, 29, 350, 436
Neal, 368, 378, 379
Nellie Hill, 141, 145, 157
Oliver and Maria Gardner, 416
Raymond Jr., 313
Robert (Bob), 157, 368, 378–9

Callahan
Pete, 98, 117, 346
Peter and Anna, 454, 464

CalShip, 235, 245, 255

Campbell
Armanda and Martha, 438
Emma, 447
Harry, 437, 455
John, 435
Mrs. Ella G., 109
Napoleon, 437, 455
Russell, 337
Tracy, 435
Walter, 174, 193, 265, 319, 337
Walter and Katherine, 463

Camp Dalinque, 34
Camp Upton, 253, 254, 263, 407

Canada
Québec, 289, 305
Canadian Army, 210, 213, 265

Cannon, James, 370
Cantor, Eddie, 15
Cantwell, 38
Chef, 29
George, 97, 446, 454, 469
John, 315, 337
Joseph, 97, 186, 223, 367
Joseph and Catherine, 469
Margarite, 29, 41, 93, 95, 97, 103, 159, 446, 454, 463, 469

Capone, Al, 15, 83
Carbon-14, 205
Carlson, Carl and Henrietta, 454
Carmeci, Anthony Sr., 319
Carmichael, 410
Decator/Phebe Linkletter, 416
Floyd D., 416
Lewis/Mary Bunce, 376, 416

Zophar/Sarah Eldred, 416
Carnarvon, Lord, 31
Carner
George, 179, 470
George and Alice, 435, 449
Carpenter, Mrs. Myron, 55
Carroll
Dennis J., V, 356, 358
Edward and Hazel, 92–3, 129, 437, 470, 448
E.H. Carroll, 93, 223
Carter
Howard, 31
James Jr., 331
Casablanca, 289
CBS, 172, 189
Chamberlain, Neville, 177, 185, 219
Chanute Field, 270–1
Chaplin, Chaplin, 15, 219
Chiang Kai-Shek, 289
China, 31, 68, 75, 109, 117, 137, 156, 177, 180, 195, 205, 219, 255, 289, 331
Chinese Communist Party, 117
Hong Kong, 235
Nanking, 177
Chinese Restaurant (Yulan), 159
Chocolate chip cookie, 109
Churches
Congregational, 3–4, 9, 10, 13, 16, 36–7, 46, 55, 60, 73, 111, 127, 131, 144, 165, 178, 193, 242, 244, 246, 264, 333, 350, 361, 374, 390, 436
Ladies' Aide, 124, 167
Lutheran, 4
Methodist, 3–4, 14, 20, 22, 30, 43, 53, 63, 69, 70, 84, 90, 108, 109, 111, 121, 126, 137, 138, 139, 140, 156, 167, 177, 179, 192, 194, 199, 212, 214, 218, 224, 227, 231–2, 234, 240, 245–6, 250, 258, 263–4, 268, 273, 276, 296, 302, 333, 339, 340, 344, 348, 353, 368, 369, 374, 390, 463, 466
St. Ann's, 303
St. Anthony's Catholic, 4
St. Bernardine Catholic, 4
St. Jacobi, 371
Churchill, Winston, 195, 205, 219, 232, 235, 255, 289, 305, 328,

331
Civilian Conservation Corps/C.C.C., 128, 137, 146, 148–9, 167, 300
Clancy, Viola Guenther, 23, 55, 97, 177, 373, 446, 454
Clark
Carolyn Hallock, V, 373
Carrie Bogert, 43, 227, 241, 426
Clark brothers, 201, 245, 247
Elbert, 214, 267, 394, 441, 445, 453, 468
Ellsworth, 394
Ernest, 9, 43, 183, 188, 228, 247, 426, 432, 456, 459
Eunice Hallock, 9, 43, 75, 158, 160, 165, 188, 194, 199, 228, 301, 308, 426, 456
Garrett and Catharine VanAhstal, 426
George and Harriet Covert, 82, 177
George Case, 426
George Case and Mary Harding Brown, 353
George James, 157
George Malcome, 114
Hope Tinn, 333
Irvin and Laura Austin, 370, 377, 394
James and Cora Cox, 426, 440, 446
James C., V
James, 273
James Joseph, 333
Jim and Cora, 449, 469
John and Carrie Bogert, 452, 457
John Henry, 353, 426
Laura Austin, 376
Lt. Gen. Mark W., 314
Martin Dominick, 157
Mary Costello, 157
Mary Weisshaar, 318, 324, 338–9, 341, 349, 351, 358, 364, 366
Mercy Harding Brown, 43, 426
Orville, 43, 113, 160, 181, 182, 188, 191, 199, 203, 212, 214, 219, 228, 234, 241, 246, 248, 251–3, 268, 269, 276, 280, 292–3, 298, 312, 315, 318, 337, 338–9, 341, 351, 358,

424
    Patsy, 65, 69
    Robert, 76, 214, 370, 394, 441, 445, 451, 468
    Thomas W. and Phebe Hazen, 426
    Vernon, V, 113, 147, 160, 188, 194, 199–01, 219, 248, 251–2, 268, 303, 314–5, 329, 335, 349–51, 456
Classen, Bernard/Hilda, 434, 445
Click, Marnette Hart, V, 185, 376, 416
Clinton
    Henry and Net Austin, 394
    Net Austin, 396
Cloud, Sue Horton, V
Clouse
    August, 436
    E., 202
    Elsie Parker, 241, 244
    Emma Wagner, 145, 439, 451
    F., 202
    Frankie, 182
    Fred and Emma, 9, 448, 462
    George, 319, 337, 363
    Herman/Veronica, 101, 441, 444, 450, 466
    Herman Clouse family, 101–2
    Herman Jr., 337
    Herman L., 353
    Herman Sr., 101, 317, 319
    Jacob V. Clouse, 145
    Joseph, 157, 173, 265, 313, 337
    Katherine, 203
    Mrs. William, 211, 227
    Ralph, 113, 319
    Raymond, 9, 165, 173, 241, 244, 313, 337
    Theodore, 319, 337
    Veronica Clouse Jr., 261
    Veronica Pope Sr., 303
    William, 117, 145, 466
    William and Maude, 450
Clouse Brothers' store, 91
Cobb, Ty, 15, 197
Cold Spring Farm, 11, 92–3, 128, 223, 433
Cole, Mrs., 42, 49, 50, 79
Coleman, Ronald, 124
Collins
    Annie, 22

    Emma Kelso, 57, 59, 70, 73, 75, 76, 80, 434, 445
    James and Isabella, 22
    Robert, 22, 66, 69, 70, 80–1, 117
    Thomas, 9, 22, 410, 434
Collins Road, 2, 17, 22, 57, 69, 70, 71, 102, 151
Colonial, 38, 77, 93–6, 109, 129, 159, 196–7, 204, 223, 260, 309, 345–9, 454, 470
Colorado, Dunton, 34
Colville
    Charles, 10–1, 42–3, 413, 432, 435
    Leslie, 413
    Lottie Bradley, 10, 32, 35, 42, 50, 116, 119, 127, 413, 435, 446, 449
computer invented, 109
Comstock, 135
    Gordon, 157, 173, 313, 462
concentration camps, 185, 195
Connecticut
    Ansonia; Waterbury, 276
    Bridgeport, 265
Connor
    Connor family, 116, 131, 168, 170, 192, 200, 314
    Hazel Sergeant, 29, 43, 77, 82, 113, 116, 118, 123, 131, 137, 144, 167–8, 170, 178, 189–90, 192–3, 295, 308, 314, 342, 350, 358, 372, 429
    Marion, V, 77, 113, 123, 144, 150, 178, 358, 429
    Marjorie, 43, 113, 123, 144, 150, 166, 178, 429
    Walter, 29, 43, 77, 113, 123, 144, 178, 358, 429
Consiglio
    Donald Consiglio, 177
    Mildred Rixton, 177
Conway, John, II, V, 5, 19, 169
Cook, Mr., 215
Coolidge, Calvin, 31, 42
Coonskin (C. Bosch), 104, 154, 411
Cordes, Arthur, 313, 337
Corkscrew Road, VIII, 8, 87, 89, 91, 105, 169, 332
Cornell University, 16, 83, 400
Counts, Brandon, 380
Coursen, Bill and Walt, 55

Coutant, Charles D., 117
Covart, Beatrice, 22
Covert, Fred and Anna, 464
Cox
    Joseph and Julia Wilson, 443
    Mrs., 46
    William and Mary, 451
Coyne Electrical School, 127
Crabtree, 52
    Ida Emily Higginson, 370
    John and Ida Higginson, 53
Crail, Ed, 68–9, 113, 125–6, 138, 453
Crandall
    Carol, 384
    Clifford and Mary Myers, 284–5, 353, 371
    Clifford D., 285, 299, 300, 326, 327, 329, 384, 467
    Clifford Family, V
    Clifford Sr., 55, 64, 120, 137, 173, 196, 241, 242, 245, 247, 287, 299, 300–1, 310, 315, 319, 326, 327, 337, 427
    David, 22, 43, 49, 77, 432, 444
    Elizabeth, 371, 384
    George and Jennie Crawford, 385, 432, 445, 449, 460
    George Crandall (h/o Jennie), 43, 49, 193, 202, 231, 252
    George (s/o Clifford), V, 353, 384
    Jennie Crawford, 23, 49, 202–3, 210–13, 219, 231, 240, 245, 252–3, 258, 266, 273, 327, 385, 410, 461
    Ken and Emma, 454
    Ken Crandall Jr,. 113, 114
    Ken Crandall Sr., 113, 115, 118, 266
    Lawrence, 92, 128, 137, 454
    Lawrence and Matilda, 433
    Leonard, 315, 337
    L.G., 93
    Mary Myers, 11, 36, 43, 72, 82, 157, 173, 179, 241–2, 245, 284, 286–7, 299, 300, 326–7, 329, 384, 427
    Matilda, 223, 464
    Milton, 465
    Nellie Simpson, 55, 137, 211, 230, 236, 242, 244, 257–8,

280, 322–3, 327, 385, 444, 451, 457
  Robert (h/o Nellie), 55, 434
  Robert (Ken's brother), 113, 115
  Sarah Ida Clark, 43, 432
  Stanley, 55, 120
Crawford
  Elvina, 432
  Joan, 15
  Joel and Maud, 432
  Seely, 127
Crawford Road, 13, 82, 114, 132, 182, 247, 432
Crellin, Doctor, 353, 410
Crispell, Mr., 141
Cross, Guernsey T., 22
Crowe, Mrs. James, 55
Cuddeback
  Ann Eliza Gardner, 18, 193, 350
  Family, 375
  lawyer, 216
  Louis, 193, 416
Curtiss
  Agnes Darling, 18, 63, 236, 384, 427
  Charlotte, 63
Curtiss, PW-8, 42
CWA (Civil Works Administration), 138, 142
Czechoslovakia, 185, 195

D

Daiber
  Frank Jr., 113, 123, 172, 287
  Frank and Raola, 113, 188
  Lillian, 113, 123
  Raola Kelley, 115, 121, 155, 156, 157, 172, 203, 429, 430
Dailey
  Hipe, 410
  Hiram, 432
  Nate, 66, 71, 72, 75
  Nathan and Ethel, 439
Daladier, Premier, 185
Dali, Salvador, 15
Daniels, Lorraine West, V
Dankwardt, Barney, 319, 337
Darling
  Amelia, 451
  Charles, 18, 63, 384, 427
  Charlotte (Lottie) Myers, 18, 24, 36–7, 63, 236, 329, 353, 384, 427
Darriensecq, Henri, 11
Dasener, Gus and Frieda, 223, 471
Dassori, Charles, 20
Daub, Carl and Naomi, 462
Davies, Clara Hughes, 38, 41, 446
Davis, Bette, 124
Dawes Plan, 42
Day, Robert and Thalia, 442
Daylight Saving Time, 253
D-Day (Operation Overlord), 305, 307
Deats
  Mary Grace Nelson, 137
  William, 140, 141, 176, 224, 264, 303, 437, 462
  William and Mary Nelson, 436
Dede
  Ida Clinton, 394
  J., 349
Deer Head Lodge (Eggers'), 11, 38, 41, 93, 100, 102–3, 129, 163, 225, 309, 345–6, 367, 451
Deer View Lodge, 354, 355
DeFeo
  Fred Jr., 43, 94, 152, 310, 312, 315–7, 319, 323, 370, 444
  Fred Sr., 8, 43, 93, 152, 261, 312, 316, 323, 437
  Pam Fischetti, V, 370
  Pearl Owen, 8, 43, 58, 93, 147–8, 150, 152, 164–5, 166, 227, 261, 312, 316, 323, 432, 437, 446, 472
DeGaulle, Charles, 205, 289
Deissler, Adeline, 107
De Laval Company, 306
Delaware View Inn, 11, 38, 41, 92–3, 345
DeMille, Cecil B., 15
Democrats, 123, 205, 308
Dempsey
  Jack, 15, 68, 154
  Restaurant, 342
Dennehy, Mrs. M.J., 37, 41, 93, 100, 102, 104, 129, 163, 445
Derheimer, Jess, 113, 115
DeSilvey, Ralph, 410
DeValera, 283
DeVenoge, Dr. Leon, 19, 104, 411
Devine, Peter and Geraldine, 435
Devireaux, Herbert and Ruth Colville, 42, 413, 449
Devlin, John, 337
Dewey, Lottie, 227
  Mr., 224, 227
  Thomas E., 169
Dewitt, H.C., 243
D&H Canal, 5, 32, 109, 374
Dieckhoff
  Henry, 373, 471
  Henry and Reka, 436, 447
Disney
  Roy and Walt Disney, 31
  Walt Disney, 31, 177, 205, 219
Distinguished Flying Cross, 303, 311
Dixon, Joe and Linn, 147
Dobbs
  George, 117
  Gladys Avery, 34, 98, 117, 119, 413
Dodgson, Mrs., 50
Doeller, 74
  Fred Doeller, 7, 8, 91–2, 456, 472
  Gertrude Doeller, 91, 456, 472
Dolan, Margaret, 193
Donaldson, Thomas, 315
Donovan, Ruth Ann Wilson, V, 303, 350, 358
Dorney, Mary Agnes Wilson, V, 261, 350, 358, 359
Dorsett, Joan Hill, 137, 160, 251, 276, 346, 430
Douglas, Dr. and Mrs., 19, 185, 209
Downey
  Dorothy, 193
  Rose, 243
Downing, Florence Ort, 324
Doyle
  Betty Ann Mulvihill; Chris, V
Drake family, 184
Draxler
  A., 349
  Carl and Hilda, 471
  Charles and Martha, 8, 38, 78, 97, 182, 185, 223, 385, 386, 447, 455, 471
  Elsa, 38
  Martha, 182
Drew Seminary, 30, 52–3
Drum

Burton, 419
Charles and Dorothy Hickok, 418, 419
Dubois place, 248
Duchess of Bedford, 291
Dugan Bakery, 321
Dunlap
  Buddy, 215
  Carl, 113, 120, 163, 261, 313, 315, 337
  Charles, 113–4, 127, 146, 163, 263
  Charles and Selma, 434, 441, 445, 452, 465
  Dorothy, 113, 155
  Evaline, 25
  George and Elizabeth Eldred, 416
  H., 202
  Harold, 47, 55, 66, 146, 163, 168, 196, 246–7, 458
  Harry, 165, 168, 444, 453
  Harry and Evaline, 434
  Isabelle, 143, 144–5
  John, 113, 125, 132, 144, 154, 168, 170–1, 176, 194, 211, 214, 248, 275, 371–2, 434, 452, 468
  Katherine, 170, 194, 211, 214, 249, 271, 275, 279, 468
  Leslie, 145, 173
  Maggie, 39, 41, 43, 145, 146, 434
  Oliver, 120, 143, 166, 171–2, 201–3
  Oliver and Margaret, 465
  Oliver Sr., 146
  Selma, 113, 163, 172–4, 178
  Walter, 145, 146
Dunlap's Restaurant 197
Dunlop, Robert H., 303
Durr, Katherine, 435, 463
Duryea
  Edward, 337
  Edward and Dorothy, 469
Dutch East Indies, 137, 235
Dwyer, Anna, 38

E

Eadie, Verna Crandall, 55, 242, 467
Eagle House, 37, 41
Earhart, Amelia, 77, 127
earthquake, 128, 156, 195
Eastman Gaines, 20
Ebers, Karl, 387–8
ECCE Bed & Breakfast, V
Echo Hill House, XI, 10–1, 14, 26, 37, 98, 110, 112, 122, 125, 135, 175, 191, 201, 206, 214, 220, 240, 284, 345, 349, 383
Eckhart/Eckhart's, 141, 360, 361
  Albert and Anna, 448
  Charles and Annie Beyer, 361
  Herbert and Kathryn, 360–1, 448, 462
  Lewis, 173, 313, 337, 360, 462
  Mary Kerr, 173, 360, 361
eclipse, 46, 125, 268
Eden, Anthony Eden, 185
Ederle, Gertrude, 124
Edsal, Margo Austin, 404
Edwards, John and Ruth, 241
Edward VIII, 165
Eggers
  Karl, 93, 129, 309, 345, 367
  Karl and Elsie, 102, 445, 451, 467
Eggers and Rothenback, 11, 38, 41
Egypt, 31, 43, 219
Ehrets, Warren, 337
Eichmann, Adolf, 195
Eiffel Tower, 324–5, 383–4
Einstein, Albert, 15
Eisenhower, Dwight, 255, 288, 289, 331, 381, 422
El Alamein, 255
Eldred
  Abraham Mulford, 37, 287, 416
  Alfred, 231, 416
  Almira Barnes, 416
  Benjamin Franklin, 18, 145, 416
  Bertha Hill, 18, 55, 416
  C.C.P., 16, 265
  C.C.P. and Effa Van Tuyl, 276, 416
  Cecil, 78
  Cecil and Hazel Crawford, 341
  Charles C., 376
  Charles (s/o Harvey), 287, 341
  Cora Hardcastle, 370, 416
  Cora Sisson, 9, 182, 185, 416
  Delia Post, 416
  Elizabeth Hardcastle, 37, 373, 416
  Elizabeth Wheeler, 416
  Eliza Post, 9, 16, 25, 27, 29, 137, 145, 177, 416, 434
  Elsie, 78
  Emmy Draxler, 38, 97, 182, 185, 287, 416, 447, 455
  Frances Payne, 109
  George Ely, 9, 18, 416
  George W., 18, 25, 137, 145, 181, 331, 416
  George W. and Marietta West, 185, 371
  H., 349
  Hannah Hickok, XI, 14, 18, 20, 376, 396, 418–9, 420
  Harvey and Emma Draxler, 376, 471
  Harvey Jr., 287, 341, 376
  Harvey Sr., 18, 78, 97, 182, 185, 287, 341, 376, 416, 434
  Herbert, 9, 16, 18, 25, 27, 29, 137, 145, 181, 185, 341
  James I, 14, 16, 18, 20, 127, 162, 193, 208, 299, 375, 376
  James and Hannah Hickok, 418
  James and Polly V. Mulford, 416
  James Daniel, 416
  James Eldred 1830 house, 98, 210, 326, 327
  James (s/o George W.), 371, 416
  John Franklin, 18, 145, 376, 416
  Lewis Laforde, 9, 18, 25, 77, 78, 182, 185, 416
  Lisa Crane, 416
  Minnie Sears, 18, 376, 416
  Orvis, 18, 127, 157, 376, 416
  Polly Mulford, 18, 127, 375, 376, 391, 436
  Rebecca, 416
  Richard O., V, 157, 376, 416
  Ronald C., 416
  Selma Myers, 157, 376, 416
Eldred-Austin Cousins, 18, 377, 391, 396, 399
Eldred Cemetery, 14, 24–5, 81, 99, 120, 181, 232, 248, 295, 302, 339, 402, 405
Eldred High School, 44–5, 54, 61, 68, 79, 83, 106–7, 109, 112, 127, 137, 147, 152, 155, 157, 165, 173, 206, 221, 222, 252,

264, 277–8, 287, 334, 354, 370, 388, 390, 459, 464, 471
El Dorado Yearbook, 167, 278, 297
Eldred Post Office, 3, 130, 138, 231, 236, 258, 266, 268, 270, 271, 281, 388
Eldridge
   Bill and Jane Pochet, 358
   Charles, 113, 121, 259, 265, 280, 295, 315, 337, 338, 339, 347
   Florence Bloom, 348
   Jane Pochet, 346, 351, 358, 364, 366
   William, 113, 121, 259, 279, 280, 295, 317, 318, 337, 346
   William Henry, 162
Eliot, T.S., 15
Ellington, Duke, 15
Empire State Building, 108–9, 115, 117
England
   Liverpool, 195
   London, 53, 66, 109, 195, 200, 219, 283, 323, 339
      1939 children, 195, 200
   Mendlesham, 299
   Thursley, 266
England General Hospital, 306, 324
Eniwetok, 308, 311
Erie Railroad, 4, 96, 133, 184, 347, 356
Ernst
   Agnes Hill, 35, 36, 37, 165
   Edward and Agnes Hill, 429
   Louisa, 438
Ether
   Helen Ether, 34
   Rev. Fidor, 22, 25, 37
Ethiopia (Abyssinia), 157, 165
Ewart
   Albert and Edith Palmer, 55, 63, 421
   Edith Palmer, 55, 63, 303
   Elliott, 55, 379, 421
   Rolland and Rhoda Crean, 63, 379, 421
   Vera Jones, 55
   Victor, 241, 421
   Willard, 379, 421
Ewing
   George and Myra, 472
   Grace, 457

F

F4U Corsair, 205
F6Fs (Hellcats), 311
Fairbanks, Douglas, 15
Fake, Dr., 273
Federal Unemployment Act, 137
Fehling, Fred, 155
Feigenhiemer, Otto and Bertha, 463
Ferguson
   Anna Eldred, 27, 29, 137, 145, 416
   Benjamin, 29
Fermi, Enrico, 289
Ferncliff Lodge, 11, 99, 101, 133, 367, 450, 466
Fierro, R., 349
Finland, 195, 205, 305
Fischer/Fisher
   Albert, 7, 91, 456, 472
   Fischer & Doeller, 41, 92, 93, 129
   Joyce, 373
Fish, Edward and Margaret, 437
Fitzgerald, F. Scott, 15
Fitzgibbons
   David and Lillian Webb, 427
Fleiger/Flieger
   Arthur, 294, 449
   C., 349
   Catharine, 435, 449
   Charles, 117, 449
   Charles and Freida Guenther, 159, 469
   Christianna Livingstone, 12, 43, 329, 333, 430
   Dorothy, 294
   Flieger Family, 13
   Freida Guenther, 23, 55, 373
   John, 313, 337, 449
   Lillian Piatt, 241
   Ron, V
   William and Christianna (Chris) Livingstone, 429
   William and Lillian Piatt, 430
   William Jr., 12, 43, 241
   William Sr., 12
Fleming, Alexander, 15, 297
Flood, Marcella, 26–8, 112, 126

Florida
   Camp Murphy, 272
   Pensacola Naval Air Station, 294
   Floyd Bennett Field, 286
Fluhr, George J., V
Flynn, Raymond, 193
FM-2s (old Wildcat), 311
Football
   American League, 15
   Cardinals, 272
   NFL Championship Game, 219
   New York Giants, 134
   Rose Bowl, 31
   Washington Redskins, 219
Ford, Gerald R., 331
Forestal, James, 303
Forman, Laura, 42, 49, 50, 79
Forrest, Kieferle, 337
Forster, Robert, 129
Foscola
   Attilio, 163
   Attilio and Angelina, 225, 469
   Joseph, 174, 265, 317, 337
Foscola's Hunting Lodge, 163, 225
Foster
   Albert, 358
   Charles, 113, 142, 144, 152, 158, 161–2, 193, 268, 295
   Darren, V
   Dorothy Knecht, V, 287
   Doug, 157
   Flora, 241
   George, 157
   George and Jennie Hallock, 121, 372, 434
   Iva Eldridge, 137, 157, 308
   Kathleen Louise Baker, V, 371
   Perry, 150, 162, 164, 287, 441, 445, 451, 467
   Roy, 136
Four
   Emile, 154, 155, 162–3, 172, 192
   Marcel, 162, 192, 317
Frace
   Charles, 121
   Mrs., 121
Fracke
   F., 349
   Fred and Kathryn, 444
   Fred, 173, 363, 457, 460

Herman, 117, 173
Fraley, Harold, 27
France
    Asniere, 30, 37, 75
    Bastogne, 305
    Bourget Airport, 74, 308
    Champs-Élysées, 308
    Dunkirk, 205
    Dun-Sur-Meuse, 33–4
    Hotel D'Angleterre, 34
    Hôtel des Invalides/Musée de l'Armée, 33
    Le Harve, 343
    Marseilles, 310
    Metz, 318
    Omaha Beach, 305
    Paris, 15, 32–4, 42, 59, 68, 74–5, 127, 136, 177, 185, 205, 255, 295–6, 305, 308, 325, 326, 343–4
    Romagne-sous-Montfaucon, 34
    Verdun, 34
    Vichy, 255
    Villacoublay Air Base, 308, 310, 324–5
    Viroflay, 295–6, 325–6, 339
Franco, Francisco, 165
Frank, Anne, 305
Frank's Diner, 361
Fream, Donald and Warren, 337
Freeman, Fred, 435
Freud, Sigmund, 15
Frey
    Charles and Gertrude, 25, 87, 332, 443, 447, 470
    Charles, 90
    Christopher, V, 87–91, 353
    Emery and Mamie, 442, 457, 472
    Everett, 25, 174, 177, 313, 337
    Everett and Mary Ann Osborn, 353, 371
    Gertrude, 25, 87, 88, 90, 332, 443, 447
    Thomas, 371
Frier, Doc, 236
Frint
    Harold, 211, 213–5, 227, 234, 245, 250, 253, 255, 257, 259, 267–8, 273, 280
    Ruth Parker, 77, 101, 210–14, 228, 234, 245, 257, 261, 264, 280, 450, 466
Frisbie, Kathy Hulse, V
Fuller, Merle, 303

G

Gaete
    Ricardo; Tania Leigh, V
Gainer, Robert, 438
Gandhi, Mohandas, 31, 195, 289
Garbo, Greta Garbo, 15
Gardner
    Edna, 7, 18, 140, 213, 299, 303, 348–9, 416, 435, 443, 447, 463
    Ella Breen, 7, 213, 416
    James E. and Rebecca Rider, 416
    James K. and Eliza Eldred, 29, 193, 350, 416
    James K., 7, 18, 299, 303, 348, 350, 416, 435, 443, 447, 463
    Kate McElroy, 18, 373, 416, 435, 447, 463
    Louisa McElroy, 416
    Stephen St. John, 350, 416
    Stephen St. John and Louisa McElroy, 303
    Susan, 18, 436, 448
Gari River, 298
Gedeone, Anna Gedeone, 21
Gehrig, Lou, 15
Geier
    Elizabeth, V
    Joan Austin, V, 138, 145, 150–1, 178–9, 183, 192, 194, 203, 216–7, 262–3, 290, 318, 330, 340, 362, 364, 366, 379, 409, 425
    Walter, V, 290, 300, 306, 327, 408, 409
Geiger, C., 349
Geisler
    Charles, 337, 459
    Mr., 12, 265
    Mrs., 266
    Otto, 438
Genegal, Johnny, 147
General Electric, 57, 265, 306
Gentes
    C., 349
    George, VI 31, 165, 177, 195

German Hotel, 124, 440
Germany
    Berlin, 15, 165, 195, 305, 331
    Crailsheim, 310
    Hyperinflation, 31
Gershwin, George, 15, 157
Gettysburg Battle (75th ann.), 185
Getz
    Amandus and Dorothy, 472
    Betty MacIntyre, 341, 346, 370, 430
    Edgar, 317, 341, 346, 370
    Eleanor, 303
    Elmer, 313
    Emery and Margaret Weber, 346, 472
    Frank, 457
    Frank and Hannah, 442
Gibbs, William Henry, 5
Gibney, Mrs. Jos. P., 93, 104
Gibran, Kahlil, 15
Gibson
    James, 109
    Karen M., V
    Mabel Austin, 18, 109, 376–7, 394–5, 400
    Robert, 376
Gieselman, Arthur, 456
Gilbert, John, 124, 333
Gilbert Islands, 289
Gillespie, Daniel, 370 457, 472
Gilmore
    Eugene Jr,. 319
    Gilmore family, 101–2
Girl Scouts, 167
Gish
    Dorothy, 15
    Lillian, 15, 101, 133
Givens, Bill, 147
Glass Factory, 4–6, 14, 82, 140, 436
Glendella, 92–3, 129, 204, 223, 350, 448, 470
Goddard, Robert, 15, 57
Goetke, Anthony J., 317
Golden Gate Bridge, 177
Gone with the Wind, 165, 205, 289
Google, Barney, 124
Gordon, Herb, 249, 363
Gothard
    Alan, V, 165
    Esther/Peggy Hill, 142, 145, 165, 259, 280, 295, 346, 429,

430, 459
William, 429
Governor's Island, 26
Grace, Mr., 4
Graf
   Henry and Elsie, 441, 446, 450
   Henry, 93, 100, 102, 121, 128, 129
Grand Ole Opry, 57
Grand Vue, 11, 93, 223, 358, 367, 446, 454, 464
Gray, Mrs., 242
Great Lakes Illinois Training, 275
Greece, 219, 231, 235, 305
Green Acres/Green Meadows, 106, 153, 157, 184, 186–7, 225, 236, 238–40, 257, 309, 322, 365, 367, 391, 412
Green and Gold, 145, 155
Greening
   Margaret, 9, 438, 449, 470
   William and Bessie, 444, 454
Greer, Charles and Lillian, 454
Gregory
   Amelia Bradley Leavenworth (Thomas), 18, 32, 34, 50–1, 116, 118–9, 379, 413, 421
   Charlie and Nora, 18, 51, 413
   Eber, 18, 34, 118, 413
Greig
   Bennett, 16, 25
   Kate, 16, 99, 441, 444, 451
   Mrs. Robert, 165, 168
   Robert, Sarah, 16
Greig's, 11, 16, 99, 150, 410, 417
Grey, Zane, 124
Griffin, Charles, 448
Grinnell, Edgar, 36–7
Grollimund, D., 349
Grotecloss
   Bennett, 99, 259, 317
   Edward III, V, 16, 99, 134, 259, 261, 317, 337, 363, 417
   Edward Jr., 16, 29, 99, 441
   Robert, 99, 259, 303, 304, 317, 327, 337
Guadalcanal, 255, 268, 279
Guam, 305, 331
Guenther
   Clinton J. Jr., 303
   Clinton Joseph, 23, 55, 97, 241, 261, 303, 373

Joseph Guenther Sr., 22, 23, 25, 56
Marion Lass, V, 23, 29, 63, 241, 261, 303
Mrs. J., 9
Guerard, Marie Therese, 136, 383, 384, 425
Gugel,
   Andy, 367
   Game Farm, 367
Gulf Oil, 60, 62, 64, 68
Gutfruend, Dr. Joseph, 66, 98, 113, 115–6, 118–9, 121, 146, 160, 174, 182, 244, 453, 457

H

Haas
   Berniece Wells, V, 77, 82, 184, 298, 315, 326, 341, 371
   D., 202
   Darlene Sutherland, V, 358
   Donald, 184, 370
   Doris, 184
   Harry, 184, 259, 298, 315, 326, 337, 371
   Katherine Hensel, 25, 341, 358
   Louise, 63, 184
   Marion, 184, 332
   Maurice, 184, 259, 261, 317, 337
   Richard and Louise, 259, 443, 454, 465
   Richard, (Dickie), V
   Richard F., 63, 184, 259, 317, 329, 337
   Richard E., (Sr.) 63, 147, 184, 362
Haas' Orchard, 144, 354
Hadden
   Henry, 169
   Malcolm, 50
Hainzl
   Frank, 223, 256, 257, 309
   Frank and Anna Hainzl, 256
Haiti, 19
Hale
   Dorothy Calkin, IV, V, 23, 40, 44–6, 49, 50, 53, 58–9, 70, 83–4, 135, 141, 152, 185, 189, 230, 234, 236, 242, 271, 295, 368, 379, 394
   Raymond, 185, 189, 230, 236,

242, 271, 379, 394
Hallock
   Anna Buchanan, 158, 184, 206, 273, 472
   Charles, 158
   Christina Ott, 160, 193, 252, 303
   Daniel, 17, 32, 410, 434
   Don, 414
   Doris Estler, 303, 341
   Douglas, 145, 157, 160, 272, 301, 308, 459
   Edgar, 158, 165
   Edna Hill, 29, 36, 37, 165
   Eileen Wolff, 151, 157, 338, 358, 360, 414
   Elmer, 158, 165, 193
   Emily Knecht, V, 145
   Emma Schwab, 29, 63
   Eugene, 317
   Evelyn, 160, 353
   F., 202
   Gene, 166, 337
   Hazel, 166
   Howard, 165
   JoAnn, 414
   John, 341, 373
   John Merlin, 158, 165, 460
   Marge, 160
   Mary Schwarz, 55, 157–8, 165, 456
   Oliver Blizzard, 29, 37, 166
   Oliver L., 29, 43, 158, 165, 166, 303, 385, 386, 429
   P., 202
   Raymond, 55, 157–8, 160, 165, 456, 472
   Robert C., 166, 303, 317, 337, 341
   Samuel Jesse and Anna Hallock, 55, 432, 456
   Samuel Jesse, 158, 165
   Sherwood, 55, 160
   Tina, 329
   Wilbur, 158, 165
   William and Mary Brodt, 32, 37
Halpin
   Edward, 427
   Frances Fitzgibbons, 427, 428
Halstead, Oscar, 127
Hamlin, Adelaide, 110
Hammond, William, 101, 210–1,

220, 230, 249, 363, 441, 445, 450, 466
Hammond House, 101, 210, 225, 230, 441, 450
Hanck, Robert, 113, 125, 132, 133
Hancy, John and Amelia Eldred, 416
Handsome Eddy Farm, 7, 11, 38, 41, 74, 91, 92, 93, 129, 434–5, 443, 456, 472
Hankins
    Emma, 436
    Mary, 91–3, 447
Hansen
    Clara Leavenworth, 10, 28, 44, 51, 84, 111–2, 114–6, 118, 120, 122–6, 128, 130–1, 133, 134–6, 138, 142–4, 150–2, 154–5, 158, 161, 162–4, 167–8, 170–5, 178–80, 186–99, 200–2, 213–5, 218–20, 222, 224–5, 228, 230, 233–4, 236, 243, 246, 255, 261, 267, 268–71, 273, 275, 276–8, 292–3, 295, 298, 307, 314, 324, 328–9, 336, 338–9, 343, 350, 358, 362, 364, 370, 374, 380–1, 383, 421, 425, 469
    Dick, Wayne, and Lois, 293, 338, 358, 361, 381, 469
    James Didrik (Dick), 193–4, 197–8, 201, 203, 212, 214–15, 220, 230, 233–4, 269, 278, 295, 318, 336, 340, 349, 382
    Lee, 163–4, 168, 170, 173–5, 177, 178–9, 182, 183, 186–8, 190, 191, 193–4, 198–204, 206, 212–3, 218–20, 222, 224–5, 228–31, 233–4, 246, 250, 252, 253, 261, 265, 269, 276, 293, 295, 306–8, 316, 324, 329, 358, 340, 342, 362, 364, 370, 374, 380–81, 421, 425, 469
    Lois, 261, 295, 340, 381–3
    Senior Hansens, 175, 186, 190, 221
    Wayne, 213, 218–20, 230, 233, 269, 295, 340, 364, 381, 382
Harding, Warren G., 15, 31
Haring, Robert, 193
Harlow, Jean, 124

Harris, Lieutenant Cecil E., 320
Harris and Burpee, 301
Hart, Maxwell and Elizabeth Watson, 185, 416
Hartmon, Miss, 64
Hartung
    Amanda, 11, 451
    Arthur, 468
    Otto, 441
Hartung Road, 11, 17, 38, 101–2, 104, 106, 210, 249, 365, 410, 446
Hauptmann, Bruno, 157, 161
Hawaii, Pearl Harbor, 235, 248, 251, 275, 311
Hawker
    Hawker's, 173–4
    Lisa, 380
Hawk's Nest, 3, 157, 198–9, 453
Hazen
    Abel, 10–1, 43, 93, 129, 159, 164, 183–5, 446
    Abel and Viola Bradley, 43, 96, 413, 454
    Elsie Parker, 13–4, 43, 96, 109, 146, 196, 244, 371, 413, 454, 469
    Lewis, 43, 96, 97, 113, 129, 130, 146, 159, 185, 223, 244, 367, 371, 413, 454, 469
    Mabel, 413
    Marcella, 96
    Viola Bradley, 10, 32, 43, 95, 96, 116, 164, 184, 185, 244, 423, 432, 454, 469
    Viola (d/o Lewis), 96, 261
Hedden, Myrtle Austin, 404
Hellcat, 51, 311, 320
Hellman, Margaret, 98, 151, 157, 453
Hemmingway, Ernest, 15
Hendricks, Fred, 68
Henrickson, J. 349
Hensel
    Fred, 38, 81, 93, 117, 463, 454, 464
    Fred and Marion, 355, 356, 358
    Jacob and Lisette, 129, 454, 470
    Jacob (Jack), 38, 77, 93, 96, 109, 196, 309, 345, 358
    Joan, 294
    Kathryn, 38, 41, 77, 93, 95, 454

    Lisette, 38, 77, 96, 109, 129, 159, 223, 357–8, 359
    Louis, 29, 358
    Ludwig and Helen, 464
    Marion, 358, 463
Hercules Munitions, 219
Hess, Walter and Esther Colville, 117, 127, 413, 452
Hessberger
    Margaret, 455, 471
    Ralph, 81, 459, 487
    Reuben, 438
    Ruben and Mabel, 471
Heydrich, Rinehart, 195
Heyen
    Frederick and Julia, 447
    Frederick, 435
    Julia, 470
Hickok
    Arthur, 78
    Asa and Esther Hinman, 18, 78, 375, 391, 418
    Benjamin Merwin, 418
    Charles, 37
    Charles and Sarah Dehart, 418
    Clarence R., 419
    David Hinman, 418
    Justus, 37, 375, 418–9, 420
    Louisa, 418, 420
    Mary Ellen Thompson, 419
    Mary J. Russell, 418
    Mary V., 419
    Mary Wells, 37, 375, 418, 419
    Olin, 78, 418
    Robert Land and Charlotte Hulse, 418
    Sylvia, 418
    Willard, 419
    Willard and Mary Ellen Thompson, 418
    William and Almeda Drake, 418, 419
Hickok Brook, 257, 375
Highland Bridge House, 38, 41
Highlander Bowlers, 358, 362
Highland Hotel and Cottage, 10, 11, 38, 41, 93, 95, 97, 129, 159, 223, 367, 456
Highland Lake Bible Conference, 234, 265, 303
Highland Lake House, 36, 41, 102, 225

Highland Lake Inn, 11, 18–9, 37, 93, 100, 104, 129, 225, 303, 443, 449
Highland Lake Road, 17, 36, 79, 82, 99, 102, 143, 249, 275, 439, 440
Highland Serenaders, 167
Highland Villa, 37, 41, 93, 100, 102, 104, 129, 163, 445
Hill
   Alfred, 35, 36, 109, 120, 137, 160, 165, 171, 184, 194, 211, 213, 220, 224, 226, 227, 232–4, 236, 244, 248, 250–4, 258, 264, 266–7, 272, 275–6, 299, 332–3, 362, 374, 429, 430, 450, 459
   Alice Sergeant, 9, 12–3, 29, 55, 113, 131, 138, 177, 429, 435
   Alvin and Anna Crawford, 432, 455, 466
   Alvin and Harriet MacKechnie, 211, 226, 429, 453, 458
   Alvin (s/o John), 35–6, 77, 165, 275, 430
   Alvin (s/o Thomas), 55, 120, 261
   Anna Crawford, 127, 461
   Bessie MacIntyre Lass, 63, 72, 109, 137, 160, 170–1, 184, 194, 211, 214, 232, 244, 248, 251, 253–4, 258, 271–3, 275–6, 332–4, 342, 362, 374, 429–30, 457, 459
   Bill and Hilda, 470
   E., 349
   Ed, 175
   Edgar, 36, 165
   Edgar and Marjorie Wells, 429, 459
   Esther Grinnell, 35–7, 165, 429
   Frank, 113, 121, 174, 185, 317, 337
   Harriet Classen Eldridge, 47, 121, 142, 145, 165, 259, 295, 338, 341, 346, 429, 430, 459
   Harriet MacKechnie, 77
   J., 202
   John Edward and Esther Grinnell, 438
   John Edward and Harriet Classen Eldridge, 449
   John Edward, 35–7, 47, 55, 72, 142, 145, 165–6, 429, 430
   Marjorie Wells, 76, 127
   Matthew, 55
   Myrtle LaBarr, 113, 307
   N., 349
   P., 202
   R., 202, 349
   Thelma, 113, 128
   Thomas and Alice Sergeant, 435
   Thomas and Myrtle LaBarr, 435, 449, 461
   Thomas Jr., 55, 113, 121, 430
   Thomas Sr., 9, 12, 29, 55, 429, 435
   Virginia, 370
   Walter, William, 55
Hillcrest, 11, 16, 37, 41, 93, 106, 349, 385, 387, 446
Hillside Inn, 159, 354, 355
Hindenburg Line, 297
Hindenburg airship, 177
Hinkley, Mr. Hinkley, 226
Hipsman, Valentine, 22
Hirohito, 57, 235
Hirsch
   Anthony Sr., 10, 26, 43, 44, 113, 144, 154, 178, 206, 214, 220, 248–50, 251, 253, 264–5, 268, 269, 271–2, 274, 284, 286, 291–3, 295, 298, 320, 335, 345, 421, 423
   Anthony Sr. family, 26, 177, 178, 206, 212, 246, 247
   Christina Leavenworth, 10, 24, 26, 36–7, 43, 44, 47, 51, 71, 110–13, 116, 122, 135, 144, 154, 186, 206, 251, 253, 263, 269, 272, 275, 277, 280, 284–6, 288, 292–3, 299, 301, 303, 305, 307, 318, 320, 321, 325–6, 328, 335, 349, 366, 379, 381, 384, 391, 421, 423
   Lily, 265, 304
   Tony Jr., 24, 26, 113, 132, 265, 304, 329, 423
Hitchcock, Alfred, 15
Hitler, Adolph, 137, 145, 165, 177, 185, 195, 205, 219, 235, 246, 249, 255, 318, 331
Hoades, Mrs. R., 243
Hoatson, 410
   Marietta West Eldred, 18, 25, 137, 145, 185, 331, 373, 416, 440
   Samuel Hoatson, 18, 331
Hobbs, Gordon, 193
Hocker, Phyllis, 452
Hoehne, Arthur, 193
Holbrook, 113
   George and Gilbert, 125
   John, 117, 173
   Holbrook brothers, 123
Holden
   Anne Toaspern Cordes, 8, 11, 223, 366, 368, 454, 463
   David, 165, 173, 454
   William, 454
Hollywood, 31, 219
Holmes & Livingston, 38, 41, 92–3
Homestead Cottage, 2, 151
Hoover
   Herbert, 109, 115
   J. Edgar, 42
   Dam, 77
Horton
   Anne Elizabeth Stanton, 17, 76, 77, 78, 441
   Beatrice Avery, 10, 30, 34, 55, 63, 98, 117, 119, 135–7, 413
   Betty (Bessie), 426
   Carl, 203
   Catherine Sutherland, 77, 184
   Charles, 30, 55, 63, 98, 117, 136, 137, 413
   Cleta Myers, 9, 115, 138, 156, 211, 252, 265, 268, 432, 465
   Clifford, 98, 117, 119, 136, 413
   E., 202
   Ernest, 78, 211, 232, 244, 245, 339, 410
   Ernest and Georgiana, 451
   G., 349
   Helen, 9, 426
   John, 17, 78, 276, 339, 440–1, 453, 460
   LeRoy, 9, 178, 202–3, 212, 298, 317, 337, 415, 426, 434
   LeRoy and Katherine (Cappy) Ott, 201, 466
   Lucille St. Priest, 413
   Madeline and Marilyn, 202
   Theo, 9, 161, 426, 432, 453
   Walter and Alice, 460

Walter D. and Cleta Myers, 426, 432, 453, 465
Walter D. Sr., 78, 125, 181, 298, 339
Walter J. Jr., 9, 127, 426
William E., V, 30, 63, 98, 413, 414, 447
William H., 77, 78, 136, 184
Horton Memorial Hospital, 339
Hotzler
  Harry, 373
  R., 370
Houdini, Harry, 15
Houghton College, 364, 368–9, 374
Howard, Leslie, 289
Howdy Doody TV show, 353
Howe, Ella Clark, 82–3
Howlett
  Della Myers, 32, 82, 99, 143, 156, 158, 413, 444, 450, 459
  Harry, 60, 82, 99, 127, 158, 350, 413, 450, 459
Hudson River, 19, 46
Huebner, Bob, 67
Hughes
  Helen, 38, 41, 446
  Lillian, 365
Hull
  Daniel Deyo, 25, 117
  Jennie, 102, 113, 115–6, 130, 160, 170, 192–3, 267, 268–70, 272, 278, 303, 314, 441, 446, 450, 466
  John D., V, 209, 353, 370, 376
  John J., 117, 275, 341, 353, 370, 373, 376
  Josephine Lipinski, 341, 353, 370, 373, 376
  Justina Schoonover, 9, 19, 25, 117, 275, 370, 376, 394
  Loretta, 370, 376
  S. Deyo, 9, 19, 25, 117, 275
Hulse
  Abe, 249, 363, 458
  Abe and Catherine, 451
  Abraham, 127
  Ami, 127, 451, 468
  Ami and Violet, 443
  Belle and Elizabeth, 127
  Bertha, 127, 454
  Chester, 113, 128, 241, 461
  Chester and Catharine, 9, 441, 448
  Clifford, 9, 174, 193, 313, 337, 341, 353, 427
  Dewey, 127, 317, 337
  Duane, 55, 127, 437–8, 451
  Ella, 127, 193, 303, 454
  Elmer, George, Harold, 127
  Helen Zita Myers, 36, 37, 72, 179, 234, 241, 242, 300, 329, 341, 353, 427, 461
  J., 349
  James, 337
  John, 410
  Joseph, Lillian, Melvyn, 127
  Josephine Holbrook, 117, 173
  Kevin, 384
  Marie Myers, 151, 227, 252, 449
  Marion, 151, 227, 252
  Maude Wells, 55, 76, 113, 127, 437–8, 451
  Michael, 353, 384
  Millard, 178, 225, 299, 374, 461
  Nelson, 127, 132, 410, 432
  Raymond, 127, 252, 299, 315, 317, 337
  Raymond and Marie Myers, 459
  Russell, Willard, 127
Hulse boys, 113, 123
Humphries, Edith Guenther, 23, 55, 97, 373
Hungary, 145
Hurricane Diane, 388
Hurtin, Mary Isabelle Austin, 394
Huxley, Aldous, 15, 127

I

IBM, 42
Iceland, 235
Ihlo
  Bill, V, 371, 431
  John, V
  Frances Toaspern, 8, 29, 113, 131, 144, 150, 206, 245, 266, 267, 282, 310, 333, 341, 371
  Fred, 282–3, 285, 305, 310, 318, 323–4, 333, 341, 371, 373
Illinois, Chicago, 15, 52, 83, 109, 110, 137, 219, 270, 275, 283, 289
Immigration, Act of 1924, 42
Inch, Mabel Austin, 404
India, 31, 195
Indian Citizenship Act (U.S.), 42
Indochina, 219
Insulin treatment, 31
Ira Austin House, 6
Iran Summit, 289
Ireland
  Irish Civil War, 31
  Irish Free State 31, 195
Italy
  Anzio, 305
  Cassino, 289, 298, 305
  Catacombs, 307
  Messina, 290, 300
  Mount Etna, 31, 33
  Naples, 255, 289
  Nettuno, 300
  Paestum, 291
  Rome, 195, 289, 297–8, 305–7
  Salerno, 289, 291, 314
  Sicily, 259, 288–90, 292, 300
Ithaca College, 281
Iwo Jima, 331

J

Jackson, Thornton, 317
James
  Beverly, 287
  Edward and Norma Wood, 224
  Edward H., 185, 213, 269, 270, 287, 371
  Elwood and Ann Plachy, 213
  Elwood, 19
  Gary Britt, 213
  Kitty Britt, 19, 149, 183, 210, 270, 394
  Norma Wood, 19, 183, 185, 213, 224, 269, 270, 287, 371
  Richard, V, 213, 224, 269
  Will, 149
Japan/Japanese, 31, 57, 77, 109, 117, 120, 127, 137, 177, 180, 195, 205, 219, 235, 249, 255, 268, 279, 283, 286, 289, 291, 305, 308, 318, 320, 326, 330–1
  Hiroshima and Nagasaki, 331
  Tokyo, 305, 331
Java, 254
Jensen's, 361
John Harding and Erik Nelson, 42
Johnson

Anna, 433
Dr., 410
John W. and Ida, 456, 472
Lyndon B., 331
Johnson City Publishing Co., 55
Johnston
    John W. (author), 29, 121
    John W. (nephew), 29
Joint Chiefs of Staff, 235
Jolson
    Al, 15, 75
    Joyce, 15
Jung, Freda, 367

K

Kaese/Kaese's, 10, 93, 94, 97, 223
    Ahrend and Sophia Kaese, 97
    A. Kaese, 95, 159
    Albert, 97, 454
    Albert and Ethel, 223, 469
    Alfred and Sophia, 433
    Charles and Edith, 464
Kaiser, Henry, 264
Kalbfus
    Ed, 410
    Edith Miller, 10, 38, 41, 93, 95, 97, 129, 159, 223, 446, 456, 469
    Mr., 264
Kalin
    Adolph, 145, 173, 265, 319, 337
    Alberta Brodmerkel, 145, 153
    Annabelle, 157, 173
    Eugene, Harold, Robert, 17
    Herman and Adelaide, 457, 472
    Ida, 442, 457
    James, 373
    Maude, 17, 78, 441
    Orville, 337
    Reta, 297, 303, 334, 457, 467
    William and Eva, 449, 465
    William Jr., 337
Kamikaze, 305, 318
Kansas, Solomon, 19, 23, 81, 82, 402
Karg, Eric, 243
Kassner, Theodore and Thekla, 11, 441
Kayser, Fritz, 317
KDKA, 15, 31, 68
Kean

Francis, 373
Justin, 261
Mary, 332
Paul, 341
Keaton, Buster, 15
Keeley
    Gertrude Lucke, 248
    Lawrence, 248
Keil, George, 450
Keller, W., 349
Kelley
    Everett, 28, 112–3, 121–2, 124–6, 155, 157, 160, 164, 172, 210, 266, 272, 276, 290, 341, 343, 429–30, 469
    Frank, 12, 29, 112, 429, 430, 439
    Leila, 429, 430
    Luella Sergeant, 12–3, 29, 112–3, 121, 124, 128, 130–1, 138, 156–7, 172, 429, 430, 439, 444, 453
Kellogg-Brian Pact, 77
Kelly
    Kenneth, 313, 337
    Michael J., 5
Kelso
    Kelso family, 56
    Murie, 57, 72
    Robert Sr., 56
Kendall, Charles and Maria Eldred, 416
Kendrigan, Martin, 337
Kennedy, John F., 331, 381
Kern, Jerome Kern, 58
Kerr
    Charles, 9, 193, 334
    Charles and Muriel Rennard, 287, 303, 334, 335, 348, 368
    John and Katherine Greening, 9, 442, 457, 472
    John (h/o Mary), 63
    John/Jack (s/o William and Mary), 32–4, 165, 173–4, 196, 313, 337
    John Kerr (b. 1873), 261
    John (s/o John and Mary J.), 63
    Katherine Greening, 303
    Lewis, 63
    Lois, 303, 334, 348
    Mary (Ed's aunt), 463
    Mary J. (w/o John; m/o

William), 63
    Mary Kerr (1929 senior), 83
    William, 63, 92
    William and Mary Kerr, 32, 63, 437, 448, 462
Kestler
    H., 349
    Kestler Family, 154
    Mary Kestler, 150, 151
    P., 349
Kew Gardens, 173
Kewley
    Chester and Gladys, 469
    Grace, 206, 292
    Mrs. Chester, 127
Kiesek, Mildred Austin, 404
King
    Edward, 157
    Martin Luther, 83
    Millie (Pamela) Ewart, 83, 157, 379, 421
King George VI and Elizabeth, 31, 177, 195
Kinne
    Billings, 261, 457, 472
    Billings and Julia, 442
    Bill, 174
    Charles, 332
    Harriet, 77
    Herbert, 55, 211, 234, 324, 457, 472
    Mildred MacKechnie, 55
    Millard, 174
    Mr., 57, 219
    William, 241
Kirby
    Charles and Caroline, 454, 464
    Kaska, 315, 454
    Klelah, 173
    Klendin, 315
Kistner
    John, 186, 337
    Marion Doeller, V, 91, 332, 371
    Rudolph, 186, 337, 371
Kloss, Lou, 114
Knecht, Francis (Red) and Margaret Harder, 145, 287
Kniffin, Mrs. John, 43
Knight, George, 303
Knorr
    Arlene, 227
    C., 202

Frances LaBarr, 152, 164, 211, 227, 234, 236, 240, 252, 265, 278, 453
Gordon, 152, 227
Paul, 68, 112–3, 118, 120, 152, 187, 199, 211, 220, 227, 234, 245, 252, 261, 264, 453, 460
Koch
  Henry, 117, 319
  Henry and Edith, 455
  Henry Jr., 337
Kodak, 165, 285
Koenig
  Deloros, 50, 74, 77, 119, 421
  Doris Kestin, 380
  Eli, 380
  Eugene, 9, 18, 25, 34, 37, 55, 74, 77, 109, 118, 127, 421
  Gerald, V, 109, 118–9, 379–80, 421
  Hazel Leavenworth, 9, 18, 25, 34, 37, 50–1, 55, 74, 77, 109, 118, 119, 127, 379, 380, 421
  Isaiah, 380
  John E., 34, 37, 50–1, 75, 118, 120, 379, 421
  Rachel, 380
Kohler
  Joseph, 371
  Marjorie Bosch, 70, 76, 125, 190, 209, 218, 219, 220, 227, 231, 241, 247, 248, 250, 252, 254, 257, 267, 270, 278, 302, 339, 371
  Victoria, IV, V, 228
  William, 313
Kollander, William, 169
Konoye, Fujimaro, 177, 235
Kornkven
  Andrew, David, James, Jeanne, Kenneth, 380
  Marialyce Koenig, V, 118, 127, 379–80, 421
Koster, 106, 410
  Chris and Freida, 11, 442
  Christian, 16, 385, 387
  Henry, 16, 385
Kramer, Walter and Barbara, 471
Krause, Mr., 113, 125, 199
Kuen
  Edward, 113
  Edward and Kathryn

Livingstone, 429
H., 215
Kate and Arthur, 192
Kate Livingstone, 113, 166
Ku Klux Klan, 31
Kunkele, R., 349
Kyte
  Anna, 113, 130
  Audrey, 75
  Bert, 71
  Bronwyn, V
  Charles and Elizabeth Bliss, 142
  Elizabeth Terry, 83
  Felix and Eliza Gregier, 83
  Felix, 3–4, 142, 197, 210
  Frank Colony, 43, 373
  Frank Crouch, 43, 75, 113, 142
  Hazel Robinson, 43, 75
  Kyte Family, 4
  Mary A. Whitney, 193, 439, 453
  Rose Paden, 373

L

LaBarr
  Edwin and Elsie, 468
  Frank and Mabel, 433
  George, 66
  George and Henrietta Middaugh, 426, 442, 445, 491
  Jacob and Emily Harder, 185
  Webster (Webb), 17, 444
  Webb and Ida, 439, 466
Lack
  Ethel Schoonover, 19, 376, 394
  Jean; John, 376
Laing, Randolph and Tina Austin, 394
Lake DeVenoge, 252
Lake House, 10–1, 17–8, 37–8, 85, 100, 102, 104, 106, 129, 153, 157, 184, 186–7, 225, 238, 252, 391, 411–2, 446, 451
Lake Metaque, 434
Lake Shore House/Hotel, 37, 41, 93, 100, 102, 163, 193, 225, 345
Lake Side Cottage, 11
Lake View (Myers), 10–1, 16, 18–9, 37, 104, 225, 300, 322–3
  Bar, 164
  Cottage, 19, 322
Lake View Farm House, 10–1, 95, 97, 159, 446
Lake View Inn, 23, 38, 41, 93, 97, 129, 159, 243
Lakewood House, 186
Lambert, Arthur, 317
Lansmith
  Lulu Bosch, 85, 106, 109, 153, 302
  Will, 85
Lass
  Charles Howard, 8, 23, 25, 29, 55, 63, 66, 68, 71
  Harry, 8, 63, 72, 75, 76
  Helen, 8
  Jay, 8, 22, 55, 75, 76, 111, 169, 262, 313, 435, 438, 447
  J., 215
  John, 8, 23, 63, 76, 77
  John and Meta Toaspern, 435
  Lass Family, 8
  Meta Toaspern, 8, 23, 63, 76, 366, 368, 447, 470
  M., 215
  Tillie Flynn, 75, 169
  Veronica Campbell, 23, 25, 29, 63, 447
  William, 72, 160, 215, 251, 276, 332, 457, 459
Laurel Brook Cottage, 223, 309
Laurel Cottage (Hazen's), 10–1, 43, 93, 95–6, 129, 159, 185, 223, 345, 446, 454
LaValle, Walter and Edythe, 456
Layden, Mac, 248
Layman, George, 7, 124
Lazerlier/Laziliere
  Abraham and Mary Webber, 427–8
League of Nations, 15, 31, 57, 109, 137, 145
Leavenworth
  Anna Mae, 36, 51, 60, 110, 116, 125, 132, 142, 144, 154, 163, 174, 181, 201, 212–3, 220–1, 224, 227, 230–1, 233, 236, 240, 242, 244, 246–52, 257–8, 260–1, 263–6, 268–9, 271–80, 284, 286, 288, 293–6, 298–9, 301, 303, 306–8, 310, 312, 316, 318, 320–1, 324, 327–31, 333, 335–6, 338, 374, 379, 382, 421
  Charlotte (Lottie), 10, 24, 26,

36, 51, 54, 61, 70–2, 79, 83, 98, 110–14, 116, 122, 123, 125, 133, 135–6, 138, 142–5, 154, 156, 162, 168, 175–6, 178, 180, 183, 190, 194, 202–3, 251, 255, 260, 263, 265, 269–70, 278–81, 285–6, 292, 303, 304, 320, 335, 349, 379–81, 384, 421–2, 425, 439, 443, 453, 469

Clinton/Goldie, 10, 28, 44, 48, 51, 84, 110–2, 114–5, 118, 120–6, 128, 130–1, 137–8, 142, 144, 150–1, 158, 160–3, 168, 170–2, 175, 178, 180–94, 196, 199–203, 206, 212–4, 216, 219–22, 224–5, 228–30, 236, 246–8, 250, 252, 254–5, 258, 265–6, 278–80, 282–3, 286, 288, 290, 292–5, 298–9, 301–2, 307–8, 314, 318, 324–5, 328–9, 335–6, 338, 340, 342, 346, 348–51, 364, 366, 372, 381, 421, 469

David, 372, 381–3, 424–5

David and Diane, V

Ella Sergeant, 26, 82, 193, 280, 296, 299, 314, 318, 320, 322, 324, 331, 362, 366, 368, 390, 421, 423

Florence, 421

Frederick Clinton, 206, 213

Garfield, 36, 51–2, 68, 110, 120, 133, 135–6, 143, 146, 150, 164–5, 180, 182–3, 224, 228, 242, 250, 252–3, 257–8, 263, 266, 281, 291, 316, 325, 379, 382, 384

Garfield and Ella, 13, 25, 28–9, 44, 46, 52, 84, 113, 115, 122–3, 125, 128, 130–2, 134, 139, 142, 144, 151, 153, 155–6, 160, 162–3, 166, 168, 170–2, 174, 176, 178–9, 181, 183–4, 186, 188, 190–2, 194, 197, 199, 201–2, 204, 206, 211, 214, 218, 221–2, 225, 228–34, 236, 240, 246–8, 261, 267, 269, 270–9, 282, 285–8, 292–5, 298, 301, 306–8, 311–2, 328–30, 335–6, 338–40, 342–3, 346, 348–51, 354, 358, 361, 364, 370, 372, 374, 381–2, 421, 429, 444, 453, 469

Gisele Rouillon, IV, V, 25, 68, 75–6, 77, 125, 136, 292, 295–6, 310, 319, 325–6, 336, 339, 341, 343–4, 346, 349–51, 366, 370, 372, 383–6, 391, 421, 424, 425, 436

Ida May, 421

James (Jim), 25, 28–9, 30, 44, 51–2, 66–8, 84, 102, 110–16, 120–3, 125–6, 128, 130, 131–7, 142–4, 147, 150, 154–6, 158, 160–2, 164, 166–8, 170–1, 173, 174–5, 178–9, 182–3, 186–91, 194, 196–9, 201–2, 204, 212, 214, 218–21, 224–7, 229–31, 233–4, 236, 245–8, 250–1, 254, 258, 262–3, 265, 266–90, 292–6, 298–9, 301, 307–8, 310, 316–9, 322, 324–5, 328–31, 335–44, 349–51, 361, 366, 370, 372, 374, 381, 383, 387, 391, 421, 424, 436

Jim and Gisele, 325, 336, 339, 343–4, 349–51, 353–4, 358, 362, 364, 366, 370, 372, 374, 381, 385–6, 424

John Ellis, 34, 118, 379, 421

Maria Myers, 110, 111, 236, 379, 384, 427

Martin D., 10, 24, 26, 36, 51, 98, 110, 113, 116, 122, 151, 154, 167, 176, 181, 183, 206, 258, 279, 304, 306, 329, 379, 421

Sherman B. and Charlotte Ingram, 20, 111, 240, 303, 379, 421

Sherman S., 10, 22, 26, 43, 51, 56, 60, 70–2, 83, 98, 110–2, 116–7, 267, 379, 384, 410, 421, 427, 439, 443, 453

Sherman S. and Maria Myers, 381, 421

Stella Clark, 9, 158, 160, 177, 181, 183–5, 188, 190–2, 194, 196, 199–203, 206, 212–4, 216, 218–22, 224, 227–31, 234, 246–7, 249–50, 252, 255, 266–80, 283, 286, 288, 292–3, 295, 298, 301, 307,–8, 314, 318, 324–5, 328–30, 335, 336, 338, 342, 344, 346, 348–9, 350, 364, 366, 372, 381, 421, 456, 459, 469

Truman E., 10, 26, 36, 51, 98, 110, 113, 120, 122, 162, 178, 182, 193, 201, 421

Legion of Merit, 314, 407

Lend-Lease, 235

Lenin, Vladimir, 42

Leo, Nancy Leavenworth, V, 381, 383, 424

Lewis
  Charles E., 54
  Frederick J., 16, 22, 83, 117, 121, 385, 438–9, 448, 460
  Mary Twichell, 83, 211, 234, 245, 248, 448

Leyte Island, 305

Libbey Glass, 5

Libya, 235, 255, 289

Liebla
  Elma, 34
  George, 4
  Hattie Austin, 48, 437, 449
  John and Catherine, 437
  Orville and Ward, 337
  Peddler, 55
  Stanley, 461
  Sylvan, 313, 337

Liefert
  Barbara, 294, 468
  Helen Guenther, 23, 55, 97, 165, 173, 373, 423, 454
  John, 313, 337

Lilley
  Alfred and Bessie Sutherland, 184
  Earl and Sharon Stewart, V
  Earl Louis Lilley, 213
  Eleanor Ort, 145, 213, 324
  Emerson, 145, 213

Lincoln Memorial, 31

Lindbergh
  Anne Morrow, 127, 161
  Charles Jr., 121, 123, 127, 157, 161
  Charles, 74, 124, 127, 161

Lithuania, 195, 205

Livingston(e)
  Evelyn MacIntyre, 206, 317,

346, 353
Joe Livingston, 353
Livingston(e) Family, 13
Ralph and Fanny, 463
Unita Jane Sergeant, 12–3, 113, 128, 130–1, 429, 434
William, 12
William H., 429
Lloyd, Margaret, 261
Locarno Pact, 57
Lochner
    Family, 234, 236
    Fred and Gertrude, 465
    L., 202
    Mr., 252, 307
Lock 68, 32
Lockheed Vega 5B, 127
Loerch
    Matilda, 102, 104, 441
    Mrs. H.J., 93
Lorphelin
    Joseph and Juliette, 341, 346, 354
    Juliette, 355, 372
Love
    John, 4, 17, 72, 112–3, 116, 120–3, 127–8, 130, 136, 138, 182–3, 185, 410, 438, 443, 453
    Katherine (Kate), 113, 114, 115, 116, 118, 120, 122, 123, 128, 144, 166, 175, 196, 199, 453
    sawmill, 173
Lovelace, J., 215
Lowell Observatory, 109
Lucke, Clement, 248
Luckenback Steamship Lines, 173
Lufburrow
    Laurence, 341
    Mildred Briggs, 25, 30, 52–3, 86, 139, 140, 161, 177, 227, 246, 341, 368, 415, 457, 464
Lutz, K., 345, 367
Lynn Brook Farm, 39, 41

M

Maas, Ben, 243
MacArthur, Douglas A., 331
MacIntyre
    Adeline, 459
    Charles and Lena Hill, 450, 458
    Charles, 25, 194, 196, 257, 275, 346, 429
    Edward and Helen Lass, 29, 385–6, 448, 462–3
    James and Adaline, 442, 457
    Lena Hill, 25, 36, 37, 165, 346, 429
    MacIntyre family, 113, 114
    Mrs. James, 63
MacKechnie
    Charles and Edith, 443
    Charles, 12, 438, 460, 494
    Joseph, 471
    Peggy Gilmore, 101–2, 243
    Russell and Edith, 442, 456, 472
    Russell and Peggy Gilmore, V, 370
    Wallace MacKechnie, 177
Mackinder, Mary Ellen Busse, V, 414
Mac's Hill, 249
Macy's Thanksgiving Parade, 42
Maglione
    Andy and Margie Austin, V
    Margie Austin, 3, 43, 70–1, 76, 77, 113, 116, 123, 125, 150, 165, 178–80, 192, 214, 216–7, 219, 227, 263, 278, 318, 330, 340, 346, 366–7, 379, 408, 429, 436, 445, 454, 456, 460, 472
Maier
    Annie, 13, 114–5, 182, 185, 253, 455
    Joseph, 13, 63, 432, 438
    Julius, 13, 50, 115, 182, 186, 188, 241, 247–8, 278, 353, 410, 432, 442, 455, 466
Mallison
    Henry and Catherine, 447, 462
    Henry, 147, 263
Manchuria, 117, 127, 137
Maney
    D., 349
    Edith Horton, 78
Mangan, Thomas, 169
Many, Mrs. Robert, 243
Mapes, Polly V. Eldred, 416
Maplecrest, 96, 196–7, 223, 309, 356, 358, 367, 469
Maple Grove Farm, 8, 11, 86–9, 91, 93, 129, 159, 213, 223, 332, 367, 443, 447, 470
Margolin, Dave Margolin, 169
Mariana Islands, 305
Marion
    C., 202
    Josette, 215
Markle
    Anna, 341
    Violet, 303
Marren, John J., 117
Marrinan
    Kevin, V, 204
    Mary, 204
Marshall Islands, 305, 308
Massachusetts
    Auburn, 57
    Easthampton, 10, 82
    Squantum, 267, 282
Master's Golf Tournament, 145
Matter, Walter, 243
Maudsley
    Amy, 371
    Ellis S. and Edna Rauner, 43
    Louis and Edith Rutledge, 43, 333, 341, 366, 371
    Mary, 333, 341
Maughan, Russell, 42
Maunz, George, 471
Mautz, Charles, 435
Maver, Hazel Austin, 404
Maxwell, Claude, 456
McAuliffe, General Anthony C., 305
McBride, 410
    Bill, 130, 178
    Buck (Ezra), 43, 98, 119, 231, 245, 246, 247, 303, 307, 308, 413, 444
    Emerson and Julia, 465
    Emerson McBride, 451
    Kenneth, 43, 51, 98, 113, 116, 119, 128, 130–1, 135, 144, 278, 335, 413–4
    Laura Avery, 10, 34, 43, 51, 98, 113, 116, 119, 120, 126, 137, 144, 148, 332, 413–4, 444, 453, 469
    Sandra Sergeant, V, 430
    Sherman Jr., 302, 341, 342, 432, 452, 465
    Sherman Sr., 287
    Sherman Sr. and Eliza, 432,

452, 465
Skeet, 291
Viola Webber, 287
Walter, 120, 248, 288, 301
William, 113, 121, 287, 317, 337
W. McBride, 202
McCaffrey, Alice, 456
McCann
   Alfred, 117
   Carol, 165, 173
   Vouletti, 469
McCormack/McCormick, M.A., 11, 38, 41, 93, 95, 97, 129, 159, 223, 446
Mr. McCormack (publisher), 283
McDonald
   Joseph, 315
   restaurant, 205
McGinnis, Ernest, 438
McKeon, Beatrice, 236, 244, 245–6
McQuirk, 8, 11, 435, 443
Meiritz
   John and Evelyn, 468
   Vivian, 370
Melconian, Mr., 212
Mellan
   Anna, 269
   Ed, V
   George Sr., 74
   Joe and Mary Paulik, 74, 249, 269, 303, 348, 354, 363
   Joe Jr., V, 249
   Mary Paulik, V, 73
   Mellan's, 230, 249, 354, 363
Memorial/Decoration Day, 22, 131, 164, 233, 262, 264
Mercedes-Benz, 42
Merchant Marines, 117, 165
Mercury Theater, 189
Merrill, Mrs. D., 243
Mertz, Johnny, 147
Methodist Hospital (Brooklyn), 277, 287, 290, 296, 333, 334, 340
Metro Goldwyn Mayer (MGM), 42
Metzger, 410
   Fred, 177
   John, 177, 438, 454, 464
   John C. and Matilda Wilson, 177
   Richard, 370
Mexico, 15, 68
Meyer
   Anna, 18

   C., 349
   Christian and Meta, 6, 11, 92, 172, 223, 435, 443, 463, 447
   Christian and Delores, 462
   Florence van Eastenbridge, 18, 25, 104, 258, 259
   Fred, 25, 143, 206, 259, 319, 337, 347, 353, 373
   Joanna Smith, V
   Joseph, 18, 25, 104, 106, 113, 258, 263
   John, 18, 258, 259, 319, 337
   Joseph and Florence van Eastenbridge, 18, 104, 259, 333, 441, 446, 451, 467
   Joseph Jr., 319
   Judy, 373
   Margo Bosch, 37, 58, 322, 323, 347, 353, 373
   Raymond, 18, 172, 259, 319, 333, 337
Meyers
   Anna Leavenworth, 10, 28, 44, 51–2, 84, 111–2, 114–5, 120–1, 123–6, 128, 130–1, 133, 134–8, 142–3, 147, 151, 154–6, 158, 161–2, 168, 171–5, 178–9, 181, 183–4, 187–8, 190, 192, 194, 196–7, 198–204, 206, 214, 219, 220, 222, 224, 227–8, 230–1, 233, 243, 247, 264–5, 270–3, 276–8, 293, 295, 298–9, 302, 307–8, 325, 330, 335–6, 338, 340, 344, 350, 354, 358, 364, 366, 370, 372, 380–1, 413, 421, 465
   Bill Jr., 13, 28, 82, 113–5, 118, 120–1, 123, 126, 138, 142–3, 146–8, 156, 158, 161–2, 170, 172, 174–5, 178–9, 181, 183–4, 186, 188, 190–4, 196, 197–8, 200–4, 206, 219–20, 224, 230, 236, 247, 252, 266, 272, 276, 278, 293, 295, 299, 301–2, 325, 335–6, 339, 364, 372, 380, 413, 421, 465
   Bill Sr., 13, 18, 28, 82, 113–5, 118, 150, 156, 183, 186, 202, 236, 262–3, 278, 338, 339, 371–2, 413, 414, 438, 444
   Florence Meyer, 83, 153

   James W. (Jimmy), 191–4, 197–9, 201–3, 212, 214, 221, 230, 233, 247, 272, 274, 276–8, 293, 295, 299, 308, 335–6, 338, 339–40, 349–50, 353, 358, 361, 364, 372, 380, 382
   Lottie Scott, 13, 28, 32, 51, 82, 113–4, 121, 142–3, 148, 150, 156, 158, 167, 179, 188, 194, 198–9, 201, 202–4, 206, 216, 233, 255, 298, 338, 413–4, 438, 444
   William and Lottie Scott, 453, 469
Michell
   Frank, 193
   Helen, 177
Mickey and Minnie Mouse, 77
Middaugh
   Chester, 113, 115, 146, 148, 151, 164, 178, 183, 188, 190, 194, 197, 211–2, 232, 240, 253, 268, 272, 279, 339, 368, 381, 383, 410, 426, 438, 444, 453, 466, 469
   Dennis and Sarah Maria Myers, 426
   Florence Hammond, 143, 146–8, 150, 185, 189, 190, 381, 426, 453
   Herbert, 150–1, 164, 170
   Middaugh's, 143
Miller
   Arthur and Frederick, 313
   Edna Beufve, 159
   Glenn, 318
   Harry, 159
   Katherine Wiest, 63, 106, 229, 411
   Louis, 19
   Mary DeVenoge, 19, 20, 37
   Titus Leonhard, 411
Mills, 410
   Agnes, 225, 308, 446, 467
   Alexander and Margaret Gillies, 102
   Alexander and Minnie Meyer, 303, 332, 451, 467
   Alexander (h/o Minnie), 172, 178, 200, 308
   D., 202

Dr. George, 170–3, 196, 252, 286, 308, 341, 446
Elizabeth Gillespie, 11, 73, 93, 102, 172, 303, 308, 441, 446, 451
James, 41, 93, 102, 147, 192, 225, 252, 308, 314
James and Sophia Stellwagen, 36, 145, 185, 341, 450, 446, 466
Kenneth, 185, 303, 341
Meta, 332
Minnie Meyer, 172, 200
R., 349
Mills House, 11, 18, 93, 102, 172, 225, 446, 451
Milne, A.A., 15
Minisink Battlefield, 77
Minisink Lodge, 11, 38, 41, 93, 95, 97, 129, 159, 223, 367, 446
Minisink Sesquicentennial, 77
Mississippi, Camp Shelby, 260, 263–4, 269, 279, 285, 304
Mitchell, Alvin, 165
Mix, Tom, 15
Mohr
   Carl, 449
   Frederick, 337
Mondrian, Piet, 15
Mongaup Falls, 53
Moniserra, Louie, 23
Montgomery
   Gen. Bernard, 255, 289
   Lake, 2, 39, 41, 49, 92–3, 95–6, 121, 132, 156, 167, 201, 203, 255, 280, 314, 452
   Ward, 67, 156, 280, 314
Moore
   Elijah, 84, 113–4, 150, 245, 247
   Howard, 72, 79, 127, 145, 157, 167
   Mr., 175, 183
   Mrs. (Austin researcher), 274
Morgan
   Fred, 69, 244, 267
   Fred and Charlotte, 449, 459
   Harold, 265, 317, 337
   James, 432
   J.P., 58
   John and Emily, 444, 452
   Mrs., 263
   Pat, 27
   Raymond, 317, 337
   John and Emily, 444, 452
Morganstern, Betty Ihlo, V
Morton, Jelly Roll, 15
Mountain Grove House, XI, 1–2, 11, 17, 20–1, 26, 39, 42, 59, 66, 99, 107, 134, 150–1, 405, 433, 450, 453
Mountain Lake House, 11, 37–8, 100, 102, 104, 129, 163, 225, 451, 467
Mount Pleasant House, 129
Mount Rushmore, 75, 235
Mud Pond, 322, 329, 363, 411
Mueller, Ernest, 337
Muller, Ben and Nick, 411
Mulvihill, Joseph and Elizabeth Ford, 63, 92, 94
Murder, Inc., Brownsville Boys, 169
Murray
   Gladys Van Tuyl, 472
   Joyce, 373
Mussolini, Benito, 31, 77, 145, 165, 185, 195, 205, 289
Myers
   Abel Sprague, 3, 14, 45, 54, 80, 107, 115, 117, 374, 410, 426
   Alberta, 227
   Archibald and Minnie Sergeant, 426, 439, 451, 459
   Archibald (Archie), 13, 63, 72, 81, 113, 114, 115, 304
   Atwell, 413
   Augustus (Gus), 17, 24–5, 36, 410, 427, 441
   Benjamin, 427, 428
   Bertha Eldred, 18, 166, 327, 416
   Bradley, 13, 413
   Celia, 327
   Charles and Elizabeth, 441, 445, 451, 467
   Charles C. (Charlie), 9, 11, 16, 18–9, 36, 61, 72, 93, 104, 113, 120–1, 164, 166, 216, 225, 229, 300–1, 322, 326, 384, 427, 428
   Charles (Chuck), II, V, 13, 63, 99, 133, 215, 283–4, 304, 317, 337, 341, 344, 374–5, 429
   Charlotte Middaugh, 150, 165, 213, 227, 459
   Chuck and Ruth Worzel, V, 386
   Clifford, 26, 229, 271, 290, 298, 304, 348, 351, 353, 362, 426
   Edwin Van Schoick, 26, 64, 78, 108, 134, 175, 179–80, 187, 190, 204, 211, 215, 217, 227, 229–30, 249–52, 266, 271, 304, 362, 410, 426, 436, 438, 443, 449, 460
   Elizabeth Ferguson, 9, 19, 72, 104, 216, 300, 301, 427
   Emily Christene (Teenie) Stevens, II, IV, V, 9, 14, 26, 27, 28, 81, 98–9, 101, 112, 126, 130, 133, 174, 193, 196, 208–9, 211, 220, 222, 241, 243, 250, 253, 258, 261, 264, 268, 270–1, 276, 280, 286–7, 326–7, 367, 369, 385–6, 427, 455, 458
   Francis, 165, 166, 426
   Fred, 11, 13, 32, 35, 37, 82–3, 413
   Fred and Mary Frances, 432
   Fred Jr., 32
   George W.T., 24, 428
   George W.T. and Martha Mills, 19, 36, 303, 384, 427
   Gladys (Jake) Hill, 9, 25–6, 36, 165, 180, 183, 426, 429, 443
   Harold (Bud), 19, 38, 104, 113, 120, 127, 427
   Harvey, 32
   Hugh, 120, 131, 144, 426, 459
   Jackson, 11, 73, 83, 101, 113, 115, 144, 145, 209, 426
   Jackson and Jessie, 434
   Jake, 183
   James, 426
   Jane Ann Van Pelt Webb, 17–8, 20, 24–5, 36–7, 109, 240, 353, 384, 391, 427–8
   Jerry, 327
   Jessie Dunlap, 113, 125, 144, 145, 426, 444, 453
   John E., 25, 60
   Lena (d/o Jackson), 113, 125, 144, 157, 173, 426
   Lena Schoonmaker, 120, 427
   Leversa (Lee) Beisel, 26, 127, 174, 214, 426
   Lynn, 113, 120, 128, 144–5, 173, 426, 146

Mabel Owen, 26, 426
Maria Hankins, 113, 115, 117, 426, 444, 453
Maria Van Schoick, 426
Martin D. I, 20, 25, 427
Martin D. and Jane Ann Van Pelt Webb, 353, 384
Martin D. and Mary Fee, 441
Martin D. and Sarah Lake, 427
Martin D. Jr., 9, 72, 98, 179, 185, 250, 261, 270–1, 276, 281, 286, 290, 299, 300, 317, 326–7, 329, 337, 385–6, 427, 443, 459
Martin D. Sr., 9, 19, 24, 36–7, 61, 72, 98, 104, 127, 177, 179, 234, 245, 270, 280, 286–7, 299, 300–1, 384, 421, 443, 449, 459
Mary Fee, 9, 37, 55, 72, 177, 179, 427
Mary Frances Bradley Scott, 11, 13, 32, 34, 36–7, 82, 118, 157, 241–2, 245, 300, 413, 427
Mildred Hill, 113, 128, 145, 173, 335, 413, 460
Minnie Sergeant, 13, 22, 63, 113–4, 304, 344, 439, 444
Moses and Phebe Hazen Clark, 426
Mr., 289
Norma, 426
Norman B. and Bertha Eldred, 426, 434, 456, 466
Norman H., 173, 337, 426
Norman B., 18, 72–3, 115, 145, 153, 166, 190, 236, 245, 265, 278, 317, 327, 410, 416
Orville, 26, 73, 117, 120, 127, 174, 214, 304, 362, 426
Patsy (d/o Orville and Lee), 174
Raymond, 9, 26, 362, 426, 429, 443, 456
Robert (s/o Chuck and Ruth), 370
Rose Straub, 131, 312, 368
Ruth Worzel, 43, 206, 215, 266–7, 341, 344, 370, 385, 429, 467
S., 202
Stanley, 113, 120–1, 153, 227, 459

Stephen and Charlotte Middaugh, 11, 426, 441, 449
Steven H. (s/o Martin and Teenie), 384
Thomas, 72, 179, 287, 290, 299, 300, 317, 329, 337, 427
Tracey, 98, 127, 443, 450, 460

N

Nancy Lee, 38, 41, 96–7, 446
Napoleon Bonaparte, 33
Narrowsburg
   Feed Company, 132
   Lumber, 68–9, 128, 184, 225, 226, 234, 236, 240, 243, 247–8, 273, 358, 360, 374, 387
Naval Treaties, 31, 109, 145, 157, 205
Nazi Party, 15, 109, 127
NBA, 339
NBC, 57, 172, 205, 235
Nelson
   Mary, 83, 436
   Minnie, 140, 227, 436, 462
   Robert (h/o Ruth), 32, 193
   Ruth Kerr, 32, 145, 193
Neutrality Act, 157, 195
Newburgh-Cochecton Turnpike, 411
New Deal, 137, 148, 168
New Guinea, 255, 289, 305
New Jersey
   Atlantic City, 31, 257, 269, 306, 324, 326
   High Point, 133, 143, 218
   Jersey City, 34, 185, 356, 444
Newman, Paul, 124
New Mexico
   Alamogordo, 331
   Los Alamos, 255
New Paltz Normal School, 40
New York
   56th Infantry, 111
   Barryville, *references throughout the book*
   Binghamton, 18, 24, 43, 55, 66, 133, 231, 236, 304, 443
   Bloomingburg, 49
   Bronx, 10, 26, 43–4, 109–10, 204
   Brooklyn, 10, 11, 41, 66, 76, 91, 93, 95, 99, 123, 149, 163, 169, 180, 187, 203–4, 213, 241, 248–9, 259, 267, 270, 277, 282, 286–7, 290, 296, 333–4, 341, 347, 353, 357, 365, 458, 470
   Cairo, 19, 77, 145, 149, 210, 270, 371
   Callicoon, 22, 43, 162, 178, 183, 186, 204, 325, 342, 349, 353, 364, 366, 453
   Camp Shanks, 300
   Coney Island, 123
   Cooperstown, 195, 197
   Eldred (Village), *references throughout the book*
   Fort Jay, 262
   Fosterdale, 50, 53, 59, 173
   Glen Spey, 1, 17, 22, 61, 63, 81, 99, 108–9, 123, 142, 173, 243, 246, 261, 370, 457, 460
   Hancock, 157, 193, 198, 199, 356, 453
   Highland Lake, *references throughout the book*
   Hopewell Junction, 28, 39, 42, 44–50, 53–6, 58, 59, 64, 69, 76, 82
   Hurleyville, 121, 169
   Jeffersonville, 39, 188
   Liberty, 43, 127, 141, 188, 219, 220, 231, 235, 245, 255, 264, 272, 276, 343, 418
   Lordville, 293, 307
   Middletown, 18, 25, 27, 34, 55, 83, 127, 130–1, 146–7, 156, 169, 181, 210, 215, 272, 336, 339
   Minisink Ford, 1, 2, 8, 11, 18, 38, 41, 78, 91, 97–8, 109, 173, 182, 223, 319, 375–6, 447
   Mongaup, 47, 184
   Monticello, 9, 30, 34, 49, 55, 60, 63, 83, 135, 148, 151, 162, 171, 173, 179, 189, 200, 202, 214, 230, 364
   Narrowsburg, 43, 67–9, 81, 128, 132, 145, 171, 184, 219, 224, 225–7, 234, 236, 240–1, 243, 247, 248, 267, 273, 349, 358, 360, 374, 387

Newburgh, 49, 246, 266–7
New Paltz, 40, 42, 44–49, 53
New York City, 1, 8, 10, 16, 17, 26, 42, 45, 68, 72, 74, 81, 94, 96, 99, 101, 108, 117, 141, 148, 152, 157, 173, 175, 176, 189, 203–5, 212, 215, 227, 247, 251, 257, 282, 309, 312, 340, 344, 350, 355–6, 365, 396, 444, 446, 462, 465
Ossining, 82, 83, 110, 135, 141, 142, 151, 152, 161, 168, 179, 200, 230, 236, 240, 245, 404
Pond Eddy, 4, 6, 20, 34, 43, 53, 139, 143, 197, 200, 213, 265, 266, 267, 453, 456, 457
Port Jervis, 3, 43, 48, 56, 73, 77, 83, 91, 111, 120, 125, 131, 138, 141, 144, 156, 157, 170, 182, 188–9, 192–3, 198–201, 206, 214–6, 224, 228, 230–1, 236, 241, 244, 246, 252, 257, 264–5, 275, 280, 338, 340, 346–7, 349, 356, 366, 390, 453
Poughkeepsie, 20, 42, 46, 266, 306, 307
Queens, 87, 93, 316, 322, 468
Ridgebury, 13
Salamanca, 30
Sidney, 240, 242, 271, 280, 368, 379
Sparrowbush, 173
Staten Island, 45, 47, 49, 108, 148, 178-2, 203, 215–7, 221, 227, 251, 260, 268–9, 272, 276, 279, 283, 293, 303, 316, 324, 327, 330, 333, 340
Town of Highland, *references throughout the book*
Town of Lumberland, 1, 4, 61, 63, 243, 375, 390, 457, 465
Tusten, XII, 63, 68, 117, 165, 350, 453
Tuxedo, 209
Wellstown, 232, 468
White Sulphur Springs, 43, 141
Youngsville, 43
Yulan, 1–4, 8, 11, 14, 20, 22, 25–6, 29, 35, 38, 41, 67–8, 77, 81, 91–7, 102, 117, 129, 159, 173, 196, 213, 220, 223, 236, 237, 243–4, 294–5, 309, 315, 331, 345, 347, 350, 355–6, 358–60, 367, 375, 432, 434–5, 438, 446, 448, 454, 463–5, 469–71
N.Y. Route 97 (3A), 109, 128, 131, 157, 193, 198–9, 213, 243, 350, 360–1, 453
Niagara Falls, 253, 405
Nieke
    Barbara, 471
    George and Leona, 470
    G. Nieke, 349
    James, V
    L., 349
    William, 313, 318, 327–8, 337, 456
Nielsen family, 137
Nifenecker, Camille, 455, 471
Nikolaus
    Celina, 346, 371, 372
    John and Celina, 335, 341, 354
Nikolaus Restaurant, 355
Nitzsche
    Fred, 87, 213, 332, 443, 447, 470
    Minnie, 87, 89, 90, 91, 213, 332, 443, 447, 470
    Nitzsche and Frey, 87–8, 93, 129, 159, 223, 367
Nixon, Richard M., 331
Nobel Prize, 31
Noble, Margaret, 446
Noble House, 129
Noe, Mrs. Louis, 66
Nolan, Rose, 365
Nooy, Lt. J.G. (Connie), 311-2
North Africa, 205, 219, 255, 275, 276, 283, 289, 291, 295, 297
North Carolina, Aberdeen, 24
Norway, 137, 205
Nugent, Maurice, 313
Nuremberg Trials, 157, 331

O

Oakdene, 8, 10–1, 93–4, 159, 312, 432, 446, 454
Oakland Hotel, 63
Oanna Mountain Farm, 38, 41
O'Connor, James, 317
Odell, Clinton, 54
O'Donnell, Frank (Mac), 230, 249, 275, 280, 319, 337, 363, 450, 458
Oellrich, Anna, 243
O'Gara, Tom, 243
O'Keefe, Georgia, 15
Oklahoma, Oklahoma City, 117, 272
Old House at Home, 92–3
Olympic House, 186
Olympics, 42, 165
O'Neil/O'Neill
    Clara, 193
    John, 193, 265
    Robert, 313
Oneonta College, 83, 143, 173
Operation Catapult, 205
Orchard Terrace, 3, 14, 44–6, 54, 78, 107, 374
Ort
    Anna Sergeant Brague, 58, 157, 166, 182–3, 185, 188, 194, 197, 204, 211, 218, 230, 274–5, 278, 307, 385, 459
    Bertha LaBarr, 29, 324, 468
    Charles, 43, 144, 157, 166, 182, 185, 218, 249, 274–5, 278, 385, 444, 459
    Frank Jr., 43, 385
    Frank and Lena, 439
    Frank Sr., 43, 432
    George, 43, 385
    John, 251, 279, 303, 317, 324, 337
    Mary Crandall, 43, 75, 166, 275, 308, 384, 385, 432, 444, 459
    Milton, 29, 317, 324, 325, 333, 337
    M., 215
    William, 29, 43, 229, 324
    William and Bertha, 434, 444, 451
    William Jr., 214, 324, 337, 385
Orwell, George, 371
Osborne, James, 449
Oset
    Chester, 93, 259, 313, 315, 337, 353, 357, 370
    Helen Hensel, V, 109, 159, 353, 357–8, 370
    Henry, 93, 353, 370
    Joseph, 93, 259, 315, 337, 464
    Stanley Sr., 93

Stanley Jr., 93, 259, 315, 337
Walter, 93, 259, 303, 307, 315, 337
Osler
   Dr. Jay Osler, 262
   Mary Murray Schoonover, 19, 262, 394
Osterhoudt/Osterhout
   Charles and Margaret, 449
   George and Clara, 472
   Homer, 457
Ott
   Charles and Christina, 341, 466
   Christine, 185, 215
   Cynthia, 241
   Katherine, 185
Ottoman Empire, 31
Outlook Cottage, 38, 41, 92, 93
Owen
   Barry, 117, 371, 463
   Basil, 8, 93, 165–6, 219, 261, 277, 432, 446
   Catherine Jr. and Sr., 117
   Earl, 117
   Elizabeth Tether, 193
   Ernest, 117, 137, 173
   Frank, 11, 93, 94, 117, 432
   Frank and Katherine, 455
   Ina, 83, 117, 166, 177, 454, 470
   Jesse, 165
   Mrs. K., 129
   Phoebe Middaugh, 8, 11, 93, 94, 152, 159, 164, 165, 168, 426, 432, 446, 454
   Richard, 164
   Robert and Elizabeth Tether, 117
   Russell, 8, 83, 93–4, 101, 117, 151, 166, 177, 249, 261, 310, 319, 323, 370, 432, 437–8, 446, 449, 451, 454, 458
   William, 8–10, 177, 426, 432
   William (s/o Russell), 463
Ozenbaugh
   Ella, 437, 449
   Lillian, 437, 449, 461

P

Pacific Ocean Theatre, 308
Page, Thad S., 24
Palmer
   Dick (Pat), 147
   Earl and Catherine, 449
   Earl and Kate, 6
   Earl, 6, 313, 438
   Harriet Leavenworth, 83, 379
   Henry and Harriet Leavenworth 421
   Pat, 4
   Richard, 83, 173, 265, 313
   Virginia West, V
Panama, 61, 122, 173
Pancho Villa, 15, 31
Pankow
   Adolph and Agnes Ozanich, 187
   Agnes, 184, 239, 468
   Charles, 184, 186, 187, 225, 238, 239, 365, 367, 373, 468
   Charlie and Millie, 365
   Diane, V, 187, 365
   Millie (Ann) Hughes, 365, 373
Paramount Manor Hotel, 169
Park Hotel (Yulan Hotel), 10–1, 38, 41, 93, 95–7, 129, 159, 223, 446, 454
Parker
   Andrew, 13–4, 113, 131, 208, 244, 263, 281, 317, 337, 385
   Andy and Marge, 208–9, 458
   Anna, 27, 29, 444, 455
   Beatrice, 185, 441, 466
   Blanche, 127, 173
   Edith, 220, 232
   Eleanora Alston, 14, 29, 37, 63, 77, 79, 98, 242, 244, 443, 450, 459, 461
   Elsie Hazen, 43, 96, 206
   Emily Christene Payne, 3, 11, 14, 27, 81, 98, 109, 164, 165, 271, 388, 432
   George Jr., 210, 216
   George (s/o Mary Murray), 19, 145, 149, 394
   Harvey, 27, 113, 133–5, 157, 337, 341, 411, 441, 467
   Hazel, 63, 98, 244
   Howard, 98, 134, 337
   James and Mabel Hazen, 456, 469
   James Y. I, 3, 14, 109, 433
   James Y. (s/o William), 13–4, 109, 244, 433
   John H., 313
   Kate, 19, 25, 149, 183, 185, 207, 394
   Leon, 69
   Mabel Hazen, 223
   Mae Hammond, 64, 101, 210–6, 219, 224, 225, 227–8, 230, 245–7, 250, 252–4, 258, 261, 264, 273, 278, 280, 441, 445, 450, 466
   Marge, 208, 209, 244, 263
   Mary Whalen, 281, 303
   Phoebe Simpson, 432, 443
   Sandy and Sue, V
   Shirley, 77, 98, 244
   Victoria Simpson, 13–4, 27, 98, 109, 137, 242, 244, 257, 280, 322–3, 327, 370, 432, 443, 450, 458
   Warren and Anna, 27, 29, 439
   Warren Parker, 27, 145, 173, 265, 290, 317, 337, 410
   William H. (1), 13–4, 98, 109, 432, 450
   William H. (2), 13, 14, 27, 29, 37, 43, 63, 77, 79, 96, 98, 109, 117, 244, 433, 450, 459
   William H. Jr. (3), V, 37, 79, 80, 98, 133–4, 147, 196, 241, 244, 281–2, 303, 315, 317, 337
Parker Hotel, 3, 11, 14, 27, 44, 80, 81, 130, 133, 138, 196, 208, 280, 432, 440, 450
Parker's Store, 208, 369
Parkers Glen geyser, 455
Parmenter
   Henry, 23, 81
   Sophorina, 23, 57
Paton
   Archibald R. and Mabel Slagle, 394, 401
   Archie C., 377, 395
   Archie H. and Rand Austin, 18, 377, 394, 401
   Archie R. and Mabel Slagle, 18, 261, 377
   Rand Austin, 18, 377, 395, 397, 401
Pat's Stand, 107, 108
Patterson
   Edmund, 436
   Rev. and Mrs., 73
Patton, G.S. Jr., 289, 318, 327–8

Paulik, Josef and Theresa, 73–4
Paulus
    Charles, V, 373, 452
    Shirley, 371
Paye, Andrew Paye, 457
Pegg
    Albert Jr., 245, 299, 333
    Albert Sr., 245, 255, 333, 335
    Julia Straub, 16, 245, 255, 333, 335, 368, 445
Pelton
    Asher and Carrie, 63, 77
    Edith, 47, 63
    Edward, 63, 77
    Howard, 4, 63, 68, 71, 220, 436
penicillin, 297
Penney
    J.C. Penney store, 83
    J.C. and Carolyn Autenrieth, 59
Pennsylvania
    Hawley, 5, 10, 158, 191, 202, 241, 338
    Honesdale, 5, 9, 25, 37, 81, 161, 170, 226, 262–3, 299, 354, 387
    Lackawaxen, 22, 98, 109, 117, 262
    Matamoras, 63, 83, 166, 241, 339
    Pittsburgh, 5, 15, 68
    Scranton, 20, 226, 227, 404
    White Mills, 5
Pepper, Edmund, 313
Perkins, Alvin, 173
Pershing, Gen. John J., 99
Petkus, Dr., 364, 410
Petterson, Sophia, 433
Philippines, 235, 291, 305, 308, 310–1, 318, 339, 419
    Manila, 251, 255, 291
Philips/Phillips
    Annie, 463
    Gertrude Peirano, 117, 173
Picasso, Pablo, 15
Pickford, Mary, 15, 124
Pierce, Charles C., 61, 64
Piermont Hotel, 11, 19, 93, 100, 104, 326, 445
Pine, Leon D. and Anna, 442
Pine Beach Inn, 93, 100, 104, 166
Pine Crest, 225
Pine Grove Cottage, 11, 93–4, 117, 129
Pine Grove House, 13, 93, 100, 102, 128–9, 137, 446, 450
Pine Hill Lodge, 104, 345, 367
Pinehurst, 37, 92–3, 102, 129, 147, 163, 193, 225, 345, 367, 445, 450
Pinehurst Cottage, 92–3
Pine Terrace, 61
Pisarski, Helen Crandall, V, 384
Poell, Emil, 345, 470
Poland, 15, 145, 195, 198, 453, 465
Polishook, Joan, V, 237, 360
Polk, Jack, 337
Polley, George, 433
Porter, Cole, 15
Portz, Mary, 456
Posse Nissen School, 135
Poth
    Anthony, 350, 373
    J., 349
    Nellie, 373, 464
Prairie Mound Cemetery, 82, 402
Prange, Ed, 97
Proctor/Proctor's, 134, 180, 234, 236, 251, 253, 381
Proctor Road, 2, 14, 16, 17, 48, 79, 82, 99, 104, 112, 171, 208, 210, 275, 366, 376, 433, 434, 460
Proper, Hilda, 193
Protz, 223, 367
    Herman and Mathilde, 237, 470
Public Works Project, 109
Purcell
    Andrew, 74, 259, 261, 306, 313, 337
    Edward, 74, 174, 185, 259, 303, 306, 313, 337
    Eva, 74, 259, 447, 462
    Gladys (Billie) Billings, 303
    Jack, 74, 290
    James, V, 74, 174, 193, 259, 304, 306, 313, 337
    James (son of Ed), V
    James Sr., 74
    John, 165, 173, 259, 265, 313, 337
    Rita Cantwell, 177, 332
Purple Heart, 323–4, 306, 333
Putnam
    Edward and Blanch, 462
    Richard, 206, 215, 313, 337
Puycher
    Ted, 313
    Thaddeus, 337
Pyle, Ernie, 331

Q

Quick
    Ami and Anna, 437, 448
    Eleanor, 157, 173
    Fannie, 472
    Harold, 4, 66, 71
    Irving, 4
    Irving and Pearl, 437, 449
    Johnnie, 274
    Millard and Ethel, 448
    Mrs., 32, 227
    Napoleon B. and Frances White, 267, 456
    Roger, 127, 173, 271
    Will, 227, 438
Quinlan, *History of Sullivan County*, 248
Quinn Place, 229, 243, 323, 410, 411
Quota Act, 31

R

Rachmaninoff, Sergei, 145
Racine, 410
    Hiram and Prudence, 55
    Lawrence, 182, 185, 459
    Truman, 443, 449
radar, 157, 272, 286
Ralph, Rev. John, 109, 111
Ramberg Dry Dock, 259
Ramsey, Madeleine, 193
Rowland, 157, 173, 317, 337
    William and Clara, 454
Randolph
    Alexander, 79, 192, 198, 208, 209, 274, 276, 458
    Kay Myers, 209, 227, 275, 458
Randolph's, 79, 176, 192, 198, 208, 209, 240, 254, 263, 264, 275
Rasmussen, 171
    Margaret (Peggy), 308
Rathbone, Basil, 219
Rationing, 261, 296
Rauer, Robert, 319

Rauscher, Theodore and Ruth, 385
Rave, Anna Rave, 341
Henry, 332, 466
Ray, Magdala Trautsch, V, 428
RCA, 57, 117
Reber/Reber's, 6, 7, 213, 358, 360, 361, 373, 374
    Hermann and Matilda, 361
    Mr. Reber, 43
Red Army, 15, 177, 205, 235, 305
Redman's Hall, 261
Reed, D., 349
Reid, Charles, 446
Reiser,
    A., 349
    Henrietta, 373
    James, 371
Reles, Abe, 169
Rennenberg, Anton and Mary, 11, 104, 441, 445, 450, 467
Republican Party, 205
Reuther
    Fred, 317, 413
    Virginia McBride, 98, 119, 120, 144, 183, 335
Revi, Albert C. 5
Ricciardi, Barone Roberto, 291, 407
Rider, Ed, 202
Riker
    Alice DeFeo, 94, 152, 166, 312
    Robert and Alice DeFeo, 261
Riverside Cottage (Warshauer's), 11, 38, 41, 92, 93, 95, 129, 159, 166, 223, 367, 443, 447
Riviera Theater, 7, 360, 361, 362
Rixton
    Claudia Hickok Freeman, 145
    Harriet, 177, 437
    Henry G., 177
    Herman and Catharine, 436, 447
    Herman, 22, 29, 117, 241
    Joseph, 145, 157, 463, 447
Rizzuto
    Eleanor Myers, 9, 19, 36, 61, 62, 72, 79, 104, 120, 121, 176, 177, 300–1, 353, 427
    Elizabeth and Roberta, 384
    Sam, 300, 353, 427
    Timothy C., V, 384
RMS Queen Elizabeth, 31, 205, 284
RMS Queen Mary, 205, 336, 343

Roberts
    Eugene, 315, 337
    Eugene and Gertrude, 464
    Marie, 83, 173
Robertson, Dick, 124
Robinson, Harvey G., 313
Rockefeller, Nelson, 381
Rockne, Knute, 15
Roebling Bridge, 98, 374
Roebling Sons, 74
Rogers, Will, 15
Rohman/Rohman's, 124, 147, 241, 282, 358, 390
    Art, 113, 124, 147, 165, 241, 282, 350
    Gwen, 157, 173
    Kate Hess, 124, 137
    Nick, 113, 121, 123–4, 142, 144
Rollenetz
    Ernest and Bessie, 469
    Helen, 370
Romania, 74, 205, 219, 269, 305
Rommel, Erwin, 235, 255, 276, 289, 290, 305
Roosevelt
    Fireside Chats, 137, 198
    Franklin D., 124, 126, 127–8, 137, 157, 168, 195, 198, 200, 205, 216, 219, 224, 235, 253, 288–9, 305, 316, 326, 331, 453
    Four essential freedoms, 235
Rosemary Lodge, 91–3
Ross, Lawrence H., 313
Rothacker, John A., 313
Rothman/Rothman's, 99, 236, 242, 244
    Anna, 99, 445, 453
Rouillon
    Blanche Olga Malinge, 25, 75, 76, 125, 127
    Cyrus, 30, 68, 125, 136, 425, 436
    Jean Charles, 25
    Jeanne Marguerite Lair, 30, 37, 68, 75, 77
Royal Greenwich Observatory, 42
Royal Scarlet, 179, 192, 198, 208, 209, 243, 369, 458, 459
Rudolph
    Joseph and Blanche, 463
    M., 349

Ruether, Virginia McBride, 120, 183, 332, 413–4
Rundle
    Abe, 410
    D., 349
    Delbert, 211, 240, 451
    Jane, 232, 241
    Robert, 189, 443, 465
    Robert and Jennie, 451
    Sadie, 273
Rupp
    Henry and Minnie, 455
    Mimie, 471
Russel/Russell
    Abraham, 121
    Geraldine Mills, 145, 202, 252, 341, 373
    Stuart and Geraldine Mills, V
Ruth, Babe, 15, 124, 157, 197
Ryman
    Mabel Boyd, 211, 450, 467
    Ray, 138, 445, 450, 467

S

Samyn, Arthur, 345
San Antonio Aviation Cadet Center, 306
Sand Beach, 101–2, 104, 168
Sanders, Shirley, 116, 118, 453
Sand Hill Fruit Growers, 24
Sardone, Barbara Ihlo, V, 341, 431
Schapals, Elizabeth Whitmarsh, 29, 37, 63, 384, 427
Scheniman
    Charles, 63
    Charles and Sara, 73, 440
    Lulu Myers, 115, 426
Schick, Jacob, 77
Schmalze, Lewis, 241, 243
Schmerfeld
    William and Katherine, 322
    William, 261
Schmid
    Agnes Pankow, 184, 187, 239, 365
    Catherine and Lillian, 187
    Henry/Henny, 187, 239, 365
Schmidt
    Frances McBride, 98, 119, 120, 144, 332, 335, 413
    Otto, 333, 335, 341, 350, 413,

INDEX • 499

437
Schneider
　Genevieve, 370
　Mrs., 50
Schoner, Alvin, 447
Schoonmaker
　Caroline, 443
　Robert, 437
Schoonover
　Ann Mary Austin, 19, 376, 394–5
　Emily Banner, 19, 117, 149, 209, 210, 214, 219, 232, 242, 258, 268, 370, 376–7, 394, 457
　Mary Murray Parker, 19, 145, 149, 183, 185, 376–7, 394
　Perry, 19, 149, 270, 376, 394–6, 377
　Rowlee, 9, 19, 117, 149, 207, 209–11, 219–20, 224, 228, 230, 232, 242, 246, 254, 258, 262–3, 268, 275, 370, 376–7, 394, 457, 461
　William, 19, 185, 394
Schoverling
　Albert, 17, 38, 93, 106, 446
　Annette, 385
　Fred, 16, 37, 38, 93, 349, 385
　Fred and Annette, 41, 106, 446, 451
Schreib, Otto and Maria, 18, 446
Schroedel
　Charlee Hirsch, V, 37, 43–4, 51, 71–2, 110–1, 113, 144, 154–5, 171, 176, 206, 240, 250–1, 261, 264–5, 269, 277, 284, 299, 301, 304–5, 325, 328–9, 334–5, 336, 381, 421
　Charles (Chuck), 380, 381
　Ed and Charlee Hirsch, 380
　Edward, 381, 421
　Matt, V, 221, 380–1
　Ric, V, 380–1
　Tony, 380–1
Schroeder
　Alan and Charles Jr., 373
　Bill Jr., 153, 365
　Charlie Sr., 341, 373
　George, 153
　Hank, 365
　Hattie, 211, 243
　Henry, 153

Mrs., 226
Norma Ott, 303, 341, 373
Otto and Hattie, 73, 453
William Sr., 153, 186
Schumacher
　Dora, 434
　Ed and Catharine, 434, 454
　Edward, 464
　Henry and Kate, 456
　Katie, 470
　Mrs., 183, 185
　Mrs. Edward, 92–3
Schwab
　Agnes, 7, 443, 448
　Fred and Marjory, 435
　Margery Kerr, 77
　Schwab Family, 7, 11, 37, 63, 77
Schwarz
　Anna Eckstein, 63
　Augusta, 442, 457
　Ella Getz, 177, 297, 319
　Frank V, V, 61
　Franz A., 22, 61, 63
　Franz and Anna, 442
　Irena, 63
　Joseph and Augusta, 442
　Margarett, Victor, Walter, 63
　Walter, 457
Scintilla Magneto, 240, 242, 271
Scofield, Kathy Wilson, V, 358, 370
Scopes, John T., 57
Scotland, 77, 252, 298
Scott
　Chris, 33, 37, 100, 102, 129, 163, 225, 445
　Chris and Kathryn, 37, 445
　Chris Jr., 193
　George, 413
　Virginia, 177
Sears
　Edith Darling, 18, 63, 384, 427
　Henry, 427
Sears and Roebuck, 116, 125, 156, 158, 164, 356
Seel, Otto, 17, 106, 367
Segarra, Dawn Lee Austin, 213–6, 268, 292, 318, 330, 340, 366, 368, 379
Seibert, George W., 111
Seitz, 92–3
　Carl, 129, 315, 337
　Carl and Borghild, 451

Lillian, 117, 173
Selassie, Haile, 165
Selective Training Service, 213, 219
Sergeant
　Alice Spiers, 9, 353, 362, 429, 439
　Alvah and Margaret Clemens, 430, 438
　Alvah (Charles A.) and Mary Hulse, 120, 128, 156, 191, 194, 336, 429–30, 439, 444, 454, 466
　Alvah and Phebe Owen, 13, 63, 131, 157, 177, 429
　Alvah (Charles A. b. 1882), 113–4, 120, 136, 156, 226, 329, 338
　Alvah T. (d. 1921), 12–3, 25
　Anna Hull, 12, 36, 102, 113, 115–6, 123, 137, 144, 168, 170–1, 181, 192–3, 303, 314, 441, 450
　Charles A. (b. 1913), 112–4, 117, 118, 128, 147, 166–7, 168, 170, 173, 177–8, 190, 193, 202, 276, 429
　Charles E. (baby), 190, 192–3
　(Charles) Edgar, 12–3, 29, 57–9, 63, 127, 190, 429, 440, 445
　Charlie and Clareta Kuen, 118, 190, 193, 212–3, 466
　Clarence and Claudia, 466
　Clarence, 211, 218, 248, 267, 342, 441, 444, 450
　Clareta Kuen, 113, 165–6, 173, 177–8, 190, 192–3, 292
　Clarissa Clark, 82, 114
　Claudia, 211, 218, 268, 273
　Elizabeth Clark, 29, 429
　Ethel B. and Lettie Gardner, 429
　Ethel, 13
　Family, 4, 12, 429–30
　Frank and Anna Hull, 102, 113, 116, 123, 130–1, 256–7, 441, 446, 450
　Frank and Clarissa Clark, 29, 429
　Frank, 12–3, 17, 36, 43, 67, 102, 113, 115–6, 118, 121, 123–4, 126, 128, 130–1, 137, 382
　Grant, 113–4, 121, 166, 197,

203, 254, 264, 273, 280, 293, 299, 312, 317, 324–5, 328–9, 337–8, 353, 364, 429, 466
  Helen Kuen, 113, 166, 193, 317, 353, 372, 461
  Henrietta Halstead Crawford, 12, 63, 127, 455
  Isaac and Elizabeth Persbacher, 12, 13, 429
  James Gardner and Emma Myers, 429
  Lettie Gardner, 13
  Lettie Hait, 429
  Lillie, 268
  Margaret Clemens, 12, 213
  Mary Richards, 4, 13, 429
  Mary Hulse, 58, 113–5, 118, 120, 125, 142, 156, 194, 202, 211, 229, 230, 232, 264, 299, 307, 328–9, 335–6, 338, 366, 429, 439
  Mauna Lee, 213
  Morgan, 9, 12–3, 113, 131, 138, 156, 362, 429, 439, 444, 453
  Morgan and Alice, 469
  Phebe Owen, 12
  Rev. Isaac, 4, 10, 13, 131, 391, 429
  Stephen and Anna Penney, 429
Seven Oaks, 11, 16, 99, 442
Shadler, Edward and Antonia, 437
Sharkey, Charles A., 313
Sharpe, William, 457
Shaw, George Bernard, 15
Sheen
  Elias A., 117
  Elias and Rachel, 463
  Kenneth, 34, 117, 173
  Mr., 199
  Roger, 83, 173
  Thorne, 174, 193
Shell Cottage, 58
Shostakovich, Dmitri, 255
Shotwell, Stephen, 438, 448
Shubert, Mr., 55, 60–1, 64
Siberia, 177
Side Hill Farm, 38, 41, 92, 129
Sidwell
  Family, 125
  Mr., 113, 123
  Mrs., 121
  Music, 410

Siegel, Harry, 450
Simon, Frederick, 437
Simpson
  Sam, 137
  Wallis, 165
Singer Machine Co., 250
Singing Pines, 17, 106, 367
Sinsheimer Store, 66
Sir Humphrey Davy Club, 167
Slonek
  Emily, 444
  House, 2, 116
Smith
  Abby H., 418, 420
  Al and Jane, 282
  Albert, 147
  Al (ran for Pres.), 71
  Austin, 5–7, 113, 121–3, 126–8, 130, 135, 137–8, 158, 160–1, 166, 203, 321–2, 448, 461
  Austin and Dot Kuen, 194
  Cyrinthia, 418
  Dale, 322
  Dale and Tricia McDowell, V
  Dorothy (Dot) Kuen, 113, 121, 123, 127, 161, 166, 203
  Dr., 21, 47, 66, 119, 128, 410
  Edward, 5–7, 113, 122, 158, 192, 243, 353, 437
  Edward and Mabel Austin, 437, 448, 461
  Gary, V, 371
  Hannah Haddasseh Hickok, 418
  James, 265, 313, 337
  Julia and Zephina, 418
  Laurilla, 418, 420
  Louise Austin, 371–2, 374, 375, 379, 430
  Mabel Austin, 6, 7, 113, 122, 126, 127, 192, 194, 370, 373
  Margaret, 206
  Mrs. (wife of Dr. Smith), 71
  Olliamus D., 117, 255, 272, 371
  Wilna, 117, 371
  Zephaniah H., 418
Social Security, 157, 205
Solomon Islands, 268, 289, 291
Somaliland, 219, 235
South America
  Brazil, 246
  Venezuela, Maracaibo, 60, 62, 64, 68, 70, 79

Spangenberg, Oren, 460
Sparks
  John, 3, 81, 107, 145, 443, 450
  Martha, 443, 459
  Mrs., 211, 236, 265, 274
Spaudling, Dr., 158
Spock, Benjamin, 339
Spring House, 6–7, 11, 38, 92, 172, 200–1, 212, 223, 303, 435, 443, 447, 463
Spring House Garage, 6, 212
S.S. Athenia, 195
S.S. Cleveland, 163
S.S. Christobal, 173
S.S. Edwin Markham, 235
S.S. John C. Fremont, 255
S.S. Nick Stoner, 341, 343, 344
S.S. President Harding, 117
S.S. President Monroe, 117
S.S. President Van Buren, 117
Stage, Charlie, 410
Stalin, Joseph, 31, 75, 77, 83, 165, 177, 235, 255, 289, 331
Stalker
  Belle Mills, 77, 308, 446
  Tom, 77
Standard Oil Co., 78
Stanley, Ralph, 83, 107, 456
Stanton
  Betty, 241
  Lillian, 157, 173
  Mary, 145, 173
Staubes
  Art and Irene, 471
  Arthur, 319, 337, 341
  Charles E., 337
  Gustave and Hattie, 451, 467
  Irene Theuer, 163, 186, 341, 347
  Staubes family, 2, 11, 37, 38, 100, 102, 104, 127, 129, 163, 173, 225, 341, 471
Steel/Steele
  Edwin and Anna, 447, 463
  John Edwin, 287
  William, 459
Stege
  Ed, 158
  Edward and Kate, 444, 451
  Kate 16, 98, 158, 165, 189
Stege property, 16, 161, 162, 189, 219, 227, 247, 253, 374, 387, 388

Stege Road, 14, 38, 99, 104, 446
Stege's Lake, 143, 387
Steinbeck, John, 177
Steiner, Walter, 219, 224
Stevens
    Charles, 337
    Emily Christene Parker, IV, 3, 9, 14, 27, 98, 109, 126, 130, 133, 150, 208, 209, 220, 231, 234, 236, 250, 257, 258, 276, 286, 341, 355, 385, 450, 460
    H., 349
    Harold, 337
    Howard, IV, 4, 9, 14, 27, 63, 68, 71–2, 79, 98, 127, 130, 134, 137–8, 145–6, 157, 167, 196, 203, 208–9, 211–2, 220, 231–2, 240, 244, 247, 263, 270–1, 274, 286, 315, 317, 341, 370, 387, 432, 436, 442–3, 450, 457, 460
Steward, Johnny, 29
Stewart
    Jim, 124
    Mr., 141
Stickel, Fritz and Ella, 367, 459
Stidd
    Lillian, 93, 95, 452, 458
    William and Mary Hickok, 418
Still Story, 133
St. Joseph's Seminary, 204
Stolt, Joseph and Sadie, 101, 106, 446
Stolte
    Christiane Lorphelin, V, 341, 346, 354
    George, 317
Stowell, Barbara Kate James, V, 371
Straub
    Fridolin and Juliana, 8, 434
    Fridolin (Fred) Jr., 16, 99, 366, 370, 450, 459
    Fridolin Sr., 9, 16
    Ida, 225
    Juliana, 11, 16, 61, 63
Straub's Hotel, 8, 11, 14, 16, 46, 99, 225, 245, 291–2, 369, 445, 450, 458–9
Street, Mr., 4
Strenglein
    Adelaide, 225, 466
    Dave, 417
    Frank, 319, 337
    Harry, 288, 319
    Kate, 284, 462
Sturgis Motorcycle Rally, 205
Stuyvesant, Peter, 99
St. Valentine's Day Massacre, 83
Styles, 410
    Charles, 17, 55
    Georgia Clark, 17, 60, 64, 82, 83, 113–4, 121, 131, 210–1, 366, 450
    Sarah, 17
    Walter, 17, 37, 55, 211, 219, 264, 265, 275, 349, 366, 370, 433, 445, 458
Suessman, Fritz, 22–3, 448
Sullivan
    Bertha, 211–2, 225, 227, 263, 273, 434
    Bill, 230, 241
    Cecelia, 160, 459
    Charles, 211
    Charles and Bertha, 434, 451, 468
    F., 202
    Mrs., 254
    Peter, 211, 232, 434
    V., 291
    William, 469
Sulzbach, 102
    Clifford, 157, 173, 193, 319, 337
    Dorothy Barker, 193, 390, 462
    Edward, 193
    Frances, 163, 193, 225, 445, 466
    Harry, 37, 127, 173, 193, 363
    Harry and Frances, 445, 450
    Margaret Olsen, 193
    Mary, 241
    Mrs. H., 93
    P., 349
    Robert, 332
Sunday, Billy, 79
Sunset Bar, 104, 163, 186, 347
Sunset Cottage, 96–7, 129–31, 159, 196, 223, 309, 356, 367, 454, 469
Sunset View House, 11, 63, 93, 102, 104, 163, 186, 225, 345, 445
Sunshine Hall, 16, 22, 58, 78–9, 145, 234, 274
Sunshine Hall Free Library, 16, 39, 40, 46, 58, 439
Sutherland
    Arthur and Annie, 402
    Barbara and Norman, 358, 360
    Gracie, 402
    Margaret Myers, 184–5, 358, 385, 386
    Norman H., 184–5, 358, 385–6
    Norman W., 373
    Norman W. and Barbara Bridge, 184
    Sutherland family, 184
    William G., 402
Swanson, Gloria, 15, 124
Swartz, Ellsworth, 447
Sweeny, Judge, 329
Switzerland, Geneva, 15

T

Taeterow, William, 38, 41
Tallwood Lodge, 223, 256, 257, 309, 349
Task Force 58, 308
Taylor
    George Washington, 427, 428
    Mary Webber Lazerlier, 428
    Robert and Mary Webber Lazerlier, 427
    Sarah, 427, 428
Taylor University, 20, 30, 139
Teed, Clara Austin, 376
Temperance Tavern, 14
Ten Mile River Scout Camp, 68, 84, 113–5, 120, 128, 132, 146, 245, 247, 266, 307, 324, 335–6, 346, 364
    Camp Manhattan, 144, 364
Terpening, Vera, 459
Tesla, Nikola, 15
Tessmer, Rudolph, 315
Testa, Judy Guamer, V
Tether
    Anne, 10
    Helen Jayne, 353
    Ivan and Helen Jayne, 371
    Ivan J., 371
    Ivan J. and Jana, V
    Ivan s/o Walter, 10, 80, 295, 325, 353
    Joseph, 10, 38, 109, 193, 358
    Meda Breen, 10, 80, 96, 370

Walter, 10, 38, 41, 80, 93, 95, 96, 109, 113, 116–7, 129, 142, 159, 190, 194, 201, 223, 295, 309, 325, 353
Walter and Meda Breen, 432, 446, 448, 463
Texas, Camp Bowie, 283
Thailand, 235
The Pines, 98, 151, 162, 180, 182, 203, 232, 237, 453
Theuer, 2, 102, 104, 163, 225
   Alfons and Johanna, 163, 186, 345, 347, 471
Thiele, Henry and Anna, 442
Thiesen, Veronica, 127, 173
Thomas
   Chauncey, 124, 350
   Lowell, 172, 175, 283
Thompson
   Addie Austin, 18, 395, 397
   Augustus A., 18, 377, 394, 398
   Augustus A. and Gertrude Cotton, 395
   Augustus Austin Family, V
   Elbert Paul, 18, 377, 394
   Elward Austin, 18, 377, 394–5
   Gertrude Cotton, 18, 377, 394
   Isaac and Rufus, 419
   Thomas E., 75, 394
   Thomas J. and Addie Austin, 18, 75, 377, 394
Thorpe, Jim, 15
Time Magazine, 31
Timmerhoff
   Betty and Charles, 112, 113
   Bud, 134
   Edith Sergeant, 29, 112, 264, 266, 273
   Ernest, 29, 77
   Ernest and Edith Sergeant, 113, 450, 466
   Ernest Jr., 337
   Joyce, 353
Tito, 289
Titus, Mr., 155, 174
Toaspern
   Arthur and Emma, 449
   Arthur C., 8, 55, 350, 460
   Barbara Wickus, 341, 373, 431
   Dennis, 287
   Doris Boudman, 241, 287
   Doris Doeller, V, 91, 92, 206, 287
   Edward, 8, 43, 113, 123, 131, 142, 144, 162, 170, 172, 178, 243, 261, 266–7, 282, 294, 304, 306, 308, 310–2, 315, 316, 318, 320, 324, 330–1, 335, 337, 373, 431
   Emma Rueger, 8
   Emma Straub, 266–7, 278, 282, 368, 435, 443
   Henry Christian (Chris) and Ida Heyen, 8
   Mr. Toaspern, 114
   Pat Myers, V, 286–7, 326–7, 384
   Royden, 8, 34, 123, 241, 287, 435, 449, 460
   Toaspern family, 8, 87
   Walt C. and Emma Straub, 8, 25, 29, 43, 131, 155, 267, 311, 366, 373, 449, 460
   Walter (Bub), 8, 157, 173, 287, 315, 337, 435, 449
   Walter C., 147, 261
Toaspern's Pond, 41, 97
Tojo, Prime Minister, 305
Tolkien, J.R.R., 177
Tolstoy, 15
Torwood Farm, 11, 38, 41
Toth, Lotsey, 74, 363
Transylvania, 73, 74
Traver
   Charles and Jennie, 435, 462
   J., 349
   John, 143, 263, 315, 337, 462
Travis, G.W., 28, 30
Traxler, Katherine Calkin, IV, V, 254, 287, 295, 368, 378–9
Trotsky, Leon, 219
Truman, Harry S., 326, 328, 331
Turash
   Hilko and Sadie, 445
   William, 319, 337
Turkey, 31
Turner
   Betty, 303
   Ida, 341
   Jeanie Staubes, V
   Mamie, 371
Turney, Gene, 68
Tutankhamun, 31
Tuthill
   Harry L., 315
   Virginia, 241
Tuzza, Mrs., 26, 32, 48, 66
Twichell, John and Edith, 457
Twin Oak Cottage, 159, 345, 356
Tyler, Harry, 50

U

U-boat, 195, 235
Ukraine, Kiev, 15
Umbreit, Herman, 367
Under the Pines, 116, 132
United Nations, 289, 305, 331, 339
U.S. Cadet Nurses Corps, 296–7
U.S. gold standard, 137
U.S.S. Akron, 130
U.S.S. Arizona, 275
U.S.S. Belleau Wood, 324, 431
U.S.S. Cabot, 308
U.S.S. Chateau Thierry, 122, 407
U.S.S. Franklin D. Roosevelt, 329
U.S.S. Greer, 235
U.S.S. Intrepid, 316, 318
U.S.S. Langley, 31
U.S.S. Missouri, 331
U.S.S. Panay, 177
U.S.S.R. (Soviet Union), 31, 77, 145, 157, 165, 195, 205, 235, 289, 331
   Moscow, 42, 235, 255
   Soviet Communist Party, 31
   Stalingrad, 255, 276
U.S.S. Wasp, 329

V

Valentino, Rudolph, 15
Vallée, Rudy, 15
van Eastenbridge
   John, 4, 446
Van Etten
   Donald, 241, 337
   Stella Boyd, 9, 273
   Stoddard, 9
Vannatta, O.E., 243
Van Ness, Walt, 417
Van Pelt
   Elizabeth Laserlier, 124, 427–428
   John, 427–8
Van Schoick, Arthur, 68
Van Tuyl

Alfred and Katherine, 442
Alfred Van Tuyl, 457
John and Angie, 472
Van Tuyl Cemetery, 63
Versailles, Treaty of, 15, 165
VF-18, 316
VF-31, 311, 324, 335, 431
Victory in Europe day, 328
Victory Mail, 285
Virginia
    Camp Eustis, 258–60, 264–5
    Natural Bridge, 321, 349
    Richmond, 85
Vitanza, Theodore, 315
VJ Day, 330–1
Vogt, 124
    Carl J., 55
    Doris, 127, 173
    Janith, V, 99, 118, 177
    John, 174, 177, 440
    William and Anna, 463
    William and Margarite, 436
Vollmer
    Cecil, 319, 337
    Clara, 241
    George, 438
    Matthew and Hazel, 471
    Vera, 206
Von Blascom, John, 179, 181, 182, 185
Vonderhorst
    Carl, 23, 173, 177, 271, 362
    Carl and Anna, 41, 97, 223, 456, 464
    Charles, 337
    Eleanor, 177, 271
    Elsie, 23, 176, 177
    Eric, 23, 25
    Louise, 22–3, 38, 41, 93, 97, 446
    Max and Minnie, 11, 435
    Mrs., 129
    Mrs. A., 93
    Nancy, V
    Walter, 23
von Hindenburg, Paul, 57, 145
Von Ohlen
    Archie, 47, 120, 265, 319, 337, 426
    Henry and Lila Myers, 439, 450, 459
    Henry, 113, 126, 144, 150–1, 370, 426
    Lila Myers, 115, 426
Von Ohlen Store, 2, 16, 46, 192

W

Wade
    James (Jim), 98, 107, 190, 196, 208, 254, 255, 263, 286, 335, 414, 443, 451, 458
    Rev. J.J., 120
Wageman, Louis, 165, 173
Wagermann, August and Margaret, 449, 470
    August, 435
Wagner, Mac, 147
Wagner and Adler Company, 17, 85
Waidler
    Emma Schoonover, 19, 77, 149, 183, 207, 209–11, 224, 228, 242, 268–71, 394
    Will, 19, 77, 149, 183
Wait
    Alex, 137, 190, 211, 214, 224, 236, 248, 254, 262, 275–6, 294, 314, 353, 450
    Alexander and Ida, 441, 445, 450, 459
    Bill, 410
    Carrie, 137
    Dorothy, 118, 190, 261
    George, 137
    Lucille, 118, 145, 173
    Marie, 137, 173
    Mary Mills, 11, 137, 441, 445, 450
    William and Carrie, 432
Wait & Boyd, 17, 77, 80–1, 107, 135, 163–4, 190, 196, 208, 209, 264, 286, 369, 372, 432, 459
Wake Island, 235
Wall, W.W., 24
Wallace, 410
Wallace Place, 74
Waller, Fats, 15
Walter
    Cyrus, 94, 96, 157, 446
    Cyrus and Ella, 38, 196, 455
    Donald, 38, 83, 96, 173, 196, 315, 337
    Ella, 470
    Joyce, 196
    Reginald, 38, 96, 117, 173, 196, 223, 309, 358, 362, 367
    Reginald and Joyce, 469
Walters, Carl and Annie, 263
Warden
    Archie, 137, 173, 265, 315, 337
    John Sr. family, 435, 464, 449
    John (Ian) Jr., 165, 173, 265, 298, 315, 337
    Robert, 294
    William, 123, 127, 173
Warner Brothers, 57, 109
War, Spanish Civil, 165, 195
Warshauer, Louis and Mildred, 11, 41, 92–3, 443, 447, 471
Washington Beach Hotel, 10–1, 38, 41, 93, 95–6, 103, 116, 129, 159, 223, 309, 449, 463
Washington D.C. Class Trip, 72, 79, 83
Washington Lake, 2, 10, 11, 23, 38, 41, 43, 81, 92–6, 98, 132, 159, 196, 204, 223, 345
    Casino, 95, 159
    House, 10, 38, 94, 196, 358
Waterman, Estella, 41
Watson
    Ella, 435, 447
    Frank and Lina Carmichael, 376, 416
    Leonard and Daisy, 416
    Maxwell and Elizabeth Watson, 376
Watts, Christina, V
Webb
    Charles Cripps, 427, 428
    Emma Jane, 427, 428
    Henry Cripps, 427, 428
    Henry G., 18, 109, 384, 427
    John Henry, 427, 428
    Mary Ellen Paye, 427
    Sarah Shotwell, 427
Weber
    Arthur, 337
    Caroline, 145, 173
    Dave, 342
    Dorothy Brodmerkel, 117, 153, 373
    Eva Kalin, 29
    Fred, 373
    Gail, 294
    Jeannette, 294

John, 29, 117
John and Katie, 433, 454
John H. and Eva, 454, 464
Joseph, 345
Louise, 472
Michael, 93, 100, 104
Mr. Weber (at HL), 166
Raymond, 157, 173, 265
Roger, 294
Weidner, David, V
Weigele, Calvina E., 315
Weismuller, Johnny, 15
Weller, Marjorie Paton, 377
Welles, Orson, 189
Wells
   Ada Myers, 13, 19, 25, 32, 37, 77, 82, 149, 183, 184, 185, 210, 269, 270, 303, 325, 385, 386, 394, 413, 434, 457
   Dorothy, 292, 298
   Earl, 25, 76–7, 82, 127, 184, 200, 279, 298, 301–2, 335, 349, 350, 385–6, 413
   Earl and Ada Myers, 455, 466
   Emil, Everitt, Mabel, 127
   George, 341
   H.G., 189
   Minerva Racine, 55, 76
   Norma, 303
   Raymond, 127, 142, 146, 163, 194, 196, 233, 444
   Raymond and Marion, 449, 459
   Troward, 157, 173
   Willard, 55, 76, 127, 410, 451, 469
   Willard and Minerva, 434
Weltner, Max and Anna, 470
Wendt, George and Anna, 470
Werman, Edey LaBarr, V, 185
Werneke, William, 281, 315
Werner, Selma, 94
West
   Charles, 194
   Charles and Selma, 94, 95, 223, 331, 432, 454, 470
   Daniel, 94, 290, 315, 332, 337
   Paul, 94
   Ralph, 94, 241, 313, 315, 331–2, 337, 371
   Selma, 332
   Selma Jr., 94
   Sophie Zepka, 371

Theodore and Phoebe, 432
Theodore (s/o Charles), 94
Theodore Sr., 22, 94, 137, 331, 454
Westerfield
   Edythe King, V, 157
   Laurence, 466
   Pamela, V
West Farm, 11, 94–5, 223, 331, 432
Westinghouse, 15, 57, 432
Westminster Abbey, 31
West Shore Cottages/Lodge, 38, 41, 93, 95, 97, 103, 159, 186, 223, 367
White
   Clara Wolff, 25, 114, 158
   Gordon, 319
   Lena, 261
   Samuel, 165, 173
White Lake, 23
Whitiak, Nicky, 147
Whitmarsh
   Ida Darling, 18, 29, 37, 63, 384, 427
   Walt, 29, 427
Whitney
   Al, 319
   Edward (Rev.), 410
Wicks
   Daniel, 258–9, 303
   Doug, 258–9
   Ted Jr., 108, 110, 258–9
   Ted Sr., 108, 110, 258–9
   Tillie Bosch, 63, 106, 108–9, 153, 258, 259, 302
Wilder, Thorton, 15, 185
Wilkinson, Barbara Waite, V
Williams
   Betty, 38
   Charles, 315, 337
   Eleanor, 34, 157, 173
   Frances, 34
   Francis, 315, 337
   Frank and Gracie, 448
   Fred and Charlotte, 456
   Frederick, 337
   Fritz, 147
   Jack, 134
   John, 142, 315, 337
   John Daton, 34
   Ted, 235
   W., 202

Williamson, Randy Drum, V, 419
Willis, Alice, V
Willkie, Wendell, 205
Wilson
   Abigail, 193
   Agnes, 442, 457, 472
   Agnes Mary Lucke, 204, 213, 241, 248, 261, 303, 350, 358, 370, 464, 474
   Albert, 436
   Arthur, 2, 14, 114
   Arthur and Abby, 443
   Bertha Boyd, XI, 14, 107, 113–5, 444, 459
   Charles, 2, 9, 14, 81, 114, 410, 440
   C. Wilson, 202
   Edward, 165, 204, 213, 241, 248, 261, 303, 350, 358, 360, 362, 370, 458, 460, 464, 474
   Ed Wilson family, 360, 456
   Elizabeth Hoatson Clark, 18, 113–4, 121, 126, 155, 162–3, 172, 210–1, 236, 244, 253, 331, 349, 366, 370, 439, 443, 451
   Forrest, 14, 83, 107, 120, 173, 254, 319, 337, 434, 459
   Gladys Moran, V
   H., 349
   Julia Cox, 114
   Louis, 461
   Robert, 319
   Samuel and Helen, 472
   William G., 303
   William H. and Bertha Boyd, 434
   Wm. H. Wilson Store, 3, 14, 16, 107, 163, 196, 410
Wilson's Taxi, 204, 358, 360
Winecoop, Miss, 141
Winter
   Bertha, 210–1, 215, 218–9, 234, 236, 244–5, 247–8, 258, 261, 265–6, 271, 273, 441, 450, 466
   Charlie and Catherine Schmerfeld, 347
   Charlie Jr., 373
Winter (Gustav) Line, 297–8
Wizlankas/ Wizlankus
   Louis, 350

Joseph, 337
Wolfe
    Mrs. Charles, 63
    Mrs. Henry, 177
    Ray, 279
Wolff
    Albert, 4, 6, 114, 121–3, 127, 185, 372, 462
    Alfred, 113
    Alfred and Helen, 159, 237, 354, 355, 470
    Amy, 370
    Arlene, V, 294, 373
    Carl, 25, 113, 114, 117, 138, 146, 154, 158, 162, 164, 173, 183, 194, 196, 197, 203, 281, 339
    Carl and Frieda Kloss, 451, 470
    Charles, 6, 114, 372, 435, 448
    Clara, 25, 206, 243, 307
    Dorothy Meyers, 13, 28, 82, 113, 118, 120, 123, 127, 138, 151, 157, 178, 188, 193, 199, 203, 204, 214, 358, 413, 414, 462
    Edward, 185, 358, 360, 372
    Frank, 4, 6, 113, 114, 437
    Frank and Mary, 448, 462
    Freida Kloss, 25, 55, 77, 114, 158, 281
    Henry and Matilda, 432, 454, 464
    Herb, V, 77, 113, 158, 161, 162
    Janette Kerr, 6, 75, 114, 435, 440, 445
    Lillian Hainzl, V, 256, 349
    Norman, 4, 6, 114, 120, 121, 122, 123, 127, 151, 157, 160, 252, 253, 273, 275, 358, 413, 414, 448, 462
    Raymond, 319, 337
    Robert, 113–4, 154, 158, 161, 162, 196, 271, 280–1, 313, 315, 337
    Ruth Foster, 121, 123, 127, 185, 358, 371, 372, 447
    William and Mary, 470
    Wolff brothers, 114
    Yolanda Foscola, 353
Wood
    Ada Britt, 19, 149, 183
    Arthur, 19, 149, 185, 269, 270, 303
    Lawrence, 315, 337
    Mr. (music teacher), 214
    Rev., 113, 125
    Smokey Joe, 124
Woodland Cottage(s), 10–1, 119, 223, 237, 360, 367, 470
    Stern Cottage, 237
Woodruff
    Bernis, 261
    Carlton, 241, 337
    E. and J., 202
Woodstock Music Festival, 23, 378
Woolsey, Edna, 107
Worden, Bill, 147
Works Project Adm. (WPA), 157
World's Fair, 110, 137, 177, 195, 214
Wormuth
    Eva, 146
    Harry and Mary Kyte, 453, 457
    Harry/Mill, 4, 72, 113, 117, 130, 183, 186–8, 190–1, 197, 202–3, 211–2, 218, 226, 233, 245, 247–8, 258, 267, 410, 439, 445
    Mabel Horton, 6–7, 18, 26, 78, 81, 83, 108–9, 126–7, 185, 192, 236, 244, 261–2, 370, 376–7, 391, 394–5, 400–1, 432, 434, 438, 445, 449, 451, 453, 469
    Mary Kyte, 73, 113, 130, 138, 193, 197, 210–1, 221, 233
Worzel
    E., 215
    Ervin and Dorothy, 471
    Gordon, 370, 456
    Herman and Blanche Quick, 43, 266–7, 344, 456, 472
    Irving, 315, 337
    Louisa, 456
    Marjorie Hess, V, 127, 452
    Martha Eldred, V, 287, 341, 376
    Oakie, 215, 297, 303
    Oscar, 462
    Raymond and Emma Williams, 287
    William, 287
Wright, Frank Lloyd, 15
Wright Aeronautics, 259, 275, 287
WWI, 31, 48
WWJ, 15

Y

Yangtze River, 177
Yeager, Chuck, 353
York Lake Mountain House, 8, 11, 38, 78, 97, 223, 455
Young, Cousin Van Wyck, 86
Yozag, Prosper, 55
Yugoslavia, 235, 289
Yulan Cottage, 11, 25, 29, 38, 41, 77, 93, 95, 356, 358, 454
Yulan Dairy, 91
Yutz, Frank, 319, 337

Z

Zauner, Anna, 38, 41
Zedong, Mao, 117
Zimmerman, Paul, 319
Zurkowsky, John, 137, 173

Clearface

Farewell to Eldred is set in Clearface, an Old Style, serif typeface designed by Morris Fuller Benton with the collaboration of his father Linn Boyd Benton, produced at American Type Founders in 1907.

Family Info Online

HalfwayBrook.com
Halfway Brook community blog, on-going projects, resources.

Weezy.info
Stories and information about the Crabtree-Higginson, Austin-Leavenworth, Smith-Corbridge, and Fallin-Williams families.

About the Author

Louise Elizabeth (Austin) Smith grew up on treeless Peach Street (in a suburb south of Detroit, Michigan). She never remembers a time she did not love to read—both biographies and classics. Louise inherited a deep appreciation of words from her father; and a love of music from her mother.

As a ten year old she wanted to write fiction, but it would be another 45 years before Louise discovered that researching and writing family stories were more her style.

Louise received a bachelor's degree in music education from Western Michigan University and a master's degree in elementary education from Eastern Michigan University.

After teaching music and fifth grade classroom for ten years, Louise met and married the love of her life, Gary, then a car designer for General Motors. She applied her educational and musical skills to homeschooling their four children, now all grown and on their own.

In the fall of 2004, Louise ran across some favorite stories her grandmother Myrtle Crabtree Briggs had told and a few photos from an aunt.

Using her interest in research (with the help of the internet) and the family collections that were soon shared, Louise began to compile the story of her grandparents and their ancestors.

The story of the new friends and "long lost" relatives she has met in doing research for the *Memoirs from Eldred* Series and the colossal amount of photos and family information they shared could be its own book.

Louise Elizabeth Smith with husband Gary.

Farewell to Eldred is the fifth book published with the help of Gary who designed the covers, interiors, prepared all of the photos, and added his much needed professional touch. Louise and Gary reside in Cave Creek, Arizona.

Other Books by Louise E. Smith

Aida Austin's 1881 Diary
Aida Austin started a diary at the beginning of 1881, the year she turned 20 in November. Whether in New York City with her Austin cousins or at her home in Eldred, New York, Aida wrote about her daily life: plumbers fixing pipes, dentist and doctor visits, going to Central Park, skating, sailing, shopping, getting the mail, holidays, daily visits with relatives, President Garfield's assassination, drinking tea, and raking hay.

Included at the end of the Diary are photos of Aida's parents, brothers, and some of her Eldred-Austin relatives mentioned in her diary.
ISBN 978-0-9826374-1-8, 6.7 × 9.6, 108 pages, Softcover

Grandma and Me
Amanda Myrtie Crabtree Briggs was born in 1891 in a sodhouse on her father's Nebraska homestead farm. Over the years she told her children and grandchildren the stories of her growing up as well as those of her parents and her Crabtree and Higginson grandparents—real pioneers of the west. This book is a collection of those stories and includes almost 600 photos and documents.
8-1/2 × 11, 246 pages, Softcover

Memoirs from Eldred Series by Louise E. Smith

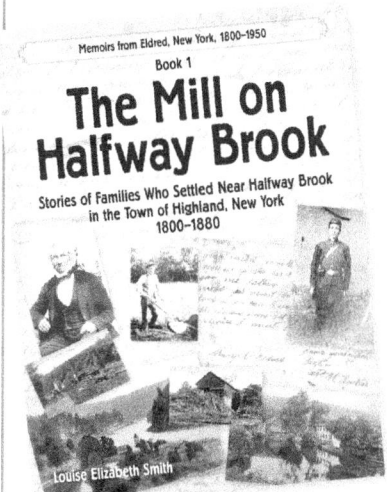

Book 1: The Mill on Halfway Brook
The Mill on Halfway Brook tells of the Eldred, Austin, Myers, and Leavenworth families, their neighbors, friends, and kinsfolk that settled in what was once the Town of Lumberland, in the villages of Halfway Brook (Eldred), The River (Barryville), Ten Mile River (Tusten), and South Lebanon (Glen Spey).

The narrative weaves vignettes of townsfolk, preachers, churches, regional and national events with historical information, land documents, censuses, an 1875 biography, Congregational and Methodist Church records, over 300 photos and postcards, old and new maps, and at least 200 family letters (1845–1880).

The Mill on Halfway Brook is fully indexed with names of over 900 people, places, and events. It is the first in the series, *Memoirs from Eldred, New York, 1800–1950*.

ISBN 978-0-9826374-0-1, 8.3 × 11, 284 pages, Softcover

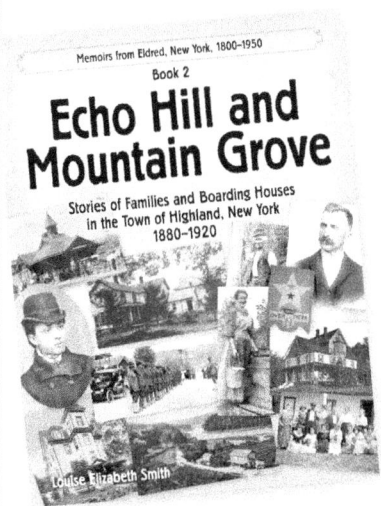

Book 2: Echo Hill and Mountain Grove
Jennie Louisa Leavenworth and her future husband Charles Mortimer Austin lived near brooks on opposite sides of the charming village of Eldred, Town of Highland, Sullivan County, New York. The Leavenworth home near Blind Pond Brook on the west, would become Echo Hill Farm House. The Austin family would build Mountain Grove House near Halfway Brook, on the east side.

Echo Hill and Mountain Grove is an account of the change from lumbering, rafting, and bluestone quarrying to that of running boarding houses in the picturesque and healthy hamlets of Barryville, Minisink Ford, Yulan, Eldred, and Venoge, located near the Delaware River. It tells the history of the Town of Highland and its townsfolk (Austin, Leavenworth, Eldred, Myers, Bodine, Bradley, Bosch, Clark, Gardner, Hallock, Mills, Boyd, Horton, Parker, Greig, Stege, Sergeant, Tether, and others), many of whom owned boarding houses.

Echo Hill and Mountain Grove is bursting with anecdotes and stories of townsfolk, boarding houses, occupations, and events in the years 1880 to 1920. It includes visits to Colorado, Kansas, Nebraska, New York City, and France. The narrative also gives details on the Shohola Depot, Shohola Glen, Shohola House, the Pelton Soda Factory, the Roebling Bridge, the Congregational Church Centennial, Zane Grey, two presidential assassinations, and World War I.

Echo Hill and Mountain Grove contains almost 900 images (photos, postcards, documents), several first person accounts, an 1881 Diary, 446 letters (150 WWI letters, including some from Lone Scout readers in 1918), nine original maps, and an index of 1,500 people, places, and events. It is the second book in the series, *Memoirs from Eldred, New York, 1800–1950*.

ISBN 978-0-9826374-2-5, 8.3 × 11, 512 pages, Softcover

Available at HalfwayBrook.com

www.ingramcontent.com/pod-product-compliance
Lightning Source LLC
Chambersburg PA
CBHW080531300426
44111CB00017B/2674